W9-AEN-161

HENRY JAMES

HENRY JAMES

AUTOBIOGRAPHIES

A Small Boy and Others
Notes of a Son and Brother
The Middle Years
Other Autobiographical Writings

Philip Horne, *editor*

THE LIBRARY OF AMERICA

Visit our website at www.loa.org.

The paper meets the requirements of
ANSI/NISO Z39.48–1992 (Permanence of Paper).

Distributed to the trade in the United States
by Penguin Random House Inc.
and in Canada by Penguin Random House Canada Ltd.

Library of Congress Control Number: 2015935692
ISBN 978–1–59853–471–9

First Printing
The Library of America—274

Manufactured in the United States of America

Contents

A Small Boy and Others 1

Notes of a Son and Brother 251

The Middle Years 571

Other Autobiographical Writings, 1881–1910 633

From the Notebooks, 1881–82 635
Wolcott Balestier 661
Dumas the Younger 670
The Late James Payn 687
From the Notebooks, March 29, 1905 690
An American Art-Scholar: Charles Eliot Norton 695
The Turning Point of My Life 704
Is There a Life After Death? 706

Appendix: "Henry James at Work" by Theodora Bosanquet 723

Chronology 753
Note on the Texts 767
Notes 773
Index 831

A SMALL BOY AND OTHERS

Henry James and his Father

From a daguerreotype taken in 1854

I

IN THE attempt to place together some particulars of the early life of William James and present him in his setting, his immediate native and domestic air, so that any future gathered memorials of him might become the more intelligible and interesting, I found one of the consequences of my interrogation of the past assert itself a good deal at the expense of some of the others. For it was to memory in the first place that my main appeal for particulars had to be made; I had been too near a witness of my brother's beginnings of life, and too close a participant, by affection, admiration and sympathy, in whatever touched and moved him, not to feel myself in possession even of a greater quantity of significant truth, a larger handful of the fine substance of history, than I could hope to express or apply. To recover anything like the full treasure of scattered, wasted circumstance was at the same time to live over the spent experience itself, so deep and rich and rare, with whatever sadder and sorer intensities, even with whatever poorer and thinner passages, after the manner of every one's experience; and the effect of this in turn was to find discrimination among the parts of my subject again and again difficult—so inseparably and beautifully they seemed to hang together and the comprehensive case to decline mutilation or refuse to be treated otherwise than handsomely. This meant that aspects began to multiply and images to swarm, so far at least as they showed, to appreciation, as true terms and happy values; and that I might positively and exceedingly rejoice in my relation to most of them, using it for all that, as the phrase is, it should be worth. To knock at the door of the past was in a word to see it open to me quite wide—to see the world within begin to "compose" with a grace of its own round the primary figure, see it people itself vividly and insistently. Such then is the circle of my commemoration and so much these free and copious notes a labour of love and loyalty. We were, to my sense, the blest group of us, such a company of characters and such a picture of differences, and withal so fused and united and interlocked, that each of us, to that fond fancy, pleads for preservation, and that in respect to what I speak of myself as possessing I think I shall be ashamed, as of a cold impiety, to find any element altogether negligible. To which I may add perhaps that I struggle under the drawback, innate and inbred, of seeing the whole content of memory and affection in each enacted and recovered moment, as who should say, in the vivid image and the very scene; the light of the only terms in which life has treated me to experience. And I cherish the moment and evoke the image and repaint the scene; though meanwhile indeed scarce able to convey how prevailingly and almost exclusively, during years and years, the field was animated and the adventure conditioned for me by my brother's nearness and that play of genius in him of which I had never had a doubt from the first.

The "first" then—since I retrace our steps to the start, for the pleasure, strangely mixed though it be, of feeling our small feet plant themselves afresh and artlessly stumble forward again—the first began long ago, far off, and yet glimmers at me there as out of a thin golden haze, with all the charm, for imagination and memory, of pressing pursuit rewarded, of distinctness in the dimness, of the flush of life in the grey, of the wonder of consciousness in everything; everything having naturally been all the while but the abject little matter of course. Partly doubtless as the effect of a life, now getting to be a tolerably long one, spent in the older world, I see the world of our childhood as very young indeed, young with its own juvenility as well as with ours; as if it wore the few and light garments and had gathered in but the scant properties and breakable toys of the tenderest age, or were at the most a very unformed young person, even a boisterous hobbledehoy. It exhaled at any rate a simple freshness, and I catch its pure breath, at our infantile Albany, as the very air of long summer afternoons—occasions tasting of ample leisure, still bookless, yet beginning to be bedless, or cribless; tasting of accessible garden peaches in a liberal backward territory that was still almost part of a country town; tasting of many-sized uncles, aunts, cousins, of strange legendary domestics, inveterately but archaically Irish, and whose familiar remarks and "criticism of life" were handed down, as well as of dim family ramifications and local allusions—mystifications always—that flowered into anecdote as into small hard plums; tasting above all of a big much-shaded savoury house in which a softly-sighing widowed grandmother, Catherine Barber by birth, whose attitude was a resigned consciousness of complications and accretions, dispensed an hospitality seemingly as joyless as it was certainly boundless. What she *liked*, dear gentle lady of many cares and anxieties, was the "fiction of the day," the novels, at that time promptly pirated, of Mrs. Trollope and Mrs. Gore, of Mrs. Marsh, Mrs. Hubback and the Misses Kavanagh and Aguilar, whose very names are forgotten now, but which used to drive her away to quiet corners whence her figure comes back to me bent forward on a table with the book held out at a distance and a tall single candle placed, apparently not at all to her discomfort, in that age of sparer and braver habits, straight between the page and her eyes. There is a very animated allusion to one or two of her aspects in the fragment of a "spiritual autobiography," the reminiscences of a so-called Stephen Dewhurst printed by W. J. (1885) in The Literary Remains of Henry James; a reference which has the interest of being very nearly as characteristic of my father himself (which his references in almost any connection were wont to be) as of the person or the occasion evoked. I had reached my sixteenth year when she died, and as my only remembered grandparent she touches the chord of attachment to a particular vibration. She represented for us in our generation the only English blood—that of both her own parents—flowing in our veins; I confess that out of that association, for reasons and reasons, I feel her image most beneficently bend. We were, as to three parts, of two other stocks; and I recall how from far back I reflected—for I see I must have been always reflecting—that, mixed as such a mixture, our Scotch with our Irish, might be, it had had still a grace to borrow from the third infusion or dimension. If I could freely have chosen moreover it was precisely from my father's mother that, fond votary of the finest faith in the vivifying and characterising force of mothers, I should have wished to borrow it; even while conscious that Catherine Barber's own people had drawn breath in American air for at least two generations before her. Our father's father, William James, an Irishman and a Protestant born (of county Cavan) had come to America, a very young man and then sole of his family, shortly after the Revolutionary War; my father, the second son of the third of the marriages to which the country of his adoption was liberally to help him, had been born in Albany in 1811. Our maternal greatgrandfather on the father's side, Hugh Walsh, had reached our shores from a like Irish home, Killyleagh, county Down, somewhat earlier, in 1764, he being then nineteen; he had settled at Newburgh-on-the-Hudson, half way to Albany, where some of his descendants till lately lingered. Our maternal greatgrandfather on the mother's side—that is our mother's mother's father, Alexander Robertson of Polmont near Edinburgh—had likewise crossed the sea in the mid-century and prospered in New York very much as Hugh Walsh was prospering and William James was still more markedly to prosper, further up the Hudson; as unanimous and fortunate beholders of the course of which admirable stream I like to think of them. I find Alexander Robertson inscribed in a wee New York directory of the close of the century as Merchant; and our childhood in that city was passed, as to some of its aspects, in a sense of the afterglow, reduced and circumscribed, it is true, but by no means wholly inanimate, of his shining solidity.

The sweet taste of Albany probably lurked most in its being our admired antithesis to New York; it was holiday, whereas New York was home; at least that presently came to be the relation, for to my very very first fleeting vision, I apprehend, Albany itself must have been the scene exhibited. Our parents had gone there for a year or two to be near our grandmother on their return from their first (that is our mother's first) visit to Europe, which had quite immediately followed my birth, which appears to have lasted some year and a half, and of which I shall have another word to say. The Albany experiment would have been then their first founded housekeeping, since I make them out to have betaken themselves for the winter following their marriage to the ancient Astor House—not indeed at that time ancient, but the great and appointed modern hotel of New York, the only one of such pretensions, and which somehow continued to project its massive image, that of a great square block of granite with vast dark warm interiors, across some of the later and more sensitive stages of my infancy. Clearly—or I should perhaps rather say dimly—recourse to that hospitality was again occasionally had by our parents; who had originally had it to such a happy end that on January 9th, 1842, my elder brother had come into the world there. It remained a tradition with him that our father's friend from an early time, R. W. Emerson, then happening to be in New York and under that convenient roof, was proudly and pressingly "taken upstairs" to admire and give his blessing to the lately-born babe who was to become the second American William James. The blessing was to be renewed, I may mention, in the sense that among the impressions of the next early years I easily distinguish that of the great and urbane Emerson's occasional presence in Fourteenth Street, a centre of many images, where the parental tent was before long to pitch itself and rest awhile. I am interested for the moment, however, in identifying the scene of our very first perceptions—of my very own at least, which I can here best speak for.

One of these, and probably the promptest in order, was that of my brother's occupying a place in the world to which I couldn't at all aspire—to any approach to which in truth I seem to myself ever conscious of having signally forfeited a title. It glimmers back to me that I quite definitely and resignedly thought of him as in the most exemplary manner already beforehand with me, already seated at his task when the attempt to drag me crying and kicking to the first hour of my education failed on the threshold of the Dutch House in Albany after the fashion I have glanced at in a collection of other pages than these (just as I remember to have once borrowed a hint from our grandmother's "interior" in a work of imagination). That failure of my powers or that indifference to them, my retreat shrieking from the Dutch House, was to leave him once for all already there an embodied demonstration of the possible—already wherever it might be that there was a question of my arriving, when arriving at all, belatedly and ruefully; as if he had gained such an advance of me in his sixteen months' experience of the world before mine began that I never for all the time of childhood and youth in the least caught up with him or overtook him. He was always round the corner and out of sight, coming back into view but at his hours of extremest ease. We were never in the same schoolroom, in the same game, scarce even in step together or in the same phase at the same time; when our phases overlapped, that is, it was only for a moment—he was clean out before I had got well in. How far he had really at any moment dashed forward it is not for me now to attempt to say; what comes to me is that I at least hung inveterately and woefully back, and that this relation alike to our interests and to each other seemed proper and pre-appointed. I lose myself in wonder at the loose ways, the strange process of waste, through which nature and fortune may deal on occasion with those whose faculty for application is all and only in their imagination and their sensibility. There may be during those bewildered and brooding years so little for them to "show" that I liken the individual dunce—as he so often must appear—to some commercial traveller who has lost the key to his packed case of samples and can but pass for a fool while other exhibitions go forward.

I achieve withal a dim remembrance of my final submission, though it is the faintest ghost of an impression and consists but of the bright blur of a dame's schoolroom, a mere medium for small piping shuffling sound and suffered heat, as well as for the wistfulness produced by "glimmering squares" that were fitfully screened, though not to any revival of cheer, by a huge swaying, yet dominant object. This dominant object, the shepherdess of the flock, was Miss Bayou or Bayhoo—I recover but the alien sound of her name, which memory caresses only because she may have been of like race with her temple of learning, which faced my grandmother's house in North Pearl Street and really justified its exotic claim by its yellow archaic gable-end: I think of the same as of brick baked in the land of dykes and making a series of small steps from the base of the gable to the point. These images are subject, I confess, to a soft confusion—which is somehow consecrated, none the less, and out of which, with its shade of contributory truth, some sort of scene insists on glancing. The very flush of the uneven bricks of the pavement lives in it, the very smell of the street cobbles, the imputed grace of the arching umbrage—I see it all as from under trees; the form of Steuben Street, which crossed our view, as steep even to the very essence of adventure, with a summit, and still more with a nethermost and riskiest incline, very far away. There lives in it the aspect of the other house—the other and much smaller than my grandmother's, conveniently near it and within sight; which was pinkish-red picked out with white, whereas my grandmother's was greyish-brown and very grave, and which must have stood back a little from the street, as I seem even now to swing, or at least to perch, on a relaxed gate of approach that was conceived to work by an iron chain weighted with a big ball; all under a spreading tree again and with the high, oh so high white stone steps (mustn't they have been marble?) and fan-lighted door of the pinkish-red front behind me. I lose myself in ravishment before the marble and the pink. There were other houses too—one of them the occasion of the first "paid" visit that struggles with my twilight of social consciousness; a call with my father, conveying me presumably for fond exhibition (since if my powers were not exhibitional my appearance and my long fair curls, of which I distinctly remember the lachrymose sacrifice, suppositiously were), on one of our aunts, the youngest of his three sisters, lately married and who, predestined to an early death, hovers there for me, softly spectral, in long light "front" ringlets, the fashion of the time and the capital sign of all our paternal aunts seemingly; with the remembered enhancement of her living in Elk Street, the name itself vaguely portentous, as through beasts of the forest not yet wholly exorcised, and more or less under the high brow of that Capitol which, as aloft somewhere and beneath the thickest shades of all, loomed, familiar yet impressive, at the end of almost any Albany vista of reference. I have seen other capitols since, but the whole majesty of the matter must have been then distilled into my mind—even though the connection was indirect and the concrete image, that of the primitive structure, long since pretentiously and insecurely superseded—so that, later on, the impression was to find itself, as the phrase is, discounted. Had it not moreover been reinforced at the time, for that particular Capitoline hour, by the fact that our uncle, our aunt's husband, was a son of Mr. Martin Van Buren, and that *he* was the President? This at least led the imagination on—or leads in any case my present imagination of that one; ministering to what I have called the soft confusion.

The confusion clears, however, though the softness remains, when, ceasing to press too far backward, I meet the ampler light of conscious and educated little returns to the place; for the education of New York, enjoyed up to my twelfth year, failed to blight its romantic appeal. The images I really distinguish flush through the maturer medium, but with the sense of them only the more wondrous. The other house, the house of my parents' limited early sojourn, becomes that of those of our cousins, numerous at that time, who pre-eminently figured for us; the various brood presided over by my father's second sister, Catherine James, who had married at a very early age Captain Robert Temple, U.S.A. Both these parents were to die young, and their children, six in number, the two eldest boys, were very markedly to people our preliminary scene; this being true in particular of three of them, the sharply differing brothers and the second sister, Mary Temple, radiant and rare, extinguished in her first youth, but after having made an impression on many persons, and on ourselves not least, which was to become in the harmonious circle, for all time, matter of sacred legend and reference, of associated piety. Those and others with them were the numerous dawnings on which in many cases the deepening and final darknesses were so soon to follow: our father's family was to offer such a chronicle of early deaths, arrested careers, broken promises, orphaned children. It sounds cold-blooded, but part of the charm of our grandmother's house for us—or I should perhaps but speak for myself—was in its being so much and so sociably a nurseried and playroomed orphanage. The children of her lost daughters and daughters-in-law overflowed there, mainly as girls; on whom the surviving sons-in-law and sons occasionally and most trustingly looked in. Parentally bereft cousins were somehow more thrilling than parentally provided ones; and most thrilling when, in the odd fashion of that time, they were sent to school in New York as a preliminary to their being sent to school in Europe. They spent scraps of holidays with us in Fourteenth Street, and I think my first childish conception of the enviable lot, formed amid these associations, was to be so little fathered or mothered, so little sunk in the short range, that the romance of life seemed to lie in some constant improvisation, by vague overhovering authorities, of new situations and horizons. We were intensely domesticated, yet for the very reason perhaps that we felt our young bonds easy; and they were *so* easy compared to other small plights of which we had stray glimpses that my first assured conception of true richness was that we should be sent separately off among cold or even cruel aliens in order to be there thrillingly homesick. Homesickness was a luxury I remember craving from the tenderest age—a luxury of which I was unnaturally, or at least prosaically, deprived. Our motherless cousin Augustus Barker came up from Albany to the Institution Charlier—unless it was, as I suspect, a still earlier specimen, with a name that fades from me, of that type of French establishment for boys which then and for years after so incongruously flourished in New York; and though he professed a complete satisfaction with pleasures tasted in our innocent society I felt that he was engaged in a brave and strenuous adventure while we but hugged the comparatively safe shore.

II

WE WERE day-boys, William and I, at dispensaries of learning the number and succession of which to-day excite my wonder; we couldn't have changed oftener, it strikes me as I look back, if our presence had been inveterately objected to, and yet I enjoy an inward certainty that, my brother being vividly bright and I quite blankly innocuous, this reproach was never brought home to our house. It was an humiliation to me at first, small boys though we were, that our instructors kept being instructresses and thereby a grave reflection both on our attainments and our spirit. A bevy of these educative ladies passes before me, I still possess their names; as for instance that of Mrs. Daly and that of Miss Rogers (previously of the "Chelsea Female Institute," though at the moment of Sixth Avenue this latter), whose benches indeed my brother didn't haunt, but who handled us literally with gloves—I still see the elegant objects as Miss Rogers beat time with a long black ferule to some species of droning chant or chorus in which we spent most of our hours; just as I see her very tall and straight and spare, in a light blue dress, her firm face framed in long black glossy ringlets and the stamp of the Chelsea Female Institute all over her. Mrs. Daly, clearly the immediate successor to the nebulous Miss Bayou, remains quite substantial—perhaps because the sphere of her small influence has succeeded in not passing away, up to this present writing; so that in certain notes on New York published a few years since I was moved to refer to it with emotion as one of the small red houses on the south side of Waverly Place that really carry the imagination back to a vanished social order. They carry mine to a stout red-faced lady with grey hair and a large apron, the latter convenience somehow suggesting, as she stood about with a resolute air, that she viewed her little pupils as so many small slices cut from the loaf of life and on which she was to dab the butter of arithmetic and spelling, accompanied by way of jam with a light application of the practice of prize-giving. I recall an occasion indeed, I must in justice mention, when the jam really was thick—my only memory of a schoolfeast, strange to say, throughout our young annals: something uncanny in the air of the schoolroom at the unwonted evening or late afternoon hour, and tables that seemed to me prodigiously long and on which the edibles were chunky and sticky. The stout red-faced lady must have been Irish, as the name she bore imported—or do I think so but from the indescribably Irish look of her revisited house? It refers itself at any rate to a New York age in which a little more or a little less of the colour was scarce notable in the general flush.

Of pure unimported strain, however, were Miss Sedgwick and Mrs. Wright (Lavinia D.), the next figures in the procession—the procession that was to wind up indeed with two foreign recruits, small brown snappy Mademoiselle Delavigne, who plied us with the French tongue at home and who had been introduced to us as the niece—or could it have been the grandniece?—of the celebrated Casimir, and a large Russian lady in an extraordinarily short cape (I like to recall the fashion of short capes) of the same stuff as her dress, and Merovingian sidebraids that seemed to require the royal crown of Frédégonde or Brunéhaut to complete their effect. This final and aggravational representative of the compromising sex looms to my mind's eye, I should add, but as the creature of an hour, in spite of her having been domiciled with us; whereas I think of Mademoiselle Delavigne as flitting in and out on quick, fine, more or less cloth-shod feet of exemplary neatness, the flat-soled feet of Louis Philippe and of the female figures in those volumes of Gavarni then actual, then contemporaneous, which were kept in a piece of furniture that stood between the front-parlour windows in Fourteenth Street, together with a set of Béranger enriched by steel engravings to the strange imagery of which I so wonderingly responded that all other art of illustration, ever since, has been for me comparatively weak and cold. These volumes and the tall entrancing folios of Nash's lithographed Mansions of England in the Olden Time formed a store lending itself particularly to distribution on the drawingroom carpet, with concomitant pressure to the same surface of the small student's stomach and relieving agitation of his backward heels. I make out that it had decidedly been given to Mlle. Delavigne to represent to my first perception personal France; she was, besides not being at all pink or shy, oval and fluent and mistress somehow of the step—the step of levity that involved a whisk of her short skirts; there she was, to the life, on the page of Gavarni, attesting its reality, and there again did that page in return (I speak not of course of the unplumbed depths of the appended text) attest her own felicity. I was later on to feel—that is I was to learn—how many impressions and appearances, how large a sense of things, her type and tone prefigured. The evanescence of the large Russian lady, whom I think of as rather *rank*, I can't express it otherwise, may have been owing to some question of the purity of her accent in French; it was one of her attributes and her grounds of appeal to us that she had come straight from Siberia, and it is distinct to me that the purity was challenged by a friend of the house, and without—pathetically enough!—provoking the only answer, the plea that the missing Atticism would have been wasted on young barbarians. The Siberian note, on our inmate's part, may perhaps have been the least of her incongruities; she was above all too big for a little job, towered over us doubtless too heroically; and her proportions hover but to lose themselves—with the successors to her function awaiting us a little longer.

Meanwhile, to revert an instant, if the depressed consciousness of our still more or less quailing, educationally, beneath the female eye—and there was as well the deeper depth, there was the degrading fact, that with us literally consorted and contended Girls, that we sat and strove, even though we drew the line at playing with them and at knowing them, when not of the swarming cousinship, at home—if that felt awkwardness didn't exactly coincide with the ironic effect of "Gussy's" appearances, his emergence from rich mystery and his return to it, our state was but comparatively the braver: he always had so much more to tell us than we could possibly have to tell him. On reflection I see that the most completely rueful period couldn't after all greatly have prolonged itself; since the female eye last bent on us would have been that of Lavinia D. Wright, to our connection with whom a small odd reminiscence attaches a date. A little schoolmate displayed to me with pride, while the connection lasted, a beautiful coloured, a positively iridescent and gilded card representing the first of all the "great exhibitions" of our age, the London Crystal Palace of 1851—his father having lately gone out to it and sent him the dazzling memento. In 1851 I was eight years old and my brother scarce more than nine; in addition to which it is distinct to me in the first place that we were never faithful long, or for more than one winter, to the same studious scene, and in the second that among our instructors Mrs. Lavinia had no successor of her own sex unless I count Mrs. Vredenburg, of New Brighton, where we spent the summer of 1854, when I had reached the age of eleven and found myself bewildered by recognition of the part that "attendance at school" was so meanly to play in the hitherto unclouded long vacation. This was true at least for myself and my next younger brother, Wilky, who, under the presumption now dawning of his "community of pursuits" with my own, was from that moment, off and on, for a few years, my extremely easy yokefellow and playfellow. On William, charged with learning—I thought of him inveterately from our younger time as charged with learning—no such trick was played; he rested or roamed, that summer, on his accumulations; a fact which, as I was sure I saw these more and more richly accumulate, didn't in the least make me wonder. It comes back to me in truth that I had been prepared for anything by his having said to me toward the end of our time at Lavinia D.'s and with characteristic authority—his enjoyment of it coming from my character, I mean, quite as much as from his own—that that lady was a very able woman, as shown by the Experiments upstairs. He was upstairs of course, and I was down, and I scarce even knew what Experiments were, beyond their indeed requiring capability. The region of their performance was William's natural sphere, though I recall that I had a sense of peeping into it to a thrilled effect on seeing our instructress illustrate the proper way to extinguish a candle. She firmly pressed the flame between her thumb and her two forefingers, and, on my remarking that I didn't see how she could do it, promptly replied that I of course couldn't do it myself (as *he* could) because I should be afraid.

That reflection on my courage awakes another echo of the same scant season—since the test involved must have been that of our taking our way home through Fourth Avenue from some point up town, and Mrs. Wright's situation in East Twenty-first Street was such a point. The Hudson River Railroad was then in course of construction, or was being made to traverse the upper reaches of the city, through that part of which raged, to my young sense, a riot of explosion and a great shouting and waving of red flags when the gunpowder introduced into the rocky soil was about to take effect. It was our theory that our passage there, in the early afternoon, was beset with danger, and our impression that we saw fragments of rock hurtle through the air and smite to the earth another and yet another of the persons engaged or exposed. The point of honour, among several of us, was of course nobly to defy the danger, and I feel again the emotion with which I both hoped and feared that the red flags, lurid signals descried from afar, would enable or compel us to renew the feat. That I didn't for myself inveterately renew it I seem to infer from the memory of other perambulations of the period—as to which I am divided between their still present freshness and my sense of perhaps making too much of these tiny particles of history. My stronger rule, however, I confess, and the one by which I must here consistently be guided, is that, from the moment it is a question of projecting a picture, no particle that counts for memory or is appreciable to the spirit *can* be too tiny, and that experience, in the name of which one speaks, is all compact of them and shining with them. There was at any rate another way home, with other appeals, which consisted of getting straight along westward to Broadway, a sphere of a different order of fascination and bristling, as I seem to recall, with more vivid aspects, greater curiosities and wonderments. *The* curiosity was of course the country-place, as I supposed it to be, on the northeast corner of Eighteenth Street, if I am not mistaken; a big brown house in "grounds" peopled with animal life, which, little as its site may appear to know it to-day, lingered on into considerably later years. I have but to close my eyes in order to open them inwardly again, while I lean against the tall brown iron rails and peer through, to a romantic view of browsing and pecking and parading creatures, not numerous, but all of distinguished appearance: two or three elegant little cows of refined form and colour, two or three nibbling fawns and a larger company, above all, of peacocks and guineafowl, with, doubtless—though as to this I am vague—some of the commoner ornaments of the barnyard. I recognise that the scene as I evoke it fails of grandeur; but it none the less had for me the note of greatness—all of which but shows of course what a very town-bred small person I was, and was to remain.

I see myself moreover as somehow always alone in these and like New York *flâneries* and contemplations, and feel how the sense of my being so, being at any rate master of my short steps, such as they were, through all the beguiling streets, was probably the very savour of each of my chance feasts. Which stirs in me at the same time some wonder at the liberty of range and opportunity of adventure allowed to my tender age; though the puzzle may very well drop, after all, as I ruefully reflect that I couldn't have been judged at home reckless or adventurous. What I look back to as my infant license can only have had for its ground some timely conviction on the part of my elders that the only form of riot or revel ever known to me would be that of the visiting mind. Wasn't I myself for that matter even at that time all acutely and yet resignedly, even quite fatalistically, aware of what to think of this? I at any rate watch the small boy dawdle and gape again, I smell the cold dusty paint and iron as the rails of the Eighteenth Street corner rub his contemplative nose, and, feeling him foredoomed, withhold from him no grain of my sympathy. He is a convenient little image or warning of all that was to be for him, and he might well have been even happier than he was. For there was the very pattern and measure of all he was to demand: just to *be* somewhere—almost anywhere would do—and somehow receive an impression or an accession, feel a relation or a vibration. He was to go without many things, ever so many—as all persons do in whom contemplation takes so much the place of action; but everywhere, in the years that came soon after, and that in fact continued long, in the streets of great towns, in New York still for some time, and then for a while in London, in Paris, in Geneva, wherever it might be, he was to enjoy more than anything the so far from showy practice of wondering and dawdling and gaping: he was really, I think, much to profit by it. What it at all appreciably gave him—that is gave him in producible form—would be difficult to state; but it seems to him, as he even now thus indulges himself, an education like another: feeling, as he has come to do more and more, that no education avails for the intelligence that doesn't stir in it some subjective passion, and that on the other hand almost anything that does so act is largely educative, however small a figure the process might make in a scheme of training. Strange indeed, furthermore, are some of the things that *have* stirred a subjective passion—stirred it, I mean, in young persons predisposed to a more or less fine inspired application.

III

BUT I positively dawdle and gape here—I catch myself in the act; so that I take up the thread of fond reflection that guides me through that mystification of the summer school, which I referred to a little way back, at the time when the Summer School as known in America to-day was so deep in the bosom of the future. The seat of acquisition I speak of must have been contiguous to the house we occupied—I recall it as most intimately and objectionably near—and carried on in the interest of those parents from New York who, in villeggiatura under the queer conditions of those days, with the many modern mitigations of the gregarious lot still unrevealed and the many refinements on the individual one still undeveloped, welcomed almost any influence that might help at all to form their children to civility. Yet I remember that particular influence as more noisy and drowsy and dusty than anything else—as to which it must have partaken strongly of the general nature of New Brighton; a neighbourhood that no apt agency whatever had up to that time concerned itself to fashion, and that was indeed to remain shabbily shapeless for years; since I recall almost as dire an impression of it received in the summer of 1875. I seem more or less to have begun life, for that matter, with impressions of New Brighton; there comes back to me another, considerably more infantile than that of 1854, so infantile indeed that I wonder at its having stuck—that of a place called the Pavilion, which must have been an hotel sheltering us for July and August, and the form of which to childish retrospect, unprejudiced by later experience, was that of a great Greek temple shining over blue waters in the splendour of a white colonnade and a great yellow pediment. The elegant image remained, though imprinted in a child so small as to be easily portable by a stout nurse, I remember, and not less easily duckable; I gasp again, and was long to gasp, with the sense of salt immersion received at her strong hands. Wonderful altogether in fact, I find as I write, the quantity, the intensity of picture recoverable from even the blankest and tenderest state of the little canvas.

I connect somehow with the Pavilion period a visit paid with my father—who decidedly must have liked to take me about, I feel so rich in that general reminiscence—to a family whom we reached in what struck me as a quite lovely embowered place, on a very hot day, and among whom luxuries and eccentricities flourished together. They were numerous, the members of this family, they were beautiful, they partook of their meals, or were at the moment partaking of one, out of doors, and the then pre-eminent figure in the group was a very big Newfoundland dog on whose back I was put to ride. That must have been my first vision of the liberal life—though I further ask myself what my age could possibly have been when my weight was so fantastically far from hinting at later developments. But the romance of the hour was particularly in what I have called the eccentric note, the fact that the children, my entertainers, riveted my gaze to stockingless and shoeless legs and feet, conveying somehow at the same time that they were not poor and destitute but rich and provided—just as I took their garden-feast for a sign of overflowing food—and that their state as of children of nature was a refinement of freedom and grace. They were to become great and beautiful, the household of that glimmering vision, they were to figure historically, heroically, and serve great public ends; but always, to my remembering eyes and fond fancy, they were to move through life as with the bare white feet of that original preferred fairness and wildness. This is rank embroidery, but the old surface itself insists on spreading—it waits at least with an air of its own. The rest is silence; I can—extraordinary encumbrance even for the most doating of parents on a morning call—but have returned with my father to "our hotel"; since I feel that I must not only to this but to a still further extent face the historic truth that we were for considerable periods, during our earliest time, nothing less than hotel children. Between the far-off and the later phases at New Brighton stretched a series of summers that had seen us all regularly installed for a couple of months at an establishment passing in the view of that simpler age for a vast caravansery—the Hamilton House, on the south Long Island shore, so called from its nearness to the Fort of that name, which had Fort Lafayette, the Bastille of the Civil War, out in the channel before it and which probably cast a stronger spell upon the spirit of our childhood, William's and mine at least, than any scene presented to us up to our reaching our teens.

I find that I draw from the singularly unobliterated memory of the particulars of all that experience the power quite to glory in our shame; of so entrancing an interest did I feel it at the time to *be* an hotel child, and so little would I have exchanged my lot with that of any small person more privately bred. We were private enough in all conscience, I think I must have felt, the rest of the year; and at what age mustn't I quite have succumbed to the charm of the world seen in a larger way? For there, incomparably, was the chance to dawdle and gape; there were human appearances in endless variety and on the exhibition-stage of a piazza that my gape measured almost as by miles; it was even as if I had become positively conscious that the social scene so peopled would pretty well always say more to me than anything else. What it did say I of course but scantly understood; but I none the less knew it spoke, and I listened to its voice, I seem to recall, very much as "young Edwin," in Dr. Beattie's poem, listened to the roar of tempests and torrents from the nobler eminence of beetling crags and in exposure to still deeper abysses. I cling for the moment, however, to the small story of our Vredenburg summer, as we were for long afterwards invidiously to brand it; the more that it so plays its part in illustration, under the light of a later and happier age, of the growth, when not rather of the arrest, of manners and customs roundabout our birthplace. I think we had never been so much as during these particular months disinherited of the general and public amenities that reinforce for the young private precept and example—disinherited in favour of dust and glare and mosquitoes and pigs and shanties and rumshops, of no walks and scarce more drives, of a repeated no less than of a strong emphasis on the more sordid sides of the Irish aspect in things. There was a castellated residence on the hill above us—very high I remember supposing the hill and very stately the structure; it had towers and views and pretensions and belonged to a Colonel, whom we thought very handsome and very costumed, (as if befrogged and high-booted, which he couldn't have been at all, only *ought* to have been, would even certainly have been at a higher pitch of social effect,) and whose son and heir, also very handsome and known familiarly and endearingly as Chick, had a velvet coat and a pony and I think spurs, all luxuries we were without, and was cousin to boys, the De Coppets, whom we had come to know at our school of the previous winter and who somehow —doubtless partly as guests of the opulent Chick—hovered again about the field of idleness.

The De Coppets, particularly in the person of the first-born Louis, had been a value to us, or at any rate to me—for though I was, in common with my elders then, unacquainted with the application of that word as I use it here, what was my incipient sense of persons and things, what were my first stirred observant and imaginative reactions, discriminations and categories, but a vague groping for it? The De Coppets (again as more especially and most impressively interpreted by the subtle Louis) enjoyed the pre-eminence of being European; they had dropped during the scholastic term of 1853–4 straight from the lake of Geneva into the very bosom of Mr. Richard Pulling Jenks's select resort for young gentlemen, then situated in Broadway below Fourth Street; and had lately been present at an historic pageant—whether or no celebrating the annals of the town of Coppet I know not—in which representatives of their family had figured in armour and on horseback as the Barons (to our comprehension) de Coup or Cou. Their father was thus of the Canton de Vaud—only their mother had been native among ourselves and sister to the Colonel of the castellations. But what was the most vivid mark of the brothers, and vividest on the part of the supersubtle Louis, was his French treatment of certain of our native local names, Ohio and Iowa for instance, which he rendered, as to their separate vowels, with a daintiness and a delicacy invidious and imperturbable, so that he might have been Chateaubriand declaiming Les Natchez at Madame Récamier's—O-ee-oh and Ee-o-wah; a proceeding in him, a violence offered to his serried circle of little staring and glaring New Yorkers supplied with the usual allowance of fists and boot-toes, which, as it was clearly conscious, I recollect thinking unsurpassed for cool calm courage. Those *were* the right names—which we owed wholly to the French explorers and Jesuit Fathers; so much the worse for us if we vulgarly didn't know it. I lose myself in admiration of the consistency, the superiority, the sublimity, of the not at all game-playing, yet in his own way so singularly sporting, Louis. He was naturally and incorruptibly French—as, so oddly, I have known other persons of both sexes to be whose English was naturally and incorruptibly American; the appearance being thus that the possession of indigenous English alone forms the adequate barrier and the assured racial ground. (Oh the queer reversions observed on the part of Latinized compatriots in the course of a long life—the remarkable drops from the quite current French or Italian to the comparatively improvised native idiom, with the resulting effect of the foreign tongue used as a domestic and the domestic, that is the original American, used as a foreign tongue, or without inherited confidence!)

Louis De Coppet, though theoretically American and domiciled, was *naturally* French, and so pressed further home to me that "sense of Europe" to which I feel that my very earliest consciousness waked—a perversity that will doubtless appear to ask for all the justification I can supply and some of which I shall presently attempt to give. He opened vistas, and I count ever as precious anyone, everyone, who betimes does that for the small straining vision; performing this office never so much, doubtless, as when, during that summer, he invited me to collaborate with him in the production of a romance which *il se fit fort* to get printed, to get published, when success, or in other words completion, should crown our effort. Our effort, alas, failed of the crown, in spite of sundry solemn and mysterious meetings—so much devoted, I seem to remember, to the publishing question that others more fundamental dreadfully languished; leaving me convinced, however, that my friend *would* have got our fiction published if he could only have got it written. I think of my participation in this vain dream as of the very first gage of visiting approval offered to the exercise of a gift—though quite unable to conceive my companion's ground for suspecting a gift of which I must at that time quite have failed to exhibit a single in the least "phenomenal" symptom. It had none the less by his overtures been handsomely *imputed* to me; that was in a manner a beginning—a small start, yet not wholly unattended with bravery. Louis De Coppet, I must add, brought to light later on, so far as I know, no compositions of his own; we met him long after in Switzerland and eventually heard of his having married a young Russian lady and settled at Nice. If I drop on his memory this apology for a bay-leaf it is from the fact of his having given the earliest, or at least the most personal, tap to that pointed prefigurement of the manners of "Europe," which, inserted wedge-like, if not to say peg-like, into my young allegiance, was to split the tender organ into such unequal halves. His the toy hammer that drove in the very point of the golden nail.

It was as if there had been a mild magic in that breath, however scant, of another world; but when I ask myself what element of the pleasing or the agreeable may have glimmered through the then general, the outer and enveloping conditions, I recover many more of the connections in which forms and civilities lapsed beyond repair than of those in which they struggled at all successfully. It is for some record of the question of taste, of the consciousness of an æsthetic appeal, as reflected in forms and aspects, that I shall like best to testify; as the promise and the development of these things on our earlier American scene are the more interesting to trace for their doubtless demanding a degree of the finer attention. The plain and happy profusions and advances and successes, as one looks back, reflect themselves at every turn; the quick beats of material increase and multiplication, with plenty of people to tell of them and throw up their caps for them; but the edifying matters to recapture would be the adventures of the "higher criticism" so far as there was any—and so far too as it might bear on the real quality and virtue of things; the state of manners, the terms of intercourse, the care for excellence, the sense of appearances, the intellectual reaction generally. However, any breasting of those deep waters must be but in the form for me of an occasional dip. It meanwhile fairly overtakes and arrests me here as a contributive truth that our general medium of life in the situation I speak of was such as to make a large defensive verandah, which seems to have very stoutly and completely surrounded us, play more or less the part of a raft of rescue in too high a tide—too high a tide there beneath us, as I recover it, of the ugly and the graceless. My particular perspective may magnify a little wildly—when it doesn't even more weirdly diminish; but I read into the great hooded and guarded resource in question an evidential force: as if it must really have played for us, so far as its narrowness and its exposure permitted, the part of a buffer-state against the wilderness immediately near, that of the empty, the unlovely and the mean. Interposing a little ease, didn't it interpose almost all the ease we knew?—so that when amiable friends, arriving from New York by the boat, came to see us, there was no rural view for them but that of our great shame, a view of the pigs and the shanties and the loose planks and scattered refuse and rude public ways; never even a field-path for a gentle walk or a garden nook in afternoon shade. I recall my prompt distaste, a strange precocity of criticism, for so much aridity—since of what lost Arcadia, at that age, had I really had the least glimpse?

Our scant margin must have affected me more nobly, I should in justice add, when old Mrs. L. passed or hovered, for she sometimes caustically joined the circle and sometimes, during the highest temperatures, which were very high that summer, but flitted across it in a single flowing garment, as we amazedly conceived; one of the signs of that grand impertinence, I supposed, which belonged to "dowagers"—dowagers who were recognised characters and free speakers, doing and saying what they liked. This ancient lady was lodged in some outlying tract of the many-roomed house, which in more than one quarter stretched away into mystery; but the piazza, to which she had access, was unbroken, and whenever she strayed from her own territory she swam afresh into ours. I definitely remember that, having heard and perhaps read of dowagers, who, as I was aware, had scarce been provided for in our social scheme, I said to myself at first sight of our emphatic neighbour, a person clearly used to exceptional deference, "This must be a perfect specimen;" which was somehow very wonderful. The absolute first sight, however, had preceded the New Brighton summer, and it makes me lose myself in a queer dim vision, all the obscurities attendant on my having been present, as a very small boy indeed, at an evening entertainment where Mrs. L. figured in an attire that is still vivid to me: a blue satin gown, a long black lace shawl and a head-dress consisting in equally striking parts of a brown wig, a plume of some sort waving over it and a band or fillet, whether of some precious metal or not I forget, keeping it in place by the aid of a precious stone which adorned the centre of her brow. Such was my first view of the *féronnière* of our grandmothers, when not of our greatgrandmothers. I see its wearer at this day bend that burdened brow upon me in a manner sufficiently awful, while her knuckly white gloves toyed with a large fan and a vinaigrette attached to her thumb by a chain; and as she was known to us afterwards for a friend of my Albany grandmother's it may have been as a tribute to this tie that she allowed me momentarily to engage her attention. *Then* it predominantly must have been that I knew her for a dowager—though this was a light in which I had never considered my grandmother herself; but what I have quite lost the clue to is the question of my extraordinary footing in such an assembly, the occasion of a dance of my elders, youthful elders but young married people, into which, really, my mother, as a participant, must have introduced me.

IV

It took place in the house of our cousins Robert and Kitty Emmet the elder—for we were to have two cousin Kittys of that ilk and yet another consanguineous Robert at least; the latter name being naturally, among them all, of a pious, indeed of a glorious, tradition, and three of my father's nieces marrying three Emmet brothers, the first of these the Robert aforesaid. Catherine James, daughter of my uncle Augustus, his then quite recent and, as I remember her, animated and attractive bride, whose fair hair framed her pointed smile in full and far-drooping "front" curls, I easily evoke as my first apprehended image of the free and happy young woman of fashion, a sign of the wondrous fact that ladies might live for pleasure, pleasure always, pleasure alone. She was distinguished for nothing whatever so much as for an insatiable love of the dance; that passion in which I think of the "good," the best, New York society of the time as having capered and champagned itself away. Her younger sister Gertrude, afterwards married to James—or more inveterately Jim—Pendleton, of Virginia, followed close upon her heels, literally speaking, and though emulating her in other respects too, was to last, through many troubles, much longer (looking extraordinarily the while like the younger portraits of Queen Victoria) and to have much hospitality, showing it, and showing everything, in a singularly natural way, for a considerable collection of young hobbledehoy kinsmen. But I am solicited a moment longer by the queer little issues involved—as if a social light would somehow stream from them—in my having been taken, a mere mite of observation, to Kitty Emmet's "grown-up" assembly. Was it that my mother really felt that to the scrap that I was other scraps would perhaps strangely adhere, to the extent thus of something to distinguish me by, nothing else probably having as yet declared itself—such a scrap for instance as the fine germ of this actual ferment of memory and play of fancy, a retroactive vision almost intense of the faded hour and a fond surrender to the questions with which it bristles? All the female relatives on my father's side who reappear to me in these evocations strike me as having been intensely and admirably, but at the same time almost indescribably, *natural*; which fact connects itself for the brooding painter and fond analyst with fifty other matters and impressions, his vision of a whole social order—if the American scene might indeed have been said at that time to be positively ordered. Wasn't the fact that the dancing passion was so out of proportion to any social resource just one of the signs of the natural?—and for that matter in both sexes alike of the artless kindred. It was shining to us that Jim Pendleton had a yacht—though I was not smuggled aboard it; there the line was drawn—but the deck must have been more used for the "German" than for other manœuvres, often doubtless under the lead of our cousin Robert, the eldest of the many light irresponsibles to whom my father was uncle: distinct to me still being the image of that phenomenally lean and nimble choreographic hero, "Bob" James to us always, who, almost ghost-fashion, led the cotillion on from generation to generation, his skull-like smile, with its accent from the stiff points of his long moustache and the brightly hollow orbits of his eyes, helping to make of him an immemorial elegant skeleton.

It is at all events to the sound of fiddles and the popping of corks that I see even young brides, as well as young grooms, originally so formed to please and to prosper as our hosts of the restless little occasion I have glanced at, vanish untimely, become mysterious and legendary, with such unfathomed silences and significant headshakes replacing the earlier concert; so that I feel how one's impression of so much foredoomed youthful levity received constant and quite thrilling increase. It was of course an impression then obscurely gathered, but into which one was later on to read strange pages—to some of which I may find myself moved to revert. Mere mite of observation though I have dubbed myself, I won't pretend to have deciphered any of them amid the bacchanal sounds that, on the evening so suggestively spent, floated out into the region of Washington Place. It is round that general centre that my richest memories of the "gay" little life in general cluster—as if it had been, for the circle in which I seem justified in pretending to have "moved," of the finer essence of "town"; covering as it did the stretch of Broadway down to Canal Street, with, closer at hand, the New York Hotel, which figured somehow inordinately in our family annals (the two newer ones, the glory of their brief and discredited, their flouted and demolished age, the brown Metropolitan and the white St. Nicholas, were much further down) and rising northward to the Ultima Thule of Twenty-third Street, only second then in the supposedly ample scheme of the regular ninth "wide" street. I can't indeed have moved much on that night of revelations and yet of enigmas over which I still hang fascinated; I must have kept intensely still in my corner, all wondering and all fearing—fearing notice most; and in a definite way I but remember the formidable interest of my so convincing dowager (to hark back for a second to *her*) and the fact that a great smooth white cloth was spread across the denuded room, converted thus into a field of frolic the prospect of which much excited my curiosity. I but recover the preparations, however, without recovering the performance; Mrs. L. and I must have been the only persons not shaking a foot, and premature unconsciousness clearly in my case supervened. Out of it peeps again the riddle, the so quaint *trait de mœurs*, of my infant participation. But I set that down as representative and interesting, and have done with it.

The manners of the time had obviously a *bonhomie* of their own—certainly so on our particularly indulgent and humane little field; as to which general proposition the later applications and transformations of the bonhomie would be interesting to trace. It has lingered and fermented and earned other names, but I seem on the track of its prime evidence with that note of the sovereign ease of all the young persons with whom we grew up. In the after time, as our view took in, with new climes and new scenes, other examples of the class, these were always to affect us as more formed and finished, more tutored and governessed, warned and armed at more points for, and doubtless often against, the social relation; so that this prepared state on their part, and which at first appeared but a preparation for shyness or silence or whatever other ideal of the unconversable, came to be for us the normal, since it was the relative and not the positive, still less the superlative, state. No charming creatures of the growing girl sort were ever to be natural in the degree of these nearer and remoter ornaments of our family circle in youth; when after intervals and absences the impression was renewed we saw how right we had been about it, and I feel as if we had watched it for years under the apprehension and the vision of some inevitable change, wondering with an affectionate interest what effect the general improvement in manners might, perhaps all unfortunately, have upon it. I make out as I look back that it was really to succumb at no point to this complication, that it was to keep its really quite inimitable freshness to the end, or, in other words, when it had been the first free growth of the old conditions, was to pass away but with the passing of those themselves for whom it had been the sole possible expression. For it was as of an altogether special shade and sort that the New York young naturalness of our prime was touchingly to linger with us—so that to myself, at present, with only the gentle ghosts of the so numerous exemplars of it before me, it becomes the very stuff of the soft cerements in which their general mild mortality is laid away. We used to have in the after-time, amid fresh recognitions and reminders, the kindest "old New York" identifications for it. The special shade of its identity was thus that it was not conscious—really not conscious of anything in the world; or was conscious of so few possibilities at least, and these so immediate and so a matter of course, that it came almost to the same thing. That was the testimony that the slight subjects in question strike me as having borne to their surrounding medium—the fact that their unconsciousness could be so preserved. They played about in it so happily and serenely and sociably, as unembarrassed and loquacious as they were unadmonished and uninformed—only aware at the most that a good many people within their horizon were "dissipated"; as in point of fact, alas, a good many *were*. What it was to be dissipated—that, however, was but in the most limited degree a feature of their vision; they would have held, under pressure, that it consisted more than anything else in getting tipsy.

Infinitely queer and quaint, almost incongruously droll, the sense somehow begotten in ourselves, as very young persons, of our being surrounded by a slightly remote, yet dimly rich, outer and quite kindred circle of the tipsy. I remember how, once, as a very small boy, after meeting in the hall a most amiable and irreproachable gentleman, all but closely consanguineous, who had come to call on my mother, I anticipated his further entrance by slipping in to report to that parent that I thought *he* must be tipsy. And I was to recall perfectly afterwards the impression I so made on her—in which the general proposition that the gentlemen of a certain group or connection might on occasion be best described by the term I had used sought to destroy the particular presumption that our visitor wouldn't, by his ordinary measure, show himself for one of those. He didn't, to all appearance, for I was afterwards disappointed at the lapse of lurid evidence: that memory remained with me, as well as a considerable subsequent wonder at my having leaped to so baseless a view. The truth was indeed that we had too, in the most innocent way in the world, our sense of "dissipation" as an abounding element in family histories; a sense fed quite directly by our fondness for making our father—I can at any rate testify for the urgency of my own appeal to him—tell us stories of the world of his youth. He regaled us with no scandals, yet it somehow rarely failed to come out that each contemporary on his younger scene, each hero of each thrilling adventure, had, in spite of brilliant promise and romantic charm, ended badly, as badly as possible. This became our gaping generalisation—it gaped even under the moral that the anecdote was always, and so familiarly, humanly and vividly, designed to convey: everyone in the little old Albany of the Dutch houses and the steep streets and the recurrent family names—Townsends, Clintons, Van Rensselaers, Pruyns: I pick them up again at hazard, and all uninvidiously, out of reverberations long since still—everyone without exception had at last taken a turn as far as possible from edifying. And what they had most in common, the hovering presences, the fitful apparitions that, speaking for myself, so engaged my imagination, was just the fine old Albany drama—in the light of which a ring of mystery as to their lives (mainly carried on at the New York Hotel aforesaid) surrounded them, and their charm, inveterate, as I believed, shone out as through vaguely-apprehended storm-clouds. Their charm was in various marks of which I shall have more to say—for as I breathe all this hushed air again even the more broken things give out touching human values and faint sweet scents of character, flushes of old beauty and good-will.

The grim little generalisation remained, none the less, and I may speak of it—since I speak of everything—as still standing: the striking evidence that scarce aught but disaster *could*, in that so unformed and unseasoned society, overtake young men who were in the least exposed. Not to have been immediately launched in business of a rigorous sort was to *be* exposed—in the absence I mean of some fairly abnormal predisposition to virtue; since it was a world so simply constituted that whatever wasn't business, or exactly an office or a "store," places in which people sat close and made money, was just simply pleasure, sought, and sought only, in places in which people got tipsy. There was clearly no mean, least of all the golden one, for it was just the ready, even when the moderate, possession of gold that determined, that hurried on, disaster. There were whole sets and groups, there were "sympathetic," though too susceptible, races, that seemed scarce to recognise or to find possible any practical application of moneyed, that is of transmitted, ease, however limited, but to go more or less rapidly to the bad with it—which meant even then going as often as possible to Paris. The bright and empty air was as void of "careers" for a choice as of cathedral towers for a sketcher, and I passed my younger time, till within a year or two of the Civil War, with an absolute vagueness of impression as to how the political life of the country was carried on. The field was strictly covered, to my young eyes, I make out, by three classes, the busy, the tipsy, and Daniel Webster. This last great man must have represented for us a class in himself; as if to be "political" was just to *be* Daniel Webster in his proper person and with room left over for nobody else. That he should have filled the sky of public life from pole to pole, even to a childish consciousness not formed in New England and for which that strenuous section was but a name in the geography-book, is probably indeed a sign of how large, in the general air, he comparatively loomed. The public scene was otherwise a blank to our young vision, I discern, till, later on, in Paris, I saw—for at that unimproved period we of the unfledged didn't suppose ourselves to "meet"—Charles Sumner; with whose name indeed there further connects itself the image of a thrilled hour in the same city some months before: the gathering of a group of indignant persons on the terrace of a small old-world *hôtel* or pavilion looking out on the Avenue des Champs Elysées, slightly above the Rond-Point and just opposite the antediluvian Jardin d'Hiver (who remembers the Jardin d'Hiver, who remembers the ancient lodges of the *octroi*, the pair of them facing each other at the Barrière de l'Étoile?) and among them a passionate lady in tears over the news, fresh that morning, of the assault on Sumner by the South Carolina ruffian of the House. The wounded Senator, injured in health, had come to Europe later on to recuperate, and he offered me my first view, to the best of my belief, not only of a "statesman," but of any person whomsoever concerned in political life. I distinguish in the earlier twilight of Fourteenth Street my father's return to us one November day—we knew he had been out to vote—with the news that General Winfield Scott, his and the then "Whig" candidate, had been defeated for the Presidency; just as I rescue from the same limbo my afterwards proud little impression of having "met" that high-piled hero of the Mexican War, whom the Civil War was so soon and with so little ceremony to extinguish, literally met him, at my father's side, in Fifth Avenue, where he had just emerged from a cross-street. I remain vague as to what had then happened and scarce suppose I was, at the age probably of eight or nine, "presented"; but we must have been for some moments face to face while from under the vast amplitude of a dark blue military cloak with a big velvet collar and loosened silver clasp, which spread about him like a symbol of the tented field, he greeted my parent—so clear is my sense of the time it took me to gape *all* the way up to where he towered aloft.

V

THE NOT very glorious smoke of the Mexican War, I note for another touch, had been in the air when I was a still smaller boy, and I have an association with it that hovers between the definite and the dim, a vision of our uncle (Captain as he then was) Robert Temple, U.S.A., in regimentals, either on his way to the scene of action or on the return from it. I see him as a person half asleep sees some large object across the room and against the window-light—even if to the effect of my now asking myself why, so far from the scene of action, he was in panoply of war. I seem to see him cock-hatted and feathered too—an odd vision of dancing superior plumes which doesn't fit if he was only a captain. However, I cultivate the wavering shade merely for its value as my earliest glimpse of any circumstance of the public order—unless indeed another, the reminiscence to which I owe to-day my sharpest sense of personal antiquity, had already given me the historic thrill. The scene of this latter stir of consciousness is, for memory, an apartment in one of the three Fifth Avenue houses that were not long afterward swallowed up in the present Brevoort Hotel, and consists of the admired appearance of my uncles "Gus" and John James to announce to my father that the Revolution had triumphed in Paris and Louis Philippe had fled to England. These last words, the flight of the king, linger on my ear at this hour even as they fell there; we had somehow waked early to a perception of Paris, and a vibration of my very most infantine sensibility under its sky had by the same stroke got itself preserved for subsequent wondering reference. I had been there for a short time in the second year of my life, and I was to communicate to my parents later on that as a baby in long clothes, seated opposite to them in a carriage and on the lap of another person, I had been impressed with the view, framed by the clear window of the vehicle as we passed, of a great stately square surrounded with high-roofed houses and having in its centre a tall and glorious column. I had naturally caused them to marvel, but I had also, under cross-questioning, forced them to compare notes, as it were, and reconstitute the miracle. They knew what my observation of monumental squares had been—and alas hadn't; neither New York nor Albany could have offered me the splendid perspective, and, for that matter, neither could London, which moreover I had known at a younger age still. Conveyed along the Rue St.-Honoré while I waggled my small feet, as I definitely remember doing, under my flowing robe, I had crossed the Rue de Castiglione and taken in, for all my time, the admirable aspect of the Place and the Colonne Vendôme. I don't now pretend to measure the extent to which my interest in the events of 1848—I was five years old—was quickened by that *souvenir*, a tradition further reinforced, I should add, by the fact that some relative or other, some member of our circle, was always either "there" ("there" being of course generally Europe, but particularly and pointedly Paris) or going there or coming back from there: I at any rate revert to the sound of the rich words on my uncles' lips as to my positive initiation into History. It was as if I had been ready for them and could catch on; I had heard of kings presumably, and also of fleeing: but that kings had sometimes to flee was a new and striking image, to which the apparent consternation of my elders added dramatic force. So much, in any case, for what I may claim—perhaps too idly—on behalf of my backward reach.

It has carried me far from my rather evident proposition that if we saw the "natural" so happily embodied about us—and in female maturity, or comparative maturity, scarce less than in female adolescence—this was because the artificial, or in other words the complicated, was so little there to threaten it. The complicated, as we were later on to define it, was but another name for those more massed and violent assaults upon the social sense that we were to recognise subsequently by their effects—observing thus that a sense more subtly social had so been created, and that it quite differed from that often almost complete inward blankness, in respect to any circumjacent, any constituted, order to the exhibition of which our earlier air and our family scene had inimitably treated us. We came more or less to see that our young contemporaries of another world, the trained and admonished, the disciplined and governessed, or in a word the formed, relatively speaking, had been made aware of many things of which those at home hadn't been; yet we were also to note—so far as we may be conceived as so precociously "noting," though we were certainly incorrigible observers—that, the awareness in question remaining at the best imperfect, our little friends as distinguished from our companions of the cousinship, greater and less, advanced and presumed but to flounder and recede, elated at once and abashed and on the whole but *feebly* sophisticated. The cousinship, on the other hand, all unalarmed and unsuspecting and unembarrassed, lived by pure serenity, sociability and loquacity; the oddest fact about its members being withal that it didn't make them bores, I seem to feel as I look back, or at least not worse bores than sundry specimens of the other growth. There can surely never have been anything like their good faith and, generally speaking, their amiability. I should have but to let myself go a little to wish to cite examples—save that in doing so I should lose sight of my point; which is to recall again that whether we were all amiable or not (and, frankly, I claim it in a high degree for most of us) the scene on which we so freely bloomed does strike me, when I reckon up, as extraordinarily unfurnished. How came it then that for the most part so simple we yet weren't more inane? This was doubtless by reason of the quantity of our inward life—ours of our father's house in especial I mean—which made an excellent, in some cases almost an incomparable, *fond* for a thicker civility to mix with when growing experience should begin to take that in. It was also quaint, among us, I may be reminded, to have *begun* with the inward life; but we began, after the manner of all men, as we could, and I hold that if it comes to that we might have begun much worse.

I was in my seventeenth year when the raid and the capture of John Brown, of Harper's Ferry fame, enjoyed its sharp reverberation among us, though we were then on the other side of the world; and I count this as the very first reminder that reached me of our living, on our side, in a political order: I had perfectly taken in from the pages of "Punch," which contributed in the highest degree to our education, that the peoples on the other side so lived. As there was no American "Punch," and to this time has been none, to give small boys the sense and the imagination of living with their public administrators, Daniel Webster and Charles Sumner had never become, for my fancy, members of a class, a class which numbered in England, by John Leech's showing, so many other members still than Lords Brougham, Palmerston and John Russell. The war of Secession, soon arriving, was to cause the field to bristle with features and the sense of the State, in our generation, infinitely to quicken; but that alarm came upon the country like a thief at night, and we might all have been living in a land in which there seemed at least nothing save a comparatively small amount of quite private property to steal. Even private property in other than the most modest amounts scarce figured for our particular selves; which doubtless came partly from the fact that amid all the Albany issue there was ease, with the habit of ease, thanks to our grandfather's fine old ability—he had decently provided for so large a generation; but our consciousness was positively disfurnished, as that of young Americans went, of the actualities of "business" in a world of business. As to that we all formed together quite a monstrous exception; business in a world of business was the thing we most agreed (differ as we might on minor issues) in knowing nothing about. We touched it and it touched us neither directly nor otherwise, and I think our fond detachment, not to say our helpless ignorance and on occasion (since I can speak for one fine instance) our settled density of understanding, made us an unexampled and probably, for the ironic "smart" gods of the American heaven, a lamentable case. Of course even the office and the "store" leave much of the provision for an approximately complete scheme of manners to be accounted for; still there must have been vast numbers of people about us for whom, under the usages, the assault on the imagination from without was much stronger and the filling-in of the general picture much richer. It was exactly by the lack of that filling-in that we—we more especially who lived at near view of my father's admirable example—had been thrown so upon the inward life. No one could ever have taken to it, even in the face of discouragement, more kindly and naturally than he; but the situation had at least that charm that, in default of so many kinds of the outward, people had their choice of as many kinds of the inward as they would, and might practise those kinds with whatever consistency, intensity and brilliancy. Of our father's perfect gift for practising *his* kind I shall have more to say; but I meanwhile glance yet again at those felicities of destitution which kept us, collectively, so genially interested in almost nothing but each other and which come over me now as one of the famous blessings in disguise.

There were "artists" in the prospect—didn't Mr. Tom Hicks and Mr. Paul Duggan and Mr. C. P. Cranch and Mr. Felix Darley, this last worthy of a wider reputation, capable perhaps even of a finer development, than he attained, more or less haunt our friendly fireside, and give us also the sense of others, landscapist Cropseys and Coles and Kensetts, and bust-producing Iveses and Powerses and Moziers, hovering in an outer circle? There were authors not less, some of them vague and female and in this case, as a rule, glossily ringletted and monumentally breastpinned, but mostly frequent and familiar, after the manner of George Curtis and Parke Godwin and George Ripley and Charles Dana and N. P. Willis and, for brighter lights or those that in our then comparative obscurity almost deceived the morn, Mr. Bryant, Washington Irving and E. A. Poe—the last-named of whom I cite not so much because he was personally present (the extremity of personal absence had just overtaken him) as by reason of that predominant lustre in him which our small opening minds themselves already recognised and which makes me wonder to-day at the legend of the native neglect of him. Was he not even at that time on all lips, had not my brother, promptly master of the subject, beckoned on my lagging mind with a recital of The Gold-Bug and The Pit and the Pendulum?—both of which, however, I was soon enough to read for myself, adding to them The Murders in the Rue Morgue. Were we not also forever mounting on little platforms at our infant schools to "speak" The Raven and Lenore and the verses in which we phrased the heroine as Annabell*ee*?—falling thus into the trap the poet had so recklessly laid for us, as he had laid one for our interminable droning, not less, in the other pieces I have named. So far from misprizing our ill-starred magician we acclaimed him surely at every turn; he lay upon our tables and resounded in our mouths, while we communed to satiety, even for boyish appetites, over the thrill of his choicest pages. Don't I just recognise the ghost of a dim memory of a children's Christmas party at the house of Fourteenth Street neighbours—they come back to me as "the Beans": who and what and whence and whither the kindly Beans?—where I admired over the chimneypiece the full-length portrait of a lady seated on the ground in a Turkish dress, with hair flowing loose from a cap which was not as the caps of ladies known to me, and I think with a tambourine, who was somehow identified to my enquiring mind as the wife of the painter of the piece, Mr. Osgood, and the so ministering friend of the unhappy Mr. Poe. There she throned in honour, like Queen Constance on the "huge firm earth"—all for *that* and her tambourine; and surely we could none of us have done more for the connection.

Washington Irving I "met," with infant promptitude, very much as I had met General Scott; only this time it was on a steamboat that I apprehended the great man; my father, under whose ever-patient protection I then was—during the summer afternoon's sail from New York to Fort Hamilton—having named him to me, for this long preservation, before they greeted and talked, and having a fact of still more moment to mention, with the greatest concern, afterwards: Mr. Irving had given him the news of the shipwreck of Margaret Fuller in those very waters (Fire Island at least was but just without our big Bay) during the great August storm that had within the day or two passed over us. The unfortunate lady was essentially of the Boston connection; but she must have been, and probably through Emerson, a friend of my parents—mustn't she have held "conversations," in the finest exotic Bostonese, in New York, Emerson himself lecturing there to admiration?—since the more I squeeze the sponge of memory the more its stored secretions flow, to remind me here again that, being with those elders late one evening at an exhibition of pictures, possibly that of the National Academy, then confined to scant quarters, I was shown a small full-length portrait of Miss Fuller, seated as now appears to me and wrapped in a long white shawl, the failure of which to do justice to its original my companions denounced with some emphasis. Was this work from the hand of Mr. Tom Hicks aforesaid, or was that artist concerned only with the life-sized, the enormous (as I took it to be) the full-length, the violently protruded accessories in which come back to me with my infant sense of the wonder and the beauty of them, as expressed above all in the image of a very long and lovely lady, the new bride of the artist, standing at a window before a row of plants or bulbs in tall coloured glasses. The light of the window playing over the figure and the "treatment" of its glass and of the flower-pots and the other furniture, passed, by my impression, for the sign of the master hand; and *was* it all brave and charming, or was it only very hard and stiff, quite ugly and helpless? I put these questions as to a vanished world and by way of pressing back into it only the more clingingly and tenderly—wholly regardless in other words of whether the answers to them at all matter. They matter doubtless but for fond evocation, and if one tries to evoke one must neglect none of the arts, one must do it with all the forms. Why I *should* so like to do it is another matter—and what "outside interest" I may suppose myself to create perhaps still another: I fatuously proceed at any rate, I make so far as I can the small warm dusky homogeneous New York world of the mid-century close about us.

VI

I SEE a small and compact and ingenuous society, screened in somehow conveniently from north and west, but open wide to the east and comparatively to the south and, though perpetually moving up Broadway, none the less constantly and delightfully walking down it. Broadway was the feature and the artery, the joy and the adventure of one's childhood, and it stretched, and prodigiously, from Union Square to Barnum's great American Museum by the City Hall—or only went further on the Saturday mornings (absurdly and deplorably frequent alas) when we were swept off by a loving aunt, our mother's only sister, then much domesticated with us and to whom the ruthless care had assigned itself from the first, to Wall Street and the torture chamber of Dr. Parkhurst, our tremendously respectable dentist, who was so old and so empurpled and so polite, in his stock and dress-coat and dark and glossy wig, that he had been our mother's and our aunt's haunting fear in *their* youth as well, since, in their quiet Warren Street, not far off, they were, dreadful to think, comparatively under his thumb. He extremely resembles, to my mind's eye, certain figures in Phiz's illustrations to Dickens, and it was clear to us through our long ordeal that our elders must, by some mistaken law of compensation, some refinement of the vindictive, be making us "pay" for what they in like helplessness had suffered from him: as if *we* had done them any harm! Our analysis was muddled, yet in a manner relieving, and for us too there were compensations, which we grudged indeed to allow, but which I could easily, even if shyly, have named. One of these was Godey's Lady's Book, a sallow pile of which (it shows to me for sallow in the warmer and less stony light of the Wall Street of those days and through the smell of ancient anodynes) lay on Joey Bagstock's table for our beguilement while we waited: I was to encounter in Phiz's Dombey and Son that design for our tormentor's type. There is no doubt whatever that I succumbed to the spell of Godey, who, unlike the present essences, was an anodyne before the fact as well as after; since I remember poring, in his pages, over tales of fashionable life in Philadelphia while awaiting my turn in the chair, not less than doing so when my turn was over and to the music of my brother's groans. This must have been at the hours when we were left discreetly to our own fortitude, through our aunt's availing herself of the relative proximity to go and shop at Stewart's and then come back for us; the ladies' great shop, vast, marmorean, plate-glassy and notoriously fatal to the female nerve (we ourselves had wearily trailed through it, hanging on the skirts, very literally, of indecision) which bravely waylaid custom on the Broadway corner of Chambers Street. Wasn't part of the charm of life—since I assume that there *was* such a charm—in its being then (I allude to life itself) so much more down-towny, on the supposition at least that our young gravitation in that sense for most of the larger joys consorted with something of the general habit? The joy that had to be fished out, like Truth, from the very bottom of the well was attendance at Trinity Church, still in that age supereminent, pointedly absolute, the finest feature of the southward scene; to the privilege of which the elder Albany cousins were apt to be treated when they came on to stay with us; an indulgence making their enjoyment of our city as down-towny as possible too, for I seem otherwise to see them but as returning with the familiar Stewart headache from the prolonged strain of selection.

The great reward dispensed to us for our sessions in the house of pain—as to which it became our subsequent theory that we had been regularly dragged there on alternate Saturdays—was our being carried on the return to the house of delight, or to one of them, for there were specifically two, where we partook of ice-cream, deemed sovereign for sore mouths, deemed sovereign in fact, all through our infancy, for everything. Two great establishments for the service of it graced the prospect, one Thompson's and the other Taylor's, the former, I perfectly recall, grave and immemorial, the latter upstart but dazzling, and having together the effect that whichever we went to we wondered if we hadn't better have gone to the other—with that capacity of childhood for making the most of its adventures after a fashion that may look so like making the least. It is in our father's company indeed that, as I press the responsive spring, I see the bedizened saucers heaped up for our fond consumption (they bore the Taylor-title painted in blue and gilded, with the Christian name, as parentally pointed out to us, perverted to "Jhon" for John, whereas the Thompson-name scorned such vulgar and above all such misspelt appeals;) whence I infer that still other occasions for that experience waited on us—as almost any would serve, and a paternal presence so associated with them was not in the least conceivable in the Wall Street *repaire.* That presence is in fact not associated for me, to any effect of distinctness, with the least of our suffered shocks or penalties—though partly doubtless because our acquaintance with such was of the most limited; a conclusion I form even while judging it to have been on the whole sufficient for our virtue. This sounds perhaps as if we had borne ourselves as prodigies or prigs—which was as far as possible from being the case; we were bred in horror of *conscious* propriety, of what my father was fond of calling "flagrant" morality; what I myself at any rate read back into our rare educational ease, for the memory of some sides of which I was ever to be thankful, is, besides the *general* humanisation of our apprehended world and our "social" tone, the unmistakeable appearance that my father was again and again accompanied in public by his small second son: so many young impressions come back to me as gathered at his side and in his personal haunts. Not that he mustn't have offered his firstborn at least equal opportunities; but I make out that he seldom led us forth, such as we were, together, and my brother must have had in *his* turn many a mild adventure of which the secret—I like to put it so—perished with him. He was to remember, as I perceived later on, many things that I didn't, impressions I sometimes wished, as with a retracing jealousy, or at least envy, that I might also have fallen direct heir to; but he professed amazement, and even occasionally impatience, at my reach of reminiscence—liking as he did to brush away old moral scraps in favour of new rather than to hoard and so complacently exhibit them. If in my way I collected the new as well I yet cherished the old; the ragbag of memory hung on its nail in my closet, though I learnt with time to control the habit of bringing it forth. And I say that with a due sense of my doubtless now appearing to empty it into these pages.

I keep picking out at hazard those passages of our earliest

age that help to reconstruct for me even by tiny touches the experience of our parents, any shade of which seems somehow to signify. I cherish, to the extent of here reproducing, an old daguerreotype all the circumstances of the taking of which I intensely recall—though as I was lately turned twelve when I figured for it the feat of memory is perhaps not remarkable. It documents for me in so welcome and so definite a manner my father's cultivation of my company. It documents at the same time the absurdest little legend of my small boyhood—the romantic tradition of the value of being taken up from wherever we were staying to the queer empty dusty smelly New York of midsummer: I apply that last term because we always arrived by boat and I have still in my nostril the sense of the *abords* of the hot town, the rank and rubbishy waterside quarters, where big loose cobbles, for the least of all the base items, lay wrenched from their sockets of pungent black mud and where the dependent streets managed by a law of their own to be all corners and the corners to be all groceries; groceries indeed largely of the "green" order, so far as greenness could persist in the torrid air, and that bristled, in glorious defiance of traffic, with the overflow of their wares and implements. Carts and barrows and boxes and baskets, sprawling or stacked, familiarly elbowed in its course the bumping hack (the comprehensive "carriage" of other days, the only vehicle of hire then known to us) while the situation was accepted by the loose citizen in the garb of a freeman save for the brass star on his breast—and the New York garb of the period was, as I remember it, an immense attestation of liberty. Why the throb of romance should have beat time for me to such visions I can scarce explain, or can explain only by the fact that the squalor was a squalor wonderfully mixed and seasoned, and that I should wrong the whole impression if I didn't figure it first and foremost as that of some vast succulent cornucopia. What did the stacked boxes and baskets of our youth represent but the boundless fruitage of that more bucolic age of the American world, and what was after all of so strong an assault as the rankness of such a harvest? Where is that fruitage now, where in particular are the peaches *d'antan*? where the mounds of Isabella grapes and Seckel pears in the sticky sweetness of which our childhood seems to have been steeped? It was surely, save perhaps for oranges, a more informally and familiarly fruit-eating time, and bushels of peaches in particular, peaches big and peaches small, peaches white and peaches yellow, played a part in life from which they have somehow been deposed; every garden, almost every bush and the very boys' pockets grew them; they were "cut up" and eaten with cream at every meal; domestically "brandied" they figured, the rest of the year, scarce less freely—if they were rather a "party dish" it was because they made the party whenever they appeared, and when ice-cream was added, or they were added *to* it, they formed the highest revel we knew. Above all the public heaps of them, the high-piled receptacles at every turn, touched the street as with a sort of southern plenty; the note of the rejected and scattered fragments, the memory of the slippery skins and rinds and kernels with which the old dislocated flags were bestrown, is itself endeared to me and contributes a further pictorial grace. We ate everything in those days by the bushel and the barrel, as from stores that were infinite; we handled water-melons as freely as cocoanuts, and the amount of stomach-ache involved was negligible in the general Eden-like consciousness.

The glow of this consciousness even in so small an organism was part of the charm of these retreats offered me cityward upon our base of provisions; a part of the rest of which, I disengage, was in my fond perception of that almost eccentrically home-loving habit in my father which furnished us with half the household humour of our childhood—besides furnishing *him* with any quantity of extravagant picture of his so prompt pangs of anguish in absence for celebration of his precipitate returns. It was traditional for us later on, and especially on the European scene, that for him to leave us in pursuit of some advantage or convenience, some improvement of our condition, some enlargement of our view, was for him breathlessly to reappear, after the shortest possible interval, with no account at all to give of the benefit aimed at, but instead of this a moving representation, a far richer recital, of his spiritual adventures at the horrid inhuman inns and amid the hard alien races which had stayed his advance. He reacted, he rebounded, in favour of his fireside, from whatever brief explorations or curiosities; these passionate spontaneities were the pulse of his life and quite some of the principal events of ours; and, as he was nothing if not expressive, whatever happened to him for inward intensity happened abundantly to us for pity and terror, as it were, as well as for an ease and a quality of amusement among ourselves that was really always to fail us among others. Comparatively late in life, after his death, I had occasion to visit, in lieu of my brother, then in Europe, an American city in which he had had, since his own father's death, interests that were of importance to us all. On my asking the agent in charge when the owner had last taken personal cognisance of his property that gentleman replied only half to my surprise that he had never in all his years of possession performed such an act. Then it was perhaps that I most took the measure of his fine faith in human confidence as an administrative function. He had to have a *relation*, somehow expressed—and as he was the vividest and happiest of letter-writers it rarely failed of coming; but once it was established it served him, in every case, much better than fussy challenges, which had always the drawback of involving lapses and inattentions in regard to solicitudes more pressing. He incurably took for granted—incurably because whenever he did so the process succeeded; with which association, however, I perhaps overdrench my complacent vision of our summer snatches at town. Through a grave accident in early life country walks on rough roads were, in spite of his great constitutional soundness, tedious and charmless to him; he liked on the other hand the peopled pavement, the thought of which made him restless when away. Hence the fidelities and sociabilities, however superficial, that he couldn't *not* reaffirm—if he could only reaffirm the others, the really intimate and still more communicable, soon enough afterwards.

It was these of the improvised and casual sort that I shared with him thus indelibly; for truly if we took the boat to town to do things I did them quite as much as he, and so that a little boy could scarce have done them more. My part may indeed but have been to surround his part with a thick imaginative aura; but that constituted for me an activity than which I could dream of none braver or wilder. We went to the office of The New York Tribune—my father's relations with that journal were actual and close; and that was a wonderful world indeed, with strange steepnesses and machineries and noises and hurrying bare-armed, bright-eyed men, and amid the agitation clever, easy, kindly, jocular, partly undressed gentlemen (it was always July or August) some of whom I knew at home, taking it all as if it were the most natural place in the world. It was big to me, big to me with the breath of great vague connections, and I supposed the gentlemen very old, though since aware that they must have been, for the connections, remarkably young; and the conversation of one of them, the one I saw oftenest up town, who attained to great local and to considerable national eminence afterwards, and who talked often and thrillingly about the theatres, I retain as many bright fragments of as if I had been another little Boswell. It was as if he had dropped into my mind the germ of certain interests that were long afterwards to flower—as for instance on his announcing the receipt from Paris of news of the appearance at the Théâtre Français of an actress, Madame Judith, who was formidably to compete with her coreligionary Rachel and to endanger that artist's laurels. Why should Madame Judith's name have stuck to me through all the years, since I was never to see her and she is as forgotten as Rachel is remembered? Why should that scrap of gossip have made a date for my consciousness, turning it to the Comédie with an intensity that was long afterwards to culminate? Why was it equally to abide for me that the same gentleman had on one of these occasions mentioned his having just come back from a wonderful city of the West, Chicago, which, though but a year or two old, with plank sidewalks when there were any, and holes and humps where there were none, and shanties where there were not big blocks, and everything where there had yesterday been nothing, had already developed a huge energy and curiosity, and also an appetite for lectures? I became aware of the Comédie, I became aware of Chicago; I also became aware that even the most alluring fiction was not always for little boys to read. It was mentioned at the Tribune office that one of its reporters, Mr. Solon Robinson, had put forth a novel rather oddly entitled "Hot Corn" and more or less having for its subject the career of a little girl who hawked that familiar American luxury in the streets. The volume, I think, was put into my father's hand, and I recall my prompt desire to make acquaintance with it no less than the remark, as promptly addressed to my companion, that the work, however engaging, was not one that should be left accessible to an innocent child. The pang occasioned by this warning has scarcely yet died out for me, nor my sense of my first wonder at the discrimination—so great became from that moment the mystery of the tabooed book, of whatever identity; the question, in my breast, of why, if it was to be so right for others, it was only to be wrong for me. I remember the soreness of the thought that it was I rather who was wrong for the book—which was somehow humiliating: in that amount of discredit one couldn't but be involved. Neither then nor afterwards was the secret of "Hot Corn" revealed to me, and the sense of privation was to be more prolonged, I fear, than the vogue of the tale, which even as a success of scandal couldn't have been great.

VII

DIMLY QUEER and "pathetic" to me were to remain through much of the after time indeed most of those early indigenous vogues and literary flurries: so few of those that brushed by my childhood had been other than a tinkling that suddenly stopped. I am afraid I mean that what was touching was rather the fact that the tinkle *could* penetrate than the fact that it died away; the light of criticism might have beat so straight—if the sense of proportion and the fact of compassion hadn't waved it away—on the æsthetic phase during which the appeal was mainly *by* the tinkle. The Scarlet Letter and The Seven Gables had the deep tone as much as one would; but of the current efforts of the imagination they were alone in having it till Walt Whitman broke out in the later fifties—and I was to know nothing of that happy genius till long after. An absorbed perusal of The Lamplighter was what I was to achieve at the fleeting hour I continue to circle round; that romance was on every one's lips, and I recollect it as more or less thrust upon me in amends for the imposed sacrifice of a ranker actuality—that of the improper Mr. Robinson, I mean, as to whom there revives in me the main question of where his impropriety, in so general a platitude of the bourgeois, could possibly have dwelt. It was to be true indeed that Walt Whitman achieved an impropriety of the first magnitude; that success, however, but showed us the platitude returning in a genial rage upon itself and getting out of control by generic excess. There was no rage at any rate in The Lamplighter, over which I fondly hung and which would have been my first "grown-up" novel—it had been soothingly offered me for that—had I consented to take it as really and truly grown-up. I couldn't have said what it lacked for the character, I only had my secret reserves, and when one blest afternoon on the New Brighton boat I waded into The Initials I saw how right I had been. The Initials *was* grown-up and the difference thereby exquisite; it came over me with the very first page, assimilated in the fluttered little cabin to which I had retired with it—all in spite of the fact too that my attention was distracted by a pair of remarkable little girls who lurked there out of more public view as to hint that they weren't to be seen for nothing.

That must have been a rich hour, for I mix the marvel of the Boon Children, strange pale little flowers of the American theatre, with my conscious joy in bringing back to my mother, from our forage in New York, a gift of such happy promise as the history of the long-legged Mr. Hamilton and his two Bavarian beauties, the elder of whom, Hildegarde, was to figure for our small generation as the very type of the haughty as distinguished from the forward heroine (since I think our categories really came to no more than those). I couldn't have got very far with Hildegarde in moments so scant, but I memorably felt that romance was thick round me—everything, at such a crisis, seeming to make for it at once. The Boon Children, conveyed thus to New Brighton under care of a lady in whose aspect the strain of the resolute triumphed over the note of the battered, though the showy in it rather succumbed at the same time to the dowdy, were already "billed," as infant phenomena, for a performance that night at the Pavilion, where our attendance, it was a shock to feel, couldn't be promised; and in gazing without charge at the pair of weary and sleepy little mountebanks I found the histrionic character and the dramatic profession for the first time revealed to me. They filled me with fascination and yet with fear; they expressed a melancholy grace and a sort of peevish refinement, yet seemed awfully detached and indifferent, indifferent perhaps even to being pinched and slapped, for art's sake, at home; they honoured me with no notice whatever and regarded me doubtless as no better than one of the little louts peeping through the tent of the show. In return I judged their appearance dissipated though fascinating, and sought consolation for the memory of their scorn and the loss of their exhibition, as time went on, in noting that the bounds of their fame seemed somehow to have been stayed. I neither "met" them nor heard of them again. The little Batemans must have obscured their comparatively dim lustre, flourishing at the same period and with a larger command of the pictorial poster and the other primitive symbols in Broadway—such posters and such symbols as they were at that time!—the little Batemans who were to be reserved, in maturer form, for my much later and more grateful appreciation.

This weak reminiscence has obstructed, however, something more to the purpose, the retained impression of those choicest of our loiterings that took place, still far down-town, at the Bookstore, home of delights and haunt of fancy. It was at the Bookstore we had called on the day of The Initials and the Boon Children —and it was thence we were returning with our spoil, of which the charming novel must have been but a fragment. My impression composed itself of many pieces; a great and various practice of burying my nose in the half-open book for the strong smell of paper and printer's ink, known to us as the English smell, was needed to account for it. *That* was the exercise of the finest sense that hung about us, my brother and me—or of one at least but little less fine than the sense for the satisfaction of which we resorted to Thompson's and to Taylor's: it bore me company during all our returns from forages and left me persuaded that I had only to snuff up hard enough, fresh uncut volume in hand, to taste of the very substance of London. All our books in that age were English, at least all our down-town ones—I personally recall scarce any that were not; and I take the perception of that quality in them to have associated itself with more fond dreams and glimmering pictures than any other one principle of growth. It was all a result of the deeply *infected* state: I had been prematurely poisoned—as I shall presently explain. The Bookstore, fondest of my father's resorts, though I remember no more of its public identity than that it further enriched the brave depth of Broadway, was overwhelmingly and irresistibly English, as not less tonically English was our principal host there, with whom we had moreover, my father and I, thanks to his office, such personal and genial relations that I recall seeing him grace our board at home, in company with his wife, whose vocal strain and complexion and coiffure and flounces I found none the less informing, none the less "racial," for my not being then versed in the language of analysis.

The true inwardness of these rich meanings—those above all of the Bookstore itself—was that a tradition was thus fed, a presumption thus created, a vague vision thus filled in: all expression is clumsy for so mystic a process. What else can have happened but that, having taken over, under suggestion and with singular infant promptitude, a particular throbbing consciousness, I had become aware of the source at which it could best be refreshed? That consciousness, so communicated, was just simply of certain impressions, certain *sources* of impression again, proceeding from over the sea and situated beyond it—or even much rather of my parents' own impression of such, the fruit of a happy time spent in and about London with their two babies and reflected in that portion of their talk with each other to which I best attended. Had *all* their talk for its subject, in my infant ears, that happy time?—did it deal only with London and Piccadilly and the Green Park, where, over against their dwelling, their two babies mainly took the air under charge of Fanny of Albany, their American nurse, whose remark as to the degree to which the British Museum fell short for one who had had the privilege of that of Albany was handed down to us? Did it never forbear from Windsor and Richmond and Sudbrook and Ham Common, amid the rich complexity of which, crowding their discourse with echoes, they had spent their summer?—all a scattering of such pearls as it seemed that their second-born could most deftly and instinctively pick up. Our sole maternal aunt, already mentioned as a devoted and cherished presence during those and many later years, was in a position to share with them the treasure of these mild memories, which strike me as having for the most part, through some bright household habit, overflowed at the breakfast-table, where I regularly attended with W. J.; she had imbibed betimes in Europe the seeds of a long nostalgia, and I think of her as ever so patiently communicative on that score under pressure of my artless appeal. That I should have been so inquiring while still so destitute of primary data was doubtless rather an anomaly; and it was for that matter quite as if my infant divination proceeded by the light of nature: I divined that it would matter to me in the future that "English life" should be of this or that fashion. My father had subscribed for me to a small periodical of quarto form, covered in yellow and entitled The Charm, which shed on the question the softest lustre, but of which the appearances were sadly intermittent, or then struck me as being; inasmuch as many of our visits to the Bookstore were to ask for the new number—only to learn with painful frequency that the last consignment from London had arrived without it. I feel again the pang of that disappointment—as if through the want of what I needed most for going on; the English smell was exhaled by The Charm in a peculiar degree, and I see myself affected by the failure as by that of a vital tonic. It was not, at the same time, by a Charm the more or the less that my salvation was to be, as it were, worked out, or my imagination at any rate duly convinced; conviction was the result of the very air of home, so far as I most consciously inhaled it. This represented, no doubt, a failure to read into matters close at hand all the interest they were capable of yielding; but I had taken the twist, had sipped the poison, as I say, and was to feel it to that end the most salutary cup. I saw my parents homesick, as I conceived, for the ancient order and distressed and inconvenienced by many of the more immediate features of the modern, as the modern pressed upon us, and since their theory of our better living was from an early time that we should renew the quest of the ancient on the very first possibility I simply grew greater in the faith that somehow to manage that would constitute success in life. I never found myself deterred from this fond view, which was implied in every question I asked, every answer I got, and every plan I formed.

Those are great words for the daydream of infant ignorance, yet if success in life may perhaps be best defined as the performance in age of some intention arrested in youth I may frankly put in a claim to it. To press my nose against the sources of the English smell, so different for young bibliophiles from any American, was to adopt that sweetness as the sign of my "atmosphere"; roundabout might be the course to take, but one was in motion from the first and one never lost sight of the goal. The very names of places and things in the other world—the marked opposite in most ways of that in which New York and Albany, Fort Hamilton and New Brighton formed so fallacious a maximum—became to me values and secrets and shibboleths; they were probably often on my tongue and employed as ignorance determined, but I quite recall being ashamed to use them as much as I should have liked. It was New Brighton, I reconstruct (and indeed definitely remember) that "finished" us at last—that and our final sordid school, W. J.'s and mine, in New York: the ancient order *had* somehow to be invoked when such "advantages" as those were the best within our compass and our means. Not further to anticipate, at all events, that climax was for a while but vaguely in sight, and the illusion of felicity continued from season to season to shut us in. It is only of what I took for felicity, however few the years and however scant the scene, that I am pretending now to speak; though I shall have strained the last drop of romance from this vision of our towny summers with the quite sharp reminiscence of my first sitting for my daguerreotype. I repaired with my father on an August day to the great Broadway establishment of Mr. Brady, supreme in that then beautiful art, and it is my impression—the only point vague with me—that though we had come up by the Staten Island boat for the purpose we were to keep the affair secret till the charming consequence should break, at home, upon my mother. Strong is my conviction that our mystery, in the event, yielded almost at once to our elation, for no tradition had a brighter household life with us than that of our father's headlong impatience. He moved in a cloud, if not rather in a high radiance, of precipitation and divulgation, a chartered rebel against cold reserves. The good news in his hand refused under any persuasion to grow stale, the sense of communicable pleasure in his breast was positively explosive; so that we saw those "surprises" in which he had conspired with our mother for our benefit converted by him in every case, under our shamelessly encouraged guesses, into common conspiracies against her—against her knowing, that is, how thoroughly we were all compromised. He had a special and delightful sophistry at the service of his overflow, and never so fine a fancy as in defending it on "human" grounds. He was something very different withal from a parent of weak mercies; weakness was never so positive and plausible, nor could the attitude of sparing you be more handsomely or on occasion even more comically aggressive.

My small point is simply, however, that the secresy of our conjoined portrait was probably very soon, by his act, to begin a public and shining life and to enjoy it till we received the picture; as to which moreover still another remembrance steals on me, a proof of the fact that our adventure was improvised.

Sharp again is my sense of not being so adequately dressed as I should have taken thought for had I foreseen my exposure; though the resources of my wardrobe as then constituted could surely have left me but few alternatives. The main resource of a small New York boy in this line at that time was the little sheath-like jacket, tight to the body, closed at the neck and adorned in front with a single row of brass buttons—a garment of scant grace assuredly and compromised to my consciousness, above all, by a strange ironic light from an unforgotten source. It was but a short time before those days that the great Mr. Thackeray had come to America to lecture on The English Humourists, and still present to me is the voice proceeding from my father's library, in which some glimpse of me hovering, at an opening of the door, in passage or on staircase, prompted him to the formidable words: "Come here, little boy, and show me your extraordinary jacket!" My sense of my jacket became from that hour a heavy one—further enriched as my vision is by my shyness of posture before the seated, the celebrated visitor, who struck me, in the sunny light of the animated room, as enormously big and who, though he laid on my shoulder the hand of benevolence, bent on my native costume the spectacles of wonder. I was to know later on why he had been so amused and why, after asking me if this were the common uniform of my age and class, he remarked that in England, were I to go there, I should be addressed as "Buttons." It had been revealed to me thus in a flash that we were somehow *queer*, and though never exactly crushed by it I became aware that I at least felt so as I stood with my head in Mr. Brady's vise. Beautiful most decidedly the lost art of the daguerreotype; I remember the "exposure" as on this occasion interminably long, yet with the result of a facial anguish far less harshly reproduced than my suffered snapshots of a later age. Too few, I may here interject, were to remain my gathered impressions of the great humourist, but one of them, indeed almost the only other, bears again on the play of his humour over our perversities of dress. It belongs to a later moment, an occasion on which I see him familiarly seated with us, in Paris, during the spring of 1857, at some repast at which the younger of us too, by that time, habitually flocked, in our affluence of five. Our youngest was beside him, a small sister, then not quite in her eighth year, and arrayed apparently after the fashion of the period and place; and the tradition lingered long of his having suddenly laid his hand on her little flounced person and exclaimed with ludicrous horror: "Crinoline?—I was suspecting it! So young and so depraved!"

A fainter image, that of one of the New York moments, just eludes me, pursue it as I will; I recover but the setting and the fact of his brief presence in it, with nothing that was said or done beyond my being left with my father to watch our distinguished friend's secretary, who was also a young artist, establish his easel and proceed to paint. The setting, as I recall it, was an odd, oblong, blank "private parlour" at the Clarendon Hotel, then the latest thing in hotels, but whose ancient corner of Fourth Avenue and—was it Eighteenth Street?—long ago ceased to know it; the gentle, very gentle, portraitist was Mr. Eyre Crowe and the obliging sitter my father, who sat in response to Mr. Thackeray's desire that his protégé should find employment. The protector after a little departed, blessing the business, which took the form of a small full-length of the model seated, his arm extended and the hand on the knob of his cane. The work, it may at this time of day be mentioned, fell below its general possibilities; but I note the scene through which I must duly have gaped and wondered (for I had as yet seen no one, least of all a casual acquaintance in an hotel parlour, "really paint" before,) as a happy example again of my parent's positive cultivation of my society, it would seem, and thought for my social education. And then there are other connections; I recall it as a Sunday morning, I recover the place itself as a featureless void—bleak and bare, with its developments all to come, the hotel parlour of other New York days—but vivid still to me is my conscious assistance for the first time at operations that were to mean much for many of my coming years. Those of quiet Mr. Crowe held me spellbound—I was to circle so wistfully, as from that beginning, round the practice of his art, which in spite of these earnest approaches and intentions never on its own part in the least acknowledged our acquaintance; scarcely much more than it was ever to respond, for that matter, to the overtures of the mild aspirant himself, known to my observation long afterwards, in the London years, as the most touchingly resigned of the children of disappointment. Not only by association was he a Thackerayan figure, but much as if the master's hand had stamped him with the outline and the value, with life and sweetness and patience—shown, as after the long futility, seated in a quiet wait, very long too, for the end. That was sad, one couldn't but feel; yet it was in the oddest way impossible to take him for a failure. He might have been one of fortune's, strictly; but what was that when he was one of Thackeray's own successes?—in the minor line, but with such a grace and such a truth, those of some dim second cousin to Colonel Newcome.

VIII

I FEEL that at such a rate I remember too much, and yet this mild apparitionism is only part of it. To look back at all is to meet the apparitional and to find in its ghostly face the silent stare of an appeal. When I fix it, the hovering shade, whether of person or place, it fixes me back and seems the less lost—not to my consciousness, for that is nothing, but to its own—by my stopping however idly for it. The day of the daguerreotype, the August afternoon, what was it if not one of the days when we went to Union Square for luncheon and for more ice-cream and more peaches and even more, even most, enjoyment of ease accompanied by stimulation of wonder? It may have been indeed that a visit to Mrs. Cannon rather on that occasion engaged us—memory selects a little confusedly from such a wealth of experience. For the wonder was the experience, and that was everywhere, even if I didn't so much find it as take it with me, to be sure of not falling short. Mrs. Cannon lurked near Fourth Street—*that* I abundantly grasp, not more definitely placing her than in what seemed to me a labyrinth of grave bye-streets westwardly "back of" Broadway, yet at no great distance from it, where she must have occupied a house at a corner, since we reached her not by steps that went up to a front door but by others that went slightly down and formed clearly an independent side access, a feature that affected me as rich and strange. What the steps went down to was a spacious room, light and friendly, so that it couldn't have been compromised by an "area," which offered the brave mystification, amid other mystifications, of being at once a parlour and a shop, a shop in particular for the relief of gentlemen in want of pockethandkerchiefs, neckties, collars, umbrellas and straw-covered bottles of the essence known in old New York as "Cullone"—with a very long and big O. Mrs. Cannon was always seated at some delicate white or other needlework, as if she herself made the collars and the neckties and hemmed the pockethandkerchiefs, though the air of this conflicts with the sense of importation from remoter centres of fashion breathed by some of the more thrilling of the remarks I heard exchanged, at the same time that it quickened the oddity of the place. For the oddity was in many things—above all perhaps in there being no counter, no rows of shelves and no vulgar till for Mrs. Cannon's commerce; the parlour clearly dissimulated the shop—and positively to that extent that I might uncannily have wondered what the shop dissimulated. It represented, honestly, I made out in the course of visits that seem to me to have been delightfully repeated, the more informal of the approaches to our friend's brave background or hinterland, the realm of her main industry, the array of the furnished apartments for gentlemen—gentlemen largely for whom she imported the Eau de Cologne and the neckties and who struck me as principally consisting of the ever remarkable Uncles, desirous at times, on their restless returns from Albany or wherever, of an intimacy of comfort that the New York Hotel couldn't yield. Fascinating thus the implications of Mrs. Cannon's establishment, where the talk took the turn, in particular, of Mr. John and Mr. Edward and Mr. Howard, and where Miss Maggie or Miss Susie, who were on the spot in other rocking chairs and with other poised needles, made their points as well as the rest of us. The interest of the place was that the uncles were somehow always under discussion—as to where they at the moment might be, or as to when they were expected, or above all as to how (the "how" was the great matter and the fine emphasis) they had last appeared and might be conceived as carrying themselves; and that their consumption of neckties and Eau de Cologne was somehow inordinate: I might have been judging it in my innocence as their only *consommation*. I refer to those sources, I say, the charm of the scene, the finer part of which must yet have been that it didn't, as it regularly lapsed, dispose of *all* mystifications. If I didn't understand, however, the beauty was that Mrs. Cannon understood (that was what she did most of all, even more than hem pockethandkerchiefs and collars) and my father understood, and each understood that the other did, Miss Maggie and Miss Susie being no whit behind. It was only I who didn't understand—save in so far as I understood *that*, which was a kind of pale joy; and meanwhile there would be more to come from uncles so attachingly, so almost portentously, discussable. The vision at any rate was to stick by me as through its old-world friendly grace, its light on the elder amenity; the prettier manners, the tender personal note in the good lady's importations and anxieties, that of the hand-made fabric and the discriminating service. Fit to figure as a value anywhere—by which I meant in the right corner of any social picture, I afterwards said to myself—that refined and composed significance of Mrs. Cannon's scene.

Union Square was a different matter, though with the element there also that I made out that I *didn't* make out (my sense of drama was in this case, I think, rather more frightened off than led on;) a drawback for which, however, I consoled myself by baked apples and custards, an inveterate feature of our Sunday luncheon there (those of weekdays being various and casual) and by a study of a great store, as it seemed to me, of steel-plated volumes, devoted mainly to the heroines of Romance, with one in particular, presenting those of Shakespeare, in which the plates were so artfully coloured and varnished, and complexion and dress thereby so endeared to memory, that it was for long afterwards a shock to me at the theatre not to see just those bright images, with their peculiar toggeries, come on. I was able but the other day, moreover, to renew almost on the very spot the continuity of contemplation; large lumpish presences, precarious creations of a day, seemed to have elbowed out of the Square all but one or two of the minor monuments, pleasant appreciable things, of the other time; yet close to University Place the old house of the picture-books and the custards and the domestic situation had, though disfigured and overscored, not quite received its death-stroke; I disengaged, by a mere identification of obscured window and profaned portico, a whole chapter of history; which fact should indeed be a warning to penetration, a practical plea here for the superficial—by its exhibition of the rate at which the relations of any gage of experience multiply and ramify from the moment the mind begins to handle it. I pursued a swarm of such relations, on the occasion I speak of, up and down West Fourteenth Street and over to Seventh Avenue, running most of them to earth with difficulty, but finding them at half a dozen points quite confess to a queer stale sameness. The gage of experience, as I say, had in these cases been strangely spared—the sameness had in two or three of them held out as with conscious craft. But these are impressions I shall presently find it impossible not to take up again at any cost.

I first "realised" Fourteenth Street at a very tender age, and I perfectly recall that flush of initiation, consisting as it did of an afternoon call with my father at a house there situated, one of an already fairly mature row on the south side and quite near Sixth Avenue. It was as "our" house, just acquired by us, that he thus invited my approval of it—heaping as that does once more the measure of my small adhesiveness. I thoroughly approved—quite as if I had foreseen that the place was to become to me for ever so long afterwards a sort of anchorage of the spirit, being at the hour as well a fascination for the eyes, since it was there I first fondly gaped at the process of "decorating." I saw charming men in little caps ingeniously formed of folded newspaper—where in the roaring city are those quaint badges of the handicrafts now?—mounted on platforms and casting plaster into moulds; I saw them in particular paste long strips of yellowish grained paper upon walls, and I vividly remember thinking the grain and the pattern (for there was a pattern from waist-high down, a complication of dragons and sphinxes and scrolls and other fine flourishes) a wonderful and sumptuous thing. I would give much, I protest, to recover its lost secret, to see what it really was—so interesting ever to retrace, and sometimes so difficult of belief, in a community of one's own knowing, is the general æsthetic adventure, are the dangers and delusions, the all but fatal accidents and mortal ailments, that Taste has smilingly survived and after which the fickle creature may still quite brazenly look one in the face. Our quarter must have bristled in those years with the very worst of the danger-signals—though indeed they figured but as coarse complacencies; the age of "brown stone" had just been ushered in, and that material, in deplorable, in monstrous form, over all the vacant spaces and eligible sites then numerous between the Fifth and Sixth Avenues, more and more affronted the day. We seemed to have come up from a world of quieter harmonies, the world of Washington Square and thereabouts, so decent in its dignity, so instinctively unpretentious. There were even there spots of shabbiness that I recall, such as the charmless void reaching westward from the two houses that formed the Fifth Avenue corner to our grandfather's, our New York grandfather's house, itself built by him, with the happiest judgment, not so long before, and at no distant time in truth to be solidly but much less pleasingly neighboured. The ancient name of the Parade-ground still hung about the central space, and the ancient wooden palings, then so generally accounted proper for central spaces—the whole image infinitely recedes—affected even my innocent childhood as rustic and mean. Union Square, at the top of the Avenue—or what practically then counted for the top—was encased, more smartly, in iron rails and further adorned with a fountain and an aged amateur-looking constable, awful to my generation in virtue of his star and his switch. I associate less elegance with the Parade-ground, into which we turned for recreation from my neighbouring dame's-school and where the parades deployed on no scale to check our own evolutions; though indeed the switch of office abounded there, for what I best recover in the connection is a sense and smell of perpetual autumn, with the ground so muffled in the leaves and twigs of the now long defunct ailanthus-tree that most of our own motions were a kicking of them up—the semi-sweet rankness of the plant was all in the air—and small boys pranced about as cavaliers whacking their steeds. There were bigger boys, bolder still, to whom this vegetation, or something kindred that escapes me, yielded long black beanlike slips which they lighted and smoked, the smaller ones staring and impressed; I at any rate think of the small one I can best speak for as constantly wading through an Indian summer of these *disjecta*, fascinated by the leaf-kicking process, the joy of lonely trudges, over a course in which those parts and the slightly more northward pleasantly confound themselves. These were the homely joys of the nobler neighbourhood, elements that had their match, and more, hard by the Fourteenth Street home, in the poplars, the pigs, the poultry, and the "Irish houses," two or three in number, exclusive of a very fine Dutch one, seated then, this last, almost as among gardens and groves—a breadth of territory still apparent, on the spot, in that marginal ease, that spread of occupation, to the nearly complete absence of which New York aspects owe their general failure of "style."

But there were finer vibrations as well—for the safely-prowling infant, though none perhaps so fine as when he stood long and drank deep at those founts of romance that gushed from the huge placards of the theatre. These announcements, at a day when advertisement was contentedly but information, had very much the form of magnified playbills; they consisted of vast oblong sheets, yellow or white, pasted upon tall wooden screens or into hollow sockets, and acquainting the possible playgoer with every circumstance that might seriously interest him. These screens rested sociably against trees and lamp-posts as well as against walls and fences, to all of which they were, I suppose, familiarly attached; but the sweetest note of their confidence was that, in parallel lines and the good old way, characters facing performers, they gave the whole cast, which in the "palmy days" of the drama often involved many names. I catch myself again in the fact of endless stations in Fifth Avenue near the southwest corner of Ninth Street, as I think it must have been, since the dull long "run" didn't exist then for the young *badaud* and the poster there was constantly and bravely renewed. It engaged my attention, whenever I passed, as the canvas of a great master in a great gallery holds that of the pious tourist, and even though I can't at this day be sure of its special reference I was with precocious passion "at home" among the theatres—thanks to our parents' fond interest in them (as from this distance I see it flourish for the time) and to the liberal law and happy view under which the addiction was shared with us, they never caring much for things we couldn't care for and generally holding that what was good to them would be also good for their children. It had the effect certainly of preparing for these, so far as we should incline to cherish it, a strange little fund of theatrical reminiscence, a small hoard of memories maintaining itself in my own case for a lifetime and causing me to wonder to-day, before its abundance, on how many evenings of the month, or perhaps even of the week, we were torn from the pursuits of home.

IX

THE TRUTH is doubtless, however, much less in the wealth of my experience than in the tenacity of my impression, the fact that I have lost nothing of what I saw and that though I can't now quite divide the total into separate occasions the various items surprisingly swarm for me. I shall return to some of them, wishing at present only to make my point of when and how the seeds were sown that afterwards so thickly sprouted and flowered. I was greatly to love the drama, at its best, as a "form"; whatever variations of faith or curiosity I was to know in respect to the infirm and inadequate theatre. There was of course anciently no question for us of the drama at its best; and indeed while I lately by chance looked over a copious collection of theatrical portraits, beginning with the earliest age of lithography and photography as so applied, and documentary in the highest degree on the personalities, as we nowadays say, of the old American stage, stupefaction grew sharp in me and scepticism triumphed, so vulgar, so barbarous, seemed the array of types, so extraordinarily provincial the note of every figure, so less than scant the claim of such physiognomies and such reputations. Rather dismal, everywhere, I admit, the histrionic image with the artificial lights turned off—the fatigued and disconnected face reduced to its mere self and resembling some closed and darkened inn with the sign still swung but the place blighted for want of custom. That consideration weighs; but what a "gang," all the same, when thus left to their own devices, the performers, men and women alike, of that world of queer appreciations! I ought perhaps to bear on them lightly in view of what in especial comes back to me; the sense of the sacred thrill with which I began to watch the green curtain, the particular one that was to rise to The Comedy of Errors on the occasion that must have been, for what I recall of its almost unbearable intensity, the very first of my ever sitting at a play. I should have been indebted for the momentous evening in that case to Mr. William Burton, whose small theatre in Chambers Street, to the rear of Stewart's big shop and hard by the Park, as the Park was at that time understood, offered me then my prime initiation. Let me not complain of my having owed the adventure to a still greater William as well, nor think again without the right intensity, the scarce tolerable throb, of the way the torment of the curtain was mixed, half so dark a defiance and half so rich a promise. One's eyes bored into it in vain, and yet one knew it *would* rise at the named hour, the only question being if one could exist till then. The play had been read to us during the day; a celebrated English actor, whose name I inconsistently forget, had arrived to match Mr. Burton as the other of the Dromios; and the agreeable Mrs. Holman, who had to my relentless vision too retreating a chin, was so good as to represent Adriana. I regarded Mrs. Holman as a friend, though in no warmer light than that in which I regarded Miss Mary Taylor—save indeed that Mrs. Holman had the pull, on one's affections, of "coming out" to sing in white satin and quite irrelevantly between the acts; an advantage she shared with the younger and fairer and more dashing, the dancing, Miss Malvina, who footed it and tambourined it and shawled it, irruptively, in lonely state. When not admiring Mr. Burton in Shakespeare we admired him as Paul Pry, as Mr. Toodles and as Aminadab Sleck in The Serious Family, and we must have admired him very much—his huge fat person, his huge fat face and his vast slightly pendulous cheek, surmounted by a sort of elephantine wink, to which I impute a remarkable baseness, being still perfectly present to me.

We discriminated, none the less; we thought Mr. Blake a much finer comedian, much more of a gentleman and a scholar—"mellow" Mr. Blake, whom with the brave and emphatic Mrs. Blake (*how* they must have made their points!) I connect partly with the Burton scene and partly with that, of slightly subsequent creation, which, after flourishing awhile slightly further up Broadway under the charmlessly commercial name of Brougham's Lyceum (we had almost only Lyceums and Museums and Lecture Rooms and Academies of Music for playhouse and opera then,) entered upon a long career and a migratory life as Wallack's Theatre. I fail doubtless to keep *all* my associations clear, but what is important, or what I desire at least to make pass for such, is that when we most admired Mr. Blake we also again admired Miss Mary Taylor; and it was at

Brougham's, not at Burton's, that we rendered *her* that tribute—reserved for her performance of the fond theatrical daughter in the English version of Le Père de la Débutante, where I see the charming panting dark-haired creature, in flowing white classically relieved by a gold tiara and a golden scarf, rush back from the supposed stage to the represented green-room, followed by thunders of applause, and throw herself upon the neck of the broken-down old gentleman in a blue coat with brass buttons who must have been after all, on second thoughts, Mr. Placide. Greater flights or more delicate shades the art of pathetic comedy was at that time held not to achieve; only I straighten it out that Mr. and Mrs. Blake, not less than Miss Mary Taylor (who preponderantly haunts my vision, even to the disadvantage of Miss Kate Horn in Nan the Good-for-Nothing, until indeed she is displaced by the brilliant Laura Keene) did migrate to Brougham's, where we found them all themselves as Goldsmith's Hardcastle pair and other like matters. We rallied especially to Blake as Dogberry, on the occasion of my second Shakespearean night, for as such I seem to place it, when Laura Keene and Mr. Lester—the Lester Wallack that was to be—did Beatrice and Benedick. I yield to this further proof that we had our proportion of Shakespeare, though perhaps antedating that rapt vision of Much Ado, which may have been preceded by the dazzled apprehension of A Midsummer Night's Dream at the Broadway (there *was* a confessed Theatre;) this latter now present to me in every bright particular. It supplied us, we must have felt, our greatest conceivable adventure—I cannot otherwise account for its emerging so clear. Everything here is as of yesterday, the identity of the actors, the details of their dress, the charm imparted by the sisters Gougenheim, the elegant elder as the infatuated Helena and the other, the roguish "Joey" as the mischievous Puck. Hermia was Mrs. Nagle, in a short salmon-coloured peplum over a white petticoat, the whole bulgingly confined by a girdle of shining gilt and forming a contrast to the loose scarves of Helena, while Mr. Nagle, not devoid, I seem to remember, of a blue chin and the latency of a fine brogue, was either Lysander or Demetrius; Mr. Davidge (also, I surmise, with a brogue) was Bottom the weaver and Madame Ponisi Oberon—Madame Ponisi whose range must have been wide, since I see her also as the white-veiled heroine of The Cataract of the Ganges, where, preferring death to dishonour, she dashes up the more or less perpendicular waterfall on a fiery black steed and with an effect only a little blighted by the chance flutter of a drapery out of which peeps the leg of a trouser and a big male foot; and then again, though presumably at a somewhat later time or, in strictness, *after* childhood's fond hour, as this and that noble matron or tragedy queen. I descry her at any rate as representing all characters alike with a broad brown face framed in bands or crowns or other heavy headgear out of which cropped a row of very small tight black curls. The Cataract of the Ganges is all there as well, a tragedy of temples and idols and wicked rajahs and real water, with Davidge and Joey Gougenheim again for comic relief—though all in a coarser radiance, thanks to the absence of fairies and Amazons and moonlit mechanical effects, the charm above all, so seen, of the play within the play; and I rank it in that relation with Green Bushes, despite the celebrity in the latter of Madame Céleste, who came to us straight out of London and whose admired walk up the stage as Miami the huntress, a wonderful majestic and yet voluptuous stride enhanced by a short kilt, black velvet leggings and a gun haughtily borne on the shoulder, is vividly before me as I write. The piece in question was, I recall, from the pen of Mr. Bourcicault, as he then wrote his name—he was so early in the field and must have been from long before, inasmuch as he now appears to me to have supplied Mr. Brougham, of the Lyceum aforesaid, with his choicest productions.

I sit again at London Assurance, with Mrs. Wallack—"Fanny" Wallack, I think, not that I quite know who she was—as Lady Gay Spanker, flushed and vociferous, first in a riding-habit with a tail yards long and afterwards in yellow satin with scarce a tail at all; I am present also at Love in a Maze, in which the stage represented, with primitive art I fear, a supposedly intricate garden-labyrinth, and in which I admired for the first time Mrs. Russell, afterwards long before the public as Mrs. Hoey, even if opining that she wanted, especially for the low-necked ordeal, less osseous a structure. There are pieces of that general association, I admit, the clue to which slips from me; the drama of modern life and of French origin—though what was then not of French origin?—in which Miss Julia Bennett, fresh from triumphs at the Haymarket, made her first appearance, in a very becoming white bonnet, either as a brilliant adventuress or as the innocent victim of licentious design, I forget which, though with a sense somehow that the white bonnet, when of true elegance, was the note at that period of the adventuress; Miss Julia Bennett with whom at a later age one was to renew acquaintance as the artful and ample Mrs. Barrow, full of manner and presence and often Edwin Booth's Portia, Desdemona and Julie de Mortemer. I figure her as having in the dimmer phase succeeded to Miss Laura Keene at Wallack's on the secession thence of this original charmer of our parents, the flutter of whose prime advent is perfectly present to me, with the relish expressed for that "English" sweetness of her speech (I already wondered why it *shouldn't* be English) which was not as the speech mostly known to us. The Uncles, within my hearing, even imitated, for commendation, some of her choicer sounds, to which I strained my ear on seeing her afterwards as Mrs. Chillington in the refined comedietta of A Morning Call, where she made delightful game of Mr. Lester as Sir Edward Ardent, even to the point of causing him to crawl about on all fours and covered with her shawl after the fashion of a horse-blanket. That delightful impression was then unconscious of the blight to come—that of my apprehending, years after, that the brilliant comedietta was the tribute of our Anglo-Saxon taste to Alfred de Musset's elegant proverb of the Porte Ouverte ou Fermée, in which nothing could find itself less at home than the horseplay of the English version. Miss Laura Keene, with a native grace at the start, a fresh and delicate inspiration, I infer from the kind of pleasure she appears to have begun with giving, was to live to belie her promise and, becoming hard and raddled, forfeit (on the evidence) all claim to the higher distinction; a fact not surprising under the lurid light projected by such a sign of the atmosphere of ineptitude as an accepted and condoned perversion to vulgarity of Musset's perfect little work. How *could* quality of talent consort with so dire an absence of quality in the material offered it? where could such lapses lead but to dust and desolation and what happy instinct not be smothered in an air so dismally non-conducting? Is it a foolish fallacy that these matters may have been on occasion, at that time, worth speaking of? is it only presumable that everything was perfectly cheap and common and everyone perfectly bad and barbarous and that even the least corruptible of our typical spectators were too easily beguiled and too helplessly kind? The beauty of the main truth as to any remembered matter looked at in due detachment, or in other words through the haze of time, is that comprehension has then become one with criticism, compassion, as it may really be called, one with musing vision, and the whole company of the anciently restless, with their elations and mistakes, their sincerities and fallacies and vanities and triumphs, embalmed for us in the mild essence of their collective submission to fate. We needn't be strenuous about them unless we particularly want to, and are glad to remember in season all that this would imply of the strenuous about our own *origines*, our muddled initiations. If nothing is more certain for us than that many persons, within our recollection, couldn't help being rather generally unadmonished and unaware, so nothing is more in the note of peace than that such a perceived state, pushed to a point, makes our scales of judgment but ridiculously rattle. *Our* admonition, our superior awareness, is of many things—and, among these, of how infinitely, at the worst, they lived, the pale superseded, and how much it was by their virtue.

Which reflections, in the train of such memories as those just gathered, may perhaps seem overstrained—though they really to my own eyes cause the images to multiply. Still others of these break in upon me and refuse to be slighted; reconstituting as I practically am the history of my fostered imagination, for whatever it may be worth, I won't pretend to a disrespect for *any* contributive particle. I left myself just above staring at the Fifth Avenue poster, and I can't but linger there while the vision it evokes insists on swarming. It was the age of the arrangements of Dickens for the stage, vamped-up promptly on every scene and which must have been the roughest theatrical tinkers' work, but at two or three of which we certainly assisted. I associate them with Mr. Brougham's temple of the art, yet am at the same time beset with the Captain Cuttle of Dombey and Son in the form of the big Burton, who never, I earnestly conceive, graced that shrine, so that I wander a trifle confusedly. Isn't it he whom I remember as a monstrous Micawber, the coarse parody of a charming creation, with the entire baldness of a huge Easter egg and collar-points like the sails of Mediterranean feluccas? Dire of course for all temperance in these connections was the need to conform to the illustrations of Phiz, himself already an improvising parodist and happy only so long as not imitated, not literally reproduced. Strange enough the "æsthetic" of artists who could desire but literally to reproduce. I give the whole question up, however, I stray too in the dust, and with a positive sense of having, in the first place, but languished at home when my betters admired Miss Cushman—terribly out of the picture and the frame we should to-day pronounce her, I fear—as the Nancy of Oliver Twist: as far away this must have been as the lifetime of the prehistoric "Park," to which it was just within my knowledge that my elders went for opera, to come back on us sounding those rich old Italian names, Bosio and Badiali, Ronconi and Steffanone, I am not sure I have them quite right; signs, of a rueful sound to us, that the line as to our infant participation *was* somewhere drawn. It had not been drawn, I all the more like to remember, when, under proper protection, at Castle Garden, I listened to that rarest of infant phenomena, Adelina Patti, poised in an armchair that had been pushed to the footlights and announcing her incomparable gift. She was about of our own age, she was one of us, even though at the same time the most prodigious of fairies, of glittering fables. That principle of selection was indeed in abeyance while I sat with my mother either at Tripler Hall or at Niblo's—I am vague about the occasion, but the names, as for fine old confused reasons, plead alike to my pen—and paid a homage quite other than critical, I dare say, to the then slightly worn Henrietta Sontag, Countess Rossi, who struck us as supremely elegant in pink silk and white lace flounces and with whom there had been for certain members of our circle some contact or intercourse that I have wonderingly lost. I learned at that hour in any case what "acclamation" might mean, and have again before me the vast high-piled auditory thundering applause at the beautiful pink lady's clear bird-notes; a thrilling, a tremendous experience and my sole other memory of concert-going, at that age, save the impression of a strange huddled hour in some smaller public place, some very minor hall, under dim lamps and again in my mother's company, where we were so near the improvised platform that my nose was brushed by the petticoats of the distinguished amateur who sang "Casta Diva," a very fine fair woman with a great heaving of bosom and flirt of crinoline, and that the ringletted Italian gentleman in black velvet and a romantic voluminous cloak who represented, or rather who professionally and uncontrollably was, an Improvisatore, had for me the effect, as I crouched gaping, of quite bellowing down my throat. That occasion, I am clear, was a concert for a charity, with the volunteer performance and the social patroness, and it had squeezed in where it would—at the same time that I somehow connect the place, in Broadway, on the right going down and not much below Fourth Street (except that everything seems to me to have been just below Fourth Street when not just above,) with the scene of my great public exposure somewhat later, the wonderful exhibition of Signor Blitz, the peerless conjurer, who, on my attending his entertainment with W. J. and our frequent comrade of the early time "Hal" Coster, practised on my innocence to seduce me to the stage and there plunge me into the shame of my sad failure to account arithmetically for his bewilderingly subtracted or added or divided pockethandkerchiefs and playing-cards; a paralysis of wit as to which I once more, and with the same wan despair, feel my companions' shy telegraphy of relief, their snickerings and mouthings and raised numerical fingers, reach me from the benches.

The second definite matter in the Dickens connection is the Smike of Miss Weston—whose prænomen I frivolously forget (though I fear it was Lizzie,) but who was afterwards Mrs. E. L. Davenport and then, sequently to some public strife or chatter, Mrs. Charles Matthews—in a version of Nicholas Nickleby that gracelessly managed to be all tearful melodrama, long-lost foundlings, wicked Ralph Nicklebys and scowling Arthur Grides, with other baffled villains, and scarcely at all Crummleses and Kenwigses, much less Squeerses; though there must have been something of Dotheboys Hall for the proper tragedy of Smike and for the broad Yorkshire effect, a precious theatrical value, of John Brodie. The ineffaceability was the anguish, to my tender sense, of Nicholas's starved and tattered and fawning and whining protégé; in face of my sharp retention of which through all the years who shall deny the immense authority of the theatre, or that the stage is the mightiest of modern engines? Such at least was to be the force of the Dickens imprint, however applied, in the soft clay of our generation; it was to resist so serenely the wash of the waves of time. To be brought up thus against the author of it, or to speak at all of the dawn of one's early consciousness of it and of his presence and power, is to begin to tread ground at once sacred and boundless, the associations of which, looming large, warn us off even while they hold. He did too much for us surely ever to leave us free—free of judgment, free of reaction, even should we care to be, which heaven forbid: he laid his hand on us in a way to undermine as in no other case the power of detached appraisement. We react against other productions of the general kind without "liking" them the less, but we somehow liked Dickens the more for having forfeited half the claim to appreciation. That process belongs to the fact that criticism, roundabout him, is somehow futile and tasteless. His own taste is easily impugned, but he entered so early into the blood and bone of our intelligence that it always remained better than the taste of overhauling him. When I take him up to-day and find myself holding off, I simply stop: not holding off, that is, but holding on, and from the very fear to do so; which sounds, I recognise, like perusal, like renewal, of the scantest. I don't renew, I wouldn't renew for the world; wouldn't, that is, with one's treasure so hoarded in the dusty chamber of youth, let in the intellectual air. Happy the house of life in which such chambers still hold out, even with the draught of the intellect whistling through the passages. We were practically contemporary, contemporary with the issues, the fluttering monthly numbers—that was the point; it made for us a good fortune, constituted for us in itself romance, on which nothing, to the end, succeeds in laying its hands.

The whole question dwells for me in a single small reminiscence, though there are others still: that of my having been sent to bed one evening, in Fourteenth Street, as a very small boy, at an hour when, in the library and under the lamp, one of the elder cousins from Albany, the youngest of an orphaned brood of four, of my grandmother's most extravagant adoption, had begun to read aloud to my mother the new, which must have been the first, instalment of David Copperfield. I had feigned to withdraw, but had only retreated to cover close at hand, the friendly shade of some screen or drooping table-cloth, folded up behind which and glued to the carpet, I held my breath and listened. I listened long and drank deep while the wondrous picture grew, but the tense cord at last snapped under the strain of the Murdstones and I broke into the sobs of sympathy that disclosed my subterfuge. I was this time effectively banished, but the ply then taken was ineffaceable. I remember indeed just afterwards finding the sequel, in especial the vast extrusion of the Micawbers, beyond my actual capacity; which took a few years to grow adequate—years in which the general contagious consciousness, and our own household response not least, breathed heavily through Hard Times, Bleak House and Little Dorrit; the seeds of acquaintance with Chuzzlewit and Dombey and Son, these coming thickly on, I had found already sown. I was to feel that I had been born, born to a rich awareness, under the very meridian; there sprouted in those years no such other crop of ready references as the golden harvest of Copperfield. Yet if I was to wait to achieve the happier of these recognitions I had already pored over Oliver Twist—albeit now uncertain of the relation borne by that experience to the incident just recalled. When Oliver was new to me, at any rate, he was already old to my betters; whose view of his particular adventures and exposures must have been concerned, I think, moreover, in the fact of my public and lively wonder about them. It was an exhibition deprecated—to infant innocence I judge; unless indeed my remembrance of enjoying it only on the terms of fitful snatches in another, though a kindred, house is due mainly to the existence there of George Cruikshank's splendid form of the work, of which our own foreground was clear. It perhaps even seemed to me more Cruikshank's than Dickens's; it was a thing of such vividly terrible images, and all marked with that peculiarity of Cruikshank that the offered flowers or goodnesses, the scenes and figures intended to comfort and cheer, present themselves under his hand as but more subtly sinister, or more suggestively queer, than the frank badnesses and horrors. The nice people and the happy moments, in the plates, frightened me almost as much as the low and the awkward; which didn't however make the volumes a source of attraction the less toward that high and square old back-parlour just westward of Sixth Avenue (as we in the same street were related to it) that formed, romantically, half our alternative domestic field and offered to our small inquiring steps a larger range and privilege. If the Dickens of those years was, as I have just called him, the great actuality of the current imagination, so I at once meet him in force as a feature even of conditions in which he was but indirectly involved.

For the other house, the house we most haunted after our own, was that of our cousin Albert, still another of the blest orphans, though this time of our mother's kindred; and if it was my habit, as I have hinted, to attribute to orphans *as* orphans a circumstantial charm, a setting necessarily more delightful than our father'd and mother'd one, so there spread about this appointed comrade, the perfection of the type, inasmuch as he alone was neither brother'd nor sister'd, an air of possibilities that were none the less vivid for being quite indefinite. He was to embody in due course, poor young man, some of these possibilities—those that had originally been for me the vaguest of all; but to fix his situation from my present view is not so much to wonder that it spoke to me of a wild freedom as to see in it the elements of a rich and rounded picture. The frame was still there but a short time since, cracked and empty, broken and gaping, like those few others, of the general overgrown scene, that my late quest had puzzled out; and this has somehow helped me to read back into it the old figures and the old long story, told as with excellent art. We knew the figures well while they lasted and had with them the happiest relation, but without doing justice to their truth of outline, their felicity of character and force of expression and function, above all to the compositional harmony in which they moved. That lives again to my considering eyes, and I admire as never before the fine artistry of fate. Our cousin's guardian, the natural and the legal, was his aunt, his only one, who was the cousin of our mother and our own aunt, virtually *our* only one, so far as a felt and adopted closeness of kinship went; and the three, daughters of two sole and much-united sisters, had been so brought up together as to have quite all the signs and accents of the same strain and the same nest. The cousin Helen of our young prospect was thus all but the sister Helen of our mother's lifetime, as was to happen, and was scarcely less a stout brave presence and an emphasised character for the new generation than for the old; noted here as she is, in particular, for her fine old-time value of clearness and straightness. I see in her strong simplicity, that of an earlier, quieter world, a New York of better manners and better morals and homelier beliefs, the very elements of some portrait by a grave Dutch or other truth-seeking master; she looks out with some of the strong marks, the anxious honesty, the modest humour, the folded resting hands, the dark handsome serious attire, the important composed cap, almost the badge of a guild or an order, that hang together about the images of past worthies, of whichever sex, who have had, as one may say, the courage of their character, and qualify them for places in great collections. I note with appreciation that she was strenuously, actively good, and have the liveliest impression both that no one was ever better, and that her goodness somehow testifies for the whole tone of a society, a remarkable cluster of private decencies. Her value to my imagination is even most of all perhaps in her mere local consistency, her fine old New York ignorance and rigour. Her traditions, scant but stiff, had grown there, close to her—they were all she needed, and she lived by them candidly and stoutly. That there have been persons so little doubtful of duty helps to show us how societies grow. A proportionately small amount of absolute conviction about it will carry, we thus make out, a vast dead weight of mere comparative. She was as anxious over hers indeed as if it had ever been in question—which is a proof perhaps that being void of imagination, when you are quite entirely void, makes scarcely more for comfort than having too much, which only makes in a manner for a homeless freedom or even at the worst for a questioned veracity. With a big installed conscience there is virtue in a grain of the figurative faculty—it acts as oil to the stiff machine.

Yet this life of straight and narrow insistences seated so clearly in our view didn't take up all the room in the other house, the house of the pictured, the intermittent Oliver, though of the fewer books in general than ours, and of the finer proportions and less peopled spaces (there were but three persons to fill them) as well as of the more turbaned and powdered family portraits, one of these, the most antique, a "French pastel," which must have been charming, of a young collateral ancestor who had died on the European tour. A vast marginal range seemed to me on the contrary to surround the adolescent nephew, who was some three years, I judge, beyond me in age and had other horizons and prospects than ours. No question of "Europe," for him, but a patriotic preparation for acquaintance with the South and West, or what was then called the West—he was to "see his own country first," winking at us while he did so; though he was, in spite of differences, so nearly and naturally neighbour'd and brother'd with us that the extensions of his range and the charms of his position counted somehow as the limits and the humilities of ours. He went neither to our schools nor to our hotels, but hovered out of our view in some other educational air that I can't now point to, and had in a remote part of the State a vast wild property of his own, known as the Beaverkill, to which, so far from his aunt's and his uncle's taking him there, he affably took them, and to which also he vainly invited W. J. and me, pointing thereby to us, however, though indirectly enough perhaps, the finest childish case we were to know for the famous acceptance of the inevitable. It was apparently not to be thought of that instead of the inevitable we should accept the invitation; the place was in the wilderness, incalculably distant, reached by a whole day's rough drive from the railroad, through every danger of flood and field, with prowling bears thrown in and probable loss of limb, of which there were sad examples, from swinging scythes and axes; but we of course measured our privation just by those facts, and grew up, so far as we did then grow, to believe that pleasures beyond price had been cruelly denied us. I at any rate myself grew up sufficiently to wonder if poor Albert's type, as it developed to the anxious elder view from the first, mightn't rather have undermined countenance; his pleasant foolish face and odd shy air of being suspected or convicted on grounds less vague to himself than to us may well have appeared symptoms of the course, of the "rig," he was eventually to run. I could think of him but as the *fils de famille* ideally constituted; not that I could then use for him that designation, but that I felt he must belong to an important special class, which he in fact formed in his own person. Everything was right, truly, for these felicities—to speak of them only as dramatic or pictorial values; since if we were present all the while at more of a drama than we knew, so at least, to my vague divination, the scene and the figures were there, not excluding the chorus, and I must have had the instinct of their being as right as possible. I see the actors move again through the high, rather bedimmed rooms—it is always a matter of winter twilight, firelight, lamplight; each one appointed to his or her part and perfect for the picture, which gave a sense of fulness without ever being crowded.

That composition had to wait awhile, in the earliest time, to find its proper centre, having been from the free point of view I thus cultivate a little encumbered by the presence of the most aged of our relatives, the oldest person I remember to have familiarly known—if it can be called familiar to have stood off in fear of such strange proofs of accomplished time: our Great-aunt Wyckoff, our maternal grandmother's elder sister, I infer, and an image of living antiquity, as I figure her to-day, that I was never to see surpassed. I invest her in this vision with all the idol-quality that may accrue to the venerable—solidly seated or even throned, hooded and draped and tucked-in, with big protective protrusive ears to her chair which helped it to the effect of a shrine, and a large face in which the odd blackness of eyebrow and of a couple of other touches suggested the conventional marks of a painted image. She signified her wants as divinities do, for I recover from her presence neither sound nor stir, remembering of her only that, as described by her companions, the pious ministrants, she had "said" so and so when she hadn't spoken at all. Was she really, as she seemed, so tremendously old, so old that her daughter, our mother's cousin Helen and ours, would have had to come to her in middle life to account for it, or did antiquity at that time set in earlier and was surrender of appearance and dress, matching the intrinsic decay, only more complacent, more submissive and, as who should say, more abject? I have my choice of these suppositions, each in its way of so lively an interest that I scarce know which to prefer, though inclining perhaps a little to the idea of the backward reach. If Aunt

Wyckoff was, as I first remember her, scarce more than seventy, say, the thought fills me with one sort of joy, the joy of our modern, our so generally greater and nobler effect of duration: who *wouldn't* more subtly strive for that effect and, intelligently so striving, reach it better, than such non-questioners of fate?—the moral of whose case is surely that if they gave up too soon and too softly we wiser witnesses can reverse the process and fight the whole ground. But I apologise to the heavy shade in question if she had really drained her conceivable cup, and for that matter rather like to suppose it, so rich and strange is the pleasure of finding the past—the Past above all—answered for to one's own touch, this being our only way to be sure of it. It was the Past that one touched in her, the American past of a preponderant unthinkable queerness; and great would seem the fortune of helping on the continuity at some other far end.

X

IT WAS at all events the good lady's disappearance that more markedly cleared the decks—cleared them for that long, slow, sustained action with which I make out that nothing was afterwards to interfere. She had sat there under her stiff old father's portrait, with which her own, on the other side of the chimney, mildly balanced; but these presences acted from that time but with cautious reserves. A brave, finished, clear-eyed image of such properties as the last-named, in particular, our already-mentioned Alexander Robertson, a faint and diminished replica of whose picture (the really fine original, as I remember it, having been long since perverted from our view) I lately renewed acquaintance with in a pious institution of his founding, where, after more than one push northward and some easy accommodations, he lives on into a world that knows him not and of some of the high improvements of which he can little enough have dreamed. Of the world he had personally known there was a feature or two still extant; the legend of his acres and his local concerns, as well as of his solid presence among them, was considerably cherished by us, though for ourselves personally the relics of his worth were a lean feast to sit at. They were by some invidious turn of fate all to help to constitute the heritage of our young kinsman, the orphaned and administered *fils de famille*, whose father, Alexander Wyckoff, son of our great-aunt and one of the two brothers of cousin Helen, just discernibly flushes for me through the ominous haze that preceded the worst visitation of cholera New York was to know. Alexander, whom, early widowed and a victim of that visitation, I evoke as with something of a premature baldness, of a blackness of short whisker, of an expanse of light waistcoat and of a harmless pomp of manner, appeared to have quite predominantly "come in" for the values in question, which he promptly transmitted to his small motherless son and which were destined so greatly to increase. There are clues I have only lost, not making out in the least to-day why the sons of Aunt Wyckoff should have been so happily distinguished. Our great-uncle of the name isn't even a dim ghost to me—he had passed away beyond recall before I began to take notice; but I hold, rightly, I feel, that it was not to his person these advantages were attached. They could have descended to our grandmother but in a minor degree—we should otherwise have been more closely aware of them. It comes to me that so far as we had at all been aware it had mostly gone off in smoke: I have still in my ears some rueful allusion to "lands," apparently in the general country of the Beaverkill, which had come to my mother and her sister as their share of their grandfather Robertson's amplitude, among the further-apportioned shares of their four brothers, only to be sacrificed later on at some scant appraisement. It is in the nature of "lands" at a distance and in regions imperfectly reclaimed to be spoken of always as immense, and I at any rate entertained the sense that we should have been great proprietors, in the far wilderness, if we had only taken more interest. Our interests were peculiarly urban—though not indeed that this had helped us much. Something of the mystery of the vanished acres hung for me about my maternal uncle, John Walsh, the only one who appeared to have been in respect to the dim possessions much on the spot, but I too crudely failed of my chance of learning from him what had become of them.

Not that they had seen *him*, poor gentleman, very much further, or that I had any strong sense of opportunity; I catch at but two or three projections of him, and only at one of his standing much at his ease: I see him before the fire in the Fourteenth Street library, sturdy, with straight black hair and as if the Beaverkill had rather stamped him, but clean-shaven, in a "stock" and a black frock-coat—I hear him perhaps still more than I see him deliver himself on the then great subject of Jenny Lind, whom he seemed to have emerged from the wilderness to listen to and as to whom I remember thinking it (strange small critic that I must have begun to be) a note of the wilderness in him that he spoke of her as "Miss Lind"; albeit I scarce know, and must even less have known then, what other form he could have used. The rest of my sense of him is tinged with the ancient pity—that of our so exercised response in those years to the general sad case of uncles, aunts and cousins obscurely afflicted (the uncles in particular) and untimely gathered. Sharp to me the memory of a call, one dusky wintry Sunday afternoon, in Clinton Place, at the house of my uncle Robertson Walsh, then the head of my mother's family, where the hapless younger brother lay dying; whom I was taken to the top of the house to see and of the sinister twilight grimness of whose lot, stretched there, amid odours of tobacco and of drugs, or of some especial strong drug, in one of the chambers of what I remember as a remote and unfriended arching attic, probably in fact the best place of prescribed quiet, I was to carry away a fast impression. All the uncles, of whichever kindred, were to come to seem sooner or later to be dying, more or less before our eyes, of melancholy matters; and yet their general story, so far as one could read it, appeared the story of life. I conceived at any rate that John Walsh, celibate, lonely and good-naturedly black-browed, had been sacrificed to the far-off Robertson acres, which on their side had been sacrificed to I never knew what. The point of my divagation, however, is that the Barmecide banquet of another tract of the same *provenance* was always spread for us opposite the other house, from which point it stretched, on the north side of the street, to Sixth Avenue; though here we were soon to see it diminished at the corner by a structure afterwards known to us as our prosiest New York school. This edifice, devoted to-day to other uses, but of the same ample insignificance, still left for exploitation at that time an uncovered town-territory the transmitted tale of which was that our greatgrandfather, living down near the Battery, had had his country villa or, more strictly speaking, his farm there, with free expanses roundabout. Shrunken though the tract a part of it remained—in particular a space that I remember, though with the last faintness, to have seen appeal to the public as a tea-garden or open-air café, a haunt of dance and song and of other forms of rather ineffective gaiety. The subsequent conversion of the site into the premises of the French Theatre I was to be able to note more distinctly; resorting there in the winter of 1874–5, though not without some wan detachment, to a series of more or less exotic performances, and admiring in especial the high and hard virtuosity of Madame Ristori, the unfailing instinct for the wrong emphasis of the then acclaimed Mrs. Rousby (I still hear the assured "Great woman, great woman!" of a knowing friend met as I went out,) and the stout fidelity to a losing game, as well as to a truth not quite measurable among us, of the late, the but lugubriously-comic, the blighted John Toole.

These are glimmering ghosts, though that drama of the scene hard by at which I have glanced gives me back its agents with a finer intensity. For the long action set in, as I have hinted, with the death of Aunt Wyckoff, and, if rather taking its time at first to develop, maintained to the end, which was in its full finality but a few years since, the finest consistency and unity; with cousin Helen, in rich prominence, for the heroine; with the pale adventurous Albert for the hero or young protagonist, a little indeed in the sense of a small New York Orestes ridden by Furies; with a pair of confidants in the form first of the heroine's highly respectable but quite negligible husband and, second, of her close friend and quasi-sister our own admirable Aunt; with Alexander's younger brother, above all, the odd, the eccentric, the attaching Henry, for the stake, as it were, of the game. So for the spectator did the figures distribute themselves; the three principal, on the large stage—it became a field of such spreading interests—well in front, and the accessory pair, all sympathy and zeal, prompt comment and rich resonance, hovering in the background, responsive to any call and on the spot at a sign: this most particularly true indeed of our anything but detached Aunt, much less a passive recipient than a vessel constantly brimming, and destined herself to become the outstanding agent, almost the *dea ex machina*, in the last act of the story. Her colleague of the earlier periods (though to that title she would scarce have granted his right) I designate rather as our earnest cousin's husband than as our kinsman even by courtesy; since he was "Mr." to his own wife, for whom the dread of liberties taken in general included even those that might have been allowed to herself: he had not in the least, like the others in his case, married into the cousinship with us, and this apparently rather by his defect than by ours. His christian name, if certainly not for use, was scarce even for ornament—which consorted with the felt limits roundabout him of aids to mention and with the fact that no man could on his journey through life well have been less eagerly designated or apostrophised. If there are persons as to whom the "Mr." never comes up at all, so there are those as to whom it never subsides; but some of them all keep it by the greatness and others, oddly enough, by the smallness of their importance. The subject of my present reference, as I think of him, nevertheless—by which I mean in spite of his place in the latter group—greatly helps my documentation; he must have been of so excellent and consistent a shade of nullity. To that value, if value it be, there almost always attaches some question of the degree and the position: with adjuncts, with a relation, the zero may figure as a numeral—and the neglected zero is mostly, for that matter, endowed with a consciousness and subject to irritation. For this dim little gentleman, so perfectly a gentleman, no appeal and no redress, from the beginning to the end of his career, were made or entertained or projected; no question of how to treat him, or of how *he* might see it or feel it, could ever possibly rise; he was blank from whatever view, remaining so under application of whatever acid or exposure to whatever heat; the one identity he could have was to be part of the consensus.

Such a case is rare—that of being no case at all, that of not having even the interest of the grievance of not being one: we as a rule catch glimpses in the down-trodden of such resentments—they have at least sometimes the importance of feeling the weight of our tread. The phenomenon was here quite other—that of a natural platitude that had never risen to the level of sensibility. When you have been wronged you can be righted, when you have suffered you can be soothed; if you have that amount of grasp of the "scene," however humble, the drama of your life to some extent enacts itself, with the logical consequence of your being proportionately its hero and *having* to be taken for such. Let me not dream of attempting to say for what cousin Helen took her spectral spouse, though I think it the most marked touch in her portrait that she kept us from ever knowing. She was a person about whom you knew everything else, but there she was genially inscrutable, and above all claimed no damages on the score of slights offered him. She knew nothing whatever of these, yet could herself be much wounded or hurt—which latter word she sounded in the wondrous old New York manner so irreducible to notation. She covered the whole case with a mantle which was yet much more probably that of her real simplicity than of a feigned unconsciousness; I doubt whether she *knew* that men could be amiable in a different manner from that which had to serve her for supposing her husband amiable; when the mould and the men cast in it were very different she failed, or at least she feared, to conclude to amiability—though *some* women (as different themselves as such stranger men!) might take it for that. Directly interrogated she might (such was the innocence of these long-extinct manners) have approved of male society in stronger doses or more vivid hues—save where consanguinity, or indeed relationship by marriage, to which she greatly deferred, had honestly imposed it. The singular thing for the drama to which I return was that there it was just consanguinity that had made the burden difficult and strange and of a nature to call on great decisions and patient plans, even though the most ominous possibilities were not involved. I reconstruct and reconstruct of course, but the elements had to my childish vision at least nothing at all portentous; if any light of the lurid played in for me just a little it was but under much later information. What my childish vision was really most possessed of, I think, was the figure of the spectral spouse, the dim little gentleman, as I have called him, pacing the whole length of the two big parlours, in prolonged repetition, much as if they had been the deck of one of those ships anciently haunted by him, as "supercargo" or whatever, in strange far seas—according to the only legend connected with him save that of his early presumption in having approached, such as he was, so fine a young woman, and his remarkable luck in having approached her successfully; a luck surprisingly renewed for him, since it was also part of the legend that he had previously married and lost a bride beyond his deserts.

XI

I AM, strictly speaking, at this point, on a visit to Albert, who at times sociably condescended to my fewer years—I still appreciate the man-of-the-world ease of it; but my host seems for the minute to have left me, and I am attached but to the rich perspective in which "Uncle" (for Albert too he was only all namelessly Uncle) comes and goes; out of the comparative high brownness of the back room, commanding brave extensions, as I thought them, a covered piazza over which, in season, Isabella grapes accessibly clustered and beyond which stretched, further, a "yard" that was as an ample garden compared to ours at home; I keep in view his little rounded back, at the base of which his arms are interlocked behind him, and I know how his bald head, yet with the hair bristling up almost in short-horn fashion at the sides, is thrust inquiringly, not to say appealingly, forward; I assist at his emergence, where the fine old mahogany doors of separation are rolled back on what used to seem to me silver wheels, into the brighter yet colder half of the scene, and attend him while he at last looks out awhile into Fourteenth Street for news of whatever may be remarkably, objectionably or mercifully taking place there; and then I await his regular return, preparatory to a renewed advance, far from indifferent as I innocently am to his discoveries or his comments. It is cousin Helen however who preferentially takes them up, attaching to them the right importance, which is for the moment the very greatest that could possibly be attached to anything in the world; I for my part occupied with those marks of character in our pacing companion—his long, slightly equine countenance, his eyebrows ever elevated as in the curiosity of alarm, and the so limited play from side to side of his extremely protrusive head, as if somehow through tightness of the "wash" neckcloths that he habitually wore and that, wound and re-wound in their successive stages, made his neck very long without making it in the least thick and reached their climax in a proportionately very small knot tied with the neatest art. I scarce can have known at the time that this was as complete a little old-world figure as any that might then have been noted there, far or near; yet if I didn't somehow "subtly" feel it, why am I now so convinced that I must have had familiarly before me a masterpiece of the great Daumier, say, or Henri Monnier, or any other then contemporary projector of Monsieur Prudhomme, the timorous Philistine in a world of dangers, with whom I was later on to make acquaintance? I put myself the question, of scant importance though it may seem; but there is a reflection perhaps more timely than any answer to it. I catch myself in the act of seeing poor anonymous "Dear," as cousin Helen confined herself, her life long, to calling him, in the light of an image arrested by the French genius, and this in truth opens up vistas. I scarce know what it *doesn't* suggest for the fact of sharpness, of intensity of type; which fact in turn leads my imagination almost any dance, making me ask myself quite most of all whether a person so marked by it mustn't really have been a highly finished figure.

That degree of finish was surely rare among us—rare at a time when the charm of so much of the cousinship and the uncleship, the kinship generally, had to be found in their so engagingly dispensing with any finish at all. They happened to be amiable, to be delightful; but—I think I have already put the question—what would have become of us all if they hadn't been? a question the shudder of which could never have been suggested by the presence I am considering. He too was gentle and bland, as it happened—and I indeed see it all as a world quite unfavourable to arrogance or insolence or any hard and high assumption; but the more I think of him (even at the risk of thinking too much) the more I make out in him a tone and a manner that deprecated crude ease. Plenty of this was already in the air, but if he hadn't so spoken of an order in which forms still counted it might scarce have occurred to one that there had ever been any. It comes over me therefore that he testified—and perhaps quite beautifully; I remember his voice and his speech, which were not those of *that* New York at all, and with the echo, faint as it is, arrives the wonder of where he could possibly have picked such things up. They were, as forms, adjusted and settled things; from what finer civilisation therefore had they come down to him? To brood on this the least little bit is verily, as I have said, to open up vistas—out of the depths of one of which fairly glimmers the queerest of questions. Mayn't we accordingly have been, the rest of us, all wrong, and the dim little gentleman the only one among us who was right? May not his truth to type have been a matter that, as mostly typeless ourselves, we neither perceived nor appreciated?—so that if, as is conceivable, he felt and measured the situation and simply chose to be bland and quiet and keep his sense to himself, he was a hero without the laurel as well as a martyr without the crown. The light of which possibility is, however, too fierce; I turn it off, I tear myself from the view—noting further but the one fact in his history that, by my glimpse of it, quite escapes ambiguity. The youthful Albert, I have mentioned, was to resist successfully through those years that solicitation of "Europe" our own response to which, both as a general and a particular solution, kept breaking out in choral wails; but the other house none the less nourished projects so earnest that they could invoke the dignity of comparative silence and patience. The other house didn't aspire to the tongues, but it aspired to the grand tour, of which ours was on many grounds incapable. Only after years and when endless things had happened—Albert having long before, in especial, quite taken up his stake and ostensibly dropped out of the game—did the great adventure get itself enacted, with the effect of one of the liveliest illustrations of the irony of fate. What had most of all flushed through the dream of it during years was the legend, at last quite antediluvian, of the dim little gentleman's early Wanderjahre, that experience of distant lands and seas which would find an application none the less lively for having had long to wait. It had had to wait in truth half a century, yet its confidence had apparently not been impaired when New York, on the happy day, began to recede from view. Europe had surprises, none the less, and who knows to what extent it may after half a century have had shocks? The coming true of the old dream produced at any rate a snap of the tense cord, and the ancient worthy my imagination has, in the tenderest of intentions, thus played with, disembarked in England only to indulge in the last of his startled stares, only to look about him in vague deprecation and give it all up. He just landed and died; but the grand tour was none the less proceeded with—cousin Helen herself, aided by resources personal, social and financial that left nothing to desire, triumphantly performed it, though as with a feeling of delicacy about it firmly overcome.

But it has taken me quite out of the other house, so that I patch up again, at a stroke, that early scene of her double guardianship at which my small wonder assisted. It even then glimmered on me, I think, that if Albert was, all so romantically, in charge of his aunt—which was a perfectly nondescript relation—so his uncle Henry, her odd brother, was her more or less legal ward, not less, despite his being so very much Albert's senior. In these facts and in the character of each of the three persons involved resided the drama; which must more or less have begun, as I have hinted, when simple-minded Henry, at a date I seem to have seized, definitely emerged from rustication—the Beaverkill had but for a certain term protected, or promoted, his simplicity—and began, on his side, to pace the well-worn field between the Fourteenth Street windows and the piazza of the Isabella grapes. I see him there less vividly than his fellow-pedestrian only because he was afterwards to loom so much larger, whereas his companion, even while still present, was weakly to shrink and fade. At this late day only do I devise for that companion a possible history; the simple-minded Henry's annals on the other hand grew in interest as soon as they became interesting at all. This happened as soon as one took in the ground and some of the features of his tutelage. The basis of it all was that, harmless as he appeared, he was not to be trusted; I remember how portentous that truth soon looked, both in the light of his intense amiability and of sister Helen's absolute certitude. He wasn't to be trusted—it was the sole very definite fact about him except the fact that he had so kindly come down from the far-off Beaverkill to regale us with the perfect demonstration, dutifully, resignedly setting himself among us to point the whole moral himself. He appeared, from the moment we really took it in, to be doing, in the matter, no more than he ought; he exposed himself to our invidious gaze, on this ground, with a humility, a quiet courtesy and an instinctive dignity that come back to me as simply heroic. He had himself accepted, under strenuous suggestion, the dreadful view, and I see him to-day, in the light of the grand dénouement, deferred for long years, but fairly dazzling when it came, as fairly sublime in his decision not to put anyone in the wrong about him a day sooner than he could possibly help. The whole circle of us would in that event be so dreadfully "sold," as to our wisdom and justice, he proving only noble and exquisite. It didn't so immensely matter to him as that, the establishment of his true character didn't; so he went on as if for all the years—and they really piled themselves up: his passing for a dangerous idiot, or at least for a slave of his passions from the moment he was allowed the wherewithal in the least to indulge them, was a less evil for him than seeing us rudely corrected. It was in truth an extraordinary situation and would have offered a splendid subject, as we used to say, to the painter of character, the novelist or the dramatist, with the hand to treat it. After I had read David Copperfield an analogy glimmered—it struck me even in the early time: cousin Henry was more or less another Mr. Dick, just as cousin Helen was in her relation to him more or less another Miss Trotwood. There were disparities indeed: Mr. Dick was the harmless lunatic on that lady's premises, but she admired him and appealed to him; lunatics, in her generous view, might be oracles, and there is no evidence, if I correctly remember, that she kept him low. Our Mr. Dick was suffered to indulge his passions but on ten cents a day, while his fortune, under conscientious, under admirable care—cousin Helen being no less the wise and keen woman of business than the devoted sister—rolled up and became large; likewise Miss Trotwood's inmate hadn't at all the perplexed brooding brow, with the troubled fold in it, that represented poor Henry's only form of criticism of adverse fate. They had alike the large smooth open countenance of those for whom life has been simplified, and if Mr. Dick had had a fortune he would have remained all his days as modestly vague about the figure of it as our relative consented to remain. The latter's interests were agricultural, while his predecessor's, as we remember, were mainly historical; each at any rate had in a general way his Miss Trotwood, not to say his sister Helen.

The good Henry's Miss Trotwood lived and died without an instant's visitation of doubt as to the due exercise of her authority, as to what would happen if it faltered; her victim waiting in the handsomest manner till she had passed away to show us all—all who remained, after so long, to do him justice—that nothing but what was charming and touching could possibly happen. This was, in part at least, the dazzling dénouement I have spoken of: he became, as soon as fortunate dispositions could take effect, the care of our admirable Aunt, between whom and his sister and himself close cousinship, from far back, had practically amounted to sisterhood: by which time the other house had long been another house altogether, its ancient site relinquished, its contents planted afresh far northward, with new traditions invoked, though with that of its great friendliness to all of us, for our mother's sake, still confirmed. Here with brief brightness, clouded at the very last, the solution emerged; we became aware, not without embarrassment, that poor Henry at large and supplied with funds was exactly as harmless and blameless as poor Henry stinted and captive; as to which if anything had been wanting to our confusion or to his own dignity it would have been his supreme abstinence, his suppression of the least "Didn't I tell you?" He didn't even pretend to have told us, when he so abundantly might, and nothing could exceed the grace with which he appeared to have noticed nothing. He "handled" dollars as decently, and just as profusely, as he had handled dimes; the only light shade on the scene—except of course for its being so belated, which did make it pathetically dim—was the question of how nearly he at all measured his resources. Not his heart, but his imagination, in the long years, had been starved; and though he was now all discreetly and wisely encouraged to feel rich, it was rather sadly visible that, thanks to almost half a century of over-discipline, he failed quite to rise to his estate. He did feel rich, just as he felt generous; the misfortune was only in his weak sense for meanings. That, with the whole situation, made delicacy of the first importance; as indeed what was perhaps most striking in the entire connection was the part played by delicacy from the first. It had all been a drama of the delicate: the consummately scrupulous and successful administration of his resources for the benefit of his virtue, so that they could be handed over, in the event, without the leakage of a fraction, what was that but a triumph of delicacy? So delicacy conspired, delicacy surrounded him; the case having been from the early time that, could he only be regarded as sufficiently responsible, could the sources of his bounty be judged fairly open to light pressure (there was question of none but the lightest) that bounty might blessedly flow. This had been Miss Trotwood's own enlightened view, on behalf of one of the oddest and most appealing collections of wistful wondering single gentlewomen that a great calculating benevolence perhaps ever found arrayed before it—ornaments these all of the second and third cousinship and interested spectators of the almost inexpressible facts.

I should have liked completely to express them, in spite of the difficulty—if not indeed just by reason of that; the difficulty of their consisting so much more of "character" than of "incident" (heaven save the artless opposition!) though this last element figured bravely enough too, thanks to some of the forms taken by our young Albert's wild wilfulness. He was so weak—after the most approved fashion of distressing young men of means—that his successive exhibitions of it had a fine high positive effect, such as would have served beautifully, act after act, for the descent of the curtain. The issue, however (differing in this from the common theatrical trick) depended less on who should die than on who should live; the younger of cousin Helen's pair of wards—putting them even only as vessels of her attempted earnestness—had violently broken away, but a remedy to this grief, for reasons too many to tell, dwelt in the possible duration, could it only not be arrested, of two other lives, one of these her own, the second the guileless Henry's. The single gentlewomen, to a remarkable number, whom she regarded and treated as nieces, though they were only daughters of cousins, were such objects of her tender solicitude that, she and Henry and Albert being alike childless, the delightful thing to think of was, on certain contingencies, the nieces' prospective wealth. There were contingencies of course—and they exactly produced the pity and terror. Her estate would go at her death to her nearest of kin, represented by her brother and nephew; it would be only of her savings—fortunately, with her kind eye on the gentlewomen, zealous and long continued—that she might dispose by will; and it was but a troubled comfort that, should he be living at the time of her death, the susceptible Henry would profit no less than the wanton Albert. Henry was at any cost to be kept in life that he *might* profit; the woeful question, the question of delicacy, for a woman devoutly conscientious, was how could anyone else, how, above all, could fifteen other persons, be made to profit by his profiting? She had been as earnest a steward of her brother's fortune as if directness of pressure on him, in a sense favourable to her interests—that is to her sympathies, which were her only interests—had been a matter of course with her; whereas in fact she would have held it a crime, given his simplicity, to attempt in the least to guide his hand. If he didn't outlive his nephew—and he was older, though, as would appear, so much more virtuous—his inherited property, she being dead, would accrue to that unedifying person. *There* was the pity; and as for the question of the disposition of Henry's savings without the initiative of Henry's intelligence, in that, alas, was the terror. Henry's savings—there had been no terror for her, naturally, in beautifully husbanding his resources *for* him—dangled, naturally, with no small vividness, before the wistful gentlewomen, to whom, if he had but *had* the initiative, he might have made the most princely presents. Such was the oddity, not to say the rather tragic drollery, of the situation: that Henry's idea of a present was ten cents' worth of popcorn, or some similar homely trifle; and that when one had created for him a world of these proportions there was no honest way of inspiring him to write cheques for hundreds; all congruous though these would be with the generosity of his nature as shown by the exuberance of his popcorn. The ideal solution would be his flashing to intelligence just long enough to apprehend the case and, of his own magnanimous movement, sign away everything; but that was a fairy-tale stroke, and the fairies here somehow stood off.

Thus between the wealth of her earnestness and the poverty of her courage—her dread, that is, of exposing herself to a legal process for undue influence—our good lady was not at peace; or, to be exact, was only at such peace as came to her by the free bestowal of her own accumulations during her lifetime and after her death. She pre-deceased her brother and had the pang of feeling that if half her residuum would be deplorably diverted the other half would be, by the same stroke, imperfectly applied; the artless Henry remained at once so well provided and so dimly inspired. Here was suspense indeed for a last "curtain" but one; and my fancy glows, all expertly, for the disclosure of the final scene, than which nothing could well have been happier, on all the premises, save for a single flaw: the installation in Forty-fourth Street of our admirable aunt, often, through the later years, domiciled there, but now settled to community of life with a touching charge and representing near him his extinguished, *their* extinguished, sister. The too few years that followed were the good man's Indian summer and a very wonderful time—so charmingly it shone forth, for all concerned, that he was a person fitted to adorn, as the phrase is, almost any position. Our admirable aunt, not less devoted and less disinterested than his former protectress, had yet much more imagination; she had enough, in a word, for perfect confidence, and under confidence what remained of poor Henry's life bloomed like a garden freshly watered. Sad alas the fact that so scant a patch was now left. It sufficed, however, and he rose, just in time, to every conception; it was, as I have already noted, as if he had all the while known, as if he had really been a conscious victim to the superstition of his blackness. His final companion recognised, as it were, his powers; and it may be imagined whether when he absolutely himself proposed to benefit the gentlewomen she passed him, or not, the blessed pen. He had taken a year or two to publish by his behaviour the perfection of his civility, and so, on that safe ground, made use of the pen. His competence was afterwards attacked, and it emerged triumphant, exactly as his perfect charity and humility and amenity, and his long inward loneliness, of half a century, did. He had bowed his head and sometimes softly scratched it during that immense period; he had occasionally, after roaming downstairs with the troubled fold in his brow and the difficult, the smothered statement on his lips (his vocabulary was scant and stiff, the vocabulary of pleading explanation, often found too complicated by the witty,) retired once more to his room sometimes indeed for hours, to think it all over again; but had never failed of sobriety or propriety or punctuality or regularity, never failed of one of the virtues his imputed indifference to which had been the ground of his discipline. It was very extraordinary, and of all the stories I know is I think the most beautiful—so far at least as *he* was concerned! The flaw I have mentioned, the one break in the final harmony, was the death of our admirable aunt too soon, shortly before his own and while, taken with illness at the same time, he lay there deprived of her attention. He had that of the gentlewomen, however, two or three of the wisest and tenderest being deputed by the others; and if his original estate reverted at law they presently none the less had occasion to bless his name.

XII

I TURN round again to where I last left myself gaping at the old ricketty bill-board in Fifth Avenue; and am almost as sharply aware as ever of the main source of its spell, the fact that it most often blazed with the rich appeal of Mr. Barnum, whose "lecture-room," attached to the Great American Museum, overflowed into posters of all the theatrical bravery disavowed by its title. It was my rueful theory of those days —though tasteful I may call it too as well as rueful—that on all the holidays on which we weren't dragged to the dentist's we attended as a matter of course at Barnum's, that is when we were so happy as to be able to; which, to my own particular consciousness, wasn't every time the case. The case was too often, to my melancholy view, that W. J., quite regularly, on the non-dental Saturdays, repaired to this seat of joy with the easy Albert—*he* at home there and master of the scene to a degree at which, somehow, neither of us could at the best arrive; he quite moulded, truly, in those years of plasticity, as to the æsthetic bent and the determination of curiosity, I seem to make out, by the general Barnum association and revelation. It was not, I hasten to add, that I too didn't, to the extent of my minor chance, drink at the spring; for how else should I have come by the whole undimmed sense of the connection?—the weary waiting, in the dusty halls of humbug, amid bottled mermaids, "bearded ladies" and chill dioramas, for the lecture-room, the true centre of the seat of joy, to open: vivid in especial to me is my almost sick wondering of whether I mightn't be rapt away before it did open. The impression appears to have been mixed; the drinking deep and the holding out, holding out in particular against failure of food and of stage-fares, provision for transport to and fro, being questions equally intense: the appeal of the lecture-room, in its essence a heavy extra, so exhausted our resources that even the sustaining doughnut of the refreshment-counter would mock our desire and the long homeward crawl, the length of Broadway and further, seem to defy repetition. Those desperate days, none the less, affect me now as having flushed with the very complexion of romance; their aches and inanitions were part of the adventure; the homeward straggle, interminable as it appeared, flowered at moments into rapt contemplations—that for instance of the painted portrait, large as life, of the celebrity of the hour, then "dancing" at the Broadway Theatre, Lola Montes, Countess of Lansfeldt, of a dazzling and unreal beauty and in a riding-habit lavishly open at the throat.

It was thus quite in order that I should pore longest, there at my fondest corner, over the Barnum announcements—my present inability to be superficial about which has given in fact the measure of my contemporary care. These announcements must have been in their way marvels of attractive composition, the placard bristling from top to toe with its analytic "synopsis of scenery and incidents"; the synoptical view cast its net of fine meshes and the very word savoured of incantation. It is odd at the same time that when I question memory as to the living hours themselves, those of the stuffed and dim little hall of audience, smelling of peppermint and orange-peel, where the curtain rose on our gasping but rewarded patience, two performances only stand out for me, though these in the highest relief. Love, or the Countess and the Serf, by J. Sheridan Knowles—I see that still as the blazonry of one of them, just as I see Miss Emily Mestayer, large, red in the face, coifed in a tangle of small, fine, damp-looking short curls and clad in a light-blue garment edged with swans-down, shout at the top of her lungs that a "pur-r-r-se of gold" would be the fair guerdon of the minion who should start on the spot to do her bidding at some desperate crisis that I forget. I forget Huon the serf, whom I yet recall immensely admiring for his nobleness; I forget everyone but Miss Mestayer, who gave form to my conception of the tragic actress at her highest. She had a hooked nose, a great play of nostril, a vast protuberance of bosom and always the "crop" of close moist ringlets; I say always, for I was to see her often again, during a much later phase, the midmost years of that Boston Museum which aimed at so vastly higher a distinction than the exploded lecture-room had really done, though in an age that snickered even abnormally low it still lacked the courage to call itself a theatre. She must have been in comedy, which I believe she also usefully and fearlessly practised, rather unimaginable; but there was no one like her in the Boston time for cursing queens and eagle-beaked mothers; the Shakespeare of the Booths and other such would have been unproducible without her; she had a rusty, rasping, heaving and tossing "authority" of which the bitterness is still in my ears. I am revisited by an outer glimpse of her in that after age when she had come, comparatively speaking, into her own—the sight of her, accidentally incurred, one tremendously hot summer night, as she slowly moved from her lodgings or wherever, in the high Bowdoin Street region, down to the not distant theatre from which even the temperature had given her no reprieve; and well remember how, the queer light of my young impression playing up again in her path, she struck me as the very image of mere sore histrionic habit and use, a worn and weary, a battered even though almost sordidly smoothed, *thing* of the theatre, very much as an old infinitely-handled and greasy violoncello of the orchestra might have been. It was but an effect doubtless of the heat that she scarcely seemed clad at all; slippered, shuffling and, though somehow hatted and vaguely veiled or streamered, wrapt in a gauzy sketch of a dressing-gown, she pointed to my extravagant attention the moral of thankless personal service, of the reverse of the picture, of the cost of "amusing the public" in a case of amusing it, as who should say, every hour. And I had thrilled before her as the Countess in "Love"—such contrasted combinations! But she carried her head very high, as with the habit of crowns and trains and tirades—had in fact much the air of some deposed and reduced sovereign living on a scant allowance; so that, all invisibly and compassionately, I took off my hat to her.

To which I must add the other of my two Barnumite scenic memories, my having anciently admired her as the Eliza of Uncle Tom's Cabin, her swelling bust encased in a neat cotton gown and her flight across the ice-blocks of the Ohio, if I rightly remember the perilous stream, intrepidly and gracefully performed. We lived and moved at that time, with great intensity, in Mrs. Stowe's novel—which, recalling my prompt and charmed acquaintance with it, I should perhaps substitute for The Initials, earlier mentioned here, as my first experiment in grown-up fiction. There was, however, I think, for that triumphant work no classified condition; it was for no sort of reader as distinct from any other sort, save indeed for Northern as differing from Southern: it knew the large felicity of gathering in alike the small and the simple and the big and the wise, and had above all the extraordinary fortune of finding itself, for an immense number of people, much less a book than a state of vision, of feeling and of consciousness, in which they didn't sit and read and appraise and pass the time, but walked and talked and laughed and cried and, in a manner of which Mrs. Stowe was the irresistible cause, generally conducted themselves. Appreciation and judgment, the whole impression, were thus an effect for which there had been no process—any process so related having in other cases *had* to be at some point or other critical; nothing in the guise of a written book, therefore, a book printed, published, sold, bought and "noticed," probably ever reached its mark, the mark of exciting interest, without having at least groped for that goal *as* a book or by the exposure of some literary side. Letters, here, languished unconscious, and Uncle Tom, instead of making even one of the cheap short cuts through the medium in which books breathe, even as fishes in water, went gaily roundabout it altogether, as if a fish, a wonderful "leaping" fish, had simply flown through the air. This feat accomplished, the surprising creature could naturally fly anywhere, and one of the first things it did was thus to flutter down on every stage, literally without exception, in America and Europe. If the amount of life represented in such a work is measurable by the ease with which representation is taken up and carried further, carried even violently furthest, the fate of Mrs. Stowe's picture was conclusive: it simply sat down wherever it lighted and made itself, so to speak, at home; thither multitudes flocked afresh and there, in each case, it rose to its height again and went, with all its vivacity and good faith, through all its motions.

These latter were to leave me, however, with a fonder vision still than that of the comparatively jejune "lecture-room" version; for the first exhibition of them to spring to the front was the fine free rendering achieved at a playhouse till then ignored by fashion and culture, the National Theatre, deep down on the East side, whence echoes had come faintest to ears polite, but where a sincerity vivid though rude was now supposed to reward the curious. Our numerous attendance there under this spell was my first experience of the "theatre party" as we have enjoyed it in our time—each emotion and impression of which is as fresh to me as the most recent of the same family. Precious through all indeed perhaps is the sense, strange only to later sophistication, of my small encouraged state as a free playgoer—a state doubly wondrous while I thus evoke the full contingent from Union Square; where, for that matter, I think, the wild evening must have been planned. I am lost again in all the goodnature from which small boys, on wild evenings, could dangle so unchidden—since the state of unchiddenness is what comes back to me well-nigh clearest. How without that complacency of conscience could every felt impression so live again? It is true that for my present sense of the matter snubs and raps would still tingle, would count double; just wherefore it is exactly, however, that I mirror myself in these depths of propriety. The social scheme, as we knew it, was, in its careless charity, worthy of the golden age—though I can't sufficiently repeat that we knew it both at its easiest and its safest: the fruits dropped right upon the board to which we flocked together, the least of us and the greatest, with differences of appetite and of reach, doubtless, but not with differences of place and of proportionate share. My appetite and my reach in respect to the more full-bodied Uncle Tom might have brooked certainly any comparison; I must have partaken thoroughly of the feast to have left the various aftertastes so separate and so strong. It was a great thing to have a canon to judge by—it helped conscious criticism, which was to fit on wings (for use ever after) to the shoulders of appreciation. In the light of that advantage I could be *sure* my second Eliza was less dramatic than my first, and that my first "Cassy," that of the great and blood-curdling Mrs. Bellamy of the lecture-room, touched depths which made the lady at the National prosaic and placid (I could already be "down" on a placid Cassy;) just as on the other hand the rocking of the ice-floes of the Ohio, with the desperate Eliza, infant in arms, balancing for a leap from one to the other, had here less of the audible creak of carpentry, emulated a trifle more, to my perception, the real water of Mr. Crummles's pump. They can't, even at that, have emulated it much, and one almost envies (quite making up one's mind not to denounce) the simple faith of an age beguiled by arts so rude.

However, the point exactly was that we attended this spectacle just in order *not* to be beguiled, just in order to enjoy with ironic detachment and, at the very most, to be amused ourselves at our sensibility should it prove to have been trapped and caught. To have become thus aware of our collective attitude constituted for one small spectator at least a great initiation; he got his first glimpse of that possibility of a "free play of mind" over a subject which was to throw him with force at a later stage of culture, when subjects had considerably multiplied, into the critical arms of Matthew Arnold. So he is himself at least interested in seeing the matter—as a progress in which the first step was taken, before that crude scenic appeal, by his wondering, among his companions, where the absurd, the absurd for *them*, ended and the fun, the real fun, which was the gravity, the tragedy, the drollery, the beauty, the thing itself, briefly, might be legitimately and tastefully held to begin. Uncanny though the remark perhaps, I am not sure I wasn't thus more interested in the pulse of our party, under my tiny recording thumb, than in the beat of the drama and the shock of its opposed forces—vivid and touching as the contrast was then found for instance between the tragi-comical Topsy, the slave-girl clad in a pinafore of sackcloth and destined to become for Anglo-Saxon millions the type of the absolute in the artless, and her little mistress the blonde Eva, a figure rather in the Kenwigs tradition of pantalettes and pigtails, whom I recall as perching quite suicidally, with her elbows out and a preliminary shriek, on that bulwark of the Mississippi steamboat which was to facilitate her all but fatal immersion in the flood. Why should I have duly noted that no little game on her part could well less have resembled or simulated an accident, and yet have been no less moved by her reappearance, rescued from the river but perfectly dry, in the arms of faithful Tom, who had plunged in to save her, without either so much as wetting his shoes, than if I had been engaged with her in a reckless romp? I could count the white stitches in the loose patchwork, and yet could take it for a story rich and harmonious; I could know we had all intellectually condescended and that we had yet had the thrill of an æsthetic adventure; and this was a brave beginning for a consciousness that was to be nothing if not mixed and a curiosity that was to be nothing if not restless.

The principle of this prolonged arrest, which I insist on prolonging a little further, is doubtless in my instinct to grope for our earliest æsthetic seeds. Careless at once and generous the hands by which they were sown, but practically appointed none the less to cause that peculiarly flurried hare to run—flurried because over ground so little native to it—when so many others held back. Is it *that* air of romance that gilds for me then the Barnum background—taking it as a symbol; that makes me resist, to this effect of a passionate adverse loyalty, any impulse to translate into harsh terms any old sordidities and poverties? The Great American Museum, the down-town scenery and aspects at large, and even the up-town improvements on them, as then flourishing?—why, they must have been for the most part of the last meanness: the Barnum picture above all ignoble and awful, its blatant face or frame stuck about with innumerable flags that waved, poor vulgar-sized ensigns, over spurious relics and catchpenny monsters in effigy, to say nothing of the promise within of the still more monstrous and abnormal living—from the total impression of which things we plucked somehow the flower of the ideal. It grew, I must in justice proceed, much more sweetly and naturally at Niblo's, which represented in our scheme the ideal evening, while Barnum figured the ideal day; so that I ask myself, with that sense of our resorting there under the rich cover of night (which was the supreme charm,) how it comes that this larger memory hasn't swallowed up all others. For here, absolutely, *was* the flower at its finest and grown as nowhere else—grown in the great garden of the Ravel Family and offered again and again to our deep inhalation. I see the Ravels, French acrobats, dancers and pantomimists, as representing, for our culture, pure grace and charm and civility; so that one doubts whether any candid community was ever so much in debt to a race of entertainers or had so happy and prolonged, so personal and grateful a relation with them. They must have been, with their offshoots of Martinettis and others, of three or four generations, besides being of a rich theatrical stock generally, and we had our particular friends and favourites among them; we seemed to follow them through every phase of their career, to assist at their tottering steps along the tight-rope as very small children kept in equilibrium by very big balancing-poles (caretakers here walking under in case of falls;) to greet them as Madame Axel, of robust maturity and in a Spanish costume, bounding on the same tense cord more heavily but more assuredly; and finally to know the climax of the art with them in Raoul or the Night-Owl and Jocko or the Brazilian Ape—and all this in the course of our own brief infancy. My impression of them bristles so with memories that we seem to have rallied to their different productions with much the same regularity with which we formed fresh educational connections; and they were so much our property and our pride that they supported us handsomely through all fluttered entertainment of the occasional Albany cousins. I remember how when one of these visitors, wound up, in honour of New York, to the very fever of perception, broke out one evening while we waited for the curtain to rise, "Oh don't you hear the cries? They're *beating* them, I'm sure they are; can't it be stopped?" we resented the charge as a slur on our very honour; for what our romantic relative had heatedly imagined to reach us, in a hushed-up manner from behind, was the sounds attendant on the application of blows to some acrobatic infant who had "funked" his little job. Impossible such horrors in the world of pure poetry opened out to us at Niblo's, a temple of illusion, of tragedy and comedy and pathos that, though its *abords* of stony brown Metropolitan Hotel, on the "wrong side," must have been bleak and vulgar, flung its glamour forth into Broadway. What more pathetic for instance, so that we publicly wept, than the fate of wondrous Martinetti Jocko, who, after befriending a hapless French family wrecked on the coast of Brazil and bringing back to life a small boy rescued from the waves (I see even now, with every detail, this inanimate victim supine on the strand) met his death by some cruel bullet of which I have forgotten the determinant cause, only remembering the final agony as something we could scarce bear and a strain of our sensibility to which our parents repeatedly questioned the wisdom of exposing us.

These performers and these things were in all probability but of a middling skill and splendour—it was the pre-trapèze age, and we were caught by mild marvels, even if a friendly good faith in them, something sweet and sympathetic, was after all a value, whether of their own humanity, their own special quality, or only of our innocence, never to be renewed; but I light this taper to the initiators, so to call them, whom I remembered, when we had left them behind, as if they had given us a silver key to carry off and so to refit, after long years, to sweet names never thought of from then till now. Signor Léon Javelli, in whom the French and the Italian charm appear to have met, who was he, and what did he brilliantly do, and why of a sudden do I thus recall and admire him? I am afraid he but danced the tight-rope, the most domestic of our friends' resources, as it brought them out, by the far stretch of the rope, into the bosom of the house and against our very hearts, where they leapt and bounded and wavered and recovered closely face to face with us; but I dare say he bounded, brave Signor Léon, to the greatest height of all: let this vague agility, in any case, connect him with that revelation of the ballet, the sentimental-pastoral, of other years, which, in The Four Lovers for example, a pantomimic lesson as in words of one syllable, but all quick and gay and droll, would have affected us as classic, I am sure, had we then had at our disposal that term of appreciation. When we read in English story-books about the pantomimes in London, which somehow cropped up in them so often, those were the only things that didn't make us yearn; so much we felt we were masters of the type, and so almost sufficiently was that a stop-gap for London constantly deferred. We hadn't the transformation-scene, it was true, though what this really seemed to come to was clown and harlequin taking liberties with policemen—these last evidently a sharp note in a picturesqueness that we lacked, our own slouchy "officers" saying nothing to us of that sort; but we had at Niblo's harlequin and columbine, albeit of less pure a tradition, and we knew moreover all about clowns, for we went to circuses too, and so repeatedly that when I add them to our list of recreations, the good old orthodox circuses under tents set up in vacant lots, with which New York appears at that time to have bristled, time and place would seem to have shrunken for most other pursuits, and not least for that of serious learning. And the case is aggravated as I remember Franconi's, which we more or less haunted and which, aiming at the grander style and the monumental effect, blazed with fresh paint and rang with Roman chariot-races up there among the deserts of Twenty-ninth Street or wherever; considerably south, perhaps, but only a little east, of the vaster desolations that gave scope to the Crystal Palace, second of its name since, following—not *passibus æquis*, alas—the London structure of 1851, this enterprise forestalled by a year or two the Paris Palais de l'Industrie of 1855. Such as it was I feel again its majesty on those occasions on which I dragged—if I must here once more speak for myself only—after Albany cousins through its courts of edification: I remember being very tired and cold and hungry there, in a little light drab and very glossy or shiny "talma" breasted with rather troublesome buttonhole-embroideries; though concomitantly conscious that I was somehow in Europe, since everything about me had been "brought over," which ought to have been consoling, and seems in fact to have been so in some degree, inasmuch as both my own pain and the sense of the cousinly, the Albany, headaches quite fade in that recovered presence of big European Art embodied in Thorwaldsen's enormous Christ and the Disciples, a shining marble company ranged in a semicircle of dark maroon walls. If this was Europe then Europe was beautiful indeed, and we rose to it on the wings of wonder; never were we afterwards to see great showy sculpture, in whatever profuse exhibition or of whatever period or school, without some renewal of that charmed Thorwaldsen hour, some taste again of the almost sugary or confectionery sweetness with which the great white images had affected us under their supper-table gaslight. The Crystal Palace was vast and various and dense, which was what Europe was going to be; it was a deep-down jungle of impressions that were somehow challenges, even as we might, helplessly defied, find foreign words and practices; over which formidably towered Kiss's mounted Amazon attacked by a leopard or whatever, a work judged at that day sublime and the glory of the place; so that I felt the journey back in the autumn dusk and the Sixth Avenue cars (established just in time) a relapse into soothing flatness, a return to the Fourteenth Street horizon from a far journey and a hundred looming questions that would still, tremendous thought, come up for all the personal answers of which one cultivated the seed.

XIII

LET ME hurry, however, to catch again that thread I left dangling from my glance at our small vague spasms of school—my personal sense of them being as vague and small, I mean, in contrast with the fuller and stronger cup meted out all round to the Albany cousins, much more privileged, I felt, in every stroke of fortune; or at least much more interesting, though it might be wicked to call them more happy, through those numberless bereavements that had so enriched their existence. I mentioned above in particular the enviable consciousness of our little red-headed kinsman Gus Barker, who, as by a sharp prevision, snatched what gaiety he might from a life to be cut short, in a cavalry dash, by one of the Confederate bullets of 1863: he blew out at us, on New York Sundays, as I have said, sharp puffs of the atmosphere of the Institution Charlier—strong to us, that is, the atmosphere of whose institutions was weak; but it was above all during a gregarious visit paid him in a livelier field still that I knew myself merely mother'd and brother'd. It had been his fate to be but scantly the latter and never at all the former—our aunt Janet had not survived his birth; but on this day of our collective pilgrimage to Sing-Sing, where he was at a "military" school and clad in a fashion that represented to me the very panoply of war, he shone with a rare radiance of privation. Ingenuous and responsive, of a social disposition, a candour of gaiety, that matched his physical activity—the most beautifully made athletic little person, and in the highest degree appealing and engaging—he not only did us the honours of his dazzling academy (dazzling at least to me) but had all the air of showing us over the great State prison which even then flourished near at hand and to which he accompanied us; a party of a composition that comes back to me as wonderful, the New York and Albany cousinships appearing to have converged and met, for the happy occasion, with the generations and sexes melting together and moving in a loose harmonious band. The party must have been less numerous than by the romantic tradition or confused notation of my youth, and what I mainly remember of it beyond my sense of our being at once an attendant train to my aged and gentle and in general most unadventurous grandmother, and a chorus of curiosity and amusement roundabout the vivid Gussy, is our collective impression that State prisons were on the whole delightful places, vast, bright and breezy, with a gay, free circulation in corridors and on stairs, a pleasant prevalence of hot soup and fresh crusty rolls, in tins, of which visitors admiringly partook, and for the latter, in chance corners and on sunny landings, much interesting light brush of gentlemen remarkable but for gentlemanly crimes—that is defalcations and malversations to striking and impressive amounts.

I recall our coming on such a figure at the foot of a staircase and his having been announced to us by our conductor or friend in charge as likely to be there; and what a charm I found in his cool loose uniform of shining white (as I was afterwards to figure it,) as well as in his generally refined and distinguished appearance and in the fact that he was engaged, while exposed to our attention, in the commendable act of paring his nails with a smart penknife and that he didn't allow us to interrupt him. One of my companions, I forget which, had advised me that in these contacts with illustrious misfortune I was to be careful not to stare; and present to me at this moment is the wonder of whether he would think it staring to note that *he* quite stared, and also that his hands were fine and fair and one of them adorned with a signet ring. I was to have later in life a glimpse of two or three dismal penitentiaries, places affecting me as sordid, as dark and dreadful; but if the revelation of Sing-Sing had involved the idea of a timely warning to the young mind my small sensibility at least was not reached by the lesson. I envied the bold-eyed celebrity in the array of a planter at his ease—we might have been *his* slaves—quite as much as I envied Gussy; in connection with which I may remark here that though in that early time I seem to have been constantly eager to exchange my lot for that of somebody else, on the assumed certainty of gaining by the bargain, I fail to remember feeling jealous of such happier persons—in the measure open to children of spirit. I had rather a positive lack of the passion, and thereby, I suppose, a lack of spirit; since if jealousy bears, as I think, on what one sees one's companions able to do—as against one's own falling short—envy, as I knew it at least, was simply of what they *were*, or in other words of a certain sort of richer consciousness supposed, doubtless often too freely supposed, in them. They were so *other*—that was what I felt; and to *be* other, other almost anyhow, seemed as good as the probable taste of the bright compound wistfully watched in the confectioner's window; unattainable, impossible, of course, but as to which just this impossibility and just that privation kept those active proceedings in which jealousy seeks relief quite out of the question. A platitude of acceptance of the poor actual, the absence of all vision of how in any degree to change it, combined with a complacency, an acuity of perception of alternatives, though a view of them as only through the confectioner's hard glass—that is what I recover as the nearest approach to an apology, in the soil of my nature, for the springing seed of emulation. I never dreamed of competing—a business having in it at the best, for my temper, if not for my total failure of temper, a displeasing ferocity. If competing was bad snatching was therefore still worse, and jealousy was a sort of spiritual snatching. With which, nevertheless, all the while, one might have been "like" So-and-So, who had such horizons. A helpless little love of horizons I certainly cherished, and could sometimes even care for my own. These always shrank, however, under almost any suggestion of a further range or finer shade in the purple rim offered to other eyes—and that is what I take for the restlessness of envy. It wasn't that I wished to change with everyone, with anyone at a venture, but that I saw "gifts" everywhere but as mine and that I scarce know whether to call the effect of this miserable or monstrous. It was the effect at least of self-abandonment—I mean to visions.

There must have been on that occasion of the Sing-Sing day—which it deeply interests me to piece together—some state of connection for some of us with the hospitalities of Rhinebeck, the place of abode of the eldest of the Albany uncles—that is of the three most in our view; for there were two others, the eldest of all a half-uncle only, who formed a class quite by himself, and the very youngest, who, with lively interests of his own, had still less attention for us than either of his three brothers. The house at Rhinebeck and all its accessories (which struck our young sense as innumerable,) in especial the great bluff of the Hudson on which it stood, yields me images scarcely dimmed, though as the effect but of snatches of acquaintance; there at all events the gently-groaning—ever so gently and dryly—Albany grandmother, with the Albany cousins as to whom I here discriminate, her two adopted daughters, maturest and mildest of the general tribe, must have paused for a stay; a feature of which would be perhaps her juncture with the New York contingent, somewhere sociably achieved, for the befriending of juvenile Gussy. It shimmers there, the whole circumstance, with I scarce know what large innocence of charity and ease; the Gussy-pretext, for reunion, all so thin yet so important an appeal, the simplicity of the interests and the doings, the assumptions and the concessions, each to-day so touching, almost so edifying. We were surely all gentle and generous together, floating in such a clean light social order, sweetly proof against ennui—unless it be a bad note, as is conceivable, never, *never* to feel bored—and thankful for the smallest æsthetic or romantic mercies. My vision loses itself withal in vaster connections—above all in my general sense of the then grand newness of the Hudson River Railroad; so far at least as its completion to Albany was concerned, a modern blessing that even the youngest of us were in a position to appraise. The time had been when the steamboat had to content us—and I feel how amply it must have done so as I recall the thrill of docking in dim early dawns, the whole hour of the Albany waterside, the night of huge strange paddling and pattering and shrieking and creaking once ended, and contrast with it all certain long sessions in the train at an age and in conditions when neither train nor traveller had suffered chastening; sessions of a high animation, as I recast them, but at the same time of mortal intensities of lassitude. The elements here indeed are much confused and mixed—I must have known that discipline of the hectic interest and the extravagant strain in relation to Rhinebeck only; an *étape*, doubtless, on the way to New York, for the Albany kinship, but the limit to our smaller patiences of any northward land-journey. And yet not the young fatigue, I repeat, but the state of easy wonder, is what most comes back: the stops too repeated, but perversely engaging; the heat and the glare too great, but the river, by the window, making reaches and glimpses, so that the great swing of picture and force of light and colour were themselves a constant adventure; the uncles, above all, too pre-eminent, too recurrent, to the creation of a positive soreness of sympathy, of curiosity, and yet constituting by their presence half the enlargement of the time. For the presence of uncles, incoherent Albany uncles, is somehow what most gives these hours their stamp for memory. I scarce know why, nor do I much, I confess, distinguish occasions—but I see what I see: the long, the rattling car of the old open native form and the old harsh native exposure; the sense of arrival forever postponed, qualified however also by that of having in my hands a volume of M. Arsène Houssaye, Philosophes et Comédiennes, remarkably submitted by one of my relatives to my judgment. I see them always, the relatives, in slow circulation; restless and nervous and casual their note, not less than strikingly genial, but with vaguenesses, lapses, eclipses, that deprived their society of a tactless weight. They cheered us on, in their way; born optimists, clearly, if not logically determined ones, they were always reassuring and sustaining, though with a bright brevity that must have taken immensities, I think, for granted. They wore their hats slightly toward the nose, they strolled, they hung about, they reported of progress and of the company, they dropped suggestions, new magazines, packets of the edible deprecated for the immature; they figured in fine to a small nephew as the principal men of their time and, so far as the two younger and more familiar were concerned, the most splendid as to aspect and apparel. It was none the less to the least shining, though not essentially the least comforting, of this social trio that, if I rightly remember, I owed my introduction to the *chronique galante* of the eighteenth century.

There tags itself at any rate to the impression a flutter as of some faint, some recaptured, grimace for another of his kindly offices (which I associate somehow with the deck of a steamboat:) his production for our vague benefit of a literary classic, the Confessions, as he called our attention to them, of the celebrated "Rosseau." I catch again the echo of the mirth excited, to my surprise, by this communication, and recover as well my responsive advance toward a work that seemed so to promise; but especially have I it before me that some play of light criticism mostly attended, on the part of any circle, this speaker's more ambitious remarks. For all that, and in spite of oddities of appearance and type, it was Augustus James who spread widest, in default of towering highest, to my wistful view of the larger life, and who covered definite and accessible ground. This ground, the house and precincts of Linwood, at Rhinebeck, harboured our tender years, I surmise, but at few and brief moments; but it hadn't taken many of these to make it the image of an hospitality liberal as I supposed great social situations were liberal; suppositions on this score having in childhood (or at least they had in mine) as little as possible to do with dry data. Didn't Linwood bristle with great views and other glories, with gardens and graperies and black ponies, to say nothing of gardeners and grooms who were notoriously and quotedly droll; to say nothing, in particular, of our aunt Elizabeth, who had been Miss Bay of Albany, who was the mother of the fair and free young waltzing-women in New York, and who floats back to me through the Rhinebeck picture, aquiline but easy, with an effect of handsome high-browed, high-nosed looseness, of dressing-gowns or streaming shawls (the dowdy, the delightful shawl of the period;) and of claws of bright benevolent steel that kept nipping for our charmed advantage: roses and grapes and peaches and currant-clusters, together with turns of phrase and scraps of remark that fell as by quite a like flash of shears. These are mere scrapings of gold-dust, but my mind owes her a vibration that, however tiny, was to insist all these years on *marking*—on figuring in a whole complex of picture and drama, the clearest note of which was that of worry and woe: a crisis prolonged, in deep-roofed outer galleries, through hot August evenings and amid the dim flare of open windows, to the hum of domesticated insects. All but inexpressible the part played, in the young mind naturally even though perversely, even though inordinately, arranged as a stage for the procession and exhibition of appearances, by matters all of a usual cast, contacts and impressions not arriving at the dignity of shocks, but happening to be to the taste, as one may say, of the little intelligence, happening to be such as the fond fancy could assimilate. One's record becomes, under memories of this order—and that is the only trouble—a tale of assimilations small and fine; out of which refuse, directly interesting to the subject-victim only, the most branching vegetations may be conceived as having sprung. Such are the absurdities of the poor dear inward life—when translated, that is, and perhaps ineffectually translated, into terms of the outward and trying at all to flourish on the lines of the outward; a reflection that might stay me here weren't it that I somehow feel morally affiliated, tied as by knotted fibres, to the elements involved.

One of these was assuredly that my father had again, characteristically, suffered me to dangle; he having been called to Linwood by the dire trouble of his sister, Mrs. Temple, and brought me with him from Staten Island—I make the matter out as of the summer of '54. We had come up, he and I, to New York; but our doings there, with the journey following, are a blank to me; I recover but my sense, on our arrival, of being for the first time in the presence of tragedy, which the shining scene, roundabout, made more sinister—sharpened even to the point of my feeling abashed and irrelevant, wondering why I had come. My aunt, under her brother's roof, had left her husband, wasted with consumption, near death at Albany; gravely ill herself—she had taken the disease from him as it was taken in those days, and was in the event very scantly to survive him—she had been ordered away in her own interest, for which she cared no scrap, and my father, the person in all his family most justly appealed and most anxiously listened to, had been urged to come and support her in a separation that she passionately rejected. Vivid to me still, as floating across verandahs into the hot afternoon stillness, is the wail of her protest and her grief; I remember being scared and hushed by it and stealing away beyond its reach. I remember not less what resources of high control the whole case imputed, for my imagination, to my father; and how, creeping off to the edge of the eminence above the Hudson, I somehow felt the great bright harmonies of air and space becoming one with my rather proud assurance and confidence, that of my own connection, for life, for interest, with such sources of light. The great impression, however, the one that has brought me so far, was another matter: only that of the close, lamp-tempered, outer evening aforesaid, with my parent again, somewhere deep within, yet not too far to make us hold our breath for it, tenderly opposing his sister's purpose of flight, and the presence at my side of my young cousin Marie, youngest daughter of the house, exactly of my own age, and named in honour of her having been born in Paris, to the influence of which fact her shining black eyes, her small quickness and brownness, marking sharply her difference from her sisters, so oddly, so almost extravagantly testified. It had come home to me by some voice of the air that she was "spoiled," and it made her in the highest degree interesting; we ourselves had been so associated, at home, without being in the least spoiled (I think we even rather missed it:) so that I knew about these subjects of invidious reflection only by literature—mainly, no doubt, that of the nursery—in which they formed, quite by themselves, a romantic class; and, the fond fancy always predominant, I prized even while a little dreading the chance to see the condition at work. This chance was given me, it was clear—though I risk in my record of it a final anticlimax—by a remark from my uncle Augustus to his daughter: seated duskily in our group, which included two or three dim dependent forms, he expressed the strong opinion that Marie should go to bed—expressed it, that is, with the casual cursory humour that was to strike me as the main expressional resource of outstanding members of the family and that would perhaps have had under analysis the defect of making judgment very personal without quite making authority so. Authority they hadn't, of a truth, these all so human outstanding ones; they made shift but with light appreciation, sudden suggestion, a peculiar variety of happy remark in the air. It had been remarked but in the air, I feel sure, that Marie should seek her couch—a truth by the dark wing of which I ruefully felt myself brushed; and the words seemed therefore to fall with a certain ironic weight. What I have retained of their effect, at any rate, is the vague fact of some objection raised by my cousin and some sharper point to his sentence supplied by her father; promptly merged in a visible commotion, a flutter of my young companion across the gallery as for refuge in the maternal arms, a protest and an appeal in short which drew from my aunt the simple phrase that was from that moment so preposterously to "count" for me. "Come now, my dear; don't make a scene—I *insist* on your not making a scene!" That was all the witchcraft the occasion used, but the note was none the less epoch-making.

The expression, so vivid, so portentous, was one I had never heard—it had never been addressed to us at home; and who should say now what a world one mightn't at once read into it? It seemed freighted to sail so far; it told me so much about life. Life at these intensities clearly became "scenes"; but the great thing, the immense illumination, was that we could make them or not as we chose. It was a long time of course before I began to distinguish between those within our compass more particularly as spoiled and those producible on a different basis and which should involve detachment, involve presence of mind; just the qualities in which Marie's possible output was apparently deficient. It didn't in the least matter accordingly whether or no a scene *was* then proceeded to—and I have lost all count of what immediately happened. The mark had been made for me and the door flung open; the passage, gathering up *all* the elements of the troubled time, had been itself a scene, quite enough of one, and I had become aware with it of a rich accession of possibilities.

XIV

It must have been after the Sing-Sing episode that Gussy came to us, in New York, for Sundays and holidays, from scarce further off than round the corner—his foreign Institution flourishing, I seem to remember, in West Tenth Street or wherever—and yet as floated by exotic airs and with the scent of the spice-islands hanging about him. He was being educated largely with Cubans and Mexicans, in those New York days more than half the little flock of the foreign Institutions in general; over whom his easy triumphs, while he wagged his little red head for them, were abundantly credible; reinforced as my special sense of them was moreover by the similar situation of his sister, older than he but also steeped in the exotic medium and also sometimes bringing us queer echoes of the tongues. I remember being deputed by my mother to go and converse with her, on some question of her coming to us, at the establishment of Madame Reichhardt (pronounced, à la française, Réchard,) where I felt that I had crossed, for the hour, the very threshold of "Europe"; it being impressed on me by my cousin, who was tall and handsome and happy, with a laugh of more beautiful sound than any laugh we were to know again, that French only was speakable on the premises. I sniffed it up aromatically, the superior language, in passage and parlour—it took the form of some strong savoury soup, an educational *potage Réchard* that must excellently have formed the taste: that was again, I felt as I came away, a part of the rich experience of being thrown in tender juvenile form upon the world. This genial girl, like her brother, was in the grand situation of having no home and of carrying on life, such a splendid kind of life, by successive visits to relations; though neither she nor Gussy quite achieved the range of their elder brother, "Bob" of that ilk, a handsome young man, a just blurred, attractive, illusive presence, who hovered a bit beyond our real reach and apparently displayed the undomesticated character at its highest. *He* seemed exposed, for his pleasure—if pleasure it was!—and my wonder, to every assault of experience; his very name took on, from these imputations, a browner glow;

and it was all in the right key that, a few years later, he should, after "showing some talent for sculpture," have gone the hapless way of most of the Albany youth, have become a theme for sad vague headshakes (kind and very pitying in his case) and died prematurely and pointlessly, or in other words, by my conception, picturesquely. The headshakes were heavier and the sighs sharper for another slim shade, one of the younger and I believe quite the most hapless of those I have called the outstanding ones; he too, several years older than we again, a tormenting hoverer and vanisher; he too charmingly sister'd, though sister'd only, and succumbing to monstrous early trouble after having "shown some talent" for music. The ghostliness of these æsthetic manifestations, as I allude to them, is the thinnest conceivable chip of stray marble, the faintest far-off twang of old chords; I ask myself, for the odd obscurity of it, under what inspiration music and sculpture may have tinkled and glimmered to the Albany ear and eye (as we at least knew those organs) and with what queer and weak delusions our unfortunates may have played. Quite ineffably quaint and *falot* this proposition of *that* sort of resource for the battle of life as it then and there opened; and above all beautifully suggestive of our sudden collective disconnectedness (ours as the whole kinship's) from *the* American resource of those days, Albanian or other. That precious light was the light of "business" only; and we, by a common instinct, artlessly joining hands, went forth into the wilderness without so much as a twinkling taper.

Our consensus, on all this ground, was amazing—it brooked no exception; the word had been passed, all round, that we didn't, that we couldn't and shouldn't, understand these things, questions of arithmetic and of fond calculation, questions of the counting-house and the market; and we appear to have held to our agreement as loyally and to have accepted our doom as serenely as if our faith had been mutually pledged. The rupture with my grandfather's tradition and attitude was complete; we were never in a single case, I think, for two generations, guilty of a stroke of business; the most that could be said of us was that, though about equally wanting, all round, in any faculty of acquisition, we happened to pay for the amiable weakness less in some connections than in others. The point was that we moved so oddly and consistently—as it was our only form of consistency—over our limited pasture, never straying to nibble in the strange or the steep places. What was the matter with us under this spell, and what the moral might have been for our case, are issues of small moment, after all, in face of the fact of our mainly so brief duration. It was given to but few of us to be taught by the event, to be made to wonder with the last intensity what *had* been the matter. This it would be interesting to worry out, might I take the time; for the story wouldn't be told, I conceive, by any mere rueful glance at other avidities, the preference for ease, the play of the passions, the appetite for pleasure. These things have often accompanied the business imagination; just as the love of life and the love of other persons, and of many of the things of the world, just as quickness of soul and sense, have again and again not excluded it. However, it comes back, as I have already hinted, to the manner in which the "things of the world" could but present themselves; there were not enough of these, and they were not fine and fair enough, to engage happily so much unapplied, so much loose and crude attention. We hadn't doubtless at all a complete play of intelligence—if I may not so far discriminate as to say *they* hadn't; or our lack of the instinct of the market needn't have been so much worth speaking of: other curiosities, other sympathies might have redressed the balance. I make out our young cousin J. J. as dimly aware of this while composing the light melodies that preluded to his extinction, and which that catastrophe so tried to admonish us to think of as promising; but his image is more present to me still as the great incitement, during the few previous years, to our constant dream of "educational" relief, of some finer kind of social issue, through Europe.

It was to Europe J. J. had been committed; he was over there forging the small apologetic arms that were so little to avail him, but it was quite enough for us that he pointed the way to the Pension Sillig, at Vevey, which shone at us, from afar, as our own more particular solution. It was true that the Pension Sillig figured mainly as the solution in cases of recognised wildness; there long flourished among New York parents whose view of such resources had the proper range a faith in it for that complaint; and it was as an act of faith that, failing other remedies, our young wifeless uncle, conscious himself of no gift for control or for edification, had placed there his difficult son. He returned with delight from this judicious course and there was an hour when we invoked, to intensity, a similar one in our own interest and when the air of home did little but reflect from afar the glitter of blue Swiss lakes, the tinkle of cattle-bells in Alpine pastures, the rich *bonhomie* that M. Sillig, dispensing an education all of milk and honey and edelweiss and ranz-des-vaches, combined with his celebrated firmness for tough subjects. Poor J. J. came back, I fear, much the same subject that he went; but he had verily performed his scant office on earth, that of having brought our then prospect, our apparent possibility, a trifle nearer. He seemed to have been wild even beyond M. Sillig's measure—which was highly disappointing; but if we might on the other hand be open to the reproach of falling too short of it there were establishments adapted to every phase of the American predicament; so that our general direction could but gain in vividness. I think with compassion, altogether, of the comparative obscurity to which our eventual success in gathering the fruits, few and scant though they might be, thus relegates those to whom it was given but to toy so briefly with the flowers. They make collectively their tragic trio: J. J. the elder, most loved, most beautiful, most sacrificed of the Albany uncles; J. J. the younger—they were young together, they were luckless together, and the combination was as strange as the disaster was sweeping; and the daughter and sister, amplest of the "natural," easiest of the idle, who lived on to dress their memory with every thread and patch of her own perfect temper and then confirm the tradition, after all, by too early and woeful an end.

If it comes over me under the brush of multiplied memories that we might well have invoked the educational "relief" I just spoke of, I should doubtless as promptly add that my own case must have been intrinsically of the poorest, and indeed make the point once for all that I should be taken as having seen and felt much of the whole queerness through the medium of rare inaptitudes. I can only have been inapt, I make out, to have retained so positively joyless a sense of it all, to be aware of most of it now but as dim confusion, as bewildered anxiety. There was interest always, certainly—but it strikes me to-day as interest in everything that wasn't supposedly or prescriptively of the question at all, and in nothing that *was* so respectably involved and accredited. Without some sharpness of interest I shouldn't now have the memories; but these stick to me somehow with none of the hard glue of recovered "spirits," recovered vivacities, assurances, successes. I can't have had, through it all, I think, a throb of assurance or success; without which, at the same time, absurdly and indescribably, I lived and wriggled, floundered and failed, lost the clue of everything but a general lucid consciousness (lucid, that is, for my tender years;) which I clutched with a sense of its value. What happened all the while, I conceive, was that I imagined things—and as if quite on system—wholly other than as they were, and so carried on in the midst of the actual ones an existence that somehow floated and saved me even while cutting me off from any degree of direct performance, in fact from any degree of direct participation, at all. *There* presumably was the interest—in the intensity and plausibility and variety of the irrelevance: an irrelevance which, for instance, made all pastors and masters, and especially all fellow-occupants of benches and desks, all elbowing and kicking presences within touch or view, so many monsters and horrors, so many wonders and splendours and mysteries, but never, so far as I can recollect, realities of relation, dispensers either of knowledge or of fate, playmates, intimates, mere coævals and coequals. They were something better—better above all than the coequal or coæval; they were so thoroughly figures and characters, divinities or demons, and endowed in this light with a vividness that the mere reality of relation, a commoner directness of contact, would have made, I surmise, comparatively poor. This superior shade of interest was not, none the less, so beguiling that I recall without unmitigated horror, or something very like it, a winter passed with my brother at the Institution Vergnès; our sorry subjection to which argues to my present sense an unmitigated surrounding aridity. To a "French school" must have been earnestly imputed the virtue of keeping us in patience till easier days should come; infinitely touching our parents' view of that New York fetish of our young time, an "acquisition of the languages"—an acquisition reinforcing those opportunities which we enjoyed at home, so far as they mustered, and at which I have briefly glanced. Charming and amusing to me indeed certain faint echoes, wavering images, of this superstition as it played about our path: ladies and gentlemen, dimly foreign, mere broken syllables of whose names come back to me, attending there to converse in tongues and then giving way to others through failures of persistence—whether in pupils or preceptors I know not. There hovers even Count Adam Gurowski, Polish, patriotic, exiled, temporarily famous, with the vision of *his* being invoked for facility and then relinquished for difficulty; though I scarce guess on which of his battle-grounds—he was so polyglot that he even had a rich command of New Yorkese.

XV

It is to the Institution Vergnès that my earliest recovery of the sense of being in any degree "educated with" W. J. attaches itself; an establishment which occupied during the early 'fifties a site in the very middle of Broadway, of the lower, the real Broadway, where it could throb with the very pulse of the traffic in which we all innocently rejoiced—believing it, I surmise, the liveliest conceivable: a fact that is by itself, in the light of the present, an odd rococo note. The lower Broadway—I allude to the whole Fourth Street and Bond Street (where now *is* the Bond Street of that antiquity?)—was then a seat of education, since we had not done with it, as I shall presently show, even when we had done with the Institution, a prompt disillusionment; and I brood thus over a period which strikes me as long and during which my personal hours of diligence were somehow more than anything else hours of the pavement and the shopfront, or of such contemplative exercise as the very considerable distance, for small legs, between those regions and the westward Fourteenth Street might comprise. Pedestrian gaping having been in childhood, as I have noted, prevailingly my line, fate appeared to have kindly provided for it on no small scale; to the extent even that it must have been really my sole and single form of athletics. Vague heated competition and agitation in the then enclosed Union Square would seem to point a little, among us all, to nobler types of motion; but of any basis for recreation, anything in the nature of a playground or a breathing space, the Institution itself was serenely innocent. This I take again for a note extraordinarily mediæval. It occupied the first and second floors, if I rightly remember, of a wide front that, overhanging the endless thoroughfare, looked out on bouncing, clattering "stages" and painfully dragged carts and the promiscuous human shuffle—the violence of repercussions from the New York pavement of those years to be further taken into account; and I win it back from every side as, in spite of these aspects of garish publicity, a dark and dreadful, and withal quite absurd, scene. I see places of that general time, even places of confinement, in a dusty golden light that special memories of small misery scarce in the least bedim, and this holds true of our next and quite neighbouring refuge; the establishment of M. Vergnès alone darkles and shrinks to me—a sordidly *black* interior is my main image for it; attenuated only by its having very soon afterwards, as a suffered ordeal, altogether lapsed and intermitted. Faintly, in the gloom, I distinguish M. Vergnès himself—quite "old," very old indeed as I supposed him, and highly irritated and markedly bristling; though of nothing in particular that happened to me at his or at anyone's else hands have I the scantest remembrance. What really most happened no doubt, was that my brother and I should both come away with a mind prepared for a perfect assimilation of Alphonse Daudet's chronicle of "Jack," years and years later on; to make the acquaintance in that work of the "petits pays chauds" among whom Jack learnt the first lessons of life was to see the Institution Vergnès at once revive, swarming as it did with small homesick Cubans and Mexicans; the complete failure of blondness that marks the memory is doubtless the cumulative effect of so many of the New York "petits pays chauds," preponderantly brown and black and conducing to a greasy gloom. Into this gloom I fear I should see all things recede together but for a certain salient note, the fact that the whole "staff" appears to have been constantly in a rage; from which naturally resulted the accent of shrillness (the only accent we could pick up, though we were supposed to be learning, for the extreme importance of it, quantities of French) and the sound of high vociferation. I remember infuriated ushers, of foreign speech and flushed complexion—the tearing across of hapless "exercises" and *dictées* and the hurtle through the air of dodged volumes; only never, despite this, the extremity of smiting. There can have been at the Institution no blows instructionally dealt—nor even from our hours of ease do any such echoes come back to me. Little Cubans and Mexicans, I make out, were not to be vulgarly whacked—in deference, presumably, to some latent relic or imputed survival of Castilian pride; which would impose withal considerations of quite practical prudence. Food for reflection and comparison might well have been so suggested; interesting at least the element of contrast between such opposed conceptions of tone, temper and manner as the passion without whacks, or with whacks only of inanimate objects, ruling the scene I have described, and the whacks without passion, the grim, impersonal, strictly penal applications of the rod, which then generally represented what was still involved in our English tradition. It was the two theories of sensibility, of personal dignity, that so diverged; but with such other divergences now on top of those that the old comparison falls away. We to-day go unwhacked altogether—though from a pride other than Castilian: it is difficult to say at least what ideal has thus triumphed. In the Vergnès air at any rate I seem myself to have sat unscathed and unterrified—not alarmed even by so much as a call to the blackboard; only protected by my insignificance, which yet covered such a sense of our dusky squalor. Queer for us the whole affair, assuredly; but how much queerer for the poor petits pays chauds who had come so far for their privilege. *We* had come, comparatively, but from round the corner—and that left the "state of education" and the range of selection all about as quaint enough. What could these things then have been in the various native climes of the petits pays chauds?

It was by some strong wave of reaction, clearly, that we were floated next into the quieter haven of Mr. Richard Pulling Jenks—where cleaner waters, as I feel their coolness still, must have filled a neater though, it was true, slightly more contracted trough. Yet the range of selection had been even on this higher plane none too strikingly exemplified; our jumping had scant compass—we still grubbed with a good conscience in Broadway and sidled about Fourth Street. But I think of the higher education as having there, from various causes, none the less begun to glimmer for us. A diffused brightness, a kind of high cross-light of conflicting windows, rests for me at all events on the little realm of Mr. Pulling Jenks and bathes it as with positively sweet limitations. Limited must it have been, I feel, with our couple of middling rooms, front and back, our close packing, our large unaccommodating stove, our grey and gritty oilcloth, and again our importunate Broadway; from the aggregation of which elements there distils itself, without my being able to account for it, a certain perversity of romance. I speak indeed here for myself in particular, and keen for romance must I have been in such conditions, I admit; since the sense of it had crept into a recreational desert even as utter as that of the Institution Vergnès. Up out of Broadway we still scrambled—I can smell the steep and cold and dusty wooden staircase; straight into Broadway we dropped—I feel again the generalised glare of liberation; and I scarce know what tenuity of spirit it argues that I should neither have enjoyed nor been aware of missing (speaking again for myself only) a space wider than the schoolroom floor to react and knock about in. I literally conclude that we must have knocked about in Broadway, and in Broadway alone, like perfect little men of the world; we must have been let loose there to stretch our legs and fill our lungs, without prejudice either to our earlier and later freedoms of going and coming. I as strictly infer, at the same time, that Broadway must have been then as one of the alleys of Eden, for any sinister contact or consequence involved for us; a circumstance that didn't in the least interfere, too, as I have noted, with its offer of an entrancing interest. The interest verily could have been a *calculated* thing on the part of our dear parents as little as on that of Mr. Jenks himself. Therefore let it be recorded as still most odd that we should all have assented to such deficiency of landscape, such exiguity of sport. I take the true inwardness of the matter to have been in our having such short hours, long as they may have appeared at the time, that the day left margin at the worst for private inventions. I think we found landscape, for ourselves—and wherever I at least found vision I found such sport as I was capable of—even between the front and back rooms and the conflicting windows; even by the stove which somehow scorched without warming, and yet round which Mr. Coe and Mr. Dolmidge, the drawing-master and the writing-master, arriving of a winter's day, used notedly, and in the case of Mr. Coe lamentedly, to draw out their delays. Is the dusty golden light of retrospect in this connection an effluence from Mr. Dolmidge and Mr. Coe, whose ministrations come back to me as the sole directly desired or invoked ones I was to know in my years, such as they were, of pupilage?

I see them in any case as old-world images, figures of an antique stamp; products, mustn't they have been, of an order in which some social relativity or matter-of-course adjustment, some transmitted form and pressure, were still at work? Mr.

Dolmidge, inordinately lean, clean-shaved, as was comparatively uncommon then, and in a swallow-tailed coat and I think a black satin stock, was surely perfect in his absolutely functional way, a pure pen-holder of a man, melancholy and mild, who taught the most complicated flourishes—great scrolls of them met our view in the form of surging seas and beaked and beady-eyed eagles, the eagle being so calligraphic a bird—while he might just have taught resignation. He was not at all funny—no one out of our immediate family circle, in fact almost no one but W. J. himself, who flowered in every waste, seems to have struck me as funny in those years; but he was to remain with me a picture of somebody in Dickens, one of the Phiz if not the Cruikshank pictures. Mr. Coe was another affair, bristling with the question of the "hard," but somehow too with the revelation of the soft, the deeply attaching; a worthy of immense stature and presence, crowned as with the thick white hair of genius, wearing a great gathered or puckered cloak, with a vast velvet collar, and resembling, as he comes back to me, the General Winfield Scott who lived so much in our eyes then. The oddity may well even at that hour have been present to me of its taking so towering a person to produce such small "drawing-cards"; it was as if some mighty bird had laid diminutive eggs. Mr. Coe, of a truth, laid his all over the place, and though they were not of more than handy size—very small boys could set them up in state on very small desks—they had doubtless a great range of number and effect. They were scattered far abroad and I surmise celebrated; they represented crooked cottages, feathery trees, browsing and bristling beasts and other rural objects; all rendered, as I recall them, in little detached dashes that were like stories told in words of one syllable, or even more perhaps in short gasps of delight. It must have been a stammering art, but I admired its fluency, which swims for me moreover in richer though slightly vague associations. Mr. Coe practised on a larger scale, in colour, in oils, producing wondrous neat little boards that make me to this day think of them and more particularly smell them, when I hear of a "panel" picture: a glamour of greatness attends them as brought home by W. J. from the master's own place of instruction in that old University building which partly formed the east side of Washington Square and figures to memory, or to fond imagination, as throbbing with more offices and functions, a denser chiaroscuro, than any reared hugeness of to-day, where character is so lost in quantity. Is there any present structure that plays such a part in proportion to its size?—though even as I ask the question I feel how nothing on earth is proportioned to present sizes. These alone are proportioned—and to mere sky-space and mere amount, amount of steel and stone; which is comparatively uninteresting. Perhaps our needs and our elements were then absurdly, were then provincially few, and that the patches of character in that small grey granite compendium were all we had in general to exhibit. Let me add at any rate that some of them were exhibitional—even to my tender years, I mean; since I respond even yet to my privilege of presence at some Commencement or Commemoration, such as might be natural, doubtless, to any "university," where, as under a high rich roof, before a Chancellor in a gown and amid serried admirers and impressive applause, there was "speaking," of the finest sort, and where above all I gathered in as a dazzling example the rare assurance of young Winthrop Somebody or Somebody Winthrop, who, though still in jackets, held us spellbound by his rendering of Serjeant Buzfuz's exposure of Mr. Pickwick. Long was I to marvel at the high sufficiency of young Winthrop Somebody or Somebody Winthrop—in which romantic impression it is perhaps after all (though with the consecration of one or two of the novels of the once-admired Theodore of that name, which so remarkably insists, thrown in) the sense of the place is embalmed.

I must not forget indeed that I throw in also Mr. Coe—even if with less assured a hand; by way of a note on those higher flights of power and promise that I at this time began to see definitely determined in my brother. As I catch W. J.'s image, from far back, at its most characteristic, he sits drawing and drawing, always drawing, especially under the lamplight of the Fourteenth Street back parlour; and not as with a plodding patience, which I think would less have affected me, but easily, freely and, as who should say, infallibly: always at the stage of finishing off, his head dropped from side to side and his tongue rubbing his lower lip. I recover a period during which to see him at all was so to see him—the other flights and faculties removed him from my view. These were a matter of course—he recurred, he passed nearer, but in his moments of ease, and I clearly quite accepted the ease of his disappearances. Didn't he always when within my view light them up and justify them by renewed and enlarged vividness? so that my whole sense of him as formed for assimilations scarce conceivable made our gaps of contact too natural for me even to be lessons in humility. Humility had nothing to do with it—as little even as envy would have had; I was below humility, just as we were together outside of competition, mutually "hors concours." *His* competitions were with others—in which how wasn't he, how could he not be, successful? while mine were with nobody, or nobody's with me, which came to the same thing, as heaven knows I neither braved them nor missed them. That winter, as I recover it, represents him as sufficiently within view to make his position or whereabouts in the upper air definite—I must have taken it for granted before, but could now in a manner measure it; and the freshness of this sense, something serene in my complacency, had to do, I divine, with the effect of our moving, with the rest of our company, which was not numerous but practically, but appreciably "select," on a higher and fairer plane than ever yet. Predominantly of course we owed this benefit to Richard Pulling himself; of whom I recall my brother's saying to me, at a considerably later time, and with an authority that affected me as absolute, that he had been of all our masters the most truly genial, in fact the only one to whom the art of exciting an interest or inspiring a sympathy could be in any degree imputed. I take this to have meant that he would have adorned a higher sphere—and it may have been, to explain his so soon swimming out of our ken, that into a higher sphere he rapidly moved; I can account at least for our falling away from him the very next year and declining again upon baser things and a lower civilisation but by some probability of his flight, just thereafter effected, to a greater distance, to one of the far upper reaches of the town. Some years must have elapsed and some distinction have crowned him when, being briefly in New York together, W. J. and I called on him of a Sunday afternoon, to find—what I hadn't been at all sure of—that he still quite knew who we were, or handsomely pretended to; handsomely in spite of his markedly confirmed identity of appearance with the Punch, husband to Judy, of the funny papers and the street show. Bald, rotund, of ruddy complexion, with the nose, the chin, the arched eye, the paunch and the *barbiche*, to say nothing of the ferule nursed in his arms and with which, in the show, such free play is made, Mr. Jenks yet seems to me to have preserved a dignity as well as projected an image, and in fact have done other things besides. He whacked occasionally—he must have been one of the last of the whackers; but I don't remember it as ugly or dreadful or droll—don't remember, that is, either directly feeling or reflectively enjoying it: it fails somehow to break the spell of our civilisation; my share in which, however, comes back to me as merely contemplative. It is beyond measure odd, doubtless, that my main association with my "studies," whether of the infant or the adolescent order, should be with almost anything but the fact of learning—of learning, I mean, what I was supposed to learn. I could only have been busy, at the same time, with other pursuits—which must have borne some superficial likeness at least to the acquisition of knowledge of a free irresponsible sort; since I remember few either of the inward pangs or the outward pains of a merely graceless state. I recognise at the same time that it was perhaps a sorry business to be so interested in one didn't know what. Such are, whether at the worst or at the best, some of the aspects of that season as Mr. Jenks's image presides; in the light of which I *may* perhaps again rather wonder at my imputation to the general picture of so much amenity. Clearly the good man was a civiliser—whacks and all; and by some art not now to be detected. He was a complacent classic—which was what my brother's claim for him, I dare say, mostly represented; though that passed over the head of my tenth year. It was a good note for him in this particular that, deploring the facile text-books of Doctor Anthon of Columbia College, in which there was even more crib than text, and holding fast to the sterner discipline of Andrews and Stoddard and of that other more conservative commentator (he too doubtless long since superseded) whose name I blush to forget. I think in fine of Richard Pulling's small but sincere academy as a consistent little protest against its big and easy and quite out-distancing rival, the Columbia College school, apparently in those days quite the favourite of fortune.

XVI

I MUST in some degree have felt it a charm there that we were not, under his rule, inordinately prepared for "business," but were on the contrary to remember that the taste of Cornelius Nepos in the air, even rather stale though it may have been, had lacked the black bitterness marking our next ordeal and that I conceive to have proceeded from some rank predominance of the theory and practice of book-keeping. It had consorted with this that we found ourselves, by I know not what inconsequence, a pair of the "assets" of a firm; Messrs. Forest and Quackenboss, who carried on business at the northwest corner of Fourteenth Street and Sixth Avenue, having for the winter of 1854–5 taken our education in hand. As their establishment had the style, so I was conscious at the time of its having the general stamp and sense, of a shop—a shop of long standing, of numerous clients, of lively bustle and traffic. The structure itself was to my recent recognition still there and more than ever a shop, with improvements and extensions, but dealing in other wares than those anciently and as I suppose then quite freshly purveyed; so far at least as freshness was imputable to the senior member of the firm, who had come down to our generation from a legendary past and with a striking resemblance of head and general air to Benjamin Franklin. Mr. Forest, under whose more particular attention I languished, had lasted on from a plainer age and, having formed, by the legend, in their youth, the taste of two or three of our New York uncles—though for what it could have been goodness only knew—was still of a *trempe* to whack in the fine old way at their nephews and sons. I see him aloft, benevolent and hard, mildly massive, in a black dress coat and trousers and a white neckcloth that should have figured, if it didn't, a frill, and on the highest rostrum of our experience, whence he comes back to me as the dryest of all our founts of knowledge, though quite again as a link with far-off manners and forms and as the most "historic" figure we had ever had to do with. W. J., as I distinguish, had in truth scarcely to do with him—W. J. lost again on upper floors, in higher classes, in real pursuits, and connecting me, in an indirect and almost deprecated manner, with a strange, curly, glossy, an anointed and bearded, Mr. Quackenboss, the junior partner, who conducted the classical department and never whacked—only sent down his subjects, with every confidence, to his friend. I make out with clearness that Mr. Forest was awful and arid, and yet that somehow, by the same stroke, we didn't, under his sway, go in terror, only went exceedingly in want; even if in want indeed of I scarce (for myself) know what, since it might well have been enough for me, in so resounding an air, to escape with nothing worse than a failure of thrill. If I didn't feel that interest I must clearly not have inspired it, and I marvel afresh, under these memories, at the few points at which I appear to have touched constituted reality. That, however, is a different connection altogether, and I read back into the one I have been noting much of the chill, or at least the indifference, of a foreseen and foredoomed detachment: it was during that winter that I began to live by anticipation in another world and to feel our uneasy connection with New York loosen beyond recovery. I remember for how many months, when the rupture took place, we had been to my particular consciousness virtually in motion; though I regain at the same time the impression of more experience on the spot than had marked our small previous history: this, however, a branch of the matter that I must for the moment brush aside. For it would have been meanwhile odd enough to hold us in arrest a moment—that quality of our situation that could suffer such elements as those I have glanced at to take so considerably the place of education as more usually and conventionally understood, and by that understanding more earnestly mapped out; a deficiency, in the whole thing, that I fail at all consistently to deplore, however—struck as I am with the rare fashion after which, in any small victim of life, the inward perversity may work.

It works by converting to its uses things vain and unintended, to the great discomposure of their prepared opposites, which it by the same stroke so often reduces to naught; with the result indeed that one may most of all see it—so at least have I quite exclusively seen it, the little life out for its chance—as proceeding by the inveterate process of conversion. As I reconsider both my own and my brother's early start—even his too, made under stronger propulsions—it is quite for me as if the authors of our being and guardians of our youth had virtually said to us but one thing, directed our course but by one word, though constantly repeated: Convert, convert, convert! With which I have not even the sense of any needed appeal in us for further apprehension of the particular precious metal our chemistry was to have in view. I taste again in that pure air no ghost of a hint, for instance, that the precious metal was the refined gold of "success"—a reward of effort for which I remember to have heard at home no good word, nor any sort of word, ever faintly breathed. It was a case of the presumption that we should hear words enough abundantly elsewhere; so that any dignity the idea might claim was in the first place not worth insisting on, and in the second might well be overstated. We were to convert and convert, success—in the sense that was in the general air—or no success; and simply everything that should happen to us, every contact, every impression and every experience we should know, were to form our soluble stuff; with only ourselves to thank should we remain unaware, by the time our perceptions were decently developed, of the substance finally projected and most desirable. That substance might be just consummately Virtue, as a social grace and value—and as a matter furthermore on which pretexts for ambiguity of view and of measure were as little as possible called upon to flourish. This last luxury therefore quite failed us, and we understood no whit the less what was suggested and expected because of the highly liberal way in which the pill, if I may call it so, was gilded. it had been made up—to emphasise my image—in so bright an air of humanity and gaiety, of charity and humour. What I speak of is the medium itself, of course, that we were most immediately steeped in—I am glancing now at no particular turn of our young attitude in it, and I can scarce sufficiently express how little it could have conduced to the formation of prigs. Our father's prime horror was of *them*—he only cared for virtue that was more or less ashamed of itself; and nothing could have been of a happier whimsicality than the mixture in him, and in all his walk and conversation, of the strongest instinct for the human and the liveliest reaction from the literal. The literal played in our education as small a part as it perhaps ever played in any, and we wholesomely breathed inconsistency and ate and drank contradictions. The presence of paradox was so bright among us—though fluttering ever with as light a wing and as short a flight as need have been—that we fairly grew used to allow, from an early time, for the so many and odd declarations we heard launched, to the extent of happily "discounting" them; the moral of all of which was that we need never fear not to be good enough if we were only social enough: a splendid meaning indeed being attached to the latter term.

Thus we had ever the amusement, since I can really call it nothing less, of hearing morality, or moralism, as it was more invidiously worded, made hay of in the very interest of character and conduct; these things suffering much, it seemed, by their association with the conscience—that is the *conscious* conscience—the very home of the literal, the haunt of so many pedantries. Pedantries, on all this ground, were anathema; and if our dear parent had at all minded his not being consistent, and had entertained about us generally less passionate an optimism (not an easy but an arduous state in him moreover,) he might have found it difficult to apply to the promotion of our studies so free a suspicion of the inhumanity of Method. Method certainly never quite raged among us; but it was our fortune nevertheless that everything had its turn, and that such indifferences were no more pedantic than certain rigours might perhaps have been; of all of which odd notes of our situation there would, and possibly will, be more to say—my present aim is really but to testify to what most comes up for me to-day in the queer educative air I have been trying to breathe again. That definite reflection is that if we had not had in us to some degree the root of the matter no method, however confessedly or aggressively "pedantic," would much have availed for us; and that since we apparently did have it, deep down and inert in our small patches of virgin soil, the fashion after which it struggled forth was an experience as intense as any other and a record of as great a dignity. It may be asked me, I recognise, of the root of "what" matter I so complacently speak, and if I say "Why, of the matter of our having with considerable intensity *proved* educable, or, if you like better, teachable, that is accessible to experience," it may again be retorted: "That won't do for a decent account of a young consciousness; for think of all the things that the failure of method, of which you make so light, didn't put into yours; think of the splendid economy of a real—or at least of a planned and attempted education, a 'regular course of instruction'—and then think of the waste involved in the so inferior substitute of which the pair of you were evidently victims." An admonition this on which I brood, less, however, than on the still other sense, rising from the whole retrospect, of my now feeling sure, of my having mastered the particular history of just that waste—to the point of its actually affecting me as blooming with interest, to the point even of its making me ask myself how in the world, if the question is of the injection of more things into the consciousness (as would seem the case,) mine could have "done" with more: thanks to its small trick, perhaps vicious I admit, of having felt itself from an early time almost uncomfortably stuffed. I see my critic, by whom I mean my representative of method at any price, take in this plea only to crush it with his confidence—that without the signal effects of method one must have had by an inexorable law to resort to shifts and ingenuities, and can therefore only have been an artful dodger more or less successfully dodging. I take full account of the respectability of the prejudice against one or two of the uses to which the intelligence may at a pinch be put—the criminal use in particular of falsifying its history, of forging its records even, and of appearing greater than the traceable grounds warrant. One can but fall back, none the less, on the particular *un*traceability of grounds—when it comes to that: cases abound so in which, with the grounds all there, the intelligence itself is not to be identified. I contend for nothing moreover but the lively interest of the view, and above all of the measure, of almost any mental history after the fact. Of less interest, comparatively, is that sight of the mind *before*—before the demonstration of the fact, that is, and while still muffled in theories and presumptions (purple and fine linen, and as such highly becoming though these be) of what shall prove best for it.

Which doubtless too numerous remarks have been determined by my sense of the tenuity of some of my clues: I had begun to count our wavering steps from so very far back, and with a lively disposition, I confess, not to miss even the vaguest of them. I can scarce indeed overstate the vagueness that quite *had* to attend a great number in presence of the fact that our father, caring for our spiritual decency unspeakably more than for anything else, anything at all that might be or might become ours, would have seemed to regard this cultivation of it as profession and career enough for us, had he but betrayed more interest in our mastery of *any* art or craft. It was not certainly that the profession of virtue would have been anything less than abhorrent to him, but that, singular though the circumstance, there were times when he might have struck us as having after all more patience with it than with this, that or the other more technical thrifty scheme. Of the beauty of his dissimulated anxiety and tenderness on these and various other suchlike heads, however, other examples will arise; for I see him now as fairly afraid to recognise certain anxieties, fairly declining to dabble in the harshness of practical precautions or impositions. The effect of his attitude, so little thought out as shrewd or as vulgarly providential, but in spite of this so socially and affectionally founded, could only be to make life interesting to us at the worst, in default of making it extraordinarily "paying." He had a theory that it would somehow or other always be paying enough—and this much less by any poor conception of our wants (for he delighted in our wants and so sympathetically and sketchily and summarily wanted *for* us) than by a happy and friendly, though slightly nebulous, conception of our resources. Delighting ever in the truth while generously contemptuous of the facts, so far as we might make the difference—the facts having a way of being many and the truth remaining but one—he held that there would always be enough; since the truth, the true truth, was never ugly and dreadful, and we didn't and wouldn't depart from it by any cruelty or stupidity (for he wouldn't have had us stupid,) and might therefore depend on it for due abundance even of meat and drink and raiment, even of wisdom and wit and honour. It is too much to say that our so preponderantly humanised and socialised adolescence was to make us look out for these things with a subtle indirectness; but I return to my proposition that there may still be a charm in seeing such hazards at work through a given, even if not in a systematised, case. My cases are of course given, so that economy of observation after the fact, as I have called it, becomes inspiring, not less than the amusement, or whatever it may be, of the question of what might happen, of what in point of fact did happen, to several very towny and domesticated little persons, who were confirmed in their towniness and fairly enriched in their sensibility, instead of being chucked into a scramble or exposed on breezy uplands under the she-wolf of competition and discipline. Perhaps any success that attended the experiment—which was really, as I have hinted, no plotted thing at all, but only an accident of accidents—proceeded just from the fact that the small subjects, a defeated Romulus, a prematurely sacrificed Remus, had in their very sensibility an asset, as we have come to say, a principle of life and even of "fun." Perhaps on the other hand the success would have been greater with less of that particular complication or facilitation and more of some other which I shall be at a loss to identify. What I find in my path happens to be the fact of the sensibility, and from the light it sheds the curious, as also the common, things that did from occasion to occasion play into it seem each to borrow a separate and vivifying glow.

As at the Institution Vergnès and at Mr. Pulling Jenks's, however this might be, so at "Forest's," or in other words at the more numerous establishment of Messrs. Forest and Quackenboss, where we spent the winter of 1854, reality, in the form of multitudinous mates, was to have swarmed about me increasingly: at Forest's the prolonged roll-call in the morning, as I sit in the vast bright crowded smelly smoky room, in which rusty black stove-shafts were the nearest hint of architecture, bristles with names, Hoes and Havemeyers, Stokeses, Phelpses, Colgates and others, of a subsequently great New York salience. It was sociable and gay, it was sordidly spectacular, one was then, by an inch or two, a bigger boy—though with crushing superiorities in that line all round; and when I wonder why the scene was sterile (which was what I took it for at the worst) the reason glooms out again in the dreadful blight of arithmetic, which affected me at the time as filling all the air. The quantity imposed may not in fact have been positively gross, yet it is what I most definitely remember—not, I mean, that I have retained the dimmest notion of the science, but only of the dire image of our being in one way or another always supposedly addressed to it. I recall strange neighbours and deskfellows who, not otherwise too objectionable, were uncanny and monstrous through their possession, cultivation, imitation of ledgers, daybooks, double-entry, tall pages of figures, interspaces streaked with oblique ruled lines that weirdly "balanced," whatever that might mean, and other like horrors. Nothing in truth is more distinct to me than the tune to which they were, without exception, at their ease on such ground—unless it be my general dazzled, humiliated sense, through those years, of the common, the baffling, mastery, all round me, of a hundred handy arts and devices. Everyone did things and had things—everyone knew how, even when it was a question of the small animals, the dormice and grasshoppers, or the hoards of food and stationery, that they kept in their desks, just as they kept in their heads such secrets for how to do sums—those secrets that I must even then have foreseen I should even so late in life as this have failed to discover. I may have known things, have by that time learnt a few, myself, but I didn't know *that*—what I did know; whereas those who surrounded me were all agog, to my vision, with the benefit of their knowledge. I see them, in this light, across the years, fairly grin and grimace with it; and the presumable vulgarity of some of them, certain scattered shades of baseness still discernible, comes to me as but one of the appearances of an abounding play of genius. Who was it I ever thought stupid?—even when knowing, or at least feeling, that sundry expressions of life or force, which I yet had no name for, represented somehow art without grace, or (what after a fashion came to the same thing) presence without type. All of which, I should add, didn't in the least prevent my moving on the plane of the remarkable; so that if, as I have noted, the general blank of consciousness, in the conditions of that winter, rather tended to spread, this could perhaps have but had for its best reason that I was fairly gorged with wonders. They were too much of the same kind; the result, that is, of everyone's seeming to know everything—to the effect, a little, that everything suffered by it. There was a boy called Simpson my juxtaposition to whom I recall as uninterruptedly close, and whose origin can only have been, I think, quite immediately Irish—and Simpson, I feel sure, was a friendly and helpful character. Yet even he reeked, to my sense, with strange accomplishment—no single show of which but was accompanied in him by a smart protrusion of the lower lip, a crude complacency of power, that almost crushed me to sadness. It is as if I had passed in that sadness most of those ostensibly animated months; an effect however doubtless in some degree proceeding, for later appreciation, from the more intelligible nearness of the time—it had brought me to the end of my twelfth year; which helps not a little to turn it to prose. How I gave to that state, in any case, such an air of occupation as to beguile not only myself but my instructors—which I infer I did from their so intensely letting me alone—I am quite at a loss to say; I have in truth mainly the remembrance of *being* consistently either ignored or exquisitely considered (I know not which to call it;) even if without the belief, which would explain it, that I passed for generally "wanting" any more than for naturally odious. It was strange, at all events—it could only have been—to be so stupid without being more brutish and so perceptive without being more keen. Here were a case and a problem to which no honest master with other and better cases could have felt justified in giving time; he would have had at least to be morbidly curious, and I recall from that sphere of rule no instance whatever of the least refinement of inquiry. I should even probably have missed one of these more flattering shades of attention had I missed attention at all; but I think I was never really aware of how little I got or how much I did without. I read back into the whole connection indeed the chill, or at least the indifference, of a foreseen and foredoomed detachment: I have noted how at this desperate juncture the mild forces making for our conscious relief, pushing the door to Europe definitely open, began at last to be effective. Nothing seemed to matter at all but that I should become personally and incredibly acquainted with Piccadilly and Richmond Park and Ham Common. I regain at the same time the impression of more experience on the spot than had marked our small previous history.

Pitiful as it looks to these ampler days the mere little fact that a small court for recreation was attached to our academy added something of a grace to life. We descended in relays, for "intermission," into a paved and walled yard of the scantest size; the only provision for any such privilege—not counting the street itself, of which, at the worst of other conditions, we must have had free range—that I recover from those years. The ground is built over now, but I could still figure, on a recent occasion, our small breathing-space; together with my then abject little sense that it richly sufficed—or rather, positively, that nothing could have been more romantic. For within our limit we freely conversed, and at nothing did I assist with more interest than at free conversation. Certain boys hover before me, the biggest, the fairest, the most worthy of freedom, dominating the scene and scattering upon fifty subjects the most surprising lights. One of these heroes, whose stature and complexion are still there for me to admire, did tricks of legerdemain, with the scant apparatus of a handkerchief, a key, a pocketknife—as to some one of which it is as fresh as yesterday that I ingenuously invited him to show me how to do it, and then, on his treating me with scorn, renewed without dignity my fond solicitation. Fresher even than yesterday, fadelessly fresh for me at this hour, is the cutting remark thereupon of another boy, who certainly wasn't Simpson and whose identity is lost for me in his mere inspired authority: "Oh, oh, oh, I should think you'd be too proud—!" I had neither been too proud nor so much as conceived that one might be, but I remember well how it flashed on me with this that I had failed thereby of a high luxury or privilege—which the whole future, however, might help me to make up for. To what extent it *has* helped is another matter, but so fine was the force of the suggestion that I think I have never in all the years made certain returns upon my spirit without again feeling the pang from the cool little voice of the Fourteenth Street yard. Such was the moral exercise it at least allowed us room for. It also allowed us room, to be just, for an inordinate consumption of hot waffles retailed by a benevolent black "auntie" who presided, with her husband's aid as I remember, at a portable stove set up in a passage or recess opening from the court; to which we flocked and pushed, in a merciless squeeze, with all our coppers, and the products of which, the oblong farinaceous compound, faintly yet richly brown, stamped and smoking, not crisp nor brittle, but softly absorbent of the syrup dabbed upon it for a finish, revealed to me I for a long time, even for a very long time supposed, the highest pleasure of sense. We stamped about, we freely conversed, we ate sticky waffles by the hundred—I recall no worse acts of violence unless I count as such our intermissional rushes to Pynsent's of the Avenue, a few doors off, in the particular interest of a confection that ran the waffle close, as the phrase is, for popularity, while even surpassing it for stickiness. Pynsent's was higher up in the row in which Forest's had its front—other and dearer names have dropped from me, but Pynsent's adheres with all the force of the strong saccharine principle. This principle, at its highest, we conceived, was embodied in small amber-coloured mounds of chopped cocoanut or whatever other substance, if a finer there be; profusely, lusciously endued and distributed on small tin trays in the manner of haycocks in a field. We acquired, we appropriated, we transported, we enjoyed them, they fairly formed perhaps, after all, our highest enjoyment; but with consequences to our pockets—and I speak of those other than financial, with an intimacy, a reciprocity of contact at any, or at every, personal point, that I lose myself in the thought of.

XVII

I LOSE myself, of a truth, under the whole pressure of the spring of memory proceeding from recent revisitings and recognitions—the action of the fact that time until lately had spared hereabouts, and may still be sparing, in the most exceptional way, by an anomaly or a mercy of the rarest in New York, a whole cluster of landmarks, leaving me to "spot" and verify, right and left, the smallest preserved particulars. These things, at the pressure, flush together again, interweave their pattern and quite thrust it at me, the absurd little fusion of images, for a history or a picture of the time—the background of which I see after all so much less as the harsh Sixth Avenue corner than as many other matters. Those scant shades claimed us but briefly and superficially, and it comes back to me that oddly enough, in the light of autumn afternoons, our associates, the most animated or at any rate the best "put in" little figures of our landscape, were not our comparatively obscure schoolmates, who seem mostly to have swum out of our ken between any day and its morrow. Our other companions, those we practically knew "at home," ignored our school, having better or worse of their own, but peopled somehow for us the social scene, which, figuring there for me in documentary vividness, bristles with Van Burens, Van Winkles, De Peysters, Costers, Senters, Norcoms, Robinsons (these last composing round a stone-throwing "Eugene,") Wards, Hunts and *tutti quanti*—to whose ranks I must add our invariable Albert, before-mentioned, and who swarm from up and down and east and west, appearing to me surely to have formed a rich and various society. Our salon, it is true, was mainly the street, loose and rude and crude in those days at best—though with a rapid increase of redeeming features, to the extent to which the spread of micaceous brown stone could redeem: as exhibited especially in the ample face of the Scotch Presbyterian church promptly rising just opposite our own peculiar row and which it now marks for me somewhat grimly a span of life to have seen laboriously rear itself, continuously flourish and utterly disappear. While in construction it was only less interesting than the dancing-academy of Mr. Edward Ferrero, slightly west of it and forming with it, in their embryonic stage, a large and delightfully dangerous adjunct to our playground, though with the distinction of coming much to surpass it for interest in the final phase. While we clambered about on ladders and toyed with the peril of unfloored abysses, while we trespassed and pried and pervaded, snatching a scant impression from sorry material enough, clearly, the sacred edifice enjoyed a credit beyond that of the profane; but when both were finished and opened we flocked to the sound of the fiddle more freely, it need scarce be said, than to that of the psalm. "Freely" indeed, in our particular case, scarce expresses the latter relation; since our young liberty in respect to church-going was absolute and we might range at will, through the great city, from one place of worship and one form of faith to another, or might on occasion ignore them all equally, which was what we mainly did; whereas we rallied without a break to the halls of Ferrero, a view of the staringly and, as I supposed dazzlingly, frescoed walls, the internal economy, the high amenity, the general æsthetic and social appeal, of which still hangs in its wealth before me. Dr. McElroy, uplifting tight-closed eyes, strange long-drawn accents and gaunt scraggy chin, squirming and swaying and cushion-thumping in *his* only a shade more chastely adorned temple, is distinct enough too—just as we enjoyed this bleak intensity the more, to my personal vision, through the vague legend (and no legend was too vague for me to cherish) of his being the next pastor in succession to the one under whom our mother, thereto predirected by our good greatgrandfather, Alexander Robertson already named, who was nothing if not Scotch and Presbyterian and authoritative, as his brave old portrait by the elder Jarves attests, had "sat" before her marriage; the marriage so lamentedly diverting her indeed from this tradition that, to mark the rueful rupture, it had invoked, one evening, with the aid of India muslin and a wondrous gold head-band, in the maternal, the Washington Square "parlours," but the secular nuptial consecration of the then Mayor of the city—I think Mr. Varick.

We progeny were of course after this mild convulsion not at all in the fold; yet it strikes me as the happy note of a simple age that we were practically, of a Sunday at least, wherever we might have chosen to enter: since, going forth hand in hand into the sunshine (and I connect myself here with my next younger, not with my elder, brother, whose orbit was other and larger) we sampled, in modern phrase, as small unprejudiced inquirers obeying their inspiration, any resort of any congregation detected by us; doing so, I make out moreover, with a sense of earnest provision for any contemporary challenge. "What church do you go to?"—the challenge took in childish circles that searching form; of the form it took among our elders my impression is more vague. To which I must add as well that our "fending" in this fashion for ourselves didn't so prepare us for invidious remark—remark I mean upon our pewless state, which involved, to my imagination, much the same discredit that a houseless or a cookless would have done—as to hush in my breast the appeal to our parents, not for religious instruction (of which we had plenty, and of the most charming and familiar) but simply for instruction (a very different thing) as to where we should say we "went," in our world, under cold scrutiny or derisive comment. It was colder than any criticism, I recall, to hear our father reply that we could plead nothing less than the whole privilege of Christendom and that there was no communion, even that of the Catholics, even that of the Jews, even that of the Swedenborgians, from which we need find ourselves excluded. With the freedom we enjoyed our dilemma clearly amused him: it would have been impossible, he affirmed, to be theologically more *en règle*. How as mere detached unaccompanied infants we enjoyed such impunity of range and confidence of welcome is beyond comprehension save by the light of the old manners and conditions, the old local bonhomie, the comparatively primal innocence, the absence of complications; with the several notes of which last beatitude my reminiscence surely shines. It was the theory of the time and place that the young, were they but young enough, could take publicly no harm; to which adds itself moreover, and touchingly enough, all the difference of the old importances. It wasn't doubtless that the social, or call it simply the human, position of the child was higher than to-day—a circumstance not conceivable; it was simply that other dignities and values and claims, other social and human positions, were less definite and settled, less prescriptive and absolute. A rich sophistication is after all a gradual growth, and it would have been sophisticated to fear for us, before such bright and vacant vistas, the perils of the way or to see us received anywhere even with the irony of patronage. We hadn't in fact seats of honour, but that justice was done us—that is that we were placed to our advantage—I infer from my having liked so to "go," even though my grounds may have been but the love of the *exhibition* in general, thanks to which figures, faces, furniture, sounds, smells and colours became for me, wherever enjoyed, and enjoyed most where most collected, a positive little orgy of the senses and riot of the mind. Let me at the same time make the point that—such may be the snobbery of extreme youth—I not only failed quite to rise to the parental reasoning, but made out in it rather a certain sophistry; such a prevarication for instance as if we had habitually said we kept the carriage we observably didn't keep, kept it because we sent when we wanted one to University Place, where Mr. Hathorn had his livery-stable: a connection, this last, promoted by my father's frequent need of the aid to circulate (his walks were limited through an injury received in youth) and promoting in turn and at a touch, to my consciousness, the stir of small, the smallest remembered things. I recall the adventure, no infrequent one, of being despatched to Mr. Hathorn to bespeak a conveyance, and the very air and odour, the genial warmth, at a fine steaming Irish pitch, of the stables and their stamping and backing beasts, their resounding boardedness, their chairs tipped up at such an angle for lifted heels, a pair of which latter seek the floor again, at my appeal, as those of big bearded Mr Hathorn himself: an impression enriched by the drive home in lolling and bumping possession of the great vehicle and associated further with Sunday afternoons in spring, with the question of distant Harlem and remoter Bloomingdale, with the experience at one of these junctures of far-away Hoboken, if it wasn't Williamsburg, which fits in fancifully somewhere; when the carriage was reinforced by a ferry and the ferry by something, something to my present vision very dim and dusty and archaic, something quite ragged and graceless, in the nature of a public tea-garden and ices. The finest link here, however, is, for some reason, with the New York Hotel, and thereby with Albany uncles; thereby also with Mr. Hathorn in person waiting and waiting expensively on his box before the house and somehow felt as attuned to Albany uncles even as Mrs. Cannon had subtly struck me as being.

Intenser than these vague shades meanwhile is my vision of the halls of Ferrero—where the orgy of the senses and even the riot of the mind, of which I have just spoken, must quite literally have led me more of a dance than anywhere. Let this sketch of a lost order note withal that under so scant a general provision for infant exercise, as distinguished from infant ease, our hopping and sliding in tune had to be deemed urgent. It was the sense for this form of relief that clearly was general, superseding as the ampler Ferrero scene did previous limited exhibitions; even those, for that matter, coming back to me in the ancient person of M. Charriau—I guess at the writing of his name—whom I work in but confusedly as a professional visitor, a subject gaped at across a gulf of fear, in one of our huddled schools; all the more that I perfectly evoke him as resembling, with a difference or two, the portraits of the aged Voltaire, and that he had, fiddle in hand and *jarret tendu*, incited the young agility of our mother and aunt. Edward Ferrero was another matter; in the prime of life, good-looking, romantic and moustachio'd, he was suddenly to figure, on the outbreak of the Civil War, as a General of volunteers—very much as if he had been one of Bonaparte's improvised young marshals; in anticipation of which, however, he wasn't at all fierce or superior, to my remembrance, but most kind to sprawling youth, in a charming man of the world fashion and as if *we* wanted but a touch to become also men of the world. Remarkably good-looking, as I say, by the measure of that period, and extraordinarily agile—he could so gracefully leap and bound that his bounding into the military saddle, such occasion offering, had all the felicity, and only wanted the pink fleshings, of the circus—he was still more admired by the mothers, with whom he had to my eyes a most elegant relation, than by the pupils; among all of whom, at the frequent and delightful soirées, he caused trays laden with lucent syrups repeatedly to circulate. The scale of these entertainments, as I figured it, and the florid frescoes, just damp though they were with newness, and the free lemonade, and the freedom of remark, equally great, with the mothers, were the lavish note in him—just as the fact that he never himself fiddled, but was followed, over the shining parquet, by attendant fiddlers, represented doubtless a shadow the less on his later dignity, so far as that dignity was compassed. Dignity marked in full measure even at the time the presence of his sister Madame Dubreuil, a handsome authoritative person who instructed us equally, in fact preponderantly, and who, though comparatively not sympathetic, so engaged, physiognomically, my wondering interest, that I hear to this hour her shrill Franco-American accent: "Don't look at *me*, little boy—look at my feet." I see them now, these somewhat fat members, beneath the uplifted skirt, encased in "bronzed" slippers, without heels but attached, by graceful cross-bands over her white stockings, to her solid ankles—an emphatic sign of the time; not less than I recover my surprised sense of their supporting her without loss of balance, substantial as she was, in the "first position"; her command of which, her ankles clapped close together and her body very erect, was so perfect that even with her toes, right and left, fairly turning the corner backward, she never fell prone on her face.

It consorted somehow with this wealth of resource in her that she appeared at the soirées, or at least at the great fancy-dress soirée in which the historic truth of my experience, free lemonade and all, is doubtless really shut up, as the "genius of California," a dazzling vision of white satin and golden flounces—her brother meanwhile maintaining that more distinctively European colour which I feel to have been for my young presumption the convincing essence of the scene in the character of a mousquetaire de Louis Quinze, highly consonant with his type. There hovered in the background a flushed, full-chested and tawnily short bearded M. Dubreuil, who, as a singer of the heavy order, at the Opera, carried us off into larger things still—the Opera having at last about then, after dwelling for years, down town, in shifty tents and tabernacles, set up its own spacious pavilion and reared its head as the Academy of Music: all at the end, or what served for the end, of our very street, where, though it wasn't exactly near and Union Square bristled between, I could yet occasionally gape at the great bills beside the portal, in which M. Dubreuil always so serviceably came in at the bottom of the cast. A subordinate artist, a "grand utility" at the best, I believe, and presently to become, on that scene, slightly ragged I fear even in its freshness, permanent stage-manager or, as we say nowadays, producer, he had yet eminently, to my imagination, the richer, the "European" value; especially for instance when our air thrilled, in the sense that our attentive parents re-echoed, with the visit of the great Grisi and the great Mario, and I seemed, though the art of advertisement was then comparatively so young and so chaste, to see our personal acquaintance, as he could almost be called, thickly sandwiched between them. Such was one's strange sense for the connections of things that they drew out the halls of Ferrero till these too seemed fairly to resound with Norma and Lucrezia Borgia, as if opening straight upon the stage, and Europe, by the stroke, had come to us in such force that we had but to enjoy it on the spot. That could never have been more the case than on the occasion of my assuming, for the famous fancy-ball—not at the operatic Academy, but at the dancing-school, which came so nearly to the same thing—the dress of a débardeur, whatever that might be, which carried in its puckered folds of dark green relieved with scarlet and silver such an exotic fragrance and appealed to me by such a legend. The legend had come round to us, it was true, by way of Albany, whence we learned at the moment of our need, that one of the adventures, one of the least lamentable, of our cousin Johnny had been his figuring as a débardeur at some Parisian revel; the elegant evidence of which, neatly packed, though with but vague instructions for use, was helpfully sent on to us. The instructions for use were in fact so vague that I was afterward to become a bit ruefully conscious of having sadly dishonoured, or at least abbreviated, my model. I fell, that is I stood, short of my proper form by no less than half a leg; the essence of the débardeur being, it appeared, that he emerged at the knees, in white silk stockings and with neat calves, from the beribboned breeches which I artlessly suffered to flap at my ankles. The discovery, after the fact, was disconcerting—yet had been best made withal, too late; for it would have seemed, I conceive, a less monstrous act to attempt to lengthen my legs than to shorten Johnny's *culotte*. The trouble had been that we hadn't really known what a débardeur *was*, and I am not sure indeed that I know to this day. It had been more fatal still that even fond Albany couldn't tell us.

XVIII

I HAVE nevertheless the memory of a restless relish of all that time—by which I mean of those final months of New York, even with so scant a record of other positive successes to console me. I had but one success, always—that of endlessly supposing, wondering, admiring: I was sunk in that luxury, which had never yet been so great, and it might well make up for anything. It made up perfectly, and more particularly as the stopgap as which I have already defined it, for the scantness of the period immediately round us; since how could I have wanted richer when the limits of reality, as I advanced upon them, seemed ever to recede and recede? It is true that but the other day, on the scene revisited, I was to be struck rather as by their weird immobility: there on the north side, still untenanted after sixty years, a tremendous span in the life of New York, was the vacant lot, undiminished, in which a friendly goat or two used to browse, whom we fed perversely with scraps of paper, just as perversely appreciated indeed, through the relaxed wooden palings. There hovers for me an impression of the glass roofs of a florist, a suffered squatter for a while; but florists and goats have alike disappeared and the barrenness of the place is as sordid as only untended gaps in great cities can seem. One of its boundaries, however, still breathes associations—the home of the Wards, the more eastward of a pair of houses then and still isolated has remained the same through all vicissitudes, only now quite shabbily mellow and, like everything else, much smaller than one had remembered it; yet this too without prejudice to the large, the lustrous part played in our prospect by that interesting family. I saddle their mild memory a bit "subjectively" perhaps with the burden of that character—making out that they were interesting really in spite of themselves and as unwittingly as M. Jourdain expressed himself in prose; owing their wild savour as they did to that New England stamp which we took to be strong upon them and no other exhibition of which we had yet enjoyed. It made them different, made them, in their homely grace, rather aridly romantic: I pored in those days over the freshness of the Franconia Stories of the brothers Abbott, then immediately sequent to the sweet Rollo series and even more admired; and there hung about the Wards, to my sense, that atmosphere of apples and nuts and cheese, of pies and jack-knives and "squrruls," of domestic Bible-reading and attendance at "evening lecture," of the fear of parental discipline and the cultivated art of dodging it, combined with great personal toughness and hardihood, an almost envied liability to warts on hard brown hands, a familiarity with garments domestically wrought, a brave rusticity in short that yet hadn't prevented the annexation of whole tracts of town life unexplored by ourselves and achieved by the brothers since their relatively recent migration from Connecticut—which State in general, with the city of Hartford in particular, hung as a hazy, fruity, rivery background, the very essence of Indian summer, in the rear of their discourse. Three in number, Johnny and Charley and Freddy, with castigating elders, even to the second and third generation back, dimly discerned through closed window-panes, they didn't at all haunt the halls of Ferrero—it was a part of their homely grace and their social tone, if not of their want of the latter, that this couldn't in the least be in question for them; on the other hand they frequented, Charley and Freddy at least, the Free School, which was round in Thirteenth Street—Johnny, the eldest, having entered the Free Academy, an institution that loomed large to us and that I see as towered or castellated or otherwise impressively embellished in vague vignettes, in stray representations, perhaps only of the grey schoolbook order, which are yet associated for me with those fond images of lovely ladies, "hand-painted," decorating at either end the interior of the old omnibusses. We must have been in relation with no other feeders at the public trough of learning—I can't account otherwise for the glamour as of envied privilege and strange experience that surrounded the Wards; they mixed, to the great sharpening of the edge of their wit, in the wild life of the people, beside which the life at Mr. Pulling Jenks's and even at the Institution Vergnès was colourless and commonplace. Somehow they were *of* the people, and still were full of family forms—which seemed, one dimly made out through the false perspective of all the cousinships, the stronger and clearer note of New England; the note that had already determined a shy yearning under perusal of the Rollo and Franconia chronicles. The special mark of these friends was perhaps however that of being socially young while they were annually old; little Freddy in particular, very short, very inured and very popular, though less curiously wrinkled about eyes and mouth than Charley, confessed to monstrous birthdays even while crouching or hopping, even while racing or roaring, as a high superiority in the games of the street prescribed. It was to strike me later on, when reading or hearing of young Americans of those parts who had turned "hard" or reckless by reaction from excessive discipline, theologic and economic, and had gone to sea or to California or to the "bad," that Freddy and Charley were typical of the race, even if their fortunes had taken, as I hoped, a happier form. That, I said to myself for the interest of it, *that*, the stuff of the Wards, their homely grace, was all New England —so far at least as New England wasn't Emerson and Margaret Fuller and Mr. Channing and the "best Boston" families. Such, in small very plastic minds, is the intensity, if not the value, of early impressions.

And yet how can such visions not have paled in the southern glow of the Norcoms, who had lately arrived *en masse* from Louisville and had improvised a fine old Kentucky home in the last house of our row—the one to be occupied so differently, after their strange and precipitate flight, as I dimly make out, by the Ladies of the Sacred Heart; those who presently, if I mistake not, moved out to Bloomingdale, if they were not already in part established there. Next us westward were the Ogdens, three slim and fair sisters, who soared far above us in age and general amenity; then came the Van Winkles, two sisters, I think, and a brother—he much the most serious and judicious, as well as the most educated, of our friends; and so at last the Norcoms, during their brief but concentrated, most vivid and momentous, reign, a matter, as I recall it, of a couple of breathless winters. We were provided by their presence with as happy a foil as we could have wished to the plainness and dryness of the Wards; their homely grace was all their own and was also embodied in three brothers, Eugene, Reginald, Albert, whose ages would have corresponded, I surmise, with those of Johnny, Charley and Freddy if these latter hadn't, in their way, as I have hinted, defied any close notation. Elder sons—there were to my recollection no daughters—moved too as with their heads in the clouds; notably "Stiffy," eldest of all, whom we supposed gorgeous, who affected us as sublime and unapproachable and to whom we thus applied the term in use among us before we had acquired for reference to such types the notion of the *nuance*, the dandy, the dude, the masher. (Divided I was, I recall, between the dread and the glory of being so greeted, "Well, Stiffy—!" as a penalty of the least attempt at personal adornment.) The higher intensity for our sense of the Norcoms came from the large, the lavish, ease of their hospitality; whereas our intercourse with the Wards was mainly in the street or at most the "yard"—and it was a wonder how intimacy *could* to that degree consort with publicity. A glazed southern gallery, known to its occupants as the "poo'ch" and to the rake of which their innermost penetralia seemed ever to stand open, encompasses my other memories. Everything took place on the poo'ch, including the free, quite the profuse, consumption of hot cakes and molasses, including even the domestic manufacture of sausages, testified to by a strange machine that was worked like a hand-organ and by the casual halves, when not the wholes, of stark stiff hogs fresh from Kentucky stores. We must have been for a time constantly engaged with this delightful group, who never ceased to welcome us or to feed us, and yet of the presence of whose members under other roofs than their own, by a return of hospitality received, I retain no image. They didn't count and didn't grudge—the sausage-mill kept turning and the molasses flowing for all who came; that was the expression of their southern grace, especially embodied in Albert, my exact contemporary and chosen friend (Reggie had but crushed my fingers under the hinge of a closing door, the mark of which act of inadvertence I was to carry through life,) who had profuse and tightly-crinkled hair, and the moral of whose queer little triangular brown teeth, casting verily a shade on my attachment to him, was pointed for me, not by himself, as the error of a Kentucky diet.

The great Kentucky error, however, had been the introduction into a free State of two pieces of precious property which our friends were to fail to preserve, the pair of affectionate black retainers whose presence contributed most to their exotic note. We revelled in the fact that Davy and Aunt Sylvia (pronounced An'silvy,) a light-brown lad with extraordinarily shining eyes and his straight, grave, deeper-coloured mother, not radiant as to anything but her vivid turban, had been born and kept in slavery of the most approved pattern and such as this intensity of their condition made them a joy, a joy to the curious mind, to consort with. Davy mingled in our sports and talk, he enriched, he adorned them with a personal, a pictorial lustre that none of us could emulate, and servitude in the absolute thus did more for him socially than we had ever seen done, above stairs or below, for victims of its lighter forms. What was not our dismay therefore when we suddenly learnt—it must have blown right up and down the street—that mother and son had fled, in the dead of night, from bondage? had taken advantage of their visit to the North simply to leave the house and not return, covering their tracks, successfully disappearing. They had never been for us so beautifully slaves as in this achievement of their freedom; for they did brilliantly achieve it—they escaped, on northern soil, beyond recall or recovery. I think we had already then, on the spot, the sense of some degree of presence at the making of history; the question of what persons of colour and of their condition might or mightn't do was intensely in the air; this was exactly the season of the freshness of Mrs. Stowe's great novel. It must have come out at the moment of our fondest acquaintance with our neighbours, though I have no recollection of hearing them remark upon it—any remark they made would have been sure to be so strong. I suspect they hadn't read it, as they certainly wouldn't have allowed it in the house; any more indeed than they had read or were likely ever to read any other work of fiction; I doubt whether the house contained a printed volume, unless its head had had in hand a law-book or so: I to some extent recover Mr. Norcom as a lawyer who had come north on important, difficult business, on contentious, precarious grounds—a large bald political-looking man, very loose and ungirt, just as his wife was a desiccated, depressed lady who mystified me by always wearing her nightcap, a feebly-frilled but tightly-tied and unmistakable one, and the compass of whose maternal figure beneath a large long collarless cape or mantle defined imperfectly for me of course its connection with the further increase of Albert's little brothers and sisters, there being already, by my impression, two or three of these in the background. Had Davy and An'silvy at least read Uncle Tom?—that question might well come up for us, with the certainty at any rate that they ignored him less than their owners were doing. These latter good people, who had been so fond of their humble dependents and supposed this affection returned, were shocked at such ingratitude, though I remember taking a vague little inward Northern comfort in their inability, in their discreet decision, not to raise the hue and cry. Wasn't one even just dimly aware of the heavy hush that, in the glazed gallery, among the sausages and the johnny-cakes, had followed the first gasp of resentment? I think the honest Norcoms were in any case astonished, let alone being much incommoded; just as *we* were, for that matter, when the genial family itself, installed so at its ease, failed us with an effect of abruptness, simply ceased, in their multitude, to be there. I don't remember their going, nor any pangs of parting; I remember only knowing with wonderment that they had gone, that obscurity had somehow engulfed them; and how afterwards, in the light of later things, memory and fancy attended them, figured their history as the public complication grew and the great intersectional plot thickened; felt even, absurdly and disproportionately, that they had helped one to "know Southerners." The slim, the sallow, the straight-haired and dark-eyed Eugene in particular haunted my imagination; he had not been my comrade of election—he was too much my senior; but I cherished the thought of the fine fearless young fire-eater he would have become and, when the War had broken out, I know not what dark but pitying vision of him stretched stark after a battle.

All of which sounds certainly like a meagre range—which heaven knows it was; but with a plea for the several attics, already glanced at, and the positive æsthetic reach that came to us through those dim resorts, quite worth making. They were scattered and they constituted on the part of such of our friends as had license to lead us up to them a ground of authority and glory proportioned exactly to the size of the field. This extent was at cousin Helen's, with a large house and few inmates, vast and free, so that no hospitality, under the eaves, might have matched that offered us by the young Albert—if only that heir of all the ages had had rather more imagination. He had, I think, as little as was possible—which would have counted in fact for an unmitigated blank had not W. J., among us, on that spot and elsewhere, supplied this motive force in any quantity required. He imagined—that was the point—the comprehensive comedies we were to prepare and to act; comprehensive by the fact that each one of us, even to the God-fearing but surreptitiously law-breaking Wards, was in fairness to be enabled to figure. Not one of us but was somehow to be provided with a part, though I recall my brother as the constant comic star. The attics were thus in a word our respective temples of the drama—temples in which the stage, the green-room and the wardrobe, however, strike me as having consumed most of our margin. I remember, that is, up and down the street—and the association is mainly with its far westward reaches—so much more preparation than performance, so much more conversation and costume than active rehearsal, and, on the part of some of us, especially doubtless on my own, so much more eager denudation, both of body and mind, than of achieved or inspired assumption. We shivered unclad and impatient both as to our persons and to our aims, waiting alike for ideas and for breeches; we were supposed to make our dresses no less than to create our characters, and our material was in each direction apt to run short. I remember how far ahead of us my brother seemed to keep, announcing a "motive," producing a figure, throwing off into space conceptions that I could stare at across the interval but couldn't appropriate; so that my vision of him in these connections is not so much of his coming toward me, or toward any of us, as of his moving rapidly away in fantastic garb and with his back turned, as if to perform to some other and more assured public. There were indeed other publics, publics downstairs, who glimmer before me seated at the open folding-doors of ancient parlours, but all from the point of view of an absolute supernumerary, more or less squashed into the wing but never coming on. Who were the copious Hunts?—whose ample house, on the north side, toward Seventh Avenue, still stands, next or near that of the De Peysters, so that I perhaps confound some of the attributes of each, though clear as to the blond Beekman, or "Beek," of the latter race, not less than to the robust George and the stout, the very stout, Henry of the former, whom I see bounding before a gathered audience for the execution of a *pas seul*, clad in a garment of "Turkey red" fashioned by his own hands and giving way at the seams, to a complete absence of *dessous*, under the strain of too fine a figure: this too though I make out in those connections, that is in the twilight of Hunt and De Peyster garrets, our command of a comparative welter of draperies; so that I am reduced to the surmise that Henry indeed had contours.

I recover, further, some sense of the high places of the Van Winkles, but think of them as pervaded for us by the upper air of the proprieties, the proprieties that were so numerous, it would appear, when once one had had a glimpse of them, rather than by the crude fruits of young improvisation. Wonderful must it clearly have been still to feel amid laxities and vaguenesses such a difference of *milieux* and, as they used to say, of atmospheres. This was a word of those days—atmospheres were a thing to recognise and cultivate, for people really wanted them, gasped for them; which was why they took them, on the whole, on easy terms, never exposing them, under an apparent flush, to the last analysis. Did we at any rate really vibrate to one social tone after another, or are these adventures for me now but fond imaginations? No, we vibrated—or I'll be hanged, as I may say, if *I* didn't; little as I could tell it or may have known it, little as anyone else may have known. There were shades, after all, in our democratic order; in fact as I brood back to it I recognise oppositions the sharpest, contrasts the most intense. It wasn't given to us all to have a social tone, but the Costers surely had one and kept it in constant use; whereas the Wards, next door to them, were possessed of no approach to any, and indeed had the case been other, had they had such a consciousness, would never have employed it, would have put it away on a high shelf, as they put the last-baked pie, out of Freddy's and Charley's reach—heaven knows what *they* two would have done with it. The Van Winkles on the other hand were distinctly so provided, but with the special note that their provision was one, so to express it, with their educational, their informational, call it even their professional: Mr. Van Winkle, if I mistake not, was an eminent lawyer, and the note of our own house was the absence of any profession, to the quickening of our general as distinguished from our special sensibility. There was no Turkey red among those particular neighbours at all events, and if there had been it wouldn't have gaped at the seams. I didn't then know it, but I sipped at a fount of culture; in the sense, that is, that, our connection with the house being through Edgar, he knew about things—inordinately, as it struck me. So, for that matter, did little public Freddy Ward; but the things one of them knew about differed wholly from the objects of knowledge of the other: all of which was splendid for giving one exactly a sense of things. It intimated more and more how many such there would be altogether. And part of the interest was that while Freddy gathered his among the wild wastes Edgar walked in a regular maze of culture. I didn't then know about culture, but Edgar must promptly have known. This impression was promoted by his moving in a distant, a higher sphere of study, amid scenes vague to me; I dimly descry him as appearing at Jenks's and vanishing again, as if even that hadn't been good enough—though I may be here at fault, and indeed can scarce say on what arduous heights I supposed him, as a day-scholar, to dwell. I took the unknown always easily for the magnificent and was sure only of the limits of what I saw. It wasn't that the boys swarming for us at school were not often, to my vision, unlimited, but that those peopling our hours of ease, as I have already noted, were almost inveterately so—they seemed to describe always, out of view, so much larger circles. I linger thus on Edgar by reason of its having somehow seemed to us that he described—was it at Doctor Anthon's?—the largest of all. If there was a bigger place than Doctor Anthon's it was there he would have been. I break down, as to the detail of the matter, in any push toward vaster suppositions. But let me cease to stir this imponderable dust.

XIX

I TRY at least to recover here, however, some closer notation of W. J.'s aspects—yet only with the odd effect of my either quite losing him or but apprehending him again at seated play with his pencil under the lamp. When I see him he is intently, though summarily, rapidly drawing, his head critically balanced and his eyebrows working, and when I don't see him it is because I have resignedly relinquished him. I can't have been often for him a deprecated, still less an actively rebuffed suitor, because, as I say again, such aggressions were so little in order for me; but I remember that on my once offering him my company in conditions, those of some planned excursion, in which it wasn't desired, his putting the question of our difference at rest, with the minimum of explanation, by the responsible remark: "*I* play with boys who curse and swear!" I had sadly to recognise that I didn't, that I couldn't pretend to have come to that yet—and truly, as I look back, either the unadvisedness and inexpertness of my young contemporaries on all that ground must have been complete (an interesting note on our general manners after all,) or my personal failure to grasp must have been. Besides which I wonder scarce less now than I wondered then in just what company my brother's privilege was exercised; though if he had but richly wished to be discouraging he quite succeeded. It wasn't that I mightn't have been drawn to the boys in question, but that I simply wasn't qualified. All boys, I rather found, were difficult to play with—unless it was that they rather found *me*; but who would have been so difficult as these? They account but little, moreover, I make out, for W. J.'s eclipses; so that I take refuge easily enough in the memory of my own pursuits, absorbing enough at times to have excluded other views. I also plied the pencil, or to be more exact the pen—even if neither implement critically, rapidly or summarily. I was so often engaged at that period, it strikes me, in literary—or, to be more precise in dramatic, accompanied by pictorial composition—that I must again and again have delightfully lost myself. I had not on any occasion personally succeeded, amid our theatric strife, in reaching the footlights; but how could I have doubted, nevertheless, with our large theatrical experience, of the nature, and of my understanding, of the dramatic form? I sacrificed to it with devotion —by the aid of certain quarto sheets of ruled paper bought in Sixth Avenue for the purpose (my father's store, though I held him a great fancier of the article in general, supplied but the unruled;) grateful in particular for the happy provision by which each fourth page of the folded sheet was left blank. When the drama itself had covered three pages the last one, over which I most laboured, served for the illustration of what I had verbally presented. Every scene had thus its explanatory picture, and as each act—though I am not positively certain I arrived at acts—would have had its vivid climax. Addicted in that degree to fictive evocation, I yet recall, on my part, no practice whatever of narrative prose or any sort of verse. I cherished the "scene"—as I had so vibrated to the idea of it that evening at Linwood; I thought, I lisped, at any rate I composed, in scenes; though how much, or how far, the scenes "came" is another affair. Entrances, exits, the indication of "business," the animation of dialogue, the multiplication of designated characters, were things delightful in themselves—while I panted toward the canvas on which I should fling my figures; which it took me longer to fill than it had taken me to write what went with it, but which had on the other hand something of the interest of the dramatist's casting of his *personæ*, and must have helped me to believe in the validity of my subject.

From where on these occasions that subject can have dropped for me I am at a loss to say, and indeed have a strong impression that I didn't at any moment quite know what I was writing about: I am sure I couldn't otherwise have written so much. With scenes, when I think, what certitude did I want more?—scenes being the root of the matter, especially when they bristled with proper names and noted movements; especially, above all, when they flowered at every pretext into the very optic and perspective of the stage, where the boards diverged correctly, from a central point of vision, even as the lashes from an eyelid, straight down to the footlights. Let this reminiscence remind us of how rarely in those days the real stage was carpeted. The difficulty of composition was naught;

the one difficulty was in so placing my figures on the fourth page that these radiations could be marked without making lines through them. The odd part of all of which was that whereas my cultivation of the picture was maintained my practice of the play, my addiction to scenes, presently quite dropped. I was capable of learning, though with inordinate slowness, to express ideas in scenes, and was not capable, with whatever patience, of making proper pictures; yet I aspired to this form of design to the prejudice of any other, and long after those primitive hours was still wasting time in attempts at it. I cared so much for nothing else, and that vaguely redressed, as to a point, my general failure of acuteness. I nursed the conviction, or at least I tried to, that if my clutch of the pencil or of the watercolour brush should once become intense enough it would make up for other weaknesses of grasp—much as that would certainly give it to do. This was a very false scent, which had however the excuse that my brother's example really couldn't but act upon me—the scent was apparently so true for *him*; from the moment my small "interest in art," that is my bent for gaping at illustrations and exhibitions, was absorbing and genuine. There were elements in the case that made it natural: the picture, the representative design, directly and strongly appealed to me, and was to appeal all my days, and I was only slow to recognise the *kind*, in this order, that appealed most. My face was turned from the first to the idea of representation—that of the gain of charm, interest, mystery, dignity, distinction, gain of importance in fine, on the part of the represented thing (over the thing of accident, of mere actuality, still unappropriated;) but in the house of representation there were many chambers, each with its own lock, and long was to be the business of sorting and trying the keys. When I at last found deep in my pocket the one I could more or less work, it was to feel, with reassurance, that the picture was still after all in essence one's aim. So there had been in a manner continuity, been not so much waste as one had sometimes ruefully figured; so many wastes are sweetened for memory as by the taste of the economy they have led to or imposed and from the vantage of which they could scarce look better if they had been current and blatant profit. Wasn't the very bareness of the field itself moreover a challenge, in a degree, to design?—not, I mean, that there seemed to one's infant eyes too few things to paint: as to that there were always plenty—but for the very reason that there were more than anyone noticed, and that a hunger was thus engendered which one cast about to gratify. The gratification nearest home was the imitative, the emulative—that is on my part: W. J., I see, needed no reasons, no consciousness other than that of being easily able. So he drew because he could, while I did so in the main only because he did; though I think we cast about, as I say, alike, making the most of every image within view. I doubt if he made more than I even then did, though earlier able to account for what he made. Afterwards, on other ground and in richer air, I admit, the challenge was in the fulness and not in the bareness of aspects, with their natural result of hunger appeased; exhibitions, illustrations abounded in Paris and London—the reflected image hung everywhere about; so that if there we daubed afresh and with more confidence it was not because no-one but because everyone did. In fact when I call our appetite appeased I speak less of our browsing vision, which was tethered and insatiable, than of our sense of the quite normal character of our own proceedings. In Europe we knew there was Art, just as there were soldiers and lodgings and concierges and little boys in the streets who stared at us, especially at our hats and boots, as at things of derision—just as, to put it negatively, there were practically no hot rolls and no iced water. Perhaps too, I should add, we didn't enjoy the works of Mr. Benjamin Haydon, then clustered at the Pantheon in Oxford Street, which in due course became our favourite haunt, so infinitely more, after all, than we had enjoyed those arrayed at the Düsseldorf collection in Broadway; whence the huge canvas of the Martyrdom of John Huss comes back to me in fact as a revelation of representational brightness and charm that pitched once for all in these matters my young sense of what should be.

Ineffable, unsurpassable those hours of initiation which the Broadway of the 'fifties had been, when all was said, so adequate to supply. If one wanted pictures there *were* pictures, as large, I seem to remember, as the side of a house, and of a bravery of colour and lustre of surface that I was never afterwards to see surpassed. We were shown without doubt, under our genial law here too, everything there was, and as I cast up the items I wonder, I confess, what ampler fare we could have dealt with. The Düsseldorf school commanded the market, and I think of its exhibition as firmly seated, going on from year to year—New York, judging now to such another tune, must have been a brave patron of that manufacture; I believe that scandal even was on occasion not evaded, rather was boldly invoked, though of what particular sacrifices to the pure plastic or undraped shocks to bourgeois prejudice the comfortable German genius of that period may have been capable history has kept no record. New accessions, at any rate, vividly new ones, in which the freshness and brightness of the paint, particularly lustrous in our copious light, enhanced from time to time the show, which I have the sense of our thus repeatedly and earnestly visiting and which comes back to me with some vagueness as installed in a disaffected church, where gothic excrescences and an ecclesiastical roof of a mild order helped the importance. No impression here, however, was half so momentous as that of the epoch-making masterpiece of Mr. Leutze, which showed us Washington crossing the Delaware in a wondrous flare of projected gaslight and with the effect of a revelation to my young sight of the capacity of accessories to "stand out." I live again in the thrill of that evening—which was the greater of course for my feeling it, in my parents' company, when I should otherwise have been in bed. We went down, after dinner, in the Fourteenth Street stage, quite as if going to the theatre; the scene of exhibition was near the Stuyvesant Institute (a circumstance stirring up somehow a swarm of associations, echoes probably of lectures discussed at home, yet at which my attendance had doubtless conveniently lapsed,) but Mr. Leutze's drama left behind any paler proscenium. We gaped responsive to every item, lost in the marvel of the wintry light, of the sharpness of the ice-blocks, of the sickness of the sick soldier, of the protrusion of the minor objects, that of the strands of the rope and the nails of the boots, that, I say, on the part of everything, of its determined purpose of standing out; but that, above all, of the profiled national hero's purpose, as might be said, of standing *up*, as much as possible, even indeed of doing it almost on one leg, in such difficulties, and successfully balancing. So memorable was that evening to remain for me that nothing could be more strange, in connection with it, than the illustration by the admired work, on its in after years again coming before me, of the cold cruelty with which time may turn and devour its children. The picture, more or less entombed in its relegation, was lividly dead—and that was bad enough. But half the substance of one's youth seemed buried with it. There were other pictorial evenings, I may add, not all of which had the thrill. Deep the disappointment, on my own part, I remember, at Bryan's Gallery of Christian Art, to which also, as for great emotions, we had taken the omnibus after dinner. It cast a chill, this collection of worm-eaten diptychs and triptychs, of angular saints and seraphs, of black Madonnas and obscure Bambinos, of such marked and approved "primitives" as had never yet been shipped to our shores. Mr. Bryan's shipment was presently to fall, I believe, under grave suspicion, was to undergo in fact fatal exposure; but it appealed at the moment in apparent good faith, and I have not forgotten how, conscious that it was fresh from Europe—"fresh" was beautiful in the connection!—I felt that my yearning should all have gone out to it. With that inconsequence to handle I doubt whether I proclaimed that it bored me—any more than I have ever noted till now that it made me begin badly with Christian art. I like to think that the collection consisted without abatement of frauds and "fakes" and that if these had been honest things my perception wouldn't so have slumbered; yet the principle of interest had been somehow compromised, and I think I have never since stood before a real Primitive, a primitive of the primitives, without having first to shake off the grey mantle of that night. The main disconcertment had been its ugly twist to the name of Italy, already sweet to me for all its dimness—even could dimness have prevailed in my felt measure of the pictorial testimony of home, testimony that dropped for us from the ample canvas of Mr. Cole, "the American Turner" which covered half a side of our front parlour, and in which, though not an object represented in it began to stand out after the manner of Mr. Leutze, I could always lose myself as soon as look. It depicted Florence from one of the neighbouring hills—I have often since wondered which, the picture being long ago lost to our sight; Florence with her domes and towers and old walls, the old walls Mr. Cole had engaged for, but which I was ruefully to miss on coming to know and love the place in after years. Then it was I felt how long before my attachment had started on its course—that closer vision was no beginning, it only took up the tale; just as it comes to me again to-day, at the end of time, that the contemplative monk seated on a terrace in the foreground, a constant friend of my childhood, must have been of the convent of San Miniato, which gives me the site from which the painter wrought. We had Italy again in the corresponding room behind—a great abundance of Italy I was free to think while I revolved between another large landscape over the sofa and the classic marble bust on a pedestal between the two back windows, the figure, a part of the figure, of a lady with her head crowned with vine-leaves and her hair disposed with a laxity that was emulated by the front of her dress, as my next younger brother exposed himself to my derision by calling the bit of brocade (simulated by the chisel) that, depending from a single shoulder-strap, so imperfectly covered her. This image was known and admired among us as the Bacchante; she had come to us straight from an American studio in Rome, and I see my horizon flush again with the first faint dawn of conscious appreciation, or in other words of the critical spirit, while two or three of the more restrictive friends of the house find our marble lady very "cold" for a Bacchante. Cold indeed she must have been—quite as of the tombstone temperament; but that objection would drop if she might only be called a Nymph, since nymphs were mild and moderate, and since discussion of a work of art mainly hung in those days on that issue of the producible *name.* I fondly recall, by the same token, that playing on a certain occasion over the landscape above the sofa, restrictive criticism, uttered in my indulged hearing, introduced me to what had probably been my very first chance, on such ground, for active participation. The picture, from the hand of a French painter, M. Lefèvre, and of but slightly scanter extent than the work of Mr. Cole, represented in frank rich colours and as a so-called "view in Tuscany" a rural scene of some exuberance, a broken and precipitous place, amid mountains and forests, where two or three bare-legged peasants or woodmen were engaged, with much emphasis of posture, in felling a badly gashed but spreading oak by means of a tense rope attached to an upper limb and at which they pulled together. "Tuscany?—are you sure it's Tuscany?" said the voice of restrictive criticism, that of the friend of the house who in the golden age of the precursors, though we were still pretty much precursors, had lived longest in Italy. And then on my father's challenge of this demur: "Oh in Tuscany, you know, the colours are much softer—there would be a certain haze in the atmosphere." "Why, of course," I can hear myself now blushingly but triumphantly intermingle—"the softness and the haze of our Florence there: isn't Florence in Tuscany?" It had to be parentally admitted that Florence was—besides which our friend had been there and knew; so that thereafter, within our walls, a certain *malaise* reigned, for if the Florence was "like it" then the Lefèvre couldn't be, and if the Lefèvre was like it then the Florence couldn't: a lapse from old convenience—as from the moment we couldn't name the Lefèvre where were we? All of which it might have been open to me to feel I had uncannily promoted.

XX

MY OWN sense of the great matter, meanwhile—that is of our possibilities, still more than of our actualities, of Italy in general and of Florence in particular—was a perfectly recoverable little awareness, as I find, of certain mild soft irregular breathings thence on the part of an absent pair in whom our parents were closely interested and whose communications, whose Roman, Sorrentine, Florentine letters, letters in especial from the Baths of Lucca, kept open, in our air, more than any other sweet irritation, that "question of Europe" which was to have after all, in the immediate years, so limited, so shortened, a solution. Mary Temple the elder had, early in our Fourteenth Street period, married Edmund Tweedy, a haunter of that neighbourhood and of our house in it from the first, but never more than during a winter spent with us there by that quasi-relative, who, by an extension of interest and admiration—she was in those years quite exceedingly handsome—ranked for us with the Albany aunts, adding so a twist, as it were, to our tie with the Temple cousins, her own close kin. This couple must have been, putting real relatives aside, my parents' best friends in Europe, twitching thereby hardest the fine firm thread attached at one end to our general desire and at the other to their supposed felicity. The real relatives, those planted out in the same countries, are a chapter by themselves, whose effect on us, whose place in our vision, I should like to trace: that of the Kings, for instance, of my mother's kin, that of the Masons, of my father's—the Kings who cultivated, for years, the highest instructional, social and moral possibilities at Geneva, the Masons, above all, less strenuous but more sympathetic, who reported themselves to us hauntingly, during a considerable period, as enjoying every conceivable *agrément* at Tours and at the then undeveloped Trouville, even the winter Trouville, on the lowest possible terms. Fain would I, as for the "mere pleasure" of it, under the temptation to delineate, gather into my loose net the singularly sharp and rounded image of our cousin Charlotte of the former name, who figured for us, on the field of Europe, wherever we looked, and all the rest of time, as a character of characters and a marvel of placid consistency; through my vague remembrance of her return from China after the arrest of a commercial career there by her husband's death in the Red Sea—which somehow sounded like a dreadful form of death, and my scarce less faint recovery of some Christmas treat of our childhood under her roof in Gramercy Park, amid dim chinoiseries and, in that twilight of time, dimmer offspring, Vernon, Anne, Arthur, marked to us always, in the distincter years, as of all our young relatives the most intensely educated and most pointedly proper—an occasion followed by her permanent and invidious withdrawal from her own country. I would keep her in my eye through the Genevese age and on to the crisis of the Civil War, in which Vernon, unforgiven by her stiff conservatism for his Northern loyalty, laid down before Petersburg a young life of understanding and pain, uncommemorated as to the gallantry of its end—he had insistently returned to the front, after a recovery from first wounds, as under his mother's malediction—on the stone beneath which he lies in the old burial ground at Newport, the cradle of his father's family. I should further pursue my subject through other periods and places, other constantly "quiet" but vivid exhibitions, to the very end of the story—which for myself was the impression, first, of a little lonely, soft-voiced, gentle, relentless lady, in a dull Surrey garden of a summer afternoon, more than half blind and all dependent on the *dame de compagnie* who read aloud to her that Saturday Review which had ever been the prop and mirror of her opinions and to which she remained faithful, her children estranged and outworn, dead and ignored; and the vision, second and for a climax, of an old-world rez-de-chaussée at Versailles, goal of my final pilgrimage, almost in presence of the end (end of her very personal career, I mean, but not of her perfectly firm spirit or of her charmingly smooth address).

I confess myself embarrassed by my very ease of re-capture of my young consciousness; so that I perforce try to encourage lapses and keep my abundance down. The place for the lapse consents with difficulty, however, to be *any* particular point of the past at which I catch myself (easily caught as I am) looking about me; it has certainly nothing in common with that coign of vantage enjoyed by me one June afternoon of 1855 in the form of the minor share of the box of a carriage that conveyed us for the first time since our babyhood, W. J.'s and mine, through so much of a vast portentous London. I was an item in the overflow of a vehicle completely occupied, and I thrilled with the spectacle my seat beside the coachman so amply commanded—without knowing at this moment why, amid other claims, I had been marked for such an eminence. I so far justify my privilege at least as still to feel that prime impression, of extreme intensity, underlie, deep down, the whole mass of later observation. There are London aspects which, so far as they still touch me, after all the years, touch me as just sensible reminders of this hour of early apprehension, so penetrated for me as to have kept its ineffaceable stamp. For at last we had come to Europe—we had disembarked at Liverpool, but a couple of days before, from that steamer Atlantic, of the Collins line, then active but so soon to be utterly undone, of which I had kept a romantic note ever since a certain evening of a winter or two before. I had on that occasion assisted with my parents at a varied theatrical exhibition—the theatre is distinct to me as Brougham's—one of the features of which was the at that time flourishing farce of Betsy Baker, a picture of some predicament, supposed droll, of its hero Mr. Mouser, whose wife, if I am correct, carries on a laundry and controls as she may a train of young assistants. A feature of the piece comes back to me as the pursuit of Mr. Mouser round and round the premises by the troop of laundresses, shouting his name in chorus, capture by them being abject, though whether through fear of their endearments or of their harsher violence I fail to remember. It was enough that the public nerve had at the moment been tried by the non-arrival of the Atlantic, several days overdue, to the pitch at last of extreme anxiety; so that, when after the fall of the curtain on the farce the distracted Mr. Mouser, still breathless, reappeared at the footlights, where I can see him now abate by his plight no jot of the dignity of his announcement, "Ladies and gentlemen, I rejoice to be able to tell you that the good ship Atlantic is safe!" the house broke into such plaudits, so huge and prolonged a roar of relief, as I had never heard the like of and which gave me my first measure of a great immediate public emotion—even as the incident itself today reminds me of the family-party smallness of the old New York, those happy limits that could make us all care, and care to fond vociferation, for the same thing at once. It was a moment of the golden age—representing too but a snatch of elation, since the wretched Arctic had gone down in mortal woe and her other companion, the Pacific, leaving England a few months later and under the interested eyes of our family group, then temporarily settled in London, was never heard of more. Let all of which show again what traps are laid about me for unguarded acute reminiscence.

I meet another of these, though I positively try to avoid it, in the sense of a day spent on the great fusty curtained bed, a mediæval four-poster such as I had never seen, of the hotel at the London and North-Western station, where it appeared, to our great inconvenience, that I had during the previous months somewhere perversely absorbed (probably on Staten Island upwards of a year before) the dull seed of malaria, which now suddenly broke out in chills and fever. This condition, of the intermittent order, hampered our movements but left alternate days on which we could travel, and as present to me as ever is the apprehended interest of my important and determinant state and of our complicated prospect while I lay, much at my ease—for I recall in particular certain short sweet times when I could be left alone—with the thick and heavy suggestions of the London room about me, the very smell of which was ancient, strange and impressive, a new revelation altogether, and the window open to the English June and the far off hum of a thousand possibilities. I consciously took them in, these last, and must then, I think, have first tasted the very greatest pleasure perhaps I was ever to know—that of almost holding my breath in presence of certain aspects to the end of so taking in. It was as if in those hours that precious fine art had been disclosed to me—scantly as the poor place and the small occasion might have seemed of an order to promote it. We seize our property by an avid instinct wherever we find it, and I must have kept seizing mine at the absurdest little rate, and all by this deeply dissimulative process of taking in, through the whole succession of those summer days. The next application of it that stands out for me, or the next that I make room for here, since I note after all so much less than I remember, is the intensity of a fond apprehension of Paris, a few days later, from the balcony of an hotel that hung, through the soft summer night, over the Rue de la Paix. I hung with the balcony, and doubtless with my brothers and my sister, though I recover what I felt as so much relation and response to the larger, the largest appeal only, that of the whole perfect Parisianism I seemed to myself always to have possessed mentally—even if I had but just turned twelve!—and that now filled out its frame or case for me from every lighted window, up and down, as if each of these had been, for strength of sense, a word in some immortal quotation, the very breath of civilised lips. How I had anciently gathered such stores of preconception is more than I shall undertake an account of—though I believe I should be able to scrape one together; certain it is at any rate that half the beauty of the whole exposed second floor of a *modiste* just opposite, for instance, with the flittings and figurings, as well as the intent immobilities, of busy young women descried through frank, and, as it were, benignant apertures, and of such bright fine strain that they but asked to work far into the night, came from the effect on the part of these things of so exactly crowning and comforting I couldn't have said what momentous young dream. I might have been *right* to myself—as against some danger of being wrong, and if I had uttered my main comment on it all this must certainly have been "I told you so, I told you so!" What I had told myself was of course that the impression would be of the richest and at the same time of the most insinuating, and this after all didn't sail very close; but I had had before me from far back a picture (which might have been hung in the very sky,) and here was every touch in it repeated with a charm. Had I ever till then known what a charm *was*?—a large, a local, a social charm, leaving out that of a few individuals. It was at all events, this mystery, one's property—that of one's mind; and so, once for all, I helped myself to it from my balcony and tucked it away. It counted all immensely for practice in taking in.

I profited by that, no doubt, still a few days later, at an hour that has never ceased to recur to me all my life as crucial, as supremely determinant. The travelling-carriage had stopped at a village on the way from Lyons to Geneva, between which places there was then no railway; a village now nameless to me and which was not yet Nantua, in the Jura, where we were to spend the night. I was stretched at my ease on a couch formed by a plank laid from seat to seat and covered by a small mattress and other draperies; an indulgence founded on my visitation of fever, which, though not now checking our progress, assured me, in our little band, these invidious luxuries. It may have been that as my body was pampered so I was moved equally to pamper my spirit, for my appropriative instinct had neglected no item of our case from the first—by which I mean from the moment of our getting under way, that morning, with much elaboration, in the court of the old Hôtel de l'Univers at Lyons, where we had arrived two days before and awaited my good pleasure during forty-eight hours that overflowed for us perhaps somewhat less than any pair of days yet, but as regards which it was afterwards my complacent theory that my contemplative rest at the ancient inn, with all the voices and graces of the past, of the court, of the French scheme of manners in general and of ancient inns, as such, in particular, had prepared me not a little, when I should in due course hear of it, for what was meant by the *vie de province*—that expression which was to become later on so *toned*, as old fine colour and old fine opinion are toned. It was the romance of travel, and it was the *suggested* romance, flushed with suppositions and echoes, with implications and memories, memories of one's "reading," save the mark! all the more that our proper bestowal required two carriages, in which we were to "post," ineffable thought, and which bristled with every kind of contradiction of common experience. The postilion, in a costume rather recalling, from the halls of Ferrero, that of my débardeur, bobbed up and down, the Italian courier, Jean Nadali, black-whiskered and acquired in London, sat in the rumble along with Annette Godefroi of Metz, fresh-coloured, broad-faced and fair-braided, a "bonne Lorraine" if ever there was, acquired in New York: I enjoy the echo of their very names, neither unprecedented nor irreproducible, yet which melt together for me, to intensification, with all the rest; with the recovered moment, above all, of our pause at the inn-door in the cool sunshine—we had mounted and mounted—during which, in my absurdly cushioned state, I took in, as I have hinted, by a long slow swig that testified to some power of elbow, a larger draught of the wine of perception than any I had ever before owed to a single throb of that faculty. The village street, which was not as village streets hitherto known to me, opened out, beyond an interval, into a high place on which perched an object also a fresh revelation and that I recognised with a deep joy—though a joy that was doubtless partly the sense of fantastic ease, of abated illness and of cold chicken—as at once a castle and a ruin. The only castle within my ken had been, by my impression, the machicolated villa above us the previous summer at New Brighton, and as I had seen no structure rise beyond that majesty so I had seen none abased to the dignity of ruin. Loose boards were no expression of this latter phase, and I was already somehow aware of a deeper note in the crumbled castle than any note of the solid one—little experience as I had had either of solidity. At a point in the interval, at any rate, below the slope on which this memento stood, was a woman in a black bodice, a white shirt and a red petticoat, engaged in some sort of field labour, the effect of whose intervention just then is almost beyond my notation. I knew her for a peasant in sabots—the first peasant I had ever beheld, or beheld at least to such advantage. She had in the whole aspect an enormous value, emphasising with her petticoat's tonic strength the truth that sank in as I lay—the truth of one's embracing there, in all the presented character of the scene, an amount of character I had felt no scene present, not even the one I had raked from the Hôtel Westminster; the sort of thing that, even as mere fulness and mere weight, would sit most warmly in the mind. Supremely, in that ecstatic vision, was "Europe," sublime synthesis, expressed and guaranteed to me—as if by a mystic gage, which spread all through the summer air, that I should now, only now, never lose it, hold the whole consistency of it: up to that time it might have been but mockingly whisked before me. Europe mightn't have been flattered, it was true, at my finding her thus most signified and summarised in a sordid old woman scraping a mean living and an uninhabitable tower abandoned to the owls; that was but the momentary measure of a small sick boy, however, and the virtue of the impression was proportioned to my capacity. It made a bridge over to more things than I then knew.

XXI

How shall I render certain other impressions coming back to me from that summer, which were doubtless involved in my having still for a time, on the alternate days when my complaint was active, to lie up on various couches and, for my main comfort, consider the situation? I considered it best, I think, gathering in the fruits of a quickened sensibility to it, in certain umbrageous apartments in which my parents had settled themselves near Geneva; an old house, in ample grounds and among great spreading trees that pleasantly brushed our windows in the summer heats and airs, known, if I am not mistaken, as the Campagne Gerebsoff—which its mistress, an invalid Russian lady, had partly placed at our disposition while she reclined in her own quarter of the garden, on a chaise longue and under a mushroom hat with a green veil, and I, in the course of the mild excursions appointed as my limit, considered her from afar in the light of the legends supplied to me, as to her identity, history, general practices and proceedings, by my younger brother Wilkey, who, according to his nature, or I may say to his genius, had made without loss of time great advances of acquaintance with her and quickened thereby my sense of his superior talent for life. Wilky's age followed closely on mine, and from that time on we conversed and consorted, though with lapses and disparities; I being on the whole, during the succession of those years, in the grateful, the really fortunate position of having one exposure, rather the northward, as it were, to the view of W. J., and the other, perhaps the more immediately sunned surface, to the genial glow of my junior. Of this I shall have more to say, but to meet in memory meanwhile even this early flicker of him is to know again something of the sense that I attached all along our boyhood to his successful sociability, his instinct for intercourse, his genius (as I have used the word) for making friends. It was the only genius he had, declaring itself from his tenderest years, never knowing the shadow of defeat, and giving me, above all, from as far back and by the very radiation of the fact, endlessly much to think of. For I had in a manner, thanks to the radiation, much of the benefit; his geniality was absolutely such that the friends he made were made almost less for himself, so to speak, than for other friends—of whom indeed we, his own adjuncts, were easily first—so far at least as he discriminated. At night all cats are grey, and in this brother's easy view all his acquaintance were his family. The trail of his sociability was over us all alike—though it here concerns me but to the effect, as I recover it, of its weight on my comparatively so indirect faculty for what is called taking life. I must have already at the Campagne Gerebsoff begun to see him take it with all his directness—begun in fact to be a trifle tormentedly aware that, though there might be many ways of so doing, we are condemned practically to a choice, not made free of them all; reduced to the use of but one, at the best, which it is to our interest to make the most of, since we may indeed sometimes make much. There was a small sad charm, I should doubtless add, in this operation of the contrast of the case before me with my own case; it was positively as if Wilky's were supplying me on occasion with the most immediate matter for my own. That was particularly marked after he had, with our elder brother, been placed at school, the Pensionnat Roediger, at Châtelaine, then much esteemed and where I was supposedly to join them on my complete recovery: I recall sociable, irrepressibly sociable *sorties* thence on the part of the pair as promptly breaking out, not less than I recall sociable afternoon visits to the establishment on the part of the rest of us: it was my brothers' first boarding school, but as we had in the New York conditions kept punctually rejoining our family, so in these pleasant Genevese ones our family returned the attention. Of this also more anon; my particular point is just the wealth of Wilky's contribution to my rich current consciousness—the consciousness fairly *made* rich by my taking in, as aforesaid, at reflective hours, hours when I was in a manner alone with it, our roomy and shadowy, our almost haunted interior.

Admirable the scale and solidity, in general, of the ancient villas planted about Geneva, and our house affected me as so massive and so spacious that even our own half of it seemed vast. I had never before lived so long in anything so old and, as I somehow felt, so deep; depth, depth upon depth, was what came out for me at certain times of my waiting above, in my immense room of thick embrasures and rather prompt obscurity, while the summer afternoon waned and my companions, often below at dinner, lingered and left me just perhaps a bit overwhelmed. That was the sense of it—the *character*, in the whole place, pressed upon me with a force I hadn't met and that was beyond my analysis—which is but another way of saying how directly notified I felt that such material conditions as I *had* known could have had no depth at all. My depth was a vague measure, no doubt, but it made space, in the twilight, for an occasional small sound of voice or step from the garden or the rooms of which the great homely, the opaque green shutters opened there softly to echo in—mixed with reverberations finer and more momentous, personal, experimental, if they might be called so; which I much encouraged (they borrowed such tone from our new surrounding medium) and half of which were reducible to Wilky's personalities and Wilky's experience: these latter, irrepressibly communicated, being ever, enviably, though a trifle bewilderingly and even formidably, *of* personalities. There was the difference and the opposition, as I really believe I was already aware—that one way of taking life was to go in for everything and everyone, which kept you abundantly occupied, and the other way was to be as occupied, quite as occupied, just with the sense and the image of it all, and on only a fifth of the actual immersion: a circumstance extremely strange. Life was taken almost equally both ways—that, I mean, seemed the strangeness; mere brute quantity and number being so much less in one case than the other. These latter were what I should have *liked* to go in for, had I but had the intrinsic faculties; that more than ever came home to me on those occasions when, as I could move further and stay out longer, I accompanied my parents on afternoon visits to Châtelaine and the Campagne Roediger, a scene that has remained with me as nobly placid and pastoral. The great trees stood about, casting afternoon shadows; the old thick-walled green-shuttered villa and its dépendances had the air of the happiest home; the big bearded bonhomie of M. Roediger among his little polyglot charges—no petits pays chauds these—appeared to justify, and more, the fond New York theory of Swiss education, the kind *à la portée* of young New

Yorkers, as a beautifully genialised, humanised, civilised, even romanticised thing, in which, amid lawny mountain slopes, "the languages" flowed into so many beaming recipients on a stream of milk and honey, and "the relation," above all, the relation from master to pupil and back again, was of an amenity that wouldn't have been of this world save for the providential arrangement of a perfect pedagogic Switzerland. "Did you notice the relation—how charming it was?" our parents were apt to say to each other after these visits, in reference to some observed show of confidence between instructor and instructed; while, as for myself, I was lost in the wonder of *all* the relations —my younger brother seemed to live, and to his own ingenuous relish as well, in such a happy hum of them. The languages had reason to prosper—they were so copiously represented; the English jostled the American, the Russian the German, and there even trickled through a little funny French.

A great Geneva school of those days was the Institution Haccius, to which generations of our young countrymen had been dedicated and our own faces first turned—under correction, however, by the perceived truth that if the languages *were* in question the American reigned there almost unchallenged. The establishment chosen for our experiment must have appealed by some intimate and insinuating side, and as less patronised by the rich and the sophisticated—for even in those days some Americans were rich and several sophisticated; little indeed as it was all to matter in the event, so short a course had the experiment just then to run. What it mainly brings back to me is the fine old candour and queerness of the New York state of mind, begotten really not a little, I think, under our own roof, by the mere charmed perusal of Rodolphe Toeppfer's Voyages en Zigzag, the two goodly octavo volumes of which delightful work, an adorable book, taken with its illustrations, had come out early in the 'fifties and had engaged our fondest study. It is the copious chronicle, by a schoolmaster of endless humour and sympathy—of what degree and form of "authority" it never occurred to one even to ask—of his holiday excursions with his pupils, mainly on foot and with staff and knapsack, through the incomparable Switzerland of the time before the railways and the "rush," before the monster hotels, the desecrated summits, the vulgarised valleys, the circular tours, the perforating tubes, the funiculars, the hordes, the horrors. To turn back to Toeppfer's pages to-day is to get the sense of a lost paradise, and the effect for me even yet of having pored over them in my childhood is to steep in sweetness and quaintness some of the pictures—his own illustrations are of the pleasantest and drollest, and the association makes that faded Swiss master of landscape Calame, of the so-called calamités, a quite sufficient Ruysdael. It must have been conceived for us that we would lead in these conditions—always in pursuit of an education—a life not too dissimilar to that of the storied exiles in the forest of Arden; though one would fain not press, after all, upon ideals of culture so little organised, so little conscious, up to that moment, of our ferocities of comparison and competition, of imposed preparation. This particular loose ideal reached out from the desert—or what might under discouragement pass for such; it invoked the light, but a simplicity of view which was somehow one with the beauty of other convictions accompanied its effort; and though a glance at the social "psychology" of some of its cheerful estimates, its relative importances, assumed and acted upon, might here seem indicated, there are depths of the ancient serenity that nothing would induce me to sound.

I need linger the less, moreover, since we in fact, oddly enough, lingered so little; so very little, for reasons doubtless well known to ourselves at the time but which I at present fail to recapture, that what next stands vividly out for me is our renewed passage through Paris on the way to London for the winter; a turn of our situation invested at the time with nothing whatever of the wonderful, yet which would again half prompt me to soundings were I not to recognise in it that mark of the fitful, that accent of the improvised, that general quality of earnest and reasoned, yet at the same time almost passionate, impatience which was to devote us for some time to variety, almost to incoherency, of interest. We had fared across the sea under the glamour of the Swiss school in the abstract, but the Swiss school in the concrete soon turned stale on our hands; a fact over which I remember myself as no further critical than to feel, not without zest, that, since one was all eyes and the world decidedly, at such a pace, all images, it ministered to the panoramic. It ministered, to begin with, through our very early start for Lyons again in the October dawn—without Nadali or the carriages this time, but on the basis of the malle-poste, vast, yellow and rumbling, which we availed wholly to fill and of which the high haughtiness was such that it could stop, even for an instant, only at appointed and much dissevered places—to the effect, I recall, of its vainly attempted arrest by our cousin Charlotte King, beforementioned, whom I see now suddenly emerge, fresh, confident and pretty, from some rural retreat by the road, a scene of simple villeggiatura, "rien que pour saluer ces dames," as she pleaded to the conductor; whom she practically, if not permittedly, overmastered, leaving with me still the wonder of her happy fusion of opposites. The coach had not, in the event, paused, but so neither had she, and as it ignored flush and flurry quite as it defied delay, she was equally a match for it in these particulars, blandly achieving her visit to us while it rumbled on, making a perfect success and a perfect grace of her idea. She dropped as elegantly out as she had gymnastically floated in, and "ces dames" must much have wished they could emulate her art. Save for this my view of that migration has faded, though to shine out again to the sense of our early morning arrival in Paris a couple of days later, and our hunt there, vain at first, for an hotel that would put us numerously up; vain till we had sat awhile, in the Rue du Helder, I think, before that of an Albany uncle, luckily on the scene and finally invoked, who after some delay descended to us with a very foreign air, I fancied, and no possibility, to his regret, of placing us under his own roof; as if indeed, I remember reflecting, we could, such as we were, have been desired to share his foreign interests—such as *they* were. He espoused our cause, however, with gay goodnature—while I wondered, in my admiration for him and curiosity about him, how he really liked us, and (a bit doubtfully) whether I should have liked us had I been in his place; and after some further adventure installed us at the Hôtel de la Ville de Paris in the Rue de la Ville-l'Evèque, a resort now long since extinct, though it lingered on for some years, and which I think of as rather huddled and disappointingly private, to the abatement of spectacle, and standing obliquely beyond a wall, a high gateway and a more or less cobbled court.

XXII

Little else of that Parisian passage remains with me—it was probably of the briefest; I recover only a visit with my father to the Palais de l'Industrie, where the first of the great French Exhibitions, on the model, much reduced, of the English Crystal Palace of 1851, was still open, a fact explaining the crowded inns; and from that visit win back but the department of the English pictures and our stopping long before The Order of Release of a young English painter, J. E. Millais, who had just leaped into fame, and my impression of the rare treatment of whose baby's bare legs, pendent from its mother's arms, is still as vivid to me as if from yesterday. The vivid yields again to the vague—I scarce know why so utterly—till consciousness, waking up in London, renews itself, late one evening and very richly, at the Gloucester Hotel (or Coffee-House, as I think it was then still called,) which occupied that corner of Piccadilly and Berkeley Street where more modern establishments have since succeeded it, but where a fatigued and famished American family found on that occasion a fine old British virtue in cold roast beef and bread and cheese and ale; their expert acclamation of which echoes even now in my memory. It keeps company there with other matters equally British and, as we say now, early Victorian; the thick gloom of the inn rooms, the faintness of the glimmering tapers, the blest inexhaustibility of the fine joint, surpassed only by that of the grave waiter's reserve—plain, immutably plain fare all; but prompting in our elders an emphasis of relief and relish, the "There's nothing like it after all!" tone, which re-excited expectation, which in fact seemed this time to re-announce a basis for faith and joy.

That basis presently shrank to the scale of a small house hard by the hotel, at the entrance of Berkeley Square—expeditiously lighted on, it would thus appear, which again has been expensively superseded, but to the ancient little facts of which I fondly revert, since I owe them what I feel to have been, in the far past, the prime faint revelation, the small broken expression, of the London I was afterwards to know. The place wears on the spot, to this day, no very different face; the house that has risen on the site of ours is still immediately neighboured at the left by the bookseller, the circulating-librarian and news-agent, who modestly flourished in our time under the same name; the great establishment of Mr. Gunter, just further along, is as soberly and solidly seated; the mews behind the whole row, from the foot of Hay Hill at the right, wanders away to Bruton Street with the irregular grace that spoke to my young fancy; Hay Hill itself is somehow less sharply precipitous, besides being no longer paved, as I seem to recall its having been, with big boulders, and I was on the point of saying that its antique charm in some degree abides. Nothing, however, could be further from the truth; its antique charm quite succumbed, years ago, to that erection of lumpish "mansions" which followed the demolition of the old-world town-residence, as the house-agents say, standing, on the south side, between court and I suppose garden, where Dover Street gives way to Grafton; a house of many histories, of vague importances and cold reserves and deep suggestions, I used to think after scaling the steep quite on purpose to wonder about it. A whole chapter of life was condensed, for our young sensibility, I make out, into the couple of months—they can scarce have been more—spent by us in these quarters, which must have proved too narrow and too towny; but it can have had no passage so lively as the occurrences at once sequent to my father's having too candidly made known in some public print, probably The Times, that an American gentleman, at such an address, desired to arrange with a competent young man for the tuition at home of his three sons. The effect of his rash failure to invite application by letter only was the assault of an army of visitors who filled us with consternation; they hung about the door, cumbered the hall, choked the staircase and sat grimly individual in odd corners. How they were dealt with, given my father's precipitate and general charity, I can but feebly imagine; our own concern, in the event, was with a sole selected presence, that of Scotch Mr. Robert Thompson, who gave us his care from breakfast to luncheon each morning that winter, who afterwards carried on a school at Edinburgh, and whom, in years long subsequent, I happened to help R. L. Stevenson to recognise gaily as *his* early pedagogue. He was so deeply solicitous, yet withal so mild and kind and shy, with no harsher injunction to us ever than "Come now, be getting on!" that one could but think well of a world in which so gentle a spirit might flourish; while it is doubtless to the credit of his temper that remembrance is a blank in respect to his closer ministrations. I recall vividly his fresh complexion, his very round clear eyes, his tendency to trip over his own legs or feet while thoughtfully circling about us, and his constant dress-coat, worn with trousers of a lighter hue, which was perhaps the prescribed uniform of a daily tutor then; but I ask myself in vain what I can have "studied" with him, there remaining with me afterwards, to testify—this putting any scrap of stored learning aside—no single textbook save the Lambs' Tales from Shakespeare, which was given me as (of all things in the world) a reward. A reward for what I am again at a loss to say—not certainly for having "got on" to anything like the tune plaintively, for the most part, piped to me. It is a very odd and yet to myself very rich and full reminiscence, though I remember how, looking back at it from after days, W. J. denounced it to me, and with it the following year and more spent in Paris, as a poor and arid and lamentable time, in which, missing such larger chances and connections as we might have reached out to, we had done nothing, he and I, but walk about together, in a state of the direst propriety, little "high" black hats and inveterate gloves, the childish costume of the place and period, to stare at grey street-scenery (that of early Victorian London had tones of a neutrality!) dawdle at shop-windows and buy water-colours and brushes with which to bedaub eternal drawing-blocks. We might, I dare say, have felt higher impulses and carried out larger plans—though indeed present to me for this, on my brother's so expressing himself, is my then quick recognition of the deeper stirrings and braver needs he at least must have known, and my perfect if rueful sense of having myself had no such quarrel with our conditions: embalmed for me did they even to that shorter retrospect appear in a sort of fatalism of patience, spiritless in a manner, no doubt, yet with an inwardly active, productive and ingenious side.

It was just the fact of our having so walked and dawdled and dodged that made the charm of memory; in addition to which what could one have asked more than to be steeped in a medium so dense that whole elements of it, forms of amusement, interest and wonder, soaked through to some appreciative faculty and made one fail at the most of nothing but one's lessons? My brother was right in so far as that my question—the one I have just reproduced—could have been asked only by a person incorrigible in throwing himself back upon substitutes for lost causes, substitutes that might *temporarily* have appeared queer and small; a person so haunted, even from an early age, with visions of life, that aridities, for him, were half a terror and half an impossibility, and that the said substitutes, the economies and ingenuities that protested, in their dumb vague way, against weakness of situation or of direct and applied faculty, were in themselves really a revel of spirit and thought. It *had* indeed again an effect of almost pathetic incoherence that our brave quest of "the languages," suffering so prompt and for the time at least so accepted and now so inscrutably irrecoverable a check, should have contented itself with settling us by that Christmas in a house, more propitious to our development, in St. John's Wood, where we enjoyed a considerable garden and wistful view, though by that windowed privilege alone, of a large green expanse in which ladies and gentlemen practised archery. Just *that*—and not the art even, but the mere spectacle—might have been one of the substitutes in question; if not for the languages at least for one or another of the romantic connections we seemed a little to have missed: it was such a whiff of the old world of Robin Hood as we could never have looked up from the mere thumbed "story," in Fourteenth Street at any rate, to any soft confidence of. More than I can begin to say, that is by a greater number of queer small channels, did the world about us, thus continuous with the old world of Robin Hood, steal into my sense—a constant state of subjection to which fact is no bad instance of those refinements of surrender that I just named as my fond practice. I seem to see to-day that the London of the 'fifties was even to the weak perception of childhood a much less generalised, a much more eccentrically and variously characterised place, than the present great accommodated and accommodating city; it had fewer resources but it had many more features, scarce one of which failed to help the whole to bristle with what a little gaping American could take for an intensity of difference from *his* supposed order. It was extraordinarily the picture and the scene of Dickens, now so changed and superseded; it offered to my presumptuous vision still more the reflection of Thackeray—and where is the *detail* of the reflection of Thackeray now?—so that as I trod the vast length of Baker Street, the Thackerayan vista of other days, I throbbed with the pride of a vastly enlarged acquaintance.

I dare say our perambulations of Baker Street in our little "top" hats and other neatnesses must have been what W. J. meant by our poverty of life—whereas it was probably one of the very things most expressive to myself of the charm and the colour of history and (from the point of view of the picturesque) of society. We were often in Baker Street by reason of those stretched-out walks, at the remembered frequency and long-drawn push of which I am to-day amazed; recalling at the same time, however, that save for Robert Thompson's pitching ball with us in the garden they took for us the place of all other agilities. I can't but feel them to have been marked in their way by a rare curiosity and energy. Good Mr. Thompson had followed us in our move, occupying quarters, not far off, above a baker's shop on a Terrace—a group of objects still untouched by time—where we occasionally by way of change attended for our lessons and where not the least of our inspirations was the confidence, again and again justified, that our mid-morning "break" would determine the appearance of a self-conscious stale cake, straight from below, received by us all each time as if it had been a sudden happy thought, and ushered in by a little girl who might have been a Dickens foundling or "ortling." Our being reduced to mumble cake in a suburban lodging by way of reaction from the strain of study would have been perhaps a pathetic picture, but we had field-days too, when we accompanied our excellent friend to the Tower, the Thames Tunnel, St. Paul's and the Abbey, to say nothing of the Zoological Gardens, almost close at hand and with which we took in that age of lingering forms no liberty of abbreviation; to say nothing either of Madame Tussaud's, then in our interminable but so amiable Baker Street, the only shade on the amiability of which was just that gruesome association with the portal of the Bazaar—since Madame Tussaud had, of all her treasures, most vividly revealed to me the Mrs. Manning and the Burke and Hare of the Chamber of Horrors which lurked just within it; whom, for days after making their acquaintance (and prolonging it no further than our conscientious friend thought advisable) I half expected, when alone, to meet quite dreadfully on the staircase or on opening a door. All this experience was valuable, but it was not the languages—save in so far indeed as it was the English, which we hadn't in advance so much aimed at, yet which more or less, and very interestingly, came; it at any rate perhaps broke our fall a little that French, of a sort, continued to be with us in the remarkably erect person of Mademoiselle Cusin, the Swiss governess who had accompanied us from Geneva, whose quite sharply extrusive but on the whole exhilarating presence I associate with this winter, and who led in that longish procession of more or less similar domesticated presences which was to keep the torch, that is the accent, among us, fairly alight. The variety and frequency of the arrivals and departures of these ladies—whose ghostly names, again, so far as I recall them, I like piously to preserve, Augustine Danse, Amélie Fortin, Marie Guyard, Marie Bonningue, Félicie Bonningue, Clarisse Bader—mystifies me in much the same degree as our own academic vicissitudes in New York; I can no more imagine why, sociable and charitable, we so often changed governesses than I had contemporaneously grasped the principle of our succession of schools: the whole group of phenomena reflected, I gather, as a rule, much more the extreme promptitude of the parental optimism than any disproportionate habit of impatience. The optimism begot precipitation, and the precipitation had too often to confess itself. What is instructive, what is historic, is the probability that young persons offering themselves at that time as guides and communicators—the requirements of our small sister were for long modest enough—quite conceivably lacked preparedness, and were so thrown back on the extempore, which in turn lacked abundance. One of these figures, that of Mademoiselle Danse, the most Parisian, and prodigiously so, was afterwards to stand out for us quite luridly—a cloud of revelations succeeding her withdrawal; a cloud which, thick as it was, never obscured our impression of her genius and her charm. The daughter of a political proscript who had but just escaped, by the legend, being seized in his bed on the terrible night of the Deux-Décembre, and who wrote her micawberish letters from Gallipolis, Ohio, she subsequently figured to my imagination (in the light, that is, of the divined revelations, too dreadful for our young ears,) as the most brilliant and most genial of irregular characters, exhibiting the Parisian "mentality" at its highest, or perhaps rather its deepest, and more remarkable for nothing than for the consummate little art and grace with which she had for a whole year draped herself in the mantle of our innocent air. It was exciting, it was really valuable, to have to that extent rubbed shoulders with an "adventuress"; it showed one that for the adventuress there might on occasion be much to be said.

Those, however, were later things—extensions of view hampered for the present, as I have noted, by our mere London street-scenery, which had much to build out for us. I see again that we but endlessly walked and endlessly daubed, and that our walks, with an obsession of their own, constantly abetted our daubing. We knew no other boys at all, and we even saw no others, I seem to remember, save the essentially rude ones, rude with a kind of mediæval rudeness for which our clear New York experience had given us no precedent, and of which the great and constant sign was the artless, invidious wonder produced in them, on our public appearances, by the alien stamp in us that, for our comfort, we vainly sought to dissimulate. We conformed in each particular, so far as we could, to the prevailing fashion and standard, of a narrow range in those days, but in our very plumage—putting our *ramage* aside—our wood-note wild must have seemed to sound, so sharply we challenged, when abroad, the attention of our native contemporaries, and even sometimes of their elders, pulled up at sight of us in the from-head-to-foot stare, a curiosity void of sympathy and that attached itself for some reason especially to our feet, which were not abnormally large. The London people had for themselves, at the same time, an exuberance of type; we found it in particular a world of costume, often of very odd costume—the most intimate notes of which were the postmen in their frock-coats of military red and their black beaver hats; the milkwomen, in hats that often emulated these, in little shawls and strange short, full frocks, revealing enormous boots, with their pails swung from their shoulders on wooden yokes; the inveterate footmen hooked behind the coaches of the rich, frequently in pairs and carrying staves, together with the mounted and belted grooms without the attendance of whom riders, of whichever sex—and riders then were much more numerous—almost never went forth. The range of character, on the other hand, reached rather dreadfully down; there were embodied and exemplified "horrors" in the streets beside which any present exhibition is pale, and I well remember the almost terrified sense of their salience produced in me a couple of years later, on the occasion of a flying return from the Continent with my father, by a long, an interminable drive westward from the London Bridge railway-station. It was a soft June evening, with a lingering light and swarming crowds, as they then seemed to me, of figures reminding me of George Cruikshank's Artful Dodger and his Bill Sikes and his Nancy, only with the bigger brutality of life, which pressed upon the cab, the early-Victorian fourwheeler, as we jogged over the Bridge, and cropped up in more and more gas-lit patches for all our course, culminating, somewhere far to the west, in the vivid picture, framed by the cab-window, of a woman reeling backward as a man felled her to the ground with a blow in the face. The London view at large had in fact more than a Cruikshank, there still survived in it quite a Hogarth, side—which I had of course then no name for, but which I was so sharply to recognise on coming back years later that it fixed for me the veracity of the great pictorial chronicler. Hogarth's mark is even yet not wholly overlaid; though time has *per contra* dealt with that stale servility of address which most expressed to our young minds the rich burden of a Past, the consequence of too much history. I liked for my own part a lot of history, but felt in face of certain queer old obsequiosities and appeals, whinings and sidlings and hand-rubbings and curtsey-droppings, the general play of apology and humility, behind which the great dim social complexity seemed to mass itself, that one didn't quite want so inordinate a quantity. Of that particular light and shade, however, the big broom of change has swept the scene bare; more history still has been after all what it wanted. Quite another order, in the whole connection, strikes me as reigning to-day—though not without the reminder from it that the relations in which manner, as a generalised thing, in which "tone," is *positively* pleasant, is really assured and sound, clear and interesting, are numerous and definite only when it has had in its past some strange phases and much misadventure.

XXIII

We were still being but vaguely "formed," yet it was a vagueness preferred apparently by our parents to the only definiteness in any degree open to us, that of the English school away from home (the London private school near home they would absolutely none of;) which they saw as a fearful and wonderful, though seemingly effective, preparation of the young for English life and an English career, but related to that situation only, so little related in fact to any other as to make it, in a differing case, an educational cul-de-sac, the worst of economies. They had doubtless heard claimed for it just that no other method for boys *was* so splendidly general, but they had, I judge, their own sense of the matter—which would have been that it all depended on what was meant by this. The truth was, above all, that to them the formative forces most closely bearing on us were not in the least vague, but very definite by *their* measure and intention; there were "advantages," generally much belauded, that appealed to them scantly, and other matters, conceptions of character and opportunity, ideals, values, importances, enjoying no great common credit but for which it was their belief that they, under whatever difficulties, more or less provided. In respect of which I further remind myself of the blest fewness, as yet, of our years; and I come back to my own sense, benighted though it may have been, of a highly-coloured and remarkably active life. I recognise our immediate, our practical ferment even in our decent perambulations, our discussions, W. J.'s and mine, of whether we had in a given case best apply for a renewal of our "artists' materials" to Messrs. Rowney or to Messrs. Windsor and Newton, and in our pious resort, on these determinations, to Rathbone Place, more beset by our steps, probably, than any other single corner of the town, and the short but charged vista of which lives for me again in the tempered light of those old winter afternoons. Of scarce less moment than these were our frequent visits, in the same general connection, to the old Pantheon of Oxford Street, now fallen from its high estate, but during that age a place of fine rococo traditions, a bazaar, an exhibition, an opportunity, at the end of long walks, for the consumption of buns and ginger-beer, and above all a monument to the genius of that wonderful painter B. R. Haydon. We must at one time quite have haunted the Pantheon, where we doubtless could better than elsewhere sink to contemplative, to ruminative rest: Haydon's huge canvases covered the walls—I wonder what has become now of The Banishment of Aristides, attended to the city gate by his wife and babe, every attitude and figure in which, especially that of the foreshortened boy picking up stones to shy at the all-too-just, stares out at me still. We found in these works remarkable interest and beauty, the reason of which was partly, no doubt, that we hung, to fascination, at home, over the three volumes of the hapless artist's Autobiography, then a new book, which our father, indulgent to our preoccupation, had provided us with; but I blush to risk the further surmise that the grand manner, the heroic and the classic, in Haydon, came home to us more warmly and humanly than in the masters commended as "old," who, at the National Gallery, seemed to meet us so little halfway, to hold out the hand of fellowship or suggest something that *we* could do, or could at least want to. The beauty of Haydon was just that he was new, shiningly new, and if he hinted that we might perhaps in some happy future emulate his big bravery there was nothing so impossible about it. If we adored daubing we preferred it *fresh*, and the genius of the Pantheon was fresh, whereas, strange to say, Rubens and Titian were not. Even the charm of the Pantheon yielded, however, to that of the English collection, the Vernon bequest to the nation, then arrayed at Marlborough House and to which the great plumed and draped and dusty funeral car of the Duke of Wellington formed an attractive adjunct. The ground-floor chambers there, none of them at that time royally inhabited, come back to me as altogether bleak and bare and as owing their only dignity to Maclise, Mulready and Landseer, to David Wilkie and Charles Leslie. *They* were, by some deep-seated English mystery, the real unattainable, just as they were none the less the directly inspiring and the endlessly delightful. I could never have enough of Maclise's Play-scene in Hamlet, which I supposed the finest composition in the world (though Ophelia did look a little as if cut in silhouette out of white paper and pasted on;) while as I gazed, and gazed again, at Leslie's Sancho Panza and his Duchess I pushed through the great hall of romance to the central or private apartments. Trafalgar Square had its straight message for us only in the May-time exhibition, the Royal Academy of those days having, without a home of its own, to borrow space from the National Gallery—space partly occupied, in the summer of 1856, by the first fresh fruits of the Pre-Raphaelite efflorescence, among which I distinguish Millais's Vale of Rest, his Autumn Leaves and, if I am not mistaken, his prodigious Blind Girl. The very word Pre-Raphaelite wore for us that intensity of meaning, not less than of mystery, that thrills us in its perfection but for one season, the prime hour of first initiations, and I may perhaps somewhat mix the order of our great little passages of perception. Momentous to us again was to be the Academy show of 1858, where there were, from the same wide source, still other challenges to wonder, Holman Hunt's Scapegoat most of all, which I remember finding so charged with the awful that I was glad I saw it in company—*it* in company and I the same: I believed, or tried to believe, I should have feared to face it all alone in a room. By that time moreover—I mean by 1858—we had been more fully indoctrinated, or such was the case at least with W. J., for whom, in Paris, during the winter of 1857, instruction at the atelier of M. Léon Coigniet, of a limited order and adapted to his years, had been candidly provided—that M. Léon Coigniet whose Marius meditating among the Ruins of Carthage impressed us the more, at the Luxembourg (even more haunted by us in due course than the Pantheon had been,) in consequence of this family connection.

Let me not, however, nip the present thread of our æsthetic evolution without a glance at that comparatively spare but deeply appreciated experience of the London theatric privilege which, so far as occasion favoured us, also pressed the easy spring. The New York familiarities had to drop; going to the play presented itself in London as a serious, ponderous business: a procession of two throbbing and heaving cabs over vast foggy tracts of the town, after much arrangement in advance and with a renewal of far peregrination, through twisting passages and catacombs, even after crossing the magic threshold. We sat in strange places, with still stranger ones behind or beside; we felt walls and partitions, in our rear, getting so hot that we wondered if the house was to burst into flame; I recall in especial our being arrayed, to the number of nine persons, all of our contingent, in a sort of rustic balcony or verandah which, simulating the outer gallery of a Swiss cottage framed in creepers, formed a feature of Mr. Albert Smith's once-famous representation of the Tour of Mont Blanc. Big, bearded, rattling, chattering, mimicking Albert Smith again charms my senses, though subject to the reflection that his type and presence, superficially so important, so ample, were somehow at odds with such ingratiations, with the reckless levity of his performance—a performance one of the great effects of which was, as I remember it, the very brief stop and re-departure of the train at Epernay, with the ringing of bells, the bawling of guards, the cries of travellers, the slamming of doors and the tremendous pop as of a colossal champagne-cork, made all simultaneous and vivid by Mr. Smith's mere personal resources and graces. But it is the publicity of our situation as a happy family that I best remember, and how, to our embarrassment, we seemed put forward in our illustrative châlet as part of the boisterous show and of what had been paid for by the house. Two other great evenings stand out for me as not less collectively enjoyed, one of these at the Princess's, then under the management of Charles Kean, the unprecedented (as he was held) Shakespearean revivalist, the other at the Olympic, where Alfred Wigan, the extraordinary and too short-lived Robson and the shrewd and handsome Mrs. Stirling were the high attraction. Our enjoyment of Charles Kean's presentation of Henry the Eighth figures to me as a momentous date in our lives: we did nothing for weeks afterwards but try to reproduce in water-colours Queen Katharine's dream-vision of the beckoning, consoling angels, a radiant group let down from the skies by machinery then thought marvellous—when indeed we were not parading across our schoolroom stage as the portentous Cardinal and impressively alternating his last speech to Cromwell with Buckingham's, that is with Mr. Ryder's, address on the way to the scaffold. The spectacle had seemed to us prodigious—as it was doubtless at its time the last word of costly scenic science; though as I look back from the high ground of an age that has mastered tone and fusion I seem to see it as comparatively garish and violent, after the manner of the complacently approved stained-glass church-windows of the same period. I was to have my impression of Charles Kean renewed later on—ten years later, in America—without a rag of scenic reinforcement; when I was struck with the fact that no actor so little graced by nature probably ever went so far toward repairing it by a kind of cold rage of endeavour. Were he and his wife really not *coercively* interesting on that Boston night of Macbeth in particular, hadn't their art a distinction that triumphed over battered age and sorry harshness, or was I but too easily beguiled by the old association? I have enjoyed and forgotten numberless rich hours of spectatorship, but somehow still find hooked to the wall of memory the picture of this hushed couple in the castle court, with the knocking at the gate, with Macbeth's stare of pitiful horror at his unused daggers and with the grand manner, up to the height of the argument, of Mrs. Kean's coldly portentous snatch of them. What I especially owe that lady is my sense of what she had in common, as a queer hooped and hook-nosed figure, of large circumference and archaic attire, strange tasteless toggery, with those performers of the past who are preserved for us on the small canvases of Hogarth and Zoffany; she helped one back at that time of her life to a vision of the Mrs. Cibbers and the Mrs. Pritchards—so affecting may often be such recovered links.

I see the evening at the Olympic as really itself partaking of that antiquity, even though Still Waters Run Deep, then in its flourishing freshness and as to which I remember my fine old friend Fanny Kemble's mentioning to me in the distant after-time that she had directed Tom Taylor to Charles de Bernard's novel of Un Gendre for the subject of it, passed at the moment for a highly modern "social study." It is perhaps in particular through the memory of our dismal approach to the theatre, the squalid slum of Wych Street, then incredibly brutal and barbarous as an avenue to joy, an avenue even sometimes for the muffled coach of Royalty, that the episode affects me as antedating some of the conditions of the mid-Victorian age; the general credit of which, I should add, was highly re-established for us by the consummately quiet and natural art, as we expertly pronounced it, of Alfred Wigan's John

Mildmay and the breadth and sincerity of the representative of the rash mother-in-law whom he so imperturbably puts in her place. This was an exhibition supposed in its day to leave its spectators little to envy in the highest finish reached by the French theatre. At a remarkable height, in a different direction, moved the strange and vivid little genius of Robson, a master of fantastic intensity, unforgettable for us, we felt that night, in Planché's extravaganza of The Discreet Princess, a Christmas production preluding to the immemorial harlequinade. I still see Robson slide across the stage, in one sidelong wriggle, as the small black sinister Prince Richcraft of the fairy-tale, everything he did at once very dreadful and very droll, thoroughly true and yet none the less *macabre*, the great point of it all its parody of Charles Kean in The Corsican Brothers; a vision filled out a couple of years further on by his Daddy Hardacre in a two-acts version of a Parisian piece thriftily and coarsely extracted from Balzac's Eugénie Grandet. This occasion must have given the real and the finer measure of his highly original talent; so present to me, despite the interval, is the distinctiveness of his little concentrated rustic miser whose daughter helps herself from his money-box so that her cousin and lover shall save a desperate father, her paternal uncle, from bankruptcy; and the prodigious effect of Robson's appalled descent, from an upper floor, his literal headlong tumble and rattle of dismay down a steep staircase occupying the centre of the stage, on his discovery of the rifling of his chest. Long was I to have in my ears the repeated shriek of his alarm, followed by a panting babble of wonder and rage as his impetus hurled him, a prostrate scrap of despair (he was a tiny figure, yet "so held the stage" that in his company you could see nobody else) half way across the room. I associate a little uncertainly with the same night the sight of Charles Matthews in Sheridan's Critic and in a comedy botched from the French, like everything else in those days that was not either Sheridan or Shakespeare, called Married for Money; an example above all, this association, of the heaped measure of the old bills—vast and various enumerations as they were, of the size of but slightly reduced placards and with a strange and delightful greasy feel and redolence of printer's ink, intensely theatrical ink somehow, in their big black lettering. Charles Matthews must have been then in his mid-career, and him too, wasted and aged, infinitely "marked," I was to see again, ever so long after, in America; an impression reminding me, as I recover it, of how one took his talent so thoroughly for granted that he seemed somehow to get but half the credit of it: this at least in all save parts of mere farce and "patter," which were on a footing, and no very interesting one, of their own. The other effect, that of a naturalness so easy and immediate, so friendly and intimate, that one's relation with the artist lost itself in one's relation with the character, the artist thereby somehow positively suffering while the character gained, or at least while the spectator did—this comes back to me quite as a part even of my earlier experience and as attesting on behalf of the actor a remarkable genius; since there are no more charming artistic cases than those of the frank result, when it is frank *enough*, and the dissimulated process, when the dissimulation has been deep. To drop, or appear to drop, machinery and yet keep, or at least gain, intensity, the interesting intensity separated by a gulf from a mere unbought coincidence of aspect or organ, is really to do something. In spite of which, at the same time, what I perhaps most retain, by the light of the present, of the sense of that big and rather dusky night of Drury Lane is not so much the felt degree of anyone's talent as the fact that personality and artistry, *with* their intensity, could work their spell in such a material desert, in conditions intrinsically so charmless, so bleak and bare. The conditions gave nothing of what we regard to-day as most indispensable—since our present fine conception is but to reduce and fill in the material desert, to people and carpet and curtain it. We may be right, so far as that goes, but our predecessors were, with their eye on the essence, not wrong; thanks to which they wear the crown of our now thinking of them—if we do think of them—as in their way giants and heroes. What their successors were to become is another question; very much better dressed, beyond all doubt.

XXIV

Good Robert Thompson was followed by *fin* M. Lerambert —who was surely good too, in his different way; good at least for feigning an interest he could scarce have rejoicingly felt and that he yet somehow managed to give a due impression of: that artifice being, as we must dimly have divined at the time (in fact I make bold to say that I personally did divine it,) exactly a sign of his *finesse*. Of no such uncanny engine had Mr. Thompson, luckily, known a need—luckily since to what arsenal could he possibly have resorted for it? None capable of supplying it could ever have met his sight, and we ourselves should at a pinch have had to help him toward it. He was easily interested, or at least took an easy view, on such ground as we offered him, of what it was to be so; whereas his successor attached to the condition a different value—one recognising no secondary substitute. Perhaps this was why our connection with M. Lerambert can have lasted but four or five months—time even for his sharp subterfuge to have ceased entirely to serve him; though indeed even as I say this I vaguely recall that our separation was attended with friction, that it took him unaware and that he had been prepared (or so represented himself) for further sacrifices. It could have been no great one, assuredly, to deal with so intensely living a young mind as my elder brother's, it could have been but a happy impression constantly renewed; but we two juniors, Wilky and I, were a drag—Wilky's powers most displayed at that time in his preference for ingenuous talk over any other pursuit whatever, and my own aptitude showing for nil, according to our poor gentleman's report of me when a couple of months had sped, save as to rendering La Fontaine's fables into English with a certain corresponding felicity of idiom. I remember perfectly the parental communication to me of this fell judgment, I remember as well the interest with which its so quite definite character inspired me—that character had such beauty and distinctness; yet, and ever so strangely, I recover no sense of having been crushed, and this even though destitute, utterly, of any ground of appeal. The fact leaves me at a loss, since I also remember my not having myself thought particularly well, in the connection allowed, of my "rendering" faculty. "Oh," I seem inwardly to have said, "if it were to be, if it only could be, *really* a question of rendering—!" and so, without confusion, though in vague, very vague, mystification to have left it: as if so many things, intrinsic and extrinsic, would have to change and operate, so many would have to happen, so much water have to flow under the bridge, before I could give primary application to such a thought, much more finish such a sentence.

All of which is but a way of saying that we had since the beginning of the summer settled ourselves in Paris, and that M. Lerambert—by what agency invoked, by what revelation vouchsafed, I quite forget—was at this time attending us in a so-called pavilion, of middling size, that, between the Rond-Point and the Rue du Colisée, hung, at no great height, over the Avenue des Champs-Elysées; hung, that is, from the vantage of its own considerable terrace, surmounted as the parapet of the latter was with iron railings rising sufficiently to protect the place for familiar use and covert contemplation (we ever so fondly used it,) and yet not to the point of fencing out life. A blest little old-world refuge it must have seemed to us, with its protuberantly-paved and peculiarly resonant small court and idle *communs* beside it, accessible by a high grille where the jangle of the bell and the clatter of response across the stones might have figured a comprehensive echo of all old Paris. Old Paris then even there considerably lingered; I recapture much of its presence, for that matter, within our odd relic of a house, the property of an American southerner from whom our parents had briefly hired it and who appeared to divide his time, poor unadmonished gentleman of the eve of the Revolution, between Louisiana and France. What association could have breathed more from the queer graces and the queer incommodities alike, from the diffused glassy polish of floor and perilous staircase, from the redundancy of mirror and clock and ormolu vase, from the irrepressibility of the white and gold panel, from that merciless elegance of tense red damask, above all, which made the gilt-framed backs of sofa and chair as sumptuous, no doubt, but as sumptuously stiff, as the brocaded walls? It was amid these refinements that we presently resumed our studies—even explicitly far from arduous at first, as the Champs-Elysées were perforce that year our summer habitation and some deference was due to the place and the season, lessons of any sort being at best an infraction of the latter. M. Lerambert, who was spare and tightly black-coated, spectacled, pale and prominently intellectual, who lived in the Rue Jacob with his mother and sister, exactly as he should have done to accentuate prophetically his resemblance, save for the spectacles, to some hero of Victor Cherbuliez, and who, in fine, was conscious, not unimpressively, of his authorship of a volume of meditative verse sympathetically mentioned by the Sainte-Beuve of the Causeries in a review of the young poets of the hour ("M. Lerambert too has loved, M. Lerambert too has suffered, M. Lerambert too has sung!" or words to that effect:) this subtle personality, really a high form of sensibility I surmise, and as qualified for other and intenser relations as any Cherbuliez figure of them all, was naturally not to be counted on to lead us gapingly forth as good Mr. Thompson had done; so that my reminiscence of warm somniferous mornings by the windows that opened to the clattery, plashy court is quite, so far as my record goes, relievingly unbroken.

The afternoons, however, glimmer back to me shamelessly different, for our circle had promptly been joined by the all-knowing and all-imposing Mademoiselle Danse aforesaid, her of the so flexible *taille* and the so salient smiling eyes, than which even those of Miss Rebecca Sharp, that other epic governess, were not more pleasingly green; who provided with high efficiency for our immediate looser needs—mine and Wilky's and those of our small brother Bob (l'ingénieux petit Robertson as she was to dub him,) and of our still smaller sister at least—our first fine *flâneries* of curiosity. Her brave Vaudoise predecessor had been bequeathed by us in London to a higher sphere than service with mere earnest nomads could represent; but had left us clinging and weeping and was for a long time afterwards to write to us, faithfully, in the most beautiful copper-plate hand, out of the midst of her "rise"; with details that brought home to us as we had never known it brought the material and institutional difference between the nomadic and the solidly, the spreadingly seated. A couple of years later, on an occasion of our being again for a while in London, she hastened to call on us, and, on departing, amiably invited me to walk back with her, for a gossip—it was a bustling day of June—across a long stretch of the town; when I left her at a glittering portal with the impression of my having in our transit seen much of Society (the old London "season" filled the measure, had length and breadth and thickness, to an extent now foregone,) and, more particularly, achieved a small psychologic study, noted the action of the massive English machinery directed to its end, which had been in this case effectually to tame the presumptuous and "work over" the crude. I remember on that occasion retracing my steps from Eaton Square to Devonshire Street with a lively sense of observation exercised by the way, a perfect gleaning of golden straws. Our guide and philosopher of the summer days in Paris was no such character as that; she had arrived among us full-fledged and consummate, fortunately for the case altogether—as our mere candid humanity would otherwise have had scant practical pressure to bring. Thackeray's novel contains a plate from his own expressive hand representing Miss Sharp lost in a cynical day-dream while her neglected pupils are locked in a scrimmage on the floor; but the marvel of *our* exemplar of the Becky type was exactly that though her larger, her more interested and sophisticated views had a range that she not only permitted us to guess but agreeably invited us to follow almost to their furthest limits, we never for a moment ceased to be aware of her solicitude. We might, we must, so tremendously have bored her, but no ironic artist could have caught her at any juncture in the posture of disgust: really, I imagine, because her own ironies would have been too fine for him and too numerous and too mixed. And this remarkable creature vouchsafed us all information for the free enjoyment—on the terms proper to our tender years—of her beautiful city.

It was not by the common measure then so beautiful as now; the second Empire, too lately installed, was still more or less feeling its way, with the great free hand soon to be allowed to Baron Haussmann marked as yet but in the light preliminary flourish. Its connections with the past, however, still hung thickly on; its majesties and symmetries, comparatively vague and general, were subject to the happy accident, the charming lapse and the odd extrusion, a bonhomie of chance composition and colour now quite purged away. The whole region of the Champs-Elysées, where we must after all at first have principally prowled, was another world from the actual huge centre of repeated radiations; the splendid Avenue, as we of course already thought it, carried the eye from the Tuileries to the Arch, but pleasant old places abutted on it by the way, gardens and terraces and hôtels of another time, pavilions still braver than ours, cabarets and cafés of homely, almost of rural type, with a relative and doubtless rather dusty ruralism, spreading away to the River and the Wood. What was the Jardin d'Hiver, a place of entertainment standing quite over against us and that looped itself at night with little coloured oil-lamps, a mere twinkling grin upon the face of pleasure? Dim my impression of having been admitted—or rather, I suppose, conducted, though under conductorship now vague to me—to view it by colourless day, when it must have worn the stamp of an auction-room quite void of the "lots." More distinct on the other hand the image of the bustling barrière at the top of the Avenue, on the hither side of the Arch, where the old loose-girt *banlieue* began at once and the two matched lodges of the octroi, highly, that is expressly even if humbly, architectural, guarded the entrance, on either side, with such a suggestion of the generations and dynasties and armies, the revolutions and restorations they had seen come and go. But the Avenue of the Empress, now, so much more thinly, but of the Wood itself, had already been traced, as the Empress herself, young, more than young, attestedly and agreeably *new*, and fair and shining, was, up and down the vista, constantly on exhibition; with the thrill of that surpassed for us, however, by the incomparable passage, as we judged it, of the baby Prince Imperial borne forth for his airing or his progress to Saint-Cloud in the splendid coach that gave a glimpse of appointed and costumed nursing breasts and laps, and beside which the *cent-gardes*, all light-blue and silver and intensely erect quick jolt, rattled with pistols raised and cocked. Was a public holiday ever more splendid than that of the Prince's baptism at Notre Dame, the fête of Saint-Napoléon, or was any ever more immortalised, as we say, than this one was to be by the wonderfully ample and vivid picture of it in the Eugène Rougon of Emile Zola, who must have taken it in, on the spot, as a boy of about our own number of years, though of so much more implanted and predestined an evocatory gift? The sense of that interminable hot day, a day of hanging about and waiting and shuffling in dust, in crowds, in fatigue, amid booths and pedlars and performers and false alarms and expectations and renewed reactions and rushes, all transfigured at the last, withal, by the biggest and brightest illumination up to that time offered even the Parisians, the blinding glare of the new Empire effectually symbolised—the vision of the whole, I say, comes back to me quite in the form of a chapter from the Rougon-Macquart, with its effect of something long and dense and heavy, without shades or undertones, but immensely kept-up and done. I dare say that for those months our contemplations, our daily exercise in general, strayed little beyond the Champs-Elysées, though I recall confusedly as well certain excursions to Passy and Auteuil, where we foregathered with small resident compatriots the easy gutturalism of whose French, an unpremeditated art, was a revelation, an initiation, and whence we roamed, for purposes of picnic, into parts of the Bois de Boulogne that, oddly enough, figured to us the virgin forest better than anything at our own American door had done.

It was the social aspect of our situation that most appealed to me, none the less—for I detect myself, as I woo it all back, disengaging a social aspect again, and more than ever, from the phenomena disclosed to my reflective gape or to otherwise associated strolls; perceptive passages not wholly independent even of the occupancy of two-sous chairs within the charmed circle of Guignol and of Gringalet. I suppose I should have blushed to confess it, but Polichinelle and his puppets, in the afternoons, under an umbrage sparse till evening fell, had still their spell to cast—as part and parcel, that is, of the general intensity of animation and variety of feature. The "amusement," the æsthetic and human appeal, of Paris had in those days less the air of a great shining conspiracy to please, the machinery in movement confessed less to its huge purpose; but manners and types and traditions, the detail of the scene, its pointed particulars, went their way with a straighter effect, as well as often with a homelier grace—character, temper and tone had lost comparatively little of their emphasis. These scattered accents were matter for our eyes and ears—not a little even already for our respective imaginations; though it is only as the season waned and we set up our fireside afresh and for the winter that I connect my small revolution with a wider field and with the company of W. J. Again for that summer he was to be in eclipse to me; Guignol and Gringalet failed to claim his attention, and Mademoiselle Danse, I make out, deprecated his theory of exact knowledge, besides thinking him perhaps a little of an *ours*—which came to the same thing. We adjourned that autumn to quarters not far off, a wide-faced apartment in the street then bravely known as the Rue d'Angoulême-St.-Honoré and now, after other mutations, as the Rue La Boëtie; which we were again to exchange a year later for an abode in the Rue Montaigne, this last after a summer's absence at Boulogne-sur-Mer; the earlier migration setting up for me the frame of a considerably animated picture. Animated at best it was with the spirit and the modest facts of our family life, among which I number the cold finality of M. Lerambert, reflected in still other testimonies—that is till the date of our definite but respectful rupture with him, followed as the spring came on by our ineluctable phase at the Institution Fezandié in the Rue Balzac; of which latter there will be even more to say than I shall take freedom for. With the Rue d'Angoulême came extensions—even the mere immediate view of opposite intimacies and industries, the subdivided aspects and neat ingenuities of the applied Parisian genius counting as such: our many-windowed *premier*, above an entresol of no great height, hung over the narrow and, during the winter months, not a little dusky channel, with endless movement and interest in the vivid exhibition it supplied. What faced us was a series of subjects, with the baker, at the corner, for the first—the impeccable dispenser of the so softly-crusty crescent-rolls that we woke up each morning to hunger for afresh, with our weak café-au-lait, as for the one form of "European" breakfast-bread fit to be named even with the feeblest of our American forms. Then came the small crêmerie, white picked out with blue, which, by some secret of its own keeping, afforded, within the compass of a few feet square, prolonged savoury meals to working men, white-frocked or blue-frocked, to uniformed cabmen, stout or spare, but all more or less audibly *bavards* and discernibly critical; and next the compact embrasure of the écaillère or oyster-lady, she and her paraphernalia fitted into their interstice much as the mollusc itself into its shell; neighboured in turn by the marchand-de-bois, peeping from as narrow a cage, his neat faggots and chopped logs stacked beside him and above him in his sentry-box quite as the niches of saints, in early Italian pictures, are framed with tightly-packed fruits and flowers. Space and remembrance fail me for the rest of the series, the attaching note of which comes back as the note of diffused sociability and domestic, in fact more or less æsthetic, ingenuity, with the street a perpetual parlour or household centre for the flitting, pausing, conversing little bourgeoise or ouvrière to sport, on every pretext and in every errand, her fluted cap, her composed head, her neat ankles and her ready wit. Which is to say indeed but that life and manners were more pointedly and harmoniously expressed, under our noses there, than we had perhaps found them anywhere save in the most salient passages of "stories"; though I must in spite of it not write as if these trifles were all our fare.

XXV

THAT AUTUMN renewed, I make out, our long and beguiled walks, my own with W. J. in especial; at the same time that I have somehow the sense of the whole more broken appeal on the part of Paris, the scanter confidence and ease it inspired in us, the perhaps more numerous and composite, but obscurer and more baffled intimations. Not indeed—for all my brother's later vision of an accepted flatness in it—that there was not some joy and some grasp; why else were we forever (as I seem to conceive we were) measuring the great space that separated us from the gallery of the Luxembourg, every step of which, either way we took it, fed us with some interesting, some admirable image, kept us in relation to something nobly intended? That particular walk was not prescribed us, yet we appear to have hugged it, across the Champs-Elysées to the river, and so over the nearest bridge and the quays of the left bank to the Rue de Seine, as if it somehow held the secret of our future; to the extent even of my more or less sneaking off on occasion to take it by myself, to taste of it with a due undiverted intensity and the throb as of the finest, which *could* only mean the most Parisian, adventure. The further quays, with their innumerable old bookshops and print-shops, the long cases of each of these commodities, exposed on the parapets in especial, must have come to know us almost as well as we knew them; with plot thickening and emotion deepening steadily, however, as we mounted the long, black Rue de Seine—*such* a stretch of perspective, *such* an intensity of tone as it offered in those days; where every low-browed vitrine waylaid us and we moved in a world of which the dark message, expressed in we couldn't have said what sinister way too, might have been "Art, art, art, don't you see? Learn, little gaping pilgrims, what *that* is!" Oh we learned, that is we tried to, as hard as ever we could, and were fairly well at it, I always felt, even by the time we had passed up into that comparatively short but wider and finer vista of the Rue de Tournon, which in those days more abruptly crowned the more compressed approach and served in a manner as a great outer vestibule to the Palace. Style, dimly described, looked down there, as with conscious encouragement, from the high grey-headed, clear-faced, straight-standing old houses—very much as if wishing to say "Yes, small staring jeune homme, we are dignity and memory and measure, we are conscience and proportion and taste, not to mention strong sense too: for all of which good things take us—you won't find one of them when you find (as you're going soon to begin to at such a rate) vulgarity." This, I admit, was an abundance of remark to such young ears; but it did all, I maintain, tremble in the air, with the sense that the Rue de Tournon, cobbled and a little grass-grown, might more or less have figured some fine old street *de province*: I cherished in short its very name and think I really hadn't to wait to prefer the then, the unmenaced, the inviolate Café Foyot of the left hand corner, the much-loved and so haunted Café Foyot of the old Paris, to its—well, to its roaring successor. The wide mouth of the present Boulevard Saint-Michel, a short way round the corner, had not yet been forced open to the exhibition of more or less glittering fangs; old Paris still pressed round the Palace and its gardens, which formed the right, the sober social antithesis to the "elegant" Tuileries, and which in fine, with these renewals of our young confidence, reinforced both in a general and in a particular way one of the fondest of our literary curiosities of that time, the conscientious study of Les Français Peints par Eux-Mêmes, rich in wood-cuts of Gavarni, of Grandville, of Henri-Monnier, which we held it rather our duty to admire and W. J. even a little his opportunity to copy in pen-and-ink. This gilt-edged and double-columned octavo it was that first disclosed to me, forestalling a better ground of acquaintance, the great name of Balzac, who, in common with every other "light" writer of his day, contributed to its pages: hadn't I pored over his exposition there of the contrasted types of L'Habituée des Tuileries and L'Habituée du Luxembourg?—finding it very *serré*, in fact what I didn't then know enough to call very stodgy, but flavoured withal and a trifle lubricated by Gavarni's two drawings, which had somehow so much, in general, to say.

Let me not however dally by the way, when nothing, at those hours, I make out, so much spoke to us as the animated pictured halls within the Palace, primarily those of the Senate of the Empire, but then also forming, as with extensions they still and much more copiously form, the great Paris museum of contemporary art. This array was at that stage a comparatively (though only comparatively) small affair; in spite of which fact we supposed it vast and final—so that it would have shocked us to foreknow how in many a case, and of the most cherished cases, the finality was to break down. Most of the works of the modern schools that we most admired are begging their bread, I fear, from door to door—that is from one provincial museum or dim back seat to another; though we were on much-subsequent returns to draw a long breath for the saved state of some of the great things as to which our faith had been clearest. It had been clearer for none, I recover, than for Couture's Romains de la Décadence, recently acclaimed, at that time, as the last word of the grand manner, but of the grand manner modernised, humanised, philosophised, redeemed from academic death; so that it was to this master's school that the young American contemporary flutter taught its wings to fly straightest, and that I could never, in the long aftertime, face his masterpiece and all its old meanings and marvels without a rush of memories and a stir of ghosts. William Hunt, the New Englander of genius, the "Boston painter" whose authority was greatest during the thirty years from 1857 or so, and with whom for a time in the early period W. J. was to work all devotedly, had prolonged his studies in Paris under the inspiration of Couture and of Edouard Frère; masters in a group completed by three or four of the so finely interesting landscapists of that and the directly previous age, Troyon, Rousseau, Daubigny, even Lambinet and others, and which summed up for the American collector and in the New York and Boston markets the idea of the modern in the masterly. It was a comfortable time—when appreciation could go so straight, could rise, and rise higher, without critical contortions; when we could, I mean, be both so intelligent and so "quiet." We were in our immediate circle to know Couture himself a little toward the end of his life, and I was somewhat to wonder then where he had picked up the æsthetic hint for the beautiful Page with a Falcon, if I have the designation right, his other great bid for style and capture of it—which we were long to continue to suppose perhaps the rarest of all modern pictures. The feasting Romans were conceivable enough, I mean *as* a conception; no mystery hung about them—in the sense of one's asking one's self whence they had come and by what romantic or roundabout or nobly-dangerous journey; which is that air of the poetic shaken out as from strong wings when great presences, in any one of the arts, appear to alight. What I remember, on the other hand, of the splendid fair youth in black velvet and satin or whatever who, while he mounts the marble staircase, shows off the great bird on his forefinger with a grace that shows *him* off, was that it failed to help us to divine, during that after-lapse of the glory of which I speak, by what rare chance, for the obscured old ex-celebrity we visited, the heavens had once opened. Poetry had swooped down, breathed on him for an hour and fled. Such at any rate are the see-saws of reputations—which it contributes to the interest of any observational lingering on this planet to have caught so repeatedly in their weird motion; the question of what may happen, under one's eyes, in particular cases, before that motion sinks to rest, whether at the up or at the down end, being really a bribe to one's own non-departure. Especially great the interest of having noted all the rises and falls and of being able to compare the final point—so far as any certainty may go as to that—either with the greatest or the least previous altitudes; since it is only when there have been exaltations (which is what is not commonest), that our attention is most rewarded.

If the see-saw was to have operated indeed for Eugène Delacroix, our next young admiration, though much more intelligently my brother's than mine, that had already taken place and settled, for we were to go on seeing him, and to the end, in firm possession of his crown, and to take even, I think, a harmless pleasure in our sense of having from so far back been sure of it. I was sure of it, I must properly add, but as an effect of my brother's sureness; since I must, by what I remember, have been as sure of Paul Delaroche—for whom the pendulum was at last to be arrested at a very different point. I could see in a manner, for all the queerness, what W. J. meant by that beauty and, above all, that living interest in La Barque du Dante, where the queerness, according to him, was perhaps what contributed most; see it doubtless in particular when he reproduced the work, at home, from a memory aided by a lithograph. Yet Les Enfants d'Edouard thrilled me to a different tune, and I couldn't doubt that the long-drawn odd face of the elder prince, sad and sore and sick, with his wide crimped sidelocks of fair hair and his violet legs marked by the Garter and dangling from the bed, was a reconstitution of far-off history of the subtlest and most "last word" modern or psychologic kind. I had never heard of psychology in art or anywhere else—scarcely anyone then had; but I truly felt the nameless force at play. Thus if I also in my way "subtly" admired, one's noted practice of that virtue (mainly regarded indeed, I judge, as a vice) would appear to have at the time I refer to set in, under such encouragements, once for all; and I can surely have enjoyed up to then no formal exhibition of anything as I at one of those seasons enjoyed the commemorative show of Delaroche given, soon after his death, in one of the rather bleak salles of the Ecole des Beaux-Arts to which access was had from the quay. *There* was reconstituted history if one would, in the straw-littered scaffold, the distracted ladies with three-cornered coifs and those immense hanging sleeves that made them look as if they had bath-towels over their arms; in the block, the headsman, the bandaged eyes and groping hands, of Lady Jane Grey—not less than in the noble indifference of Charles the First, compromised king but perfect gentleman, at his inscrutable ease in his chair and as if on his throne, while the Puritan soldiers insult and badger him: the thrill of which was all the greater from its pertaining to that English lore which the good Robert Thompson had, to my responsive delight, rubbed into us more than anything else and all from a fine old conservative and monarchical point of view. Yet of these things W. J. attempted no reproduction, though I remember his repeatedly laying his hand on Delacroix, whom he found always and everywhere interesting—to the point of trying effects, with charcoal and crayon, in his manner; and not less in the manner of Decamps, whom we regarded as more or less of a genius of the same rare family. They were touched with the ineffable, the inscrutable, and Delacroix in especial with the incalculable; categories these toward which we had even then, by a happy transition, begun to yearn and languish. We were not yet aware of style, though on the way to become so, but were aware of mystery, which indeed was one of its forms—while we saw all the others, without exception, exhibited at the Louvre, where at first they simply overwhelmed and bewildered me.

It was as if they had gathered there into a vast deafening chorus; I shall never forget how—speaking, that is, for my own sense—they filled those vast halls with the influence rather of some complicated sound, diffused and reverberant, than of such visibilities as one could directly deal with. To distinguish among these, in the charged and coloured and confounding air, was difficult—it discouraged and defied; which was doubtless why my impression originally best entertained was that of those magnificent parts of the great gallery simply not inviting us to distinguish. They only arched over us in the wonder of their endless golden riot and relief, figured and flourished in perpetual revolution, breaking into great high-hung circles and symmetries of squandered picture, opening into deep outward embrasures that threw off the rest of monumental Paris somehow as a told story, a sort of wrought effect or bold ambiguity for a vista, and yet held it there, at every point, as a vast bright gage, even at moments a felt adventure, of experience. This comes to saying that in those beginnings I felt myself most happily cross that bridge over to Style constituted by the wondrous Galerie d'Apollon, drawn out for me as a long but assured initiation and seeming to form with its supreme coved ceiling and inordinately shining parquet a prodigious tube or tunnel through which I inhaled little by little, that is again and again, a general sense of *glory*. The glory meant ever so many things at once, not only beauty and art and supreme design, but history and fame and power, the world in fine raised to the richest and noblest expression. The world there was at the same time, by an odd extension or intensification, the local present fact, to my small imagination, of the Second Empire, which was (for my notified consciousness) new and queer and perhaps even wrong, but on the spot so amply radiant and elegant that it took to itself, took under its protection with a splendour of insolence, the state and ancientry of the whole scene, profiting thus, to one's dim historic vision, confusedly though it might be, by the unparalleled luxury and variety of its heritage. But who shall count the sources at which an intense young fancy (when a young fancy *is* intense) capriciously, absurdly drinks?—so that the effect is, in twenty connections, that of a love-philtre or fear-philtre which fixes for the senses their supreme symbol of the fair or the strange. The Galerie d'Apollon became for years what I can only term a splendid scene of things, even of the quite irrelevant or, as might be, almost unworthy; and I recall to this hour, with the last vividness, what a precious part it played for me, and exactly by that continuity of honour, on my awaking, in a summer dawn many years later, to the fortunate, the instantaneous recovery and capture of the most appalling yet most admirable nightmare of my life. The climax of this extraordinary experience—which stands alone for me as a dream-adventure founded in the deepest, quickest, clearest act of cogitation and comparison, act indeed of life-saving energy, as well as in unutterable fear—was the sudden pursuit, through an open door, along a huge high saloon, of a just dimly-descried figure that retreated in terror before my rush and dash (a glare of inspired reaction from irresistible but shameful dread,) out of the room I had a moment before been desperately, and all the more abjectly, defending by the push of my shoulder against hard pressure on lock and bar from the other side. The lucidity, not to say the sublimity, of the crisis had consisted of the great thought that I, in my appalled state, was probably still more appalling than the awful agent, creature or presence, whatever he was, whom I had guessed, in the suddenest wild start from sleep, the sleep within my sleep, to be making for my place of rest. The triumph of my impulse, perceived in a flash as I acted on it by myself at a bound, forcing the door outward, was the grand thing, but the great point of the whole was the wonder of my final recognition. Routed, dismayed, the tables turned upon him by my so surpassing him for straight aggression and dire intention, my visitant was already but a diminished spot in the long perspective, the tremendous, glorious hall, as I say, over the far-gleaming floor of which, cleared for the occasion of its great line of priceless vitrines down the middle, he sped for *his* life, while a great storm of thunder and lightning played through the deep embrasures of high windows at the right. The lightning that revealed the retreat revealed also the wondrous place and, by the same amazing play, my young imaginative life in it of long before, the sense of which, deep within me, had kept it whole, preserved it to this thrilling use; for what in the world were the deep embrasures and the so polished floor but those of the Galerie d'Apollon of my childhood? The "scene of something" I had vaguely then felt it? Well I might, since it was to be the scene of that immense hallucination.

Of what, at the same time, in those years, were the great rooms of the Louvre almost equally, above and below, not the scene, from the moment they so wrought, stage by stage, upon our perceptions?—literally on almost all of these, in one way and another; quite in such a manner, I more and more see, as to have been educative, formative, fertilising, in a degree which no other "intellectual experience" our youth was to know could pretend, as a comprehensive, conducive thing, to rival. The sharp and strange, the quite heart-shaking little prevision had come to me, for myself, I make out, on the occasion of our very first visit of all, my brother's and mine, under conduct of the good Jean Nadali, before-mentioned, trustfully deputed by our parents, in the Rue de la Paix, on the morrow of our first arrival in Paris (July 1855) and while they were otherwise concerned. I hang again, appalled but uplifted, on brave Nadali's arm—his professional acquaintance with the splendours about us added for me on the spot to the charm of his "European" character: I cling to him while I gape at Géricault's Radeau de la Méduse, *the* sensation, for splendour and terror of interest, of that juncture to me, and ever afterwards to be associated, along with two or three other more or less contemporary products, Guérin's Burial of Atala, Prudhon's Cupid and Psyche, David's helmetted Romanisms, Madame Vigée-Lebrun's "ravishing" portrait of herself and her little girl, with how can I say what foretaste (as determined by that instant as if the hour had struck from a clock) of all the fun, confusedly speaking, that one was going to have, and the kind of life, always of the queer so-called inward sort, tremendously "sporting" in its way—though that description didn't then wait upon it, that one was going to lead. It came of itself, this almost awful apprehension in all the presences, under our courier's protection and in my brother's company—it came just there and so; there was alarm in it somehow as well as bliss. The bliss in fact I think scarce disengaged itself at all, but only the sense of a freedom of contact and appreciation really too big for one, and leaving such a mark on the very place, the pictures, the frames themselves, the figures within them, the particular parts and features of each, the look of the rich light, the smell of the massively enclosed air, that I have never since renewed the old exposure without renewing again the old emotion and taking up the small scared consciousness. *That*, with so many of the conditions repeated, is the charm—to feel afresh the beginning of so much that was to be. The beginning in short was with Géricault and David, but it went on and on and slowly spread; so that one's stretched, one's even strained, perceptions, one's discoveries and extensions piece by piece, come back, on the great premises, almost as so many explorations of the house of life, so many circlings and hoverings round the image of the world. I have dim reminiscences of permitted independent visits, uncorrectedly juvenile though I might still be, during which the house of life and the palace of art became so mixed and interchangeable—the Louvre being, under a general description, the most peopled of all scenes not less than the most hushed of all temples—that an excursion to look at pictures would have but half expressed my afternoon. I had looked at pictures, looked and looked again, at the vast Veronese, at Murillo's moon-borne Madonna, at Leonardo's almost unholy dame with the folded hands, treasures of the Salon Carré as that display was then composed, but I had also looked at France and looked at Europe, looked even at America as Europe itself might be conceived so to look, looked at history, as a still-felt past and a complacently personal future, at society, manners, types, characters, possibilities and prodigies and mysteries of fifty sorts; and all in the light of being splendidly "on my own," as I supposed it, though we hadn't then that perfection of slang, and of (in especial) going and coming along that interminable and incomparable Seine-side front of the Palace against which young sensibility felt itself almost rub, for endearment and consecration, as a cat invokes the friction of a protective piece of furniture. Such were at any rate some of the vague processes—I see for how utterly vague they must show—of picking up an education; and I was, in spite of the vagueness, so far from agreeing with my brother afterwards that we didn't pick one up and that that never *is* done, in any sense not negligible, and also that an education might, or should, in particular, have picked *us* up, and yet didn't—I was so far dissentient, I say, that I think I quite came to glorify such passages and see them as part of an order really fortunate. If we had been little asses, I seem to have reasoned, a higher intention driving us wouldn't have made us less so—to any point worth mentioning; and as we extracted such impressions, to put it at the worst, from redemptive accidents (to call Louvres and Luxembourgs nothing better) why we weren't little asses, but something wholly other: which appeared all I needed to contend for. Above all it would have been stupid and ignoble, an attested and lasting dishonour, not, with our chance, to have followed our straggling clues, as many as we could and disengaging as we happily did, I felt, the gold and the silver ones, whatever the others might have been—not to have followed them and not to have arrived by them, so far as we were to arrive. Instinctively, for any dim designs we might have nourished, we picked out the silver and the gold, attenuated threads though they must have been, and I positively feel that there were more of these, far more, casually interwoven, than will reward any present patience for my unravelling of the too fine tissue.

XXVI

I ALLUDE of course in particular here to the æsthetic clue in general, with which it was that we most (or that I at any rate most) fumbled, without our in the least having then, as I have already noted, any such rare name for it. There were sides on which it fairly dangled about us, involving our small steps and wits; though others too where I could, for my own part, but clutch at it in the void. Our experience of the theatre for instance, which had played such a part for us at home, almost wholly dropped in just the most propitious air: an anomaly indeed half explained by the fact that life in general, all round us, was perceptibly more theatrical. And there were other reasons, whether definitely set before us or not, which we grasped in proportion as we gathered, by depressing hearsay, that the French drama, great, strange and important, was as much out of relation to our time of life, our so little native strain and our cultivated innocence, as the American and English had been directly addressed to them. To the Cirque d'Eté, the Cirque d'Hiver, the Théâtre du Cirque, we were on occasion conducted—we had fallen so to the level of circuses, and that name appeared a safety; in addition to which the big theatre most bravely bearing it, the especial home at that time of the glittering and multitudinous *féerie*, did seem to lift the whole scenic possibility, for our eyes, into a higher sphere of light and grace than any previously disclosed. I recall Le Diable d'Argent as in particular a radiant revelation—kept before us a whole long evening and as an almost blinding glare; which was quite right for the *donnée*, the gradual shrinkage of the Shining One, the money-monster hugely inflated at first, to all the successive degrees of loose bagginess as he leads the reckless young man he has originally contracted with from dazzling pleasure to pleasure, till at last he is a mere shrivelled silver string such as you could almost draw through a keyhole. That was the striking moral, for the young man, however regaled, had been somehow "sold"; which *we* hadn't in the least been, who had had all his pleasures and none of his penalty, whatever this was to be. I was to repine a little, in these connections, at a much later time, on reflecting that had we only been "taken" in the Paris of that period as we had been taken in New York we might have come in for celebrities—supremely fine, perhaps supremely rank, flowers of the histrionic temperament, springing as they did from the soil of the richest romanticism and adding to its richness—who practised that braver art and finer finish which a comparatively homogenous public, forming a compact critical body, still left possible. Rachel was alive, but dying; the memory of Mademoiselle Mars, at her latest, was still in the air; Mademoiselle Georges, a massive, a monstrous antique, had withal returned for a season to the stage; but we missed her, as we missed Déjazet and Frédéric Lemaître and Mélingue and Samson; to say nothing of others of the age before the flood—taking for the flood that actual high tide of the outer barbarian presence, the general alien and polyglot, in stalls and boxes, which I remember to have heard Gustave Flaubert lament as the ruin of the theatre through the assumption of judgeship by a bench to whom the very values of the speech of author and actor were virtually closed, or at the best uncertain.

I enjoyed but two snatches of the older representational art—no particular of either of which, however, has faded from me; the earlier and rarer of these an evening at the Gymnase for a *spectacle coupé*, with Mesdames Rose Chéri, Mélanie, Delaporte and Victoria (afterwards Victoria-La-fontaine). I squeeze again with my mother, my aunt and my brother into the stuffy baignoire, and I take to my memory in especial Madame de Girardin's Une Femme qui Déteste son Mari; the thrilling story, as I judged it, of an admirable lady who, to save her loyalist husband, during the Revolution, feigns the most Jacobin opinions, represents herself a citoyenne of citoyennes, in order to keep him the more safely concealed in her house. He flattens himself, to almost greater peril of life, behind a panel of the wainscot, which she has a secret for opening when he requires air and food and they may for a fearful fleeting instant be alone together; and the point of the picture is in the contrast between these melting moments and the heroine's *tenue* under the tremendous strain of receiving on the one side the invading, investigating Terrorist commissaries, sharply suspicious but successfully baffled, and on the other her noble relatives, her husband's mother and sister if I rightly remember, who are not in the secret and whom, for perfect prudence, she keeps out of it, though alone with her, and themselves in hourly danger, they might be trusted, and who, believing him concealed elsewhere and terribly tracked, treat her, in her republican rage, as lost to all honour and all duty. One's sense of such things after so long a time has of course scant authority for others; but I myself trust my vision of Rose Chéri's fine play just as I trust that of her *physique ingrat*, her at first extremely odd and positively osseous appearance; an emaciated woman with a high bulging forehead, somewhat of the form of Rachel's, for whom the triumphs of produced illusion, as in the second, third and fourth great dramas of the younger Dumas, had to be triumphs indeed. My one other reminiscence of this order connects itself, and quite three years later, with the old dingy Vaudeville of the Place de la Bourse, where I saw in my brother's company a rhymed domestic drama of the then still admired Ponsard, Ce qui Plaît aux Femmes; a piece that enjoyed, I believe, scant success, but that was to leave with me ineffaceable images. How was it possible, I wondered, to have more grace and talent, a rarer, cooler art, than Mademoiselle Fargeuil, the heroine?—the fine lady whom a pair of rival lovers, seeking to win her hand by offering her what will most please her, treat, in the one case, to a brilliant fête, a little play within a play, at which we assist, and in the other to the inside view of an attic of misery, into which the more cunning suitor introduces her just in time to save a poor girl, the tenant of the place, from being ruinously, that is successfully, tempted by a terrible old woman, a prowling *revendeuse*, who dangles before her the condition on which so pretty a person may enjoy every comfort. Her happier sister, the courted young widow, intervenes in time, reinforces her tottering virtue, opens for her an account with baker and butcher, and, doubting no longer which flame is to be crowned, charmingly shows us that what pleases women most is the exercise of charity.

Then it was I first beheld that extraordinary veteran of the stage, Mademoiselle Pierson, almost immemorially attached, for later generations, to the Théâtre Français, the span of whose career thus strikes me as fabulous, though she figured as a very juvenile beauty in the small *féerie* or allegory forming M. Ponsard's second act. She has been playing mothers and aunts this many and many a year—and still indeed much as a juvenile beauty. Not that light circumstance, however, pleads for commemoration, nor yet the further fact that I was to admire Mademoiselle Fargeuil, in the after-time, the time after she had given all Sardou's earlier successes the help of her shining firmness, when she had passed from interesting comedy and even from romantic drama—not less, perhaps still more, interesting, with Sardou's Patrie as a bridge—to the use of the bigger brush of the Ambigu and other homes of melodrama. The sense, such as it is, that I extract from the pair of modest memories in question is rather their value as a glimpse of the old order that spoke so much less of our hundred modern material resources, matters the stage of to-day appears mainly to live by, and such volumes more of the one thing that was then, and that, given various other things, had to be, of the essence. That one thing was the quality, to say nothing of the quantity, of the actor's personal resource, technical history, tested temper, proved experience; on which almost everything had to depend, and the thought of which makes the mere starved scene and medium of the period, the *rest* of the picture, a more confessed and more heroic battleground. They have been more and more eased off, the scene and medium, for our couple of generations, so much so in fact that the rest of the picture has become almost *all* the picture: the author and the producer, among us, lift the weight of the play from the performer—particularly of the play dealing with our immediate life and manners and aspects—after a fashion which does half the work, thus reducing the "personal equation," the demand for the maximum of individual doing, to a contribution mostly of the loosest and sparest. As a sop to historic curiosity at all events may even so short an impression serve; impression of the strenuous age and its fine old masterful *assouplissement* of its victims—who were not the expert spectators. The spectators were so expert, so broken in to material suffering for the sake of their passion, that, as the suffering was only material, they found the æsthetic reward, the critical relish of the essence, all adequate; a fact that seems in a sort to point a moral of large application. Everything but the "interpretation," the personal, in the French theatre of those days, had kinds and degrees of weakness and futility, say even falsity, of which our modern habit is wholly impatient—let alone other conditions still that were detestable even at the time, and some of which, forms of discomfort and annoyance, linger on to this day. The playhouse, in short, was almost a place of physical torture, and it is still rarely in Paris a place of physical ease. Add to this the old thinness of the school of Scribe and the old emptiness of the thousand vaudevillistes; which part of the exhibition, till modern comedy began, under the younger Dumas and Augier, had for its counterpart but the terrible dead weight, or at least the prodigious prolixity and absurdity, of much, not to say of most, of the romantic and melodramatic "output." It *paid* apparently, in the golden age of acting, to sit through interminable evenings in impossible places—since to assume that the age *was* in that particular respect golden (for which we have in fact a good deal of evidence) alone explains the patience of the public. With the public the *actors* were, according to their seasoned strength, almost exclusively appointed to deal, just as in the conditions most familiar to-day to ourselves this charge is laid on almost everyone concerned in the case save the representatives of the parts. And far more other people are now concerned than of old; not least those who have learned to make the playhouse endurable. All of which leaves us with this interesting vision of a possibly great truth, the truth that you can't have more than one kind of intensity—intensity worthy of the name—at once. The intensity of the golden age of the histrion was the intensity of *his* good faith. The intensity of our period is that of the "producer's" and machinist's, to which add even that of architect, author and critic. Between which derivative kind of that article, as we may call it, and the other, the immediate kind, it would appear that you have absolutely to choose.

XXVII

I SEE much of the rest of that particular Paris time in the light of the Institution Fezandié, and I see the Institution Fezandié, Rue Balzac, in the light, if not quite of Alphonse Daudet's lean asylum for the *petits pays chauds*, of which I have felt the previous institutions of New York sketchily remind me, at least in that of certain other of his studies in that field of the precarious, the ambiguous Paris over parts of which the great Arch at the top of the Champs-Elysées flings, at its hours, by its wide protective plausible shadow, a precious mantle of "tone." They gather, these chequered parts, into its vast paternal presence and enjoy at its expense a degree of reflected dignity. It was to the big square villa of the Rue Balzac that we turned, as pupils not unacquainted with vicissitudes, from a scene swept bare of M. Lerambert, an establishment that strikes me, at this distance of time, as of the oddest and most indescribable—or as describable at best in some of the finer turns and touches of Daudet's best method. The picture indeed should not be invidious—it so little needs that, I feel, for its due measure of the vivid, the queer, the droll, all coming back to me without prejudice to its air as of an equally futile felicity. I see it as bright and loose and vague, as confused and embarrassed and helpless; I see it, I fear, as quite ridiculous, but as wholly harmless to my brothers and me at least, and as having left us with a fund of human impressions; it played before us such a variety of figure and character and so relieved us of a sense of untoward discipline or of the pursuit of abstract knowledge. It was a recreational, or at least a social, rather than a tuitional house; which fact had, I really believe, weighed favourably with our parents, when, bereft of M. Lerambert, they asked themselves, with their considerable practice, how next to bestow us. Our father, like so many free spirits of that time in New York and Boston, had been much interested in the writings of Charles Fourier and in his scheme of the "phalanstery" as the solution of human troubles, and it comes to me that he must have met or in other words heard of M. Fezandié as an active and sympathetic ex-Fourierist (I think there were only ex-Fourierists by that time,) who was embarking, not far from us, on an experiment if not absolutely phalansteric at least inspired, or at any rate enriched, by a bold idealism. I like to think of the Institution as all but phalansteric—it so corrects any fear that such places might be dreary. I recall this one as positively gay—bristling and bustling and resonant, untouched by the strenuous note, for instance, of Hawthorne's co-operative Blithedale. I like to think that, in its then still almost suburban, its pleasantly heterogeneous quarter, now oppressively uniform, it was close to where Balzac had ended his life, though I question its identity—as for a while I tried not to—with the scene itself of the great man's catastrophe. Round its high-walled garden at all events he would have come and gone—a throb of inference that had for some years indeed to be postponed for me; though an association displacing to-day, over the whole spot, every other interest. I in any case can't pretend not to have been most appealed to by that especial phase of our education from which the pedagogic process as commonly understood was most fantastically absent. It excelled in this respect, the Fezandié phase, even others exceptionally appointed, heaven knows, for the supremacy; and yet its glory is that it was no poor blank, but that it fairly creaked and groaned, heatedly overflowed, with its wealth. We were *externes*, the three of us, but we remained in general to luncheon; coming home then, late in the afternoon, with an almost sore experience of multiplicity and vivacity of contact. For the beauty of it all was that the Institution was, speaking technically, not more a *pensionnat*, with prevailingly English and American pupils, than a *pension*, with mature beneficiaries of both sexes, and that our two categories were shaken up together to the liveliest effect. This had been M. Fezandié's grand conception; a son of the south, bald and slightly replete, with a delicate beard, a quick but anxious, rather melancholy eye and a slim, graceful, juvenile wife, who multiplied herself, though scarce knowing at moments, I think, where or how to turn; I see him as a Daudet *méridional*, but of the sensitive, not the sensual, type, as something of a rolling stone, rolling rather down hill—he had enjoyed some arrested, possibly blighted, connection in America—and as ready always again for some new application of faith and funds. If fondly failing in the least to see why the particular application in the

Rue Balzac—the body of pensioners ranging from infancy to hoary eld—shouldn't have been a bright success could have made it one, it would have been a most original triumph.

I recover it as for ourselves a beautifully mixed adventure, a brave little seeing of the world on the happy pretext of "lessons." We *had* lessons from time to time, but had them in company with ladies and gentlemen, young men and young women of the Anglo-Saxon family, who sat at long boards of green cloth with us and with several of our contemporaries, English and American boys, taking *dictées* from the head of the house himself or from the aged and most remarkable M. Bonnefons, whom we believed to have been a superannuated actor (he above all such a model for Daudet!) and who interrupted our abashed readings aloud to him of the French classics older and newer by wondrous reminiscences and even imitations of Talma. He moved among us in a cloud of legend, the wigged and wrinkled, the impassioned, though I think alas underfed, M. Bonnefons: it was our belief that he "went back," beyond the first Empire, to the scenes of the Revolution—this perhaps partly by reason, in the first place, of his scorn of our pronunciation, when we met it, of the sovereign word *liberté*, the poverty of which, our deplorable "libbeté," without r's, he mimicked and derided, sounding the right, the revolutionary form out splendidly, with thirty r's, the prolonged beat of a drum. And then we believed him, if artistically conservative, politically obnoxious to the powers that then were, though knowing that those so marked had to walk, and even to breathe, cautiously for fear of the *mouchards* of the tyrant; we knew all about mouchards and talked of them as we do to-day of aviators or suffragettes—to remember which in an age so candidly unconscious of them is to feel how much history we have seen unrolled. There were times when he but paced up and down and round the long table—I see him as never seated, but always on the move, a weary Wandering Jew of the *classe*; but in particular I hear him recite to us the combat with the Moors from Le Cid and show us how Talma, describing it, seemed to crouch down on his haunches in order to spring up again terrifically to the height of "Nous nous levons alors!" which M. Bonnefons rendered as if on the carpet there fifty men at least had leaped to their feet. But he threw off these broken lights with a quick relapse to indifference; he didn't like the Anglo-Saxon—of the children of Albion at least his view was low; on his American specimens he had, I observed, more mercy; and this imperfection of sympathy (the question of Waterloo apart) rested, it was impossible not to feel, on his so resenting the dishonour suffered at our hands by his beautiful tongue, to which, as the great field of elocution, he was patriotically devoted. I think he fairly loathed our closed English vowels and confused consonants, our destitution of sounds that he recognised as sounds; though why in this connection he put up best with our own compatriots, embroiled at that time often in even stranger vocables than now, is more than I can say. I think that would be explained perhaps by his feeling in them as an old equalitarian certain accessibilities *quand même*. Besides, we of the younger persuasion at least must have done his ear less violence than those earnest ladies from beyond the sea and than those young Englishmen qualifying for examinations and careers who flocked with us both to the plausibly spread and the severely disgarnished table, and on whose part I seem to see it again an effort of anguish to "pick up" the happy idiom that we had unconsciously acquired. French, in the fine old formula of those days, so much diffused, "was the language of the family"; but I think it must have appeared to these students in general a family of which the youngest members were but scantly kept in their place. We piped with a greater facility and to a richer meed of recognition; which sounds as if we might have become, in these strange collocations, fairly offensive little prigs. That was none the less not the case, for there were, oddly enough, a few French boys as well, to whom on the lingual or the "family" ground, we felt ourselves feebly relative, and in comparison with whom, for that matter, or with one of whom, I remember an occasion of my having to sink to insignificance. There was at the Institution little of a staff—besides waiters and bonnes; but it embraced, such as it was, M. Mesnard as well as M. Bonnefons—M. Mesnard of the new generation, instructor in whatever it might be, among the arts, that didn't consist of our rolling our r's, and with them, to help us out, more or less our eyes. It is significant that this elegant branch is now quite vague to me; and I recall M. Mesnard, in fine, as no less modern and cheap than M. Bonnefons was rare and unappraiseable. He had nevertheless given me his attention, one morning, doubtless patiently enough, in some corner of the villa that we had for the moment practically to ourselves—I seem to see a small empty room looking on the garden; when there entered to us, benevolently ushered by Madame Fezandié, a small boy of very fair and romantic aspect, as it struck me, a pupil newly arrived. I remember of him mainly that he had a sort of nimbus of light curls, a face delicate and pale and that deeply hoarse voice with which French children used to excite our wonder. M. Mesnard asked of him at once, with interest, his name, and on his pronouncing it sought to know, with livelier attention, if he were then the son of M. Arsène Houssaye, lately director of the Théatre Français. To this distinction the boy confessed —all to such intensification of our répétiteur's interest that I knew myself quite dropped, in comparison, from his scheme of things. Such an origin as our little visitor's affected him visibly as dazzling, and I felt justified after a while, in stealing away into the shade. The beautiful little boy was to live to be the late M. Henry Houssaye, the shining hellenist and historian. I have never forgotten the ecstasy of hope in M. Mesnard's question —as a light on the reverence then entertained for the institution M. Houssaye the elder had administered.

XXVIII

There comes to me, in spite of these memories of an extended connection, a sense as of some shrinkage or decline in the *beaux jours* of the Institution; which seems to have found its current run a bit thick and troubled, rather than with the pleasant plash in which we at first appeared all equally to bathe. I gather, as I try to reconstitute, that the general enterprise simply proved a fantasy not workable, and that at any rate the elders, and often such queer elders, tended to outnumber the candid *jeunesse*; so that I wonder by the same token on what theory of the Castalian spring, as taught there to trickle, if not to flow, M. Houssaye, holding his small son by the heel as it were, may have been moved to dip him into our well. Shall I blush to relate that my own impression of its virtue must have come exactly from this uncanny turn taken—and quite in spite of the high Fezandié ideals—by the *invraisemblable* house of entertainment where the assimilation of no form of innocence was doubted of by reason of the forms of experience that insisted somehow on cropping up, and no form of experience too directly deprecated by reason of the originally plotted tender growths of innocence. And some of these shapes were precisely those from which our good principal may well have first drawn his liveliest reassurance: I seem to remember such ancient American virgins in especial and such odd and either distinctively long-necked or more particularly long-haired and chinless compatriots, in black frock-coats of no type or "cut," no suggested application at all as garments—application, that is, to anything in the nature of character or circumstance, function or position—gathered about in the groups that M. Bonnefons almost terrorised by his refusal to recognise, among the barbarous races, any approach to his view of the great principle of Diction. I remember deeply and privately enjoying some of his shades of scorn and seeing how, given his own background, they were thoroughly founded; I remember above all as burnt in by the impression he gave me of the creature *wholly* animated and containing no waste expressional spaces, no imaginative flatnesses, the notion of the luxury of life, though indeed of the amount of trouble of it too, when *none* of the letters of the alphabet of sensibility might be dropped, involved in being a Frenchman. The liveliest lesson I must have drawn, however, from that source makes in any case, at the best, an odd educational connection, given the kind of concentration at which education, even such as ours, is supposed especially to aim: I speak of that direct promiscuity of insights which might easily have been pronounced profitless, with their attendant impressions and quickened sensibilities—yielding, as these last did, harvests of apparitions. I positively cherish at the present hour the fond fancy that we all soaked in some such sublime element as might still have hung about there—I mean on the very spot—from the vital presence, so lately extinct, of the prodigious Balzac; which had involved, as by its mere respiration, so dense a cloud of other presences, so arrayed an army of interrelated shades, that the air was still thick as with the fumes of witchcraft, with infinite seeing and supposing and creating, with a whole imaginative traffic. The Pension Vauquer, then but lately existent, according to Le Père Goriot, on the other side of the Seine, was still to be revealed to me; but the figures peopling it are not to-day essentially more intense (that is as a matter of the marked and featured, the terrible and the touching, as compared with the paleness of the conned page in general,) than I persuade myself, with so little difficulty, that I found the more numerous and more shifting, though properly doubtless less inspiring, constituents of the Pension Fezandié. Fantastic and all "subjective" that I should attribute a part of their interest, or that of the scene spreading round them, to any competent perception, in the small-boy mind, that the general or public moment had a rarity and a brevity, a sharp intensity, of its own; ruffling all things, as they came, with the morning breath of the Second Empire and making them twinkle back with a light of resigned acceptance, a freshness of cynicism, the force of a great grimacing example. The grimace might have been legibly there in the air, to the young apprehension, and could I but simplify this record enough I should represent everything as part of it. I seemed at any rate meanwhile to think of the Fezandié young men, young Englishmen mostly, who were getting up their French, in that many-coloured air, for what I supposed, in my candour, to be appointments and "posts," diplomatic, commercial, vaguely official, and who, as I now infer, though I didn't altogether embrace it at the time, must, under the loose rule of the establishment, have been amusing themselves not a little. It was as a side-wind of their free criticism, I take it, that I felt the first chill of an apprehended decline of the establishment, some pang of prevision of what might come, and come as with a crash, of the general fine fallacy on which it rested. Their criticism was for that matter free enough, causing me to admire it even while it terrified. They expressed themselves in terms of magnificent scorn—such as might naturally proceed, I think I felt, from a mightier race; they spoke of poor old Bonnefons, they spoke of our good Fezandié himself, they spoke more or less of everyone within view, as beggars and beasts, and I remember to have heard on their lips no qualification of any dish served to us at déjeuner (and still more at the later meal, of which my brothers and I didn't partake) but as rotten. These were expressions, absent from our domestic, our American air either of fonder discriminations or vaguer estimates, which fairly extended for me the range of intellectual, or at least of social resource; and as the general tone of them to-day comes back to me it floods somehow with light the image of the fine old insular confidence (so intellectually unregenerate then that such a name scarce covers it, though inward stirrings and the growth of a *comparative* sense of things have now begun unnaturally to agitate and disfigure it,) in which the general outward concussion of the English "abroad" with the fact of being abroad took place. The Fezandié young men were as much abroad as might be, and yet figured to me—largely by the upsetting force of that confidence, all but physically exercised—as the finest, handsomest, knowingest creatures; so that when I met them of an afternoon descending the Champs-Elysées with fine long strides and in the costume of the period, for which we can always refer to contemporary numbers of "Punch," the fact that I was for the most part walking sedately either with my mother or my aunt, or even with my sister and her governess, caused the spark of my vision that they were armed for conquest, or at the least for adventure, more expansively to glow. I am not sure whether as a general thing they honoured me at such instants with a sign of recognition; but I recover in especial the sense of an evening hour during which I had accompanied my mother to the Hôtel Meurice, where one of the New York cousins aforementioned, daughter of one of the Albany uncles—that is of the Rhinebeck member of the group—had perched for a time, so incongruously, one already seemed to feel, after the sorriest stroke of fate. I see again the gaslit glare of the Rue de Rivoli in the spring or the autumn evening (I forget which, for our year of the Rue d'Angoulême had been followed by a migration to the Rue Montaigne, with a period, or rather with two periods, of Boulogne-sur-mer interwoven, and we might have made our beguiled way from either domicile); and the whole impression seemed to hang too numerous lamps and too glittering *vitrines* about the poor Pendletons' bereavement, their loss of their only, their so sturdily handsome, little boy, and to suffuse their state with the warm rich exhalations of subterraneous cookery with which I find my recall of Paris from those years so disproportionately and so quite other than stomachically charged. The point of all of which is simply that just as we had issued from the hotel, my mother anxiously urging me through the cross currents and queer contacts, as it were, of the great bazaar (of which the Rue de Rivoli was then a much more bristling avenue than now) rather than depending on me for support and protection, there swung into view the most splendid, as I at least esteemed him, of my elders and betters in the Rue Balzac, who had left the questions there supposedly engaging us far behind, and, with his high hat a trifle askew and his cigar actively alight, revealed to me at a glance what it was to be in full possession of Paris. There was speed in his step, assurance in his air, he was visibly, impatiently on the way; and he gave me thereby my first full image of what it was exactly to *be* on the way. He gave it the more, doubtless, through the fact that, with a flourish of the aforesaid high hat (from which the Englishman of that age was so singularly inseparable) he testified to the act of recognition, and to deference to my companion, but with a grand big-boy good-humour that—as I remember from childhood the so frequent effect of an easy patronage, compared with a topmost overlooking, on the part of an admired senior—only gave an accent to the difference. As if he cared, or could have, that I but went forth through the Paris night in the hand of my mamma; while he had greeted us with a grace that was as a beat of the very wings of freedom! Of such shreds, at any rate, proves to be woven the stuff of young sensibility—when memory (if sensibility has at all existed for it) rummages over our old trunkful of spiritual duds and, drawing forth ever so tenderly this, that and the other tattered web, holds up the pattern to the light. I find myself in this connection so restlessly and tenderly rummage that the tatters, however thin, come out in handsful and every shred seems tangled with another.

Gertrude Pendleton's mere name, for instance, becomes, and very preferably, the frame of another and a better picture, drawing to it cognate associations, those of that element of the New York cousinship which had originally operated to place there in a shining and even, as it were, an economic light a "preference for Paris"—which preference, during the period of the Rue d'Angoulême and the Rue Montaigne, we wistfully saw at play, the very lightest and freest, on the part of the inimitable Masons. Their earlier days of Tours and Trouville were over; a period of relative rigour at the Florence of the still encircling walls, the still so existent abuses and felicities, was also, I seem to gather, a thing of the past; great accessions, consciously awaited during the previous leaner time, had beautifully befallen them, and my own whole consciousness of the general air—so insistently I discriminate for that alone—was coloured by a familiar view of their enjoyment of these on a tremendously draped and festooned *premier* of the Rue-St.-Honoré, bristling with ormolu and Pradier statuettes and looking almost straight across to the British Embassy; rather a low premier, after the manner of an entresol, as I remember it, and where the closed windows, which but scantly distinguished between our own sounds and those of the sociable, and yet the terrible, street of records and memories, seemed to maintain an air and a light thick with a mixture of every sort of queer old Parisian amenity and reference: as if to look or to listen or to touch were somehow at the same time to probe, to recover and communicate, to behold, to taste and even to smell—to one's greater assault by suggestion, no doubt, but also to the effect of some sweet and strange repletion, as from the continued consumption, say, out of flounced and puckered boxes, of serried rows of chocolate and other bonbons. I must have felt the whole thing as something for one's developed senses to live up to and make light of, and have been rather ashamed of my own for just a little sickishly staggering under it. This goes, however, with the fondest recall of our cousins' inbred ease, from far back, in all such assumable relations; and of how, four of the simplest, sweetest, best-natured girls as they were (with the eldest, a charming beauty, to settle on the general ground, after marriage and widowhood, and still to be blooming there), they were possessed of the scene and its great reaches and resources and possibilities in a degree that reduced us to small provincialism and a hanging on their lips when they told us, that is when the gentlest of mammas and the lovely daughter who was "out" did, of presentations at the Tuileries to the then all-wonderful, the ineffable Empress: reports touchingly qualified, on the part of our so exposed, yet after all so scantily indurated relatives, by the question of whether occasions so great didn't perhaps nevertheless profane the Sundays for which they were usually appointed. There was something of an implication in the air of those days, when young Americans were more numerously lovely than now, or at least more wide-eyed, it would fairly appear, that some account of the only tradition they had ever been rumoured to observe (that of the Lord's day) might have been taken even at the Tuileries.

But what most comes back to me as the very note and fragrance of the New York cousinship in this general connection is a time that I remember to have glanced at on a page distinct from these, when the particular cousins I now speak of had conceived, under the influence of I know not what unextinguished morning star, the liveliest taste for the earliest possible rambles and researches, in which they were so good as to allow me, when I was otherwise allowed, to participate: health-giving walks, of an extraordinarily *matinal* character, at the hour of the meticulous rag-pickers and exceptionally French polishers known to the Paris dawns of the Second Empire as at no time since; which made us all feel together, under the conduct of Honorine, bright child of the pavement herself, as if *we*, in our fresh curiosity and admiration, had also something to say to the great show presently to be opened, and were free, throughout the place, as those are free of a house who know its aspects of attic and cellar or how it looks from behind. I call our shepherdess Honorine even though perhaps not infallibly naming the sociable soubrette who might, with all her gay bold confidence, have been an official inspectress in person, and to whose easy care or, more particularly, expert sensibility and candour of sympathy and curiosity, our flock was freely confided. If she wasn't Honorine she was Clémentine or Augustine—which is a trifle; since what I thus recover, in any case, of these brushings of the strange Parisian dew, is those communities of contemplation that made us most hang about the jewellers' windows in the Palais Royal and the public playbills of the theatres on the Boulevard. The Palais Royal, now so dishonoured and disavowed, was then the very Paris of Paris; the shutters of the shops seemed taken down, at that hour, for our especial benefit, and I remember well how, the "dressing" of so large a number of the compact and richly condensed fronts being more often than not a matter of diamonds and pearls, rubies and sapphires, that represented, in their ingenuities of combination and contortion, the highest taste of the time, I found open to me any amount of superior study of the fact that the spell of gems seemed for the feminine nature almost alarmingly boundless. I stared too, it comes back to me, at these exhibitions, and perhaps even thought it became a young man of the world to express as to this or that object a refined and intelligent preference; but what I really most had before me was the chorus of abjection, as I might well have called it, led, at the highest pitch, by Honorine and vaguely suggesting to me, by the crudity, so to say, of its wistfulness, a natural frankness of passion—goodness knew in fact (for my small intelligence really didn't) what depths of corruptibility. Droll enough, as I win them again, these queer dim plays of consciousness: my sense that my innocent companions, Honorine *en tête*, would have done anything or everything for the richest ruby, and that though one couldn't one's self be decently dead to that richness one didn't at all know what "anything" might be or in the least what "everything" was. The gushing cousins, at the same time, assuredly knew still less of that, and Honorine's brave gloss of a whole range alike of possibilities and actualities was in itself a true social grace.

They all enjoyed, in fine, while I somehow but wastefully mused—which was after all my form of enjoyment; I was shy for it, though it was a truth and perhaps odd enough withal, that I didn't really at all care for gems, that rubies and pearls, in no matter what collocations, left me comparatively cold; that I actually cared for them about as little as, monstrously, secretly, painfully, I cared for flowers. Later on I was to become aware that I "adored" trees and architectural marbles—that for a sufficient slab of a sufficiently rare, sufficiently bestreaked or empurpled marble in particular I would have given a bag of rubies; but by then the time had passed for my being troubled to make out what in that case would represent on a small boy's part the corruptibility, so to call it, proclaimed, before the *vitrines*, by the cousins. That hadn't, as a question, later on, its actuality; but it had so much at the time that if it had been frankly put to me I must have quite confessed my inability to say—and must, I gather, by the same stroke, have been ashamed of such inward penury; feeling that as a boy I showed more poorly than girls. There was a difference meanwhile for such puzzlements before the porticos of the theatres; all questions melted for me there into the single depth of envy—envy of the equal, the beatific command of the evening hour, in the *régime* of Honorine's young train, who were fresh for the early sparrow and the chiffonier even after shedding buckets of tears the night before, and not so much as for the first or the second time, over the beautiful story of La Dame aux Camélias. There indeed was another humiliation, but by my weakness of position much more than of nature: whatever doing of "everything" might have been revealed to me as a means to the end, I would certainly have done it for a sight of Madame Doche and Fechter in Dumas's triumphant idyll—now enjoying the fullest honours of innocuous classicism; with which, as with the merits of its interpreters, Honorine's happy charges had become perfectly and if not quite serenely, at least ever so responsively and feelingly, familiar. Of a wondrous mixed sweetness and sharpness and queerness of uneffaced reminiscence is all that aspect of the cousins and the rambles and the overlapping nights melting along the odorously bedamped and retouched streets and arcades; bright in the ineffable morning light, above all, of our peculiar young culture and candour!

All of which again has too easily led me to drop for a moment my more leading clue of that radiation of goodnature from Gertrude Pendleton and her headlong hospitalities in which we perhaps most complacently basked. The becraped passage at Meurice's alluded to a little back was of a later season, and the radiation, as I recall it, had been, that first winter, mainly from a *petit hôtel* somewhere "on the other side," as we used with a large sketchiness to say, of the Champs Elysées; a region at that time reduced to no regularity, but figuring to my fond fancy as a chaos of accidents and contrasts where *petits hôtels* of archaic type were elbowed by woodyards and cabarets, and pavilions ever so characteristic, yet ever so indefinable, snuggled between frank industries and vulgarities—all brightened these indeed by the sociable note of Paris, be it only that of chaffering or of other *bavardise*. The great consistencies of arch-refinement, now of so large a harmony, were still to come, so that it seemed rather original to live there; in spite of which the attraction of the hazard of it on the part of our then so uniformly natural young kinswoman, not so much ingeniously, or even expressively, as just gesticulatively and helplessly gay—since that earlier pitch of New York parlance scarce arrived at, or for that matter pretended to, enunciation—was quite in what I at least took to be the glitter of her very conventions and traditions themselves; exemplified for instance by a bright nocturnal christening-party in honour of the small son of all hopes whom she was so precipitately to lose: an occasion which, as we had, in our way, known the act of baptism but as so abbreviated and in fact so tacit a business, had the effect for us of one of the great "forms" of a society taking itself with typical seriousness. We were much more serious than the Pendletons, but, paradoxically enough, there was that weakness in our state of our being able to make no such attestation of it. The evening can have been but of the friendliest, easiest and least pompous nature, with small guests, in congruity with its small hero, as well as large; but I must have found myself more than ever yet in presence of a "rite," one of those round which as many kinds of circumstance as possible clustered—so that the more of these there were the more one might imagine a great social order observed. How shall I now pretend to say how many kinds of circumstance I supposed I recognised?—with the remarkable one, to begin with, and which led fancy so far afield, that the "religious ceremony" was at the same time a "party," of twinkling lustres and disposed flowers and ladies with bare shoulders (that platitudinous bareness of the period that suggested somehow the moral line, drawn as with a ruler and a firm pencil); with little English girls, daughters of a famous physician of that nationality then pursuing a Parisian career (he must have helped the little victim into the world), and whose emphasised type much impressed itself; with round glazed and beribboned boxes of multi-coloured sugared almonds, dragées de baptême above all, which we harvested, in their heaps, as we might have gathered apples from a shaken tree, and which symbolised as nothing else the ritual dignity. Perhaps this grand impression really came back but to the dragées de baptême, not strictly more immemorial to our young appreciation than the New Year's cake and the "Election" cake known to us in New York, yet immensely more official and of the nature of scattered largesse; partly through the days and days, as it seemed to me, that our life was to be furnished, reinforced and almost encumbered with them. It wasn't simply that they were so toothsome, but that they were somehow so important and so historic.

It was with no such frippery, however, that I connected the occasional presence among us of the young member of the cousinship (in this case of the maternal) who most moved me to wistfulness of wonder, though not at all, with his then marked difference of age, by inviting my free approach. Vernon King, to whom I have in another part of this record alluded, at that time doing his baccalauréat on the other side of the Seine and coming over to our world at scraps of moments (for I recall my awe of the tremendous nature, as I supposed it, of his toil), as to quite a make-believe and gingerbread place, the lightest of substitutes for the "Europe" in which he had been from the first so technically plunged. His mother and sister, also on an earlier page referred to, had, from their distance, committed him to the great city to be "finished," educationally, to the point that for our strenuous cousin Charlotte was the only proper one—and I feel sure he can have acquitted himself in this particular in a manner that would have passed for brilliant if such lights didn't, thanks to her stiff little standards, always tend to burn low in her presence. These ladies were to develop more and more the practice of living in odd places for abstract inhuman reasons—at Marseilles, at Düsseldorf (if I rightly recall their principal German sojourn), at Naples, above all, for a long stage; where, in particular, their grounds of residence were somehow not as those of others, even though I recollect, from a much later time, attending them there at the opera, an experience which, in their fashion, they succeeded in despoiling for me of every element of the concrete, or at least of the pleasantly vulgar. Later impressions, few but firm, were so to enhance one's tenderness for Vernon's own image, the most interesting surely in all the troop of our young kinsmen early baffled and gathered, that he glances at me out of the Paris period, fresh-coloured, just blond-bearded, always smiling and catching his breath a little as from a mixture of eagerness and shyness, with such an appeal to the right idealisation, or to belated justice, as makes of mere evocation a sort of exercise of loyalty. It seemed quite richly laid upon me at the time—I get it all back—that he, two or three years older than my elder brother and dipped more early, as well as held more firmly, in the deep, the refining waters the virtue of which we all together, though with our differences of consistency, recognised, was the positive and living proof of what the process, comparatively poor for ourselves, could do at its best and with clay originally and domestically kneaded to the right plasticity; besides which he shone, to my fancy, and all the more for its seeming so brightly and quietly in his very grain, with the vague, the supposititious, but the intensely accent-giving stamp of the Latin quarter, which we so thinly imagined and so superficially brushed on our pious walks to the Luxembourg and through the parts where the glamour might have hung thickest. We were to see him a little—but two or three times—three or four years later, when, just before our own return, he had come back to America for the purpose, if my memory serves, of entering the Harvard Law School; and to see him still always with the smile that was essentially as facial, as livingly and loosely fixed, somehow, as his fresh complexion itself; always too with the air of caring so little for what he had been put through that, under any appeal to give out, more or less wonderfully, some sample or echo of it, as who should say, he still mostly panted as from a laughing mental embarrassment: he had been put through too much; it was all stale to him, and he wouldn't have known where to begin. He did give out, a little, on occasion—speaking, that is, on my different plane, as it were, and by the roundabout report of my brother; he gave out, it appeared, as they walked together across shining Newport sands, some fragment, some beginning of a very youthful poem that "Europe" had, with other results, moved him to, and a faint thin shred of which was to stick in my remembrance for reasons independent of its quality:

"Harold, rememberest thou the day,
  We rode along the Appian Way?
Neglected tomb and altar cast
  Their lengthening shadow o'er the plain,
And while we talked the mighty past
  Around us lived and breathed again!"

That was European enough, and yet he had returned to America really to find himself, even with every effort made immediately near him to defeat the discovery. He found himself, with the outbreak of the War, simply as the American soldier, and not under any bribe, however dim, of the epaulette or the girt sword; but just as the common enlisting native, which he smiled and gasped—to the increase of his happy shortness of breath, as from a repletion of culture, since it suggested no lack of personal soundness—at feeling himself so *like* to be. As strange, yet as still more touching than strange, I recall the sight, even at a distance, of the drop straight off him of all his layers of educational varnish, the possession of the "advantages," the tongues, the degrees, the diplomas, the reminiscences, a saturation too that had all sunk in—a sacrifice of precious attributes that might almost have been viewed as a wild bonfire. So his prodigious mother, whom I have perhaps sufficiently presented for my reader to understand, didn't fail to view it—judging it also, sharply hostile to the action of the North as the whole dreadful situation found her, with deep and resentful displeasure. I remember how I thought of Vernon himself, during the business, as at once so despoiled, so diverted, and above all so resistantly bright, as vaguely to suggest something more in him still, some deep-down reaction, some extremity of indifference and defiance, some exhibition of a young character too long pressed and impressed, too long prescribed to and with too much expected of it, and all under too firmer a will; so that the public pretext had given him a lift, or lent him wings, which without its greatness might have failed him. As the case was to turn nothing—that is nothing he most wanted and, remarkably, most enjoyed—did fail him at all. I forget with which of the possible States, New York, Massachusetts or Rhode Island (though I think the first) he had taken service; only seeming to remember that this all went on for him at the start in McClellan's and later on in Grant's army, and that, badly wounded in a Virginia battle, he came home to be nursed by his mother, recently restored to America for a brief stay. She held, I believe, in the event, that he had, under her care, given her his vow that, his term being up, he would not, should he get sufficiently well, re-engage. The question here was between them, but it was definite that, materially speaking, she was in no degree dependent on him. The old, the irrepressible adage, however, was to live again between them: when the devil was sick the devil a saint would be; when the devil was well the devil a saint was he!

The devil a saint, at all events, was Vernon, who denied that he had passed his word, and who, as soon as he had surmounted his first disablement, passionately and quite admirably re-enlisted. At once restored to the front and to what now gave life for him its indispensable relish, he was in the thick, again, of the great carnage round about Richmond, where, again gravely wounded, he (as I figure still incorrigibly smiling) succumbed. His mother had by this time indignantly returned to Europe, accompanied by her daughter and her younger son—the former of whom accepted, for our great pity, a little later on, the office of closing the story. Anne King, young and frail, but not less firm, under stress, than the others of her blood, came back, on her brother's death, and, quietest, most colourless Electra of a lucidest Orestes, making her difficult way amid massed armies and battle-drenched fields, got possession of his buried body and bore it for reinterment to Newport, the old habitation, as I have mentioned, of their father's people, both Vernons and Kings. It must have been to see my mother, as well as to sail again for Europe, that she afterwards came to Boston, where I remember going down with her, at the last, to the dock of the English steamer, some black and tub-like Cunarder, an archaic "Africa" or "Asia" sufficing to the Boston service of those days. I saw her off drearily and helplessly enough, I well remember, and even at that moment found for her another image: what was she most like, though in a still sparer and dryer form, but some low-toned, some employed little Brontë heroine?—though more indeed a Lucy Snowe than a Jane Eyre, and with no shade of a Brontë hero within sight. To this all the fine privilege and fine culture of all the fine countries (collective matter, from far back, of our intimated envy) had "amounted"; just as it had amounted for Vernon to the bare headstone on the Newport hillside where, by his mother's decree, as I have already noted, there figured no hint of the manner of his death. So grand, so finely personal a manner it appeared to me at the time, and has indeed appeared ever since, that this brief record irrepressibly springs from that. His mother, as I have equally noted, was however, with her views, to find no grace in it so long as she lived; and his sister went back to her, and to Marseille, as they always called it, but prematurely to die.

XXIX

I FEEL that much might be made of my memories of Boulogne-sur-Mer had I but here left room for the vast little subject; in which I should probably, once started, wander to and fro as exploringly, as perceivingly, as discoveringly, I am fairly tempted to call it, as might really give the measure of my small operations at the time. I was almost wholly reduced there to operations of that mere inward and superficially idle order at which we have already so freely assisted; reduced by a cause I shall presently mention, the production of a great blur, well-nigh after the fashion of some mild domestic but quite considerably spreading grease-spot, in respect to the world of action, such as it was, more or less immediately about me. I must personally have lived during this pale predicament almost only by seeing what I could, after my incorrigible ambulant fashion—a practice that may well have made me pass for bringing home nothing in the least exhibitional—rather than by pursuing the inquiries and interests than agitated, to whatever intensity, our on the whole widening little circle. The images I speak of as matter for more evocation that I can spare them were the fruit of two different periods at Boulogne, a shorter and a longer; this second appearing to us all, at the time, I gather, too endlessly and blightingly prolonged: so sharply, before it was over, did I at any rate come to yearn for the Rue Montaigne again, the Rue Montaigne "sublet" for a term under a flurry produced in my parents' breasts by a "financial crisis" of great violence to which the American world, as a matter now of recorded history, I believe, had tragically fallen victim, and which had imperilled or curtailed for some months our moderate means of existence. We were to recover, I make out, our disturbed balance, and were to pursue awhile further our chase of the alien, the somehow repeatedly postponed *real* opportunity; and the second, the comparatively cramped and depressed connection with the classic refuge, as it then was, of spasmodic thrift, when not of settled indigence, for the embarrassed of our race in the largest sense of this matter, was to be shuffled off at last with no scant relief and reaction. This is perhaps exactly why the whole picture of our existence at the Pas-de-Calais watering place pleads to me now for the full indulgence, what would be in other words every touch of tenderness workable, after all the years, over the lost and confused and above all, on their own side, poor ultimately rather vulgarised and violated little sources of impression: items and aspects these which while they in their degree and after their sort flourished we only asked to admire, or at least to appreciate, for their rewarding extreme queerness. The very centre of my particular consciousness of the place turned too soon to the fact of my coming in there for the gravest illness of my life, an all but mortal attack of the malignant typhus of old days; which, after laying me as low as I could well be laid for many weeks, condemned me to a convalescence so arduous that I saw my apparently scant possibilities, by the measure of them then taken, even as through a glass darkly, or through the expansive blur for which I found just above a homely image.

This experience was to become when I had emerged from it the great reminiscence or circumstance of old Boulogne for me, and I was to regard it, with much intelligence, I should have maintained, as the marked limit of my state of being a small boy. I took on, when I had decently, and all the more because I had so retardedly, recovered, the sense of being a boy of other dimensions somehow altogether, and even with a new dimension introduced and acquired; a dimension that I was eventually to think of as a stretch in the direction of essential change or of living straight into a part of myself previously quite unvisited and now made accessible as by the sharp forcing of a closed door. The blur of consciousness imaged by my grease-spot was not, I hasten to declare, without its relenting edges and even, during its major insistence, fainter thicknesses; short of which, I see, my picture, the picture I was always so incurably "after," would have failed of animation altogether—quite have failed to bristle with characteristics, with figures and objects and scenic facts, particular passages and moments, the stuff, in short, of that scrap of minor gain which I have spoken of as our multiplied memories. Wasn't I even at the time, and much more later on, to feel how we had been, through the thick and thin of the whole adventure, assaulted as never before in so concentrated a way by local and social character?

Such was the fashion after which the Boulogne of long ago—I have known next to nothing of it since—could come forth, come more than half-way, as we say, to meet the imagination open to such advances. It was, taking one thing with another, so verily drenched in character that I see myself catching this fine flagrancy almost equally in everything; unless indeed I may have felt it rather smothered than presented on the comparatively sordid scene of the Collège Communal, not long afterwards to expand, I believe, into the local Lycée, to which the inimitable process of our education promptly introduced us. I was to have less of the Collège than my elder and my younger brother, thanks to the interrupting illness that placed me so long, with its trail of after-effects, half complacently, half ruefully apart; but I suffered for a few early weeks the mainly malodorous sense of the braver life, produced as this was by a deeply democratic institution from which no small son even of the most soapless home could possibly know exclusion. Odd, I recognise, that I should inhale the air of the place so particularly, so almost only, to that dismal effect; since character was there too, for whom it should concern, and my view of some of the material conditions, of the general collegiate presence toward the top of the steepish Grand' Rue, on the right and not much short, as it comes back to me, of the then closely clustered and inviolate *haute ville*, the more or less surviving old town, the idle grey rampart, the moated and towered citadel, the tree-shaded bastion for strolling and sitting "immortalised" by Thackeray, achieved the monumental, in its degree, after a fashion never yet associated for us with the pursuit of learning. Didn't the Campaigner, suffering indigence at the misapplied hands of Colonel Newcome, rage at that hushed victim supremely and dreadfully just thereabouts—by which I mean in the haute ville—over some question of a sacrificed sweetbread or a cold hacked joint that somebody had been "at"? Beside such builded approaches to an education as we had elsewhere known the Collège exhibited, with whatever reserves, the measure of style which almost any French accident of the administratively architectural order more easily rises to than fails of; even if the matter be but a question of the shyest similitude of a *cour d'honneur*, the court disconnecting the scene, by intention at least, from the basely bourgeois and giving value to the whole effect of opposed and windowed wall and important, or balanced and "placed," *perron*. These are many words for the dull precinct, as then presented, I admit, and they are perhaps half prompted by a special association, too ghostly now quite to catch again—the sense of certain Sundays, distinct from the grim, that is the flatly instructional, body of the week, when I seem to myself to have successfully flouted the whole constituted field by passing across it and from it to some quite ideally old-world little annexed *musée de province*, as inviolate in its way as the grey rampart and bare citadel, and very like them in unrelieved tone, where I repeatedly, and without another presence to hinder, looked about me at goodness knows what weird ancientries of stale academic art. Not one of these treasures, in its habit as it lived, do I recall; yet the sense and the "note" of them was at the time, none the less, not so elusive that I didn't somehow draw straight from them intimations of the interesting, that is revelations of the æsthetic, the historic, the critical mystery and charm of things (of such things taken altogether), that added to my small loose handful of the seed of culture.

That apprehension was, in its way, of our house of learning too, and yet I recall how, on the scant and simple terms I have glanced at, I quite revelled in it; whereas other impressions of my brief ordeal shrink, for anything in the nature of interest, but to three or four recovered marks of the social composition of the school. There were the sons of all the small shop-keepers and not less, by my remembrance, of certain of the mechanics and artisans; but there was also the English contingent, these predominantly *internes* and uniformed, blue-jacketed and brass-buttoned, even to an effect of odd redundancy, who by my conceit gave our association a lift. Vivid still to me is the summer morning on which, in the wide court—as wide, that is, as I liked to suppose it, and where we hung about helplessly enough for recreation—a brownish black-eyed youth, of about my own degree of youthfulness, mentioned to me with an air that comes back as that of the liveliest informational resource the outbreak, just heard of, of an awful Mutiny in India, where his military parents, who had not so long before sent him over thence, with such weakness of imagination, as I measured it, to the poor spot on which we stood, were in mortal danger of their lives; so that news of their having been killed would perhaps be already on the way. They might well have been military, these impressively exposed characters, since my friend's name was Napier, or Nappié as he was called at the school, and since, I may add also, there attached to him, in my eyes, the glamour of an altogether new emphasis of type. The English boys within our ken since our coming abroad had been of the fewest—the Fezandié youths, whether English or American, besides being but scantly boys, had been so lost, on that scene, in our heap of disparities; and it pressed upon me after a fashion of its own that those we had known in New York, and all aware of their varieties and "personalities" as one had supposed one's self, had in no case challenged the restless "placing" impulse with any such force as the finished little Nappié. They had not been, as he was by the very perversity of his finish, resultants of forces at all—or comparatively speaking; it was as if their producing elements had been simple and few, whereas behind this more mixed and, as we have learnt to say, evolved companion (his very simplicities, his gaps of possibility, being still evolved), there massed itself I couldn't have said what protective social order, what tangled creative complexity. Why I should have thought him almost Indian of stamp and hue because his English parents were of the so general Indian peril is more than I can say; yet I have his exotic and above all his bold, his imaginably even "bad," young face, finely unacquainted with law, before me at this hour quite undimmed—announcing, as I conceived it, and quite as a shock, any awful adventure one would, as well as something that I must even at the time have vaguely taken as the play of the "passions." He vanishes, and I dare say I but make him over, as I make everything; and he must have led his life, whatever it was to become, with the least possible waiting on the hour or the major consequence and no waste of energy at all in mooning, no patience with any substitute for his very own humour. We had another schoolmate, this one native to the soil, whose references were with the last vividness local and who was yet to escape with brilliancy in the aftertime the smallest shadow of effacement. His most direct reference at that season was to the principal pastry-cook's of the town, an establishment we then found supreme for little criss-crossed apple tartlets and melting *babas*—young Coquelin's home life amid which we the more acutely envied that the upward cock of his so all-important nose testified, for my fancy, to the largest range of free familiar sniffing. C.-B. Coquelin is personally most present to me, in the form of that hour, by the value, as we were to learn to put it, of this nose, the fine assurance and impudence of which fairly made it a trumpet for promises; yet in spite of that, the very gage, as it were, of his long career as the most interesting and many-sided comedian, or at least most unsurpassed dramatic *diseur* of his time, I failed to doubt that, with the rich recesses of the parental industry for his background, his subtlest identity was in his privilege, or perhaps even in his expertest trick, of helping himself well.

These images, however, were but drops in the bucket of my sense of catching character, roundabout us, as I say, at every turn and in every aspect; character that began even, as I was pleased to think, in our own habitation, the most spacious and pompous Europe had yet treated us to, in spite of its fronting on the Rue Neuve Chaussée, a street of lively shopping, by the measure of that innocent age, and with its own ground-floor occupied by a bristling exhibition of indescribably futile *articles de Paris.* Modern and commodious itself, it looked from its balcony at serried and mismatched and quaintly-named haunts of old provincial, of sedately passive rather than confidently eager, traffic; but this made, among us, for much harmless inquisitory life—while we were fairly assaulted, at home, by the scale and some of the striking notes of our fine modernity. The young, the agreeable (agreeable to anything), the apparently opulent M. Prosper Sauvage—wasn't it?—had not long before, unless I mistake, inherited the place as a monument of "family," quite modestly local yet propitious family, ambition; with an ample extension in the rear, and across the clearest prettiest court, for his own dwelling, which thus became elegant, *entre cour et jardin*, and showed all the happy symmetries and proper conventions. Here flourished, or rather, I surmise at this time of day, here languished, a domestic drama of which we enjoyed the murmurous overflow: frankly astounding to me, I confess, how I remain still in sensitive presence of our resigned proprietor's domestic drama, in and out of which I see a pair of figures quite up to the dramatic mark flit again with their air of the very rightest finish. I must but note these things, none the less, and pass; for scarce another item of the whole Boulogne concert of salient images failed, after all, of a significance either still more strangely social or more distinctively spectacular. These appearances indeed melt together for my interest, I once more feel, as, during the interminable stretch of the prescribed and for the most part solitary airings and outings involved in my slow convalescence from the extremity of fever, I approached that straitened and somewhat bedarkened issue of the Rue de l'Ecu (was it?) toward the bright-coloured, strongly-peopled Port just where Merridew's English Library, solace of my vacuous hours and temple, in its degree too, of deep initiations, mounted guard at the right. Here, frankly, discrimination drops—every particular in the impression once so quick and fresh sits interlinked with every other in the large lap of the whole. The motley, sunny, breezy, bustling Port, with its classic, its admirable fisher-folk of both sexes, models of type and tone and of what might be handsomest in the thoroughly weathered condition, would have seemed the straightest appeal to curiosity had not the old Thackerayan side, as I may comprehensively call it, and the scattered wealth of illustration of *his* sharpest satiric range, not so constantly interposed and competed with it. The scene bristled, as I look back at it, with images from Men's Wives, from the society of Mr. Deuceace and that of fifty other figures of the same creation, with Bareacreses and Rawdon Crawleys and of course with Mrs. Macks, with Roseys of a more or less crumpled freshness and blighted bloom, with battered and bent, though doubtless never quite so fine, Colonel Newcomes not less; with more reminders in short than I can now gather in. Of those forms of the seedy, the subtly sinister, the vainly "genteel," the generally damaged and desperate, and in particular perhaps the invincibly impudent, all the marks, I feel sure, were stronger and straighter than such as we meet in generally like cases under our present levelling light. Such anointed and whiskered and eked-out, such brazen, bluffing, swaggering gentlemen, such floridly repaired ladies, their mates, all looking as hard as they could as if they were there for mere harmless amusement—it was as good, among them, as just *being* Arthur Pendennis to know so well, or at least to guess so fearfully, who and what they might be. They were floated on the tide of the manners then prevailing, I judge, with a rich processional effect that so many of our own grand lapses, when not of our mere final flatnesses, leave no material for; so that the living note of Boulogne was really, on a more sustained view, the opposition between a native race the most happily tempered, the most becomingly seasoned and salted and self-dependent, and a shifting colony—so far as the persons composing it *could* either urgently or speculatively shift—inimitably at odds with any active freshness. And the stale and the light, even though so scantly rebounding, the too densely socialised, group was the English, and the "positive" and hardy and steady and wind-washed the French; and it was all as flushed with colour and patched with costume and referable to record and picture, to literature and history, as a more easily amusing and less earnestly uniform age could make it. When I speak of this opposition indeed I see it again most take effect in an antithesis that, on one side and the other, swallowed all differences at a gulp. The general British show, as we had it there, in the artless mid-Victorian desert, had, I think, for its most sweeping sign the high assurance of its dowdiness; whereas one had only to glance about at the sea-faring and fisher-folk who were the real strength of the place to feel them shed at every step and by their every instinct of appearance the perfect lesson of taste. There it was to be learnt and taken home—with never a moral, none the less, drawn from it by the "higher types." I speak of course in particular of the tanned and trussed and kerchiefed, the active and productive women, all so short-skirted and free-limbed under stress; for as by the rule of the dowdy their sex is ever the finer example, so where the sense of the suitable, of the charmingly and harmoniously right prevails, they preserve the pitch even as a treasure committed to their piety. To hit that happy mean of rightness amid the mixed occupations of a home-mother and a fishwife, to be in especial both so bravely stripped below and so perfectly enveloped above as the deep-wading, far-striding, shrimp-netting, crab-gathering matrons or maidens who played, waist-high, with the tides and racily quickened the market, was to make grace thoroughly practical and discretion thoroughly vivid. These attributes had with them all, for the eye, however, a range too great for me to follow, since, as their professional undress was a turn-out positively self-consistent, so their household, or more responsibly public, or altogether festal, array played through the varied essentials of fluted coif and folded kerchief and sober skirt and tense, dark, displayed stocking and clicking wooden slipper, to say nothing of long gold ear-drop or solid short-hung pectoral cross, with a respect for the rigour of conventions that had the beauty of self-respect.

I owe to no season of the general period such a preserved sense of innumerable unaccompanied walks—at the reason of which luxury of freedom I have glanced; which as often as not were through the steep and low-browed and brightly-daubed *ruelles* of the fishing town and either across and along the level sea-marge and sustained cliff beyond; this latter the site of the first Napoleon's so tremendously mustered camp of invasion, with a monument as futile, by my remembrance, as that enterprise itself had proved, to give it all the special accent I could ask for. Or I was as free for the *haute ville* and the ramparts and the scattered, battered benches of reverie—if I may so honour my use of them; they kept me not less complacently in touch with those of the so anciently odd and mainly contracted houses over which the stiff citadel and the ghost of Catherine de Médicis, who had dismally sojourned in it, struck me as throwing such a chill, and one of which precisely must have witnessed the never-to-be-forgotten Campaigner's passage in respect to her cold beef. Far from extinct for me is my small question of those hours, doubtless so mentally, so shamelessly wanton, as to what human life might be tucked away in such retreats, which expressed the last acceptance whether of desired or of imposed quiet; so absolutely appointed and obliged did I feel to make out, so far as I could, what, in so significant a world, they on their part *represented*. I think the force mainly sustaining me at that rather dreary time—as I see it can only show for—was this lively felt need that everything should represent something more than what immediately and all too blankly met the eye; I seem to myself to have carried it about everywhere and, though of course only without outward signs that might have betrayed my fatuity, and insistently, quite yearningly applied it. What I wanted, in my presumption, was that the object, the place, the person, the unreduced impression, often doubtless so difficult or so impossible to reduce, should give out to me something of a situation; living as I did in confused and confusing situations and thus hooking them on, however awkwardly, to almost any at all living surface I chanced to meet. My memory of Boulogne is that we had almost no society of any sort at home—there appearing to be about us but one sort, and that of far too great, or too fearful, an immediate bravery. Yet there were occasional figures that I recover from our scant circle and that I associate, whatever links I may miss, with the small still houses on the rampart; figures of the quaintest, quite perhaps the frowsiest, little English ladies in such mushroom hats, such extremely circular and bestriped scarlet petticoats, such perpetual tight gauntlets, such explicit claims to long descent, which showed them for everything that everyone else at Boulogne was not. These mid-Victorian samples of a perfect consistency "represented," by my measure, as hard as ever they could—and represented, of all things, literature and history and society. The literature was that of the three-volume novel, then, and for much after, enjoying its loosest and serenest spread; for they separately and anxiously and awfully "wrote"—and that must almost by itself have amounted in them to all the history I evoked.

The dreary months, as I am content that in their second phase especially they should be called, are subject, I repeat, to the perversion, quite perhaps to the obscuration, of my temporarily hindered health—which should keep me from being too sure of these small *proportions* of experience—I was to look back afterwards as over so grey a desert; through which, none the less, there flush as sharp little certainties, not to be disallowed, such matters as the general romance of Merridew, the English Librarian, before mentioned, at the mouth of the Port; a connection that thrusts itself upon me now as after all the truest centre of my perceptions—waylaying my steps at the time, as I came and went, more than any other object or impression. The question of what *that* spot represented, or could be encouraged, could be aided and abetted, to represent, may well have supremely engaged me—for depth within depth there could only open before me. The place "meant," on these terms, to begin with, frank and licensed fiction, licensed to my recordedly relaxed state; and what this particular luxury represented it might have taken me even more time than I had to give to make out. The blest novel in three volumes exercised through its form, to my sense, on grounds lying deeper for me to-day than my deepest sounding, an appeal that fairly made it do with me what it would. Possibly a drivelling confession, and the more drivelling perhaps the more development I should attempt for it; from which, however, the very difficulty of the case saves me. Too many associations, too much of the ferment of memory and fancy, are somehow stirred; they beset me again, they hover and whirl about me while I stand, as I used to stand, within the positively sanctified walls of the shop (so of the *vieux temps* now their aspect and fashion and worked system: by which I mean again of the frumpiest and civillest mid-Victorian), and surrender to the vision of the shelves packed with their rich individual trinities. Why should it have affected me so that my choice, so difficult in such a dazzle, could only be for a trinity? I am unable fully to say—such a magic dwelt in the mere rich fact of the trio. When the novel of that age was "bad," as it so helplessly, so abjectly and prevailingly consented to be, the three volumes still did something for it, a something that was, all strangely, not an aggravation of its case. When it was "good" (our analysis, our terms of appreciation, had a simplicity that has lingered on) they made it copiously, opulently better; so that when, after the span of the years, my relation with them became, from that of comparatively artless reader, and to the effect of a superior fondness and acuteness, that of complacent author, the tradition of infatuated youth still flung over them its mantle: this at least till *all* relation, by one of the very rudest turns of life we of the profession were to have known, broke off, in clumsy interfering hands and with almost no notice given, in a day, in an hour. Besides connecting me with the lost but unforgotten note of waiting service and sympathy that quavered on the Merridew air, they represented just for intrinsic charm more than I could at any moment have given a plain account of; they fell, by their ineffable history, every trio I ever touched, into the category of such prized phenomena as my memory, for instance, of fairly hanging about the Rue des Vieillards, at the season I speak of, through the apprehension that something vague and sweet—if I shouldn't indeed rather say something of infinite future point and application—would come of it. This is a reminiscence that nothing would induce me to verify, as for example by any revisiting light; but it was going to be good for me, good, that is, for what I was pleased to regard as my intelligence or my imagination, in fine for my obscurely specific sense of things, that I *should* so have hung about. The name of the street was by itself of so gentle and intimate a persuasion that I must have been ashamed not to proceed, for the very grace of it, to some shade of active response. And there was always a place of particular arrest in the vista brief and blank, but inclusively blank, blank *after* ancient, settled, more and more subsiding things, blank almost, in short, with all Matthew Arnold's "ennui of the middle ages," rather than, poorly and meanly and emptily, before such states, which was previously what I had most known of blankness. This determined pause was at the window of a spare and solitary shop, a place of no amplitude at all, but as of an inveterate cheerful confidence, where, among a few artists' materials, an exhibited water-colour from some native and possibly then admired hand was changed but once in ever so long. That was perhaps after all the pivot of my revolution—the question of whether or no I should at a given moment find the old picture replaced. I made this, when I had the luck, pass for an event—yet an event which would *have* to have had for its scene the precious Rue des Vieillards, and pale though may be the recital of such pleasures I lose myself in depths of kindness for my strain of ingenuity.

All of which, and to that extent to be corrected, leaves small allowance for my service to good M. Ansiot, rendered while my elder and younger brothers—the younger completing our group of the ungovernessed—were continuously subject to collegial durance. Their ordeal was, I still blush to think, appreciably the heavier, as compared with mine, during our longer term of thrifty exile from Paris—the time of stress, as I find I recall it, when we had turned our backs on the Rue Montaigne and my privilege was so to roam on the winter and the spring afternoons. Mild M. Ansiot, "under" whom I for some three hours each forenoon sat sole and underided—and actually by himself too—was a curiosity, a benignity, a futility even, I gather; but save for a felt and remembered impulse in me to open the window of our scene of study as soon as he had gone was in no degree an ideal. He might rise here, could I do him justice, as the rarest of my poor evocations; for he it was, to be frank, who most literally smelt of the vieux temps—as to which I have noted myself as wondering and musing as much as might be, with recovered scraps and glimpses and other intimations, only never yet for such a triumph of that particular sense. To be still frank, he was little less than a monster—for mere unresisting or unresilient mass of personal presence I mean; so that I fairly think of him as a form of bland porpoise, violently blowing in an age not his own, as by having had to exchange deep water for thin air. Thus he impressed me as with an absolute ancientry of type, of tone, of responsible taste, above all; this last I mean in literature, since it was literature we sociably explored, to my at once charmed and shamed apprehension of the several firm traditions, the pure proprieties, the discussabilities, in the oddest way both so many and so few, of that field as they prevailed to his pious view. I must have had hold, in this mere sovereign sample of the accidentally, the quite unconsciously and unpretentiously, the all negligibly or superfluously handed-down, of a rare case of the provincial and academic *cuistre*; though even while I record it I see the good man as too helpless and unaggressive, too smothered in his poor facts of person and circumstance, of overgrown time of life alone, to incur with justness the harshness of classification. He rested with a weight I scarce even felt—such easy terms he made, without scruple, for both of us—on the cheerful innocence of my barbarism; and though our mornings were short and subject, I think, to quite drowsy lapses and other honest aridities, we did scumble together, I make out, by the aid of the collected extracts from the truly and academically great which formed his sole resource and which he had, in a small portable and pocketed library rather greasily preserved, some patch of picture of a saving as distinguished from a losing classicism. The point remains for me that when all was said—and even with everything that might directly have counted unsaid—he discharged for me such an office that I was to remain to this far-off hour in a state of possession of him that is the very opposite of a blank: quite after the fashion again in which I had all along and elsewhere suffered and resisted, and yet so perversely and intimately appropriated, tutoring; which was with as little as ever to show for my profit of his own express showings. The blank he fills out crowds itself with a wealth of value, since I shouldn't without him have been able to claim, for whatever it may be worth, a tenth (at that let me handsomely put it), of my "working" sense of the vieux temps. How can I allow then that we hadn't planted together, with a loose felicity, some of the seed of work?—even though the sprouting was so long put off. Everything, I have mentioned, had come at this time to be acceptedly, though far from braggingly, put off; and the ministrations of M. Ansiot really wash themselves over with the weak mixture that had begun to spread for me, to immensity, during that summer day or two of our earlier residence when, betraying strange pains and apprehensions, I was with all decision put to bed. Present to me still is the fact of my sharper sense, after an hour or two, of my being there in distress and, as happened for the moment, alone; present to me are the sounds of the soft afternoon, the mild animation of the Boulogne street through the half-open windows; present to me above all the strange sense that something had begun that would make more difference to me, directly and indirectly, than anything had ever yet made. I might verily, on the spot, have seen, as in a fading of day and a change to something suddenly queer, the whole large extent of it. I must thus, much impressed but half scared, have wanted to appeal; to which end I tumbled, all too weakly, out of bed and wavered toward the bell just across the room. The question of whether I really reached and rang it was to remain lost afterwards in the strong sick whirl of everything about me, under which I fell into a lapse of consciousness that I shall conveniently here treat as a considerable gap.

THE END

NOTES OF A SON AND BROTHER

Pencil-drawn portrait of
William James by himself, about 1866

Illustrations

Pencil-drawn portrait of William James by himself, about 1866 . . . . *Frontispiece*

Louis Osborne. Sketch from a letter of William James (page 264) 265

Portrait in oils of Miss Katharine Temple, 1861 313

A leaf from the letter quoted on page 333 335

Sketch of G. W. James brought home wounded from the assault on Fort Wagner 405

"The cold water cure at Divonne—excellent for melancholia."—From a letter of William James (page 525) 527

I

IT MAY again perhaps betray something of that incorrigible vagueness of current in our educational drift which I have elsewhere[1] so unreservedly suffered to reflect itself that, though we had come abroad in 1855 with an eye to the then supposedly supreme benefits of Swiss schooling, our most resolute attempt to tap that supply, after twenty distractions, waited over to the autumn of the fourth year later on, when we in renewed good faith retraced our steps to Geneva. Our parents began at that season a long sojourn at the old Hôtel de l'Écu, which now erects a somewhat diminished head on the edge of the rushing Rhone—its only rival then was the Hôtel des Bergues opposite, considerably larger and commanding more or less the view of that profiled crest of Mont-Blanc which used to be so oddly likened to the head and face of a singularly supine Napoleon. But on that side the shooting blue flood was less directly and familiarly under the windows; in our position we lived with it and hung over it, and its beauty, just where we mainly congregated, was, I fear, my own sole happy impression during several of those months. It was of a Sunday that we congregated most; my two younger brothers had, in general, on that day their *sortie* from the Pensionnat Maquelin, a couple of miles out of town, where they were then established, and W. J., following courses at the Academy, in its present enriched and amplified form the University, mingled, failing livelier recreation, in the family circle at the hotel. Livelier recreation, during the hours of completest ease, consisted mostly, as the period drew itself out, of those *courses*, along the lake and along the hills, which offer to student-life in whatever phase, throughout that blest country, the most romantic of all forms of "a little change"; enjoyed too in some degree, but much more restrictedly, by myself—this an effect, as I remember feeling it, of my considerably greater servitude. I had been placed, separately, at still another Institution, that of M. Rochette, who carried on an École Préparatoire aux Écoles Spéciales, by

[1] *A Small Boy and Others.* New York, 1913.

which was meant in particular the Polytechnic School at Zurich, with whatever other like curricula, always "scientific," might elsewhere be aimed at; and I had been so disposed of under a flattering misconception of my aptitudes that leaves me to-day even more wonderstruck than at that immediate season of my distress.

I so feared and abhorred mathematics that the simplest arithmetical operation had always found and kept me helpless and blank—the dire discipline of the years bringing no relief whatever to my state; and mathematics unmitigated were at the Institution Rochette the air we breathed, building us up as they most officiously did for those other grim ordeals and pursuits, those of the mining and the civil engineer, those of the architectural aspirant and the technician in still other fields, to which we were supposed to be addressed. Nothing of the sort was indeed supposed of me—which is in particular my present mystification; so that my assault of the preliminaries disclosed, feeble as it strikingly remained, was mere darkness, waste and anguish. I found myself able to bite, as the phrase was, into no subject there deemed savoury; it was hard and bitter fruit all and turned to ashes in my mouth. More extraordinary however than my good parents' belief—eccentric on their part too, in the light of their usual practice and disposition, their habit, for the most part, of liking for us after a gasp or two whatever we seemed to like—was my own failure to protest with a frankness proportioned to my horror. The stiffer intellectual discipline, the discipline of physics and of algebra, invoked for the benefit of an understanding undisputedly weak and shy, had been accepted on my side as a blessing perhaps in disguise. It had come to me by I know not what perversity that if I couldn't tackle the smallest problem in mechanics or face without dismay at the blackboard the simplest geometric challenge I ought somehow in decency to make myself over, oughtn't really to be so inferior to almost everyone else. That was the pang, as it was also the marvel—that the meanest minds and the vulgarest types approached these matters without a sign of trepidation even when they approached them, at the worst, without positive appetite. My attempt not therefore to remain abnormal wholly broke down, however, and when I at last withdrew from the scene it was not even as a conspicuous, it was only as an obscure, a deeply hushed failure. I joined William, after what had seemed to me an eternity of woe, at the Academy, where I followed, for too short a time but with a comparative recovery of confidence, such literary *cours* as I might.

I puzzle it out to-day that my parents had simply said to themselves, in serious concern, that I read too many novels, or at least read them too attentively—*that* was the vice; as also that they had by the contagion of their good faith got me in a manner to agree with them; since I could almost always enter, to the gain of "horizon" but too often to the perversion of experience, into any view of my real interests, so-called, that was presented to me with a dazzling assurance. I didn't consider certainly that I was so forming my mind, and was doubtless curious to see whether it mightn't, by a process flourishing in other applications, get to some extent formed. It wasn't, I think, till I felt the rapture of that method's arrest that I knew how grotesquely little it had done for me. And yet I bore it afterwards no malice—resorting again to that early fatalistic philosophy of which the general sense was that almost anything, however disagreeable, had been worth while; so unable was I to claim that it hadn't involved impressions. I positively felt the impressional harvest rather rich, little as any item of it might have passed at the time for the sort of thing one exhibits as a trophy of learning. My small exhibition was all for myself and consisted on the whole but of a dusty, spotty, ugly picture—I took it for ugly well-nigh to the pitch of the sinister. Its being a picture at all—and I clung to that—came from the personal and material facts of the place, where I was the only scholar of English speech, since my companions, with a Genevese predominance, were variously polyglot. They wondered, I couldn't doubt, what I was doing among them, and what lost lamb, almost audibly bleating, I had been charged to figure. Yet I remember no crude chaff, no very free relation of any one with any one, no high pitch, still less any low descent, of young pleasantry or irony; our manners must have been remarkably formed, and our general tone was that of a man-of-the-world discretion, or at the worst of a certain small bourgeois circumspection. The dread in the Genevese of having definitely to "know" strangers and thereby be at costs for any sort of hospitality to them comes back to me as written clear; not less than their being of two sorts or societies, sons of the townspeople pure and simple and sons of the local aristocracy perched in certain of the fine old houses of the Cité and enjoying a background of sturdily-seated lakeside villas and deeply umbrageous campagnes. I remember thinking the difference of type, complexion and general *allure* between these groups more marked, to all the senses, than any "social distinction" I had yet encountered. But the great thing was that I could so simplify our enclosing scene itself, round it in and make it compose—the dark, the dreary Institution, squeezed into a tall, dim, stony-faced and stony-hearted house at the very top of the Cité and directly in the rear of the Cathedral, portions of the apse of which seem to me to have straggled above or protruded toward it, with other odd extraneous masses than itself pressing still nearer. This simplification, quite luxuriously for my young mind, was to mere mean blackness of an old-world sordid order. I recognised *rich* blackness in other connections, but this was somehow of a harsh tradition and a tragic economy; sordid and strong was what I had from the first felt the place, though urging myself always to rub off history from its stones, and suffering thus, after a fashion, by the fact that with history it ought to be interesting and that I ought to know just how and why it was. For that, I think, was ever both the burden and the joy—the complication, I mean, of interest, and the sense, in the midst of the ugly and the melancholy, that queer crooked silent corners behind cathedrals wrought in their way for one, did something, while one haunted them, to the imagination and the taste; and that so, once more, since the generalisation had become a habit with me, I couldn't, seeing and feeling these things, really believe I had picked up nothing.

When I sat in a dusky upper chamber and read "French literature" with blighted M. Toeppfer, son of a happier sire, as I was sure the charming writer and caricaturist, in spite of cumbrous cares, must have been; or when, a couple of times a week and in the same eternal twilight (we groped almost lampless through the winter days, and our glimmering tapers, when they sparsely appeared, smelt of a past age), I worried out Virgil and Tite-Live with M. Verchère, or Schiller and Lessing with the ruddy noisy little professor of German, who sat always, the lesson long, in a light brown talma, the sides of which he caused violently to flap for emphasis like agitated wings, I was almost conscious of the breath of culture as I modestly aspired to culture, and was at any rate safe for the time from a summons to the blackboard at the hands of awful little M. Galopin, that dispenser of the paralysing chalk who most affected me. Extremely diminutive and wearing for the most part a thin inscrutable smile, the ghost of a tribute to awkwardness happily carried off, he found in our barren interviews, I believed, a charm to curiosity, bending afresh each time as over the handful of specimen dust, unprecedented product at its finest, extracted from the scratched soil of my intelligence. With M. Toeppfer I was almost happy; with each of these instructors my hour was unshared, my exploits unwitnessed, by others; but M. Toeppfer became a friend, shewed himself a *causeur*, brightened our lesson with memories of his time in Paris, where, if I am not mistaken, he had made, with great animation, his baccalauréat, and whence it was my possibly presumptuous impression he had brought back a state of health, apparently much impaired, which represented contrition for youthful spirits. He had haunted the parterre of the Théâtre Français, and when we read Racine his vision of Rachel, whom he had seen there as often as possible, revived; he was able to say at moments how she had spoken and moved, and I recall in particular his telling me that on her entrance as Phèdre, borne down, in her languorous passion, by the weight of her royal robes—"Que ces vains ornemens, que ces voiles me pèsent!"—the long lapse of time before she spoke and while she sank upon a seat filled itself extraordinarily with her visible woe. But where he most gave me comfort was in bringing home to me that the house commemorated, immortalised, as we call it, in the first of his father's Nouvelles Genevoises, La Bibliothèque de mon Oncle, was none other than the structure facing us where we sat and which so impinged and leaned on the cathedral walls that he had but to indicate to me certain points from the window of our room to reconstitute thrillingly the scenery, the drollery, the whimsical action of the tale. *There* was a demonstration I could feel important, votary and victim of the "scene," the scene and the "atmosphere" only, that I had been formed to be. That I called interesting lore—called it so at least to myself, though feeling it at the same time of course so little *directly* producible that I could perhaps even then have fronted this actually remote circumstance of my never having produced it till this moment. There abode in me, I may add, a sense that on any subject that did appeal and that so found me ready—such subjects being indeed as yet vague, but immensely suggestive of number—I should have grasped the confident chalk, welcomed the very biggest piece, not in the least have feared the blackboard. They were inscribed, alas for me, in no recognised course. I put my hand straight on another of them, none the less, if not on a whole group of others, in my ascent, each morning of the spring or the early summer sémestre, of the admirable old Rue de la Tour de Boël, pronounced Boisl, which, dusky, steep and tortuous, formed a short cut to that part of the Grand' Rue in which the Academy was then seated.

It was a foul and malodorous way—I sniff again, during the tepid weeks, its warm close air and that near presence of rank cheese which was in those days almost everywhere, for the nostril, the note of urban Switzerland; these things blessed me as I passed, for I passed straight to freedom and away from M. Galopin; they mixed with the benediction of the exquisite spring and the rapture, constantly renewed, though for too short a period, of my now substituting literary, or in other words romantic, studies for the pursuits of the Institution Rochette. I viewed them as literary, these new branches of research, though in truth they were loose enough and followed on loose terms. My dear parents, as if to make up to me, characteristically, for my recent absurd strain to no purpose, allowed me now the happiest freedom, left me to attend such lectures as I preferred, only desiring that I should attend several a week, and content—cherished memory that it makes of their forms with me—that these should involve neither examinations nor reports. The Academic authorities, good-natured in the extreme and accustomed to the alien amateur, appear to have been equally content, and I was but too delighted, on such lines, to attend anything or everything. My whole impression now, with my self-respect re-established, was of something exquisite: I was put to the proof about nothing; I deeply enjoyed the confidence shown in my taste, not to say in my honour, and I sat out lecture after lecture as I might have sat out drama, alternate tragedy and comedy, beautifully performed—the professor in each case figuring the hero, and the undergraduates, much more numerous, though not in general maturer than those of the Institution, where I had been, to my perception, every one's junior, partaking in an odd fashion of the nature at once of troupe and spectators. The scientific subjects, in a large suggestive way, figured tragedy, I seemed to feel, and I pushed this form to the point of my following, for conscience' sake, though not with the last regularity, lurid demonstrations, as they affected me, on anatomy and physiology; these in turn leading to my earnest view, at the Medical School, of the dissection of a *magnifique gendarme*—which ordeal brought me to a stand. It was by the literary and even by the philosophic *leçons* that the office of bright comedy was discharged, on the same liberal lines; at the same time that I blush to remember with how base a blankness I must have several times listened to H. F. Amiel, admirable writer, analyst, moralist. His name and the fact of his having been then a mild grave oracle of the shrine are all that remain with me (I was fit to be coupled with my cousin Anne King, named in another place, who, on the same Genevese scene, had had early lessons from the young Victor Cherbuliez, then with all his music in him, and was to live to mention to me that he had been for her "like any one else"); the shrine, not to say the temple itself, shining for me truly, all that season, with a mere confounding blur of light. Was it an effect of my intensity of reaction from what I had hated? was it to a great extent the beguiling beauty of a wonderful Swiss spring, into which all things else soothingly melted, becoming together a harmony without parts?—whatever the cause, I owed it to some accident only to be described, I think, as happy, that I moved, those three months, in an acutely enjoying and yet, as would at present appear, a but scantly comparing or distinguishing maze of the senses and the fancy. So at least, to cover this so thin report of my intelligence and my sum of acquisition and retention, I am reduced to supposing.

What essentially most operated, I make out, however, was that force of a renewed sense of William's major activity which always made the presumption of any degree of importance or success fall, with a sort of ecstasy of resignation, from my own so minor. Whatever he might happen to be doing made him so interesting about it, and indeed, with the quickest concomitance, about everything else, that what I probably most did, all the while, was but to pick up, and to the effect not a bit of starving but quite of filling myself, the crumbs of his feast and the echoes of his life. His life, all this Geneva period, had been more of a feast than mine, and I recall the sense of this that I had got on the occasion of my accompanying him, by his invitation, toward the end of our stay, to a students' celebration or carouse, which was held at such a distance from the town, at a village or small bourg, up in the Vaud back-country, that we had, after a considerable journey by boat and in heterogeneous and primitive conveyances, tightly packed, to spend two nights there. The Genevese section of the Société de Zoffingue, the great Swiss students' organisation for brotherhood and beer, as it might summarily be defined, of which my brother had become a member, was to meet there certain other sections, now vague to me, but predominantly from the German-speaking Cantons, and, holding a Commerce, to toast their reunion in brimming bowls. It had been thought the impression might amuse, might even interest me—for it was not denied that there were directions, after all, in which I *could* perhaps take notice; and this was doubtless what after a fashion happened, though I felt out in the cold (and all the more that the cold at the moment happened to be cruel), as the only participant in view not crowned with the charming white cap of the society, becoming to most young heads, and still less girt with the parti-coloured ribbon or complementary scarf, which set off even the shabby—for shabbiness considerably figured. I participated vaguely but not too excludedly; I suffered from cold, from hunger and from scant sleeping-space; I found the Bernese and the Bâlois strange representatives of the joy of life, some of them the finest gothic grotesques—but the time none the less very long; all of which, however, was in the day's work if I might live, by the imagination, in William's so adaptive skin. To see that he was adaptive, was initiated, and to what a happy and fruitful effect, that, I recollect, was my measure of content; which was filled again to overflowing, as I have hinted, on my finding him so launched at the Academy after our stretch of virtual separation, and just fancying, with a freedom of fancy, even if with a great reserve of expression, how much he might be living and learning, enjoying and feeling, amid work that was the right work for him and comrades, consecrated comrades, that at the worst weren't the wrong. What was not indeed, I always asked myself, the right work for him, or the right thing of any kind, that he took up or looked at or played with?—failing, as I did more than ever at the time I speak of, of the least glimpse of his being below an occasion. Whatever he played with or worked at entered at once into his intelligence, his talk, his humour, as with the action of colouring-matter dropped into water or that of the turning-on of a light within a window. Occasions waited on him, had always done so, to my view; and there he was, that springtime, on a level with them all: the effect of which recognition had much, had more than aught else, to say to the charming silver haze just then wrapped about everything of which I was conscious. He had formed two or three young friendships that were to continue and to which even the correspondence of his later years testifies; with which it may have had something to do that the Swiss *jeunesse* of the day was, thanks to the political temperature then prevailing, in a highly inflamed and exalted state, and particularly sensitive to foreign sympathy, however platonic, with the national fever. It was the hour at which the French Emperor was to be paid by Victor Emmanuel the price of the liberation of Lombardy; the cession of Nice and Savoie were in the air—with the consequence, in the Genevese breast, of the new immediate neighbourhood thus constituted for its territory. Small Savoie was to be replaced, close against it, by enormous and triumphant France, whose power to absorb great mouthfuls was being so strikingly exhibited. Hence came much hurrying to and fro, much springing to arms, in the way of exercise, and much flocking to the standard—"demonstrations," in other words, of the liveliest; one of which I recall as a huge tented banquet, largely of the white caps, where I was present under my brother's wing, and, out of a sea of agitated and vociferous young heads, sprang passionate protests and toasts and vows and declaimed verses, a storm of local patriotism, though a flurry happily short-lived.

All this was thrilling, but the term of it, by our consecrated custom, already in view; we were transferred at a bound, for the rest of that summer of 1860, to the care, respectively, of a pair of kindly pedagogues at Bonn-am-Rhein; as to which rapid phase I find remembrance again lively, with a letter or two of William's to reinforce it. Yet I first pick up as I pass several young lines from Geneva, and would fain pick up too the drawing that accompanied them—this by reason of the interest of everything of the sort, without exception, that remains to us from his hand. He at a given moment, which came quite early, as completely ceased to ply his pencil as he had in his younger time earnestly and curiously exercised it; and this constitutes exactly the interest of his case. No stroke of it that I have recovered but illustrates his aptitude for drawing, his possible real mastery of the art that was yet, in the light of other interests, so utterly to drop from him; and the example is rare of being so finely capable only to become so indifferent. It was thanks to his later indifference that he made no point of preserving what he had done—a neglect that, still more lucklessly, communicated itself to his circle; so that we also let things go, let them again and again stray into the desert, and that what might be reproducible is but the handful of scraps that have happened not to perish. "Mother," he writes to his father in absence, "does nothing but sit and cry for you. She refuses to associate with us and has one side of the room to herself. She and the Aunt are now in the Aunt's room. Wilky and Bobby, at home for the day, are at church. It is a hard grey day. H. is telling a story to Louis Osborne, and I will try to make a sketch of them. There has been a terrible bise; the two Cornhill Magazines have come; Mrs. Thomas has been too sick to be at dinner, and we have seen something of some most extraordinary English people." Mrs. Thomas, of New York, was a handsome American widow with handsome children, all from the Avenue Gabriel in Paris, and with the boys enjoying life, among many little compatriots, at the admired establishment of M. Haccius, even as our small brothers were doing at that of M. Maquelin; yet with their destiny of ultimate Europeanisation, of finally complete absorption into the French system, already rather written for them—as a like history, for like foredoomed young subjects, was in those years beginning

Louis Osborne. Sketch from a letter of William James (page 264).

to be prefigured, through marriages of daughters and other such beguilements, almost wherever one looked. The extraordinary English people were perhaps an amiable family of whom I retain an image as conversing with our parents at the season when the latter were in their prompt flush of admiration for George Eliot's first novel, Adam Bede, then just given to the world and their copy of which they had rejoicingly lent to their fellow Anglo-Saxons. I catch again the echo of their consternation on receiving it back with the remark that all attempt at an interest in such people, village carpenters and Methodists, had proved vain—for that style of Anglo-Saxon; together with that of my own excited wonder about such other people, those of the style in question, those somehow prodigiously presented by so rare a delicacy, so proud a taste, and made thus to irradiate a strange historic light. It *referred* them, and to a social order, making life more interesting and more various; even while our clear democratic air, that of our little family circle, quivered as with the monstrosity. It might, this note that made us, in the parlance of to-day, sit up, fairly have opened to me that great and up to then unsuspected door of the world from which the general collection of monstrosities, its existence suddenly brought home to us, would doubtless stretch grandly away. The story I told Louis Osborne has quite passed from me, but not little Louis himself, an American child of the most charming and appealing intelligence, marked by some malady that was more or less permanently to cripple, or was even cruelly to destroy him, and whom it was a constant joy to aspire to amuse. His mother was schooling her elder son in the company of our own brothers, his father having established them all at Geneva that he might go for a tour in the East. Vivid to me still is the glimpse I happened to get one Sunday betimes of the good Maquelin couple, husband and wife, in deep mourning —a touch of the highest decency—who had come, with faces a yard long, to announce to Mrs. Osborne the death of her husband in the Holy Land, communicated to them, by slow letter, in the first instance. With little Louis on one's knee one didn't at all envy M. and Madame Maquelin; and than this small faint phantom of sociable helpless little listening Louis none more exquisite hovers before me.

With which mild memories thus stands out for me too the

lively importance, that winter, of the arrival, from the first number, of the orange-covered earlier Cornhill—the thrill of each composing item of that first number especially recoverable in its intensity. Is anything like that thrill possible to-day—for a submerged and blinded and deafened generation, a generation so smothered in quantity and number that discrimination, under the gasp, has neither air to breathe nor room to turn round? Has any like circumstance now conceivably the value, to the charmed attention, so far as anything worth naming attention, or any charm for it, is anywhere left, of the fact that Trollope's Framley Parsonage there began?—let alone the still other fact that the Roundabout Papers did and that Thackeray thus appeared to us to guarantee personally, intimately, with a present audibility that was as the accent of good company, the new relation with him and with others of company not much worse, as they then seemed, that such a medium could establish. To speak of these things, in truth, however, is to feel the advantage of being able to live back into the time of the more sovereign periodical appearances much of a compensation for any reduced prospect of living forward. For these appearances, these strong time-marks in such stretches of production as that of Dickens, that of Thackeray, that of George Eliot, had in the first place simply a genial weight and force, a direct importance, and in the second a command of the permeable air and the collective sensibility, with which nothing since has begun to deserve comparison. They were enrichments of life, they were *large* arrivals, these particular renewals of supply—to which, frankly, I am moved to add, the early Cornhill giving me a pretext, even the frequent examples of Anthony Trollope's fine middle period, looked at in the light of old affection and that of his great heavy shovelfuls of testimony to constituted English matters; a testimony of course looser and thinner than Balzac's to *his* range of facts, but charged with something of the big Balzac authority. These various, let alone numerous, deeper-toned strokes of the great Victorian clock were so many steps in the march of our age, besides being so many notes, full and far-reverberating, of our having high company to keep—high, I mean, to cover all the ground, in the sense of the genial pitch of it. So it was, I remember too, that our parents spoke of their memory of the successive surpassing attestations of the contemporary presence of Scott; to which we might have replied, and doubtless after no great space began to reply, that our state, and even their later one, allowing for a certain gap, had nothing to envy any other. I witnessed, for that matter, with all my senses, young as I was, the never-to-be-equalled degree of difference made, for what may really be called the world-consciousness happily exposed to it, by the prolonged "coming-out" of The Newcomes, yellow number by number, and could take the general civilised participation in the process for a sort of basking in the light of distinction. The process repeated itself for some years under other forms and stimuli, but the merciless change was to come—so that through whatever bristling mazes we may now pick our way it is not to find them open into any such vales of Arcady. My claim for our old privilege is that we did then, with our pace of dignity, proceed from vale to vale.

II

My point at any rate, such as it is, would be that even at the age I had reached in 1860 something of the happier time still lingered—the time in which a given product of the press might have a situation and an aspect, a considerability, so to speak, a circumscription and an *aura*; room to breathe and to show in, margin for the casting of its nets. The occasion at large was doubtless shrinking, one could note—shrinking like the unlet "house" on a night of grandest opera, but "standing room only" was not yet everywhere the sign, and the fine deliberate thing could here and there find its seat. I really indeed might have held it the golden age of letters still, and of their fond sister leisure, with that quiet swim into our ken on its appointed day, during our Bonn summer, of the charming Once a Week of the prime, the prime of George Meredith and Charles Reade and J. E. Millais and George du Maurier; which our father, to bridge our separation from him, sent us, from Paris and elsewhere, in prompt and characteristic relief of our plotted, our determined strict servitude to German, and to the embrace of the sweet slim essence of which the strain of one's muscles round a circular ton of advertisement was not a condition attached. I should like to say that I rioted, all that season, on the supreme German classics *and* on Evan Harrington, with Charles Reade's A Good Fight, the assured little prelude to The Cloister and the Hearth, thrown in; and I should indeed be ready to say it, were not the expression gross for the really hushed piety of my attitude during those weeks. It was perhaps not quite till then that I fully emerged from the black shadow of the École Préparatoire aux Écoles Spéciales, not quite till we had got off beyond the blest Rhine at Basle that I ceased to hear and feel all but just behind me, portentous perhaps of another spring, the cold breath of the monster. The guttery Bonn-Gasse was during those weeks of the year close and stale, and the house of our good Herr Doctor Humpert, professor at the Bonn Gymnasium, in which I shared a room with my brother Wilky, contracted and dim, as well as fragrant through a range of assaults that differed only in kind and not at all in number from those of the street itself; and yet I held the period and the whole situation idyllic—the slightly odd sense of which was one's being to that extent attuned to the life of letters and of (oh the great thing!) impressions "gone in for." To feel a unity, a character and a tone in one's impressions, to feel them related and all harmoniously coloured, that *was* positively to face the æsthetic, the creative, even, quite wondrously, the critical life and almost on the spot to commence author. They had begun, the impressions—that was what was the matter with them—to scratch quite audibly at the door of liberation, of extension, of projection; what they were *of* one more or less knew, but what they were *for* was the question that began to stir, though one was still to be a long time at a loss directly to answer it.

There, for the present, was the rub, the dark difficulty at which one could but secretly stare—secretly because one was somehow ashamed of its being there and would have quickly removed one's eyes, or tried to clear them, if caught in the act of watching. Impressions were not merely all right but were the dearest things in the world; only one would have gone to the stake rather than in the first place confessed to some of them, or in the second announced that one really lived by them and built on them. This failure then to take one's stand in the connection could but come from the troubled view that they were naught without a backing, a stout stiff hard-grained underside that would hold them together and of which the terrible name was simply science, otherwise learning, and learning exclusively by books, which were at once the most beautiful and the most dreadful things in the world, some of them right, strikingly, showily right, some of them disgracefully and almost unmentionably wrong, that is grossly irrelevant, as for instance a bound volume of Once a Week would be, but remarkable above all for overwhelming number and in general for defiance of comprehension. It was true that one had from time to time the rare adventure of one's surprise at understanding parts of them none the less—understanding more than a very little, more than much too little; but there was no practical support to speak of in that, even the most one could ever hope to understand being a mere drop in the bucket. Never did I quite strike it off, I think, that impressions might themselves *be* science—and this probably because I didn't then know them, when it came to the point, as anything but life. I knew them but by that collective and unpractical—many persons would have said that frivolous—name; which saw me little further. I was under the impression—this in fact the very liveliest of what might have been called the lot—that life and knowledge were simply mutual opposites, one inconsistent with the other; though hovered about, together, at the same time, by the anomaly that when knowledge impinged upon life, pushed against her, as it were, and drove her to the wall, it was all right, and such was knowledge's way and title; whereas when life played the like tricks with knowledge nothing but shame for the ruder, even if lighter, party could accrue. There was to come to me of course in time the due perception that neither was of the least use—use to myself—without the other; but meanwhile, and even for much after, the extreme embarrassment continued: to whichever of the opposites one gave one's self it was with a sense of all but basely sacrificing the other. However, the conflict and the drama involved in the question at large was doubtless what was to make consciousness—under whichever of the two names one preferred to entertain it—supremely intense and interesting.

This then is by way of saying that the idyll, as I have called it, of the happy juncture I glanced at a moment back came from the fact that I didn't at all know how much I was living, and meanwhile quite supposed I was considerably learning. When, rising at some extraordinary hour of the morning, I went forth through the unawakened town (and the Germans, at that time, heaven knows, were early afoot too), and made for the open country and the hill, in particular, of the neighbouring Venusberg, long, low and bosky, where the dews were still fresh and ancient mummies of an old cloister, as I remember it, somewhere perched and exposed, I was doing, to my sense, an attuned thing; attuned, that is, to my coming home to bend double over Schiller's Thirty Years' War in the strenuous spirit that would keep me at it, or that would vary it with Goethe's Wahlverwandtschaften, till late in the warm afternoon. I found German prose much tougher than the verse, and thereby more opposed to "life," as to which I of course couldn't really shake off the sense that it might be worked as infinitely comprehensive, comprehensive even of the finest discriminations against it. The felicity, present but naturally unanalysed, was that the whole thing, our current episode, *was* exactly comprehensive of life, presenting it in particular as characteristically German, and therein freshly vivid—with the great vividness that, by our parents' vague wish, we were all three after or out for; in spite of our comparatively restricted use, in those days, of these verbal graces. Such therefore was the bright unity of our experience, or at least of my own share in it—this luck that, through the intensity of my wanting it to, all consciousness, all my own immediate, *tasted* German, to the great and delightful quickening of my imagination. The quickening was of course no such matter as I was to know nearly ten years later on plunging for the first time over the Alps into Italy; but, letting alone that I was then so much older, I had wondered about Italy, to put it embracingly, far more than I was constitutionally capable of wondering about Germany. It was enough for me at Bonn that I felt no lack of appetite—had for the time all the illusion of being on the way to something; to something, I mean, with which the taste of German might somehow *directly* mix itself. Every aspect and object round about was a part, at all events, of the actual mixture; and when on drowsy afternoons, not a little interspaced indeed, I attempted the articulate perusal of Hermann and Dorothea with our good Professor, it was like dreaming, to the hum of bees, if not to the aftertaste of "good old Rhenish," in some homely fruity eighteenth-century garden.

The good old Rhenish is no such false note in this reconstitution; I seem to see the Frau Doctorin and her ancient mildly-scowling sister Fräulein Stamm, who reminded me of Hepzibah Pyncheon in The House of the Seven Gables, perpetually wiping green hock-glasses and holding them up to our meagre light, as well as setting out long-necked bottles, with rather chalky cakes, in that forward section of our general eating-and-living-room which formed our precinct of reception and conversation. The unbroken space was lighted at either end, from street and court, and its various effects of tempered shade or, frankly speaking, of rather greasy gloom, amid which the light touch of elegance gleamed but from the polish of the glasses and the sloping shoulders of their bottle, comes back to me as the view of an intensely internal interior.

I recall how oppressively in that apartment, how congestedly, as in some cage of which the wires had been papered over, I felt housed and disconnected; I scarce then, I think, knew what the matter was, but it could only have been that in all those summer weeks, to the best of my belief, no window was ever once opened. Still, there was the scene, the thick, the much-mixed chiaroscuro through which the two ladies of the family emerged from an exiguous retreat just off the back end of the place with ample platters of food; the almost impenetrable dusk of the middle zone, where the four or five of us, seated with our nutcracker-faced pastor, conveyed the food to our mouths with a confidence mainly borrowed from the play of his own deep-plunging knife; and then the forward, the festal extension, the privilege of occasionally lingering in which, or of returning to it for renewed refreshment, was a recognition both of our general minding of our business upstairs—left as we were to thumb our Flügel's Dictionary by the hour so long as we invoked no other oracle. Our drowsy Doctor invited no such approach; he smiled upon us as if unseen forefingers of great force had been inserted for the widening of his mouth at the corners, and I had the sense of his not quite knowing what to make of our being so very gently barbaric, or rather so informally civilised; he safely housed and quite rankly fed us, guided us to country walks and to the swimming-baths by the Rhine-side, introduced us to fruit-gardens where, on payment of the scantest tribute, we were suffered to consume off-hand bushels of cherries, plums and pears; suffered us to ascend the Drachenfels and to partake of coffee at Rolandseck and in other friendly open-air situations; but flung his gothic shadow as little as possible over my so passive page at least, and took our rate of acquisition savingly for granted.

This, in the optimism of the hour, I have no memory of resenting; the page, though slow, managed at the same time to be stirring, and I asked no more of any one or anything but that they should be with all due gothicism whatever they most easily might. The long vistas of the beeches and poplars on the other side of the Rhine, after we had crossed by the funicular ferry, gothically rustled and murmured: I fancied their saying perpetually "We are German woods, we are German woods—which makes us very wonderful, do you know? and unlike any others: don't you feel the spell of the very sound of us and of the beautiful words, 'Old German woods, old German woods,' even if you can't tell why?" I couldn't altogether tell why, but took everything on trust as mystically and valuably gothic—valuably because ministering with peculiar directness, as I gathered, to culture. I was in, or again I was "out," in my small way, for culture; which seemed quite to come, come from everywhere at once, with the most absurd conciliatory rush, pitifully small as would have been any list of the sources I tapped. The beauty was in truth that everything was a source, giving me, by the charmingest breach of logic, more than it at all appeared to hold; which was exactly what had not been the case at the Institution Rochette, where things had appeared, or at least had pretended, to hold so much more than they gave. The oddity was that about us now everything—everything but the murmur of the German woods and the great flow and magic name of the Rhine—was more ugly than beautiful, tended in fact to say at every turn: "You shall suffer, yes, indeed you *are* doing so (stick up for your right to!) in your sense of form; which however is quite compatible with culture, is really one of the finest parts of it, and may decidedly prove to you that you're getting it." I hadn't, in rubbing, with whatever weakness, against French and, so far as might be, against France, and in sinking, very sensibly, more and more into them, particularly felt that I was getting it *as* such; what I was getting as such was decidedly rather my famous "life," and without so much as thinking of the degree, with it all, of the valuable and the helpful.

Life meanwhile I had a good deal of at my side in the person of my brother Wilky, who, as I have had occasion elsewhere to say, contrived in those years to live, or to have every appearance of so doing, with an immediacy that left me far in the lurch. I was always still wondering how, while he had solved the question simply *ambulando*, which was for him but by the merest sociable stroll. This represented to me success—success of a kind, but such an assured kind—in a degree that was my despair; and I have never forgotten how, that summer, when the Herr Doctor did look in, did settle down a little to have the bristling page out with us, Wilky's share of the hour took on the spot the form of his turning at once upon our visitor the tables of earnest inquiry. He delighted, after this tribute of eagerness, to meet the Doctor's interrogative advance; but the communication so made was of anything and everything except the fruit of his reading (the act of reading was inhuman and repugnant to him), and I amazedly noted while I nursed my small hoard that anything he offered did in the event quite as well: he could talk with such charm, such drollery of candour, such unexpectedness of figure, about what he had done and what he hadn't—or talk at least before it, behind it and beside it. We had three or four house-companions, youths from other places attending the Gymnasium and committed to our Professor's care, as to whom I could somehow but infer that they were, each in his personal way, inordinately gothic—which they had to be to supply to my mind a relation, or a substitute for a relation, with them; whereas my younger brother, without a scrap of a view of them, a grain of theory or formula, tumbled straight into their confidence all round. Our air for *him* was by just so much life as it couldn't have dreamed of being culture, and he was so far right that when the son of the house and its only child, the slim and ardent Theodor, who figured to me but as a case of such classic sensibility, of the Lieder or the Werther sort, as might have made, with the toss of a yellow lock or the gleam of a green blouse, the image for an Uhland or a Heine stanza, had imparted to him an intention of instant suicide under some resentment of parental misconception, he had been able to use dissuasion, or otherwise the instinct of then most freely fraternising, with a success to which my relish for so romantic a stroke as charmingly in Theodor's character and setting mightn't at all have attained. There is a small something of each of us in a passage of an ingenuous letter addressed by him from the midst of these conditions to his parents. I fondly catch, I confess, at any of these recoverable lights; finding them at the best too scant for my commemorative purpose.

> Willy got his photograph this morning after three hours' hard work. From the post-office he was sent to the custom-house, and there was obliged to sign his name and to go to some neighbouring bookstore to buy a seal. On returning to the custom-house he

> was sent back to the post-office to get some document or other. After obtaining this article he turned his steps once more to the custom-house, where an insolent officer told him he must wait an hour. W. informed him that he would return at the end of the hour, and accordingly for the third time went to the C.H., and was conducted by the clerk to a cellar where the packages were kept, and there told to take off his hat. He obeyed, raging, and then was a fourth time sent to the P.O.—this time to pay money. Happily he is now in possession of his property. H. and he took a walk this afternoon to a fruit-garden, where plums, cherries, gooseberries and currants were abundant. After half an hour's good work H. left W. finishing merely the plums—the cherry and gooseberry course to come later. He was so enchanted that he thought H. a great fool to leave so soon. How does Paris now strike you? It can't be as nice as Bonn. You had better write to Bob.

Bob, our youngest brother, had been left at Geneva with excellent M. Maquelin and was at that time *en course*, over the Alps, with this gentleman and their young companions; a most desirable, delicious excursion, which I remember following in envious fancy, as it included a descent to the Italian Lakes and a push on as far as Genoa. In reference to which excursion I cull a line or two from a faded scrap of a letter addressed a little later by this youngest of us to his "Beloved Brother" William. "This is about our Grande Course. We started at 5 o'clock in the morning with our faces and hands all nicely washed and our nails clean. The morning was superb, and as we waited in the court the soft balmy air of the mountains came in bringing with it the melodious sound of the rappel for breakfast. This finished we bade adieu, and I could see the emotions of the kind and ever-watchful Madame Maquelin as a few silent drops trickled down her fair cheeks. We at last arrived at the boat, where we met Mr. Peters, a portly gentleman from the city of Philadelphia, with his two sweet sons, one twelve, the other seven years old, the eldest coming from Mr. E.'s school with no very good opinion of the principal—saying he had seen him in a state of tightness several times during his stay there." Mr. Peters appears to have been something of a pessimist, for, when at a later stage "it began to rain hard, and half the road was a foot deep in water, and the cocher had stopped somewhere to get lanterns and had at the same time indulged in certain potations which didn't make him drive any the straighter," this gentleman "insinuated that we had all better have been with our mothers." The letter records at some length the early phases of the affair, but under the weight of the vision of Italy it rather breaks down and artlessly simplifies. "Genoa is a most lively town, and there is a continual swarm of sailors in the street. We visited several palaces, among others that of Victor Emmanuel, which is very fine, and the fruit is very cheap. We stayed there several days, but at last started for Turin, where we spent a Sunday—a place I didn't much like, I suppose because of that reason. We left Turin the next day on foot, but lost our road and had to come back." I recover even in presence of these light accents my shade of wonder at this odd chance that made the least developed of us the subject of what seemed to me even then a privilege of the highest intensity; and there again keeps it company my sense, through all the after years, that this early glimpse of the blest old Italy, almost too early though it appears to have but just missed being, might have done something towards preparing or enriching for Bob the one little plot of consciousness in which his deeply troubled life was to find rest. He was in the event also fondly to aim at painting, like two of his brothers; but whereas they were to fumble with the lock, in their very differing degree, only in those young years, he was to keep at it most as he grew older, though always with a perfect intelligence of the inevitable limits of the relation, the same intelligence that was so sharp and sad, so extraordinarily free and fine and detached in fact, as play of mind, play of independent talk and of pen, for the limits of his relation to many other matters. Singularly intelligent all round, yet with faculties that had early declined any consummation of acquaintance with such training as under a different sort of pressure he might have enjoyed, he had an admirable hand and eye, and I have known no other such capacity for absorbing or storing up the minutest truths and shades of landscape fact and giving them out afterward, in separation from the scene, with full assurance and felicity. He could do this still better even than he cared to do; I for my part cared much more that he should than he ever did himself, and then it was, I dare say, that I made the reflection: "He took in the picture of Italy, with his firm hard gift, having the chance while William and I were still, comparatively, small untouched and gaping barbarians; and it should always be in him to do at some odd fine moment a certain honour to that." I held to it that that sensibility had played in him more than by any outward measure at the time; which was perhaps indeed one of the signs within me of the wasteful habit or trick of a greater feeling for people's potential propriety or felicity or full expression than they seemed able to have themselves. At all events I was absolutely never to cease to remember for Bob, through everything—and there was much and of the most agitated and agitating—that he had been dipped as a boy into the sacred stream; to some effect which, thanks to two or three of his most saving and often so amusing sensibilities, the turbid sea of his life might never quite wash away.

William had meanwhile come to Bonn with us, but was domiciled with another tutor, younger and fairer and more of the world, above all more ventilated and ventilating, Herr Stromberg, whose defect might in fact have seemed that, with his constant exhibition of the stamp received by him from the writings of Lord Macaulay, passages of which he could recite by heart, and the circumstance that his other pupil, William's comrade for a time, was of unmitigatedly English, that is of quasi-Byronic association, he didn't quite rise to the full gothic standard. Otherwise indeed our brother moved on the higher plane of light and air and ease, and above all of enjoyed society, that we felt he naturally must. Present to me yet is the thrill of learning from him that his English fellow-pupil was the grandson, if I remember rightly the degree of descent, of Mary Chaworth, Byron's "first love," and my sense afterwards, in gaping at young Mr. Musters himself, that this independently romantic contact would have been more to my own private purpose at least than the most emphasised gothicism. None the less do I regain it as a part of my current vision that Frau Stromberg, who was young and fair, wrote tragedies as well as made pancakes—which were served to each consumer double, a thick confiture within being the reason of this luxuriance, and being also a note beyond our experience in the Bonn-Gasse; and that with the printed five acts of a certain "Cleopatra" before me, read aloud in the first instance to her young inmates and by my brother passed on to me, I lost myself in the view of

I scarce knew what old-world Germanic grace, positively, or little court-city practice of the theatre: these things so lived in the small thick pamphlet, "grey paper with blunt type" and bristling, to my discomfiture, with descriptive stage directions, vast dense bracketed tracts, gothic enough in all conscience, as to which I could already begin to wonder whether such reinforcements of presentation proved more for or against the true expressional essence of the matter; for or against, that is, there being nothing at all so dramatic, so chargeable with meaning and picture, as speech, of whatever sort, made perfect. Such speculations, I may parenthesise, might well have been fostered, and doubtless were, by an impression that I find commemorated in a few lines of a letter of my father's to a friend in America—he having brought us on to Bonn, introduced us to our respective caretakers and remained long enough to have had an evening at the theatre, to which we accompanied him. "We had Ristori to play Mary Stuart for us last night—which was the vulture counterfeiting Jenny Wren. Every little while the hoarse exulting voice, the sanguinary beak, the lurid leer of menace, and the relentless talons looked forth from the feathery mass and sickened you with disgust. She would do Elizabeth better." I recall the performance in every feature, as well as my absence of such reserves, though quite also the point to which I was impressed by the utterance of them; not that it didn't leave me at the same time free to feel that the heroine of history represented could scarce have been at all a dove-like, much less a wren-like person. She had indeed on Madame Ristori's showing prodigious resources of militant mobility—of what in fact would be called to-day mobilisation. Several years later on I was to see the actress play the same part in America; and then, if I am not mistaken, was to note scarce more than one point; the awful effect on *any* histrionic case, even on one so guardedly artful as hers, of having been dragged round the globe and forced home, so far as might be, to imperfect comprehensions. The big brush had come fairly to daub the canvas. Let the above, however, serve in particular to lead in as many examples of my father's singularly striking and personal habit of expression and weight of thought as these pages may find room for.

The one difficulty is that to open that general door into the limbo of old letters, charged with their exquisite ghostly appeal, is almost to sink into depths of concession. I yield here for instance to the claim of a page or two from William, just contemporary and addressed to our parents in Paris—and yield perhaps but for no better reason than that of the small historic value or recoverable charm that I am moved to find in its illustrative items. The reference of its later lines is to a contemporary cousin, young and blooming, by whom I have already ever so lightly brushed[1] and who figured quite with the grand air on our young horizon; the only daughter of the brightest of the Albany uncles (by that time lost and mourned) now on the tour of Europe with a pair of protective elders for her entrance upon life and at that hour surrounding our parents, her uncle and aunt, with a notably voluminous rustle of fresh Paris clothes, the far-spreading drapery of the more and more draped and flounced and "sloped" second Empire. This friendly frou-frou almost reached our ears, so sociable for us was every sound of her, in our far-off Rhineland. She was with her stature and shape the finest possible person to carry clothes, and I thought of her, with a revival of the old yearning envy, as now quite transcendently orphaned and bereft, dowered, directed and equipped.

> Your hearts, I know, would have been melted if you had had a view of us this Sunday morning. I went directly after breakfast for the boys, and though H. had an "iron stomach-ache," as he called it, we went off together to that low wooded hill which the Aunt could see from her window when you were here, and walked about till dinner-time, H. being all the while in great pain. In one part we found a platform with a stone bench commanding a view of the whole valley, and, as we were rather tired, sat down on it, H. and Wilky each with a Once a Week, while I tried to draw the view in my pocket-book. We wondered what our beloved parents were doing at that moment, 11.30, and thought you must all have been in your salon, Alice at the window with her eyes fixed on her novel, but eating some rich fruit that Father has just brought in for her from the Palais Royal, and the lovely Mother and Aunt in armchairs, their hands crossed in front of them, listening to Father, who walks up and down talking of the

[1] *A Small Boy and Others*, 1913.

superiority of America to these countries after all, and how much better it is we should have done with them. We wished, oh we wished we could have been with you to join in the conversation and partake of the fruit. We got up from the seat and went on with a heavy sigh, but in a way so fraternal, presenting such a sweet picture of brotherly unitedness and affection, that it would have done you good to see us.

And so it is every day that we meet for our shorter walks and talks. The German gets on slowly, but I notice a very marked improvement in talking. I have not kept at it so hard this last week as before, and I prevent H. from working his eyes out, which he seems on the whole rather less inclined to do. I am going to read as much as I can the rest of the time we are here. It seems a mere process of soaking, requiring no mental effort, but only time and steady patience. My room is very comfortable now I've got used to it, and I have a pair of slippers of green plush heavy and strong enough to last all my life and then be worn by my children. The photograph of our Zoffingen group has come, which gives me a moustache big enough for three lifeguardsmen. Tell us something more about Mary Helen. How long does she expect to stay in Europe, and who is this Dr. Adams—the man she is engaged to? She directs me to write to her in his care—so that I wish you would ask her, as she says she hopes to meet me, whether I shall still address her as Miss James? Of course it would be painful, but I think I could do it if Adams weren't there. Let the delicious little grey-eyed Alice be locked up alone on the day after the receipt of this with paper and envelopes to write a letter unassisted, uncorrected and unpunctuated to her loving brothers, who would send her novels and peaches if they could. What a blessing it is to have such parents, such a perfect Mother and magnificent Father and dear good Aunt and splendid little Sister!

I may mention that Mary Helen was not "engaged" to the gentleman above-mentioned, and was eventually to marry the late Alfred Grymes, originally of Louisiana. Also that a letter subsequent to this, apparently of the first days in September, sounds to his father the first note of my brother's definite personal preference, as he seemed lately and increasingly, though not in conditions markedly propitious, to have become aware of it, for an adoption of the "artistic career." It was an odd enough circumstance, in respect to the attested blood in our veins, that no less than three of our father's children, with two of his grandsons to add to these, and with a collateral addendum representing seven, in all, of our grandfather's, William James's, descendants in three generations, should have found the artistic career in general and the painter's trade in particular irresistibly solicit them.

I wish you would as you promised set down as clearly as you can on paper what your idea of the nature of Art *is*, because I do not, probably, understand it fully, and should like to have it presented in a form that I might think over at my leisure. I wish you would do so as fully as you conveniently can, so that I may ruminate it—and I won't say more about it till I have heard from you again. As for what your last letter did contain, what can I do but thank you for every word of it and assure you that they went to the right spot. Having such a Father with us, how can we be other than in some measure worthy of him?—if not perhaps as eminently so as the distance leads his fond heart to imagine. I never value him so much as when I am away from him. At home I see only his striking defects, but here he seems all perfection, and I wonder as I write why I didn't cherish him more when he was beside me. I beg darling old Mother's forgiveness too for the rude and dastardly way in which I snub her, and the Aunt for the impatience and violence I have always shown her. I shall be a perfect sherry-cobbler to both of them, and to the small Alice too, young as she may be for such treats.

I have just got home from dining with the boys and their Humperts; where I found the Doctor as genial as ever and the two old ladies perfect characters for Dickens. They have been so shut out from the world and melting together so long by the kitchen fire that the minds of both have become fused into one, and then seem to constitute a sort of two-bodied individual. I never saw anything more curious than the way they sit mumbling together at the end of the table, each using simultaneously the same comment if anything said at our end strikes their ear. H. pegs away pretty stoutly, but I don't think you need worry about him. He and Wilky appear to get on in great harmony and enliven themselves occasionally by brotherly trials of strength, quite good-natured, in their room, when excess of labour has made them sleepy or heavy. In these sometimes one, sometimes the other is victorious. They often pay me a visit here while I am dressing, which of course is highly convenient—and I have more than once been with *them* early enough to be present at Wilky's tumble out of bed and consequent awakening, with the call on the already-at-work H.:

"Why the mischief didn't you stop me?" Wilky and I walked to Rolandseck yesterday afternoon, and after a furious race back to the station found ourselves too late for the train by a second. So we took a boat and rowed down here, which was delightful. We are going to put H. through a splashing good walk daily. A thousand thanks to the cherry-lipped, apricot-nosed, double-chinned little Sister for her strongly dashed-off letter, which inflamed the hearts of her lonely brothers with an intense longing to smack her celestial cheeks.

III

I HAVE before me another communication of about the same moment, a letter addressed to his father in Paris within that month; from which, in spite of its lively interest as I hold, I cull nothing—and precisely because of that interest, which prescribes for it a later appearance in conditions in which it may be given entire. William is from this season on, to my sense, so livingly and admirably reflected in his letters, which were happily through much of his career both numerous and highly characteristic, that I feel them particularly plead, in those cases in which they most testify to his personal history, for the separate gathered presentation that happily awaits them. *There* best may figure the serious and reasoned reply drawn from him by some assuredly characteristic enough communication of our parent's own in respect to his declared preference for a painter's life over any other. Lost is this original and, in the light of later matters, sufficiently quaint declaration, and lost the paternal protest answered by my brother from Bonn and anything *but* infelicitous, on its side, so far as the truer apprehension went, under the showing of the time to come. The only thing was that our father had a wonderful way of being essentially right without being practically or, as it were, vulgarly, determinant, and that this relegation of his grounds of contention to the sphere of the non-immediate, the but indirectly urgent, from the point of view of the thing really to *do*, couldn't but often cause impatience in young breasts conscious of gifts or desires or ideals of which the very sign and warrant, the truth they were known by, was that they were susceptible of application. It was in no world of close application that our wondrous parent moved, and his indifference at the first blush to the manifestation of special and marketable talents and faculties, restlessly outward purposes of whatever would-be "successful" sort, was apt to be surpassable only by his delight subsequently taken in our attested and visible results, the very fruits of application; as to which the possibility, perhaps even the virtual guarantee, hadn't so much left him cold in advance as made him adversely and "spiritually" hot. The sense of that word was the most living thing in the world for him—to the point that the spiritual simply meant to him the practical and the successful, so far as he could get into touch with such denominations, or so far, that is, as he could face them or care for them *a priori.* Fortunately, as he had observational powers of the happiest, perceptions—perceptions of character and value, perceptions of relation and effect, perceptions in short of the whole—turned to the ground sensibly beneath our feet, as well as a splendid, an extraordinarily animated and, so far as he himself at least was concerned, guiding and governing soul, justice and generosity always eventually played up, the case worked itself happily out, and before we knew it he had found it quite the rightest of all cases, while we on our side had had the liveliest, and certainly the most amusing and civilising, moral or, as he would have insisted, spiritual recreation by the way.

My brother challenges him, with a beautiful deference, on the imputed damage to what might be best in a man by the professional pursuit of "art"—which he appears to have set forth with characteristic emphasis; and I take the example for probably one of the rarest in all the so copious annals of parental opposition to the æsthetic as distinguished from some other more respectable course. What was marked in our father's prime uneasiness in presence of any particular form of success we might, according to our lights as then glimmering, propose to invoke was that it bravely, or with such inward assurance, dispensed with any suggestion of an alternative. What we were to do instead was just to *be* something, something unconnected with specific doing, something free and uncommitted, something finer in short than being *that*, whatever it was, might consist of. The "career of art" has again and again been deprecated and denounced, on the lips of anxiety or authority, as a departure from the career of business, of industry and respectability, the so-called regular life, but it was perhaps never elsewhere to know dissuasion on the very ground of its failing to uplift the spirit in the ways it most pretends to. I must in fairness add, however, that if the uneasiness I here refer to continued, and quite by exception as compared with the development of other like episodes, during the whole of my brother's fortunately but little prolonged studio season, it was really because more alternatives swarmed before our parent's eyes, in the cause, than he could bring himself to simplify it by naming. He apprehended ever so deeply and tenderly his eldest son's other genius—as to which he was to be so justified; though this indeed was not to alter the fact that when afterwards that subject went in, by a wondrous reaction, for the pursuit of science, first of chemistry and then of anatomy and physiology and medicine, with psychology and philosophy at last piling up the record, the rich *malaise* at every turn characteristically betrayed itself, each of these surrenders being, by the measure of them in the parental imagination, so comparatively narrowing. That was the nearest approach to any plea for some other application of the spirit—that they *were* narrowing. When I myself, later on, began to "write" it was breathed upon me with the finest bewildering eloquence, with a power of suggestion in truth which I fairly now count it a gain to have felt play over me, that this too was narrowing. On the subsequent history of which high paradox no better comment could occur to me than my find of a passage in a letter long subsequently addressed to Mr. James T. Fields, then proprietor and editor of the Atlantic Monthly magazine—a letter under date of May 1868 and referring clearly to some published remarks on a certain young writer which did violence to the blessedly quick paternal prejudice.

> I had no sooner left your sanctum yesterday than I was afflicted to remember how I had profaned it by my unmeasured talk about poor H. Please forget it utterly. I don't know how it is with better men, but the parental sentiment is so fiendish a thing with me that if anyone attempt to slay my young, especially in a clandestine way, or out of a pious regard (*e.g.*) to the welfare of the souls comprised in the diocese of the Atlantic, I can't help devoting him bag and baggage to the infernal gods. I am not aware of my animus until I catch, as yesterday, a courteous ear; then the unholy fire flames forth at such a rate as to leave me no doubt on reflection where it was originally lighted.

Almost all my dear father is there, making the faded page to-day inexpressibly touching to me; his passionate tenderness, his infinite capacity for reaction on reaction, a force in him fruitful in so many more directions than any high smoothness of *parti-pris* could be, and his beautiful fresh individual utterance, always so stamped with the very whole of him. The few lines make for me, after all the years, a sort of silver key, so exquisitely fitting, to the treasure of living intercourse, of a domestic air quickened and infinitely coloured, comprised in all our younger time. The renewed sense of which, however, has carried me for the moment too far from the straighter line of my narrative.

The author of the young letter of which I have deferred presentation met in Paris, shortly after that date, the other party to the discussion; and the impression of the endless day of our journey, my elder and my younger brothers' and mine, from Bonn to that city, has scarcely faded from me. The railway service was so little then what it has become that I even marvel at our having made our connections between our early rise in the Bonn-Gasse and our midnight tumble into bed at the Hôtel des Trois Empereurs in the Place du Palais Royal; a still-felt rapture, a revelation of the Parisian idea of bed after the rude German conception, our sore discipline for so many weeks. I remember Cologne and its cathedral almost in the bland dawn, and our fresh start thence for Strasbourg, now clearly recognised, alas, as a start back to America, to which it had been of a sudden settled that we were, still with a fine inconsequence, to return. We had seen Cologne cathedral by excursion from Bonn, but we saw Strasbourg, to my sorrow until a far later occasion soothed it, only as a mild monster behind bars, that is above chimneys, housetops and fortifications; a loss not made up to me by other impressions or particulars, vivid and significant as I found myself none the less supposing several of these. Those were the September days in which French society, so far as it was of the Empire at least, moved more or less in its mass upon Homburg and Baden-Baden; and we met it in expressive samples, and in advance and retreat, during our incessant stops, those long-time old stops, unknown to the modern age, when everyone appeared to alight and walk about with the animation of prisoners suddenly pardoned, and ask for conveniences, and clamour for food, and get mixed with the always apparently still dustier people of opposite trains drawn up for the same purposes. We appeared to be concerned with none but first-class carriages, as an effect of which our own was partly occupied, the livelong day, by the *gens* of a noble French house as to which we thus had frequent revelations—a pair of footmen and a lady's maid, types of servile impudence taking its ease, who chattered by the hour for our wonderstruck ears, treating them to their first echo of the strange underworld, the sustaining vulgarity, of existences classified as "great." They opened vistas, and I remember how when, much later, I came to consider the designed picture, first in Edmond About and then in Alphonse Daudet, of fifty features symptomatic of the social pace at which the glittering régime hurried to its end, there came back to me the breath of this sidewind of the frenzied dance that we had caught during those numerous and so far from edifying hours in our fine old deep-seated compartment. The impression, I now at any rate perfectly recover, was one that could feed full enough any optimism of the appointedly modest condition. It was true that Madame la Marquise, who was young and good-natured and pretty without beauty, and unmistakably "great," exhaling from afar, as I encouraged myself to imagine, the scented air of the Tuileries, came on occasion and looked in on us and smiled, and even pouted, through her elegant patience; so that she at least, I recollect, caused to swim before me somehow such a view of happy privilege at the highest pitch as made me sigh the more sharply, even if the less professedly, for our turning our backs on the complex order, the European, fresh to me still, in which contrasts flared and flourished and through which discrimination could unexhaustedly riot—pointing so many more morals, withal, if that was the benefit it was supposed to be, than we should find pretexts for "on the other side." We were to fall as soon as we were at home again to reading the Revue des Deux Mondes—though doubtless again I should speak here, with any emphasis, but for myself; my chin, in Europe, had scarce risen to the level of that publication; but at Newport in Rhode Island, our next following place of sojourn, I speedily shot up so as quite to bend down to it: it took its place therewith as the very headspring of culture, a mainstay in exile, and as opening wide in especial the doors of that fictive portrayal of a society which put a price, for the brooding young reader, on cases, on *cadres*, in the Revue parlance, already constituted and propitiously lighted. Then it was that the special tension of the dragged-out day from Cologne to Paris proved, on the absurdest scale, a preparation, justified itself as a vivid point of reference: I was to know what the high periodical meant when I encountered in its *études de mœurs* the blue-chinned corruptible, not to say corrupt, *larbin* and the smart soubrette; it was above all a blessing to feel myself, in the perusal of M. Octave Feuillet, an education, as I supposed, of the taste, not at a marked disadvantage; since who but the Petite Comtesse herself had swung her crinoline in and out of my prospect, or, to put it better, of my preserved past, on one of my occasions of acutest receptivity?

The truth was that acute, that quite desperate receptivity set in for me, under a law of its own—may really be described as having quite raged for me—from the moment our general face, by the restless parental decree (born not a little of parental homesickness and reinforced by a theory of that complaint on our own part, we having somehow in Europe "no companions," none but mere parents themselves), had been turned again to the quarter in which there would assuredly be welcomes and freedoms and unchecked appropriations, not to say also cousins, of both sexes and of a more and more engaging time of life, cousins kept and tended and adorned for us in our absence, together with the solicitation for our favour of possible, though oh so just barely possible, habitats before which the range of Europe paled; but which, nevertheless, to my aching fancy, meant premature abdication, sacrifice and, in one dreadful word, failure. I had had cousins, naturally, in the countries we were quitting, but to a limited degree; yet I think I already knew I had had companions in as full a measure as any I was still to know—inasmuch as my imagination made out one, in the complex order and the coloured air, almost wherever I turned; and, inasmuch as, further, to live by the imagination was to live almost only in that way, so to foresee the comparative, not to say the absolute, absence of tonic accent in the appearances complacently awaiting me, as well as to forecast in these appearances, at the best, a greater paucity, was really to enjoy a sharp prevision of dearth. Certain it is that those supreme moments of Paris, those after-days at the Trois Empereurs, were to flush for me, as they ebbed, with images and visions; judged by any achieved act of possession I hadn't assuredly much to give up, but intensity of sentiment, resting on a good disposition, makes for its own sake the most of opportunity, and I buried my associations, which had been in a manner till lately my hopes as well, with all decent dignity and tenderness. These more or less secret obsequies lent to our further brief delay a quality of suppressed excitement; the "old-world" hours were numbered too dreadfully—had shrunk but to a handful: I had waked up to that, as with a passionate even if private need for gathering in and saving, on the morrow of our reaching our final sticking-place: I had slipped from my so cushioned sleep, my canopied couch, to hang, from the balcony of our quatrième, my brothers' and mine, over that Place du Palais Royal and up against that sculptured and storied façade of the new Louvre which seemed to me then to represent, in its strength, the capacity and chiselled rim of some such potent vivifying cup as it might have been given us, under a happier arrangement, to taste now in its fulness and with a braver sense for it. Over against us on the great palace wall, as I make out—if not for that occasion then for some other—were statues of heroes, Napoleon's young generals, Hoche, Marceau, Desaix or whoever, such a galaxy as never was or should ever be again for splendid monumental reference; and what it somehow came to was that here massed itself the shining second Empire, over which they stood straight aloft and on guard, like archangels of the sword, and that the whole thing was a high-pitched wonder and splendour, which we had already, in our small gaping way, got into a sort of relation with and which would have ever so much more ever so thrillingly to give us. What it would give us loomed but vaguely enough out of the great hum and the great toned perspective, and withal the great noble expense, of which we had constant reminder; but that we were present at something it would be always after accounted a privilege to have been concerned with, and that we were perversely and inconsiderately dropping out of it, and for a reason, so far as there might be a reason, that was scarcely less than strange—all this loomed large to me as our interval shrank, and I even ask myself before the memory of it whether I was ever again in the later and more encompassing and accommodating years to have in those places so rich a weight of consciousness to carry or so grand a presumption of joy. The presumption so boldly entertained was, if you please, of what the whole thing meant. It meant, immensely, the glittering régime, and *that* meant in turn, prodigiously, something that would probably never be meant quite to any such tune again: so much one positively and however absurdly said to one's self as one stood up on the high balcony to the great insolence of the Louvre and to all the history, all the glory again and all the imposed applause, not to say worship, and not to speak of the implied inferiority, on the part of everything else, that it represented. And the sense was of course not less while one haunted at odd hours the arcades and glass galleries of the Palais Royal close at hand—as if to store up, for all the world, treasures of impression that might be gnawed, in seasons or places of want, like winter pears or a squirrel's hoard of nuts, and so perhaps keep one alive, as to one's most vital faculty above-mentioned, till one should somehow or other be able to scramble back.

The particular ground for our defection, which I obscurely pronounced mistaken, was that since William was to embrace the artistic career—and freedom for this experiment had been after all, as I repeat that it was always in like cases to be, not in the least grudgingly granted him—our return to America would place him in prompt and happy relation to William Hunt, then the most distinguished of our painters as well as one of the most original and delightful of men, and who had cordially assured us that he would welcome such a pupil. This was judged among us at large, other considerations aiding, a sound basis for action; but never surely had so odd a motive operated for a break with the spell of Paris. We named the motive generally, I think, and to the credit of our earnest good faith, with confidence—and I am of course not sure how often our dear father may not explicatively have mentioned the shy fact that he himself in any case had gradually ceased to "like" Europe. This affects me at present as in the highest degree natural: it was to be his fortune for the rest of his life to find himself, as a worker in his own field and as to what he held most dear, scantly enough heeded, reported or assimilated even in his own air, no brisk conductor at any time of his remarkable voice; but in Europe his isolation had been utter—he had there had the sense of playing his mature and ardent thought over great dense constituted presences and opaque surfaces that could by their very nature scarce give back so much as a shudder. No more admirable case of apostolic energy combined with philosophic patience, of constancy of conviction and solitary singleness of production unperturbed, can I well conceive; and I certainly came later on to rejoice in his having had after a certain date to walk, if there was a preference, rather in the thin wilderness than in the thick. I dare say that when we returned to America toward the end of 1860, some five years and a half after our departure, it may have been with illusions not a few for him about the nature of the desert, or in other words about the degree of sensibility of the public, there awaiting him; but the pretext given him by his so prized and admired eldest son was at the worst, and however eccentric our action, inspiring: I alone of the family perhaps made bold not to say quite directly or literally that we went home to learn to paint. People stared or laughed when we said it, and I disliked their thinking us so simple—though dreaming too a little perhaps that they might have been struck with our patriotism. This however conveyed but a chill the more—since we didn't in the least go to our friend, who had been Couture's and Frère's pupil, who had spent years in France and of whom it was the common belief that you couldn't for the life of you tell him from a French painter, because he was patriotic; but because he was distinguished and accomplished, charming and kind, and above all known to us and thereby in a manner guaranteed. He looked, as people get to look under such enjoyed or even suffered exposures, extremely like a Frenchman, and, what was noteworthy, still more like a sculptor of the race than a painter; which doubtless had to do with my personally, though I hope, in present cultivated anxiety, not too officiously, sighing at all the explanation the whole thing took. I am bound to add none the less that later on, repatriated and, as to my few contacts, reassured, I found this amount, the apprehension of which had haunted me, no great charge; and seem even to make out that for the first six months of our Newport phase at least we might have passed for strikingly wise. For here *was*, beyond doubt, a genial, an admirable master; and here also—at such a rate did sparse individuals, scattered notches in the long plain stick, count—was John La Farge. Here moreover—here and everywhere about me, before we could quite turn round—was the War, with its infinite, its truly quite humiliating correction of my (as I now can but so far call it) fatuous little confidence that "appearances," on the native scene, would run short. They were in the event, taking one thing with another, never to hold out for me as they held during those four years. Wondrous this force in them as I at present look back—wondrous I mean in view of that indirectness of its play which my conditions confined me, with such private, though I must add, alas, such helplessly unapplied resentment, to knowing it by. If the force was great the attenuation of its reach was none the less preappointed and constant; so that the case must have come back again but to the degree—call *it* too, frankly, the force—of one's sensibility, or in other words the blest resource, the supremely breatheable and thereby nourishing and favouring air of one's imaginative life. There were of a truth during that time probably more appearances at one's command in the way of felt aspects, images, apprehended living relations and impressions of the stress of life, than during any other season one was to know; only doubtless with more of the work of their figuring to their utmost, their giving all they could, to do by one's self and, in the last resort, deep within one's breast. The point to be made just here, in any case, is that if we had not recrossed the sea, by way, rather, of such an anticlimax, to William Hunt, we should certainly with brief delay have found ourselves doing it, on the first alarm of War, for the experience I thus too summarily glance at and which I don't pretend to speak of as all my own.

IV

NEWPORT, WITH repatriation accepted, would have been on many grounds inevitable, I think—as it was to remain inevitable for several years, and this quite apart from William's having to paint; since if I spoke just now of the sweep of our view, from over the water, of a continent, or well-nigh, waiting to receive us, the eligibility of its innumerable sites was a matter much more of our simplified, our almost distressfully uninvolved and unconnected state than of the inherent virtue of this, that or the other particular group of local conditions. Our parents had for us no definite project but to be liberally "good"—in other words so good that the presumption of our being so would literally operate anywhere and anyhow, would really amount in itself to a sort of situated state, a sufficient prime position, and leave other circumstances comparatively irrelevant. What would infallibly have occurred at the best, however, was what did punctually happen—its having to be definitely gathered that, though we might apparently be good, as I say, almost on any ground, there was but one place in which we should even at a restricted pitch be well: Newport imposed itself at that period to so remarkable a degree as the one right residence, in all our great country, for those tainted, under whatever attenuations, with the quality and the effect of detachment. The effect of detachment was the fact of the experience of Europe. Detachment might of course have come from many causes, but it truly came in most cases but from one, though that a fairly merciless: it came from the experience of Europe, and I think was on the whole regarded as—what it could only have been in the sphere of intimacy and secrecy felt to be—without an absolute remedy. As comparatively remedial Newport none the less figured, and this for sundry reasons into the detail of which I needn't go. Its rare distinction and precious attribute was that, being a watering-place, a refuge from summer heats, it had also, were the measure considerably stretched, possibilities of hibernation. We could, under stress, brave there the period from November to June; and it was to be under stress not to know what else to do. That was the pinch to which Europe reduced you; insidiously, fatally disconnected, you could but make the best, as a penalty, of the one marked point of reattachment. The philosophy of all of which was that to confess to disconnection was to confess by the same stroke to leisure—which involved also an admission, however rueful at once and deprecatory, of what might still at that time pass in our unregenerate country for something in the nature of "means." You had had the means, that is, to *become*, so awkwardly, detached—for you might then do that cheaply; but the whole basis of the winter life there, of that spare semblance of the Brighton life, the Folkestone life, the Bath or the Cheltenham or the Leamington life, was that your occupation or avocation should be vague enough; or that you shouldn't in other words be, like everyone you might know save a dozen or so at the most, in business. I remember well how when we were all young together we had, under pressure of the American ideal in that matter, then so rigid, felt it tasteless and even humiliating that the head of our little family was *not* in business, and that even among our relatives on each side we couldn't so much as name proudly anyone who was—with the sole exception of our maternal uncle Robertson Walsh, who looked, ever so benevolently, after our father's "affairs," happily for us. Such had never been the case with the father of any boy of our acquaintance; the business in which the boy's father gloriously *was* stood forth inveterately as the very first note of our comrade's impressiveness. *We* had no note of that sort to produce, and I perfectly recover the effect of my own repeated appeal to our parent for some presentable account of him that would prove us respectable. Business alone was respectable—if one meant by it, that is, the calling of a lawyer, a doctor or a minister (we never spoke of clergymen) as well; I think that if we had had the Pope among us we should have supposed the Pope in business, just as I remember my friend Simpson's telling me crushingly, at one of our New York schools, on my hanging back with the fatal truth about our credentials, that the author of *his* being (we spoke no more of "governors" than we did of "parsons") was in the business of a stevedore. That struck me as a great card to play—the word was fine and mysterious; so that "What shall we tell them you *are*, don't you see?" could but become on our lips at home a more constant appeal. It seemed wantonly to be prompted for our father, and indeed greatly to amuse him, that he should put us off with strange unheard-of attributions, such as would have made us ridiculous in our special circles; his "Say I'm a philosopher, say I'm a seeker for truth, say I'm a lover of my kind, say I'm an author of books if you like; or, best of all, just say I'm a Student," saw us so very little further. Abject it certainly appeared to be reduced to the "student" plea; and I must have lacked even the confidence of my brother Bob, who, challenged, in my hearing and the usual way, was ready not only with the fact that our parent "wrote," but with the further fact that he had written *Lectures and Miscellanies James*. I think that when we settled awhile at Newport there was no one there who had written but Mr. Henry T. Tuckerman, a genial and graceful poet of the Artless Age, as it might still be called in spite of Poe and Hawthorne and Longfellow and Lowell, the most characteristic works of the first and the two last of whom had already appeared; especially as those most characteristic of Mr. Tuckerman referred themselves to a past sufficiently ample to have left that gentleman with a certain deafness and a glossy wig and a portly presence and the reputation, positively, of the most practised and desired of diners-out. He was to be recognised at once as a social value on a scene not under that rubric densely peopled; he constituted indeed such a note as would help to keep others of the vague definability in countenance. Clearly indeed it might happen that an association of vaguenesses would arrive in time, by fondly cleaving together, at the semblance of a common identity; the nature of the case then demanding, however, that they should be methodically vague, take their stand on it and work it for all it was worth. That in truth was made easy by the fact that what I have called our common disconnectedness positively projected and proclaimed a void; disconnected from business we could only be connected with the negation of it, which had as yet no affirmative, no figurative side. This probably would come; figures, in the void, would one by one spring up; but what would be thus required for them was that the void should be ample and, as it were, established. Not to be afraid of it they would have to feel it clear of everything and everyone they knew in the air actually peopled.

William Hunt, for that matter, was already a figure unmistakable, superficially speaking unsurpassable, just as John La Farge, already mentioned, was so soon to prove to be. They were only two indeed, but they argued the possibility; and so the great thing, as I say, was that, to stand out, they should have margin and light. We couldn't all be figures—on a mere margin, the margin of business, and in the light of the general wonder of our being anything, anything *there*; but we could at least understand the situation and cultivate the possibilities, watch and protect the germs. This consciousness, this aim or ideal, had after all its own intensity—it burned with a pure flame: there is a special joy, clearly, in the hopeful conversion of the desert into the garden, of thinness into thickness, a joy to which the conversion of the thick into the mere dense, of the free into the rank or the close, perhaps gives no clue. The great need that Newport met was that of a basis of reconciliation to "America" when the habit, the taking for granted, of America had been broken or intermitted: it would be hard to say of what subtle secret or magic the place was possessed toward this end, and by a common instinct, I think, we didn't attempt to formulate it—we let it alone, only looking at each other hard, only moving gently, on the brave hypothesis, only in fine deprecating too rude and impatient, too precipitate a doubt of the spell that perhaps might work if we waited and prayed. We did wait and pray, accordingly, scantly-served though the board we might often have felt we had sat down to, and there was a fair company of us to do so, friendliest among whom to our particular effort was my father's excellent friend of many years Edmund Tweedy, already named in pages preparatory to these and who, with his admirable wife, presented himself as our main introducer and initiator. He had married, while we were all young in New York together, a manner of Albany cousin, Mary Temple the elder, aunt of the younger,[1] and had by this time "been through" more than anything, more than everything, of which there could be question for ourselves. The pair had on their marriage gone at once to Europe to live, had put in several years of Italy and yet had at last, particular reasons operating, returned to their native, that is to sterner, realities;

[1] *A Small Boy and Others*, 1913.

those as to which it was our general theory, of so touching a candour as I look back to it, that they offered themselves at Newport in a muffling mitigating air. The air, material, moral, social, was in fact clear and clean to a degree that might well have left us but dazed at the circumjacent blankness; yet as to that I hasten to add too that the blowing out of our bubble, the planting of our garden, the correction of our thinness, the discovery, under stress, of such scraps of colour and conversation, such saving echoes and redeeming references as might lurk for us in each other, all formed in themselves an active, and might at last even grow to suggest an absolutely bustling, process.

I come back with a real tenderness of memory for instance to that felicity of the personal, the social, the "literary and artistic," almost really the romantic, identity responding, after a fashion quite to bring tears to the eyes, in proportion as it might have seemed to feel by some divine insufflation what it practically could stand for. What should one call this but the brave triumph of values conscious of having to be almost missionary? There were many such that in "Europe" hadn't had to be missionary at all; in Europe, as it were, one hadn't—comparatively—seen, if not the forest for the trees, then the trees for the forest; whereas on this other great vacuous level every single stem seemed to enjoy for its distinction quite the totality of the daylight and to rise into the air with a gladness that was itself a grace. Of some of the personal importances that acted in that way I should with easier occasion have more to say—I shall as it is have something; but there could perhaps be no better sample of the effect of sharpness with which the forces of culture might emerge than, say, the fairly golden glow of romance investing the mere act of perusal of the Revue des Deux Mondes. There was the charm—though I grant of course that I speak here all for myself, constitutionally and, face to face *with* myself, quite shamelessly an inquirer, a hunter, for charm—that whereas the spell cast had more or less inevitable limits in the world to which such a quality as the best things of the Revue, such a performance of the intellectual and expressional engagement as these suggested, was native and was thereby relative to other generally like phenomena, so it represented among *us*, where it had to take upon itself what I have already alluded to as all the work, far more than its face value. Few of the forces about us reached as yet the level of representation (even if here and there some might have been felt as trying for it); and this made all the difference. Anything suggestive or significant, anything promising or interesting, anything in the least finely charming above all, immensely counted, claimed tendance and protection, almost claimed, or at any rate enjoyed, worship; as for that matter anything finely charming does, quite rightly, anywhere. But our care, our privilege, on occasion our felt felicity, was to foster every symptom and breathe encouragement to every success; to hang over the tenderest shoots that betrayed the principle of growth—or in other words to read devoutly into everything, and as straight as possible, the very fullest meaning we might hope it would learn to have. So at least quite at first—and so again very considerably after the large interval and grim intermission represented by the War; during which interest and quality, to say nothing of quantity, at the highest pitch, ceased in any degree to fail us, and what might be "read into" almost any aspect without exception paled in the light of what was inevitably read out from it. It must be added at the same time that with its long duration the War fell into its place as part of life at large, and that when it was over various other things still than the love of peace were found to have grown.

Immediately, at any rate, the Albany cousins, or a particular group of them, began again to be intensely in question for us; coloured in due course with reflections of the War as their lives, not less than our own, were to become—and coloured as well too, for all sorts of notation and appreciation, from irrepressible private founts. Mrs. Edmund Tweedy, bereft of her own young children, had at the time I speak of opened her existence, with the amplest hospitality, to her four orphaned nieces, who were also our father's and among whom the second in age, Mary Temple the younger, about in her seventeenth year when she thus renewed her appearance to our view, shone with vividest lustre, an essence that preserves her still, more than half a century from the date of her death, in a memory or two where many a relic once sacred has comparatively yielded to time. Most of those who knew and loved, I was going to say adored, her have also yielded—which is a reason the more why thus much of her, faint echo from too far off though it prove, should be tenderly saved. If I have spoken of the elements and presences round about us that "counted," Mary Temple was to count, and in more lives than can now be named, to an extraordinary degree; count as a young and shining apparition, a creature who owed to the charm of her every aspect (her aspects were so many!) and the originality, vivacity, audacity, generosity, of her spirit, an indescribable grace and weight—if one might impute weight to a being so imponderable in common scales. Whatever other values on our scene might, as I have hinted, appear to fail, she was one of the first order, in the sense of the immediacy of the impression she produced, and produced altogether as by the play of her own light spontaneity and curiosity—not, that is, as through a sense of such a pressure and such a motive, or through a care for them, in others. "Natural" to an effect of perfect felicity that we were never to see surpassed is what I have already praised all the Albany *cousinage* of those years for being; but in none of the company was the note so clear as in this rarest, though at the same time symptomatically or ominously palest, flower of the stem; who was natural at more points and about more things, with a greater range of freedom and ease and reach of horizon than any of the others dreamed of. They had that way, delightfully, with the small, after all, and the common matters—while she had it with those too, but with the great and rare ones over and above; so that she was to remain for us the very figure and image of a felt interest in life, an interest as magnanimously far-spread, or as familiarly and exquisitely fixed, as her splendid shifting sensibility, moral, personal, nervous, and having at once such noble flights and such touchingly discouraged drops, such graces of indifference and inconsequence, might at any moment determine. She was really to remain, for our appreciation, the supreme case of a taste for life as life, as personal living; of an endlessly active and yet somehow a careless, an illusionless, a sublimely forewarned curiosity about it: something that made her, slim and fair and quick, all straightness and charming tossed head, with long light and yet almost sliding steps and a large light postponing, renouncing laugh, the very muse or amateur priestess of rash speculation. To express her in the mere terms of her restless young mind, one felt from the first, was to place her, by a perversion of the truth, under the shadow of female "earnestness" —for which she was much too unliteral and too ironic; so that, superlatively personal and yet as independent, as "off" into higher spaces, at a touch, as all the breadth of her sympathy and her courage could send her, she made it impossible to say whether she was just the most moving of maidens or a disengaged and dancing flame of thought. No one to come after her could easily seem to show either a quick inward life or a brave, or even a bright, outward, either a consistent contempt for social squalors or a very marked genius for moral reactions. She had in her brief passage the enthusiasm of humanity —more, assuredly, than any charming girl who ever circled, and would fain have continued to circle, round a ballroom. This kept her indeed for a time more interested in the individual, the immediate human, than in the race or the social order at large; but that, on the other hand, made her ever so restlessly, or quite inappeasably, "psychologic." The psychology of others, in her shadow—I mean their general resort to it— could only for a long time seem weak and flat and dim, above all not at all amusing. She burned herself out; she died at twenty-four.

At the risk perhaps of appearing to make my own scant adventure the pivot of that early Newport phase I find my reference to William Hunt and his truly fertilising action on our common life much conditioned by the fact that, since W. J., for the first six months or so after our return, daily and devotedly haunted his studio, I myself did no less, for a shorter stretch, under the irresistible contagion. The clearness of the whole passage for me, the clearest impression, above all, of the vivid and whimsical master, an inspirer, during a period that began a little later on, of numberless devotions and loyalties, is what this fond memory of my permitted contact and endeavour still has to give me. Pupils at that time didn't flock to his gates—though they were to do so in Boston, during years, later on; an earnest lady or two, Boston precursors, hovered and flitted, but I remember for the rest (and I speak of a short period) no thoroughgoing *élèves* save John La Farge and my brother. I remember, for that matter, sitting quite in solitude in one of the grey cool rooms of the studio, which thus comes back to me as having several, and thinking that I really might get to copy casts rather well, and might in particular see myself congratulated on my sympathetic rendering of the sublime uplifted face of Michael Angelo's "Captive" in the Louvre. I sat over this effort and a few others for long quiet hours, and seem to feel myself again aware, just to that tune, of how happy I ought to be. No one disturbed me; the earnest workers were elsewhere; I had a chamber of the temple all to myself, with immortal forms and curves, with shadows beautiful and right, waiting there on blank-eyed faces for me to prove myself not helpless; and with two or three of Hunt's own fine things, examples of his work in France, transporting me at once and defying. I believed them great productions—thought in especial endless good of the large canvas of the girl with her back presented while she fills her bucket at the spout in the wall, against which she leans with a tension of young muscle, a general expression of back, beneath her dress, and with the pressure of her raised and extended bare arm and flattened hand: this, to my imagination, could only become the prize of some famous collection, the light of some museum, for all the odd circumstance that it was company just then for muddled *me* and for the queer figures projected by my crayon. Frankly, intensely—that was the great thing—these were hours of Art, art definitely named, looking me full in the face and accepting my stare in return—no longer a tacit implication or a shy subterfuge, but a flagrant unattenuated aim. I had somehow come into the temple by the back door, the *porte d'honneur* opened on an other side, and I could never have believed much at best in the length of my stay; but I was there, day by day, as much as any one had ever been, and with a sense of what it "meant" to be there that the most accredited of pupils couldn't have surpassed; so that the situation to this extent really hummed with promise. I fail, I confess, to reconstitute the relation borne by my privilege to that of tuition "in the higher branches," to which it was quite time I should have mounted, enjoyed at the hands of the Reverend William C. Leverett, curate to the then "rector," Doctor Mercer, of that fine old high-spired Trinity Church in which had throbbed, from long before the Revolution as they used to say, the proud episcopal heart of Newport; and feel indeed that I must pretty well have shaken off, as a proved absurd predicament, all submission to my dilemma: all submission of the mind, that is, for if my share of Mr. Leverett's attention was less stinted than my share of William Hunt's (and neither had much duration) it failed to give me the impression that anything worth naming had opened out to me, whereas in the studio I was at the threshold of a world.

It became itself indeed on the spot a rounded satisfying world, the place did; enclosed within the grounds, as we then regarded them, of the master's house, circled about with numerous trees, as we then counted them, and representing a more direct exclusion of vulgar sounds, false notes and harsh reminders than I had ever known. I fail in the least to make out where the real work of the studio went forward; it took somewhere else its earnest course, and our separation—mine from the real workers, my indulged yet ignored state—kept me somehow the safer, as if I had taken some mild and quite harmless drug through which external rubs would reach me from a distance, but which left my own rubbing power, not to say my own smearing or smutching, quite free. Into the world so beautifully valid the master would occasionally walk, inquiring as to what I had done or would do, but bearing on the question with an easy lightness, a friendliness of tact, a neglect of conclusion, which it touches me still to remember. It was impossible to me at that time not so to admire him that his just being to such an extent, as from top to toe and in every accent and motion, the living and communicating Artist, made the issue, with his presence, quite cease to be of how one got on or fell short, and become instead a mere self-sacrificing vision of the picturesque itself, the constituted picturesque or treated "subject," in efficient figure, personal form, vivid human style. I then felt the man the great mystery could mark with its stamp, when wishing the mark unmistakable, teach me just in himself the most and best about any art that I should come to find benignantly concerned with me, for moments however smilingly scant. William Hunt, all muscular spareness and brownness and absence of waste, all flagrant physiognomy, brave bony arch of handsome nose, upwardness of strong eyebrow and glare, almost, of eyes that both recognised and wondered, strained eyes that played over questions as if they were objects and objects as if they were questions, might have stood, to the life, for Don Quixote, if we could associate with that hero a far-spreading beard already a little grizzled, a manner and range of gesture and broken form of discourse that was like a restless reference to a palette and that seemed to take for granted, all about, canvases and models and charming, amusing things, the "tremendously interesting" in the seen bit or caught moment, and the general unsayability, in comparison, of anything else. He never would have perched, it must be added, on Rosinante—he was fonder of horses even than of the method of Couture, and though with a shade of resemblance, as all simple and imaginative men have, to the knight of La Mancha, he least suggested that analogy as he passed in a spinning buggy, his beard flying, behind a favourite trotter. But what he perhaps most puts before me to-day is the grim truth of the merciless manner in which a living and hurrying public educates itself, making and devouring in a day reputations and values which represent something of the belief in it that it has had in *them*, but at the memory of which we wince, almost to horror, as at the legend of victims who have been buried alive. Oh the cold grey luminaries hung about in odd corners and back passages, and that we have known shining and warm! They serve at the most now as beacons warning any step not to come *that* way, whatever it does; the various attested ways it may not with felicity come growing thus all the while in number.

John La Farge became at once, in breaking on our view, quite the most interesting person we knew, and for a time remained so; he became a great many other things beside—a character, above all, if there ever was one; but he opened up to us, though perhaps to me in particular, who could absorb all that was given me on those suggestive lines, prospects and possibilities that made the future flush and swarm. His foreignness, which seemed great at that time, had gained a sharper accent from a long stay made in France, where both on his father's and his mother's side he had relations, and had found, to our hovering envy, all sorts of charming occasions. He had spent much time in Brittany, among kindred the most romantically interesting, people and places whose very names, the De Nanteuils of Saint-Pol-de-Léon, I seem to remember for instance, cast a spell across comparatively blank Newport sands;

he had brought home with him innumerable water-colour sketches, Breton peasants, costumes, interiors, bits of villages and landscape; and I supposed him to have had on such ground the most delightful adventure in the world. How was one not to suppose it at a time when the best of one's education, such as that was, had begun to proceed almost altogether by the aid of the Revue des Deux Mondes, a periodical that supplied to us then and for several years after (or again I can but speak for myself) all that was finest in the furniture and the fittings of romance? Those beginnings of Newport were our first contact with New England—a New England already comparatively subdued and sophisticated, a Samson shorn of his strength by the shears of the Southern, and more particularly of the New York, Delilah; the result of which, still speaking for myself, was a prompt yearning and reaching out, on the part of the spirit, for some corrective or antidote to whatever it was that might be going, in the season to come, least charmingly or informingly or inspiringly to press upon us. I well recall my small anxious foresight as to a required, an indispensable provision against either assault or dearth, as if the question might be of standing an indefinite siege; and how a certain particular capacious closet in a house we were presently to occupy took on to my fond fancy the likeness at once of a store of edibles, both substantial and succulent, and of a hoard of ammunition for the defence of any breach—the Revue accumulating on its shelves at last in serried rows and really building up beneath us with its slender firm salmon-coloured blocks an alternative sphere of habitation. There will be more to say of this, bristling or rather flowering with precious particulars, if I stray so far; but the point for the moment was that one would have pushed into that world of the closet, one would have wandered or stumbled about in it quite alone if it hadn't been that La Farge was somehow always in it with us. That was in those years his admirable function and touch—that he affected me as knowing his way there as absolutely no one else did, and even as having risen of a sudden before us to bear us this quickening company. Nobody else, not another creature, was free of it to that tune; the whole mid-century New England—as a rough expression of what the *general* consciousness most signified—was utterly out of it; which made, you see, a most unequal division of our little working, or our totally cogitative, universe into the wondrous esoteric quarter peopled just by us and our friend and our common references, and the vast remainder of the public at large, the public of the innumerably uninitiated even when apparently of the most associated.

All of which is but a manner of expressing the intensity, as I felt it, of our Franco-American, our most completely accomplished friend's presence among us. Out of the safe rich home of the Revue, which opened away into the vastness of visions, he practically stepped, and into it, with all his ease, he mysteriously returned again: he came nearer to being what might have been meant concretely throughout it all—though meant most of course in its full-charged stream of fiction—than any other visiting figure. The stream of fiction was so constant an appeal to the charmed, by which I mean of course the predisposed, mind that it fairly seemed at moments to overflow its banks and take to its bosom any recognised, any congruous creature or thing that might happen to be within reach. La Farge was of the type—the "European," and this gave him an authority for me that it verily took the length of years to undermine; so that as the sense of those first of them in especial comes back to me I find it difficult, even under the appeal to me of the attempt, to tell how he was to count in my earliest culture. If culture, as I hold, is a matter of attitude quite as much as of opportunity, and of the form and substance of the vessel carried to the fountain no less than of the water-supply itself, there couldn't have been better conditions for its operating drop by drop. It operates ever much more, I think, by one's getting whatever there may happen to be out for one's use than by its conforming to any abstract standard of quantity or lustre. It may work, as between dispenser and subject, in so incalculably personal a manner that no chemical analysis shall recover it, no common estimate of forces or amounts find itself in the least apply. The case was that La Farge swam into our ingenuous ken as the figure of figures, and that such an agent, on a stage so unpeopled and before a scene so unpainted, became salient and vivid almost in spite of itself. The figure was at a premium, and fit for any glass case that its vivacity should allow to enclose it—wherein it might be surrounded by wondering, admiring and often quite inevitably misconceiving observers. It was not that these too weren't agents in their way, agents in some especial good cause without the furtherance of which we never should have done at all; but they were by that very fact specialised and stiffened, committed to their one attitude, the immediately profitable, and incapable of that play of gesture in which we recognise representation. A representative, a rounded figure, however, is as to none of its relations definable or announceable beforehand; we only know it, for good or for ill, but with something of the throb of elation always, when we see it, and then it in general sufficiently accounts for itself. We often for that matter insist on its *being* a figure, we positively make it one, in proportion as we seem to need it—or as in other words we too acutely miss the active virtue of representation. It takes some extraordinary set of circumstances or time of life, I think, either to beguile or to hustle us into indifference to some larger felt extension roundabout us of "the world"—a sphere the confines of which move on even as we ourselves move and which is always there, just beyond us, to twit us with the more it should have to show if we were a little more "of" it. Sufficiency shuts us in but till the man of the world—never prefigured, as I say, only welcomed on the spot—appears; when we see at once how much we have wanted him. When we fail of that acknowledgment, that sense as of a tension, an anxiety or an indigence relieved, it is of course but that the extraordinary set of circumstances, or above all the extraordinary time of life I speak of, has indeed intervened.

It was as a man of the world that, for all his youth, La Farge rose or, still better, bowed, before us, his inclinations of obeisance, his considerations of address being such as we had never seen and now almost publicly celebrated. This was what most immediately and most iridescently showed, the truth being all the while that the character took on in him particular values without which it often enough, though then much more grossly, flourishes. It was by these enrichments of curiosity, of taste and genius, that he became the personality, as we nowadays say, that I have noted—the full freshness of all of which was to play but through his younger time, or at least through our younger apprehension. He was so "intellectual"—that was the flower; it crowned his being personally so finished and launched. The wealth of his cultivation, the variety of his initiations, the inveteracy of his forms, the degree of his *empressement* (this in itself, I repeat, a revelation) made him, with those elements of the dandy and the cavalier to which he struck us as so picturesquely sacrificing, a cluster of bright promises, a rare original and, though not at all a direct model for simpler folk, as we then could but feel ourselves, an embodiment of the gospel of esthetics. Those more resounding forms that our age was to see this gospel take on were then still to come, but I was to owe them in the later time not half the thrill that the La Farge of the prime could set in motion. He was really an artistic, an esthetic nature of wondrous homogeneity; one was to have known in the future many an unfolding that went with a larger ease and a shrewder economy, but never to have seen a subtler mind or a more generously wasteful passion, in other words a sincerer one, addressed to the problems of the designer and painter. Of his long later history, full of flights and drops, advances and retreats, experiment and performance, of the endless complications of curiosity and perversity, I say nothing here save that if it was to contradict none of our first impressions it was to qualify them all by others still more lively; these things belonging quite to some other record. Yet I may just note that they were to represent in some degree an eclipse of the so essentially harmonious person round whom a positive grace of legend had originally formed itself. I see him at this hour again as that bright apparition; see him, jacketed in black velvet or clad from top to toe in old-time elegances of cool white and leaning much forward with his protuberant and over-glazed, his doubting yet all-seizing vision, dandle along the shining Newport sands in far-away summer sunsets on a charming chestnut mare whose light legs and fine head and great sweep of tail showed the Arab strain—quite as if (what would have been characteristic of him) he had borrowed his mount from the adorable Fromentin, whom we already knew as a painter, but whose acquaintance as a writer we were of course so promptly to owe him that when "Dominique" broke upon us out of the Revue as one of the most exquisite literary events of our time it found us doubly responsive.

So, at any rate, he was there, and there to stay—intensely among us but somehow not withal *of* us; his being a Catholic, and apparently a "real" one in spite of so many other omnisciences, making perhaps by itself the greatest difference. He had been through a Catholic college in Maryland, the name of which, though I am not assured of it now, exhaled a sort of educational elegance; but where and when he had so miraculously laid up his stores of reading and achieved his universal saturation was what we longest kept asking ourselves. Many of these depths I couldn't pretend to sound, but it was immediate and appreciable that he revealed to us Browning for instance; and this, oddly enough, long after Men and Women had begun (from our Paris time on, if I remember) to lie upon our parents' book-table. *They* had not divined in us as yet an aptitude for that author; whose appeal indeed John reinforced to our eyes by the reproduction of a beautiful series of illustrative drawings, two or three of which he was never to surpass—any more than he was to complete his highly distinguished plan for the full set, not the least faded of his hundred dreams. Most of all he revealed to us Balzac; having so much to tell me of what was within that formidably-plated door, in which he all expertly and insidiously played the key, that to re-read even after long years the introductory pages of Eugénie Grandet, breathlessly seized and earnestly absorbed under his instruction, is to see my initiator's youthful face, so irregular but so refined, look out at me between the lines as through blurred prison bars. In Mérimée, after the same fashion, I meet his expository ghost—hovering to remind me of how he started me on La Vénus d'Ille; so that nothing would do but that I should translate it, try to render it as lovingly as if it were a classic and old (both of which things it now indeed is) and send it off to the New York weekly periodical of that age of crudest categories which was to do me the honour neither of acknowledging nor printing nor, clearly, since translations did savingly appear there, in the least understanding it. These again are mild memories—though not differing in that respect from most of their associates; yet I cherish them as ineffaceable dates, sudden milestones, the first distinctly noted, on the road of so much inward or apprehensive life. Our guest—I call him our guest because he was so lingeringly, so abidingly and supersedingly present—began meanwhile to paint, under our eyes, with devotion, with exquisite perception, and above all as with the implication, a hundred times beneficent and fertilising, that if one didn't in these connections consistently take one's stand on supersubtlety of taste one was a helpless outsider and at the best the basest of vulgarians or flattest of frauds—a doctrine more salutary at that time in our world at large than any other that might be sounded. Of all of which ingenuous intensity and activity I should have been a much scanter witness than his then close condisciple, my brother, had not his personal kindness, that of the good-natured and amused elder youth to the enslaved, the yearningly gullible younger, charmed me often into a degree of participation. Occasions and accidents come back to me under their wash of that distilled old Newport light as to which we more and more agreed that it made altogether exceptionally, on our side of the world, for possibility of the *nuance*, or in other words for picture and story; such for example as my felt sense of how unutterably it was the real thing, the gage of a great future, when I one morning found my companions of the larger, the serious studio inspired to splendid performance by the beautiful young manly form of our cousin Gus Barker, then on a vivid little dash of a visit to us and who, perched on a pedestal and divested of every garment, was the gayest as well as the neatest of models. This was my first personal vision of the "life," on a pedestal and in a pose, that had half gleamed and half gloomed through the chiaroscuro of our old friend Haydon; and I well recall the crash, at the sight, of all my inward emulation—so forced was I to recognise on the spot that I might niggle for months over plaster casts and not come within miles of any such point of attack. The bravery of my brother's own in especial dazzled me out of every presumption; since nothing less than that meant drawing (they were not using colour) and since our genial kinsman's perfect gymnastic figure meant living truth, I should certainly best testify to the whole mystery by pocketing my pencil.

I secured and preserved for long William's finished rendering of the happy figure—which was to speak for the original, after his gallant death, in sharper and finer accents perhaps than aught else that remained of him; and it wanted but another occasion somewhat later on, that of the sitting to the pair of pupils under Hunt's direction of a subject presented as a still larger challenge, to feel that I had irrecoverably renounced. Very handsome were the head and shoulders of

Katharine Temple, the eldest of those Albany cousins then gathered at Newport under their, and derivatively our, Aunt Mary's wing, who afterwards was to become Mrs. Richard Emmet—the Temples and the Emmets being so much addicted to alliances that a still later generation was to bristle for us with a delightful Emmetry, each member of it a different blessing; she sat with endless patience, the serenest of models, and W. J.'s portrait of her in oils survives (as well as La Farge's, dealing with her in another view) as a really mature, an almost masterly, piece of painting, having, as has been happily suggested to me, much the air of a characteristic Manet. Such demonstrations would throw one back on regret, so far as my brother was concerned, if subsequent counter-demonstrations hadn't had it in them so much to check the train. For myself at the hour, in any case, the beautiful success with Kitty Temple did nothing but hurry on the future, just as the sight of the charming thing to-day, not less than that of La Farge's *profil perdu*, or presented ear and neck and gathered braids of hair, quite as charming and quite as painted, touchingly reanimates the past. I say touchingly because of the remembered pang of my acceptance of an admonition so sharply conveyed. Therefore if somewhat later on I could still so fondly hang about in that air of production—so far at least as it enveloped our friend, and particularly after his marriage and his setting up of his house at Newport, vivid proofs alike, as seemed to us all, of his consummate, his *raffiné* taste, even if we hadn't yet, I think, that epithet for this—it was altogether in the form of mere helpless admirer and inhaler, led captive in part by the dawning perception that the arts were after all essentially one and that even with canvas and brush whisked out of my grasp I still needn't feel disinherited. That was the luxury of the friend and senior with a literary side—that if there were futilities that he didn't bring home to me he nevertheless opened more windows than he closed; since he couldn't have meant nothing by causing my eyes to plunge so straight into the square and dense little formal garden of Mérimée. I might occasionally serve for an abundantly idle young out-of-doors model—as in fact I frequently did, the best perhaps of his early exhibitions of a rare colour-sense even now attesting it; but mightn't it become possible that Mérimée would meanwhile serve for *me*?

Portrait in oils of Miss Katharine Temple, 1861.

Didn't I already see, as I fumbled with a pen, of what the small dense formal garden might be inspiringly symbolic? It was above all wonderful in the La Farge of those years that even as he painted and painted, very slowly and intently and belatedly—his habit of putting back the clock and ignoring every time-scheme but his own was matched only by his view of the constant timeliness of talk, talk as talk, for which no moment, no suspended step, was too odd or too fleeting—he remained as referentially and unexhaustedly bookish, he turned his back by the act as little on our theory of his omniscience as he ceased to disown his job, whatever it might be, while endlessly burying his salient and reinforced eyes and his visibly active organ of scent in some minutest rarity of print, some precious ancientry of binding, mechanically plucked, by the hazard of a touch, from one of the shelves of a stored collection that easily passed with us for unapproached.

He lost himself on these occasions both by a natural ease and by his early adoption and application of the principle of the imperturbable, which promised even from those days to govern his conduct well-nigh to the exclusion of every other. We were to know surely as time went on no comparable case of consistency of attitude—no other such prompt grasp by a nature essentially entire, a settled sovereign self, of the truth of what would work for it most favourably should it but succeed in never yielding the first inch of any ground. Immense every ground thus became by its covering itself from edge to edge with the defence of his serenity, which, whatever his fathomless private dealings with it, was never consentingly, I mean publicly, to suffer a grain of abatement. The artist's serenity, by this conception, was an intellectual and spiritual capital that must never brook defeat—which it so easily might incur by a single act of abdication. That was at any rate the case for the particular artist and the particular nature he felt himself, armour-proof as they became against the appeal of sacrifice. Sacrifice was fallibility, and one could only of course be consistent if one inveterately *had* hold of the truth. There was no safety or, otherwise, no inward serenity or even outward—though the outward came secondly—unless there was no deflection; none into the question, that is, of what might make for the serenity of others, which was their own affair and which above all seemed not urgent in comparison with the supreme artistic. It wasn't that the artist hadn't to pay, to pay for the general stupidity, perversity and perfidy, from the moment he might have to deal with these things; that was the inevitable suffering, and it was always there; but it could be more or less borne if one was systematically, or rather if one was naturally, or even, better still, preternaturally, in the right; since this meant the larger, the largest serenity. That account of so fine a case of inward confidence would indeed during those very first years have sinned somewhat by anticipation; yet something of the beauty—that is of the unmatched virtuosity—of the attitude finally achieved did even at the early time colour the air of intercourse with him for those who had either few enough or many enough of their own reserves. The second of these conditions sprang from a due anxiety for one's own interests, more or less defined in advance and therefore, as might be, more or less menaced; the other proviso easily went with vagueness—vagueness as to what things *were* one's interests, seeing that the exhibited working of an esthetic and a moral confidence conjoined on that scale and at play together unhampered would perhaps prove for the time an attraction beyond any other. This reflection must verily, in our relation, have brought about my own quietus—so far as that mild ecstasy could be divorced from agitation. I recall at all events less of the agitation than of the ecstasy; the primary months, certain aspects even of the few following years, look out at me as from fine accommodations, acceptances, submissions, emotions, all melted together, that one must have taken for joys of the mind and gains of the imagination so clear as to cost one practically nothing. They are what I see, and are all I want to see, as I look back; there hangs about them a charm of thrilled good faith, the flush and throb of crowding apprehensions, that has scarce faded and of which I can only wish to give the whole picture the benefit. I bottle this imponderable extract of the loitering summers of youth, when every occasion really seemed to stay to be gathered and tasted, just for the sake of its faint sweetness.

Some time since, in Boston, I spent an hour before a commemorative cluster of La Farge's earlier productions, gathered in on the occasion of his death, with the effect as of a plummet suddenly dropped into obscure depths long unstirred, that of a remembered participation, it didn't seem too much to say, in the far-away difficult business of their getting themselves born. These things, almost all finished studies of landscape, small and fond celebrations of the modest little Newport harmonies, the spare felicities and delicacies of a range of aspects that have ceased to appeal or to "count," called back into life a hundred memories, laid bare the very footsteps of time, light and uncertain though so often the imprint. I seemed so to have been there by the projection of curiosity and sympathy, if not by having literally looked in, when the greater number of such effects worked themselves out, that they spoke to me of my own history—through the felt intensity of my commission, as it were, to speak for my old friend. The terms on which he was ever ready to draw out for us the interesting hours, terms of patience as they essentially were for the edified party, lived again in this record, but with the old supposition of profit, or in other words the old sense of pleasure, of precious acquisition and intenser experience, more vivid than anything else. There recurs to me for instance one of the smallest of adventures, as tiny a thing as could incur the name and which was of the early stage of our acquaintance, when he proposed to me that we should drive out to the Glen, some six miles off, to breakfast, and should afterwards paint—*we* paint!—in the bosky open air. It looks at this distance a mythic time, that of felt inducements to travel so far at such an hour and in a backless buggy on the supposition of rustic fare. But different ages have different measures, and I quite remember how ours, that morning, at the neat hostel in the umbrageous valley, overflowed with coffee and griddle-cakes that were not as other earthly refreshment, and how a spell of romance rested for several hours on our invocation of the genius of the scene: of such material, with the help of the attuned spirit, may great events consent to be composed. My companion, his easel and canvas, his palette and stool and other accessories happily placed, settled to his subject, while I, at a respectful distance, settled to mine and to the preparation of this strange fruit of time, my having kept the impression as if it really mattered. It did indeed matter, it was to continue to have done so, and when I ask myself the reason I find this in something as rare and deep and beautiful as a passage of old poetry, a scrap of old legend, in the vagueness of rustling murmuring green and plashing water and woodland voices and images, flitting hovering possibilities; the most retained of these last of course being the chance that one's small daub (for I too had my easel and panel and palette) might incur appreciation by the eye of friendship. This indeed was the true source of the spell, that it was in the eye of friendship, friendship full of character and colour, and full of amusement of its own, that I lived on any such occasion, and that I had come forth in the morning cool and had found our breakfast at the inn a thing of ineffable savour, and that I now sat and flurriedly and fearfully aspired. Yes, the interesting ineffectual and exquisite array of the Boston "show" smote for me most the chord of the prime questions, the admirations and expectations at first so confident, even that of those refinements of loyalty out of which the last and highest tribute was to spring; the consideration, I mean, of whether our extraordinary associate, neither promptly understood nor inveterately accepted, might not eventually be judged such a colourist and such a poet that owners of his first felicities, those very ones over which he was actually bending, and with a touch so inscrutable, such "tonalities" of his own, would find themselves envied and rich. I remember positively liking to see most people stupid about him, and to make them out, I dare say, more numerously stupid than they really were: this perhaps in some degree as a bright communication of his own spirit—which discerned from so far off that of the bitterest-sweet cup it was abundantly to taste; and partly because the case would after that fashion only have its highest interest. The highest interest, the very highest, it certainly couldn't fail to have; and the beauty of a final poetic justice, with exquisite delays, the whole romance of conscious delicacy and heroic patience intervening, was just what we seemed to see meanwhile stow itself expectantly away.

This view of the inevitable fate of distinguished work was thus, on my part, as it comes before me again, of early development, and I admit that I should appear to antedate it hadn't I in renewed presence of each of the particular predestined objects of sacrifice I have glanced at caught myself in the very act of that invidious apprehension, that fondest contemporaneity. There were the charming individual things round the production of which I had so at once elatedly and resignedly circled; and nothing remained at the end of time but to test the historic question. *Was* the quiet chamber of the Boston museum a constitution of poetic justice long awaited and at last fully cognisant?—or did the event perhaps fail to give out, after all, the essence of our far-away forecast? I think that what showed clearest, or what I, at any rate, most sharply felt, was the very difficulty of saying; which fact meant of course, I recognise, that the story fell a little short, alas, of rounding itself off. Poetic justice, when it comes, I gather, comes ever with a great shining; so that if there is any doubt about it the source of the doubt is in the very depths of the case and has been from the first at work there. It literally seems to me, besides, that there was more history and thereby more interest recoverable as the matter stood than if every answer to every question about it hadn't had a fine ambiguity. I like ambiguities and detest great glares; preferring thus for my critical no less than for my pedestrian progress the cool and the shade to the sun and dust of the way. There was an exquisite effort of which I had been peculiarly sure; the large canvas of the view of the Paradise Rocks over against Newport, but within the island and beyond the "second beach"—such were our thin designations! On the high style and the grand manner of this thing, even though a little uneasy before the absence from it of a certain *crânerie* of touch, I would have staked every grain of my grounded sensibility—in spite of which, on second thoughts, I shall let that faded fact, and no other contention at all, be my last word about it. For the prevailing force, within the Boston walls, the supreme magic anything was to distil, just melted into another connection which flung a soft mantle as over the whole show. It became, from the question of how even a man of perceptive genius had painted what we then locally regarded as our scenery, a question of how we ourselves had felt and cherished that scenery; which latter of these two memories swept for me everything before it. The scenery we cherished—by which I really mean, I fear, but four or five of us—has now been grossly and utterly sacrificed; in the sense that its range was all for the pedestrian measure, that to overwalk it was to love it and to love it to overwalk it, and that no such relation with it as either of these appears possible or thinkable to-day. We had, the four or five of us, the instinct—the very finest this must have been—of its scale and constitution, the adorable wise economy with which nature had handled it and in the light of which the whole seaward and insular extension of the comparatively futile town, untrodden, unsuspected, practically all inviolate, offered a course for the long afternoon ramble more in harmony with the invocations, or for that matter the evocations, of youth than we most of us, with appreciation so rooted, were perhaps ever to know. We knew already, we knew then, that no such range of airs would ever again be played for us on but two or three silver strings. They were but two or three—the sea so often as of the isles of Greece, the mildly but perpetually embayed promontories of mossy rock and wasted thankless pasture, bathed in a refinement of radiance and a sweetness of solitude which amounted in themselves to the highest "finish"; and little more than the feeling, with all this, or rather with no more than this, that possession, discrimination, far frequentation, were ours alone, and that a grassy rocky tide-washed, just a bare, though ever so fine-grained, toned and tinted breast of nature and field of fancy stretched for us to the low horizon's furthest rim. The vast region—it struck us then as vast—was practically roadless, but this, far from making it a desert, made it a kind of boundless empty carpeted saloon. It comes back to me that nobody in those days walked, nobody but the three or four of us—or indeed I should say, if pushed, the single pair in particular of whom I was one and the other Thomas Sargeant Perry, superexcellent and all-reading, all-engulfing friend of those days and still, sole survivor, of these, I thus found deeply consecrated that love of the long, again and again of the very longest possible, walk which was to see me, year after year, through so many of the twists and past so many of the threatened blocks of life's road, and which, during the early and American period, was to make me lone and perverse even in my own sight: so little was it ever given me then, wherever I scanned the view, to descry a fellow-pedestrian. The pedestrians came to succumb altogether, at Newport, to this virtual challenge of their strange agitation—by the circumstance, that is, of their being offered at last, to importunity, the vulgar road, under the invasion of which the old rich alternative miserably dwindled.

V

NOTHING MEANWHILE could have been less logical, yet at the same time more natural, than that William's interest in the practice of painting should have suddenly and abruptly ceased; a turn of our affair attended, however, with no shade of commotion, no repining at proved waste; with as little of any confessed ruefulness of mistake on one side as of any elation of wisdom, any resonance of the ready "I told you so" on the other. The one side would have been, with a different tone about the matter and a different domestic habit than ours, that of my brother's awkwardness, accompanying whatever intelligence, of disavowal, and the other been our father's not unemphatic return to the point that his doubts, those originally and confidently intimated, had been justified by the fact. Tempting doubtless in a heavier household air the opportunity on the latter's part to recall that if he had perfectly recognised his son's probable progress to a pitch of excellence he had exactly not granted that an attainment of this pitch was likely in the least, however uncontested, to satisfy the nature concerned; the foregone conclusion having all the while been that such a spirit was competent to something larger and less superficially calculable, something more expressive of its true inwardness. This was not the way in which things happened among us, for I really think the committed mistake was ever discriminated against—certainly by the head of the family—only to the extent of its acquiring, even if but speedily again to fade, an interest greater than was obtainable by the too obvious success. I am not sure indeed that the kind of personal history most appealing to my father would not have been some kind that should fairly proceed by mistakes, mistakes more human, more associational, less angular, less hard for others, that is less exemplary for them (since righteousness, as mostly understood, was in our parent's view, I think, the cruellest thing in the world) than straight and smug and declared felicities. The qualification here, I allow, would be in his scant measure of the difference, after all, for the life of the soul, between the marked achievement and the marked shortcoming. He had a manner of his own of appreciating failure, or of not at least piously rejoicing in displayed moral, intellectual, or even material, economies, which, had it not been that his humanity, his generosity and, for the most part, his gaiety, were always, at the worst, consistent, might sometimes have left us with our small savings, our little exhibitions and complacencies, rather on our hands. As the case stood I find myself thinking of our life in those years as profiting greatly for animation and curiosity by the interest he shed for us on the whole side of the human scene usually held least interesting—the element, the appearance, of *waste* which plays there such a part and into which he could read under provocation so much character and colour and charm, so many implications of the fine and the worthy, that, since the art of missing or of failing, or of otherwise going astray, did after all in his hands escape becoming either a matter of real example or of absolute precept, enlarged not a little our field and our categories of appreciation and perception. I recover as I look back on all this the sense as of an extraordinary young confidence, our common support, in our coming round together, through the immense lubrication of his expressed thought, often perhaps extravagantly working and playing, to plenty of unbewildered rightness, a state of comfort that would always serve—whether after strange openings into a sphere where nothing practical mattered, or after even still quainter closings in upon us of unexpected importances and values. Which means, to my memory, that we breathed somehow an air in which waste, for us at least, couldn't and didn't live, so certain were aberrations and discussions, adventures, excursions and alarms of whatever sort, to wind up in a "transformation scene" or, if the term be not profane, happy harlequinade; a figuration of each involved issue and item before the footlights of a familiar idealism, the most socialised and ironised, the most amusedly generalised, that possibly could be.

Such an atmosphere was, taking one of its elements with another, doubtless delightful; yet if it was friendly to the suggested or imagined thing it promoted among us much less directly, as I have already hinted, the act of choice—choice as to the "career" for example, with a view of the usual proceedings thereupon consequent. I marvel at the manner in which the door appears to have been held or at least left open to us for experiment, though with a tendency to close, the oddest yet most inveterately perceptible movement in that sense, before any very earnest proposition in particular. I have no remembrance at all of marked prejudices on our father's part, but I recall repeated cases, in his attitude to our young affairs, of a disparagement suggested as by stirred memories of his own; the instance most present to me being his extreme tepidity in the matter of William's, or in fact of my, going, on our then American basis, to college. I make out in him, and at the time made out, a great revulsion of spirit from that incurred experience in his own history, a revulsion I think moreover quite independent of any particular or intrinsic attributes of the seat of learning involved in it. Union College, Schenectady, New York, the scene of his personal experiment and the natural resort, in his youth, of comparatively adjacent Albanians, might easily have offered at that time no very rare opportunities—few were the American country colleges that then had such to offer; but when, after years, the question arose for his sons he saw it in I scarce know what light of associational or "subjective" dislike. He had the disadvantage—unless indeed it was much more we who had it—of his having, after many changes and detachments, ceased to believe in the Schenectady resource, or to revert to it sentimentally, without his forming on the other hand, with his boys to place, any fonder presumption or preference. There comes out to me, much bedimmed but recognisable, the image of a day of extreme youth on which, during a stay with our grandmother at Albany, we achieved, William and I, with some confused and heated railway effort, a pious pilgrimage to the small scholastic city—pious by reason, I clearly remember, of a lively persuasion on my brother's part that to Union College, at some indefinite future time, we should both most naturally and delightedly repair. We invoked, I gather, among its scattered shades, fairly vague to me now, the loyalty that our parent appeared to have dropped by the way—even though our attitude about it can scarce have been prematurely contentious; the whole vision is at any rate to-day bathed and blurred for me in the air of some charmed and beguiled dream, that of the flushed good faith of an hour of crude castle-building. We were helped to build, on the spot, by an older friend, much older, as I remember him, even than my brother, already a member of the college and, as it seemed, greatly enjoying his life and those "society" badges and trinkets with which he reappears to me as bristling and twinkling quite to the extinction of his particular identity. This is lost, like everything else, in the mere golden haze of the little old-time autumn adventure. Wondrous to our sensibility may well have been the October glamour—if October it was, and if it was not it ought to have been!—of that big brave region of the great State over which the shade of Fenimore Cooper's Mohawks and Mohicans (if this be not a pleonasm) might still have been felt to hang. The castle we had built, however, crumbled—there were plenty of others awaiting erection; these too successively had their hour, but I needn't at this time stoop to pick up their pieces. I see moreover vividly enough how it might have been that, at this stage, our parents were left cold by the various appeal, in our interest, of Columbia, Harvard and Yale. Hard by, at Providence, in the Newport time, was also "Brown"; but I recover no connection in which that mystic syllable swept our sky as a name to conjure with. Our largest licence somehow didn't stray toward Brown. It was to the same tune not conceivable that we should have been restored for educational purposes to the swollen city, the New York of our childhood, where we had then so tumbled in and out of school as to exhaust the measure, or as at least greatly to deflower the image, of our teachability on that ground. Yale, off our beat from every point of view, was as little to be thought of, and there was moreover in our father's imagination no grain of susceptibility to what might have been, on the general ground, "socially expected." Even Harvard, clearly—and it was perhaps a trifle odd—moved him in our interest as little as Schenectady could do; so that, for authority, the voice of social expectation would have had to sound with an art or an accent of which it had by no means up to that time learned roundabout us the trick. This indeed (it comes to saying) is something that, so far as our parents were concerned, it would never have learned. They were, from other preoccupations, unaware of any such pressure; and to become aware would, I think, primarily have been for them to find it out of all proportion to the general pitch of prescription. We were not at that time, when it came to such claims, in presence of persuasive, much less of impressive, social forms and precedents—at least those of us of the liberated mind and the really more curious culture were not; the more curious culture, only to be known by the positive taste of it, was nowhere in the air, nowhere seated or embodied.

Which reflections, as I perhaps too loosely gather them in, refresh at any rate my sense of how we in particular of our father's house actually profited more than we lost, if the more curious culture was in question, by the degree to which we were afloat and disconnected; since there were at least luxuries of the spirit in this quite as much as drawbacks—given a social order (so far as it *was* an order) that found its main ideal in a "strict attention to business," that is to buying and selling over a counter or a desk, and in such an intensity of the traffic as made, on the part of all involved, for close localisation. To attend strictly to business was to be invariably *there*, on a certain spot in a certain place; just as to be nowhere in particular, to *have* to be nowhere, told the queer tale of a lack or of a forfeiture, or possibly even of a state of intrinsic unworthiness. I have already expressed how few of these elements of the background we ourselves had ever had either to add to or to subtract from, and how this of itself did after a fashion "place" us in the small Newport colony of the despoiled and disillusioned, the mildly, the reminiscentially desperate. As easy as might be, for the time, I have also noted, was our footing there; but I have not, for myself, forgotten, or even now outlived, the particular shade of satisfaction to be taken in one's thus being in New England without being of it. To have originally been of it, or still to have had to be, affected me, I recall, as a case I should have regretted—unless it be more exact to say that I thought of the condition as a danger after all escaped. Long would it take to tell why it figured as a danger, and why that impression was during the several following years much more to gain than to lose intensity. The question was to fall into the rear indeed, with ever so many such secondary others, during the War, and for reasons effective enough; but it was afterwards to know a luxury of emergence—this, I mean, while one still "cared," in general, as one was sooner or later to stop caring. Infinitely interesting to recover, in the history of a mind, for those concerned, these movements of the spirit, these tides and currents of growth—though under the inconvenience for the historian of such ramifications of research that here at any rate I feel myself warned off. There appeared to us at Newport the most interesting, much, of the Albany male cousins, William James Temple—coming, oddly enough, first from Yale and then from Harvard; so that by contact and example the practicability of a like experience might have been, and doubtless was, put well before us. "Will" Temple, as we were in his short life too scantly to know him, had made so luckless, even if so lively a start under one alma mater that the appeal to a fresh parentship altogether appears to have been judged the best remedy for his case: he entered Harvard jumping, if I mistake not, a couple of years of the undergraduate curriculum, and my personal memory of these reappearances is a mere recapture of admiration, of prostration, before him. The dazzled state, under his striking good looks and his manly charm, was the common state; so that I disengage from it no presumption of a particular plea playing in our own domestic air for his temporary Cambridge setting; he was so much too radiant and gallant and personal, too much a character and a figure, a splendid importance in himself, to owe the least glamour to settings; an advantage that might have seemed rather to be shed on whatever scene by himself in consenting to light it up. He made all life for the hour a foreground, and one that we none of us would have quitted for a moment while he was there.

In that form at least I see him, and no revival of those years so puts to me the interesting question, so often aimlessly returned upon in later life, of the amount of truth in this or that case of young confidence in a glory to come—for another than one's self; of the likelihood of the wonders so flatteringly forecast. Many of our estimates were monstrous magnifications—though doing us even at that more good than harm; so that one isn't even sure that the happiest histories were to have been those of the least liberal mistakes. I like at any rate to think of our easy overstrainings—the possible flaw in many of which was not indeed to be put to the proof. That was the case for the general, and for every particular, impression of Will Temple, thanks to his early death in battle—at Chancellorsville,

1863; he having, among the quickened forces of the time, and his father's record helping him, leaped to a captaincy in the regular Army; but I cling to the idea that the siftings and sortings of life, had he remained subject to them, would still have left him the lustre that blinds and subdues. I even do more, at this hour; I ask myself, while his appearance and my personal feeling about it live for me again, what possible aftertime could have kept up the pitch of my sentiment—aftertime either of his or of mine. Blest beyond others, I think as we look back, the admirations, even the fondest (and which indeed were not of their nature fond?) that were not to know to their cost the inevitable test or strain; they are almost the only ones, of the true high pitch, that, without broken edges or other tatters to show, fold themselves away entire and secure, even as rare lengths of precious old stuff, in the scented chest of our savings. So great misadventure have too often known at all events certain of those that were to come to trial. The others are the *residual*, those we must keep when we can, so to be sure at least of a few, sacrificing as many possible mistakes and misproportions as need be to pay but for two or three of them. There could be no mistake about Gus Barker, who threw himself into the fray, that is into the cavalry saddle, as he might into a match at baseball (football being then undreamt of), and my last reminiscence of whom is the sight of him, on a brief leave for a farewell to his Harvard classmates after he had got his commission, crossing with two or three companions the expanse of Harvard Square that faced the old Law School, of which I found myself for that year (1862–63) a singularly alien member. I was afterwards sharply to regret the accident by which I on that occasion missed speech of him; but my present vision of his charming latent agility, which any motion showed, of his bright-coloured wagging head and of the large gaiety of the young smile that made his handsome teeth shine out, is after all the years but the more happily uneffaced. The point of all which connections, however, is that they somehow managed to make in the parental view no straight links for us with the matter-of-course of college. There were accidents too by the aid of which they failed of this the more easily. It comes to me that, for my own part, I thought of William at the time as having, or rather as so much more than having, already graduated; the effect of contact with his mind and talk, with the free play of his spirit and the irrepressible brush of his humour, couldn't have been greater had he carried off fifty honours. I felt in him such authority, so perpetually quickened a state of intellect and character, that the detail or the literal side of the question never so much as came up for me: I must have made out that to plenty of graduates, or of the graduating, nothing in the nature of such appearances attached. I think of our father moreover as no less affected by a like impression; so extremely, so immensely disposed do I see him to generalise his eldest son's gifts as by the largest, fondest synthesis, and not so much proceed upon them in any one direction as proceed *from* them, as it were, in all.

Little as such a view might have lent itself to application, my brother's searching discovery during the summer of 1861 that his vocation was not "after all" in the least satisfyingly for Art, took on as a prompt sequel the recognition that it was quite positively and before everything for Science, physical Science, strenuous Science in all its exactitude; with the opportunity again forthcoming to put his freshness of faith to the test. I had presumed to rejoice before at his adoption of the studio life, that offering as well possible contacts for myself; and yet I recall no pang for his tergiversation, there being nothing he mightn't have done at this or at any other moment that I shouldn't have felt as inevitable and found in my sense of his previous age some happy and striking symptom or pledge of. As certain as that he had been all the while "artistic" did it thus appear that he had been at the same time quite otherwise inquiring too—addicted to "experiments" and the consumption of chemicals, the transfusion of mysterious liquids from glass to glass under exposure to lambent flame, the cultivation of stained fingers, the establishment and the transport, in our wanderings, of galvanic batteries, the administration to all he could persuade of electric shocks, the maintenance of marine animals in splashy aquaria, the practice of photography in the room I for a while shared with him at Boulogne, with every stern reality of big cumbrous camera, prolonged exposure, exposure mostly of myself, darkened development, also interminable, and ubiquitous brown blot. Then there had been also the constant, as I fearfully felt it, the finely speculative and boldly disinterested absorption of curious drugs. No livelier remembrance have I of our early years together than this inveteracy, often appalling to a nature so incurious as mine in *that* direction, of his interest in the "queer" or the incalculable effects of things. There was apparently for him no possible effect whatever that mightn't be more or less rejoiced in as such—all exclusive of its relation to other things than merely knowing. There recurs to me withal the shamelessness of my own indifference—at which I also, none the less, I think, wondered a little; as if by so much as it hadn't been given me to care for visibly provoked or engineered phenomena, by that same amount was I open to those of the mysteriously or insidiously aggressive, the ambushed or suffered sort. Vivid to me in any case is still the sense of how quite shiningly light, as an activity and an appeal, he had seemed to make everything he gave himself to; so that at first, until the freshness of it failed, he flung this iridescent mantle of interest over the then so grey and scant little scene of the Harvard (the Lawrence) Scientific School, where in the course of the months I had had a glimpse or two of him at work. Early in the autumn of 1861 he went up from Newport to Cambridge to enter that institution; in which thin current rather than in the ostensibly more ample began to flow his long connection with Harvard, gathering in time so many affluents. His letters from Cambridge during the next couple of years, many of them before me now, breathe, I think, all the experience the conditions could have begotten at the best; they mark the beginning of those vivacities and varieties of intellectual and moral reaction which were for the rest of his life to be the more immeasurably candid and vivid, the more numerous above all, and the more interesting and amusing, the closer view one had of him. That of a certainty; yet these familiar pages of youth testify most of all for me perhaps to the forces of amenity and spontaneity, the happy working of all relations, in our family life. In such parts of them as I may cite this will shine sufficiently through—and I shall take for granted thus the interest of small matters that have perhaps but that reflected light to show. It is in a letter to myself, of that September, dated "Drear and Chill Abode," that he appears to have celebrated the first steps of his initiation.

Sweet was your letter and grateful to my eyes. I had gone in a mechanical way to the P.O. not hoping for anything (though "on espère alors qu'on désespère toujours,") and, finding nothing, was turning heavily away when a youth modestly tapped me and, holding out an envelope inscribed in your well-known character, said, "Mr. J., this was in our box!" 'Twas the young Pascoe, the joy of his mother—but the graphic account I read in the letter he gave me of the sorrow of *my* mother almost made me shed tears on the floor of the P.O. Not that on reflection I should dream——! for reflection shows me a future in which she shall regard my vacation visits as "on the whole" rather troublesome than otherwise; or at least when she shall feel herself as blest in the trouble I spare her when absent as in the glow of pride and happiness she feels at the sight of me when present. But she needn't fear I can ever think of *her* when absent with such equanimity. I oughtn't to "joke on such a serious subject," as Bobby would say though; for I have had several pangs since being here at the thought of all I have left behind at Newport—especially gushes of feeling about the *place*. I haven't for one minute had the feeling of being at home here. Something in my quarters precludes the possibility of it, though what this is I don't suppose I can describe to you.

As I write now even, writing itself being a cosy cheerful-looking amusement, and an argand gas-burner with a neat green shade merrily singing beside me, I still feel unsettled. I write on a round table in the middle of the room, with a fearful red and black cloth. Before me I see another such-covered table of oblong shape against the wall, capped by a cheap looking-glass and flanked by two windows, curtainless and bleak, whose shades of linen flout the air as the sportive wind impels them. To the left are two other such windows, with a horse-hair sofa between them, and at my back a fifth window and a vast wooden mantel-piece with nothing to relieve its nakedness but a large cast, much plumbago'd, of a bust of Franklin. On my right the Bookcase, imposing and respectable with its empty drawers and with my little array of printed wisdom covering nearly *one* of the shelves. I hear the people breathe as they go past in the street, and the roll and jar of the horse-cars is terrific. I have accordingly engaged the other room from Mrs. Pascoe, with the little sleeping-room upstairs. It looks infinitely more cheerful than this, and if I don't find the grate sufficient I can easily have a Franklin stove put up. But she says the grate will make an oven of it. . . . John Ropes I met the other day at Harry Quincy's room, and was very much pleased with him. Don't fail to send on Will Temple's letters to him and to Herbert Mason, which

I left in one of the library's mantelpiece jars, to use the Portuguese idiom. Storrow Higginson has been very kind to me, making enquiries about tables etc. We went together this morning to the house of the Curator of the Gray collection of Engravings, which is solemnly to unfold its glories to me to-morrow. He is a most serious stately German gentleman, Mr. Thies by name, fully sensible of the deep vital importance of his treasures and evidently thinking a visit to them a great affair—to *me*. Had I known how great, how tremendous and formal, I hardly think I should have ventured to call. Tom Ward pays me a visit almost every evening. Poor Tom seems a-cold too. His deafness keeps him from making acquaintances. Professor Eliot, at the School, is a fine fellow, I suspect; a man who if he resolves to do a thing won't be prevented. I find analysis very interesting *so far!* The Library has a reading-room, where they take all the magazines; so I shan't want for the Rev. des 2 M. I remain with unalterable sentiments of devotion ever, my dear H., your Big Brother Bill.

This record of further impressions closely and copiously followed.

Your letter this morning was such a godsend that I hasten to respond a line or two, though I have no business to—for I have a fearful lesson to-morrow and am going to Boston to-night to hear Agassiz lecture (12 lectures on "Methods in Nat. Hist."), so that I will only tell you that I am very well and my spirits just getting good. Miss Upham's table is much pleasanter than the other. Professor F. J. Child is a great joker—he's a little flaxen-headed boy of about 40. There is a nice old lady boarder, another man of about 50, of aristocratic bearing, who interests me much, and 3 intelligent students. At the other table was no conversation at all; the fellows had that American solemnity, called each other Sir, etc. I cannot tell you, dearest Mother, how your account of your Sunday dinner and of your feelings thereat brought tears to my eyes. Give Father my ardent love and cover with kisses the round fair face of the most kiss-worthy Alice. Then kiss the Aunt till you get tired, and get all the rest of them to kiss *you* till you cry hold enough!

This morning as I was busy over the 10th page of a letter to Wilky in he popped and made my labour of no account. I had intended to go and see him yesterday, but found Edward Emerson and Tom Ward were going, and so thought he would have too much of a good thing. But he walked over this morning with, or rather without them, for he went astray and arrived very hot and dusty. I gave him a bath and took him to dinner, and he is now gone to see Andrew Robeson and E. E. His plump corpusculus looks as always. I write in my new parlour whither I moved yesterday. You have no idea what an improvement it is on the old affair—worth double the cost, and the little bedroom under the roof is perfectly delicious, with a charming outlook on little back yards with trees and pretty old brick walls. The sun is upon *this* room from earliest dawn till late in the afternoon—a capital thing in winter. I like Miss Upham's very much. Dark "aristocratic" dining-room, with royal cheer. "Fish, roast beef, veal cutlets, pigeons!" says the splendid, tall, noble-looking, white-armed, black-eyed Juno of a handmaid as you sit down. And for dessert a choice of three, *three*, darling Mother, of the most succulent, unctuous (no, not unctuous, unless you imagine a celestial unction without the oil) pie-like confections, always 2 platesful—my eye! She has an admirable chemical, not mechanical, combination of cake and jam and cream which I recommend to Mother if she is ever at a loss; though there is no well-stored pantry like that of good old Kay Street, or if there is it exists not for miserable me.

This chemical analysis is so bewildering at first that I am "muddled and bet" and have to employ almost all my time reading up. Agassiz is evidently a great favourite with his Boston audience and feels it himself. But he's an admirable earnest lecturer, clear as day, and his accent is most fascinating. Jeffries Wyman's lectures on Comp. Anatomy of Verts. promise to be very good; prosy perhaps a little and monotonous, but plain and well-arranged and nourris. Eliot I have not seen much more of; I don't believe he is a *very* accomplished chemist, but can't tell yet. We are only about 12 in the Laboratory, so that we have a very cosy time. I expect to have a winter of "crowded life." I can be as independent as I please, and want to live regardless of the good or bad opinion of every one. I shall have a splendid chance to try, I know, and I know too that the native hue of resolution has never been of very great shade in me hitherto. I am sure that that feeling is a right one, and I mean to live according to it if I can. If I do so I think I shall turn out all right.

I stopped this letter before tea, when Wilky the rosy-gilled and Frank Higginson came in. I now resume it by the light of a taper and that of the moon. Wilky read H.'s letter and amused me "metch" by his naive interpretation of Mother's most rational request that I should "keep a memorandum of all moneys I receive from Father." He thought it was that she might know exactly what sums her prodigal philosopher really gives out, and that mistrust of his generosity caused it. The phrase has a little sound that way, as H. subtly framed it, I confess!

The first few days, the first week here, I really didn't know what to do with myself or how to fill my time. I felt as if turned out of doors. I then received H.'s and Mother's letters. Never before did I know what mystic depths of rapture lay concealed within that familiar word. Never did the same being look so like two different ones as I going in and out of the P. O. if I bring a letter with me. Gloomily, with despair written on my leaden brow I stalk the street along towards the P. O., women, children and students involuntarily shrinking against the wall as I pass—thus,[1] as if the curse of Cain were stamped upon my front. But when I come out with a letter an immense concourse of people generally attends me to my lodging, attracted by my excited wild gestures and look.

Christmas being sparely kept in the New England of those days, William passed that of 1861, as a Cambridge letter of the afternoon indicates, without opportunity for a seasonable dash to Newport, but with such compensations, nearer at hand as are here exhibited. Our brother Wilky, I should premise, had been placed with the youngest of us, Bob, for companion, at the "co-educational" school then but a short time previously established by Mr. F. B. Sanborn at Concord, Massachusetts—and of which there will be more to say. "Tom" Ward, already mentioned and who, having left the Concord school shortly before, had just entered Harvard, was quickly to become William's intimate, approved and trusted friend; the diversion of whose patient originality, whose intellectual independence, ability and curiosity from science and free inquiry to hereditary banking—consequent on the position of the paternal Samuel Gray Ward as the representative for many years in the United States of the house of Baring Brothers—he from the first much regretted: the more pertinently doubtless that this companion was of a family "connected" with ours through an intermarriage, Gus Barker, as Mrs. S. G. Ward's nephew, being Tom's first cousin as well as ours, and such links still counting, in that age of comparatively less developed ramifications, when

[1]Expressive drawing alas irreproducible.

sympathy and intercourse kept pace as it was kept between our pairs of parents.

I have been in Boston the whole blest morning, toted round by the Wards, who had as usual asked me to dine with them. I had happily provided myself with an engagement here for all such emergencies, but, as is my sportive wont, I befooled Tom with divers answers, and finally let him believe I would come (having refused several dazzling chances for the purpose) supposing of course I should see him here yesterday at Miss Upham's board and disabuse him. But the young viper went home right after breakfast—so I had to go into Boston this morning and explain. Wilky had come up from Concord to dine in said Commonwealth Avenue, and I, as it turned out, found myself in for following the innocent lamb Lily up and down the town for two hours, to hold bundles and ring bells for her; Wilky and Tom having vanished from the scene. Clear sharp cold morning, thermometer 5 degrees at sunrise, and the streets covered with one glare of ice. I had thick smooth shoes and went sliding off like an avalanche every three steps, while she, having india-rubbers and being a Bostonian, went ahead like a swan. I had among other things to keep her bundles from harm, to wipe away every three minutes the trembling jewel with which the cold *would* with persistent kindness ornament my coral nose; to keep a hypocritic watchful eye on her movements lest she fall; to raise my hat gracefully to more and more of her acquaintances every block; to skate round and round embracing lamp-posts and door-scrapers by the score to keep from falling, as well as to avoid serving old lady-promenaders in the same way; to cut capers 4 feet high at the rate of 20 a second, every now and then, for the same purpose; to keep from scooting off down hills and round corners as fast as my able-bodied companion; often to do all these at once and then fall lickety-bang like a chandelier, but *when* so to preserve an expression of placid beatitude or easy nonchalance despite the raging fiend within: oh it beggars description! When finally it was over and I stood alone I shook my companion's dust from my feet and, biting my beard with rage, sware a mighty oath unto high heaven that I would never, while reason held her throne in this distracted orb, *never* NEVER, by word, look or gesture and this without mental reservation, acknowledge a "young lady" as a human being. The false and rotten spawn might die before I would wink to save it. No more Parties now!—at last I am a Man, etc., etc.!

My enthusiasm ran very high for a few minutes, but I suddenly

letters Never before did I know
what mystic depths of rapture* lay
concealed within that familiar word.
Never did the same being look so like
two different ones as I going in and coming
out of the P. O. if I bring a letter
with me. Gloomily, with despair
written on my leaden brow I stalk
the street along towards the P. O.
women, children and students involuntarily shrinking against the wall
as I pass, —thus as if the Curse of Cain were stamped upon my front
But when I come
out with a letter an
immense concourse
of people generally
attends me
to my lodging
attracted by my
excited wild gestures
and look.

A leaf from the letter quoted on page 333.

saw that I was a great ass and became sobered instantly, so that on the whole I am better for the circumstance, being a sadder and a wiser man. I also went to the Tappans' and gave the children slight presents; then, coming home to my venal board, behaved very considerately and paternally to a young lady who sat next to me, but with a shade of subdued melancholy in my manner which could not have been noticed at the breakfast-table. Many times and bitterly to-day have I thought of home and lamented that I should have to be away at this merry Christmastide from my rare family; wondering, with Wilky, if they were missing us as we miss them. And now as I sit in the light of my kerosene, with the fire quietly consuming in the grate and the twilight on the snow outside and the melancholy old-fashioned strains of the piano dimly rising from below, I see in vision those at home just going in to dinner; my aged, silvered Mother leaning on the arm of her stalwart yet flexible H., merry and garrulous as ever, my blushing Aunt with her old wild beauty still hanging about her, my modest Father with his rippling raven locks, the genial auld Rob and the mysterious Alice, all rise before me, a glorified throng; but two other forms, one tall, intellectual, swarthy, with curved nose and eagle eye, the other having breadth rather than depth, but a goodly morsel too, are wanting to complete the harmonious whole. Eftsoons they vanish and I am again alone, *alone*—what pathos in the word! I have two companions though, most all the time—remorse and despair! T. S. Perry took their place for a little, and to-day they have not come back. T. S. seemed to enjoy his visit very much. It was very pleasant for me to have him; his rustic wonder at the commonest sights was most ludicrous, and his conversation most amusing and instructive.

The place here improves to me as I go on living in it, and if I study with Agassiz 4 or 5 years there is nothing I should like better than to have you all with me, regular and comfortable. I enclose another advertisement of a house—but which would be too small for us, I believe, though it might be looked at. I had a long talk with one of A.'s students the other night, and saw for the first time how a naturalist may feel about his trade exactly as an artist does about his. For instance Agassiz would rather take wholly uninstructed people—"for he has to unteach them all they have learnt." He doesn't let them so much as look into a book for a long while; what they learn they must learn for themselves and be *masters* of it all. The consequence is he makes Naturalists of them—doesn't merely cram them; and this student (he had been there 2 years) said he felt ready to go anywhere in the world now with nothing but his notebook and study out anything quite

> alone. A. must be a great teacher. Chemistry comes on tolerably, but not so fast as I expected. I am pretty slow with my substances, having done but 12 since Thanksgiving and having 38 more to do before the end of the term.

Comment on the abundance, the gaiety and drollery, the generous play of vision and fancy in all this, would seem so needless as to be almost officious, were not the commentator constantly, were he not infinitely, arrested and reminded and solicited; which is at once his advantage and his embarrassment. Such a letter, at all events, read over with the general key, touches its contemporary scene and hour into an intensity of life for him; making indeed the great sign of that life my brother's signal vivacity and cordiality, his endless spontaneity of mind. Every thing in it is characteristic of the genius and expressive of the mood, and not least, of course, the pleasantry of paradox, the evocation of each familiar image by its vivid opposite. Our mother, *e.g.*, was not at that time, nor for a good while yet, so venerably "silvered"; our handsome-headed father had lost, occipitally, long before, all pretence to raven locks, certainly to the effect of their "rippling"; the beauty of our admirable aunt was as happily alien either to wildness or to the "hanging" air as it could very well be; the "mystery" of our young sister consisted all in the candour of her natural bloom, even if at the same time of her lively intelligence; and H.'s mirth and garrulity appear to have represented for the writer the veriest ironic translation of something in that youth, I judge, not a little mildly—though oh *so* mildly!—morose or anxiously mute. To the same tune the aquiline in his own nose heroically derides the slightly relaxed line of that feature; and our brother Wilky's want of physical "depth" is a glance at a different proportion. Of a like tinge of pleasantry, I may add, is the imputation of the provincial gape to our friend T. S. Perry, of Newport birth and unintermitted breeding, with whom we were to live so much in the years to come, and who was then on the eve of entering Harvard—his face already uninterruptedly turned to that love of letters, that practice of them by dauntless and inordinate, though never at all vulgarly resonant, absorption which was to constitute in itself the most disinterested of careers. I had myself felt him from the first an exemplary, at once, and a discouraging friend; he had let himself loose in the world of books, pressed and roamed through the most various literatures and the most voluminous authors, with a stride that, as it carried him beyond all view, left me dismayed and helpless at the edge of the forest, where I listened wistfully but unemulously to the far-off crash from within of his felled timber, the clearing of whole spaces or periods shelf by shelf or great tree by tree. The brother-in-law of John La Farge, he had for us further, with that reviving consciousness of American annals which the War was at once so rudely and so insidiously to quicken in us, the glamour of his straight descent from the Commodores Perry of the Lake Erie in the war of 1812, respectively, and of the portentous penetration of Japan just after the mid-century, and his longer-drawn but equally direct and so clean and comfortable affiliation to the great Benjamin Franklin: as these things at least seemed to me under my habit (too musing and brooding certainly to have made for light loquacity) of pressing every wind-borne particle of personal history—once the persons were only other enough from myself—into the service of what I would fain have called picture or, less explicitly, less formulatedly, romance.

These, however, are but too fond insistences, and what mainly bears pointing out is my brother's already restless reach forth to some new subject of study. He had but lately addressed himself, not without confidence, to such an investigation of Chemistry as he might become conscious of a warrant for, yet the appeal of Agassiz's great authority, so much in the air of the Cambridge of that time, found him at once responsive; it opened up a world, the world of sentient life, in the light of which Chemistry faded. He had not, however, for the moment done with it; and what I at any rate find most to the point in the pages before me is the charm of their so witnessing to the geniality and harmony of our family life, exquisite as I look back on it and reflected almost as much in any one passage taken at hazard as in any other. He had apparently, at the date of the following, changed his lodging.

President Felton's death has been the great event of the week—two funerals and I don't know how many prayers and sermons.

To-day I thought I would go to University chapel for the sake of variety and hear Dr. Peabody's final word on him—and a very long and lugubrious one it was. The prayer was a prolonged moan in which the death (not in its consequences, but in itself) was treated as a great calamity, and the whole eulogy was almost ridiculously overcharged. What was most disagreeable throughout was the wailing tones, not a bit that of simple pagan grief at the *loss*—which would have been honest; but a whine consciously put on as from a sense of duty, and a whine at nothing definite either, only a purposeless clothing of all his words in tears. The whole style of the performance was such that I have concluded to have nothing more to do with funerals till they improve.

The walking here has been terrible with ice or slush these many weeks, but over head celestial. No new developments in this house. The maniac sometimes chills my very marrow by hoarsely whispering outside the door, "Gulielmo, Gulielmo!" Old Sweetser sits in his dressing-gown smoking his pipe all day in a little uncomfortable old *bathroom* next door to me. He may with truth be called a queer cuss. The young ladies have that very nasty immodest habit of hustling themselves out of sight precipitately whenever I appear. I dined with Mrs. ——— yesterday all alone. She was quite sick, very hoarse, and *he* was in the country, so that on the whole it was a great bore. She is very clumsy in her way of doing things, and her invitation to me was for the wife of an artist—not artistic!

I am now studying organic Chemistry. It will probably shock Mother to hear that I yesterday destroyed a pockethandkerchief—but it was an old one and I converted it into some sugar which though rather brown is very good. I believe I forgot to tell you that I am shorn of my brightest ornament. That solitary hirsute jewel which lent such a manly and martial aspect to my visage is gone, and the place thereof is naked. I don't think anyone will know the difference, and moreover it is not dead, it only sleeps and will some day rise phoenix-like from its ashes with tenfold its former beauty. When Father comes will he please bring Ganot's Physique *if H. doesn't want it*?

In none of these earlier communications from Cambridge is the element of affectionate pleasantry more at play than in those addressed to his sister.

Charmante jeune fille, I find the Tappans *really* expected me to bring you to them and were much disappointed at my failure. Ellen has grown very fat and big. Mary calls everybody "horrid."

Lyly Barker is with the Wards. I haven't seen her yet, but shall do so on Saturday, when I am also to dine with the Hunts. I hope your neuralgia, or whatever you may believe the thing was, has gone and that you are back at school instead of languishing and lolling about the house. I send you herewith a portrait of Prof. Eliot, a very fair likeness, to grace your book withal. Write me whenever you have the slightest or most fleeting inclination to do so. If you have only one sentence to say, don't grudge paper and stamps for it. You don't know how much good you may do me at an appropriate time by a little easy scratching of your graceful nimble pen.

In another apostrophe to the same correspondent, at the same season, his high spirits throw off the bonds of the vernacular.

Est-ce que tu songes jamais à moi comme moi je songe à toi?—oh je crois bien que non! Maintes fois dans la journée l'image d'une espèce d'ange vêtue de blanc avec de longs boucles noirs qui encadrent une figure telle que la plupart des mortels ne font que l'entrevoir dans leur rêves, s'impose à mes sens ravis; créature longue et fluette qui se dispose à se coucher dans une petite chambrette verte où le gaz fait un grand jour. Eh, oua, oua, oua! c'est à faire mourir de douleur. Mais je parie que tout de même pas une étincelle ne vibre pour moi dans les fibres de ton cœur endurci. Hélas, oublié de mes parents et de mes semblables, je ne vois, où que je regarde, qu'un abîme de désespoir, un gouffre noir et peuplé de démons, qui tôt ou tard va m'engloutir. Tu ne m'écris jamais sauf pour me soutirer des objets de luxe. La vaste mère me déteste, il n'y a que le frère qui me reste attaché, et lui par esprit d'opposition plus que par autre chose. Eh mon Dieu, que vais-je devenir? En tout cas je vais clore cette lettre, qui s'est allongée malgré moi. Ton frère, James William.

Of the same bright complexion is this report, addressed to his parents, of the change of lodging already noted.

The presence of the Tweedys has been most agreeable and has contributed in no small degree to break the shock of removal to these new rooms, which are not near so cosy as the old; especially with the smoking of my stove, which went on all the first two days. That has been stopped, however, and the only trouble is now to get the fire alight at all. I have generally to start it 3 or 4 times,

> and the removal of the material of each failure from the grate is a fearful business. I have also to descend to the cellar myself to get my coal, and my "hod," as Ma Sweetser, my landlady, calls it, not being very much bigger than a milk-pitcher, doesn't add to the charm. The coal is apt to drop on the stairs, and I have to pick it all up. At present the stove fills the room with a nephitic and pestilential gas, so that I have to keep the window open. I went last night with the Tweedys to the concert for which they came up, and with them this morning to hear Wendell Phillips. This Sweetser family is worthy of Dickens. It consists of a Mr. and Miss S., Mr. S.'s three gushing girls, a parrot and a maniac. The maniac is very obstreperous. Her husband left her boarding here 3 months ago and went to Cuba. When she got mad he was written to, but has sent no reply, and they are keeping her. For the Aunt's sake I keep my drawer locked against her at night. Old Sweetser is a riddle I hope to do justice to at some future time, but can't begin on now. His sister shakes like an aspen whenever she is spoken to. Oh I forgot the most important character of all, the black wench who "does" the room. She is about 20 years old and wears short frocks, but talks like Alice Robeson and has an antediluvian face about as large as the top of a flour-barrel.

I can really keep my hand from nothing, of whatever connection, that causes his intensity of animation and spontaneity of expression to revive. On a Sunday evening early in 1862 he had

> just returned from Milton, and, after removing from my person a beetle, sit down to write you immediately. Ever since 10.30 this A.M. the beetle s'est promené à l'envi sur ma peau. The first feeling I had of his becoming attached to it made me jump so as to scare an old lady opposite me in the car into fits. Finding him too hard to crush I let him run, and at last got used to him though at times he tickled me to excruciation. I ache in every limb and every cranny of my mind from my visit. . . . They had the usual number of stories, wonderful and not wonderful, to tell of their friends and relatives (of Stephen somebody, *e.g.*, who had a waggon weighing several tons run over his chest without even bruising him, and so on). They are very nice girls indeed all the same. I then went, near by, to the Forbes's in a state of profuse perspiration, and saw handsome Mrs. F. and her daughters, and a substitute for Governor Andrew in the person of his wife; after which I returned here, being driven back in the car, as I perceived on the front platform,

by our old familiar—familiar indeed!—friend William (I mean our Irish ex-coachman) whom age doesn't seem to render more veracious, as he told me several very big stories about himself: how he smashed a car to pieces the other night, how he first gave the alarm of the great fire, etc.

I went to the theatre the other night, and, asking a gentleman to make room for me, found him to be Bob Temple, who had arrived in Boston that day. He looks very well and talks in the most extraordinary way you ever heard about Slavery and the wickedness of human society, and is apparently very sincere. He sailed for Europe on Wednesday. I exhorted him to stop over at Newport, but he wouldn't. There was something quite peculiar about him—he seemed greatly changed. I can tell you more at home, but wish I might have seen more of him. I have been the last three nights running to hear John Wilkes Booth, the "young American Roscius." Rant, rant, rant of the most fearful kind. The worst parts most applauded, but with any amount of fire and energy in the passionate parts, in some of which he really becomes natural. . . . You don't know what a regular Sévigné you have in Alice. I blush for my delinquencies toward her, but bow my head with meek humility, contented to be her debtor all my life and despairing of ever repaying her the value of her letters. Mother and Aunt I pine to see, and the honest Jack Tar of the family, the rough Bob, with his rude untutored ways!

Traps for remembrance I find set at every turn here, so that I have either to dodge them or patiently to suffer catching. I try in vain for instance merely to brush past the image of our kinsman Robert Temple the younger, who made with his brother Will the eldest pair in that house of cousins: he waylays, he persuades me too much, and to fail of the few right words for him would be to leave a deep debt unrepaid—his fitful hovering presence, repeatedly vivid and repeatedly obscured, so considerably "counted" for us, pointing the sharpest moral, pointing fifty morals, and adorning a perpetual tale. He was for years, first on the nearer and then little by little on the further, the furthest, horizon, quite the most emphasised of all our wastrels, the figure bristling most with every irregular accent that we were to find ourselves in any closeness of relation with. I held him for myself at least, from far back, a pure gift of free-handed chance to the grateful imagination, the utmost limit of whose complaint of it could be but for the difficulty of rendering him the really proper tribute. I regarded him truly, for a long time, as a possession of the mind, the human image swung before us with most of the effect of strong and thick and inimitable colour. If to be orphaned and free of range had affected my young fancy as the happy, that is the romantic, lot, no member of the whole cousinship, favoured in that sense as so many of them were, enjoyed so, by my making out, the highest privilege of the case. Nothing, I could afterwards easily see, had been less inevitable and of a greater awkwardness of accident than his being, soon after the death of his parents, shipped off from Albany, in pursuit of an education, to an unheard-of school in a remote corner of Scotland; which fact it was, however, that played for me exactly the bright part of preparing to show with particular intensity what Europe again, with the opportunity so given, was going to proceed to. It thus shone out when after the lapse of several years he recurred to our more competent view that, quite richly erratic creature as he might appear, and to whatever degree of wonder and suspense, of amusement and amazement, he might wind us up, the rich alien influence, full of special queernesses and mysteries in this special connection, had complacently turned him out for us and had ever so irretrievably and ineffaceably stamped him. He rose before us, tall and goodlooking and easy, as a figure of an oddly *civilised* perversity; his irreverent challenging humour, playing at once, without mercy, over American aspects, seemed somehow not less cultivated than profane—just which note in itself caused the plot beautifully to thicken; for this was to distinguish and almost embellish him throughout a long career in which he was to neglect no occasion, however frankly forbidding, for graceless adventure, that he had the pure derisive, the loose and mocking mind, yet initiated, educated, almost elegantly impudent, in other words successfully impertinent, and which expressed itself, in particular by the pen, with a literary lightness that we used to find inimitable. He had dangled there, further off and nearer, as a character, to my attention, in the sense in which "people in books" were characters, and other people, roundabout us, were somehow not; so that I fairly thought of him (though this more, doubtless, with the lapse of time) very much as if we had owed him to Thackeray or Dickens, the creators of superior life to whom we were at that time always owing most, rather than to any set of circumstances by which we had in our own persons felt served; that he was inimitable, inimitably droll, inimitably wasted, wanton, impossible, or whatever else it might be, making him thus one with the rounded and represented creature, shining in the light of art, as distinguished from the vague handful of more or less susceptible material that had in the common air to pass for a true concretion. The promise of this had been, to my original vision, in every wind-borne echo of him, however light; I doubtless put people "into books" by very much the same turn of the hand with which I took them out, but it had tinged itself with the finely free that, proceeding in due course from his school at Fochabers to the University of Aberdeen (each sound and syllable of this general far cry from Albany had in itself an incoherence!) he had encountered while there the oddest of all occasions to embrace the Romish faith. In the same way it ministered to the vivid, even if baffled, view of him that he appeared then to have retreated upon the impenetrable stronghold of Nairn, described by him as a bleak little Scotch watering-place which yet sufficed to his cluster of predicaments: whence he began to address to his bewildered pair of Albany guardians and trustees the earlier of that series of incomparably amusing letters, as we judged them, the arrival of almost any one of which among us, out of the midst of indocilities at once more and more horrific and more and more reported with a desperate drollery, was to constitute an event so supremely beguiling that distressful meanings and expensive remedies found themselves alike salved to consciousness by the fact that such compositions could only be, for people of taste, enjoyable. I think of this hapless kinsman throughout as blest with a "form" that appealed to the finer fibres of appreciation; so that, variously misadventurous as he was ever to continue, his genius for expression again and again just saved him—saved him for bare life, left in his hand a broken piece of the effective magic wand, never perhaps waved with anything like that easy grace in an equally compromised interest.

It was at any rate as if I had from the first collected and saved up the echoes—or so at least it seems to me now: echoes of him as all sarcastically and incorrigibly mutinous, somewhat later on, while in nominal charge of a despairing *pasteur* at Neuchâtel—followed by the intensified sense of him, after I scarce remember quite what interval, on his appearing at Newport, where his sisters, as I have mentioned, had been protectively gathered in, during the year, more or less, that followed our own installation there. Then it was that we had the value of his being interesting with less trouble taken to that end—in proportion to the effect achieved—than perhaps ever served such a cause; it would perhaps scarce even be too much to say that, as the only trouble he seemed capable of was the trouble of quite positively declining to interest on any terms, his essential Dickensism, as I have called it, or his Thackerayan tint if preferred, his comedy-virtue in fine, which he could neither disown nor, practically speaking, misapply, was stronger even than his particular sardonic cynicism, strongly as that was at last to flower. I won't in the least say he dazzled—that was reserved for his so quite otherwise brilliant, his temporarily triumphant, younger brother, at whom I have already glanced, who was on no possible terms with him, and never could have been, so that the difficulty of their relation glimmers upon me as probably half the good reason for the original queer despatch of the elder to about the remotest, the most separating, point in space at which "educational advantages" could be conceived as awaiting him. I must have had no need by that time to be dazzled, or even to be charmed, in order more or less fondly, often indeed doubtless fearfully, to apprehend; what I apprehended being that here was a creature quite amusedly and perceptively, quite attentively and, after a fashion, profitably, living without a single one of the elements of life (of the inward, I mean, those one would most have missed if deprived of them) that I knew as most conducive to animation. What could have roused more curiosity than this, for the time at least, even if there hadn't been associated with it such a fine redolence, as I then supposed it, of the rich and strange places and things, as I supposed *them*, that had contributed to making him over? He had come back made—unless one was already, and too conveniently or complacently, to call it unmade: *that* was the point (and it certainly wasn't Albany that ever would have made him); he had come back charged, to my vision, with prodigious "English" impressions and awarenesses, each so thoroughly and easily assimilated that they might have played their part as convictions and standards had he pretended to anything that would in that degree have satisfied us. He never spoke of his "faith," as that might have been the thing we could have held him to; and he knew what not too gracelessly to speak of when the sense of the American grotesque in general and the largely-viewed "family" reducibility to the absurd in particular offered him such free light pasture. He had the sign of grace that he ever perfectly considered my father—so far as attitude, distinct from behaviour, went; but most members of our kinship on that side still clung to this habit of consideration even when, as was in certain cases but too visible, they had parted with all sense of any other. I have preserved no happier truth about my father than that the graceless whom, according to their own fond term, he, and he alone of all of us, "understood," returned to him as often and appealed to him as freely as those happier, though indeed scarce less importunate, in their connection, who found attraction and reason enough in their understanding *him*. My brother's impression of this vessel of intimations that evening at the Boston theatre, and of his "sincerity" and his seeming "greatly changed," doesn't at all events, I feel, fail in the least to fit into one of those amplifications upon which my incurable trick of unwillingness wholly to sacrifice any good value compromised by time tends to precipitate me with a force that my reader can scarce fear for me more than I fear it for myself. There was no "extraordinary way" in which our incalculable kinsman *mightn't* talk, and that William should have had for the hour the benefit of this general truth is but a happy note in my record. It was not always the case that one wished one "might have seen more of him," but this was only because one had had on any contact the sense of seeing so much. That produced consequences among which the desire for more might even be uncannily numbered. John Wilkes Booth, of the same evening, was of course President Lincoln's assassin-to-be, of whose crudely extravagant performance of the hero of Schiller's Robbers I recall my brother's imitative description—I never myself saw him; and it simplifies his case, I think, for distracted history, that he must have been quite an abominable actor. I appear meanwhile to have paid William at Cambridge a visit of which I have quite oddly lost remembrance—by reason doubtless of its but losing itself in like, though more prolonged, occasions that were to follow at no great distance and that await my further reference. The manner of his own allusion to it more than suffices.

> The radiance of H.'s visit has not faded yet, and I come upon gleams of it three or four times a day in my farings to and fro, but it has never a bit diminished the lustre of far-off shining Newport, all silver and blue, and of this heavenly group below[1]—all being more or less failures, especially the two outside ones. The more so as the above-mentioned H. could in no wise satisfy my craving for knowledge of family and friends—he didn't seem to have been on speaking terms with anyone for some time past, and could tell me nothing of what they did, said or thought, about any given subject. Never did I see a so-much uninterested creature in the affairs of those about him. He is a good soul, though, in his way, too; and less fatal than the light fantastic and ever-sociable Wilky, who has wrought little but disaster during his stay with me; breaking down my good resolutions about food, keeping me from all intellectual exercise, working havoc on my best hat by wearing it while dressing, while in his nightgown, while washing his face, and all but going to bed with it. He occupied my comfortable arm-chair all the morning in the position represented in the fine plate that accompanies this letter—but one more night though, and he will have gone, and no thorn shall pierce the side of the serene and hallowed felicity of expectation in which I shall revel till the time comes for returning home, home to the hearth of my infancy and budding youth. As Wilky has submitted to you a résumé of his future history for the next few years, so will I of mine, hoping it will meet your approval. Thus: one year Chemistry, then one term at home. Then one year with Wyman, followed by a medical education. Then five or six years with Agassiz; after which probably death, death, death from inflation and plethora of knowledge. This you had better seriously consider. So farewell till 8.45 some Sunday evening soon. Your bold, your beautiful, your blossom!

"I lead, as ever," he meanwhile elsewhere records, "the monotonous life of the scholar, with few variations."

> We have very general talk at our table, Miss Upham declaiming against the vulgarity of President Lincoln and complacently telling

[1]A drawing of figures in evening lamplight.

of her own ignorance as to the way the wind blows or as to the political events going on, and saying she thinks it a great waste of time and of "no practical account" to study natural history. F. J. Child impresses one as very witty and funny, but leaves it impossible to remember what he says. I took a walk with the Divinity student this splendid afternoon. He told me he had been walking yesterday with one of the Jerseymen and they had discussed the doctrine of a future state. The Jerseyman thought that if the easy Unitarian doctrines were to become popular the morals of the community would be most terribly relaxed. "Why," said the other, "here you are in the very thick of Unitarianism; look about you—people are about as good as anywhere." "Yes," replied the Jerseyman, "I confess to you that that is what has *staggered* me, and I don't understand it yet!"

I stretch over to the next year, 1863, for the sake of the following to his sister.

Chérie charmante, I am established in a cosy little room, with a large recess with a window in it containing bed and washstand, and separated from the main apartment by a rich green silk curtain and a large gilt cornice. This gives the whole establishment a splendid look. I found when I got back here that Miss Upham had raised her price; so great efforts were made by two of us to form a club. But too little enthusiasm was shown by any one else, and it fell through. I then with that fine economical instinct which distinguishes me resolved to take breakfast and tea, of my own finding and making, in my room, and only pay Miss Upham for dinners. Miss U. is now holding forth at Swampscott, so I asked to see her sister Mrs. Wood and learn the cost of the 7 dinners a week. She with true motherly instinct said that I should only make a slop with my self-made meals in my room, and that she would rather let me keep on for 4.50, seeing it was me. I said she must first consult Miss Upham. She returned from Swampscott saying that Miss U. had sworn she would rather pay *me* a dollar a week than have me go away. Ablaze with economic passion I cried "Done!"—trying to make it appear that she had made me a formal offer to that effect. But she then wouldn't admit it, and after much recrimination we separated, it being agreed that I should come for 4.50, *but tell no one*. So mind *you* don't either. I now lay my hand on my heart and confidently look to my Mother for that glance of approbation which she *must* bestow. Have I not redeemed any weaknesses of the past? Though part of my conception fails, yet it was boldly planned and would have been a noble stroke.

I have been pretty busy this week. I have a filial feeling toward Wyman already. I work in a vast museum at a table all alone, surrounded by skeletons of mastodons, crocodiles and the like, with the walls hung about with monsters and horrors enough to freeze the blood. But I have no fear, as most of them are tightly bottled up. Occasionally solemn men and women come in to see the museum, and sometimes timid little girls (reminding me of thee, my love, only they are less fashionably dressed), who whisper "Is folks allowed here?" It pains me to remark, however, that not all the little girls are of this pleasing type, many being bold-faced jades. Salter is back here, but morose. One or two new students and Prof. Goodwin, who is very agreeable. Also William Everett, son of the great Edward, very intelligent and a capital scholar, studying law. He took honours at the English Cambridge. I send a photograph of General Sickles for your and Wilky's amusement. It is a part of a great anthropomorphological collection which I am going to make. So take care of it, as well as of all the photographs you will find in the table-drawer in my room. But isn't he a bully boy? Desecrate the room as little as possible. If Wilky wants me as an extra nurse send for me without hesitation.

VI

THESE RETURNS to that first year or two at Newport contribute meanwhile to filling out as nothing in the present pages has yet done for me that vision of our father's unsurpassable patience and independence, in the interest of the convictions he cherished and the expression of them, as richly emphatic as it was scantly heeded, to which he daily gave himself. We took his "writing" infinitely for granted—we had always so taken it, and the sense of him, each long morning, at his study table either with bent considering brow or with a half-spent and checked intensity, a lapse backward in his chair and a musing lift of perhaps troubled and baffled eyes, seems to me the most constant fact, the most closely interwoven and underlying, among all our breaks and variations. He applied himself there with a regularity and a piety as little subject to sighing abatements or betrayed fears as if he had been working under pressure for his bread and ours and the question were too urgent for his daring to doubt. This play of his remarkable genius brought him in fact throughout the long years no ghost of a reward in the form of pence, and could proceed to publicity, as it repeatedly did, not only by the copious and resigned sacrifice of such calculations, but by his meeting in every single case all the expenses of the process. The untired impulse to this devotion figured for us, comprehensively and familiarly, as "Father's Ideas," of the force and truth of which in his own view we were always so respectfully, even though at times so bewilderedly and confoundedly persuaded, that we felt there was nothing in his exhibition of life that they didn't or couldn't account for. They pervaded and supported his existence, and very considerably our own; but what comes back to me, to the production of a tenderness and an admiration scarce to be expressed, is the fact that though we thus easily and naturally lived with them and indeed, as to their more general effects, the colour and savour they gave to his talk, breathed them in and enjoyed both their quickening and their embarrassing presence, to say nothing of their almost never less than amusing, we were left as free and unattacked by them as if they had been so many droppings of gold and silver coin on tables and chimney-pieces, to be "taken" or not according to our sense and delicacy, that is our felt need and felt honour. The combination in him of his different vivacities, his living interest in his philosophy, his living interest in us and his living superiority to all greed of authority, all overreaching or everemphasising "success," at least in the heated short run, gave his character a magnanimity by which it was impossible to us not to profit in all sorts of responsive and in fact quite luxurious ways. It was a luxury, I to-day see, to have all the benefit of his intellectual and spiritual, his religious, his philosophic and his social passion, without ever feeling the pressure of it to our direct irritation or discomfort. It would perhaps more truly figure the relation in which he left us to these things to have likened our opportunities rather to so many scattered glasses of the liquor of faith, poured-out cups stood about for our either sipping or draining down or leaving alone, in the measure of our thirst, our curiosity or our strength of head and heart. If there was much leaving alone in us—and I freely confess that, so far as the taking any of it all "straight" went, my lips rarely adventured—this was doubtless because we drank so largely at the source itself, the personally overflowing and irrigating. What it then comes to, for my present vision, was that he treated us most of all on the whole, as he in fact treated everything, by his saving imagination—which set us, and the more as we were naturally so inclined, the example of living as much as we might in some such light of our own. If we had been asked in our younger time for instance what *were* our father's ideas, or to give an example of one of them, I think we should promptly have answered (I should myself have hastened to do so) that the principal was a devoted attachment to the writings of Swedenborg; as to whom we were to remember betimes, with intimate appreciation, that in reply to somebody's plea of not finding him credible our parent had pronounced him, on the contrary, fairly "insipid with veracity." We liked that partly, I think, because it disposed in a manner, that is in favour of our detachment, of the great Emanuel, but when I remember the part played, so close beside us, by this latter's copious revelation, I feel almost ashamed for my own incurious conduct. The part played consisted to a large extent in the vast, even though incomplete, array of Swedenborg's works, the old faded covers of which, anciently red, actually apt to be loose, and backed with labels of impressive, though to my sense somewhat sinister London imprint, Arcana Coelestia, Heaven and Hell and other such matters—they all had, as from other days, a sort of black emphasis of dignity—ranged themselves before us wherever, and however briefly, we disposed ourselves, forming even for short journeys the base of our father's travelling library and perhaps at some seasons therewith the accepted strain on our mother's patience. I recall them as inveterately part of our very luggage, requiring proportionate receptacles; I recall them as, in a number considerable even when reduced, part of their proprietor's own most particular dependence on his leaving home, during our more agitated years, for those speculative visits to possible better places (than whatever place of the moment) from which, as I have elsewhere mentioned, he was apt to return under premature, under passionate nostalgic, reaction. The Swedenborgs were promptly out again on their customary shelves or sometimes more improvised perches, and it was somehow not till we had assured ourselves of this that we felt *that* incident closed.

Nothing could have exceeded at the same time our general sense—unless I all discreetly again confine myself to the spare record of my own—for our good fortune in never having been, even when most helpless, dragged by any approach to a faint jerk over the threshold of the inhabited temple. It stood there in the centre of our family life, into which its doors of fine austere bronze opened straight; we passed and repassed them when we didn't more consciously go round and behind; we took for granted vague grand things within, but we never paused to peer or penetrate, and none the less never had the so natural and wistful, perhaps even the so properly resentful, "Oh I say, do look in a moment for manners if for nothing else!" called after us as we went. Our admirable mother sat on the steps at least and caught reverberations of the inward mystic choir; but there were positive contemporary moments when I well-nigh became aware, I think, of something graceless, something not to the credit of my aspiring "intellectual life," or of whatever small pretensions to seriousness I might have begun to nourish, in the anything but heroic impunity of my inattention. William, later on, made up for this not a little, redeeming so, to a large extent, as he grew older, our filial honour in the matter of a decent sympathy, if not of a noble curiosity: distinct to me even are certain echoes of passages between our father and his eldest son that I assisted at, more or less indirectly and wonderingly, as at intellectual "scenes," gathering from them portents of my brother's independent range of speculation, agitations of thought and announcements of difference, which could but have represented, far beyond anything I should ever have to show, a gained and to a considerable degree an enjoyed, confessedly an interested, acquaintance with the paternal philosophic *penetralia.* That particular impression refers indeed to hours which at the point I have reached had not yet struck; but I am touched even now, after all the years, with something exquisite in my half-grasped premonitory vision of their belonging, these belated discussions that were but the flowering of the first germs of such *other*, doubtless already such opposed, perceptions and conclusions, to that order of thin consolations and broken rewards which long figured as the most and the best of what was to have been waited for on our companion's part without the escape of a plaint. Yet I feel I may claim that our awareness of all that was so serenely dispensed with—to call it missed would have been quite to falsify the story and reflect meanly on the spirit—never in the least brutally lapsed from admiration, however unuttered the sentiment itself, after the fashion of raw youth; it is in fact quite distinct to me that, had there been danger of this, there came to us from our mother's lips at intervals long enough to emphasise the final sincerity and beauty a fairly sacred reminder of that strain of almost solely self-nourished equanimity, or in other words insuperable gaiety, in her life's comrade, which she had never seen give way. This was the very gaiety that kept through the years coming out for us—to the point of inviting free jokes and other light familiarities from us at its expense. The happiest household pleasantry invested our legend of our mother's fond habit of address, "Your father's *ideas*, you know—!" which was always the signal for our embracing her with the last responsive finality (and, for the full pleasure of it, in his presence). Nothing indeed so much as his presence encouraged the licence, as I may truly call it, of the legend—that is of our treatment *en famille* of any reference to the attested public weight of his labours; which, I hasten to add, was much too esoteric a ground of geniality, a dear old family joke, not to be kept, for its value, to ourselves. But there comes back to me the impression of his appearing on occasion quite moved to the exuberance of cheer—as a form of refreshment he could draw on for a stronger and brighter spurt, I mean—by such an apology for resonance of reputation as our harmless, our of course utterly edgeless, profanity represented. It might have been for him, by a happy stretch, a sign that the world *did* know—taking us for the moment, in our selfish young babble, as a part of the noise of the world. Nothing, at the same time, could alter the truth of his case, or can at least alter it to me now: he had, intellectually, convictionally, passionally speaking, a selfless detachment, a lack of what is called the eye for effect—always I mean of the elated and interested order—which I can but marvel at in the light of the rare aptitude of his means to his end, and in that of the beauty of both, though the stamp was doubtless most vivid, for so differing, so gropingly "esthetic" a mind as my own, in his unfailingly personal and admirable style. We knew he had thoroughly his own "unconventional" form, which, by the unspeakable law of youth, we managed to feel the distinction of as not platitudinous even while we a bit sneakingly felt it as quotable, on possible occasions, against our presence of mind; the great thing was at all events that we couldn't live with him without the sense that if his books resembled his talk and his character—as we moreover felt they couldn't help almost violently doing—they might want for this, that or the other which kept the conventional true to its type, but could as little fail to flush with the strong colour, colour so remarkably given and not taken, projected and not reflected, colour of thought and faith and moral and expressional atmosphere, as they could leave us without that felt side-wind of their strong composition which made after all so much of the air we breathed and was in the last resort the gage of something perpetually fine going on.

It is not too much to say, I think, that our religious education, so far as we had any, consisted wholly in that loose yet enlightening impression: I say so far as we had any in spite of my very definitely holding that it would absolutely not have been possible to us, in the measure of our sensibility, to breathe more the air of that reference to an order of goodness and power greater than any this world by itself can show which we understand as the religious spirit. Wondrous to me, as I consider again, that my father's possession of this spirit, in a degree that made it more deeply one with his life than I can conceive another or a different case of its being, should have been unaccompanied with a single one of the outward or formal, the theological, devotional, ritual, or even implicitly pietistic signs by which we usually know it. The fact of course was that his religion was nothing if not a philosophy, extraordinarily complex and worked out and original, intensely personal as an exposition, yet not only susceptible of application, but clamorous for it, to the whole field of consciousness, nature and society, history, knowledge, all human relations and questions, every pulse of the process of our destiny. Of this vast and interesting conception, as striking an expression of the religious spirit surely as ever was put forth, his eldest son has given an account[1]—so far as this was possible at once with brevity and with full comprehension—that I should have been unable even to dream of aspiring to, and in the masterly clearness and justice of which the opportunity of the son blends with that of the critic, each character acting in perfect felicity, after a fashion of which I know elsewhere no such fine example. It conveys the whole sense of our father's philosophic passion, which was theologic, by my direct impression of it, to a degree fairly outdistancing all theologies; representing its weight, reproducing its utterance, placing it in the eye of the world, and making for it the strong and single claim it suggests, in a manner that leaves nothing to be added to the subject. I am not concerned with the intrinsic meaning of these things here, and should not be even had they touched me more directly, or more converted me from what I can best call, to my doubtless scant honour, a total otherness of contemplation, during the years when my privilege was greatest and my situation for inquiry and response amplest; but the active, not to say the obvi-

[1]Literary Remains of Henry James, Boston, 1885. The portrait accompanying the volume gave us, alas, but the scantest satisfaction.

ous, moral of them, in all our younger time, was that a life of the most richly consequent flowed straight out of them, that in this life, the most abundantly, and above all naturally, communicated *as* life that it was possible to imagine, we had an absolutely equal share, and that in fine I was to live to go back with wonder and admiration to the quantity of secreted thought in our daily medium, the quality of intellectual passion, the force of cogitation and aspiration, as to the explanation both of a thousand surface incoherences and a thousand felt felicities. A religion that was so systematically a philosophy, a philosophy that was so sweepingly a religion, being together, by their necessity, as I have said, an intensity of relation to the actual, the consciousness so determined was furnished forth in a way that met by itself the whole question of the attitude of "worship" for instance; as I have attempted a little to show that it met, with a beautiful good faith and the easiest sufficiency, every other when such came up: those of education, acquisition, material vindication, what is called success generally. In the beauty of the whole thing, again, I lose myself—by which I mean in the fact that we were all the while partaking, to our most intimate benefit, of an influence of direction and enlargement attended with scarce a single consecrated form and which would have made many of these, had we been exposed to intrusion from them, absurdly irrelevant. My father liked in our quite younger period to read us chapters from the New Testament and the Old, and I hope we liked to listen to them—though I recall their seeming dreary from their association with school practice; but that was the sole approach to a challenge of our complete freedom of inward, not less than our natural ingenuity of outward, experience. No other explicit address to us in the name of the Divine could, I see, have been made with any congruity—in face of the fact that invitations issued in all the vividest social terms, terms of living appreciation, of spiritual perception, of "human fellowship," to use the expression that was perhaps oftenest on his lips and his pen alike, were the very substance of the food supplied in the parental nest.

The freedom from pressure that we enjoyed in every direction, all those immunities and exemptions that had been, in protracted childhood, positively embarrassing to us, as I have already noted, before the framework, ecclesiastical and mercantile, squared at us as with reprobation from other households, where it seemed so to conduce to their range of resource—these things consorted with our yet being yearned over or prescribed for, by every implication, after a fashion that was to make the social organisation of such invidious homes, under my subsequent observation of life, affect me as so much bleak penury or domestic desert where these things of the spirit, these genialities of faith were concerned. Well do I remember, none the less, how I was troubled all along just by this particular crookedness of our being so extremely religious without having, as it were, anything in the least classified or striking to show for it; so that the measure of other-worldliness pervading our premises was rather a waste, though at the same time oddly enough a congestion—projecting outwardly as it did no single one of those usual symptoms of propriety any of which, gathered at a venture from the general prospect, might by my sense have served: I shouldn't have been particular, I thought, as to the selection. Religion was a matter, by this imagination, to be worked off much more than to be worked in, and I fear my real vague sentiment to have been but that life would under the common equipment be somehow more amusing; and this even though, as I don't forget, there was not an item of the detail of devotional practice that we had been so much as allowed to divine. I scarce know why I should have wanted anything more amusing, as most of our coevals would have regarded it, than that we had from as far back as I could remember indulged in no shade of an approach to "keeping Sunday"; which is one of the reasons why to speak as if piety could have borne for us any sense but the tender human, or to speak at all of devotion, unction, initiation, even of the vaguest, into the exercises or professions, as among our attributes, would falsify altogether our mere fortune of a general liberty of living, of making ourselves as brightly at home as might be, in that "spiritual world" which we were in the habit of hearing as freely alluded to as we heard the prospect of dinner or the call of the postman. The oddity of my own case, as I make it out so far as it involved a confused criticism, was that my small uneasy mind, bulging and tightening in the wrong, or at least in unnatural and unexpected, places, like a little jacket ill cut or ill sewn, attached its gaping view, as I have already more than enough noted, to things and persons, objects and aspects, frivolities all, I dare say I was willing to grant, compared with whatever manifestations of the serious, these being by need, apparently, the abstract; and that in fine I should have been thankful for a state of faith, a conviction of the Divine, an interpretation of the universe—anything one might have made bold to call it—which would have supplied more features or appearances. Feeling myself "after" persons so much more than after anything else—to recur to that side of my earliest and most constant consciousness which might have been judged most deplorable—I take it that I found the sphere of our more nobly supposititious habitation too imperceptibly peopled; whereas the religious life of every other family that could boast of any such (and what family didn't boast?) affected my fancy as with a social and material crowdedness. That faculty alone was affected—this I hasten to add; no directness of experience ever stirred for me; it being the case in the first place that I scarce remember, as to all our young time, the crossing of our threshold by any faint shade of an ecclesiastical presence, or the lightest encounter with any such elsewhere, and equally of the essence, over and above, that the clerical race, the pre-eminently restrictive tribe, as I apprehended them, couldn't very well have agreed less with the general colour of my fondest vision: if it be not indeed more correct to say that I was reduced to *supposing* they couldn't. We knew in truth nothing whatever about them, a fact that, as I recover it, also flushes for me with its fine awkwardness—the social scene in general handsomely bristling with them to the rueful view I sketch, and they yet remaining for us, or at any rate for myself, such creatures of pure hearsay that when late in my teens, and in particular after my twentieth year, I began to see them portrayed by George Eliot and Anthony Trollope the effect was a disclosure of a new and romantic species. Strange beyond my present power to account for it this anomaly that amid a civilisation replete with "ministers"—for we at least knew the word—actively, competitively, indeed as would often appear quite violently, ministering, so little sense of a brush against approved examples was ever to attend me that I had finally to draw my nearest sufficiency of a true image from pictures of a social order largely alien to our own. All of which, at the same time, I allow myself to add, didn't mitigate the simple fact of my felt—my indeed so luxuriously permitted—detachment of sensibility from everything, everything, that is, in the way of great relations, as to which our father's emphasis was richest. *There* was the dim dissociation, there my comparative poverty, or call it even frivolity, of instinct: I gaped imaginatively, as it were, to such a different set of relations. I couldn't have framed stories that would have succeeded in involving the least of the relations that seemed most present to *him*; while those most present to myself, that is more complementary to whatever it was I thought of as humanly most interesting, attaching, inviting, were the ones his schemes of importances seemed virtually to do without. Didn't I discern in this from the first a kind of implied snub to the significance of mine?—so that, in the blest absence of "pressure" which I just sought here passingly to celebrate, I could brood to my heart's content on the so conceivable alternative of a field of exposure crammed with those objective appearances that my faculty seemed alone fitted to grasp. In which there was ever the small torment of the fact—though I don't quite see to-day why it should not have been of a purely pleasant irritation—that what our parent most overflowed with was just the brave contradiction or opposition between all his parts, a thing which made for perfect variety, which he carried ever so easily and brightly, and which would have put one no less in the wrong had one accused him of knowing only the abstract (as I was so complacently and invidiously disposed to name it) than if one had foolishly remarked on his living and concluding without it. But I have already made clear his great mixed range—which of course couldn't *not* have been the sign of a mind conceiving our very own breathing humanity in its every fibre the absolute expression of a resident Divinity. No element of character, no spontaneity of life, but instantly seized his attention and incurred his greeting and his comment; which things could never possibly have been so genially alert and expert—as I have, again, before this, superabundantly recorded—if it had not fairly fed on active observation and contact. He could answer one with the radiant when one challenged him with the obscure, just as he could respond with the general when one pulled at the particular; and I needn't repeat that this made for us, during all our time, anything but a starved actuality.

None the less, however, I remember it as savouring of loss to me—which is my present point—that our so thoroughly informal scene of susceptibility seemed to result from a positive excess of familiarity, in his earlier past, with such types of the shepherd and the flock, to say nothing of such forms of the pasture, as might have met in some degree my appetite for the illustrational. This was one of the things that made me often wish, as I remember, that I might have caught him sooner or younger, less developed, as who should say; the matters that appeared, however confusedly, to have started his development being by this measure stranger and livelier than most of those that finally crowned it, marked with their own colour as many of these doubtless were. Three or four strongest pages in the fragment of autobiography gathered by his eldest son into the sheaf of his Literary Remains describe the state of soul undergone by him in England, in '44, just previous to the hour at which Mrs. Chichester, a gentle lady of his acquaintance there, brought to his knowledge, by a wondrous chance, the possibility that the great Swedenborg, from whom she had drawn much light, might have something to say to his case; so that under the impression of his talk with her he posted at once up to London from the neighbourhood of Windsor, where he was staying, possessed himself of certain volumes of the writings of the eminent mystic (so-called I mean, for to my father this description of him was grotesque), and passed rapidly into that grateful infinitude of recognition and application which he was to inhabit for the rest of his days. I saw him move about there after the fashion of the oldest and easiest native, and this had on some sides its own considerable effect, tinged even on occasion with romance; yet I felt how the *real* right thing for me would have been the hurrying drama of the original rush, the interview with the admirable Mrs. Chichester, the sweet legend of his and my mother's charmed impression of whom had lingered with us—I admired her very name, there seeming none other among us at all like it; and then the return with the tokens of light, the splendid agitation as the light deepened, and the laying in of that majestic array of volumes which were to form afterward the purplest rim of his library's horizon and which I was thus capable, for my poor part, of finding valuable, in default of other values, as coloured properties in a fine fifth act. It was all a play I hadn't "been to," consciously at least—that was the trouble; the curtain had fallen while I was still tucked in my crib, and I assisted but on a comparatively flat home scene at the echo of a great success. I could still have done, for the worst, with a consciousness of Swedenborg that should have been graced at least with Swedenborgians—aware as I was of the existence of such enrolled disciples, ornaments of a church of their own, yet known to us only as persons rather acidly mystified by the inconvenience, as we even fancied them to feel it, of our father's frankly independent and disturbingly irregular (all the more for its being so expressive) connection with their inspirer. In the light or the dusk of all this it was surely impossible to make out that he professed any faint shade of that clerical character as to his having incurred which we were, "in the world," to our bewilderment, not infrequently questioned. Those of the enrolled order, in the matter of his and their subject of study, might in their way too have raised to my regard a fretted vault or opened a long-drawn aisle, but they were never at all, in the language of a later day, to materialise to me; we neither on a single occasion sat in their circle, nor did one of them, to the best of my belief, ever stray, remonstrantly or invitingly, into ours; where Swedenborg was read not in the least as the Bible scarce more than just escaped being, but even as Shakespeare or Dickens or Macaulay was content to be—which was without our arranging or subscribing for it. I seem to distinguish that if a fugitive or a shy straggler from the pitched camp did turn up it was under cover of night or of curiosity and with much panting and putting off of the mantle, much nervous laughter above all—this safe, however, to become on the shortest order amusement easy and intimate. That *figured* something in a slight way—as at least I suppose I may infer from the faint adumbration I retain; but nothing none the less much attenuated what I suppose I should have denounced as the falsity of our position (meaning thereby of mine) had I been constitutionally at all voluble for such flights. Constructionally we had all the fun of licence, while the truth seemed really to be that fun in the religious connection closely depended on bondage. The fun was of course that I wanted in this line of diversion something of the coarser strain; which came home to me in especial, to cut the matter short, when I was present, as I yielded first and last to many an occasion for being, at my father's reading out to my mother with an appreciation of that modest grasp of somebody's attention, the brief illusion of publicity, which has now for me the exquisite grace of the touching, some series of pages from among his "papers" that were to show her how he had this time at last done it. No touch of the beautiful or the sacred in the disinterested life can have been absent from such scenes—I find every such ideally there; and my memory rejoices above all in their presentation of our mother at her very perfectest of soundless and yet absolutely all-saving service and trust. To have attempted any projection of our father's aspect without an immediate reference to her sovereign care for him and for all of us as the so widely open, yet so softly enclosing, lap of all his liberties and all our securities, all our variety and withal our harmony, the harmony that was for nine-tenths of it our sense of her gathered life in us, and of her having no other—to have so proceeded has been but to defer by instinct and by scruple to the kind of truth and of beauty before which the direct report breaks down. I may well have stopped short with what there would be to say, and yet what account of us all can pretend to have gone the least bit deep without coming to our mother at every penetration? We simply lived by her, in proportion as we lived spontaneously, with an equanimity of confidence, an independence of something that I should now find myself think of as decent compunction if I didn't try to call it instead morbid delicacy, which left us free for detachments of thought and flights of mind, experiments, so to speak, on the assumption of our genius and our intrinsic interest, that I look back upon as to a luxury of the unworried that is scarce of this world. This was a support on which my father rested with the absolute whole of his weight, and it was when I felt her listen with the whole of her usefulness, which needed no other force, being as it was the whole of her tenderness and amply sufficing by itself, that I understood most what it was so to rest and so to act. When in the fulness of the years she was to die, and he then to give us time, a few months, as with a beatific depth of design, to marvel at the manner of his acceptance of the stroke, a shown triumph of his philosophy, he simply one day consciously ceased, quietly declined to continue, as an offered measure of his loss of interest. Nothing—he had enabled himself to make perfectly sure—was in the least worth while without her; this attested, he passed away or went out, with entire simplicity, promptness and ease, for the definite reason that his support had failed. His philosophy had been not his support but his suspension, and he had never, I am sure, felt so lifted as at that hour, which splendidly crowned his faith. It showed us more intimately still what, in this world of cleft components, one human being can yet be for another, and how a form of vital aid may have operated for years with such perfection as fairly to have made recognition seem at the time a sort of excess of reaction, an interference or a pedantry. All which is imaged for me while I see our mother listen, at her work, to the full music of the "papers." She could do that by the mere force of her complete availability, and could do it with a smoothness of surrender that was like an array of all the perceptions. The only thing that I might well have questioned on these occasions was the possibility on the part of a selflessness so consistently and unabatedly active of its having anything ever left *acutely* to offer; to abide so unbrokenly in such inaptness for the personal claim might have seemed to render difficult such a special show of it as any particular pointedness of hospitality would propose to represent. I dare say it was our sense of this that so often made us all, when the explicit or the categoric, the impulse of acclamation, flowered out in her, find our happiest play of filial humour in just embracing her for the sound of it; than which I can imagine no more expressive tribute to our constant depths of indebtedness. She lived in ourselves so exclusively, with such a want of use for anything in her consciousness that was not about us and for us, that I think we almost contested her being separate enough to be proud of us—it was too like our being proud of ourselves. We were delightedly derisive with her even about pride in our father—it was the most domestic of our pastimes; for what really could exceed the tenderness of our fastening on her that she *was* he, *was* each of us, was our pride and our humility, our possibility of *any* relation, and the very canvas itself on which we were floridly embroidered? How can I better express what she seemed to do for her second son in especial than by saying that even with her deepest delicacy of attention present I could still feel, while my father read, why it was that I most of all seemed to wish we might have been either much less religious or much more so? Was not the reason at bottom that I so suffered, I might almost have put it, under the impression of his style, which affected me as somehow too philosophic for life, and at the same time too living, as I made out, for thought?—since I must weirdly have opined that by so much as you were individual, which meant personal, which meant monotonous, which meant limitedly allusive and verbally repetitive, by so much you were not literary or, so to speak, *largely* figurative. My father had terms, evidently strong, but in which I presumed to feel, with a shade of irritation, a certain narrowness of exclusion as to images otherwise—and oh, since it was a question of the pen, so multitudinously!—entertainable. Variety, variety—*that* sweet ideal, *that* straight contradiction of any dialectic, hummed for me all the while as a direct, if perverse and most unedified, effect of the parental concentration, with some of its consequent, though heedless, dissociations. I heard it, felt it, saw it, both shamefully enjoyed and shamefully denied it as form, though as form only; and I owed thus supremely to my mother that I could, in whatever obscure levity, muddle out some sense of my own preoccupation under the singular softness of the connection that she kept for me, by the outward graces, with that other and truly much intenser which I was so little framed to share.

If meanwhile my father's tone, so far as that went, was to remain the same, save for a natural growth of assurance, and thereby of amplitude, all his life, I find it already, and his very voice as we were to know them, in a letter to R. W. Emerson of 1842, without more specific date, after the loose fashion of those days, but from 2 Washington Place, New York, the second house in the row between the University building and Broadway, as he was next to note to his correspondent in expressing the hope of a visit from him. (It was the house in which, the following year, his second son was born.)

> I came home to-night from my lecture a little disposed to think, from the smart reduction of my audience, that I had about as

well not have prepared my course, especially as I get no tidings of having interested one of the sort (the religious) for whom they are wholly designed. When I next see you I want a half-hour's support from you under this discouragement, and the purpose of this letter is to secure it. When I am *with* you I get no help from you—of the sort you can give me, I feel sure; though you must know what I want before I listen to you next. Usually the temper you show, of perfect repose and candour, free from all sickening partisanship and full of magnanimous tenderness for every creature, makes me forget my wants in your lavish plenty. But I know you have the same as I have, deep down in your breast, and it is by these I would fain know you. I am led, quite without any conscious wilfulness either, to seek the *laws* of these appearances that swim round us in God's great museum, to get hold of some central facts which may make all other facts properly circumferential and orderly; and you continually dishearten me by your apparent indifference to such law and such facts, by the dishonour you seem to cast on our intelligence as if it were what stands in our way. Now my conviction is that my intelligence is the necessary digestive apparatus for my life; that there is nihil in vita—worth anything, that is—quod non prius in intellectu. Now is it not so in truth with you? Can you not report your life to me by some intellectual symbol which my intellect appreciates? Do you not know your activity? But fudge—I cannot say what I want to say, what aches to say itself in me, and so I'll hold up till I see you, and try once more to get some better furtherance by my own effort. Here I am these thirty-one years in life, ignorant in all outward science, but having patient habits of meditation which never know disgust or weariness, and feeling a force of impulsive love toward all humanity which will not let me rest wholly mute, a force which grows against all resistance that I can muster against it. What shall I do? Shall I get me a little nook in the country and communicate with my *living* kind—not my talking kind—by life only; a word perhaps of *that* communication, a fit word once a year? Or shall I follow some commoner method—learn science and bring myself first into man's respect, that I may thus the better speak to him? I confess this last theory seems rank with earthliness—to belong to days forever past.

His appeal to Emerson at this hour was, as he elsewhere then puts it, to the "invisible" man in the matter, who affected him as somewhere behind the more or less immediately visible, the beautifully but mystifyingly audible, the Emerson of honeyed lectures and addresses, suggestive and inspiring as that one might be, and who might, as we say to-day, have something, something more at least, for him. "I will tell him that I do not value his substantive discoveries, whatever they may be, perhaps half so largely as he values them, but that I chiefly cherish that erect attitude of mind in him which in God's universe undauntedly seeks the worthiest tidings of God, and calmly defies every mumbling phantom which would challenge its freedom. Should his zeal for realities and contempt of vulgar shows abide the ordeal I have thus contrived for them I shall gladly await his visit to me. So much at least is what I have been saying to myself. Now that I have told it to you also you have become a sort of confidant between me and myself, and so bound to promote harmony there." The correspondence expands, however, beyond my space for reporting of it; I but pick out a few passages.

> I am cheered by the coming of Carlyle's new book, which Greeley announces, and shall hasten off for it as soon as I have leisure.[1] The title is provokingly enigmatical, but thought enough there will be in it no doubt, whatever the name; thought heaped up to topheaviness and inevitable lopsidedness, but more interesting to me than comes from any other quarter of Europe—interesting for the man's sake whom it shows. According to my notion he is the very best interpreter of a spiritual philosophy that could be devised for *this age*, the age of transition and conflict; and what renders him so is his natural birth-and-education-place. Just to think of a Scotchman with a heart widened to German spiritualities! To have overcome his educational bigotries far enough to listen to the new ideas, this by itself was wonderful; and then to give all his native shrewdness and humour to the service of making them *tell* to the minds of his people—what more fortunate thing for the time could there be? You don't look upon Calvinism as a fact at all; wherein you are to my mind philosophically infirm—impaired in your universality. I can see in Carlyle the advantage his familiarity with it gives him over you with a general audience. What is highest in him is built upon that lowest. At least so I read; I believe Jonathan Edwards redivivus in true blue would, after an honest study of the philosophy that has grown up since his day, make the best possible reconciler and critic of this philosophy—far better than Schelling redivivus.

[1] *Past and Present*, 1843.

In the autumn of 1843 the "nook in the country" above alluded to had become a question renounced, so far at least as the American country was concerned, and never again afterwards flushed into life. "I think it probable I shall winter in some mild English climate, Devonshire perhaps, and go on with my studies as at home. I shall miss the stimulus of your candid and generous society, and I confess we don't like the aspect of the journey; but one's destiny puts on many garments as it goes shaping itself in secret—so let us not cling to any particular fashion." Very marked, and above all very characteristic of my father, in this interesting relation, which I may but so imperfectly illustrate, his constant appeal to his so inspired, yet so uninflamed, so irreducible and, as it were, inapplicable, friend for intellectual and, as he would have said, spiritual help of the immediate and adjustable, the more concretely vital, kind, the kind translatable into terms of the real, the particular human terms of action and passion. "Oh you man without a *handle*! Shall one never be able to help himself out of you, according to his needs, and be dependent only upon your fitful tippings-up?"—a remarkably felicitous expression, as it strikes me, of that difficulty often felt by the passionately-living of the earlier time, as they may be called, to draw down their noble philosopher's great overhanging heaven of universal and ethereal answers to the plane of their comparatively terrestrial and personal questions; the note of the answers and their great anticipatory spirit being somehow that they seemed to anticipate everything but the unaccommodating individual case. My father, on his side, bristled with "handles"—there could scarce be a better general account of him—and tipped himself up for you almost before you could take hold of one; of which truth, for that matter, this same letter happens to give, even if just trivially, the hint. "Can I do anything for you in the way of taking parcels, no matter how large or expensive?—or for any of your friends? If you see Margaret Fuller ask her to give me some service to render her abroad, the dear noble woman: it seems a real hardship to be leaving the country now that I have just come to talk with her." Emerson, I should add, did offer personally so solid a handle that my father appears to have taken from him two introductions to be made use of in London, one to Carlyle and the other to John Sterling, the result of which shortly afterwards was as vivid and as deeply appropriated an impression of each eminent character as it was probably to be given either of them ever to have made. The impression of Carlyle was recorded but long subsequently, I note, and is included in William's gathering-in of our father's Literary Remains (1885) ; and of the acquaintance with Sterling no reflection remains but a passage in a letter, under date of Ventnor and of the winter of 1843, from the latter to his biographer to be; Carlyle having already mentioned in the Life that "Two American gentlemen, acquaintances also of mine, had been recommended to him, by Emerson most likely"; and that "one morning Sterling appeared here with a strenuous proposal that we should come to Knightsbridge and dine with him and them. . . . And accordingly we went," it goes on. "I remember it as one of the saddest dinners; though Sterling talked copiously, and our friends, Theodore Parker one of them, were pleasant and distinguished men." My father, with Theodore Parker his friend and the date fitting, would quite seem to have been one of the pair were it not that "our conversation was waste and logical, I forget quite on what, not joyful and harmoniously effusive." It is *that* that doesn't fit with any real participation of his—nothing could well do less so; unless the occasion had but too closely conformed to the biographer's darkly and richly prophetic view of it as tragic and ominous, "sad as if one had been dining in a ruin, in the crypt of a mausoleum"—all this "painfully apparent through the bright mask (Sterling) had bound himself to wear." The end of his life was then, to Carlyle's view, in sight; but his own note, in the Isle of Wight, on "Mr. James, your New-England friend," was genial enough—"I saw him several times and liked him. They went on the 24th of last month back to London—or so purposed," he adds, "because there is no pavement here for him to walk on. I want to know where he is, and thought I should be able to learn from you. I gave him a note for Mill, who may perhaps have seen him."

My main interest in which is, I confess, for the far-off germ of the odd legend, destined much to grow later on, that—already the nucleus of a household—we were New England products; which I think my parents could then have even so much as seemed only to eyes naturally unaware of our

American "sectional" differences. My father, when considerably past his thirtieth year, if I am not mistaken, had travelled "East," within our borders, but once in his life—on the occasion of his spending two or three months in Boston as a very young man; there connecting itself with this for me a reminiscence so bedimmed at once and so suggestive as now almost to torment me. It must have been in '67 or '68 that, giving him my arm, of a slippery Boston day, up or down one of the steep streets that used to mount, from behind, and as slightly sullen with the effort, to Beacon Hill, and between which my now relaxed memory rather fails to discriminate, I was arrested by his pointing out to me opposite us a house in which he had for a while had rooms, long before and quite in his early time. I but recall that we were more or less skirting the base of an ancient town-reservoir, the seat of the water-supply as then constituted, a monument rugged and dark, massively granitic, perched all perversely, as it seemed to look, on the precipitous slope, and which—at least as I see it through the years—struck quite handsomely the Babylonian note. I at any rate mix up with this frowning object—it had somehow a sinister presence and suggestion—my companion's mention there in front of it that he had anciently taken refuge under its shadow from certain effects of a misunderstanding, if indeed not of a sharp rupture, for the time, with a highly generous but also on occasion strongly protesting parent at Albany, a parent displeased with some course he had taken or had declined to take (there was a tradition among us that he had been for a period quite definitely "wild"), and relief from further discussion with whom he had sought, and had more or less found, on that spot. It was an age in which a flight from Albany to Boston—there being then no Boston and Albany Railroad—counted as a far flight; though it wasn't to occur to me either then or afterwards that the ground of this manœuvre had been any plotted wildness in the Puritan air. What was clear at the moment, and what he remarked upon, was that the street-scene about us showed for all the lapse of time no scrap of change, and I remember well for myself how my first impression of Boston gave it to me under certain aspects as more expressive than I had supposed an American city could be of a seated and rooted social order, an order not complex but sensibly fixed—gathered in or folded back to intensity upon itself; and this, again and again, when the compass of the posture, its narrow field, might almost have made the fold excruciating. It had given however no sign of excruciation—that itself had been part of the Puritan stoicism; which perhaps was exactly why the local look, recognised to the point I speak of by the visitor, was so contained and yet comparatively so full: full, very nearly, I originally fancied, after the appraisable fashion of some composed town-face in one of Balzac's *villes de province.* All of which, I grant, is much to say for the occasion of that dropped confidence, on the sloshy hillside, to which I allude—and part of the action of which was that it had never been dropped before; this circumstance somehow a peculiar source of interest, an interest I the more regret to have lost my grasp of as it must have been sharp, or in other words founded, to account for the long reverberation here noted. I had still—as I was indeed to keep having through life—the good fortune that elements of interest easily sprang, to my incurable sense, from any ghost of a drama at all *presented*; though I of course can't in the least pretend to generalise on what may or may not have constituted living presentation. This felicity occurred, I make out, quite incalculably, just as it could or would; the effect depended on some particular touch of the spring, which was set in motion the instant the touch happened to be right. My father's was always right, to my receptive mind; as receptive, that is, of any scrap of enacted story or evoked picture as it was closed to the dry or the abstract proposition; so that I blush the deeper at not being able, in honour of his reference, to make the latter more vividly flower—I still so feel that I quite thrilled with it and with the standing background at the moment lighted by it. There were things in it, and other persons, old actualities, old meanings and furnishings of the other old Boston, as I by that time couldn't but appraise it; and the really archaic, the overhung and sombre and secret-keeping street, "socially" disconnected, socially mysterious—as I like at any rate to remember it—was there to testify (testify to the ancient time of tension, expansion, sore meditation or whatever) by its positively conscious gloom.

The moral of this, I fear, amounts to little more than that, putting aside the substance of his anecdote, my father had not set foot in New England till toward his thirty-fifth year, and my mother was not to do so till later still; circumstances not in the least preventing the birth of what I have called the falsifying legend. The allusion to the walking at Ventnor touches his inability to deal with rural roads and paths, then rougher things than now; by reason of an accident received in early youth and which had so lamed him for life that he could circulate to any convenience but on even surfaces and was indeed mainly reduced to driving—it had made him for all his earlier time an excellent whip. His constitution had been happily of the strongest, but as I look back I see his grave disability, which it took a strong constitution to carry, mainly in the light of a consistency of patience that we were never to have heard broken. The two acceptances melt together for me—that of the limits of his material action, his doing and enjoying, set so narrowly, and that of his scant allowance of "public recognition," or of the support and encouragement that spring, and spring so naturally and rightly, when the relation of effect to cause is close and straight, from any at all attested and glad understanding of a formula, as we say nowadays a message, richly and sincerely urged. Too many such reflections, however, beset me here by the way. My letters jump meanwhile to the summer of 1849, when I find in another of them, addressed to Emerson, a passage as characteristic as possible of one of the writer's liveliest and, as I confess it was ever to seem to me, most genially perverse idiosyncrasies, his distinctly low opinion of "mere" literary men. This note his letters in general again and again strike—not a little to the diversion of those who were to have observed and remembered his constant charmed subjection, in the matter of practice, to the masters, even quite the lighter, in the depreciated group. His sensibility to their spell was in fact so marked that it became from an early time a household game with us to detect him in evasive tears over their pages, when these were either real or romantic enough, and to publish without mercy that he had so been caught. There was a period in particular during which this pastime enjoyed, indeed quite revelled in, the form of our dragging to the light, with every circumstance of derision, the fact of his clandestine and deeply moved perusal of G. P. R. James, our nominal congener, at that time ceasing to be prescribed. It was his plea, in the "'fifties," that this romancer had been his idol in the 'forties and the 'thirties, and that under renewed, even if but experimental, surrender the associations of youth flocked back to life—so that *we*, profane about the unduly displaced master, were deplorably the poorer. He loved the novel in fine, he followed its constant course in the Revue with a beautiful inconsequence, and the more it was literature loved it the better, which was just how he loved, as well, criticism and journalism; the particular instance, with him, once he was in relation with it, quite sufficiently taking care of the invidiously-viewed type—as this was indeed viewed but *a priori* and at its most general—and making him ever so cheerfully forget to be consistent. Work was verily cut out for the particular instance, as against the type, in an air and at a time favouring so, again and again, and up and down the "literary world," a dire mediocrity. It was the distillers of *that* thinness, the "mere" ones, that must have been present to him when he wrote to Emerson in 1849: "There is nothing I dread so much as literary men, especially *our* literary men; catch them out of the range of mere personal gossip about authors and books and ask them for honest sympathy in your sentiment, or for an honest repugnancy of it, and you will find the company of stage-drivers sweeter and more comforting to your soul. In truth the questions which are beginning to fill the best books, and will fill the best for a long time to come, are not related to what we have called literature, and are as well judged—I think better—by those whom books have at all events not belittled. When a man *lives*, that is lives enough, he can scarcely write. He cannot read, I apprehend, at all. All his writing will be algebraicised, put into the form of sonnets and proverbs, and the community will feel itself insulted to be offered a big bunch of pages, as though it were stupid and wanted tedious drilling like a child." When I begin to quote my father, however, I hang over him perhaps even too historically; for his expression leads me on and on so by its force and felicity that I scarce know where to stop. "The fact is that I am afraid I am in a very bad way, for I cannot heartily engage in any topic in which I shall appear to advantage"—the question having been, *de part et d'autre*, of possible courses of lectures for which the appetite of New York and Boston already announced itself as of the largest. And it still more beguiles me that "my wife and I are obliged—so numerous has waxed our family—to enlarge our house in town and get a country house for the summer." Here came in that earnest dream of the solutional "Europe" with which I have elsewhere noted that my very youngest sensibility was fed. "These things look expensive and temporary to us, besides being an additional care; and so, considering with much pity our four stout boys, who have no play-room within doors and import shocking bad manners from the street, we gravely ponder whether it wouldn't be better to go abroad for a few years with them, allowing them to absorb French and German and get such a sensuous education as they can't get here."

In 1850, however, we had still not departed for Europe—as we were not to do for several years yet; one advantage of which was that my father remained for the time in intercourse by letter with his English friend Dr. J. J. Garth Wilkinson, first known during my parents' considerable stay in London of several years before, 1843–44; and whose admirable style of expression, in its way as personal and as vivid as Henry James's own, with an added and doubtless more perceptibly full-blooded massiveness, is so attested by his earlier writings,[1] to

[1]"But, Sir, we have yet one more scene to visit together, connected with all we have previously witnessed: a home scene, Sir Benjamin; and we must now ascend a mountain of pity high enough to command the dewy extense of three kingdoms. From thence we have to look down from every point of our warm hearts with a sight as multifold as the cherubic eyes. We are to see with equal penetration through the diverse thickness of castles, mansions, and cottages, through London and through hamlet, at young wives and at aged mothers, little children, brothers and sisters—all groups and ties that are; and at affianced maidens, ties that were to be. There are rents and tears to-day in the general life: the bulletin of the dead has come, and the groups of sorrow are constituted. Splendid Paris bends as a Niobe or as a Rachel while the corse of her much-enduring Hero is borne to the marble Invalides; other corses go earthward with a shorter procession, helped away by the spades of ruder but more instant sculptors; the rucked sod of the Alma is their urn and monument in one; yet every warrior among them is also buried to-day with swelling greatness of obsequies, if we could see them, in the everlasting ruby vaults of some human heart. You are touched, Sir Benjamin, and are justly religious on this summit. Struck down for a moment from worldliness, we both discourse without an afterthought on the immortal state; we hope that the brave are already welcomed in the land of peace; that our laurels they could not stop to take, and our earned promotion they seem to have missed are clad upon

say nothing of the rich collection of his letters (1845–55) lately before me—notably by The Human Body and its Connection with Man, dedicated in 1851 to my father—that I wonder at the absence of such a master, in more than one happy specimen, from the common educational exhibitions of English prose. Dr. Wilkinson was a friend of Emerson's as well, which leads the latter's New York correspondent to cite to him in February 1850 a highly characteristic passage from one of the London communications.

> Carlyle came up here (presumably to Hampstead) on Monday to see Neuberg, and spoke much of you with very kind recollections. He remembered your metaphysics also and asked with terrible solicitude whether they yet persevered. I couldn't absolutely say that they did not, though I did my best to stammer out something about the great social movement. He was suffering dreadfully from *malaise* and indigestion and gave with his usual force his usual putrid theory of the universe. All great men were most miserable; the day on which any man could say he was not miserable, that day he was a scoundrel; God was a Divine Sorrow; to no moment could he, Carlyle, ever say Linger, but only Goodbye and never let me see your face again. And all this interpolated with convulsive laughter, showing that joy would come into him were it even by the path of hysteria and disease. To me he is an unprofitable man, and though he gave me the most kind invitation I have too much respect for my stomach to go much into his company. Where hope is feeble genius and the human voice are on the way to die. By the next boat I will endeavour to send you over my thoughts on his recent pamphlet, the first of a series of Latter-Day-Tracts. He is very rapidly falling out with all his present admirers, for which I like them all the better; and indeed is driving fast toward social views—only his is to be a compulsory, not an attractive, socialism.

After quoting which my father comments: "Never was anything more false than this worship of sorrow by Carlyle; he has picked it up out of past history and spouts it for mere display,

them now by the God of battles in front of the shining armies of the just. We hope also that if their voices could now speak to the mourners, the oil of their sure gladness would heal our faithless sorrow. It is a true strain no doubt, and yet but of momentary power." War, Cholera, and the Ministry of Health. An Appeal to Sir Benjamin Hall and the British People. London, 1854.

as a virtuoso delights in the style of his grandfather. It is the merest babble in him, as everyone who has ever talked an hour with him will acquit him of the least grain of humility. A man who has once uttered a cry of despair should ever after clothe himself in sackcloth and ashes."

The writer was to have meanwhile, before our migration of 1855, a considerable lecturing activity. A confused, yet perfectly recoverable recollection, on my own part, of these years, connects itself with our knowledge that our father engaged in that practice and that he went forth for the purpose, with my mother always in earnest and confident even though slightly fluttered attendance, at about the hour of our upward procession to bed; which fact lent to the proceeding—that is to *his*—a strange air of unnatural riot, quite as of torch-lighted and wind-blown dissipation. We went to plays and to ballets, and they had comparatively speaking no mystery; but at no lecture had we ever been present, and these put on for my fancy at least a richer light and shade, very much as if we ourselves had been on the performing side of the curtain, or the wonder of admiring (in our mother's person) and of being admired (in our father's) had been rolled for us into a single glory. This glory moreover was not menaced, but only made more of a thrill by the prime admirer's anxiety, always displayed at the last, as to whether they were not starting without the feature of features, the *corpus delicti* or manuscript itself; which it was legendary with us that the admired had been known to drive back for in an abashed flurry at the moment we were launched in dreams of him as in full, though mysterious, operation. I can see him now, from the parlour window, at the door of the carriage and under the gusty street-lamp, produce it from a coat-tail pocket and shake it, for her ideal comfort, in the face of his companion. The following, to Emerson, I surmise, is of some early date in the autumn of '52.

I give three lectures in Boston at the Masonic Temple; the first and second on Nov. 5th and 8th respectively. I should be greatly appalled in some respects, but still charmed, to have you for an auditor, seeing thus a hundred empty seats obliterated; but, I beg of you, don't let any engagement suffer by such kindness to me. Looking over the lectures again they horrify me with their loud-mouthed imbecility!—but I hope they may fall upon less hardened ears in some cases. I am sure that the thought which is in them, or rather seems to me to struggle to be in them, is worthy of all men's rapturous homage, and I will trust that a glimpse of it may somehow befall my patient auditory. The fact is that a vital truth can never be transferred from one mind to another, because life alone appreciates it. The most one can do for another is to plant some rude formula of such truths in his memory, leaving his own spiritual chemistry to set free the germ whenever the demands of his life exact it. The reason why the gods seem so powerless to the sensuous understanding, and suffer themselves to be so long defamed by our crazy theologies, is that they are life, and can consequently be revealed only to life. But life is simply the passage of idea into action; and our crazy theologies forbid ideas to come into action any further than our existing institutions warrant. Hence man leads a mere limping life, and the poor gods who are dependent upon his manliness for their true revelation and for their real knowledge, are doomed to remain forever unknown, and even denied by such solemn pedants as Mr. Atkinson and Miss Martineau. However, I shall try to convert *myself* at least into an army of Goths and Huns, to overcome and destroy our existing sanctities, that the supernal splendours may at length become credible and even visible. Good-bye till we meet in Boston, and cultivate your goodnature according to my extensive needs.

I bridge the interval before our migration of 1855 exactly for the sake of certain further passages addressed to the same correspondent, from London, in the following year. The letter is a long one and highly significant of the writer's familiar frankness, but I must keep down my examples—the first of which glances at his general sense of the men he mainly met.

They are all of them depressed or embittered by the public embarrassments that beset them; deflected, distorted, somehow despoiled of their rich individual manliness by the necessity of providing for these imbecile old inheritances of church and state. Carlyle is the same old sausage, fizzing and sputtering in his own grease, only infinitely *more* unreconciled to the blest Providence which guides human affairs. He names God frequently and alludes to the highest things as if they were realities, but all only as for a picturesque effect, so completely does he seem to regard them as habitually circumvented and set at naught by the politicians. I took our friend M. to see him, and he came away greatly distressed and désillusionné, Carlyle having taken the utmost pains to deny and descry and deride the idea of his having done the least good to anybody, and to profess indeed the utmost contempt for everybody who thought he had, and poor M. being intent on giving him a plenary assurance of this fact in his own case. . . . Arthur Helps seems an amiable kindly little man with friendly offers, but I told him I had no intention to bore him, and would at most apply to him when I might want a good hatter or bootmaker. He fancied a little—at least I thought this was the case—that I was going to make a book, and might be indiscreet enough to put him in! . . . . ——— disappoints me, he is so eaten up with the "spirits" and all that. His imagination is so vast as to dwarf all the higher faculties, and his sympathy as narrow as Dr. Cheever's or Brownson's. No reasonable man, it is true, likes the clergy or the philosophers, but ———'s dislike of them seems as envenomed as that between rival tradesmen or rival beauties. One can't endure the nonsense they talk, to be sure, but when one considers the dear human meaning and effort struggling at the bottom of it all one can feel still less any personal separation from the men themselves. ———'s sarcasm is of the fiercest, and on the whole he is only now at last sowing his intellectual wild oats—he will grow more genial in good time. This is it: I think he is but now finding his youth! That which we on our side of the water find so early and exhaust so prodigally he has found thus much later—I mean an emancipation from the shackles of custom; and the kicking up of his heels consequently is proportionate to his greater maturity of muscle. Mrs. ——— is a dear little goose of a thing, who fancies the divine providence in closer league with herself than with others, giving her intimations of events about to happen and endowing her with peculiar perspicacity in the intuition of remedies for disease; and ———, the great brawny fellow, sits by and says never a word in abatement of this enormous domestic inflation, though the visitor feels himself crowded by it into the most inconsiderable of corners. A sweet, loving, innocent woman like Mrs. ——— oughtn't to grow egotistical in the company of a truly wise man, and this accordingly is another quarrel I have with ———. In short I am getting to the time of life when one values one's friends for what they are more than for what they do. I am just as much impressed as ever by his enormous power, but the goodness out of which it is born and the wisdom by which it is nurtured and bred are things I don't so much see.

The correspondence grew more interspaced, and with the year 1861 and the following, when we were at home again, became a matter of the occasional note. I have before me a series of beautiful examples of Emerson's share in it—during the earlier time copious enough; but these belong essentially to another case. I am all but limited, for any further show of the interesting relation than I have already given, to reproducing a few lines from Emerson's Diary, passages unpublished at the moment I write, and the first of them of April 1850. "I have made no note of these long weary absences at New York and Philadelphia. I am a bad traveller, and the hotels are mortifications to all sense of well-being in me. The people who fill them oppress me with their excessive virility, and would soon become intolerable if it were not for a few friends who, like women, tempered the acrid mass. Henry James was true comfort —wise, gentle, polished, with heroic manners and a serenity like the sun." The hotels of those days may well have been an ordeal—distinct to me still, from no few childish glimpses of their bareness of ease and rudeness of *acceuil*; yet that our justly fastidious friend was not wholly left to their mercy seems signified by my not less vivid remembrance of his staying with us on occasion in New York; some occasion, or occasions, I infer, of his coming on to lecture there. Do I roll several occasions into one, or amplify one beyond reason?—this last being ever, I allow, the waiting pitfall of a chronicler too memory-ridden. I "visualise" at any rate the winter firelight of our back-parlour at dusk and the great Emerson—I knew he was great, greater than any of our friends—sitting in it between my parents, before the lamps had been lighted, as a visitor consentingly housed only could have done, and affecting me the more as an apparition sinuously and, I held, elegantly slim, benevolently aquiline, and commanding a tone alien, beautifully alien, to any we heard roundabout, that he bent this benignity upon me by an invitation to draw nearer to him, off the hearth-rug, and know myself as never yet, as I was not indeed to know myself again for years, in touch with the wonder of Boston. The wonder of Boston was above all just then and there for me in the sweetness of the voice and the finish of the speech—this latter through a sort of attenuated emphasis which at the same time made sounds more important, more interesting in themselves, than by any revelation yet vouchsafed us. Was not this my first glimmer of a sense that the human tone *could*, in that independent and original way, be interesting? and didn't it for a long time keep me going, however unwittingly, in that faith, carrying me in fact more or less on to my day of recognising that it took much more than simply not being of New York to produce the music I had listened to. The point was that, however that might be, I had had given me there in the firelight an absolutely abiding measure. If I didn't know from that hour forth quite all it was to *not* utter sounds worth mentioning, I make out that I had at least the opposite knowledge. And all by the operation of those signal moments—the truth of which I find somehow reflected in the fact of my afterwards knowing one of our household rooms for the time—it must have been our only guest-chamber—as "Mr. Emerson's room." The evening firelight played so long for me upon the door—that is to the length probably of three days, the length of a child's impression. But I must not let this carry me beyond the second note of the Diary, this time of May 1852. "'I do not wish this or that thing my fortune will procure, I wish the great fortune,' said Henry James, and said it in the noblest sense." The report has a beauty to me without my quite understanding it; the union of the two voices in it signifies quite enough. The last very relevant echo of my father's by itself, in the connection, I hasten now to find in a communication that must have been of the summer of 1869, when Dr. Wilkinson paid his only visit to America—this apparently of the briefest. The letter to Emerson from Cambridge notes that his appearance there had been delayed.

> He may come to-morrow possibly: if in the morning I will telegraph you; if in the evening I shall try to keep him over Monday that you may meet him here at dinner on that day. But I fear this bothersome Sabbath and its motionless cars may play us a trick. I shall hope for a generous Monday all the same, and if that hope is baulked shall owe Sunday a black-eye—and will pay my debt on the first suitable occasion, I warrant you. What an awkward story (the letter continues) The Nation to-day tells of Charles Sumner! Charles's burly voice has always had for me a dreadfully hollow sound, as if it came from a great copper vat, and I have loved him but with fear and trembling accordingly. Is he *really*, like all American politicians, tricky, or is The Nation—so careful about facts ordinarily—only slanderous? . . . . Carlyle nowadays is a

palpable nuisance. If he holds to his present mouthing ways to the end he will find no showman là-bas to match him, for I hold Barnum a much more innocent personage. I shouldn't wonder if Barnum grew regenerate in some far off day by mere force of his democracy. But Carlyle's intellectual pride is so stupid that one can hardly imagine anything able to cope with it.

The following, in so different a key, is of some seven years earlier date—apparently '62; but I have let it stand over, for reasons, that it may figure here as the last of the communications addressed to Emerson that I shall cite. Written at an hotel, the Tremont House, in Boston, it marks his having come up from Newport for attendance at some meeting of a dining-club, highly distinguished in composition, as it still happily remains, of which he was a member—though but so occasionally present that this circumstance perhaps explains a little the even more than usual vivacity of his impression. Not indeed, I may add, that mustered reasons or apologies were ever much called for in any case of the play of that really prime note of his spontaneity.

I go to Concord in the morning, but shall have barely time to see you there, even if I do as much as that; so that I can't forbear to say to you now the word I wanted as to my impression of yesterday about Hawthorne and Ellery Channing. Hawthorne isn't to me a prepossessing figure, nor apparently at all an *enjoying* person in any way: he has all the while the look—or would have to the unknowing—of a rogue who suddenly finds himself in a company of detectives. But in spite of his rusticity I felt a sympathy for him fairly amounting to anguish, and couldn't take my eyes off him all dinner, nor my rapt attention: as that indecisive little Dr. Hedge[1] found, I am afraid, to his cost, for I hardly heard a word of what he kept on saying to me, and resented his maliciously putting his artificial person between me and the profitable object of study. (It isn't however that I *now* feel any ill-will to him—I could recommend anyone but myself to go and hear him preach. The thing was that Hawthorne seemed to me to possess human substance and not to have dissipated it all away like that culturally debauched ———, or even like good inoffensive comforting Longfellow.) John Forbes and you kept up the human balance at the other end of the table,

[1]An eminent Unitarian pastor.

but my region was a desert with H. for its only oasis. It was so pathetic to see him, contented sprawling Concord owl that he was and always has been, brought blindfold into that brilliant daylight and expected to wink and be lively, like some dapper Tommy Titmouse. I felt him bury his eyes in his plate and eat with such voracity that no one should dare to speak to him. My heart broke for him as his attenuated left-hand neighbour kept putting forth *his* long antennae to stroke his face and try whether his eyes were open. It was heavenly to see him persist in ignoring the spectral smiles—in eating his dinner and doing nothing *but* that, and then go home to his Concord den to fall upon his knees and ask his heavenly Father why it was that an owl couldn't remain an owl and not be forced into the diversions of a canary. I have no doubt that all the tenderest angels saw to his case that night and poured oil into his wounds more soothing than gentlemen ever know. W. Ellery Channing too seemed so human and good—sweet as summer and fragrant as pinewoods. He is more sophisticated than Hawthorne of course, but still he was kin; and I felt the world richer by two *men*, who had not yet lost themselves in mere members of society. This is what I suspect—that we are fast getting so fearful one to another, we "members of society" that we shall ere long begin to kill one another in self-defence and give place in that way at last to a more veracious state of things. The old world is breaking up on all hands: the glimpse of the everlasting granite I caught in H. and W. E. shows me that there is stock enough left for fifty better. Let the old impostors go, bag and baggage, for a very real and substantial one is aching to come in, in which the churl shall not be exalted to a place of dignity, in which innocence shall never be tarnished nor trafficked in, in which every man's freedom shall be respected down to its feeblest filament as the radiant altar of God. To the angels, says Swedenborg, death means resurrection to life; by that necessary rule of inversion which keeps them separate from us and us from them, and so prevents our being mutual nuisances. Let us then accept political and all other distraction that chooses to come; because what is disorder and wrath and contention on the surface is sure to be the greatest peace at the centre, working its way thus to a surface that shall never be disorderly.

But it is in the postscript that the mixture and the transition strike me as most inevitable.

Weren't you shocked at ———'s engagement? To think of that prim old snuffers imposing himself on that pure young flame!

What a world, what a world! But once we get rid of Slavery the new heavens and new earth will swim into reality.

No better example could there be, I think, of my father's remarkable and constant belief, proof against all confusion, in the imminence of a transformation-scene in human affairs —"spiritually" speaking of course always—which was to be enacted somehow without gross or vulgar visibility, or at least violence, as I have said, but was none the less straining to the front, and all by reason of the world's being, deep within and at heart, as he conceived, so achingly anxious for it. He had the happiness—though not so untroubled, all the while, doubtless, as some of his declarations would appear to represent—of being able to see his own period and environment as the field of the sensible change, and thereby as a great historic hour; that is, I at once subjoin, I more or less *suppose* he had. His measure of the imminent and immediate, of the socially and historically visible and sensible was not a thing easy to answer for, and when treated to any one of the loud vaticinations or particular revolutionary messages and promises our age was to have so much abounded in, all his sense of proportion and of the whole, of the real and the ridiculous, asserted itself with the last emphasis. In that mixture in him of faith and humour, criticism and conviction, that mark of a love of his kind which fed on discriminations and was never so moved to a certain extravagance as by an exhibited, above all by a cultivated or in the least sententious vagueness in respect to these, dwelt largely the original charm, the peculiarly social and living challenge (in that it was so straight and bright a reflection of life) of his talk and temper. Almost all of my father shines for me at any rate in the above passages, and in another that follows, with their so easy glide from discrimination, as I have called it, that is from analytic play, in the outward sphere, to serenity of synthesis and confidence and high joy in the inward. It was as if he might have liked so to see his fellow-humans, fellow-diners, fellow-celebrities or whatever, in that acuity of individual salience, in order to proceed thence to some enormous final doubt or dry renouncement—instead of concluding, on the contrary, and on the same free and familiar note, to the eminently "worth while" character of life, or its susceptibility to vast and happy conversions. With which too, more than I can say, have I the sense here of his so finely contentious or genially perverse impulse to carry his wares of observation to the market in which they would on the whole bring least rather than most—where his offering them at all would produce rather a flurry (there might have been markets in which it had been known to produce almost a scandal), and where he would in fact give them away for nothing if thereby he might show that such produce grew. Never was there more of a case of the direct friendliness to startling growths—if so they might be held—of the very soil that lies under our windows. I don't think he liked to scandalise—certainly he didn't in the least for scandal's sake; but nothing inspired him more to the act and the pleasure of appreciation for appropriation, as it might be termed, than the deprecating attitude of others on such ground—that degree of shyness of appropriation on their part which practically left appreciation vague. It was true that the appreciation for a human use, as it might be called—that is for the high optimistic transition—could here carry the writer far.

VII

I FIND markedly relevant at this point a letter from Newport in the autumn of '61 to another correspondent, one of a series several other examples of which no less successfully appeal to me, even though it involve my going back a little to place three or four of these latter, written at Geneva in 1860. Mrs. William Tappan, primarily Caroline Sturgis of Boston, was for long years and to the end of her life our very great friend and one of my father's most constant and most considered interlocutors, both on the ground of his gravity and on that of his pleasantry. She had spent in Europe with her husband and her two small daughters very much the same years, from early in the summer of '55 till late in the autumn of '60, that we had been spending; and like ourselves, though with less continuity for the time, she had come to live at Newport, where, with no shadow of contention, but with an admirable intelligence, of the incurably ironic or mocking order, she was such a light, free, somewhat intellectually perverse but socially impulsive presence (always for instance insatiably hospitable) as our mustered circle could ill have spared. If play of mind, which she carried to any point of quietly-smiling audacity that might be, had not already become a noted, in fact I think the very most noted, value among us, it would have seated itself there in her person with a nervous animation, a refinement of what might have been called soundable sincerity, that left mere plump assurance in such directions far in the lurch. And she was interesting, she became fairly historic, with the drawing-out of the years, as almost the only survivor of that young band of the ardent and uplifted who had rallied in the other time to the "transcendental" standard, the movement for organised candour of conversation on almost all conceivable or inconceivable things which appeared, with whatever looseness, to find its prime inspirer in Emerson and become more familiarly, if a shade less authentically, vocal in Margaret Fuller. Hungry, ever so cheerfully and confidently hungry, had been much of the New England, and peculiarly the Boston, of those days; but with no such outreaching of the well-scoured empty platter, it probably would have struck one, as by the occasional and quite individual agitation of it from some ruefully-observed doorstep of the best society. It was from such a doorstep that Caroline Sturgis had originally taken her restless flight, just as it was on such another that, after a course of infinite freedom of inquiry and irony, she in the later time, with a fortune inherited, an hospitality extended and a genial gravity of expression confirmed, alighted again, to the no small re-enrichment of a company of friends who had had meanwhile scarce any such intellectual adventures as she was to retain, in a delicate and casual irreverence, the just slightly sharp fragrance or fine asperity of, but who might cultivate with complacency and in support of the general claim to comprehensive culture and awareness unafraid the legend of her vicarious exposure.

Mr. Frank Sanborn's school, which I have already mentioned and to which the following alludes, was during the years immediately preceding the War, as during those of the War itself, the last word of what was then accounted the undauntedly modern, flourishing as it did under the patronage of the most "advanced" thought. The "coeducational" idea had up to that time, if I mistake not, taken on no such confident and consistent, certainly no such graceful or plausible form; small boys and big boys, boys from near and boys from far, consorted there and cohabited, so far as community of board and lodging and of study and sport went, with little girls and great girls, mainly under the earnest tutoring and elder-sistering of young women accomplished as scholarly accomplishment in such cases was then understood, but with Mr. Sanborn himself of course predominantly active and instructional, and above all with the further felicity of the participation of the generous Emerson family by sympathy and interest and the protective spread of the rich mantle of their presence. The case had been from the first a frank and high-toned experiment, a step down from the tonic air, as was so considerably felt, of radical conviction to the firm ground of radical application, that is of happy demonstration—an admittedly new and trustful thing, but all the brighter and wiser, all the more nobly and beautifully workable for that. With but the scantest direct observation of the attempted demonstration—demonstration, that is, of the excellent fruit such a grafting might produce—I yet imagine the enacted and considerably prolonged scene (it lasted a whole decade) to have heaped perfectly full the measure of what it proposed. The interesting, the curious, the characteristic thing was just, however, I seem to make out—I seemed to have made out even at the time—in the almost complete absence of difficulty. It might almost then be said of the affair that it hadn't been difficult enough for interest even should one insist on treating it as sufficiently complicated or composed for picture. The great War was to leave so many things changed, the country over, so many elements added, to say nothing of others subtracted, in the American consciousness at large, that even though the coeducational idea, taking to itself strength, has during these later years pushed its conquests to the very verge of demonstration of its inevitable limits, my memory speaks to me of the Concord school rather as of a supreme artless word on the part of the old social order than as a charged intimation or announcement on the part of the new. The later arrangements, more or less in its likeness and when on a considerable scale, have appeared, to attentive observation, I think, mere endlessly multiplied notes of the range of high spirits in the light heart of communities more aware on the whole of the size and number of their opportunity, of the boundless spaces, the possible undertakings, the uncritical minds and the absent standards about them, than of matters to be closely and preparedly reckoned with. They have been, comparatively speaking, experiments in the void—the great void that may spread so smilingly between wide natural borders before complications have begun to grow. The name of the complication before the fact is very apt to be the discovery —which latter term was so promptly to figure for the faith that living and working more intimately together than had up to then been conceived possible would infinitely improve both the condition and the performance of the brother and sister sexes. It takes long in new communities for discoveries to become complications—though complications become discoveries doubtless often in advance of this; the large vague area, with its vast marginal ease, over which confidence could run riot and new kinds of human relation, elatedly proposed, flourish in the sun, was to shift to different ground the question the

Concord school had played with, during its term of life, on its smaller stage, under the great New England elms and maples and in the preoccupied New England air.

The preoccupation had been in a large measure, it is true, exactly with such possibilities, such bright fresh answers to old stale riddles, as Mr. Sanborn and his friends clubbed together to supply; but I can only, for my argument, recover the sense of my single visit to the scene, which must have been in the winter of '62–'63, I think, and which put before me, as I seem now to make out, some suggested fit of perversity—not desperate, quite harmless rather, and almost frivolously futile, on the part of a particular little world that had been thrown back upon itself for very boredom and, after a spell of much admired talking and other beating of the air, wanted for a change to "do" something. The question it "played" with I just advisedly said—for what could my impression have been, personally if indirectly gathered, and with my admirably communicative younger brother to testify, but that if as a school, in strict parlance, the thing was scarce more than naught, as a prolonged pastime it was scarce less than charming and quite filled up in that direction its ample and original measure? I have to reckon, I here allow, with the trick of what I used irrepressibly to read into things in front of which I found myself, for gaping purposes, planted by some unquestioned outer force: it seemed so prescribed to me, so imposed on me, to read more, as through some ever-felt claim for roundness of aspect and intensity of effect in presented matters, whatever they might be, than the conscience of the particular affair itself was perhaps developed enough to ask of it. The experience of many of the Concord pupils during the freshness of the experiment must have represented for them a free and yet ever so conveniently conditioned taste of the idyllic—such possibilities of perfect good comradeship between unsuspected and unalarmed youths and maidens (on a comprehensive ground that really exposed the business to a light and put it to a test) as they were never again to see so favoured in every way by circumstance and, one may quite emphatically say, by atmosphere. It is the atmosphere that comes back to me as most of all the making of the story, even when inhaled but by an occasional whiff and from afar—the manner of my own inhaling. In that air of charmed and cultivated good faith nothing for which the beautiful might be so presumingly claimed—if only claimed with a sufficiently brave clean emphasis—wouldn't have *worked*, which was the great thing; every one must have felt that what was aspired to did work, and as I catch the many-voiced report of it again (many-voiced but pretty well suffused with one clear tone, this of inflections irreproducible now) I seem to listen in convinced admiration, though not by any means in stirred envy, to the cheerful clatter of its working. My failure of envy has, however, no mite of historic importance, proving as it does nothing at all but that if we had, in the family sense, so distinctly turned our back on Europe, the distinctness was at no point so marked as in our facing so straight to such a picture, by which I mean to such an exhibition, as my father's letter throws off. Without knowledge of the letter at the time I yet measured the situation much as he did and enjoyed it as he did, because it would have been stupid not to; but from that to any wishful vision of being in it or of it would have been a long jump, of which I was unabashedly incapable. To have broken so personally, so all but catastrophically, with Europe as we had done affected me as the jump sufficient; we had landed somewhere in quite another world or at least on the sharp edge of one; and in the single particular sense could I, as time then went on, feel myself at all moved, with the helpless, the baffled visionary way of it, to push further in. What straight solicitation *that* phase of the American scene could exert—more coercive to the imagination than any we were ever again, as Americans, to know—I shall presently try to explain; but this was an intensely different matter.

> I buried two of my children yesterday—at Concord, Mass., and feel so heartbroken this morning that I shall need to adopt two more instantly to supply their place; and lo and behold you and William present yourselves, or if you decline the honour Ellen and Baby. Mary and I trotted forth last Wednesday, bearing Wilky and Bob in our arms to surrender them to the famous Mr. Sanborn. The yellowest sunshine and an atmosphere of balm were all over the goodly land, while the maple, the oak and the dogwood showered such splendours upon the eye as made the Champs Elysées and the Bois appear parvenus and comical. Mrs. Clark is a graceless enough woman outwardly, but so tenderly feathered

inwardly, so unaffectedly kind and motherly toward the urchins under her roof, that one was glad to leave them in that provident nest. She has three or four other school-boarders, one of them a daughter of John Brown—tall, erect, long-haired and freckled, as John Brown's daughter has a right to be. I kissed her (inwardly) between the eyes, and inwardly heard the martyred Johannes chuckle over the fat inheritance of love and tenderness he had after all bequeathed to his children in all good men's minds. An arch little Miss Plumley also lives there, with eyes full of laughter and a mouth like a bed of lilies bordered with roses. How it is going to be possible for my two boys to pursue their studies in the midst of that bewilderment I don't clearly see. I am only sure of one thing, which is that if I had had such educational advantages as that in my youth I should probably have been now far more nearly ripe for this world's business. We asked to see Miss Waterman, one of the teachers quartered in the house, in order to say to her how much we should thank her if she would occasionally put out any too lively spark she might see fall on the expectant tinder of my poor boys' bosoms; but Miss W. herself proved of so siliceous a quality on inspection—with round tender eyes, young, fair and womanly—that I saw in her only new danger and no promise of safety. My present conviction is that a general conflagration is inevitable, ending in the total combustion of all that I hold dear on that spot. Yet I can't but felicitate our native land that such magnificent experiments in education go on among us.

Then we drove to Emerson's and waded up to our knees through a harvest of apples and pears, which, tired of their mere outward or carnal growth, had descended to the loving bosom of the lawn, there or elsewhere to grow inwardly meet for their heavenly rest in the veins of Ellen the saintly and others; until at last we found the cordial Pan himself in the midst of his household, breezy with hospitality and blowing exhilarating trumpets of welcome. Age has just the least in the world dimmed the lustre we once knew, but an unmistakable breath of the morning still encircles him, and the odour of primaeval woods. Pitchpine is not more pagan than he continues to be, and acorns as little confess the gardener's skill. Still I insist that he is a voluntary Pan, that it is a condition of mere wilfulness and insurrection on his part, contingent upon a mercilessly sound digestion and an uncommon imaginative influx, and I have no doubt that even he, as the years ripen, will at last admit Nature to be tributary and not supreme. However this be, we consumed juicy pears to the diligent music of Pan's pipe, while Ellen and Edith softly gathered themselves upon two low stools in the chimney-corner, saying never a word nor looking a look, but apparently hemming their handkerchiefs; and good Mrs. Stearns, who sat by the window and seemed to be the village dressmaker, ever and anon glanced at us over her spectacles as if to say that never before has she seen this wondrous Pan so glistening with dewdrops. Then and upon the waves of that friendly music we were duly wafted to our educational Zion and carefully made over our good and promising and affectionate boys to the school-master's keeping. Out into the field beside his house Sanborn incontinently took us to show how his girls and boys perform together their worship of Hygeia. It was a glimpse into that new world wherein dwelleth righteousness and which is full surely fast coming upon our children and our children's children; and I could hardly keep myself, as I saw my children's eyes drink in the mingled work and play of the inspiring scene, from shouting out a joyful Nunc Dimittis. The short of the story is that we left them and rode home robbed of our plumage, feeling sore and ugly and only hoping that they wouldn't die, any of these cold winter days, before the parental breast could get there to warm them back to life or cheer them on to a better.

Mrs. William Hunt has just come in to tell the good news of your near advent and that she has found the exact house for you; instigated to that activity by one of your angels, of the Hooper band, with whom she has been in correspondence. I don't thank angel Hooper for putting angel Hunt upon that errand, since I should like to have had the merit of it myself. I suspect the rent is what it ought to be: if it's not I will lay by something every week for you toward it, and have no doubt we shall stagger through the cold weather.

I gather from the above the very flower of my father's irrepressible utterance of his constitutional optimism, that optimism fed so little by any sense of things as they were or are, but rich in its vision of the facility with which they might become almost at any moment or from one day to the other totally and splendidly different. A less vague or vain idealist couldn't, I think, have been encountered; it was given him to catch in the fact at almost any turn right or left some flagrant assurance or promise of the state of man transfigured. The Concord school could be to him for the hour—there were hours and hours!—such a promise; could even figure in that light, to his amplifying sympathy, in a degree disproportionate to its genial, but after all limited, after all not so intensely "inflated," as he would have said, sense of itself. In which light it is that I recognise, and even to elation, how little, practically, of the idea of the Revolution in the vulgar or violent sense was involved in his seeing so many things, in the whole social order about him, and in the interest of their being more or less immediately altered, as lamentably, and yet at the same time and under such a coloured light, as amusingly and illustratively, wrong—wrong, that is, with a blundering helpless human salience that kept criticism humorous, kept it, so to speak, sociable and almost "sympathetic" even when readiest. The case was really of his rather feeling so vast a rightness close at hand or lurking immediately behind actual arrangements that a single turn of the inward wheel, one real response to pressure of the spiritual spring, would bridge the chasms, straighten the distortions, rectify the relations and, in a word, redeem and vivify the whole mass—after a far sounder, yet, one seemed to see, also far subtler, fashion than any that our spasmodic annals had yet shown us. It was of course the old story that we had only to *be* with more intelligence and faith—an immense deal more, certainly—in order to work off, in the happiest manner, the many-sided ugliness of life; which was a process that might go on, blessedly, in the quietest of all quiet ways. *That* wouldn't be blood and fire and tears, or would be none of these things stupidly precipitated; it would simply have taken place by *enjoyed* communication and contact, enjoyed concussion or convulsion even—since pangs and agitations, the very agitations of perception itself, are of the highest privilege of the soul and there is always, thank goodness, a saving sharpness of play or complexity of consequence in the intelligence completely alive. The meaning of which remarks for myself, I must be content to add, is that the optimists of the world, the constructive idealists, as one has mainly known them, have too often struck one as overlooking more of the aspects of the real than they recognise; whereas our indefeasible impression, William's and mine, of our parent was that he by his very constitution and intimate heritage recognised many more of those than he overlooked. What was the finest part of our intercourse with him—that is the most nutritive—but a positive record of that? Such a matter as that the factitious had absolutely no hold on him was the truest thing about him, and it was all the while present to us, I think, as backing up his moral authority and play of vision that never, for instance, had there been a more numerous and candid exhibition of all the human susceptibilities than in the nest of his original nurture. I have spoken of the fashion in which I still see him, after the years, attentively bent over those much re-written "papers," that we had, even at our stupidest, this warrant for going in vague admiration of that they caught the eye, even the most filially detached, with a final face of wrought clarity, and thereby of beauty, that there *could* be no thinking unimportant—and see him also fall back from the patient posture, again and again, in long fits of remoter consideration, wondering, pondering sessions into which I think I was more often than not moved to read, for the fine interest and colour of it, some story of acute inward difficulty amounting for the time to discouragement. If one wanted drama *there* was drama, and of the most concrete and most immediately offered to one's view and one's suspense; to the point verily, as might often occur, of making one go roundabout it on troubled tiptoe even as one would have held one's breath at the play.

These opposed glimpses, I say, hang before me as I look back, but really fuse together in the vivid picture of the fond scribe separated but by a pane of glass—his particular preference was always directly to face the window—from the general human condition he was so devoutly concerned with. He *saw* it, through the near glass, saw it in such detail and with a feeling for it that broke down nowhere—that was the great thing; which truth it confirmed that his very fallings back and long waits and stays and almost stricken musings witnessed exactly to his intensity, the intensity that would "come out," after all, and make his passionate philosophy and the fullest array of the appearances that couldn't be blinked fit together and harmonise. Detached as I could during all those years perhaps queerly enough believe myself, it would still have done my young mind the very greatest violence to have to suppose that any plane of conclusion for him, however rich and harmonious he might tend to make conclusion, could be in the nature of a fool's paradise. Small vague outsider as I was, I couldn't have borne *that* possibility; and I see, as I return to the case, how little I really could ever have feared it. This would have amounted to fearing it on account of his geniality—a shocking supposition; as if his geniality had been thin and *bête*, patched up and poor, and not by the straightest connections, nominal and other, of the very stuff of his genius. No, I feel myself complacently look back to *my* never having, even at my small poorest, been so *bête*, either, as to conceive he might be "wrong," wrong as a thinker-out, in his own way, of the great mysteries, because of the interest and amusement and vividness his attesting spirit could fling over the immediate ground. What he saw *there* at least could be so enlightening, so evocatory, could fall in so—which was to the most inspiring effect within the range of perception of a scant son who was doubtless, as to the essential, already more than anything else a novelist *en herbe*. If it didn't sound in a manner patronising I should say that I saw that my father saw; and that I couldn't but have given my own case away by not believing, however obscurely, in the virtue of his consequent and ultimate synthesis. Of course I never dreamed of any such name for it—I only thought of it as something very great and fine founded on those forces in him that came home to us and that touched us all the while. As these were extraordinary forces of sympathy and generosity, and that yet knew how to be such without falsifying any minutest measure, the structure raised upon them might well, it would seem, and even to the uppermost sublime reaches, be as valid as it was beautiful. If he so endeared himself wasn't it, one asked as time went on, through his never having sentimentalised or merely meditated away, so to call it, the least embarrassment of the actual about him, and having with a passion peculiarly his own kept together his stream of thought, however transcendent and the stream of life, however humanised? There was a kind of experiential authority in his basis, as he felt his basis—there being no human predicament he couldn't by a sympathy more *like* direct experience than any I have known enter into; and this authority, which concluded so to a widening and brightening of the philosophic—for him the spiritual—sky, made his character, as intercourse disclosed it, in a high degree fascinating. These things, I think, however, are so happily illustrated in his letters that they look out from almost any continuous passage in such a series for instance as those addressed in the earlier time to Mrs. Tappan. His *tone*, that is, always so effectually looks out, and the living parts of him so singularly hung together, that one may fairly say his philosophy *was* his tone. To cite a few passages here is at the same time to go back to a previous year or two—which my examples, I hold, make worth while. He had been on a visit to Paris toward the winter's end of '60, and had returned to Geneva, whence he writes early in April.

> So sleepy have I been ever since my return from Paris that I am utterly unfit to write letters. I was thoroughly poisoned by tobacco in those horrid railway carriages, and this with want of sleep knocked me down. I am only half awake still, and will not engage consequently in any of those profound inquiries which your remembrance always suggests.
>
> I am very sorry for you that you live in an excommunicated country, or next door to it; and I don't wonder at your wanting to get away. But it is provoking to think that but for your other plan Switzerland might possess you all for the summer. It is doubtless in part this disappointment that will unsettle us in our present moorings and take us probably soon to Germany. What after that I have no idea, and am always so little wilful about our movements that I am ready the young ones should settle them. So we may be in Europe a good while yet, always providing that war keep smooth his wrinkled front and allow us quiet newspapers. They must fight in Italy for some time to come, but between England and France is the main point. If *they* can hold aloof from tearing each other we shall manage; otherwise we go home at once, to escape the universal spatter that must then ensue.
>
> What is the meaning of all these wars and rumours of wars? No respectable person ever seems to occupy himself with the question, but I can't help feeling it more interesting than anything in Homer or Plato or the gallery of the Vatican. I long daily with unappeasable longing for a righteous life, such a life as I am sure is implied in every human possibility, and myriads are bearing me company. What does this show but that the issue is near out of all our existing chaos? All our evil is fossil and comes from the mere persistence of diseased institutions in pretending to rule us when we ought to be left free to be living spirits of God. There is no *fresh* evil in the world. No one now steals or commits murder or any other offence with the least relish for it, but only to revenge his poor starved opportunities. The superiority of America in respect to freedom of thought over Europe comes from this fact that she

> has so nearly achieved her deliverance from such tyrannies. All she now needs to make her right is simply an intelligent recognition of her spiritual whereabouts. If she had this she would put her hand to the work splendidly. You and I when we get home will try to quicken her intelligence in that respect, will do at any rate *our* best to put away this pestilent munching of the tree of knowledge of good and evil, and persuade to the belief of man's unmixed innocence.

Which, it will easily be seen, was optimism with a vengeance, and marked especially in the immediacy, the state of being at hand for him, of a social redemption. What made this the more signal was its being so unattended with visions the least Apocalyptic or convulsional; the better order slipping in amid the worse, and superseding it, so insidiously, so quietly and, by a fair measure, so easily. It was a faith and an accompanying philosophy that couldn't be said not to be together simplifying; and yet nothing was more unmistakable when we saw them at close range, I repeat, than that they weren't unnourished, weren't what he himself would, as I hear him, have called the "flatulent" fruit of sentimentality.

His correspondent had in a high degree, by her vivacity of expression, the art of challenging his—as is markedly apparent from a letter the date of which fails beyond its being of the same stay at Geneva and of the winter's end.

> If I had really imagined that I had bored you and your husband so very little while I was in Paris in December I should long since have repeated the experiment; the more surely that I want so much to see again my darling nieces and delight myself in the abundance of their large-eyed belief. . . . Our Alice is still under discipline—preparing to fulfil some high destiny or other in the future by reducing decimal fractions to their lowest possible rate of subsistence, where they often grow so attenuated under her rapid little fingers that my poor old eyes can no longer see them at all. I shall go before long to England, and then perhaps—! But I shan't promise anything on *her* behalf.
>
> You ask me "why I do not brandish my tomahawk and, like Walt Whitman, raise my barbaric yawp over the roofs of all the houses." It is because I am not yet a "cosmos" as that gentleman avowedly is, but only a very dim nebula, doing its modest best, no doubt, to solidify into cosmical dimensions, but still requiring an "awful

sight" of time and pains and patience on the part of its friends. You evidently fancy that cosmoses are born to all the faculty they shall ever have, like ducks: no such thing. There is no respectable cosmos but what is born to such a vapoury and even gaseous inheritance as requires long centuries of conflict on its part to overcome the same and become pronounced or educated in its proper mineral, vegetable or animal order. Ducks are born perfect; that is to say they utter the same unmodified unimproved quack on their dying pillow that they uttered on their natal day; whereas cosmoses are destined to a life of such surprising change that you may say their career is an incessant disavowal of their birth, or that their highest maturation consists in their utter renunciation of their natural father and mother. You transcendentalists make the fatal mistake of denying education, of sundering present from past and future from present. These things are indissolubly one, the present deriving its consciousness only from the past, and the future drawing all its distinctive wisdom from our present experience. The law is the same with the individual as it is with the race: none of us can dodge the necessity of regeneration, of disavowing our natural ancestry in order to come forth in our own divinely-given proportions. The secret of this necessity ought to reconcile us to it, however onerous the obligation it imposes; for that secret is nothing more nor less than this, that we cosmoses have a plenary divine origin and are bound eventually to see that divinity reproduced in our most familiar and trivial experience, even down to the length of our shoe-ties. If the Deity were an immense Duck capable only of emitting an eternal quack we of course should all have been born webfooted, each as infallible in his way as the Pope, nor ever have been at the expense and bother of swimming-schools. But He is a perfect man, incapable of the slightest quackery, capable only of every honest and modest and helpful purpose, and these are perfections to which manifestly no one is born, but only *re*-born. We come to such states not by learning, only by *unlearning*. No natural edification issues in spiritual architecture of this splendour, but only a natural demolition or undoing. I dimly recognise this great truth, and hence hold more to a present imbecility than to a too eager efficiency. I feel myself more fit to be knocked about for some time yet and vastated of my natural vigour than to commence cosmos and raise the barbaric yawp. Time enough for that when I am fairly finished. Say what we will, you and I are all the while at school just now. The genial pedagogue may give you so little of the ferule as to leave you to doubt whether you really *are* there; but this only proves what a wonderful pedagogue it is, and how capable of adapting himself to everyone.

His friend in Paris found herself at that time, like many other persons, much interested in the exercise of automatic writing, of which we have since so abundantly heard and as to which she had communicated some striking observations.

. . . Your letter is full of details that interest but don't fascinate. I haven't a doubt of a single experience you allege, and do not agree with your friend Count S. (your writing of this name is obscure) that the world of spirits is not an element in your writing. I am persuaded now for a long time of the truth of these phenomena and feel no inclination to dispute or disparage them; but at the same time I feel to such a degree my own remoteness from them that I am sure I could never get any personal contact with them. The state of mind exposing one to influences of this nature, and which makes them beneficial to it, is a sceptical state; and this I have never known for a moment. Spiritual existence has always been more real to me (I was going to say) than natural; and when accordingly I am asked to believe in the spiritual world because my senses are getting to reveal it I feel as if the ground of my conviction were going to be weakened rather than strengthened. Of course I should have very little respect for spiritual things which didn't ultimately report themselves to sense, which didn't indeed subside into things of sense as logically as a house into its foundations. But what I deny is that spiritual existence can be directly known on earth—known otherwise than by correspondence or inversely. The letter of every revelation must be directly hostile to its spirit, and only inversely accordant, because the very pretension of revelation is that it's a descent, an absolute coming down, of truth, a humiliation of it from its own elevated and habitual plane to a lower one.

Admit therefore that the facts of "spiritualism" are all true; admit that persons really deceased have been communicating with you about the state of Europe, the approaching crisis and the persons known to us whom you name; in that case I should insist that, to possess the slightest spiritual interest, their revelation should be re-translated into the spiritual tongue by correspondences; because as to any spirit knowing or caring to know those persons, or being bothered about any crisis of ours, that is to me simply incredible. Such matters have in each case doubtless some spiritual or substantial counterpart answering in every particular to its superficial features; and Wilkinson and Emerson, for instance, with the others, are of course shadows of some greater or less spiritual quantities. But I'll be hanged if there's the slightest *sensible* accord between the substance and the semblance on either hand. Your spirits, no doubt, give you the very communications you report to me; only Wilkinson spiritually interpreted and Emerson spiritually interpreted mean things so very different from our two friends of those denominations that if our spiritual eye were for a moment open to discern the difference I think it highly probable—I'm sure it is infinitely possible—we should renounce their acquaintance.

But I have harped on this string long enough; let me change the tune. Your spirits tell you to repose in what they are doing for you and, with a pathos to which I am not insensible, say "Rest now, poor child; your struggles have been great; clasp peace to your bosom at last." And as a general thing our ears are saluted by assurances that these communications are all urged by philanthropy and that everyone so addressing us wants in some way to help and elevate us. But just this is to my mind the unpleasant side of the business. I have been so long accustomed to see the most arrant deviltry transact itself in the name of benevolence that the moment I hear a profession of good-will from almost any quarter I instinctively look about for a constable or place my hand within reach of the bell-rope. My ideal of human intercourse would be a state of things in which no man will ever stand in need of any other man's help, but will derive all his satisfaction from the great social tides which own no individual names. I am sure no man can be put in a position of dependence upon another without that other's very soon becoming—if he accepts the duties of the relation—utterly degraded out of his just human proportions. No man can play the Deity to his fellow man with impunity—I mean spiritual impunity of course. For see: if I am at all satisfied with that relation, if it contents me to be in a position of generosity toward others, I must be remarkably indifferent at bottom to the gross social inequality which permits that position, and instead of resenting the enforced humiliation of my fellow man to myself, in the interests of humanity, I acquiesce in it for the sake of the profit it yields to my own self-complacency. I do hope the reign of benevolence is over; until that event occurs I am sure the reign of God will be impossible. But I have a shocking bad cold that racks my head to bursting almost; I can't think to any purpose. Let me hear soon from you that I have not been misunderstood. I wouldn't for the world seem wilfully to depreciate what you set a high value on. No, I really can't help my judgments. And I always soften them to within an inch of their life as it is.

The following, no longer from the Hotel de l'Ecu, but from 5 Quai du Mont Blanc, would indicate that his "Dear Queen Caroline," as he addresses her, was at no loss to defend her own view of the matters in discussion between them: in which warm light indeed it is that I was myself in the after years ever most amusedly to see her.

> Don't scold a fellow so! Exert your royal gifts in exalting only the lowly and humbling only the proud. Precisely what I like, to get extricated from metaphysics, is encouragement from a few persons like yourself, such encouragement as would lie in your intelligent apprehension and acknowledgment of the great *result* of metaphysics, which is a godly and spotless life on earth. If I could find anyone apt to that doctrine I should not work so hard metaphysically to convince the world of its truth. And as for being a metaphysical Jack Horner, the thing is contradictory, as no metaphysician whose studies are sincere ever felt tempted to self-complacency or disposed to reckon himself a good boy. Such exaltations are not for him, but only for the artists and poets, who dazzle the eyes of mankind and *don't* recoil from the darkness they themselves produce—as Dryden says, or Collins.

Mrs. Tappan, spending the month of June in London, continued to impute for the time, I infer (I seem to remember a later complete detachment), a livelier importance to the supernatural authors of her "writing" than her correspondent was disposed to admit; but almost anything was a quickener of the correspondent's own rich, that is always so animated, earnestness. He had to feel an interlocutor's general sympathy, or recognise a moral relation, even if a disturbed one, for the deep tide of his conviction to rise outwardly higher; but when that happened the tide overflowed indeed.

> MY DEAR CAROLINA—Neither North nor South, but an eminently free State, with no exulting shout of master and no groan of captive to be heard in all its borders, but only the cheerful hum of happy husband and children—how do you find London? Here in Geneva we are so saturate with sunshine that we would fain dive to the depths of the lake to learn coolness of the little fishes. Still, we don't envy your two weeks of unbroken rain in dear dismal London. What a preparation for doing justice to Lenox! You see I know—through Mary Tweedy, who has a hearty appreciation of

her London privileges. How are A. D. and all the rest of them? *Familiar* spirits, are they not, on a short acquaintance?—and how pleasant an aspect it gives to the middle kingdom to think you shall be sure to find there such lovers and friends! Only let us keep them at a proper distance. It doesn't do for us ever to accept another only at that other's own estimate of himself. If we do we may as well plunge into Tartarus at once. No human being can afford to commit his happiness to another's keeping, or, what is the same thing, forego his own individuality with all that it imports. The first requisite of our true relationship to each other (spiritually speaking) is that we be wholly independent of each other: then we may give ourselves away as much as we please, we shall do neither them nor ourselves any harm. But until that blessed day comes, by the advance of a scientific society among men, we shall be utterly unworthy to love each other or be loved in return. We shall do nothing but prey upon each other and turn each other's life to perfect weariness.

The more of it then just now the better! The more we bite and devour each other, the more horribly the newspapers abound in all the evidences of our disgusting disorganisation, the disorganisation of the old world, the readier will our dull ears be to listen to the tidings of the new world which is aching to appear, the world wherein dwelleth righteousness. Don't abuse the newspapers therefore publicly, but tell everybody of the use they are destined to promote, and set others upon the look-out. A. D. is a very good woman, I haven't a doubt, but will fast grow a better one if she would let herself alone, and me also, and all other mere persons, while she diligently inquires about the Lord; that is about that lustrous universal life which God's providence is now forcing upon men's attention and which will obliterate for ever all this exaggeration of our personalities. It is very well for lovers to abase themselves in this way to each other; because love is a *passion* of one's nature—that is to say the lover is not self-possessed, but is lifted for a passing moment to the level of the Lord's life in the race, and so attuned to higher issues ever after in his own proper sphere. But these experiences are purely disciplinary and not final. All passion is a mere inducement to action, and when at last activity really dawns in us we drop this faculty of hallucination that we have been under about persons and see and adore the abounding divinity which is in all persons alike. Who will then ever be caught in that foolish snare again? I did nothing but tumble into it from my boyhood up to my marriage; since which great disillusioning—yes!—I feel that the only lovable person is one who will never permit himself to be loved. But I have written on without any intention and have now no time to say what alone I intended, how charming and kind and long to be remembered you were all those Paris days. Give my love to honest William and tell my small nieces that I pine to pluck again the polished cherries of their cheeks. My wife admires and loves you.

From which I jump considerably forward, for its (privately) historic value, to a communication from Newport of the middle of August '63. My father's two younger sons had, one the previous and one at the beginning of the current, year obtained commissions in the Volunteer Army; as a sequel to which my next younger brother, as Adjutant of the Fifty-fourth Massachusetts, Colonel Robert Shaw's regiment, the first body of coloured soldiers raised in the North, had received two grave wounds in that unsuccessful attack on Fort Wagner from which the gallant young leader of the movement was not to return.

Wilky had a bad day yesterday and kept me busy or I shouldn't have delayed answering your inquiries till to-day. He is very severely wounded both in the ankle and in the side—where he doesn't heal so fast as the doctor wishes in consequence of the shell having made a pouch which collects matter and retards nature. They cut it open yesterday, and to-day he is better, or will be. The wound in the ankle was made by a cannister ball an inch and a half in diameter, which lodged eight days in the foot and was finally dislodged by cutting down through (the foot) and taking it out at the sole. He is excessively weak, unable to do anything but lie passive, even to turn himself on his pillow. He will probably have a slow and tedious recovery—the doctors say of a year at least; but he knows nothing of this himself and speaks, so far as he does talk, but of going back in the Fall. If you write please say nothing of this; he is so distressed at the thought of a long sickness. He is vastly attached to the negro-soldier cause; believes (I think) that the world has existed for it; and is sure that enormous results to civilisation are coming out of it. We heard from Bob this morning at Morris Island; with his regiment, building earthworks and mounting guns. Hot, he says, but breezy; also that the shells make for them every few minutes—while he and his men betake themselves to the trenches and holes in the earth "like so many land-crabs in distress." He writes in the highest spirits. Cabot Russell, Wilky's dearest friend, is, we fear, a prisoner and

> wounded. We hear nothing decisive, but the indications point that way. Poor Wilky cries aloud for his friends gone and missing, and I could hardly have supposed he might be educated so suddenly up to serious manhood altogether as he appears to have been. I hear from Frank Shaw this morning, and they are all well—and admirable.

This goes beyond the moment I had lately, and doubtless too lingeringly, reached, as I say; just as I shall here find convenience in borrowing a few passages from my small handful of letters of the time to follow—to the extent of its not following by a very long stretch. Such a course keeps these fragments of record together, as scattering them would perhaps conduce to some leakage in their characteristic tone, for which I desire all the fulness it can keep. Impossible moreover not in some degree to yield on the spot to *any* brush of the huge procession of those particular months and years, even though I shall presently take occasion to speak as I may of my own so inevitably contracted consciousness of what the brush, with its tremendous possibilities of violence, could consist of in the given case. I had, under stress, to content myself with knowing it in a more indirect and muffled fashion than might easily have been—even should one speak of it but as a matter of mere vision of the eyes or quickened wonder of the mind or heaviness of the heart, as a matter in fine of the closer and more inquiring, to say nothing of the more agitated, approach. All of which, none the less, was not to prevent the whole quite indescribably intensified time—intensified through all lapses of occasion and frustrations of contact—from remaining with me as a more constituted and sustained act of living, in proportion to my powers and opportunities, than any other homogeneous stretch of experience that my memory now recovers. The case had to be in a peculiar degree, alas, that of living inwardly—like so many of my other cases; in a peculiar degree compared, that is, to the immense and prolonged outwardness, outwardness naturally at the very highest pitch, that was the general sign of the situation. To which I may add that my "alas" just uttered is in the key altogether of my then current consciousness, and not in the least in that of my present appreciation of the same—so that I leave it, even while I thus put my mark against it, as I should restore tenderly to the shelf any odd rococo object that might have slipped from a reliquary. My appreciation of what I presume at the risk of any apparent fatuity to call my "relation to" the War is at present a thing exquisite to me, a thing of the last refinement of romance, whereas it had to be at the time a sore and troubled, a mixed and oppressive thing—though I promptly see, on reflection, how it must frequently have flushed with emotions, with small scraps of direct perception even, with particular sharpnesses in the generalised pang of participation, that were all but touched in themselves as with the full experience. Clear as some object presented in high relief against the evening sky of the west, at all events, is the presence for me beside the stretcher on which my young brother was to lie for so many days before he could be moved, and on which he had lain during his boat-journey from the South to New York and thence again to Newport, of lost Cabot Russell's stricken father, who, failing, up and down the searched field, in respect of his own irrecoverable boy—then dying, or dead, as afterwards appeared, well within the enemy's works—had with an admirable charity brought Wilky back to a waiting home instead, and merged the parental ache in the next nearest devotion he could find. Vivid to me still is one's almost ashamed sense of this at the hurried disordered time, and of how it was impossible not to impute to his grave steady gentleness and judgment a full awareness of the difference it would have made for him, all the same, to be doing such things with a still more intimate pity. Unobliterated for me, in spite of vaguenesses, this quasi-twilight vision of the good bereft man, bereft, if I rightly recall, of his only son, as he sat erect and dry-eyed at the guarded feast of *our* relief; and so much doubtless partly because of the image that hovers to me across the years of Cabot Russell himself, my brother's so close comrade—dark-eyed, youthfully brown, heartily bright, actively handsome, and with the arrested expression, the indefinable shining stigma, worn, to the regard that travels back to them, by those of the young figures of the fallen that memory and fancy, wanting, never ceasing to want, to "do" something for them, set as upright and clear-faced as may be, each in his sacred niche. They have each to such a degree, so ranged, the strange property or privilege—one scarce knows what to call

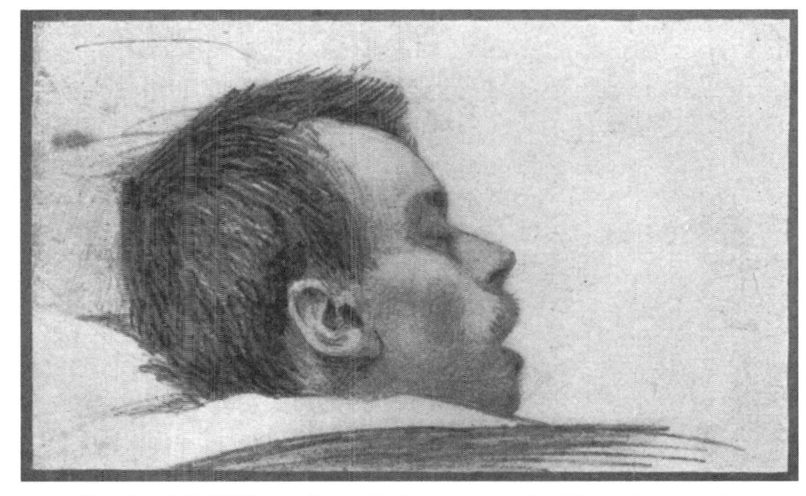

Sketch of G. W. James brought home wounded from the assault on Fort Wagner.

it—of exquisitely, for all *our* time, facing us out, quite blandly ignoring us, looking through us or straight over us at something they partake of together but that we mayn't pretend to know. We walk thus, I think, rather ruefully before them—those of us at least who didn't at the time share more happily their risk. William, during those first critical days, while the stretcher itself, set down with its load just within the entrance to our house, mightn't be moved further, preserved our poor lacerated brother's aspect in a drawing of great and tender truth which I permit myself to reproduce. It tells for me the double story—I mean both of Wilky's then condition and of the draughtsman's admirable hand.

But I find waiting my father's last letter of the small group to Mrs. Tappan. We were by that time, the autumn of 1865, settled in Boston for a couple of years.

> MY DEAR CARRY—Are you a carry*atid* that you consider yourself bound to uphold that Lenox edifice through the cold winter as well as the hot summer? Why don't you come to town? I can't *write* what I want to say. My brain is tired, and I gladly forego all writing that costs thought or attention. But I have no day forgotten your question, and am eager always to make a conquest of you; you are so full both of the upper and the nether might as always greatly to excite my interest and make me feel how little is accomplished while you are left not so. I make no prayer to you; I would have no assistance from your own vows; or the pleasure of my intercourse with you would be slain. I would rather outrage than conciliate your sympathies, that I might have all the joy of winning you over at last. Hate me on my ideal side, the side that menaces you, as much as you please meanwhile, but keep a warm corner in your regard for me personally, as I always do for you, until we meet again. It's a delight to know a person of your sense and depth; even the *gaudia certaminis* are more cheering with you than ordinary agreements with other people.

On which note I may leave the exchange in question, feeling how equal an honour it does to the parties.

VIII

I JUDGE best to place together here several passages from my father's letters belonging to this general period, even though they again carry me to points beyond my story proper. It is not for the story's sake that I am moved to gather them, but for their happy illustration, once more, of something quite else, the human beauty of the writer's spirit and the fine breadth of his expression. This latter virtue is most striking, doubtless, when he addresses his women correspondents, of whom there were many, yet it so pervades for instance various notes, longer and shorter, to Mrs. James T. Fields, wife of the eminent Boston publisher and editor, much commended to us as founder and, for a time, chief conductor of the Atlantic Monthly, our most adopted and enjoyed native *recueil* of that series of years. The Atlantic seemed somehow, while the good season lasted, to live with us, whereas our relation to the two or three other like organs, homegrown or foreign, of which there could be any question, and most of all, naturally, to the great French Revue, was that we lived with *them*. The light of literature, as we then invoked or at any rate received it, seemed to beat into the delightful Fields salon from a nearer heaven than upon any other scene, and played there over a museum of relics and treasures and apparitions (these last whether reflected and by that time legendary, or directly protrusive and presented, wearers of the bay) with an intensity, I feel again as I look back, every resting ray of which was a challenge to dreaming ambition. I am bound to note, none the less, oddly enough, that my father's communications with the charming mistress of the scene are more often than not a bright profession of sad reasons for inability to mingle in it. He mingled with reluctance in scenes designed and preappointed, and was, I think, mostly content to feel almost anything near at hand become a scene for him from the moment he had happened to cast into the arena (which he preferred without flags or festoons) the golden apple of the unexpected—in humorous talk, that is, in reaction without preparation, in sincerity which was itself sociability. It was not nevertheless that he didn't now and then "accept"—with attenuations.

> . . . If therefore you will let Alice and me come to you on Wednesday evening I shall still rejoice in the benignant fate that befalls my house—even though my wife, indisposed, "feels reluctantly constrained to count herself out of the sphere of your hospitality;" and I will bind myself moreover by solemn vows not to perplex the happy atmosphere which almost reigns in yours by risking a syllable of the incongruous polemic your husband wots of. I will listen devotedly to you and him all the evening if thereby I may early go home repaired in my own esteem, and not dilapidated, as has been hitherto too often the case.

He could resist persuasion even in the insidious form of an expressed desire that he should read something, "something he was writing," to a chosen company.

> Your charming note is irresistible at first sight, and I had almost uttered a profligate Yes!—that is a promise irrespective of a power to perform; when my good angel arrested me by the stern inquiry: What have you got to give them? And I could only say in reply to this intermeddling but blest spirit: Nothing, my dear friend, absolutely nothing! Whereupon the veracious one said again: Sit you down immediately therefore and, confessing your literary indigence to this lovely lady, pray her to postpone the fulfilment of her desire to some future flood-tide in the little stream of your inspiration, when you will be ready to serve her.

The following refers to the question of his attending with my mother at some session of a Social Club, at which a prepared performance of some sort was always offered, but of which they had lately found it convenient to cease to be members.

> I snatch the pen from my wife's hand to enjoy, myself, the satisfaction of saying to you how good and kind and charming you always are, and how we never grow tired of recounting the fact among ourselves here, and yet how we still shall be unable to accept your hospitality. Why? Simply because we have a due sense of what becomes us after our late secession, and would not willingly be seen at two successive meetings, lest the carnal observer should

argue that we had left the Club by the front door of obligation only to be readmitted at the back door of indulgence: I put it as Fields would phrase it. To speak of him always reminds me of various things, so richly endowed is the creature in all good gifts; but the dominant consideration evoked in my mind by his name is just his beautiful home and that atmosphere of faultless womanly worth and dignity which fills it with light and warmth, and makes it a blessing to one's heart whenever one enters its precincts. Please felicitate the wretch for me—!

However earnest these deprecations he could embroider them with a rare grace.

My wife—who has just received your kind note in rapid route for the Dedham Profane Asylum, or something of that sort—begs leave to say, through me as a willing and sensitive medium, that you are one of those *arva beata*, renowned in poetry, which, visit them never so often, one is always glad to *re*visit, which are attractive in all seasons by their own absolute light and without any Emersonian pansies and buttercups to make them so. This enthusiastic Dedhamite says further in effect that while she is duly grateful for your courteous offer of a seat upon your sofa to hear the conquered sage, she yet prefers the material banquet you summon us to in your dining-room, since there we should be out of the mist and able to discern between nature and cookery, between what eats and what is eaten, at all events, and feel a thankful mind that we were in solid comfortable Charles Street, instead of in the vague and wide weltering galaxy, and should be sure to deem A. and J. (*I* am sure of A., and I think my wife feels equally sure of J.), finer fireflies than ever sparkled in the old empyrean. But alas who shall control his destiny? Not my wife, whom multitudinous cares enthrall; nor yet myself, whom a couple of months' enforced idleness now constrains to a preternatural activity, lest the world fail of salvation. Please accept then our united apologies and regrets. . . .

P.S. Who contrived the comical title for E.'s lectures?—"Philosophy of the People!" May it not have been a joke of J. T. F.'s? It would be no less absurd for Emerson himself to think of philosophising than for the rose to think of botanising. He is the divinely pompous rose of the philosophic garden, gorgeous with colour and fragrance; so what a sad look-out for tulip and violet and lily, and the humbler grasses, if the rose should turn out philosophic gardener as well.

There connects itself with a passage in another letter to the same correspondent a memory of my own that I have always superlatively cherished and that remains in consequence vivid enough for some light reflection here. But I first give the passage, which is of date of November '67. "What a charming impression of Dickens the other night at the Nortons' dinner! How innocent and honest and sweet he is maugre his fame! Fields was merely superb on the occasion, but Dickens was saintly." As a young person of twenty-four I took part, restrictedly yet exaltedly, in that occasion—and an immense privilege I held it to slip in at all—from after dinner on; at which stage of the evening I presented myself, in the company of my excellent friend Arthur Sedgwick, brother to our hostess and who still lives to testify, for the honour of introduction to the tremendous guest. How tremendously it had been laid upon young persons of our generation to feel Dickens, down to the soles of our shoes, no more modern instance that I might try to muster would give, I think, the least measure of; I can imagine no actual young person of my then age, and however like myself, so ineffably agitated, so mystically moved, in the presence of any exhibited idol of the mind who should be in that character at all conceivably "like" the author of Pickwick and of Copperfield. There has been since his extinction no corresponding case—as to the relation between benefactor and beneficiary, or debtor and creditor; no other debt in our time has been piled so high, for those carrying it, as the long, the purely "Victorian" pressure of that obligation. It was the pressure, the feeling, that made it—as it made the feeling, and no operation of feeling on any such ground has within my observation so much as attempted to emulate it. So that on the evening I speak of at Shady Hill it was as a slim and shaken vessel of the feeling that one stood there—of the feeling in the first place diffused, public and universal, and in the second place all unfathomably, undemonstrably, unassistedly and, as it were, unrewardedly, proper to one's self as an already groping and fumbling, already dreaming and yearning dabbler in the mystery, the creative, that of comedy, tragedy, evocation, representation, erect and concrete before us there as in a sublimity of mastership. I saw the master—nothing could be more evident—in the light of an intense emotion, and I trembled, I remember, in every limb, while at the same time, by a blest fortune, emotion produced no luminous blur, but left him shining indeed, only shining with august particulars. It was to be remarked that those of his dress, which managed to be splendid even while remaining the general spare uniform of the diner-out, had the effect of higher refinements, of accents stronger and better placed, than we had ever in such a connection seen so much as hinted. But the offered inscrutable mask was the great thing, the extremely handsome face, the face of symmetry yet of formidable character, as I at once recognised, and which met my dumb homage with a straight inscrutability, a merciless *military* eye, I might have pronounced it, an automatic hardness, in fine, which at once indicated to me, and in the most interesting way in the world, a kind of economy of apprehension. Wonderful was it thus to see, and thrilling inwardly to note, that since the question was of personal values so great no faintest fraction of the whole could succeed in *not* counting for interest. The confrontation was but of a moment; our introduction, my companion's and mine, once effected, by an arrest in a doorway, nothing followed, as it were, or happened (what *might* have happened it remained in fact impossible to conceive); but intense though the positive perception there was an immensity more left to understand—for the long aftersense, I mean; and one, or the chief, of these later things was that if our hero neither shook hands nor spoke, only meeting us by the barest act, so to say, of the trained eye, the penetration of which, to my sense, revealed again a world, there was a grim beauty, to one's subsequently panting imagination, in that very truth of his then so knowing himself (committed to his monstrous "readings" and with the force required for them ominously ebbing) on the outer edge of his once magnificent margin. So at any rate I was to like for long to consider of it; I was to like to let the essential radiance which had nevertheless reached me measure itself by this accompaniment of the pitying vision. He couldn't loosely spend for grace what he had to keep for life—which was the awful nightly, or all but nightly, exhibition: such the economy, as I have called it, in which I was afterwards to feel sure he had been locked up—in spite of the appearance, in the passage from my father's letter, of the opened gates of the hour or two before. These were but a reason the more, really, for the so exquisitely complicated image which was to remain with me to this day and which couldn't on any other terms have made itself nearly so important. For that was the whole sense of the matter. It hadn't been in the least important that we should have shaken hands or exchanged platitudes—it had only been supremely so that one should have had the essence of the hour, the knowledge enriched by proof that whatever the multifold or absolute reason, no accession to sensibility from any other at all "similar" source could have compared, for penetration, to the intimacy of this particular and prodigious glimpse. It was as if I had carried off my strange treasure just exactly from under the merciless military eye—placed there on guard of the secret. All of which I recount for illustration of the force of action, unless I call it passion, that may reside in a single pulse of time.

I allow myself not to hang back in gathering several passages from another series for fear of their crossing in a manner the line of privacy and giving a distinctness to old intimate things. The distinctness is in the first place all to the honour of the persons and the interests thus glimmering through; and I hold, in the second, that the light touch under which they revive positively adds, by the magic of memory, a composite fineness. The only thing is that to speak of my father's correspondent here is to be more or less involved at once in the vision of her frame and situation, and that to get at all into relation with "the Nortons," as they were known to us at that period, to say nothing of all the years to follow, is to find on my hands a much heavier weight of reference than my scale at this point can carry. The relation had ripened for us with the settlement of my parents at Cambridge in the autumn of '66, and might I attempt even a sketch of the happy fashion in which the University circle consciously accepted, for its better satisfaction, or in other words just from a sense of what was, within its range, in the highest degree interesting, the social predominance of Shady Hill and the master there, and the ladies of the master's family, I should find myself rich in material. That institution and its administrators, however, became at once, under whatever recall of them, a picture of great inclusions and implications; so true is it of any community, and so true above all of one of the American communities best to be studied fifty years ago in their homogeneous form and native essence and identity, that a strong character reinforced by a great culture, a culture great in the given conditions, obeys an inevitable law in simply standing out. Charles Eliot Norton stood out, in the air of the place and time—which for that matter, I think, changed much as he changed, and couldn't change much beyond his own range of experiment—with a greater salience, granting his background, I should say, than I have ever known a human figure stand out with from any: an effect involved of course in the nature of the background as well as in that of the figure. He profited at any rate, to a degree that was a lesson in all the civilities, by the fact that he represented an ampler and easier, above all a more curious, play of the civil relation than was to be detected anywhere about, and a play by which that relation had the charming art of becoming extraordinarily multifold and various without appearing to lose the note of rarity. It is not of course through any exhibition of mere multiplicity that the instinct for relations becomes a great example and bears its best fruit; the weight of the example and the nature of the benefit depending so much as they do on the achieved and preserved terms of intercourse. Here it was that the curiosity, as I have called it, of Shady Hill was justified—so did its action prove largely humanising. This was all the witchcraft it had used—that of manners understood with all the extensions at once and all the particularisations to which it is the privilege of the highest conception of manners to lend itself. What it all came back to, naturally, was the fact that, on so happy a ground, the application of such an ideal and such a genius *could* find agents expressive and proportionate, and the least that could be said of the ladies of the house was that they had in perfection the imagination of their opportunity. History still at comparatively close range lays to its lips, I admit, a warning finger—yet how can I help looking it bravely in the face as I name in common courtesy Jane Norton? She distilled civility and sympathy and charm, she exhaled humanity and invitation to friendship, which latter she went through the world leaving at mortal doors as in effect the revelation of a new amenity altogether—something to wait, most other matters being meanwhile suspended, for her to come back on a turn of the genial tide and take up again, according to the stirred desire, with each beneficiary. All this to the extent, moreover, I confess, that it takes the whole of one's measure of her rendered service and her admirable life, cut so much too short—it takes the full list of her fond acclaimers, the shyest with the clearest, those who most waited or most followed, not to think almost more of the way her blest influence went to waste as by its mere uneconomised and selfless spread than of what would have been called (what was by the simply-seeing freely enough called) her achieved success. It was given her at once to shine for the simply-seeing and to abide forever with the subtly; which latter, so far as they survive, are left again to recognise how there plays inveterately within the beautiful, if it but go far enough, the fine strain of the tragic. The household at Shady Hill was leaving that residence early in the summer of '68 for a long stay in Europe, and the following is of that moment.

> When I heard the other day that you had been at our house to say farewell I was glad and also sorry, glad because I couldn't say before all the world so easily what I wanted to say to you in parting, and sorry because I longed for another sight of your beautiful countenance. And then I consoled myself with thinking that I should write you the next morning and be able to do my feelings better justice. But when the morning came I saw how you would, with all your wealth of friends, scarcely value a puny chirrup from one of my like, and by no means probably expect it, and so I desisted. And now comes your heavenly letter this moment to renew my happiness in showing me once more your undimmed friendly face. How delightful that face has ever been to me since first I beheld it; how your frank and gracious and healing manners have shed on my soul a celestial dew whenever I have encountered you: I despair to tell you in fitting words. You are the largest and more generous nature I know, and one that remains always, at the same time, so womanly; and while you leave behind you such a memory you needn't fear that our affectionate wishes will ever fail you for a moment. I for my part shall rest in my affection for you till we meet where to love is to live.

Shady Hill was meanwhile occupied by other friends, out of the group of which, especially as reflected in another of my father's letters to Miss Norton, there rise for me beckoning ghosts; against whose deep appeal to me to let them lead me on I have absolutely to steel myself—so far, for the interest of it, I feel that they might take me.

> We dined the other night at Shady Hill, where the Gurneys were charming and the company excellent; but there was a perpetual suggestion of the Elysian Fields about the banquet to me, and we seemed met together to celebrate a memory rather than applaud a hope. Godkin and his wife were there, and they heartily lent themselves to discourse of you all. Ever and anon his friendship gave itself such an emphatic *jerk* to your address that you might have heard it on your window-panes if you had not been asleep. As for her—what a great clot she is of womanly health, beauty and benignity! That is a most unwonted word to use in such a connection, but it came of itself, and I won't refuse it, as it means to express a wealth that seems chaotic—seems so because apparently not enough exercised or put to specific use. The Ashburners and Sedgwicks continue your tradition and even ornament or variegate it with their own original force. I go there of a Sunday afternoon, whenever possible, to read anew the gospel of their beautiful life and manners and bring away a text for the good of my own household. No one disputes the authenticity of that gospel, and I have no difficulty in spreading its knowledge.

On which follows, as if inevitably, the tragic note re-echoed; news having come from Dresden, in March '72, of the death of Mrs. Charles Norton, still young, delightful, inestimable.

> What a blow we have all had in the deeper blow that has prostrated you! I despair to tell you how keen and how real a grief is felt here by all who have heard the desolating news. With my own family the brooding presence of the calamity is almost as obvious as it is in the Kirkland Street home, and I have to make a perpetual effort to reason it down. Reflectively, I confess, I am somewhat surprised that I could have been so *much* surprised by an event of this order. I know very well that death is the secret of life spiritually, and that this outward image of death which has just obtruded itself upon our gaze is *only* an image—is wholly unreal from a spiritual point of view. I know in short that your lovely sister lives at present more livingly than she has ever lived before. And yet my life is so low, habitually, that when I am called upon to put my knowledge into practice I am as superstitious as anybody else and grovel instead of soaring. Keep me in your own sweet and fragrant memory, for nowhere else could I feel myself more

> embalmed to my own self-respect. Indeed if anything could relieve a personal sorrow to me it would be the sense that it was shared by a being so infinitely tender and true as yourself.

Of the mass of letters by the same hand that I further turn over too many are of a domestic strain inconsistent with other application; but a page here and there emerges clear, with elements of interest and notes of the characteristic that rather invite than deprecate an emphasis. From these I briefly glean, not minding that later dates are involved—no particular hour at that time being far out of touch with any other, and the value of everything gaining here, as I feel, by my keeping my examples together. The following, addressed to me in England early in '69, beautifully illustrates, to my sense, our father's close participation in any once quite positive case that either one or the other of his still somewhat undetermined, but none the less interesting sons—interesting to themselves, to each other and to *him*—might appear for the time to insist on constituting. William had in '68 been appointed to an instructorship in Psychology at Harvard.

> He gets on greatly with his teaching; his students—fifty-seven of them—are elated with their luck in having him, and I feel sure he will have next year a still larger number attracted by his fame. He came in the other afternoon while I was sitting alone, and, after walking the floor in an animated way for a moment, broke out: "Bless my soul, what a difference between me as I am now and as I was last spring at this time! Then so hypochondriachal"—he used that word, though perhaps less in substance than form—"and now with my mind so cleared up and restored to sanity. It's the difference between death and life." He had a great effusion. I was afraid of interfering with it, or possibly checking it, but I ventured to ask what especially in his opinion had produced the change. He said several things: the reading of Renouvier (particularly his vindication of the freedom of the will) and of Wordsworth, whom he has been feeding on now for a good while; but more than anything else his having given up the notion that all mental disorder requires to have a physical basis. This had become perfectly untrue to him. He saw that the mind does act irrespectively of material coercion, and could be dealt with therefore at first hand, and this was health to his bones. It was a splendid declaration, and though I had known from unerring signs of the *fact* of the change I never

> had been more delighted than by hearing of it so unreservedly from his own lips. He has been shaking off his respect for men of mere science as such, and is even more universal and impartial in his mental judgments than I have known him before.

Nothing in such a report could affect me more, at a distance, as indeed nothing shines for me more sacredly now, than the writer's perfect perception of what it would richly say to me, even if a little to my comparative confusion and bewilderment; engaged as I must rightly have appeared in working out, not to say in tentatively playing with, much thinner things. I like to remember, as I do, ineffaceably, that my attention attached itself, intensely and on the spot, to the very picture, with whatever else, conveyed, which for that matter hangs before me still: the vision of my brother, agitated by the growth of his genius, moving in his burst of confidence, his bright earnestness, about the room I knew, which must have been our admirable parent's study—with that admirable parent himself almost holding his breath for the charm and the accepted peace of it, after earlier discussions and reserves; to say nothing too, if charm was in question, of the fact of rarity and beauty I must have felt, or in any case at present feel, in the resource for such an intellectually living and fermenting son of such a spiritually perceiving and responding sire. What was the whole passage but a vision of the fine private luxury of each?—with the fine private luxury of my own almost blurred image of it superadded. Of that same spring of '69 is another page addressed to myself in Europe. My memory must at the very time have connected itself with what had remained to me of our common or certainly of my own inveterate, childish appeal to him, in early New York days, for repetition, in the winter afternoon firelight, of his most personal, most remembering and picture-recovering "story"; that of a visit paid by him about in his nineteenth year, as I make it out, to his Irish relatives, his father's nephews, nieces and cousins, with a younger brother or two perhaps, as I set the scene forth—which it conduced to our liveliest interest to see "Billy Taylor," the negro servant accompanying him from Albany, altogether rule from the point of view of effect. The dignity of this apparition indeed, I must parenthesise, would have yielded in general to the source of a glamour still more marked—the very air in which the young emissary would have moved as the son of his father and the representative of an American connection prodigious surely in its power to dazzle. William James of Albany was at that time approaching the term of his remarkably fruitful career, and as I see the fruits of it stated on the morrow of his death—in the New York Evening Post of December 20th 1832, for instance, I find myself envying the friendly youth who could bring his modest Irish kin such a fairytale from over the sea. I attach as I hang upon the passage a melancholy gaze to the cloud of images of what might have been for us all that it distractingly throws off. Our grandfather's energy, exercised in Albany from the great year 1789, appears promptly to have begun with his arrival there. "Everywhere we see his footsteps, turn where we may, and these are the results of his informing mind and his vast wealth. His plans of improvement embraced the entire city, and there is scarcely a street or a square which does not exhibit some mark of his hand or some proof of his opulence. With the exception of Mr. Astor," this delightful report goes on to declare, "no other business man has acquired so great a fortune in this State. To his enormous estate of three millions of dollars there are nine surviving heirs. His enterprises have for the last ten years furnished constant employment for hundreds of our mechanics and labourers." The enterprises appear, alas, to have definitely ceased, or to have fallen into less able hands, with his death—and to the mass of property so handsomely computed the heirs were, more exactly, not nine but a good dozen. Which fact, however, reduces but by a little the rich ambiguity of the question that was to flit before my father's children, as they grew up, with an air of impenetrability that I remember no attempt on his own part to mitigate. I doubt, for that matter, whether he could in the least have appeased our all but haunting wonder as to what had become even in the hands of twelve heirs, he himself naturally being one, of the admirable three millions. The various happy and rapid courses of most of the participants accounted for much, but did they account for the full beautiful value, and would even the furthest stretch of the charming legend of his own early taste for the amusements of the town really tell us what had been the disposition, by such a measure, of *his* share?

Our dear parent, we were later quite to feel, could have told us very little, in all probability, under whatever pressure, what had become of anything. There had been, by our inference, a general history—not on the whole exhilarating, and pressure for information could never, I think, have been applied; wherefore the question arrests me only through the brightly associated presumption that the Irish visit was made, to its extreme enlivening, in the character of a gilded youth, a youth gilded an inch thick and shining to effulgence on the scene not otherwise brilliant. Which image appeals to my filial fidelity—even though I hasten not to sacrifice the circle evoked, that for which I a trifle unassuredly figure a small town in county Cavan as forming an horizon, and which consisted, we used to delight to hear with every contributive circumstance, of the local lawyer, the doctor and the (let us hope—for we *did* hope) principal "merchant," whose conjoined hospitality appeared, as it was again agreeable to know, to have more than graced the occasion: the main definite pictorial touches that have lingered with me being that all the doors always stood open, with the vistas mostly raking the provision of whiskey on every table, and that these opportunities were much less tempting (to our narrator) than that of the quest of gooseberries in the garden with a certain beautiful Barbara, otherwise anonymous, who was not of the kin but on a visit from a distance at one of the genial houses. We liked to hear about Barbara, liked the sound of her still richer rarer surname; which in spite of the fine Irish harmony it even then struck me as making I have frivolously forgotten. She had been matchlessly fair and she ate gooseberries with a charm that was in itself of the nature of a brogue—so that, as I say, we couldn't have too much of her; yet even her measure dwindled, for our appetite, beside the almost epic shape of black Billy Taylor carrying off at every juncture alike the laurel and the bay. He singularly appealed, it was clear, to the Irish imagination, performing in a manner never to disappoint it; his young master—in those days, even in the North, young mastership hadn't too long since lapsed to have lost every grace of its tradition—had been all cordially acclaimed, but not least, it appeared, *because* so histrionically attended: he had been the ringmaster, as it were, of the American circus, the small circus of two, but the other had been the inimitable clown. My point is that we repaired retrospectively to the circus as insatiably as our Irish cousins had of old attended it in person—even for the interest of which fact, however, my father's words have led me too far. What here follows, I must nevertheless add, would carry me on again, for development of reference, should I weakly allow it. The allusion to my brother Wilky's vividly independent verbal collocations and commentative flights re-echoes afresh, for instance, as one of the fond by-words that spoke most of our whole humorous harmony. Just so might the glance at the next visitor prompt a further raising of the curtain, save that this is a portrait to which, for lack of acquaintance with the original, I have nothing to contribute—beyond repeating again that it was ever the sign of my father's portraits to supply almost more than anything else material for a vision of himself.

> Your enjoyment of England reminds me of my feelings on my first visit there forty years ago nearly, when I landed in Devonshire in the month of May or June and was so intoxicated with the roads and lanes and hedges and fields and cottages and castles and inns that I thought I should fairly expire with delight. You can't expatiate too much for our entertainment on your impressions, though you make us want consumedly to go over and follow in your footsteps. Wilky has been at home now for 2 or 3 days and is very philosophic and enthusiastic over your letters. I hoped to remember some of his turns of speech for you, but one chases another out of my memory and it is now all a blank. I will consult Alice's livelier one before I close.
>
> My friend ——— is a tropical phenomenon, a favourite of nature whatever his fellow man may say of him. His face and person are handsome rather than otherwise, and it's obvious that he is a very unsoiled and pure piece of humanity in all *personal* regards. And with such a gift of oratory—such a boundless wealth of diction set off by copious and not ungraceful gesticulation! Here is where he belongs to the tropics, where nature claims him for her own and flings him like a cascade in the face of conventional good-breeding. I can't begin to describe him, he is what I have never before met. I see that he can't help turning out excessively tiresome, but he is not at all vulgar. He has a genius for elocution, that is all; but a real genius and no mistake. In comparison with Mr. F. L. or Mr. Longfellow or the restrained Boston style of address generally, he is what the sunflower is to the snowdrop; but on the whole, if I

could kick his shins whenever I should like to and so reduce him to silence, I prefer him to the others.

What mainly commends to me certain other passages of other dates (these still reaching on a little) is doubtless the fact that I myself show in them as the object of attention and even in a manner as a claimant for esthetic aid. This latter active sympathy overflows in a letter of the spring of '70, which would be open to more elucidation than I have, alas, space for. Let the sentence with which it begins merely remind me that Forrest, the American actor, of high renown in his time, and of several of whose appearances toward the close of his career I keep a memory uneffaced—the impression as of a deep-toned thunderous organ, a prodigious instrument pounded by a rank barbarian—had been literally, from what we gathered, an early comrade of our parent: literally, I say, because the association could seem to me, at my hours of ease, so bravely incongruous. By my hours of ease I mean those doubtless too devoted to that habit of wanton dispersed embroidery for which any scrap of the human canvas would serve. From one particular peg, I at the same time allow, the strongest sense of the incongruity depended—my remembrance, long entertained, of my father's relating how, on an occasion, which must have been betimes in the morning, of his calling on the great tragedian, a man of enormous build and strength, the latter, fresh and dripping from the bath, had entered the room absolutely upside down, or by the rare gymnastic feat of throwing his heels into the air and walking, as with strides, on his hands; an extraordinary performance if kept up for more than a second or two, and the result at any rate of mere exuberance of muscle and pride and robustious joie de vivre. It had affected me, the picture, as one of those notes of high colour that the experience of a young Albany viveur, the like of which I felt I was never to come in for, alone could strike off; but what was of the finer profit in it was less the direct illustration of the mighty mountebank than of its being delightful on the part of a domestic character we so respected to have had, with everything else, a Bohemian past too—since I couldn't have borne at such moments to hear it argued as not Bohemian. What did his having dropped in after such a fashion and at a late breakfast-hour on the glory of the footlights and the idol of the town, what did it fall in with but the kind of thing one had caught glimpses and echoes of from the diaries and memoirs, so far as these had been subject to the passing peep, of the giftedly idle and the fashionably great, the Byrons, the Bulwers, the Pelhams, the Coningsbys, or even, for a nearer vividness perhaps, the N. P. Willises?—of all of whom it was somehow more characteristic than anything else, to the imagination, that they always began their day in some such fashion. Even if I cite this as a fair example of one's instinct for making much of a little—once this little, a chance handful of sand, could show the twinkle of the objective, or even the reflective, grain of gold—I still claim value for that instanced felicity, as I felt it, of being able to yearn, thanks to whatever chance support, over Bohemia, and yet to have proof in the paternal presence close at hand of how well even the real frequentation of it, when achieved in romantic youth, might enable a person at last to turn out. The lesson may now indeed seem to have been one of those that rather more strictly adorn a tale than point a moral; but with me, at that period, I think, the moral ever came first and the tale more brilliantly followed. As for the recital, in such detail, of the theme of a possible literary effort which the rest of my letter represents, how could I feel this, when it had reached me, as anything but a sign of the admirable anxiety with which thought could be taken, even though "amateurishly," in my professional interest?—since professional I by that time appeared able to pass for being. And how above all can it not serve as an exhibition again of the manner in which all my benevolent backer's inveterate original *malaise* in face of betrayed symptoms of the impulse to "narrow down" on the part of his young found its solution always, or its almost droll simplification, as soon as the case might reach for him a *personal* enough, or "social" enough, as he would have said, relation to its fruits? Then the malaise might promptly be felt as changed, by a wave of that wand, to the extremity of active and expatiative confidence.

> Horatio Alger is writing a Life of Edwin Forrest, and I am afraid will give him a Bowery appreciation. He reports his hero as a very "fine" talker—in which light I myself don't so much recall him, though he had a native breadth—as when telling Alger for example

of old Gilbert Stuart's having when in a state of dilapidation asked him to let him paint his portrait. "I consented," said Forrest, "and went to his studio. He was an old white lion, so blind that he had to ask me the colour of my eyes and my hair; but he threw his brush at the canvas, and every stroke was life." Alger talks freely about his own late insanity—which he in fact appears to enjoy as a subject of conversation and in which I believe he has somewhat interested William, who has talked with him a good deal of his experience at the Somerville Asylum. Charles Grinnell—though not à propos of the crazy—has become a great reader and apparently a considerable understander of my productions; Alger aforesaid aussi. Everyone hopes that J. G. hasn't caught a Rosamund Vincy in Miss M. I don't know whether this hope means affection to J. or disaffection to the young lady.

I have written to Gail Hamilton to send me your story; but she does it not as yet. I will renew my invitation to her in a day or two if necessary. I went to see Osgood lately about his publishing a selection from your tales. He repeated what he had told you—that he would give you 15 per cent and do all the advertising, etc., you paying for the plates; or he would pay everything and give you 10 per cent on every copy sold after the first thousand. I shall be glad (in case you would like to publish, and I think it time for you to do so) to meet the expense of your stereotyping, and if you will pick out what you would like to be included we shall set to work at once and have the book ready by next autumn. I have meanwhile the materials of a story for you which I was telling William of the other day as a regular Tourgéneff subject, and he urged me to send it off to you at once—he was so struck with it.

Matthew Henry W. was a very cultivated and accomplished young man in Albany at the time I was growing up. He belonged to a highly respectable family of booksellers and publishers and was himself bred to the law; but had such a love of literature, and more especially of the natural sciences, that he never devoted himself strictly to his profession. He was the intimate friend of my dear old tutor, Joseph Henry of the Smithsonian, and of other distinguished men of science; he corresponded with foreign scientific bodies, and his contributions to science generally were of so original a cast as to suggest great hopes of his future eminence. He was a thorough gentleman, of perfect address and perfect courage—utterly unegotistic, and one's wonder was how he had ever grown up in Albany or resigned himself to living there. One day he invested his money, of which he had a certain quantity, in a scheme much favoured by the president of the bank in which he deposited, and this adventure proved a fortune. There lived near us as well a family of the name of K———, your cousin Mary Minturn Post's stepmother being of its members; and this family reckoned upon a great social sensation in bringing out their youngest daughter, Lydia Sibyl, who had never been seen by mortal eye outside her own immediate circle, save that of a physician who reported that she was fabulously beautiful. She *was* the most beautiful girl I think I ever saw, at a little distance. Well, she made her sensation and brought Matthew Henry promptly to her feet. Her family wanted wealth above all things for her; but here was wealth and something more, very much more, and they smiled upon his suit. Everything went merrily for a while—M. H. was deeply intoxicated with his prize. Never was man so enamoured, and never was beauty better fitted to receive adoration. She was of an exquisite Grecian outline as to face, with a countenance like the tender dawn and form and manners ravishingly graceful. But W. was not content with his adventure—he embarked again and lost almost all he owned. The girl's father—or her mother rather, being the ruler of the family and as hard as the nether world at heart—gave the cue to her daughter and my friend was dismissed. He couldn't believe his senses, he raved and cursed his fate, but it was inexorable. What was to be done? With a bitterness of heart inconceivable he plucked his revenge by marrying at once a stout and blooming jade who was to Lydia Sibyl as a peony to a violet, absolutely nothing but flesh and blood. Her he bore upon his arm at fashionable hours through the streets; her he took to church, preserving his admirable ease and courtesy to everyone, as if absolutely nothing had occurred; and her he pretended to take to his bosom in private, with what a shudder one can imagine. Everybody stood aghast. He went daily about his affairs, as serene and unconscious apparently as the moon in the heavens. Soon his poverty showed itself in certain economies of his attire, which had always been most recherché. Soon again he broke his leg and went about on crutches, but neither poverty nor accident had the least power to ruffle his air of equanimity. He was always superior to his circumstances, met you exactly as he had always done, impressed you always as the best-bred man you knew, and left you wondering what a heart and what a brain lay behind such a fortune. One morning we all read in the newspaper at breakfast that Mr. M. H. W. had appealed the day before to the protection of the police against his wife, who had taken to beating him and whom as a woman he couldn't deal with by striking back; and the police responded properly to his appeal. He went about his affairs

> as usual that day and every day, never saying a word to any one of his trouble nor even indirectly asking sympathy, but making you feel that here if anywhere was a rare kind of manhood, a self-respect so eminent as to look down with scorn on the refuges open to ordinary human weakness. This lasted five or six years. He never drank or took to other vices, and lived a life of such decorum, so far as his own action was concerned, a life of such interest and science and literature, as to be the most delightful and unconscious of companions even when his coat was at the last shabbiness and you didn't dare to look at him for fear of betraying your own vulgar misintelligence. Finally Lydia Sibyl died smitten with smallpox and all her beauty gone to hideousness. He lingered awhile, his charming manners undismayed still, his eye as undaunted as at the beginning, and then he suddenly died. I never knew his equal for a manly force competent to itself in every emergency and seeking none of the ordinary subterfuges that men so often seek to hide their imbecility. I think it a good basis. . . .

Returning from Europe in June '70, after a stay there of some fifteen months, I had crossed the sea eastward again two years later, with my sister and our admirable aunt as companions—leaving them, I may mention, to return home at the end of six months while I betook myself to Italy, where I chiefly remained till the autumn of '74. The following expresses our father's liberality of recognition and constant tenderness of tone in a manner that no comment need emphasise, but at one or two of his references I allow myself to glance. I happen to remember perfectly for instance the appearance of the novel of Madame Sand's that he so invidiously alludes to in one of the first numbers of the cherished Revue that reached us after the siege of Paris had been raised—such a pathetically scant starved pale number, I quite recall, as expressed the share even of the proud periodical in the late general and so tragic dearth; with which it comes back to me that I had myself a bit critically mused on the characteristic queerness, the oddity of the light thrown on the stricken French consciousness by the prompt sprouting of *such* a flower of the native imagination in the chill air of discipline accepted and after the administration to that consciousness of a supposedly clarifying dose. But I hadn't gone the length of my father, who must have taken up the tale in its republished form, a so slim salmon-coloured volume this time: oh the repeated arrival, during those years, of the salmon-coloured volumes in their habit as they lived, a habit reserved, to my extreme appreciation, for this particular series, and that, enclosing the extraordinarily fresh fruit of their author's benign maturity, left Tamaris and Valvèdre and Mademoiselle La Quintinie in no degree ever "discounted" for us as devotees of the Revue, I make out, by their being but renewals of acquaintance. The sense of the salmon-coloured distinctive of Madame Sand was even to come back to me long years after on my hearing Edmond de Goncourt speak reminiscentially and, I permit myself to note, not at all reverently, of the *robe de satin fleur-de-pêcher* that the illustrious and infatuated lady, whose more peculiar or native tint, as Blanche Amory used to say, didn't contribute to a harmony, *s'était fait faire* in order to fix as much as possible the attention of Gustave Flaubert at the Dîner Magny; of Gustave Flaubert, who, according to this most invidious of reporters, disembroiled from each other with too scant ease his tangle of possibly incurred ridicule from the declared sentiment of so old a woman, even in a peach-blossom dress, and the glory reflected on him by his admirer's immense distinction. Which vision of a complicated past, recovered even as I write—and of a past indeed contemporary with the early complacencies I attribute to ourselves—doesn't at all blur its also coming back to me that I was to have found my parent "hard on" poor Francia in spite of my own comparative reserves; these being questions and shades that I rejoice to think of our having had so discussionally, and well at home for the most part, the social education of. I see that general period as quite flushed and toned by the salmon-coloured covers, so that a kind of domestic loyalty would ever operate, as we must have all felt, to make us take the thick with the thin and not *y regarder* for a Francia the more or the less. When I say all indeed I doubtless have in mind especially my parents and myself, with my sister and our admirable aunt (in her times of presence) thrown in—to the extent of our subjection to the charm of such matters in particular as La Famille de Germandre, La Ville Noire, Nanon and L'Homme de Neige, round which last above all we sat ranged in united ecstasy; so that I was to wonder through the after years, and I think perhaps to this day, how it could come that a case of the "story" strain at its finest and purest, a gush of imaginative force so free and yet so artfully directed, shouldn't have somehow "stood out" more in literary history. Perhaps indeed L'Homme de Neige does essentially stand out in the unwritten parts of that record—which are content to be mere tacit tender tradition; for all the world as if, since there are more or less dreadful perpetuated books, by the hundred, dreadful from whatever baseness or whatever scantness, that for shame, as it were, we never mention, so one may figure others as closeted in dimness (than which there is nothing safer) by the very scruple of respect at its richest. I hover for instance about the closet of L'Homme de Neige, I stand outside a moment as if listening for a breath from within; but I don't open the door, you see—which must mean, in all probability, that I wouldn't for the world inconsiderately finger again one of the three volumes; *that* meaning, in its turn, doubtless, that I have heard the breath I had listened for and that it can only have been what my argument wants, the breath of life unquenched. Isn't it relevant to this that when she was not reading Trollope our dear mother was reading "over" La Famille de Germandre, which, with several of its companions of the same bland period, confirmed her in the sense that there was no one like their author for a "love-story"?—a conviction, however, that when made articulate exposed her to the imputation of a larger tolerance than she doubtless intended to project; till the matter was cleared up by our generally embracing her for so sweetly not knowing about Valentine and Jacques and suchlike, and having only begun at La Mare au Diable and even thereafter been occasionally obliged to skip.

So far do I let myself go while, to recur to my letter, Chauncey Wright sits for me in his customary corner of the deep library sofa and his strange conflictingly conscious light blue eyes, appealing across the years from under the splendid arch of his fair head, one of the handsomest for representation of amplitude of thought that it was possible to see, seems to say to me with a softness more aimed at the heart than any alarm or any challenge: "But what then are you going to do for me?" I find myself simply ache, I fear, as almost the only answer to this—beyond his figuring for me as the most wasted and doomed, the biggest at once and the gentlest, of the great intending and unproducing (in anything like the just degree) bachelors of philosophy, bachelors of attitude and of life. And as he so sits, loved and befriended and welcomed, valued and invoked and vainly guarded and infinitely pitied, till the end couldn't but come, he renews that appeal to the old kindness left over, as I may say, and which must be more or less known to all of us, for the good society that was helplessly to miss a right chronicler, and the names of which, so full at the time of their fine sense, were yet to be writ in water. Chauncey Wright, of the great imperfectly-attested mind; Jane Norton, of the train, so markedly, of the distinguished, the sacrificial, devoted; exquisite Mrs. Gurney, of the infallible taste, the beautiful hands and the tragic fate; Gurney himself, for so long Dean of the Faculty at Harvard and trusted judge of all judgments (this latter pair the subject of my father's glance at the tenantship of Shady Hill in the Nortons' absence:) they would delightfully adorn a page and appease a piety that is still athirst if I hadn't to let them pass. Harshly condemned to let them pass, and looking wistfully after them as they go, how can I yet not have inconsequently asked them to turn a moment more before disappearing?

> My heart turns to you this morning, so radiant in the paternal panoply you wear toward Alice and your aunt, and I would give a great deal to see you. The enclosed scrap of a letter from William is sent to show you how vastly improved are his eyes, especially when you shall have learned that he has written us within the last four or five days twenty pages of like density to these. He would fain persuade us to go to Mount Desert; perhaps later we may go to Quebec, but we are so comfortable together reading Trollope and talking philosophy that we cheerfully drop the future from our regard. Mamma is free and active and bracing. She is a domestic nor'wester, carrying balm and bloom into every nook and corner of her empire. . . . She hangs over The Eustace Diamonds while I try vainly to read George Sand's Francia. I have come across nothing of that lady's that reflects a baser light on her personal history. What must a woman have been through to want to grovel at this time of day in such uncleanness? Don't buy it—I wish I hadn't! The new North American is out, with a not too interesting article of Chauncey Wright's on Mivart, a scandalous (in point of taste) essay of Mr. Stirling on Buckle, full of Scotch conceit, insolence

and "wut;" a very very laboured article by James Lowell on Dante, in which he determines to exhaust all knowledge; and these are all I have read. Mr. Stirling of course makes Buckle ridiculous, but he stamps himself a shabby creature.

I find the following, addressed to his daughter in August '72, so beautifully characteristic of our parents' always explicit admonition to us, in our dependent years, against too abject an impulse to be frugal in their interests, that I may fairly let it stand as a monument to this particular aspect of their affection.

Your and H.'s last letters bring tears of joy to our eyes. It's a delight above all delights to feel one's children turn out all that the heart covets in children. Your conviction is not up to the truth. Our "tender thoughts" of you are so constant that I have hardly been able to settle to anything since you have been gone. I can do little else than recount to myself "the tender mercies of the Lord" to me and my household. Still I am not wholly useless; I try to write every day, and though I haven't my daughter at hand to look after my style and occasionally after my ideas, I manage to do a little. Your conscientious economy is excessively touching, but it's a little overstrained. You needn't be afraid of putting us to any embarrassment so long as your expenses don't exceed their present rate; and you can buy all you want in Paris without stretching your tether a particle. This is Mamma's message as well as mine. Charles Atkinson wishes me to say that Monte Genneroso above Lugano Lake—the P.O. Mendrisio—offers a wondrous climate; and Mamma thinks—so fearful is she that you will descend into Italy before the warm weather is over and so compromise your strength—that you had either better go there awhile first or else be ready to retreat on it in case you find the summer heat in Venice impossible.

Nor does this scrap from a letter to myself at the same season breathe a spirit less liberal—so far as the sympathy with whatever might pass for my fondest preoccupations was concerned. These were now quite frankly recognised as the arduous attempt to learn somehow or other to write.

I send you The Nation, though there seems nothing in it of your own, and I think I never fail to recognise you. A notice of

> Gustave Droz's Babolain (by T. S. P., I suppose) there is; which book I read the other day. This fumbling in the cadaver of the old world, however, only disgusts me when so unrelieved as in this case by any contrast or any souffle of inspiration such as you get in Tourguéneff. It's curious to observe how uncertain the author's step is in this story—how he seems always on the look-out for some chance to break away. But it has mastered him, he can't lay the ghost he has conjured.

To which I should limit myself for the commemoration of that group of years by the gentle aid of the always vivid excerpt, were it not that I have before me a considerable cluster of letters addressed by the writer of the foregoing to Mr. J. Eliot Cabot, most accomplished of Bostonians, most "cultivated" even among the cultivated, as we used to say, and of a philosophic acuteness to which my father highly testified, with which indeed he earnestly contended. The correspondence in question covered, during the years I include, philosophic ground and none other; but though no further exhibition of it than this reference may convey is to my purpose I lay it under contribution to the extent of a passage or two just for the pleasure of inviting recognition, as I invite it wherever we meet an instance, of the fashion after which the intensely animated soul can scarce fail of a harmony and a consistency of expression that are nothing less than interesting, that in fact become at once beautiful, in themselves. By which remark I nevertheless do not mean to limit the significance of the writer's side of his long argument with Mr. Eliot Cabot, into which I may not pretend to enter, nor the part that in any such case a rare gift for style must inveterately play.

> I grant then that I am often tempted to conceive, as I read your letters, that we differ only in your terms being more abstract, mine more concrete; and yet I really don't think this difference is exhaustive. If I thought Philosophy capable ever of being reduced to logical compass or realising itself as science, I should give in at once. But this is just what I cannot think. Philosophy is the doctrine exclusively of the infinite in the finite, and deals with the latter therefore only as a mask, only as *harbouring* the former. But if you formulate it scientifically your terms are necessarily all finite, as furnished by experience, and the infinite is excluded or at most

creeps in as the indefinite—Hegel's *becoming* for example. Thus Hegel's dialectic modulates only in the sphere of his distance. His *being* is universal existence, and, as universals have only a logical truth, being in se is equivalent to Nothing. But Nothing hasn't even a logical basis. Lithe as human thought is it can't compass the conception. It is a mere brutum fulmen devised to disguise the absence of thought or its inanition; and Hegel, if he had been wise, would have said no-thought instead of no-thing. For no-thing doesn't express the complete absence of existence. Existence is of two sorts, real and personal, sensible and conscious, quantitative and qualitative. The most you are entitled to say therefore when existence disappears in quantitative, real or sensible, form is that it has been taken up into purely qualitative, personal or conscious form; no-thing being the logical equivalent of all-person. Thus I, who in Hegel's formula presumably extract existence from being, survive the operation as person, and though I am most clearly no-thing I am yet not *being*. Indeed I am not even existence any longer, since by knocking thing out of being I have forfeited my own reality, and consent henceforth to be pure personality, *i.e.* phenomenality. And personal or phenomenal existence is constituted by referring itself to a foreign source, or, what is the same thing, confessing itself created: so that the fundamental word of Philosophy, by Hegel's own formula, is creation; which, however, as I understand him, he denies in any objective sense of the word. This then is what I complain of in him—with deference of course to your better knowledge, which, however, you do not urge as yet in what seems to me a silencing way—that he makes existence *essential* to being, so that take existence away and being becomes nothing. It would not be a whit less preposterous in me to say that thought is essential to thing, subject to object, marble to statue, canvas to picture, woman to wife, mother to child. It is literally putting the cart before the horse and converting Philosophy to a practical quagmire. Being implies existence of course just as picture implies canvas, or as personality implies reality, or as chick implies egg; but it implies it only to a lower intelligence than itself, an unspiritual intelligence to wit, which has no direct or inward intuition of being, and requires to be agitated to discerning it. When I recognise the spiritual life of Art I never think of marble or canvas as entering even conditionally into its manifestations.

But I hold my case for a rare command of manner thus proved, and need go no further; the more that I have dropped too many of those threads of my rather niggled tapestry that belong but to the experience of my own weaving hand and the interplay of which represents thereby a certain gained authority. I disentangle these again, if the term be not portentous, though reflecting too, and again with complacency, that though I thus prize them as involved most in my own consciousness, this is just because of their attachment somewhere else to other matters and other lives.

IX

I WENT up from Newport to Cambridge early in the autumn of '62, and on one of the oddest errands, I think, that, given the several circumstances, I could possibly have undertaken. I was nineteen years old, and it had seemed to me for some time past that some such step as my entering for instance the Harvard Law School more or less urgently concerned what I could but try to help myself out by still putting forward as my indispensable education—I am not sure indeed that the claim didn't explicitly figure, or at least successfully dangle, as that of my possibly graceful mere "culture." I had somehow—by which I mean for reasons quite sufficient—to fall back on the merciful "mere" for any statement of my pretensions even to myself: so little they seemed to fit into any scheme of the conventional maximum as compared with those I saw so variously and strongly asserted about me, especially since the outbreak of the War. I am not sure whether I yet made bold to say it, but I should surely be good for nothing, all my days, if not for projecting into the concrete, by hook or by crook—that is my imagination shamelessly aiding—some show of (again) mere life. This impression was not in the least the flag I publicly brandished; in fact I must have come as near as possible to brandishing none whatever, a sound instinct always hinting to me, I gather, that the time for such a performance was much more after than before—before the perfect place had been found for the real planting of the standard and the giving of its folds to the air. No such happy spot had been marked, decidedly, at that period, to my inquiring eye; in consequence of which the emblazoned morsel (hoisted sooner or later by all of us, I think, somehow and somewhere), might have passed for the hour as a light extravagant bandanna rolled into the tight ball that fits it for hiding in the pocket. There it considerably stayed, so far as I was concerned; and all the more easily as I can but have felt how little any particular thing I might meanwhile "do" would matter—save for some specious appearance in it. This last, I recognise, had for me a virtue—principally that of somehow gaining time; though I hasten to add that my approach to the Law School can scarcely, as a means to this end, in the air of it that comes back to me, have been in the least deceptive. By which I mean that my appearance of intentions, qualifications, possibilities, or whatever else, in the connection, hadn't surely so much as the grace of the specious. I spoke above of the assumed "indispensability" of some show of my being further subject to the "education" theory, but this was for the moment only under failure to ask to whom, or for what, such a tribute *was* indispensable. The interest to myself would seem to have been, as I recover the sense of the time, that of all the impossibilities of action my proceeding to Cambridge on the very vaguest grounds that probably ever determined a residence there might pass for the least flagrant; as I breathe over again at any rate the comparative confidence in which I so moved I feel it as a confidence in the positive saving virtue of vagueness. Could I but work that force as an ideal I felt it must see me through, for the beauty of it in that form was that it should absolutely superabound. I wouldn't have allowed, either, that it was vaguer to do nothing; for in the first place just staying at home when everyone was on the move couldn't in any degree show the right mark: to be properly and perfectly vague one had to be vague *about* something; mere inaction quite lacked the note—it was nothing but definite and dull. I thought of the Law School experiment, I remember, in all sorts of conceivable connections, but in the connection of dulness surely never for an hour. I thought of it under the head of "life"—by which term at the same time, I blush to confess, I didn't in the least mean free evening access to Boston in a jangling horse-car, with whatever extension this might give to the joy of the liberated senses. I simply meant—well, what was monstrously to happen; which I shall be better inspired here to deal with as a demonstration made in its course than as a premonition relatively crude and at the time still to be verified. Marked in the whole matter, however these things might be, was that irony of fate under the ugly grin of which I found my father reply in the most offhand and liberal manner to my remark that the step in question—my joining, in a sense, my brother at Cambridge—wouldn't be wholly unpracticable. It might have been, from his large assent to it, a masterstroke of high policy. A certain inconsequence in this left me wondering why then if the matter was now so natural it hadn't been to his mind a year before equally simple that I should go to college, and to *that* College, after a more showy, even though I see it would have been at the same time a less presumptuous, fashion. To have deprecated the "college course" with such emphasis only so soon afterwards to forswear all emphasis and practically smile, in mild oblivion, on *any* Harvard connection I might find it in me to take up, was to bring it home, I well recall, that the case might originally have been much better managed.

All of which would seem to kick up more dust than need quite have hung about so simple a matter as my setting forth to the Cambridge scene with no design that I could honourably exhibit. A superficial account of the matter would have been that my father had a year or two earlier appeared to think so ill of it as to reduce me, given the "delicacy," the inward, not then the outward, which I have glanced at, to mild renunciation—mild I say because I remember in fact, rather to my mystification now, no great pang of disappointment, no soreness of submission. I didn't want anything so much as I wanted a certain good (or wanted thus supremely *to* want it, if I may say so), with which a conventional going to college wouldn't have so tremendously much to do as for the giving it up to break my heart—or an unconventional not-going so tremendously much either. What I "wanted to want" to be was, all intimately, just *literary*; a decent respect for the standard hadn't yet made my approach so straight that there weren't still difficulties that might seem to meet it, questions it would have to depend on. Passing the Harvard portal positively failed in fact to strike me as the shorter cut to literature; the sounds that rose from the scene as I caught them appeared on the contrary the most detached from any such interest that had ever reached my ear. Merely to open the door of the big square closet, the ample American closet, to the like of which Europe had never treated us, on the shelves and round the walls of which the pink Revues sat with the air, row upon row, of a choir of breathing angels, was to take up that particular, that sacred connection in a way that put the coarser process to shame. The drop of the Harvard question had of a truth really meant, as I recover it, a renewed consecration of the rites of that chapel where the taper always twinkled—which circumstance I mention as not only qualifying my sense of loss, but as symbolising, after a queer fashion, the independence, blest vision (to the extent, that is, of its being a closer compact with the life of the imagination), that I should thus both luckily come in for and designingly cultivate: cultivate in other words under the rich cover of obscurity. I have already noted how the independence was, ever so few months later, by so quaint a turn, another mere shake of the tree, to drop into my lap in the form of a great golden apple—a value not a simple windfall only through the fact that my father's hand had after all just lightly loosened it. This accession pointed the moral that there was no difficulty about anything, no intrinsic difficulty; so that, to re-emphasise the sweet bewilderment, I was to "go" where I liked in the Harvard direction and do what I liked in the Harvard relation. Such was the situation as offered me; though as I had to take it and use it I found in it no little difference. Two things and more had come up—the biggest of which, and very wondrous as bearing on any circumstance of mine, as having a grain of weight to spare for it, was the breaking out of the War. The other, the infinitely small affair in comparison, was a passage of personal history the most entirely personal, but between which, as a private catastrophe or difficulty, bristling with embarrassments, and the great public convulsion that announced itself in bigger terms each day, I felt from the very first an association of the closest, yet withal, I fear, almost of the least clearly expressible. Scarce at all to be stated, to begin with, the queer fusion or confusion established in my consciousness during the soft spring of '61 by the firing on Fort Sumter, Mr. Lincoln's instant first call for volunteers and a physical mishap, already referred to as having overtaken me at the same dark hour, and the effects of which were to draw themselves out incalculably and intolerably. Beyond all present notation the interlaced, undivided way in which what had happened to me, by a turn of fortune's hand, in twenty odious minutes, kept company of the most unnatural—I can call it nothing less—with my view of what was happening, with the question of what might still happen, to everyone about me, to the country at large: it so made of these marked disparities a single vast visitation. One had the sense, I mean, of a huge comprehensive ache, and there were hours at which one could scarce have told whether it came most from one's own poor organism, still so young and so meant for better things, but which had suffered particular wrong, or from the enclosing social body, a body rent with a thousand wounds and that thus treated one to the honour of a sort of tragic fellowship. The twenty minutes had sufficed, at all events, to establish a relation—a relation to everything occurring round me not only for the next four years but for long afterward—that was at once extraordinarily intimate and quite awkwardly irrelevant. I must have felt in some befooled way in presence of a crisis—the smoke of Charleston Bay still so acrid in the air—at which the likely young should be up and doing or, as familiarly put, lend a hand much wanted; the willing youths, all round, were mostly starting to their feet, and to have trumped up a lameness at such a juncture could be made to pass in no light for graceful. Jammed into the acute angle between two high fences, where the rhythmic play of my arms, in tune with that of several other pairs, but at a dire disadvantage of position, induced a rural, a rusty, a quasi-extemporised old engine to work and a saving stream to flow, I had done myself, in face of a shabby conflagration, a horrid even if an obscure hurt; and what was interesting from the first was my not doubting in the least its duration—though what seemed equally clear was that I needn't as a matter of course adopt and appropriate it, so to speak, or place it for increase of interest on exhibition. The interest of it, I very presently knew, would certainly be of the greatest, would even in conditions kept as simple as I might make them become little less than absorbing. The shortest account of what was to follow for a long time after is therefore to plead that the interest never did fail. It was naturally what is called a painful one, but it consistently declined, as an influence at play, to drop for a single instant. Circumstances, by a wonderful chance, overwhelmingly favoured it—*as* an interest, an inexhaustible, I mean; since I also felt in the whole enveloping tonic atmosphere a force promoting its growth. Interest, the interest of life and of death, of our national existence, of the fate of those, the vastly numerous, whom it closely concerned, the interest of the extending War, in fine, the hurrying troops, the transfigured scene, formed a cover for every sort of intensity, made tension itself in fact contagious—so that almost any tension would do, would serve for one's share.

I have here, I allow, not a little to foreshorten—have to skip sundry particulars, certain of the steps by which I came to think of my relation to my injury as a *modus vivendi* workable for the time. These steps had after the first flush of reaction inevitably *had* to be communications of my state, recognitions and admissions; which had the effect, I hasten to add, of producing sympathies, supports and reassurances. I gladly took these things, I perfectly remember, at that value; distinct to me as it still is nevertheless that the indulgence they conveyed lost part of its balm by involving a degree of publication. Direfully distinct have remained to me the conditions of a pilgrimage to Boston made that summer under my father's care for consultation of a great surgeon, the head of his profession there; whose opinion and advice—the more that he was a guaranteed friend of my father's—had seemed the best light to invoke on the less and less bearable affliction with which I had been for three or four months seeking to strike some sort of bargain: mainly, up to that time, under protection of a theory of temporary supine "rest" against which everything inward and outward tended equally to conspire. Agitated scraps of rest, snatched, to my consciousness, by the liveliest violence, were to show for futile almost to the degree in which the effort of our interview with the high expert was afterwards so to show; the truth being that this interview settled my sad business, settled it just in that saddest sense, for ever so long to come. This was so much the case that, as the mere scene of our main appeal, the house from which we had after its making dejectedly emerged put forth to me as I passed it in many a subsequent season an ironic smug symbolism of its action on my fate. That action had come from the complete failure of our approached oracle either to warn, to comfort or to command—to do anything but make quite unassistingly light of the bewilderment exposed to him. In default of other attention or suggestion he might by a mere warning as to gravities only too possible, and already well advanced, have made such a difference; but I have little forgotten how I felt myself, the warning absent, treated but to a comparative pooh-pooh—an impression I long looked back to as a sharp parting of the ways, with an adoption of the wrong one distinctly determined. It was not simply small comfort, it was only a mystification the more, that the inconvenience of my state had to reckon with the strange fact of there being nothing to speak of the matter with me. The graceful course, on the whole ground again (and where moreover was delicacy, the proposed, the intended, without grace?) was to behave accordingly, in good set terms, as if the assurance were true; since the time left no margin at all for one's gainsaying with the right confidence so high an authority. There were a hundred ways to behave—in the general sense so freely suggested, I mean; and I think of the second half of that summer of '62 as my attempt at selection of the best. The best still remained, under closer comparisons, very much what it had at first seemed, and there was in fact this charm in it that to prepare for an ordeal essentially intellectual, as I surmised, might justly involve, in the public eye, a season of some retirement. The beauty was—I can fairly see it now, through the haze of time, even as beauty!—that studious retirement and preparatory hours did after all supply the supine attitude, did invest the ruefulness, did deck out the cynicism of lying down book in hand with a certain fine plausibility. This was at least a negative of combat, an organised, not a loose and empty one, something definitely and firmly parallel to action in the tented field; and I well recall, for that matter, how, when early in the autumn I had in fact become the queerest of forensic recruits, the bristling horde of my Law School comrades fairly produced the illusion of a mustered army. The Cambridge campus was tented field enough for a conscript starting so compromised; and I can scarce say moreover how easily it let me down that when it came to the point one had still fine fierce young men, in great numbers, for company, there being at the worst so many such who hadn't flown to arms. I was to find my fancy of the merely relative right in any way to figure, or even on such terms just to exist, I was to find it in due course quite drop from me as the Cambridge year played itself out, leaving me all aware that, full though the air might be of stiffer realities, one had yet a rare handful of one's own to face and deal with.

At Cambridge of course, when I got there, I was further to find my brother on the scene and already at a stage of possession of its contents that I was resigned in advance never to reach; so thoroughly I seemed to feel a sort of quickening savoury meal in any cold scrap of his own experience that he might pass on to my palate. This figure has definite truth, that is, but for association at the board literally yielding us nourishment —the happiest as to social composition and freedom of supply of all the *tables d'hôte* of those days, a veritable haunt of conversation ruled by that gently fatuous Miss Upham something of whose angular grace and antique attitude has lived again for us in William's letters. I place him, if not at the moment of my to that extent joining him then at least from a short time afterwards, in quarters that he occupied for the next two or three years—quiet cloistered rooms, as they almost appeared to me, in the comparatively sequestered Divinity Hall of that still virtually rustic age; which, though mainly affected to the use of post-graduates and others, of a Unitarian colour, enrolled under Harvard's theological Faculty, offered chance accommodation, much appreciated for a certain supposedly separate charm, not to say a finer dignity, by the more maturely studious in other branches as well. The superstition or aftertaste of Europe had then neither left me nor hinted that it ever might; yet I recall as a distinct source of interest, to be desperately dealt with, and dealt with somehow to my inward advantage, the special force of the circumstance that I was now for the first time in presence of matters normally, entirely, consistently American, and that more particularly I found myself sniff up straight from the sources, such as they unmistakably were, the sense of that New England which had been to me till then but a name. This from the first instant was what I most took in, and quite apart from the question of what one was going to make of it, of whether one was going, in the simple formula, to like it, and of what would come, could the impression so triumph, of such monstrous assimilations. Clear to me in the light thus kindled that my American consciousness had hitherto been after all and at the best singularly starved, and that Newport for instance, during the couple of years, had fed it but with sips of an adulterated strain. Newport, with its opera-glass turned for ever across the sea—for Newport, or at least *our* Newport, even during the War, lived mainly, and quite visibly, by the opera-glass—was comparatively, and in its degree incurably, cosmopolite; and though on our first alighting there I had more or less successfully, as I fancied, invited the local historic sense to vibrate, it was at present left me to feel myself a poor uninitiated creature. However, an initiation, at least by the intelligence, into some given thing—almost anything really given would do—was essentially what I was, as we nowadays say, after; the fault with my previous data in the American kind had been that they weren't sufficiently given; so that here would be Boston and Cambridge giving as with absolute authority. The War had by itself of course, on the ground I speak of, communicated something of the quality, or rather of the quantity, otherwise deficient; only this was for my case, of which alone I speak, an apprehension without a language or a channel—a revelation as sublime as one would like to feel it, but spreading abroad as a whole and not, alas, by any practice of mine, reducible to parts. What I promptly made out at Cambridge was that "America" would be given, as I have called it, to a tune altogether fresh, so that to hear this tune wholly played out might well become on the spot an inspiring privilege. If I indeed, I should add, said to myself "wholly," this was of course not a little straining a point; since, putting my initiation, my grasp of the exhibition, at its conceivable liveliest, far more of the supposed total was I inevitably to miss than to gather to my use. But I might gather what I could, and therein was exactly the adventure. To rinse my mouth of the European aftertaste *in order* to do justice to whatever of the native bitter-sweet might offer itself in congruous vessels—such a brave dash for discovery, and such only, would give a sense to my posture. With which it was unmistakable that I shouldn't in the least have painfully to strive; of such a force of impact was each impression clearly capable that I had much rather to steady myself, at any moment, where I stood, and quite to a sense of the luxury of the occasion, than to cultivate inquiry at the aggressive pitch. There was no need for curiosity—it was met by every object, I seemed to see, so much more than half way; unless indeed I put it better by saying that as *all* my vision partook of that principle the impulse and the object perpetually melted together. It wasn't for instance by the faintest process of inquiry that the *maison* Upham, where I three times daily sat at meat, had scarce to wait an hour to become as vivid a translation into American terms of Balzac's

Maison Vauquer, in Le Père Goriot, as I could have desired to deal with.

It would have been at once uplifting to see in the American terms a vast improvement on the prime version, had I not been here a bit baffled by the sense that the correspondence was not quite, after all, of like with like, and that the main scene of Balzac's action was confessedly and curiously sordid and even sinister, whereas its equivalent under the Harvard elms would rank decidedly as what we had *de mieux*, or in other words of most refined, in the "boarding" line, to show. I must have been further conscious that what we had de mieux in the social line appeared quite liable, on occasion, to board wherever it might—the situation in Balzac's world being on this head as different as possible. No one not deeply distressed or dismally involved or all but fatally compromised could have taken the chances of such an establishment at all; so that any comparison to our own particular advantage had to be, on reflection, nipped in the bud. There was a generic sameness, none the less, I might still reason; enough of that at least to show the two pictures as each in its way interesting—which was all that was required. The Maison Vauquer, its musty air thick with heavier social elements, might have been more so, for the Harvard elms overhung no strange Vautrin, no old Goriot, no young Rastignac; yet the interest of the Kirkland Street company couldn't, so to speak, help itself either, any more than I could help taking advantage of it. In one respect certainly, in the matter of talk as talk, we shone incomparably brighter; and if it took what we had de mieux to make our so regular resort a scene essentially of conversation, the point was none the less that our materials were there. I found the effect of this, very easily, as American as I liked—liked, that is, to think of it and to make all I might of it for being; about which in truth all difficulty vanished from the moment the local colour of the War broke in. So of course this element did at that season come back to us through every outward opening, and mean enough by contrast had been the questions amid which the Vauquer boarders grubbed. Anything even indirectly touched by our public story, stretching now into volume after volume of the very biggest print, took on that reflected light of dignity, of importance, or of mere gross salience, which passion charged with criticism, and criticism charged with the thousand menaced affections and connections, the whole of the reaction—charged in short with immediate intimate life—have a power, in such conditions, to fling as from a waving torch. The torch flared sufficiently about Miss Upham's board—save that she herself, ancient spinster, pushed it in dismay from her top of the table, blew upon it with vain scared sighs, and would have nothing to do with a matter so disturbing to the right temperature of her *plats*. We others passed it from hand to hand, so that it couldn't go quite out—since I must in fairness add that the element of the casual and the more *generally* ironic, the play of the studious or the irrepressibly social intelligence at large, couldn't fail to insist pretty constantly on its rights. There were quarters as well, I should note, in which the sense of local colour proceeding at all straight from the source I have named—reflected, that is, from camp and field—could but very soon run short; sharply enough do I recall for instance the felt, even if all so privately felt, limits of *my* poor stream of contributive remark (despite my habit, so fondly practised in the connection, of expatiating *in petto*). My poor stream would have trickled, truly, had it been able to trickle at all, from the most effective of my few occasions of "realising," up to that time, as to field and camp; literally as to camp in fact, since the occasion had consisted of a visit paid, or a pilgrimage, rather, ever so piously, so tenderly made, one August afternoon of the summer just ended, to a vast gathering of invalid and convalescent troops, under canvas and in roughly improvised shanties, at some point of the Rhode Island shore that figures to my memory, though with a certain vagueness, as Portsmouth Grove. (American local names lend themselves strangely little to retention, I find, if one has happened to deal for long years with almost any group of European designations—these latter springing, as it has almost always come to seem, straight from the soil where natural causes were anciently to root them, each with its rare identity. The bite into interest of the borrowed, the imposed, the "faked" label, growing but as by a dab of glue on an article of trade, is inevitably much less sharp.) Vagueness at best attends, however, the queer experience I glance at; what lives of it, in the ineffaceable way, being again, by my incurable perversity, my ambiguous economy, much less a matter of the "facts of the case," as they should, even though so dead and buried now, revive to help me through an anecdote, than the prodigiously subjective side of the experience, thanks to which it still presumes to flush with the grand air of an adventure. If I had not already so often brazened out my confession of the far from "showy" in the terms on which impressions could become indelibly momentous to me I might blush indeed for the thin tatter dragged in thus as an affair of record. It consisted at the time simply of an emotion—though the emotion, I should add, appeared to consist of everything in the whole world that my consciousness could hold. By *that* intensity did it hang as bravely as possible together, and by the title so made good has it handed itself endlessly down.

Owing to which it is that I don't at all know what troops were in question, a "mere" couple of Rhode Island regiments (nothing in those days could be too big to escape the application of the "mere,") or a congeries of the temporarily incapacitated, the more or less broken, picked from the veterans—so far as there already were such—of the East at large and directed upon the Grove as upon a place of stowage and sanitation. Discriminations of the prosaic order had little to do with my first and all but sole vision of the American soldier in his multitude, and above all—for that was markedly the colour of the whole thing—in his depression, his wasted melancholy almost; an effect that somehow corresponds for memory, I bethink myself, with the tender elegiac tone in which Walt Whitman was later on so admirably to commemorate him. The restrictions I confess to are abject, but both my sense and my after sense of the exhibition I here allude to had, thanks to my situation, to do all the work they could in the way of representation to me of what was most publicly, most heroically, most wastefully, tragically, terribly going on. It had so to serve for my particular nearest approach to a "contact" with the active drama—I mean of course the collectively and scenically active, since the brush of interest against the soldier single and salient was an affair of every day—that were it not for just one other strange spasm of awareness, scarce relaxed to this hour, I should have been left all but pitifully void of any scrap of a substitute for the concrete experience. The long hot July 1st of '63, on which the huge battle of Gettysburg had begun, could really be—or rather couldn't possibly not be—a scrap of concrete experience for any group of united persons, New York cousins and all, who, in a Newport garden, restlessly strolling, sitting, neither daring quite to move nor quite to rest, quite to go in nor quite to stay out, actually *listened* together, in their almost ignobly safe stillness, as to the boom of far-away guns. This *was*, as it were, the War—the War palpably in Pennsylvania; not less than my hour of a felt rage of repining at my doomed absence from the sight of that march of the 54th Massachusetts out of Boston, "Bob" Shaw at its head and our exalted Wilky among its officers, of which a great sculptor was, on the spot of their vividest passing, to set the image aloft forever. Poor other visitations, comparatively, had had to suffice for me; I could take in fact for amusing, most of all (since that, thank goodness, was high gaiety), a couple of impressions of the brief preliminary camp life at Readville during which we admired the charming composition of the 44th of the same State, under Colonel Frank Lee, and which fairly made romantic for me Wilky's quick spring out of mere juvenility and into such brightly-bristling ranks. He had begun by volunteering in a company that gave him half the ingenuous youth of the circle within our social ken for brothers-in-arms, and it was to that pair of Readville afternoons I must have owed my all so emphasised vision of handsome young Cabot Russell, who, again to be his closest brother-in-arms in the 54th, irrecoverably lost himself, as we have seen, at Fort Wagner. A dry desert, one must suppose, the life in which, for memory and appreciation made one, certain single hours or compressed groups of hours have found their reason for standing out through everything, for insistently living on, in the cabinet of intimate reference, the museum, as it were, of the soul's curiosities—where doubtless at the same time an exhibition of them to mere other eyes or ears or questioning logical minds may effect itself in no plain terms. We recognise such occasions more and more as we go on, and are surely, as a general thing, glad when, for the interest of memory—which it's such a business to *keep* interesting—they constitute something of a cluster. In my queer cluster, at any rate, that flower of the connection which answers to the name of Portsmouth Grove still overtops other members of its class, so that to finger it again for a moment is to make it perceptibly exhale its very principle of life. This was, for me, at the time, neither more nor less than that the American soldier in his multitude was the most attaching and affecting and withal the most amusing figure of romance conceivable; the great sense of my vision being thus that, as the afternoon light of the place and time lingered upon him, both to the seeming enhancement of his quality and of its own, romance of a more confused kind than I shall now attempt words for attended his every movement. It was the charmingest, touchingest, dreadfullest thing in the world that my impression of him should have to be somehow of his abandonment to a rueful humour, to a stoic reserve which could yet melt, a relation with him once established, into a rich communicative confidence; and, in particular, all over the place, of his own scanted and more or less baffled, though constantly and, as I couldn't not have it, pathetically, "knowing" devices.

The great point remained for me at all events that I could afterwards appear to myself to have done nothing but establish with him a relation, that I established it, to my imagination, in several cases—and all in the three or four hours—even to the pitch of the last tenderness of friendship. I recover that, strolling about with honest and so superior fellow-citizens, or sitting with them by the improvised couches of their languid rest, I drew from each his troubled tale, listened to his plaint on his special hard case—taking form, this, in what seemed to me the very poetry of the esoteric vernacular—and sealed the beautiful tie, the responsive sympathy, by an earnest offer, in no instance waved away, of such pecuniary solace as I might at brief notice draw on my poor pocket for. Yet again, as I indulge this memory, do I feel that I might if pushed a little rejoice in having to such an extent coincided with, not to say perhaps positively anticipated, dear old Walt—even if I hadn't come armed like him with oranges and peppermints. I ministered much more summarily, though possibly in proportion to the time and thanks to my better luck more pecuniarily; but I like to treat myself to making out that I can scarce have brought to the occasion (in proportion to the time again and to other elements of the case) less of the consecrating sentiment than he. I like further to put it in a light that, ever so curiously, if the good Walt was most inwardly stirred to his later commemorative accents by his participating in the common Americanism of his hospital friends, the familiar note and shared sound of which formed its ground of appeal, I found myself victim to a like moving force through quite another logic. It was literally, I fear, because our common Americanism carried with it, to my imagination, such a disclosed freshness and strangeness, working, as I might say, over such gulfs of dissociation, that I reached across to *their*, these hospital friends', side of the matter, even at the risk of an imperilled consistency. It had for me, the state in question, colour and form, accent and quality, with scarce less "authority" than if instead of the rough tracks or worn paths of my casual labyrinth I had trod the glazed halls of some school of natural history. What holds me now indeed is that such an institution might have exemplified then almost nothing but the aspects strictly native to our social and seasonal air; so simply and easily conceivable to the kindly mind were at that time these reciprocities, so great the freedom and pleasure of them compared with the restrictions imposed on directness of sympathy by the awful admixtures of to-day, those which offer to the would-be participant among us, on returns from sojourns wherever homogeneity and its entailed fraternity, its easy contacts, still may be seen to work, the strange shock of such amenities declined on any terms. Really not possible then, I think, the perception now accompanying, on American ground, this shock—the recognition, by any sensibility at all reflective, of the point where our national theory of absorption, assimilation and conversion appallingly breaks down; appallingly, that is, for those to whom the *consecrated* association, of the sort still at play where community has not been blighted, strongly speaks. Which remarks may reinforce the note of my unconsciousness of any difficulty for knowing in the old, the comparatively brothering, conditions what an American at least *was*. Absurd thus, no doubt, that the scant experience over which I perversely linger insists on figuring to me as quite a revel of the right confidence.

The revel, though I didn't for the moment yet know it, was to be renewed for me at Cambridge with less of a romantic intensity perhaps, but more usefully, so to put it, and more informingly; surrounded as I presently found myself at the Law School with young types, or rather with young members of a single type, not one of whom but would have enriched my imagined hall of congruous specimens. *That*, with the many months of it, was to be the real disclosure, the larger revelation; that was to be the fresh picture for a young person reaching the age of twenty in wellnigh grotesque unawareness of the properties of the atmosphere in which he but wanted to claim that he had been nourished. Of what I mean by this I shall in a moment have more to say—after pointing a trifle more, for our patience, the sense of my dilatation upon Portsmouth Grove. Perfectly distinct has remained the sail back to Newport by that evening's steamboat; the mere memory of which indeed—and I recall that I felt it inordinately long—must have been for me, just above, the spring of the whole reference. The sail was long, measured by my acute consciousness of paying physically for my excursion—which hadn't answered the least little bit for my impaired state. This last disobliging fact became one, at the same time, with an intensity, indeed a strange rapture, of reflection, which I may not in the least pretend to offer as a clear or coherent or logical thing, and of which I can only say, leaving myself there through the summer twilight, in too scant rest on a deck stool and against the bulwark, that it somehow crowned my little adventure of sympathy and wonder with a shining round of resignation—a realisation, as we nowadays put it, that, measuring wounds against wounds, or the compromised, the particular taxed condition, at the least, against all the rest of the debt then so generally and enormously due, one was no less exaltedly than wastefully engaged in the common fact of endurance. There are memories in truth too fine or too peculiar for notation, too intensely individual and supersubtle—call them what one will; yet which one may thus no more give up confusedly than one may insist on them vainly. Their kind is nothing ever to a present purpose unless they are in a manner statable, but is at the same time ruefully aware of threatened ridicule if they are overstated. Not that I in the least mind such a menace, however, in just adding that, soothed as I have called the admirable ache of my afternoon with that inward interpretation of it, I felt the latter—or rather doubtless simply the entire affair—absolutely overarched by the majestic manner in which the distress of our return drew out into the lucid charm of the night. To which I must further add that the hour seemed, by some wondrous secret, to know itself marked and charged and unforgettable—hinting so in its very own terms of cool beauty at something portentous in it, an exquisite claim then and there for lasting value and high authority.

X

All of which foregoing makes, I grant, a long parenthesis in my recovery of the more immediate Cambridge impressions. I have left them awaiting me, yet I am happy to say not sensibly the worse for it, in their cluster roundabout Miss Upham and her board of beneficiary images; which latter start up afresh and with the softest submission to any convenient neglect—that ineffably touching and confessed dependence of such apparitions on one's "pleasure," save the mark! for the flicker of restorative light. The image most vividly restored is doubtless that of Professor F. J. Child, head of the "English Department" at Harvard and master of that great modern science of folk-lore to his accomplishment in which his vast and slowly-published collection of the Ballad literature of our language is a recognised monument; delightful man, rounded character, passionate patriot, admirable talker, above all thorough humanist and humorist. He was the genial autocrat of that breakfast-table not only, but of our symposia otherwise timed, and as he comes back to me with the fresh and quite circular countenance of the time before the personal cares and complications of life had gravely thickened for him, his aspect *all* finely circular, with its close rings of the fairest hair, its golden rims of the largest glasses, its finished rotundity of figure and attitude, I see that *there* was the American spirit since I was "after" it—of a quality deeply inbred, beautifully adjusted to all extensions of knowledge and taste and, as seemed to me, quite sublimely quickened by everything that was at the time so tremendously in question. That vision of him was never afterwards to yield to other lights—though these, even had occasion for them been more frequent with me, couldn't much have interfered with it; so that what I still most retain of him is the very flush and mobility, the living expansion and contraction, the bright comedy and almost lunar eclipse, of his cherubic face according as things appeared to be going for the country. I was always just across from him, as my brother, beside whom I took my place, had been, and I remember well how vivid a clock-face it became to me; I found still, as in my younger time, matter enough everywhere for gaping, but greatest of all, I think, while that tense season lasted, was my wonder for the signs and portents, the quips and cranks, the wreathed smiles, or otherwise the candid obscurations, of our prime talker's presented visage. I set, as it were, the small tick of my own poor watch by it—which private register would thump or intermit in agreement with these indications. I recover it that, thanks to the perpetual play of his sympathy and irony, confidence and scorn, as well as to that of my own less certainly directed sensibility, he struck me on the bad days, which were then so many, as fairly august, cherubism and all, for sincerity of association with every light and shade, every ebb and flow, of our Cause. Where he most shone out, indeed, so that depression then wasn't a gloom in him but a darting flame, was in the icy air of the attitude of the nations to us, that of the couple, the most potent, across the sea, with which we were especially concerned and which, as during the whole earlier half of the War and still longer it more and more defined itself, drew from him at once all the drolleries and all the asperities of his sarcasm. Nothing more particularly touched me in him, I make out—for it lingers in a light of its own—than the fashion after which he struck me as a fond grave guardian, not so much of the memory and the ashes yet awhile, as of the promise, in all its flower, of the sacrificial young men whom the University connection had passed through his hands and whom he looked out for with a tenderness of interest, a nursing pride, that was as contagious as I could possibly have wished it. I didn't myself know the young men, save three or four, and could only, at our distance, hold my tongue and do them homage; never afterwards (as I even then foreknew would be the case) missing, when I could help it, or failing to pick up, a single brush, a scattered leaf, of their growing or their riper legend. Certain of them whom I had neither seen nor, as they fell in battle, was destined ever to see, have lived for me since just as communicated images, figures created by his tone about them—which, I admit, mightn't or needn't have mattered to me for all the years, yet which couldn't help so doing from the moment the right touch had handed them over to my restless claim.

It was not meanwhile for want of other figures that these

were gathered in, for I have again to grant that in those days figures became such for me on easy terms, and that in particular William had only to let the light of *his* attention, his interest, his curiosity, his aversion even (could he indeed have passingly lived in the helplessness of mere aversion) visibly rest on them for me entirely to feel that they must count for as much as might be—so far at least as my perception was concerned, contact being truly another affair. That was the truth at that season, if it wasn't always to remain the truth; I felt his interpretations, his personal allowances, so largely and inveterately liberal, always impose themselves: it was not till ever so much later, and then only little by little, that I came to accept the strange circumstance of my not invariably "liking," in homely parlance, his people, and his not invariably liking mine. The process represented by that word was for each of us, I think, a process so involved with other operations of the spirit, so beautifully complicated and deformed by them, that our results in this sort doubtless eventually lost themselves in the labyrinth of our reasons; which latter, eventually—the labyrinth, I mean—could be a frequent and not other than animated meeting-place in spite of the play of divergence. The true case, I all the while plentifully felt, and still more feel now, was that *I* diverged and my brother almost never; in the sense, that is, that no man can well have cared less for the question, or made less of the consciousness, of dislike—have valued less their developments and comforts. Even the opposite of that complacency scarce seemed a recognised, or at least in any degree a cultivated, state with him; his passion, and that a passion of the intelligence, was justice unafraid—and this, as it were, almost unformulatedly, altogether unpedantically: it simply made him utterly not "mind" numberless things that with most people serve as dim lights, warnings or attractions, in the grope of appreciation or the adventure of instinct. His luminous indifference kept his course thus, as I was later to recognise, extraordinarily straight—to the increase, as I have noted, of my own poor sense of weakly straggling, unaccompanied as this at the same time was by the least envy of such a deficiency in what is roughly called prejudice, and what I, to save my face, in my ups and downs of sociability or curiosity, could perhaps have found no better term for than the play of taste as taste.

Wonderful, and to me in the last resort admirable, was William's fine heritage and awareness of that principle without its yet affecting him on the human, the more largely social, just the conversable and workable ground—in presence of some other principle that might do so, whether this validly or but speciously interfered. The triumph over *dis*taste, in one's relations, one's exposures, one's judgments, *that* I could understand as high virtue, strained heroism, the ideal groaningly applied; but what left me always impressed, to put it mildly, was the fact that in my brother's case the incorruptibility of his candour would have had to be explained to him, and with scant presumption too of his taking it in or having patience while one spoke. Such an enterprise, I was well aware, would at any rate have left *me* a sorry enough figure afterwards. What one would have had to be, what one could in the least decently be, *except* candid without alternative—this, with other like matters, I should have had to be prepared to set forth; and, more and more addressed as I eventually found myself to a cultivation of the absolute in taste as taste, to repeat my expression, I was far from the wish to contend for it as against any appearance whatever of a better way. Such was part of the experience, or call it even the discipline, of association with a genius so marked for the process known as giving the benefit of the doubt—and giving it (for that was the irritating charm), not in smug charity or for a pointed moral, but through the very nature of a mind incapable of the shut door in any direction and of a habit of hospitality so free that it might again and again have been observed, in contact and intercourse, to supply weaker and less graced vessels with the very means of bringing in response, often absolutely in retort. This last of course was not so much the benefit of the doubt as the displayed unconsciousness of any doubt, a perpetual aid rendered the doubtful, especially when incarnate in persons, to be more right or more true, more clever or more charming or whatever, than mere grudging love of "form," standing by, could at all see it entitled to become. Anything like William's unawareness of exertion after having helped the lame dog of converse over stile after stile I have in no other case met. Together with which, however, I may not forbear to add, the very occasional and comparatively small flare in him of some blest perversity of prejudice that one might enjoy on one's own side the vulgar luxury of naming as such was a thing which, conformably to that elation, one reached out for as one might for the white glint of the rare edelweiss on some high Alpine ledge.

If these remarks illustrate in their number the inevitable bent of the remark to multiply within me as an effect of fraternal evocation I thereby but stick the more to my subject, or in other words to the much-peopled scene, as I found it; which I should scarce have found without him. Peopled as it was with *his* people, which they at first struck me as markedly being, it led me then to take the company, apart from F. J. Child, for whatever he all vividly and possessively pronounced it; I having for a long time but the scantest company of my own, even at the Law School, where my fellow-disciples could bear the name for me only as a troop of actors might have done on that further side of footlights to which I never went round. This last at least with few exceptions, while there were none to the exquisite rule, as I positively to-day feel it, of my apprehension of William's cluster as a concern of his—interesting exactly because of that reference. Any concern of his was thus a thing already charged with life, *his* life over and above its own, if it happened by grace to have any comparable; which, as I pick out the elements again from the savoury Upham shades, could indeed be claimed for several of these. I pick out the ardent and delicate and firm John May, son, as he comes back to me, of a distinguished Abolitionist of New York State—rare bird; and seen by that fact in a sort of glamour of picturesque justification, an air deriving colour from the pre-established gallantry, yet the quiet and gentlemanly triumph, of his attitude. So at least do I read back into blurred visions the richest meanings they could have. I pick out for a not less baffled tribute a particular friend of my brother's and a comrade of May's, whom I identify on the superficial side but by his name of Salter and the fact of his studentship in theology; which pursuit, it comes over me as I write, he must have shared, of homely, almost of sickly, New England type as he was, with May of the fine features, the handsome smile, by my resolute recollection, the developed moustache and short dark pointed beard, the property of vaguely recalling in fine some old portrait supposedly Spanish (supposedly, and perhaps to a fantastic tune, by *me*—for I dare say it was by no one else). Salter had no such references—it even appalled me to have a bit intelligently to imagine to what origins starved of amenity or colour his aspect and air, the slope of his shoulders, the mode of growth of his hair, the relation of his clothes to his person and the relation of his person to the inevitable needs of intercourse, might refer him; but there played about him a bright force in the highest and extraordinarily quick flares of which one felt nothing, while the exhibition lasted, but his intellectual elegance. He had the distinction of wit—so rare, we ever feel it to be, when we see it beautifully act; and I remember well how, as that was indeed for me almost the whole of intellectual elegance, I fell back on the idea that such an odd assortment of marks in him was at least picturesque, or much in the Maison Vauquer line: pinched as I must have been by the question of whether a person of that type and cut had the "right" to be witty. On what else but the power the right rested I couldn't doubtless have said; I but recall my sense that wit was somehow the finest of all social matters and that it seemed impossible to be less connected with such than this product of New England at its sparest and dryest; which fact was a sort of bad mark for the higher civilisation. I was prepared to recognise that you might be witty and ugly, ugly with the highest finish of ugliness—hadn't the celebrated Voltaire been one of the scrappiest of men as well as of the most immortally quoted?—but it cost a wrench to have to take it that you could shine to admiration out of such a platitude of the mere "plain." It was William in especial who guaranteed to me Salter's superior gift, of which in the free commerce of Divinity Hall he had frequent illustration—so that what I really most apprehended, I think, was the circumstance of *his* apprehending: this too with a much finer intellectual need and competence than mine, after all, and in the course of debates and discussions, ardent young symposia of the spirit, which struck me as falling in with all I had ever curiously conceived of those hours that foster the generous youth of minds preappointed to greatness. *There* was the note of the effective quaint on which I could put my finger: catch a poor student only dreary enough and then light in him the flame of irony at its intensest, the range of question and the command of figure at their bravest, and one might, with one's appetite for character, feed on the bold antithesis. I had only to like for my brother, and verily almost with pride, his assured experience of any queer concretion—his experience of abstractions I was to rise to much more feebly and belatedly, scarce more indeed ever than most imperfectly—to find the very scene of action, or at least of passion, enjoyed by these my elders and betters, enriched and toned and consecrated after the fashion of places referred to in literature and legend.

I thus live back of a sudden—for I insist on just yielding to it—into the odd hours when the poor little old Divinity Hall of the overgrown present faced me as through the haze of all the past Indian summers it had opened its brooding study-windows to; when the "avenue" of approach to it from the outer world was a thing of dignity, a positive vista in a composition; when the Norton woods, near by, massed themselves in scarlet and orange, and when to penetrate and mount a stair and knock at a door and, enjoying response, then sink into a window-bench and inhale at once the vague golden November and the thick suggestion of the room where nascent "thought" had again and again piped or wailed, was to taste as I had never done before the poetry of the prime initiation and of associated growth. With cards of such pale pasteboard could the trick, to my vision, play itself—by which I mean that I admire under this memory the constant "dodges" of an imagination reduced to such straits for picking up a living. It was as if one's sense of "Europe," sufficiently sure of itself to risk the strategic retreat, had backed away on tiptoe just to see how the sense of what was there facing one would manage without it—manage for luxury, that is, with the mere indispensable doubtless otherwise provided for. That the sense in question did manage beautifully, when at last so hard pressed, and that the plasticity and variety of my vision draw from me now this murmur of elation, are truths constituting together for me the perhaps even overloaded moral of my tale. With which I scarce need note that so elastic a fancy, so perverse a little passion for finding good in everything—good for what I thought of as history, which was the consideration of life, while the given thing, whatever it was, had only to be before me—was inevitably to work a storage of other material for memory close-packed enough to make such disengagement as I thus attempt at the end of time almost an act of violence. I couldn't do without the *scene*, as I have elsewhere had occasion to hint, whether actually or but possibly peopled (the people always calling for the background and the background insisting on the people); and thanks to this harmless extravagance, or thanks in other words to the visionary liberties I constantly took (so that the plate of sense was at the time I speak of more overscored and figured for me than sense was in the least practically required to have it), my path is even now beset to inconvenience with the personal image unextinct. It presents itself, I feel, beyond reason, and yet if I turn from it the ease is less, and I am divided when I further press the spring between compunction at not pausing before some shade that seems individually and even hopefully to wait, and the fear of its feeling after all scanted of service should I name it only to leave it. I name for instance, just to hover a little, silent Vanderpool, the mutest presence at the Upham board, and quite with no sense of the invidious in so doing. He was save for myself, by my remembrance, the only member of the Law School there present; I see him moreover altogether remarkably, just incorruptibly and exquisitely dumb, though with a "gentlemanly" presence, a quasi-conservative New Jersey finish (so delicate those dim discriminations!) that would have seemed naturally to go with a certain forensic assurance. He looked so as if he came from "good people"—which was no very common appearance on the Harvard scene of those days, as indeed it is to a positive degree no so very common appearance on any scene at any time: it was a note of aspect which one in any case found one's self, to whatever vague tune, apt quite to treasure or save up. So it was impossible not to recognise in our soundless *commensal* the very finest flower of shyness, the very richest shade of the deprecating blush, that one had perhaps ever encountered; one ended in fact by fairly hanging on the question of whether the perfection of his modesty—for it was all a true welter of modesty, not a grain of it anything stiffer—would beautifully hold out or would give way to comparatively brute pressure from some point of our circle. I longed to bet on him, to see him through without a lapse; and this in fact was so thoroughly reserved to me that my eventual relief and homage doubtless account for the blest roundness of my impression.

He had so much "for" him, was tall and fine, equipped and appointed, born, quite to an effect of ultimately basking, in the light of the Law, acquainted, one couldn't fail of seeing, with a tradition of manners, not to mention that of the forensic as aforesaid, and not to name either the use of "means," equally imputable: how rare accordingly would be the *quality*, letting even the quantity alone, of his inhibitions, and how interesting in the event the fact that he was absolutely never to have deviated! He disappeared without having spoken, and yet why should I now be noting it if he hadn't nevertheless admirably expressed himself? What this consisted of was that there was scarce anything he wouldn't have done for us had it been possible, and I think, in view of the distinctness with which he still faces me, the tenderness with which he inspires my muse and the assurance with which I have "gone into" him, that I can never in all my life since have seen so precious a message delivered under such difficulties. Admirable, ineffaceable, because so essentially all *decipherable*, Vanderpool!

It wasn't either that John Bancroft tossed the ball of talk—which but for the presence of the supremely retentive agent just commemorated would have appeared on occasion to remain in his keeping by a preference, on its own part, not to be outwitted; this more or less at all times too, but especially during the first weeks of his dawning on us straight out of Germany and France, flushed with the alarm, as one might have read it, of having to justify rare opportunities and account for the time he had inordinately, obscurely, or at least not a little mysteriously, spent—the implication of every inch of him being that he had spent it seriously. Odd enough it certainly was that we should have been appointed to unveil, so far as we might, a *pair* of such marked monuments to modesty, marble statues, as they might have been, on either side of the portal of talk; what I at any rate preserve of my immediate vision of Bancroft—whose very promptest identity indeed had been his sonship to the eminent historian of our country and earlier and later diplomatist—was an opposition, trying to me rather than engaging as its like had been in the composition of Vanderpool, between what we somehow wanted from him (or what I at least did) and what we too scantly gathered. This excellent friend, as he was later on to become, with his handsome high head, large colourable brow and eyes widely divided—brave contribution ever to a fine countenance—sat there in a sort of glory of experience which, had he been capable of anything so akin to a demonstration, he would have appeared all unsociably to repudiate. It was bruited of him that, like John La Farge, whose friend he was admiringly to become—for he too had a Newport connection—he "painted," that is persisted (which was the wondrous thing!) in painting; and that this practice had grown upon him in France, where, *en province*, his brother had entirely taken root and where the whole art-life, as well as the rural life, of the country had been opened to him; besides its a little later coming to light that he had romantically practised at Dusseldorf, where too he had personally known and tremendously liked George du Maurier, whose first so distinguished appearances as an illustrator had already engaged our fondest attention—were they most dawningly in the early Cornhill, or in Punch, or in Once a Week? They glimmer upon me, darkly and richly, as from the pages of the last named. Not to be rendered, I may again parenthesise, our little thrilled awareness, William's and mine, though mine indeed but panting after his, of such peeping phenomena of the European day as the outbreak of a "new man" upon our yearning view of the field of letters and of the arts. I am moved to wonder at how we came by it, shifting all for ourselves, and with the parental *flair*, so far as the sensibility of home was concerned, turned but to directions of its own and much less restless on the whole than ours. More touching to me now than I can say, at all events, this recapture of the hour at which Du Maurier, consecrated to much later, to then still far-off intimate affection, became the new man so significantly as to make a great importance of John Bancroft's news of him, which already bore, among many marvels, upon the supreme wonder of his working, as he was all his life bravely to work, under impaired and gravely menaced eyesight. When I speak, as just above, of what, through so many veils, "came to light," I should further add, I use a figure representing a considerable lapse of time and shading off, for full evocation, into more associations than I can here make place for. Nothing in this connection came *soon* to light at least but that endless amazement might lie in the strange facts of difference between our companion and his distinguished sire—the latter so supremely, so quaintly yet so brilliantly, social a figure, I apprehended, when gaped at, a still more angular, but more polished and pacific Don Quixote, on the sleekest of Rosinantes, with white-tipped chin protrusive, with high sharp elbows raised and long straight legs beautifully pointed, all after the gallantest fashion, against the clear sunset sky of old Newport cavalcades. Mr. Bancroft the elder, the "great," was a comfort, that is a fine high identity, a cluster of strong accents, the sort of thing one's vision followed, in the light of history, if not of mere misguided fancy, for illustration of conceived type—type, say in this case, of superior person of the ancient and the more or less alien public order, the world of affairs transacted at courts and *chancelleries*, in which renown, one had gathered from the perusal of memoirs, allowed for much development of detail and much incision of outline, when not even directly resting on them. As it had been a positive bliss to me that words and names might prove in extremity sources of support, so it comes back to me that I had drawn mystic strength from just obscurely sighing "Metternich!" or "Talleyrand!" as Mr. Bancroft bounced by me—so far as a pair of widely-opened compasses might bounce—in the August gloaming. The value of which, for reflection, moreover, was not in the least in its being that if his son remained so long pleadingly inscrutable any derived Metternich suggestion had contributed to keep him so—for quite *there* was the curiosity of the case, that among the imputations John appeared most to repudiate was that of having at any moment breathed the air either of records or of protocols. If he persisted in painting for years after his return to America without, as the legend grew, the smallest disclosure of his work or confession of his progress to human eye or ear, he drew the rigour of this course wholly from his singleness of nature, in the aftertime to be so much approved to us. However, I pause before the aftertime, into the lap of which more than one sort of stored soundness and sweetness was to fall from him drop by drop.

I scarce know whether my impulse to lead forth these most shrinking of my apparitions be more perverse or more natural—mainly feeling, I confess, however it appear, that the rest of my impression of the animated Cambridge scene, so far as I could take it in, was anything but a vision of unasserted forces. It was only I, as now appears to me, who, ready as yet to assert nothing, hung back, and for reasons even more appreciable to me to-day than then; wondering, almost regretting as I do, that I didn't with a still sharper promptness throw up the sponge for stoppage of the absurd little boxing-match within me between the ostensible and the real—this I mean because I might afterwards thereby have winced a couple of times the less in haunting remembrance of exhibited inaptitude. My condition of having nothing to exhibit was blessedly one that there was nobody to quarrel with—and I couldn't have sufficiently let it alone. I didn't in truth, under a misleading light, reconsider it much; yet I have kept to this hour a black little memory of my having attempted to argue one afternoon, by way of exercise and under what seemed to me a perfect glare of publicity, the fierce light of a "moot-court," some case proposed to me by a fellow-student—who can only have been one of the most benign of men unless he was darkly the designingest, and to whom I was at any rate to owe it that I figured my shame for years much in the image of my having stood forth before an audience with a fiddle and bow and trusted myself to rub them together desperately enough (after the fashion of Rousseau in a passage of the Confessions,) to make some appearance of music. My music, I recall, before the look on the faces around me, quavered away into mere collapse and cessation, a void now engulfing memory itself, so that I liken it all to a merciful fall of the curtain on some actor stricken and stammering. The sense of the brief glare, as I have called the luckless exposure, revives even on this hither side of the wide gulf of time; but I must have outlived every witness—I was so obviously there the very youngest of all aspirants—and, in truth, save for one or two minor and merely comparative miscarriages of the sacrificial act before my false gods, my connection with the temple was to remain as consistently superficial as could be possible to a relation still restlessly perceptive through all its profaneness. Perceiving, even with its accompaniments of noting, wondering, fantasticating, kicked up no glare, but went on much rather under richest shades or in many-coloured lights—a *tone* of opportunity that I look back on as somehow at once deliciously soothing to myself and favourable to the clearness of each item of the picture even as the cool grey sky of a landscape is equalising. That was of course especially when I had let everything slide—everything but the mere act of rather difficultly living (by reason of my scant physical ease,) and fallen back again on the hard sofa of certain ancient rooms in the Winthrop Square, contracted nook, of a local order now quite abolished, and held to my nose for long and sustaining sniffs the scented flower of independence. I took my independence for romantic, or at least for a happy form of yawning vessel into which romance, even should it perforce consist but of mere loose observational play, might drop in the shape of ripe fruit from a shaken tree. Winthrop Square, as I had occasion to note a couple of years since, is a forgotten name, and the disappearance of my lodging spares me doubtless a reminder, possibly ironic, of the debility of those few constructional and pictorial elements that, mustering a wondrous good-will, I had invited myself to rejoice in as "colonial." The house was indeed very old, as antiquity in Cambridge went, with everything in it slanting and gaping and creaking, but with humble antique "points" and a dignity in its decay; above all with the deep recess or alcove, a sweet "irregularity" (so could irregularities of architectural conception then and there count,) thrust forth from its sitting-room toward what I supposed to be the Brighton hills and forming, by the aid of a large window and that commanding view, not to mention the grace of an ancient expansive bureau or secretary-desk (this such a piece, I now venture to figure, as would to-day be pounced on at any cunning dealer's,) a veritable bower toward which even so shy a dreamer as I still then had to take myself for might perhaps hope to woo the muse. The muse was of course the muse of prose fiction—never for the briefest hour in my case the presumable, not to say the presuming, the much-taking-for-granted muse of rhyme, with whom I had never had, even in thought, the faintest flirtation; and she did, in the event, I note, yield to the seduction of so appointed a nook—as to which romantic passage, however, I may not here anticipate. I but lose myself in the recovered sense of what it richly "meant" to me just to *have* a place where I could so handsomely receive her, where I could remark with complacency that the distant horizon, an horizon long since rudely obliterated, was not, after all, too humble to be blue, purple, tawny, changeable in short, everything an horizon should be, and that over the intervening marshes of the Charles (if I don't go astray in so much geography) there was all the fine complicated cloud-scenery I could wish—so extravagantly did I then conceive more or less associational cloud-scenery, after the fashion, I mean, of that feature of remembered English and Boulognese water-colours, to promote the atmosphere of literary composition as the act had begun to glimmer for me.

Everything, however, meant, as I say, more quite other things than I can pretend now to treat of. The mere fact of a sudden rupture, as by the happiest thought, with the "form" of bringing home from the Law-library sheepskin volumes that might give my table, if not, for sufficiency of emphasis, my afflicted self, a temporary countenance, heaped up the measure of my general intention—from the moment I embraced instead of it the practice of resorting to Gore Hall exclusively for my reading-matter; a practice in the light of which my general intention took on the air of absolutely basking. To get somehow, and in spite of everything, in spite especially of being so much disabled, at life, *that* was my brooding purpose, straight out of which the College library, with its sparse bristle of aspiring granite, stood open to far more enchanted distances than any represented by the leathery walls, with never a breach amid their labelled and numbered blocks, that I might pretend to beat against in the other quarter. Yet, happily enough, on this basis of general rather than of special culture, I still loosely rejoiced in being where I was, and by way of proof that it was all right the swim into my ken of Sainte-Beuve, for whose presence on my table, in still other literary company, Gore Hall aiding, I succeeded in not at all blushing, became in the highest degree congruous with regular attendance at lectures. The forenoon lectures at Dane Hall I never in all my time missed, that I can recollect, and I look back on it now as quite prodigious that I should have been so systematically faithful to them without my understanding the first word of what they were about. They contrived—or at least my attendance at them did, inimitably—to be "life;" and as my wondering dips into the vast deep well of the French critic to whom all my roused response went out brought up that mystery to me in cupfuls of extraordinary savour, where was the incongruity of the two rites? That the Causeries du Lundi, wholly fresh then to my grateful lips, should so have overflowed for me was certainly no marvel—that prime acquaintance absolutely *having*, by my measure, to form a really sacred date in the development of any historic or aesthetic consciousness worth mentioning; but that I could be to the very end more or less thrilled by simply sitting, all stupid and sentient, in the thick company of my merely nominal associates and under the strange ministrations of Dr. Theophilus Parsons, "Governor" Washburn and Professor Joel Parker, would have appeared to defy explanation only for those by whom the phenomena of certain kinds of living and working sensibility are unsuspected. For myself at any rate there was no anomaly—the anomaly would have been much rather in any prompter consciousness of a sated perception; I knew why I liked to "go," I knew even why I could unabashedly keep going in face of the fact that if I had learned my reason I had learned, and was still to learn, absolutely nothing else; and that sufficiently supported me through a stretch of bodily overstrain that I only afterwards allowed myself dejectedly to measure. The mere sitting at attention for two or three hours—such attention as I achieved—was paid for by sorry pain; yet it was but later on that I wondered how I could have found what I "got" an equivalent for the condition produced. The condition was one of many, and the others for the most part declared themselves with much of an equal, though a different, sharpness. It was acute, that is, that one was so incommoded, but it had broken upon me with force from the first of my taking my seat—which had the advantage, I acknowledge, of the rim of the circle, symbolising thereby all the detachment I had been foredoomed to—that the whole scene was going to be, and again and again, as "American," and above all as suffused with New England colour, however one might finally estimate that, as I could possibly have wished. Such was the effect of one's offering such a plate for impressions to play on at their will; as well as of one's so failing to ask in advance what they would matter, so taking for granted that they would all matter somehow. It would matter somehow for instance that just a queer dusky half smothered light, as from windows placed too low, or too many interposing heads, should hang upon our old auditorium—long since voided of its then use and, with all its accessory chambers, seated elsewhere afresh and in much greater state; which glimpse of a scheme of values might well have given the measure of the sort of profit I was, or rather wasn't, to derive. It doubtless quite ought to have confounded me that I had come up to *faire mon droit* by appreciations predominantly of the local chiaroscuro and other like quantities; but I remember no alarm—I only remember with what complacency my range of perception on those general lines was able to spread.

It mattered, by the same law, no end that Dr. Theophilus Parsons, whose rich, if slightly quavering, old accents were the first to fall upon my ear from the chair of instruction beneath a huge hot portrait of Daniel Webster should at once approve himself a vivid and curiously-composed person, an *illustrative* figure, as who should say—exactly with all the marks one might have wished him, marks of a social order, a general air, a whole history of things, or in other words of people; since there was nothing one mightn't, by my sentiment, do with such a subject from the moment it gave out character. Character thus was all over the place, as it could scarce fail to be when the general subject, the one gone in for, had become identical with the persons of all its votaries. Such was the interest of the source of edification just named, not one ray of whose merely professed value so much as entered my mind. Governor Washburn was of a different, but of a no less complete consistency—queer, ingenuous, more candidly confiding, especially as to his own pleasant fallibility, than I had ever before known a chaired dispenser of knowledge, and all after a fashion that endeared him to his young hearers, whose resounding relish of the frequent tangle of his apologetic returns upon himself, quite, almost always, to inextricability, was really affectionate in its freedom. I could understand and admire that—it seemed to have for me legendary precedents; whereas of the third of our instructors I mainly recall that he represented dryness and hardness, prose unrelieved, at their deadliest—partly perhaps because he was most master of his subject. He was none the less placeable for these things withal, and what mainly comes back to me of him is the full sufficiency with which he made me ask myself how I *could* for a moment have seen myself really browse in any field where the marks of the shepherd were such an oblong dome of a bare cranium, such a fringe of dropping little ringlets toward its base, and a mouth so meanly retentive, so ignorant of style, as I made out, above a chin so indifferent to the duty, or at least to the opportunity, of chins. If I had put it to myself that there was no excuse for the presence of a young person so affected by the idea of how people looked on a scene where the issue was altogether what they usefully taught, as well as intelligently learned and wanted to learn, I feel I should, after my first flush of confusion, have replied assuredly enough that just the beauty of the former of these questions was in its being of equal application everywhere; which was far from the case with the latter. The question of how people looked, and of how their look counted for a thousand relations, had risen before me too early and kept me company too long for me not to have made a fight over it, from the very shame of appearing at all likely to give it up, had some fleeting delusion led me to cast a slur upon it. It would do, I was already sure, half the work of carrying me through life, and where was better proof of all it would have to give than just in the fact of what it was then and there doing? It worked for appreciation—not one of the uses of which as an act of intelligence had, all round, finer connections; and on the day, in short, when one should cease to live in large measure by one's eyes (with the imagination of course all the while waiting on this) one would have taken the longest step towards not living at all. My companions—however scantly indeed they were to become such—were subject to my so practising in a degree which represented well nigh the whole of my relation with them, small reciprocity for them as there may have been in it; since vision, and nothing but vision, was from beginning to end the fruit of my situation among them. There was not one of them as to whom it didn't matter that he "looked," by my fancy of him, thus or so; the key to this disposition of the accents being for me to such an extent that, as I have said, I was with all intensity taking in New England and that I knew no better *immediate* way than to take it in by my senses. What that name really comprehended had been a mystery, daily growing less, to which everything that fell upon those senses referred itself, making the innumerable appearances hang together ever so densely. Theophilus Parsons, with his tone, his unction, his homage still to some ancient superstition, some standard of manners, reached back as to a state of provincialism rounded and compact, quite self-supporting, which gave it serenity and quality, something comparatively rich and urban; the good ex-Governor, on the other hand, of whom I think with singular tenderness, opened through every note of aspect and expression straight into those depths of rusticity which more and more unmistakably underlay the social order at large and out of which one felt it to have emerged in any degree but at scattered points. Where it did emerge, I seemed to see, it held itself as high as possible, conscious, panting a little, elate with the fact of having cleared its skirts, saved its life, consolidated its Boston, yet as with wastes unredeemed, roundabout it, propping up and pushing in—all so insistently that the light in which one for the most part considered the scene was strongly coloured by their action. This was one's clue to the labyrinth, if labyrinth it was to be called—a generalisation into which everything fitted, first to surprise and then indubitably to relief, from the moment one had begun to make it. Under its law the Puritan capital, however visibly disposed to spread and take on new disguises, affected me as a rural centre even to a point at which I had never known anything as rural; there being involved with this too much further food for curiosity and wonder. Boston was in a manner of its own stoutly and vividly urban, not only a town, but a town of history—so that how did it manage to be such different things at the same time? That was doubtless its secret—more and more interesting to study in proportion as, on closer acquaintance, yet an acquaintance before which the sense of one's preferred view from outside never gave way, one felt the equilibrium attained as on the whole an odd fusion and intermixture, of the chemical sort as it were, and not a matter of elements or aspects sharply alternating. There was in the exhibition at its best distinctly a savour—an excellent thing for a community to have, and part of the savour was, as who should say, the breath of the fields and woods and waters, though at their domesticated and familiarised stage, or the echo of a tone which had somehow become that of the most educated of our societies without ceasing to be that of the village.

Of so much from the first I felt sure, and this all the more that by my recollection of New York, even indeed by my recollection of Albany, we had been aware in those places of no such strain. New York at least had been whatever disagreeable, not to say whatever agreeable, other thing one might have declared it—it might even have been vulgar, though that cheap substitute for an account of anything didn't, I think, in the connection, then exist for me; but the last reference to its nature likely to crop up in its social soil was beyond question the flower of the homely. New England had, by one's impression, cropped up there, but had done so just *as* New England, New England unabsorbed and unreconciled; which was exactly a note in the striated, the piebald or, more gracefully, cosmopolite local character. I am not sure that the comparatively—I say comparatively—market-town suggestion of the city by the Charles came out for me as a positive richness, but it did essentially contribute to what had become so highly desirable, the reinforcement of my vision of American life by the idea of variety. I apparently required of anything I should take to my heart that it should be, approached at different angles, "like" as many other things as possible—in accordance with which it made for a various "America" that Boston should seem really strong, really quaint and amusing and beguiling or whatever, in not having, for better or worse, the same irrepressible likenesses as New York. I invoked, I called down the revelation of, new likenesses by the simple act of threading the Boston streets, whether by garish day (the afterglow of the great snowfalls of winter was to turn in particular to a blinding glare, an unequalled hardness of light,) or under that mantle of night which draped as with the garb of adventure our long-drawn townward little rumbles in the interest of the theatre or of Parker's—oh the sordid, yet never in the least deterrent conditions of transit in that age of the unabbreviated, the dividing desert and the primitive horse-car! (The desert is indeed, despite other local developments and the general theory of the rate at which civilisation spreads and ugliness wanes, still very much what it was in the last mid-century, but the act of passage through it has been made to some extent easier.) Parker's played in the intercourse of Cambridge with Boston a part of a preponderance that I look back upon, I confess, as the very condition of the purest felicity we knew—I knew at any rate myself none, whether of a finer or a grosser strain, that competed with this precious relation. Competition has thickened since and proportions have altered—to no small darkening of the air, but the time was surely happier; a single such *point de repère* not only sufficed but richly heaped up the measure. Parker's, on the whole side of the joy of life, *was* Boston—speaking as under the thrill of early occasions recaptured; Boston could be therefore, in the acutest connections, those of young comradeship and young esthetic experience, heaven save the mark, fondly prepared or properly crowned, but the enjoyed and shared repast, literally the American feast, as I then appraised such values; a basis of native abundance on which everything else rested. The theatre, resorted to whenever possible, rested indeed doubtless most, though with its heaviest weight thrown perhaps at a somewhat later time; the theatre my uncanny appetite for which strikes me as almost abnormal in the light of what I braved to reach it from the studious suburb, or more particularly braved to return from it. I touch alas no spring that doesn't make a hum of memories, and pick them over as I will three or four of that scenic strain linger on my sense. The extraordinary fact about these—which plays into my generalisation a little way back—was that, for all the connection of such occasions with the great interest of the theatre at large, there was scarce an impression of the stage wrung from current opportunity that didn't somehow underscore itself with the special Boston emphasis; and this in spite of the fact that plays and performers in those days were but a shade less raggedly itinerant over the land than they are now. The implication of the provincial in the theatric air, and of the rustic in the provincial, may have been a matter of the "house" itself, with its twenty kinds of redolence of barbarism—with the kind determined by the very audience perhaps indeed plainest; vivid to me at all events is it how I felt even at the time, in repairing to the Howard Atheneum to admire Miss Maggie Mitchell and Miss Kate Bateman, that one would have had only to scratch a little below the surface of the affair to come upon the but half-buried Puritan curse not so very long before devoted to such perversities. Wasn't the curse still in the air, and could anything less than a curse, weighing from far back on the general conscience, have accounted for one could scarce say what want of self-respect in the total exhibition?—for that intimation more than anything else perhaps of the underhand snicker with which one sat so oddly associated. By the blest law of youth and fancy withal one did admire the actress—the young need to admire as flatly as one could broke through all crowding apprehensions. I like to put it down that nothing in the world qualified my wonder at the rendering by the first of the performers I have named of the figure of "Fanchon the Cricket" in a piece so entitled, an artless translation from a German original, if I rightly remember, which original had been an arrangement for the stage of La Petite Fadette, George Sand's charming rustic idyll. I like to put it down that Miss Maggie Mitchell's having for years, as I gathered, twanged that one string and none other, every night of her theatric life, over the huge country, before she was revealed to us—just as Mr. Joe Jefferson, with no word of audible reprehension ever once addressed to him, was to have twanged his—did nothing to bedim the brightness of our vision or the apparent freshness of her art, and that above all it seemed a privilege critically to disengage the delicacy of this art and the rare effect of the natural in it from the baseness in which it was framed: so golden a glimmer is shed, as one looks back, from any shaky little torch lighted, by whatever fond stretch, at the high esthetic flame. Upon these faint sparks in the night of time would I gently breathe, just to see them again distinguishably glow, rather than leave their momentary function uncommemorated. Strange doubtless were some of the things that represented these momentary functions—strange I mean in proportion to the fires they lighted. The small bower of the muse in Winthrop Square was first to know the fluttered descent of the goddess to my appeal for her aid in the composition of a letter from which the admired Miss Maggie should gather the full force of my impression. Particularly do I incline even now to mention that she testified to her having gratefully gathered it by the despatch to me in return of a little printed copy of the play, a scant pamphlet of "acting edition" humility, addressed in a hand which assumed a romantic cast as soon as I had bethought myself of finding for it a happy precedent in that of Pendennis's Miss Fotheringay.

It had been perhaps to the person of this heroine that Pendennis especially rendered homage, while I, without illusions, or at least without confusions, was fain to discriminate in favour of the magic of method, that is of genius, itself; which exactly, more than anything else could have done (success, as I considered, crowning my demonstration,) contributed to consecrate to an exquisite use, *the* exquisite, my auspicious *réduit* aforesaid. For an esthetic vibration to whatever touch had but to be intense enough to tremble on into other reactions under other blest contacts and commotions. It was by the operation again of the impulse shaking me up to an expression of what the elder star of the Howard Atheneum had artistically "meant" to me that I first sat down beside my view of the Brighton hills to enrol myself in the bright band of the fondly hoping and fearfully doubting who count the days after the despatch of manuscripts. I formally addressed myself under the protection, not to say the inspiration, of Winthrop Square to the profession of literature, though nothing would induce me now to name the periodical on whose protracted silence I had thus begun to hang with my own treasures of reserve to match it. The bearing of which shy ecstasies—shy of exhibition then, that is, save as achievements recognised—is on their having thus begun, at any rate, to supply all the undertone one needed to whatever positive perfunctory show; the show proceeding as it could, all the while, thanks to much help from the undertone, which felt called upon at times to be copious. It is not, I allow, that memory may pretend for me to keep the two elements of the under and the over always quite distinct—it would have been a pity all round, in truth, should they have altogether escaped mixing and fraternising. The positive perfunctory show, at all events, to repeat my term, hitched itself along from point to point, and could have no lack of outside support to complain of, I reflect, from the moment I could make my own every image and incitement—those, as I have noted, of the supply breaking upon me with my first glimpse of the Cambridge scene. If I seem to make too much of these it is because I at the time made still more, more even than my pious record has presumed to set down. The air of truth doubtless hangs uneasy, as the matter stands, over so queer a case as my having, by my intimation above, found appreciability in life at the Law School even under the failure for me of everything generally drawn upon for it, whether the glee of study, the ardour of battle or the joy of associated adventure. Not to have felt earlier sated with the mere mechanic amusement or vain form of regularity at lectures would strike me to-day as a fact too "rum" for belief if certain gathered flowers by the way, flowers of perverse appreciation though they might but be, didn't give out again as I turn them over their unspeakable freshness. They were perforce gathered (what makes it still more wondrous) all too languidly; yet they massed themselves for my sense, through the lapsing months, to the final semblance of an intimate secret garden. Such was the odd, the almost overwhelming consequence—or one of these, for they are many—of an imagination to which literally everything obligingly signified. One of the actual penalties of this is that so few of such ancient importances remain definable or presentable. It may in the fulness of time simply sound *bête* that, with the crash of greater questions about one, I should have been positively occupied with such an affair as the degree and the exact shade to which the blest figures in the School array, each quite for himself, might settle and fix the weight, the interest, the function, as it were, of his Americanism. I could scarce have cleared up even for myself, I dare say, the profit, or more pertinently the charm, of that extravagance—and the fact was of course that I didn't feel it as extravagance, but quite as homely thrift, moral, social, esthetic, or indeed, as I might have been quite ready to say, practical and professional. It was practical at least in the sense that it probably more helped to pass the time than all other pursuits together. The real proof of which would be of course my being able now to string together for exhibition some of these pearls of differentiation—since it was to differentiation exactly that I was then, in my innocence, most prompted; not dreaming of the stiff law by which, on the whole American ground, division of *type*, in the light of opposition and contrast, was more and more to break down for me and fail: so that verily the recital of my mere concomitant efforts to pick it up again and piece its parts together and make them somehow show and serve would be a record of clinging courage. I may note at once, however, as a light on the anomaly, that there hung about *all* young appearances at that period something ever so finely derivative and which at this day rather defies re-expression—the common character or shared function of the precious clay so largely making up the holocausts of battle; an advantage working for them circuitously or perhaps ambiguously enough, I grant, but still placing them more or less under the play of its wing even when the arts of peace happened for the hour to engage them. They potentially, they conceivably, they indirectly paid, and nothing was for the most part more ascertainable of them individually than that, with brothers or other near relatives in the ranks or in commands, they came, to their credit, of paying families. All of which again may represent the high pitch of one's associated sensibility—there having been occasions of crisis, were they worth recovering, when under its action places, persons, objects animate or not, glimmered alike but through the grand idealising, the generalising, blur. At moments of less fine a strain, it may be added, the sources of interest presented themselves in looser formation. The young appearances, as I like to continue to call them, could be pleasingly, or at least robustly homogeneous, and yet, for livelier appeal to fancy, flower here and there into special cases of elegant deviation—"sports," of exotic complexion, one enjoyed denominating these (or would have enjoyed had the happy figure then flourished) thrown off from the thick stem that was rooted under our feet. Even these rare exceptions, the few apparitions referring themselves to other producing conditions than the New England, wrought by contrast no havoc in the various quantities for which that section was responsible; it was certainly refreshing—always to the fond imagination—that there were, for a change, imprints in the stuff of youth that didn't square with the imprint, virtually *one* throughout, imposed by Springfield or Worcester, by Providence or Portland, or whatever rural wastes might lie between; yet the variations, I none the less gather as I strive to recall them, beguiled the spirit (talking always of my own) rather than coerced it, and this even though fitting into life as one had already more or less known it, fitting in, that is, with more points of contact and more reciprocation of understanding than the New England relation seemed able to produce. It could in fact fairly blind me to the implication of an inferior immediate *portée* that such and such a shape of the New York heterogeneity, however simplified by silliness, or at least by special stupidity (though who was I to note *that*?) pressed a certain spring of association, waiting as I always was for such echoes, rather than left it either just soundless or bunglingly touched.

It was for example a link with the larger life, as I am afraid I must have privately called it, that a certain young New Yorker, an outsider of still more unmistakable hue than I could suppose even myself, came and went before us with an effect of cultivated detachment that I admired at the time for its perfect consistency, and that caused him, it was positively thrilling to note, not in the least to forfeit sympathy, but to shine in the high light of public favour. The richest reflections sprang for me from this, some of them inspiring even beyond the promptly grasped truth, a comparative commonplace, that the variation or opposition sufficiently embodied, the line of divergence sharply enough drawn, always achieves some triumph by the fact of its emphasis, by its putting itself through at any cost, any cost in particular of ridicule. So much one had often observed; but what really enriched the dear induction and made our friend's instance thus remain with me was the part played by the utter blandness itself of his protest, such an exhibition of the sweet in the imperturbable. This it was that enshrined him, by my vision, in a popularity than which nothing could have seemed in advance less indicated, and that makes me wonder to day whether he was simply the luckiest of gamblers or just a conscious and consummate artist. He reappears to me as a finished fop, finished to possibilities we hadn't then dreamt of, and as taking his stand, or rather taking all his walks, on *that*, the magician's wand of his ideally tight umbrella under his arm and the magician's familiar of his bristling toy-terrier at his heels. He became thus an apparition entrancing to the mind. His clothes were of a perfection never known nor divined in that sphere, a revelation, straight and blindingly authentic, of Savile Row in its prime; his single eyeglass alone, and his inspired, his infinite use of it as at once a defensive crystal wall and a lucid window of hospitality, one couldn't say most which, might well have foredoomed him, by all likelihood, to execration and destruction. He became none the less, as I recover him, our general pride and joy; his entrances and exits were acclaimed beyond all others, and it was his rare privilege to cause the note of derision and the note of affection to melt together, beyond separation, in vague but virtual homage to the refreshment of felt type. To see it dawn upon rude breasts (for rude, comparatively, *were* the breasts of the typeless, or at the best of the typed but in one character, throughout the same,) that defiant and confident difference carried far enough might avert the impulse to slay, was to muse ever so agreeably on the queer means by which great morals, picking up a life as they may, can still get themselves pointed. The "connotation" of the trivial, it was thus attaching to remark, could perfectly serve when that of the important, roughly speaking, failed for a grateful *connection*—from the moment some such was massed invitingly in view. The difficulty with the type about me was that, in its monotony, beginning and ending with itself, it *had* no connections and suggested none; whereas the grace of the salient apparition I have perhaps too earnestly presented lay in its bridging over our separation from worlds, from great far-off reservoirs, of a different mixture altogether, another civility and complexity. Young as I was, I myself clearly recognised that ground of reference, saw it even to some extent in the light of experience—so could I stretch any scrap of contact; kept hold of it by fifty clues, recalls and reminders that dangled for me mainly out of books and magazines and heard talk, things of picture and story, things of prose and verse and anecdotal vividness in fine, and, as I have elsewhere allowed, for the most part hoardedly English and French. Our "character man" of the priceless monocle and the trotting terrier was "like" some type in a collection of types—that was the word for it; and, there being no collection, nor the ghost of one, roundabout us, was a lone courageous creature in the desert of our bald reiterations. The charm of which conclusion was exactly, as I have said, that the common voice did, by every show, bless him for rendered service, his dropped hint of an ideal containing the germ of other ideals—and confessed by that fact to more appetites and inward yearnings than it the least bit consciously counted up.

Not quite the same service was rendered by G. A. J., who had no ridicule to brave, and I can speak with confidence but of the connections, rather confused if they were, opened up to me by his splendid aspect and which had absolutely nothing in common with the others that hung near. It was brilliant to a degree that none other had by so much as a single shade the secret of, and it carried the mooning fancy to a further reach even, on the whole, than the figure of surprise I have just commemorated; this last comparatively scant in itself and rich only by what it made us read into it, and G. A. J. on the other hand intrinsically and actively ample and making us read wonders, as it were, into whatever it might be that was, as we used to say, "back of" him. He had such a flush of life and presence as to make that reference mysteriously and inscrutably loom—and the fascinating thing about this, as we again would have said, was that it could strike me as so beguilingly American. That too was part of the glamour, that its being so could kick up a mystery which one might have pushed on to explore, whereas our New York friend only kicked up a certainty (for those properly prepared) and left not exploration, but mere assured satisfaction, the mark of the case. G. A. J. reached westward, westward even of New York, and southward at least as far as Virginia; teeming facts that I discovered, so to speak, by my own unaided intelligence—so little were they responsibly communicated. Little was communicated that I recover—it would have had to drop from too great a personal height; so that the fun, as I may call it, was the greater for my opening all by myself to perceptions. I was getting furiously American, in the big sense I invoked, through this felt growth of an ability to reach out westward, southward, anywhere, everywhere, on that apprehension of finding myself but patriotically charmed. Thus there dawned upon me the grand possibility that, charm for charm, the American, the assumed, the postulated, would, in the particular case of its really acting, count double; whereas the European paid for being less precarious by being also less miraculous. It counted single, as one might say, and only made up for that by counting almost always. It mightn't be anything like almost always, even at the best, no doubt, that an American-grown value of aspect would so entirely emerge as G. A. J.'s seemed to do; but what did this exactly point to unless that the rarity so implied would be in the nature of the splendid? That at least was the way the cultivation of patriotism as a resource was the cultivation of workable aids to the same, however ingenious these. (Just to glow belligerently with one's country was no resource, but a primitive instinct breaking through; and besides this resources were cooling, not heating.) It might have seemed that I might after all perfectly dispense with friends when simple acquaintances, and rather feared ones at that, though feared but for excess of lustre, could kindle in the mind such bonfires of thought, feeding the flame with gestures and sounds and light accidents of passage so beyond their own supposing. In spite of all which, however, G. A. J. was marked for a friend and taken for a kinsman from the day when his blaze of colour should have sufficiently cleared itself up for me to distinguish the component shades.

XI

I AM fully aware while I go, I should mention, of all that flows from the principle governing, by my measure, these recoveries and reflections—even to the effect, hoped for at least, of stringing their apparently dispersed and disordered parts upon a fine silver thread; none other than the principle of response to a long-sought occasion, now gratefully recognised, for making trial of the recording and figuring act on behalf of some case of the imaginative faculty under cultivation. The personal history, as it were, of an imagination, a lively one of course, in a given and favourable case, had always struck me as a task that a teller of tales might rejoice in, his advance through it conceivably causing at every step some rich precipitation—unless it be rather that the play of strong imaginative passion, passion strong enough to *be*, for its subject or victim, the very interest of life, constitutes in itself an endless crisis. Fed by every contact and every apprehension, and feeding in turn every motion and every act, wouldn't the light in which it might so cause the whole scene of life to unroll inevitably become as fine a thing as possible to represent? The idea of some pretext for such an attempt had again and again, naturally, haunted me; the man of imagination, and of an "awfully good" one, showed, as the creature of that force or the sport of that fate or the wielder of that arm, for the hero of a hundred possible fields—if one could but first "catch" him, after the fashion of the hare in the famous receipt. Who and what might he prove, when caught, in respect to *other* signs and conditions? He might take, it would seem, some finding and launching, let alone much handling—which itself, however, would be exactly part of the pleasure. Meanwhile, it no less appeared, there were other subjects to go on with, and even if one had to wait for him he would still perhaps come. It happened for me that he *was* belatedly to come, but that he was to turn up then in a shape almost too familiar at first for recognition, the shape of one of those residual substitutes that engage doubting eyes the day after the fair. He had been with me all the while, and only too obscurely and intimately—I had not found him in the market as an exhibited or *offered* value. I had in a word to draw him forth from within rather than meet him in the world before me, the more convenient sphere of the objective, and to make him objective, in short, had to turn nothing less than myself inside out. What was *I* thus, within and essentially, what had I ever been and could I ever be but a man of imagination at the active pitch?—so that if it was a question of treating *some* happy case, any that would give me what, artistically speaking, I wanted, here on the very spot was one at hand in default of a better. It wasn't what I should have preferred, yet it was after all the example I knew best and should feel most at home with—granting always that objectivity, the prize to be won, shouldn't just be frightened away by the odd terms of the affair. It is of course for my reader to say whether or no what I have done *has* meant defeat; yet even if this should be his judgment I fall back on the interest, at the worst, of certain sorts of failure. I shall have brought up from the deep many things probably not to have been arrived at for the benefit of these pages without my particular attempt. Sundry of such I seem still to recognise, and not least just now those involved in that visionary "assistance" at the drama of the War, from however far off, which had become a habit for us without ceasing to be a strain. I am sure I thought more things under that head, with the fine visionary ache, than I thought in all other connections together; for the simple reason that one had to *ask* leave—of one's own spirit—for these last intermissions, whereas one but took it, with both hands free, for one's sense of the bigger cause. There was not in that the least complication of consciousness. I have sufficiently noted how my apprehension of the bigger cause was at the same time, and this all through, at once quickened and kept low; to the point that positively my whole acquaintance of the personal sort even with such a matter as my brother Wilky's enrolment in the 44th Massachusetts was to reduce itself to but a single visit to him in camp.

I recall an afternoon at Readville, near Boston, and the fashion in which his state of juniority gave way, for me, on the spot, to immensities of superior difference, immensities that were at the same time intensities, varieties, supremacies, of the enviable in the all-difficult and the delightful in the impossible: such a fairy-tale seemed it, and withal such a flat revolution, that this soft companion of my childhood should have such romantic chances and should have mastered, by the mere aid of his native gaiety and sociability, such mysteries, such engines, such arts. To become first a happy soldier and then an easy officer was in particular for G. W. J. an exercise of sociability —and that above all was my extract of the Readville scene, which most came home to me as a picture, an interplay of bright breezy air and high shanty-covered levels with blue horizons, and laughing, welcoming, sunburnt young men, who seemed mainly to bristle, through their welcome, with Boston genealogies, and who had all alike turned handsome, only less handsome than their tawny-bearded Colonel, under I couldn't have said what common grace of clear blue toggery imperfectly and hitchingly donned in the midst of the camp labours that I gaped at (by the blessing of heaven I could in default of other adventures still gape) as at shining revels. I couldn't "do things," I couldn't indefinitely hang about, though on occasion I did so, as it comes back to me, verily to desperation; which had to be my dim explanation—dim as to my ever insisting on it—of so rare a snatch at opportunity for gapings the liveliest, or in better terms admirations the crudest, that I could have presumed to encumber the scene with. Scarce credible to me now, even under recall of my frustrations, that I was able in all this stretch of time to respond but to a single other summons to admire at any cost, which I think must have come again from Readville, and the occasion of which, that of my brother's assumed adjutancy of the so dramatically, so much more radically recruited 54th involved a view superficially less harmonious. The whole situation was more wound up and girded then, the formation of negro regiments affected us as a tremendous War measure, and I have glanced in another place at the consequence of it that was at the end of a few months most pointedly to touch ourselves. That second aspect of the weeks of preparation before the departure of the regiment can not at all have suggested a frolic, though at the time I don't remember it as grim, and can only gather that, as the other impression had been of something quite luminous and beautiful, so this was vaguely sinister and sad—perhaps simply through the fact that, though our sympathies, our own as a family's, were, in the current phrase, all enlisted on behalf of the race that had sat in bondage, it was impossible for the mustered presence of more specimens of it, and of stranger, than I had ever seen together, not to make the young men who were about to lead them appear sacrificed to the general tragic need in a degree beyond that of their more orthodox appearances. The air of sacrifice was, however, so to brighten as to confound itself with that of splendid privilege on the day (May 28th, '63) of the march of the 54th out of Boston, its fairest of young commanders at its head, to great reverberations of music, of fluttering banners, launched benedictions and every public sound; only from that scene, when it took place, I had to be helplessly absent—just as I see myself in a like dismal manner deprived of any nearness of view of my still younger brother's military metamorphosis and contemporary initiation. I vainly question memory for some such picture of *him*, at this stage of his adventure, as would have been certain to hang itself, for reasons of wonder and envy again, in my innermost cabinet. Our differently compacted and more variously endowed Bob, who had strained much at every tether, was so eager and ardent that it made for him a positive authority; but what most recurs to me of his start in the 45th, or of my baffled vision of it, is the marvel of our not having all just wept, more than anything else, either for his being so absurdly young or his being so absurdly strenuous—we might have had our choice of pretexts and protests. It seemed so short a time since he had been l'ingénieux petit Robertson of the domestic schoolroom, pairing with our small sister as I paired with Wilky. We didn't in the least weep, however—we smiled as over the interest of childhood at its highest bloom, and that my parents, with their consistent tenderness, should have found their surrender of their latest born so workable is doubtless a proof that we were all lifted together as on a wave that might bear us where it would. Our ingenious Robertson was but seventeen years old, but I suspect his ingenuity of having, in so good a cause, anticipated his next birthday by a few months. The 45th was a nine-months regiment, but he got himself passed out of it, in advance of its discharge, to a lieutenancy in the 55th U.S.C.T., Colonel A. P. Hallowell (transferred from lieutenant-colonelcy of the 54th) commanding; though not before he had been involved in the siege of Charleston, whence the visionary, the quite Edgar Poeish look, for my entertainment, of the camp-covered "Folly Island" of his letters. While his regiment was engaged in Seymour's raid on Florida he suffered a serious sunstroke, with such consequences that he was recommended for discharge; of which he declined to avail himself, obtaining instead a position on General Ames's staff and enjoying thus for six months the relief of being mounted. But he returned to his regiment in front of Charleston (after service with the Tenth Army Corps, part of the Army of the James, before Petersburg and Richmond); and though I have too scant an echo of his letters from that scene one of the passages that I do recover is of the happiest. "It was when the line wavered and I saw Gen'l Hartwell's horse on my right rear up with a shell exploding under him that I rammed my spurs into my own beast, who, maddened with pain, carried me on through the line, throwing men down, and over the Rebel works some distance ahead of our troops." For this action he was breveted captain; and the 55th, later on, was the first body of troops to enter Charleston and march through its streets—which term of his experience, as it unfolded, presents him to my memory as again on staff duty; with Brigadier-Generals Potter, Rufus Hatch and his old superior and, at my present writing, gallant and vivid survivor, Alfred Hartwell, who had been his captain and his lieut.-colonel in the 45th and the 55th respectively.[1]

I can at all events speak perfectly of my own sense of the uplifting wave just alluded to during the couple of years that the "boys'" letters from the field came in to us—with the one abatement of glamour for them the fact that so much of their substance was in the whole air of life and their young reports of sharp experience but a minor pipe in the huge mixed concert always in our ears. Faded and touching pages, these letters are in some abundance before me now, breathing confidence

[1]My youngest brother's ingenuity was to know as little rest during much of his life as his strong faculty of agitation—to the employment of which it was indeed not least remarkably applied. Many illustrations of it would be to give, had I more margin; and not one of them anything less than striking, thanks to the vivacity of his intelligence, the variety of his gifts and the native ability in which he was himself so much less interested than was the case with everyone he met, however casually, that he became, many years before his death in

and extraordinary cheer—though surviving principally but in Wilky's admirable hand, of all those I knew at that time the most humiliating to a feebler yet elder fist; and with their liveliest present action to recompose for me not by any means so much the scenes and circumstances, the passages of history

1910, our one gentleman of leisure: so far as this condition might consort with the easiest aptitude for admirable talk, charged with natural life, perception, humour and colour, that I have perhaps ever known. There were times when Bob's spoken overflow struck me as the equivalent, for fine animation, of William's epistolary. The note of the ingenious in him spent itself as he went, but I find an echo of one of its many incidents in the passage of verse that I am here moved to rescue from undue obscurity. It is too "amateurish" and has too many irregular lines, but images admirably the play of spirit in him which after ranging through much misadventure could at last drop to an almost effective grasp of the happiest relation.

Although I lie so low and still
Here came I by the Master's will;
He smote at last to make me free,
As He was smitten on the tree
And nailèd there. He knew of old
The human heart, and mine is cold;
And I know now that all we gain
Until we come to Him is vain.
Thy hands have never wrought a deed,
Thy heart has never known a need,
That went astray in His great plan
Since far-off days when youth began.
For in that vast and perfect plan
Where time is but an empty span
Our Master waits. He knows our want,
We know not his—till pale and gaunt
With weariness of life we come
And say to Him, What shall I be?
Oh Master, smite, but make me free
Perchance in these far worlds to know
The better thing we sought to be.

And then upon thy couch lie down
And fold the hands which have not sown;
And as thou liest there alone
Perhaps some breath from seraph blown
As soft as dew upon the rose
Will fall upon thee at life's close.
So thou wilt say, At last, at last!
All pain is love when pain is past!

concerned, as to make me know again and reinhabit the places, the hours, the stilled or stirred conditions through which I took them in. These conditions seem indeed mostly to have settled for me into the single sense of what I missed, compared to what the authors of our bulletins gained, in wondrous opportunity of vision, that is *appreciation of the thing seen*—there being clearly such a lot of this, and all of it, by my conviction, portentous and prodigious. The key to which assurance was that I longed to live by my eyes, in the midst of such far-spreading chances, in greater measure than I then had help to, and that the measure in which *they* had it gloriously overflowed. This capacity in them to deal with such an affluence of life stood out from every line, and images sprung up about them at every turn of the story. The story, the general one, of the great surge of action on which they were so early carried, was to take still other turns during the years I now speak of, some of these not of the happiest; but with the same relation to it on my own part too depressingly prolonged—that of seeing, sharing, envying, applauding, pitying, all from too far-off, and with the queer sense that, whether or no they would prove to have had the time of their lives, it seemed that the only time I should have had would stand or fall by theirs. This was to be yet more deplorably the case later on—I like to give a twitch to the curtain of a future reduced to the humility of a past: when, the War being over and we confronted with all the personal questions it had showily muffled up only to make them step forth with their sharper angles well upon us, our father, easily beguiled, acquired by purchase and for the benefit of his younger sons divers cotton-lands in Florida; which scene

And to the Master once again:
Oh keep my heart too weak to pray;
I ask no longer questions vain
Of life and love, of loss and gain—
These for the living are and strong;
I go to Thee, to Thee belong.
Once was I wakened by Thy light,
But years have passed, and now the night
Takes me to Thee. I am content;
So be it in Thy perfect plan
A mansion is where I am sent
To dwell among the innocent.

of blighted hopes it perhaps was that cast upon me, at its defiant distance, the most provoking spell. There was provocation, at those subsequent seasons, in the very place-name of Serenola, beautiful to ear and eye; unforgettable were to remain the times, while the vain experiment dragged on for our anxiety and curiosity, and finally to our great discomfiture, when my still ingenuous young brothers, occupied in raising and selling crops that refused alike, it seemed, to come and to go, wafted northward their fluctuating faith, their constant hospitality and above all, for one of the number at home, their large unconscious evocations. The mere borrowed, and so brokenly borrowed, impression of southern fields basking in a light we didn't know, of scented sub-tropic nights, of a situation suffused with economic and social drama of the strangest and sharpest, worked in me, I dare say most deceptively, as a sign of material wasted, my material not being in the least the crops unproduced or unsold, but the precious store of images ungathered. However, the vicarious sensation had, as I say, been intense enough, from point to point, before that; a series of Wilky's letters of the autumn of '62 and the following winter during operations in North Carolina intended apparently to clear an approach to Charleston overflow with the vivacity of his interest in whatever befell, and still more in whatever promised, and reflect, in this freshness of young assurances and young delusions, the general public fatuity. The thread of interest for me here would certainly be much more in an exhibition of some such artless notes of the period, with their faded marks upon them, than in that of the spirit of my own poor perusal of them—were it not that those things shrink after years to the common measure when not testifying to some rarity of experience and expression. All experience in the field struck me indeed as then rare, and I wondered at both my brothers' military mastery of statement, through which played, on the part of the elder, a whimsicality of "turn," an oddity of verbal collocation, that we had ever cherished, in the family circle, as the sign of his address. "The next fight we have, I expect," he writes from Newberne, N. C., on New Year's Day '63, "will be a pretty big one, but I am confident that under Foster and our gunboats we will rid the State of these miserable wretches whom the Divine Providence has created in its wisdom to make men wish —— ! Send on then, open yourselves a recruiting establishment if necessary—all we want is numbers! *They* are the greatest help to the individual soldier on the battle-field. If he feels he has 30,000 men behind him pushing on steadily to back him he is in much more fighting trim than when away in the rear with 10,000 ahead of him fighting like madmen. It seems that Halleck told Foster when F. was in Washington that he scarcely slept for a week after learning that we were near Goldsboro', having heard previously that a reinforcement of 40,000 Rebels were coming down there to whip us. Long live Foster!"

"It was so cold this morning," he writes at another and earlier date, "that Divine service was held in our barracks instead of out-of-doors, as it generally is, and it was the most impressive that I have ever heard. The sermon was on profanity, and the chaplain, after making all the observations and doing by mouth and action as much as he could to rid the regiment of the curse, sat down, credulous being, thinking he had settled the question for ever. Colonel Lee then rose and said that the chaplain the other day accused him—most properly—of profanity and of its setting a very bad example to the regiment; also that when he took the command he had felt how very bad the thing would be in its influence on all around him. He felt that it would be the great conflict of his life. At this point his head drooped and he lifted his handkerchief to his face; but he went on in conclusion: 'Now boys, let us try one and all to vindicate the sublime principles our chaplain has just so eloquently expressed, and I will do *my* best. I hope to God I have wounded no man's feelings by an oath; if I have I humbly beg his pardon.' Here he finished." How this passage impressed me at the time signifies little; but I find myself now feel in its illustration of what could then happen among soldiers of the old Puritan Commonwealth a rich recall of some story from Cromwellian ranks. Striking the continuity, and not unworthy of it my brother's further comment. "I leave you to imagine which of these appeals did most good, the conventional address of the pastor or the honest manly heart-touching acknowledgment of our Colonel. That is the man through and through, and I heard myself say afterwards: 'Let him swear to all eternity if he *is* that sort of man, and if profanity makes such, for goodness' sake let us all swear.' This may be a bad doctrine, but is one that might after all undergo discussion." From which letter I cull further: "I really begin to think you've been hard in your judgments of McClellan. You don't know what an enemy we have to conquer. Every secesh I've seen, and all the rebel prisoners here, talk of the War with such callous earnestness." A letter from Newberne of December 2nd contains a "pathetic" record of momentary faith, the sort so abundant at the time in what was not at all to be able to happen. Moreover a name rings out of it which it is a kind of privilege to give again to the air—when one can do so with some approach to an association signified; so much did Charles Lowell's virtue and value and death represent at the season soon to come for those who stood within sight of them, and with such still unextinct emotion may the few of these who now survive turn to his admirably inspired kinsman's Harvard Commemoration Ode and find it infinitely and tenderly suffused with pride. Two gallantest nephews, particularly radiant to memory, had James Russell Lowell to commemorate.

> I sweep for them a pæan, but they wane
> Again and yet again
> Into a dirge and die away in pain.
> In these brave ranks I only see the gaps,
> Thinking of dear ones whom the dumb turf wraps,
> Dark to the triumph which they died to gain.

> Cabot has had news that Mr. Amos Lawrence of Boston is getting up a cavalry regiment (Wilky writes), and he has sent home to try for a commission as 2nd lieutenant. Now if we could only *both* get such a commission in that regiment you can judge yourself how desirable it would be. Perkins will probably have one in the Massachusetts 2nd and our orderly stands a pretty good chance of one in the 44th. This cavalry colonelcy will probably be for Cabot's cousin, Charles Lowell.
>
> There is a report that we start this week for Kinston, and if so we shall doubtless have a good little fight. We have just received 2 new Mass. Regiments, the 8th and the 51st. We have absolutely no time to ourselves; and what time we do have we want much more to give to lying down than to anything else. But try your best for me now, and I promise you to do *my* best wherever I am.

A homelier truth is in a few lines three weeks later.

> The men as a general thing think war a mean piece of business as it's carried on in this State; we march 20 or 30 miles and find the enemy entrenched in rifle-pits or hidden away in some out-of-the-way place; we send our artillery forward, and after a brisk skirmish ahead the foe is driven back into the woods, and we march on for 20 miles more to find the same luck. We were all on the last march praying for a fight, so that we might halt and throw off our knapsacks. I don't pretend I am eager to make friends with bullets, but at Whitehall, after marching some 20 miles, I was on this account really glad when I heard cannonading ahead and the column was halted and the fight began.

The details of this engagement are missing from the letter, but we found matter of interest in two or three other passages —one in particular recording a December day's march with 15,000 men, "not including artillerymen," 70 pieces of artillery and 1100 cavalry; which, "on account of obstructions on the roads," had achieved by night but seventeen miles and resulted in a bivouac "in 3 immense cotton-fields, one about as large as Easton's Pond at Newport."

> We began to see the camp fires of the advance brigade about 4 miles ahead of us, and I assure you those miles were soon got over. I think Willy's artistic eye would have enjoyed the sight—it seemed so as if the world were on fire. When we arrived on the field the stacks were made, the ranks broken and the men sent after rail fences, which fortunately abound in this region and are the only comfort we have at night. A long fire is made, the length of the stacks, and one rank is placed on one side of it and the other opposite. I try to make a picture you see, but scratch it out in despair. The fires made, we sit down and make our coffee in our tin dippers, and often is one of these pushed over by some careless wretch who hasn't noticed it on the coals or has been too tired to look. The coffee and the hard tack consumed we spread our rubber blankets and sleep as sound as any house in Christendom. At about 5 the fearful réveillé calls us to our feet, we make more coffee, drink it in a hurry, sling our knapsacks and spank down the road in one of Foster's regular old quicksteps.

Thrilling at our fireside of course were the particulars of the

Kinston engagement, and still more, doubtless, the happy freshness of the writer.

> At 8 A.M. we were on the road, and had hardly marched 3 miles when we knew by sounds ahead that the ball had opened. We were ordered up and deployed in an open field on the right of the road, where we remained some half an hour. Then we were moved some hundred yards further, but resumed our former position in another field. Here Foster came up to the Major, who was directly in the rear of our company and told him to advance our left wing to support Morrison's battery, which was about half a mile ahead. He also said he was pressing the Rebs hard and that they were retiring at every shell from our side. On we went, the left flank company taking the lead, and many a bullet and shell whizzed over our heads in that longest half-mile of my life. We seemed to be nearing the fun, for wounded men were being carried to the rear and dead ones lay on each side of us in the woods. We were taken into another field on the left of the road, and before us were deployed the 23rd Mass., who were firing in great style. First we were ordered to lie down, and then in 5 or 10 minutes ordered up again, when we charged down that field in a manner creditable to any Waterloo legion. I felt as if this moment was the greatest of my life and as if all the devils of the Inferno were my benighted system. We halted after having charged some 60 yards, when what should we see on our left, just out of the woods and stuck up on a rail, but a flag of truce, placing under its protecting wing some 50 or 60 poor cowering wretches who, in their zeal for recognition, not only pulled out all their pocket handkerchiefs, but in the case of one man spread out his white shirt-flaps and offered them pacifically to the winds. The most demonic shouts and yells were raised by the 23rd ahead of us at this sight, in which the 44th joined; while the regiments on our right, and that of the road, greeted in the same frightful manner 200 prisoners they had cut off from retreat by the bridge. So far I was alive and the thing had lasted perhaps 3 hours; all the enemy but the 200 just named had got away over the bridge to Kinston and our cavalry were in hot pursuit. I don't think Sergeant G. W. has ever known greater glee in all his born days. At about 3 P.M. we crossed the bridge and got into the town. All along the road from bridge to town Rebel equipments, guns and cartridge-boxes lay thick, and within the place dead men and horses thickened too. We were taken ahead through the town to support the New York 3rd Artillery beyond, where it was shelling the woods around and ridding the place for the night of any

troublesome wanderers. The Union pickets posted out ahead that night said the shrieks of women and children further on in the wood could be heard perfectly all night long, these unfortunates having taken refuge there from the threatened town. That night we lived like fighting-cocks—molasses, pork, butter, cheese and all sorts of different delicacies being foraged for and houses entered regardless of the commonest dues of life, and others set on fire to show Kinston was our own. She belonged to our army, and almost every man claimed a house. If I had only had your orders beforehand for trophies I could have satisfied you with anything named, from a gold watch to an old brickbat. This is the ugly part of war. A too victorious army soon goes down; but we luckily didn't have time for big demoralisation, as the next day in the afternoon we found ourselves some 17 miles away and bivouacking in a single prodigious cornfield.

To which I don't resist subjoining another characteristic passage from the same general scene as a wind-up to that small chapter of history.

The report has gained ground to-day that we leave to-morrow, and if so I suppose the next three months will be important ones in the history of the War. Four ironclads and a great many gunboats are in Beaufort Harbour; we have at present a force of 50,000 infantry, an immense artillery and upwards of 800 cavalry. Transports innumerable are filling up every spare inch of our harbour, and every man's pity and charity are exercised upon Charleston, Mobile or Wilmington. We are the only nine-months regiment going, a fact which to the sensitive is highly gratifying, showing Foster's evident high opinion of us. The expedition, I imagine, will be pretty interesting, for we shall have excitement enough without the fearful marches. To-day is Sunday, and I've been reading Hugo's account of Waterloo in Les Misérables and preparing my mind for something of the same sort at Wilmington. God grant the battle may do as much harm to the Rebels as Waterloo did to the French. If it does the fight will be worth the dreadful carnage it may involve, and the experience for the survivors an immense treasure. Men will fight forever if they are well treated. Give them little marching and keep the wounded away from them, and they'll do anything. I am very well and in capital spirits, though now and then rather blue about home. But only 5 months more and then heaven! General Foster has just issued an order permitting us to inscribe Goldsboro, Kinston and Whitehall on our banner.

On the discharge of the 44th after the term of nine months for which it had engaged and my brother's return home, he at once sought service again in the Massachusetts 54th, his connection with which I have already recorded, as well as his injuries in the assault on Fort Wagner fruitlessly made by that regiment in the summer of '63. He recovered with difficulty, but at last sufficiently, from his wounds (with one effect of which he had for the rest of his short life grievously to reckon), and made haste to rejoin his regiment in the field—to the promotion of my gathering a few more notes. From "off Graham's point, Tillapenny River, Headquarters 2nd Brigade," he writes in December '64.

> We started last night from the riflepits in the front of Deveaux Neck to cross the Tillapenny and make a reconnaissance on this side and try and get round the enemy's works. It is now half-past 10 A.M., and I have been trying to wash some of my mud off. We are all a sorry crowd of beggars—I don't look as I did the night we left home. I am much of the time mud from head to foot, and my spirit is getting muddled also. But I am in excellent condition as regards my wounds and astonish myself by my powers. I rode some 26 miles yesterday and walked some 3 in thick mud, but don't feel a bit the worse for it. We're only waiting here an hour or two to get a relief of horses, when we shall start again. We shan't have a fight of any kind to-day, but to-morrow expect to give them a little trouble at Pocotaligo. Colonel Hallowell commands this reconnaissance. We have only 4 regiments and a section of artillery from the 2nd Brigade with us. We heard some fine music from the Rebel lines yesterday. They have got a stunning band over there. Prisoners tell us it's a militia band from Georgia. Most all the troops in our front are militia composed of old men and boys, the flower of the chivalry being just now engaged with Sherman at Savannah. We hear very heavy firing in that direction this morning, and I guess the chivalry is getting the worst of it. The taking of Fort McAllister the other day was a splendid thing—we got 280 prisoners and made them go out and pick up the torpedoes round the fort. Sherman was up at Oguchee and Ossahaw yesterday on another consultation with Foster. We had called our whole army out the night before in front of our works to give him three cheers. This had a marvellous effect upon the Rebs. About 20 men came in the night into our lines, thinking we had got reinforcements and were going to advance. Later. A scout has just come in and

tells us the enemy are intrenched about 4 miles off, so that we *shall* have to-day a shindy of some kind. Our headquarters are now in a large house once owned by Judge Graham. The coloured troops are in high spirits and have done splendidly this campaign.

The high spirits of the coloured troops appear naturally to have been shared by their officers—"in the field, Tillapenny River," late at night on December 23rd, '64.

We have just received such bully news to comfort us that I can't help rising from my slumbers to drop you a line. A despatch just received tells us that Sherman has captured 150 guns, 250,000 dols. worth of cotton at Savannah, that Forrest is killed and routed by Rousseau, and that Thomas has walked into Hood and given him the worst kind of fits. I imagine the poor Rebel outposts in our front feel pretty blue to-night, for what with that and the thermometer at about zero I guess the night won't pass without robbing their army of some of its best and bravest. We suffer a good deal from the cold, but are now sitting round our camp fire in as good spirits as men could possibly be. A despatch received early this evening tells us to look out sharp for Hardee, but this latest news knocks that to a cocked hat, and we are only just remembering that that gentleman is round. My foot is bully.

As regards that impaired member, on which he was ever afterwards considerably to limp, he opines three days later, on Christmas evening, that "even in the palmy days of old it never *felt* better than now." And he goes on:

Though Savannah is taken I fear we shan't get much credit for having helped to take it. Yet night and day we have been at it hammer and tongs, and as we are away from the main army and somewhat isolated and cut off our work has been pretty hard. We have had only 1,200 effective men in our brigade, and out of that number have had regularly 400 on picket night and day, and the fatigue and extra guard duty have nearly used them up. Twice we have been attacked and both times held our own. Twice we attacked and once have been driven. The only prisoners we have captured on the whole expedition have been taken by this part of the column, and on the whole though we didn't march into Savannah I know you will give us a little credit for having hastened its downfall. Three prisoners that we took the other night slept at our Hdqrs, and we had a good long talk with them. We could get out of them nothing at all that helps from a military point of view, but their stories about the Confederacy were most hopeless. They were 3 officers and gentlemen of a crack S.C. cavalry company which has been used during the War simply to guard this coast, and their language and state of mind were those of the true Southern chevalier. They confessed to a great scare on finding themselves hemmed in by coloured troops, and all agree that the niggers are the worst enemies they have had to face. On Thursday we turned them over to the Provost-Marshal at Deveaux Neck, who took them to Gen'l Hatch. The General had got our despatch announcing we could get nothing at all out of them, and he came down on them most ruthlessly and told them to draw lots, as one would have to swing before night. He told them he had got the affidavit of an escaped Union prisoner, a man captured at Honey Hill and who had come into our lines the day previous, to the effect that he had witnessed the hanging of a negro soldier belonging to the 26th U.S.C.T., and that he had determined one of them should answer for it. Two seemed very much moved, but the third, Lee by name (cousin of Gen'l Stephen Lee of the cavalry), said he knew nothing about it, but if it was so, so it might be. The other two were taken from each other and Gen'l Hatch managed to draw a good deal of information from them about our position, that is the force and nature of the enemy and works in our front. Lee refused to the last to answer any question whatever, and they all 3 now await at Hilton Head the issue of the law. The hanging of the negro seems a perfectly ascertained fact—he was hung by the 48th Georgia Infty, and the story has naturally much stirred up our coloured troops. If Hardee should decide to come down on us I believe he would get the worst of it, and only hope now that our men won't take a prisoner alive. They certainly make a great mistake at Washington in not attending to these little matters, and I am sure the moral effect of an order from the President announcing that such things have happened, and that the coloured troops have taken them thoroughly to heart, would be greater on the Rebels than any physical blow we can deal them.

When I read again, "in the field before Pocotaligo," toward the middle of January '65, that "Sherman leaves to-night from Beaufort with Logan's Corps to cross Beaufort Ferry and come up on our right flank and push on to Pocotaligo bridge," the stir as from great things rises again for me, wraps about Sherman's name as with the huge hum that then surrounded it, and in short makes me give the passage such honour as I may. "We are waiting anxiously for the sound of his musketry announcing him." I was never in my life to wait for any such sound, but *how* at that juncture I hung about with privileged Wilky! "We all propose at Hdqrs to take our stores out and ride up to the bank of the river and watch the fight on the other side. We are praying to be relieved here—our men are dying for want of clothing; and when we see Morris Island again we shall utterly rejoice." He writes three days later from headquarters established in a plantation the name of which, as well as that of the stream, of whatever magnitude, that they had crossed to reach it, happens to be marked by an illegibility quite unprecedented in his splendid script—to the effect of a still intenser evocation (as was then to be felt at any rate) of all the bignesses involved. "Sherman's whole army is in our front, and they expect to move on Charleston at any moment." Sherman's whole army!—it affected me from afar off as a vast epic vision. The old vibration lives again, but with it also that of the smaller and nearer, the more intimate notes—such for instance as: "I shall go up to the 20th Corps to-morrow and try for a sight of Billy Perkins and Sam Storrow in the 2nd Mass." Into which I somehow read, under the touch of a ghostly hand no more "weirdly" laid than *that*, more volumes than I can the least account for or than I have doubtless any business to.

My visionary yearning must however, I think, have drawn most to feed on from the first of a series of missives dated from Headquarters, Department of the South, Hilton Head S.C., this particular one of the middle of February. "I write in a great hurry to tell you I have been placed on General Gillmore's staff as A.D.C. It is just the very thing for my foot under present circumstances, and I consider myself most fortunate. I greatly like the General, who is most kind and genial and very considerate. My duties will be principally the carrying of orders to Savannah, Morris Island, Fortress Monroe, Combalee (?) Florida, and the General's correspondence. Charleston is ours," he goes on two days later: "it surrendered to a negro regiment yesterday at 9 A.M. We have just come up from Sumter, where we have hoisted the American flag. We were lying off Bull's Bay yesterday noon waiting for this when the General saw through his glass the stars and stripes suddenly flown from the town hall. We immediately steamed up to

Sumter and ran up the colours there. Old Gillmore was in fine feather and I am in consummate joy." The joy nevertheless, I may add, doesn't prevent the remark after a couple of days more that "Charleston isn't on the whole such a very great material victory; in fact the capture of the place is of value only in that its moral effect tends to strengthen the Union cause." After which he proceeds:

> Governor Aiken of S.C. came up to Hdqrs to-day to call on the Gen'l, and they had a long talk. He is a "gradual Emancipationist" and says the worst of the President's acts was his sweeping Proclamation. Before that every one in this State was ready to come back on the gradual system, and would have done so if Lincoln's act hadn't driven them to madness. This is all fine talk, but there is nothing in it. They had at least 5 months' warning and could have in that time perfectly returned within the fold; in fact the strong Abolitionists of the North were afraid the President had made the thing but too easy for them and that they would get ahead of us and themselves emancipate. This poor gentleman is simple crazy and weakminded. Between Davis and us he is puzzled beyond measure, and doesn't know what line to take. One thing though troubled him most, namely the ingratitude of the negro. He can't conceive how the creatures he has treated with such extraordinary kindness and taken such care of should all be willing to leave him. He says he was the first man in the South to introduce religion among the blacks and that his plantation of 600 of them was a model of civilisation and peace. Just think of this immense slaveholder telling me as I drove him home that the coat he had on had been turned three times and his pantaloons the only ones he possessed. He stated this so simply and touchingly that I couldn't help offering him a pair of mine—which he refused, however. There are some 10,000 people in the town, mostly women and negroes, and it's tremendously ravaged by our shell, about which they have naturally lied from beginning to end.

"Bob has just come down from Charleston," he writes in March—"he has been commissioned captain in the 103rd U.S.C.T. I am sorry he has left his regiment, still he seemed bent on doing so and offers all kinds of reasons for it. He may judge rightly, but I fear he's hasty;" and indeed this might appear from a glimpse of our younger brother at his ease given by him in a letter of some days before, written at two o'clock in the morning and recording a day spent in a somewhat arduously performed visit to Charleston. "I drove out to the entrenchments to-day to see B., and found him with Hartwell (R. J.'s colonel) smoking their long pipes on the verandah of a neat country cottage with a beautiful garden in front of them and the birds chirping and rambling around. Bob looks remarkably well and seemed very nice indeed. He speaks very highly of Hartwell, and the latter the same of him. They seemed settled in remarkable comfort at Charleston and to be taking life easy after their 180 miles march through South Carolina." He mentions further that his visit to the captured city, begun the previous day, had been made in interesting conditions; there is in fact matter for quotation throughout the letter, the last of the small group from which I shall borrow. He had, with his general, accompanied a "large Senatorial delegation from Washington and shown them round the place." He records the delegation's "delight" in what they saw; how "a large crowd of young ladies" were of the party, so that the Senatorial presences were "somewhat relieved and lightened to the members of the staff;" and also that they all went over to Forts Sumter and Moultrie and the adjacent works. The pleasure of the whole company in the scene of desolation thus presented is one of those ingenuous historic strokes that the time-spirit, after a sufficient interval, permits itself to smile at—and is not the only such, it may be noted, in the sincere young statement.

> To-morrow they go to Savannah, returning here in the evening, when there is to be a grand reception for them at Hdqrs. We expect Gen'l Robert Anderson (the loyalist commandant at Sumter when originally fired upon) by the next steamer, with Gideon Welles (secretary of the Navy) and a number of other notables from Washington. Anderson is going to raise the old flag on Sumter, and of course there will be a great shindy here—I only wish you were with us to join in it. I never go to Sumter without the deepest exhilaration—so many scenes come to my mind. It's the centre of the nest, and for one to *be* there is to feel that the whole game is up. These people have always insisted that there the last gun should be fired. But the suffering and desolation of this land

> is the worst feature of the whole thing. If you could see what they are reduced to you couldn't help being touched. The best people are in utter penury; they look like the poorest of the poor and they talk like them also. They are deeply demoralised, in fact degraded. Charleston is more forsaken and stricken than I can describe; it reminds me when I go through the streets of some old doomed city on which the wrath of God has rested from far back, and if it ever revives will do so simply through the infinite mercy and charity of the North. But for this generation at least the inhabitants are done for. Can't H. come down and pay us a visit of 2 or 3 weeks? I can get him a War Dept. pass approved by General Gillmore.

H. knew and well remembers the pang of his inability to accept this invitation, to the value of which for emphasis of tragic life on the scene of the great drama the next passage adds a touch. Mrs. William Young, the lady alluded to, was a friend we had known almost only on the European stage and amid the bright associations of Paris in particular. Whom did we suppose he had met on the arrival of a steamer from the North but this more or less distracted acquaintance of other days?—who had come down "to try and get her stepmother into our lines and take her home. She is accompanied by a friend from New York, and expects to succeed in her undertaking. I hardly think she will, however, as her mother is 90 miles out of our lines and a very old woman. We have sent a negro out to give her Mrs. Young's news, but how can this poor old thing travel such a distance on foot and sleep in the swamp besides? It's an absurd idea, but I shall do everything in my power to facilitate it." Of what further befell I gather no account; but I remember how a later time was to cause me to remark on the manner in which even dire tragedy may lapse, in the individual life, and leave no trace on the ground it has ravaged—none at least apparent unless pushingly searched for. The last thing to infer from appearances, on much subsequent renewal of contact with Mrs. Young in Paris again, was that this tension of a reach forth across great war-wasted and swamp-smothered spaces for recovery of an aged and half-starved pedestrian female relative counted for her as a chapter of experience: the experience of Paris dressmakers and other like matters had so revived and supervened. But let me add that I speak here of mere appearances, and have ever inclined to the more ironic and more complicating vision of them. It would doubtless have been too simple for wonder that our elegant friend should have lived, as it were, under the cloud of reminiscence—and wonder had always somewhere to come in.

XII

IT HAD been, however, neither at Newport nor at Cambridge —the Cambridge at least of that single year—that the plot began most to thicken for me: I figure it as a sudden stride into conditions of a sort to minister and inspire much more, all round, that we early in 1864 migrated, as a family, to Boston, and that I now seem to see the scene of our existence there for a couple of years packed with drama of a finer consistency than any I had yet tasted. We settled for the interesting time in Ashburton Place—the "sympathetic" old house we occupied, one of a pair of tallish brick fronts based, as to its ground floor, upon the dignity of time-darkened granite, was lately swept away in the interest of I know not what grander cause; and when I wish to think of such intercourse as I have enjoyed with the good city at its closest and, as who should say its kindest, though this comes doubtless but to saying at its freshest, I live over again the story of that sojourn, a period bristling, while I recover my sense of it, with an unprecedented number of simultaneous particulars. To stick, as I can only do, to the point from which my own young outlook worked, the things going on for me so tremendously all at once were in the first place the last impressions of the War, a whole social relation to it crowding upon us there as for many reasons, all of the best, it couldn't have done elsewhere; and then, more personally speaking, the prodigious little assurance I found myself gathering as from one day to another that fortune had in store some response to my deeply reserved but quite unabashed design of becoming as "literary" as might be. It was as if, our whole new medium of existence aiding, I had begun to see much further into the question of how that end was gained. The vision, quickened by a wealth, a great mixture, of new appearances, became such a throbbing affair that my memory of the time from the spring of '64 to the autumn of '66 moves as through an apartment hung with garlands and lights—where I have but to breathe for an instant on the flowers again to see them flush with colour, and but tenderly to snuff the candles to see them twinkle afresh. Things happened, and happened repeatedly, the mere brush or side-wind of which was the stir of life; and the fact that I see, when I consider, how it was mostly the mere side-wind I got, doesn't draw from the picture a shade of its virtue. I literally, and under whatever felt restriction of my power to knock about, formed independent relations—several; and two or three of them, as I then thought, of the very most momentous. I may not attempt just here to go far into these, save for the exception of the easiest to treat, which I also, by good fortune, win back as by no means the least absorbing—the beautiful, the entrancing presumption that I should have but to write with sufficient difficulty and sufficient felicity to get once for all (that was the point) into the incredibility of print. I see before me, in the rich, the many-hued light of my room that overhung dear Ashburton Place from our third floor, the very greenbacks, to the total value of twelve dollars, into which I had changed the cheque representing my first earned wage. I had earned it, I couldn't but feel, with fabulous felicity: a circumstance so strangely mixed with the fact that literary composition of a high order had, at that very table where the greenbacks were spread out, quite viciously declined, and with the air of its being also once for all, to "come" on any save its own essential terms, which it seemed to distinguish in the most invidious manner conceivable from mine. It was to insist through all my course on this distinction, and sordid gain thereby never again to seem so easy as in that prime handling of my fee. Other guerdons, of the same queer, the same often rather greasy, complexion followed; for what had I done, to the accompaniment of a thrill the most ineffable, an agitation that, as I recapture it, affects me as never exceeded in all my life for fineness, but go one beautiful morning out to Shady Hill at Cambridge and there drink to the lees the offered cup of editorial sweetness?—none ever again to be more delicately mixed. I had addressed in trembling hope my first fond attempt at literary criticism to Charles Eliot Norton, who had lately, and with the highest, brightest competence, come to the rescue of the North American Review, submerged in a stale tradition and gasping for life, and he had not only published it in his very next number—the interval for me of breathless brevity—but had expressed the liveliest further hospitality, the gage of which was thus at once his welcome to me at home. I was to grow fond of regarding as a positive consecration to letters that half-hour in the long library at Shady Hill, where the winter sunshine touched serene bookshelves and arrayed pictures, the whole embrowned composition of objects in my view, with I knew not what golden light of promise, what assurance of things to come: there was to be nothing exactly like it later on—the conditions of perfect rightness for a certain fresh felicity, certain decisive pressures of the spring, *can* occur, it would seem, but once. This was on the other hand the beginning of so many intentions that it mattered little if the particular occasion was not repeated; for what did I do again and again, through all the years, but handle in plenty what I might have called the small change of it?

I despair, however, as I look back, of rendering the *fusions* in that much-mixed little time, every feature of which had something of the quality and interest of every other, and the more salient, the more "epoch-making"—I apply with complacency the portentous term—to drape themselves romantically in the purple folds of the whole. I think it must have been the sense of the various climaxes, the enjoyed, because so long postponed, revenges of the War, that lifted the moment in the largest embrace: the general consciousness was of such big things at last in sight, the huge national emergence, the widening assurance, however overdarkened, it is true, by the vast black cost of what General Grant (no light-handed artist he!) was doing for us. He was at all events working to an end, and something strange and immense, even like the light of a new day rising above a definite rim, shot its rays through the chinks of the immediate, the high-piled screen of sacrifice behind which he wrought. I fail to seize again, to my wonder, the particular scene of our acclamation of Lee's surrender, but I feel in the air the exhalation of our relief, which mingled, near and far, with the breath of the springtime itself and positively seemed to become over the land, over the world at large in fact, an element of reviving Nature. Sensible again are certain other sharpest vibrations then communicated from the public consciousness: Ashburton Place resounds for me with a wild cry, rocks as from a convulsed breast, on that early morning of our news of Lincoln's death by murder; and, in a different order, but also darkening the early day, there associates itself with my cherished chamber of application the fact that of a sudden, and while we were always and as much as ever awaiting him, Hawthorne was dead. What I have called the fusion strikes me as indeed beyond any rendering when I think of the peculiar assault on my private consciousness of *that* news: I sit once more, half-dressed, late of a summer morning and in a bedimmed light which is somehow at once that of dear old green American shutters drawn to against openest windows and that of a moral shadow projected as with violence—I sit on my belated bed, I say, and yield to the pang that made me positively and loyally cry. I didn't rise early in those days of scant ease—I now even ask myself how sometimes I rose at all; which ungrudged license withal, I thus make out, was not less blessedly effective in the harmony I glance at than several showier facts. To tell at all adequately why the pang was fine would nevertheless too closely involve my going back, as we have learned to say, on the whole rich interpenetration. I fondly felt it in those days invaluable that I had during certain last and otherwise rather blank months at Newport taken in for the first time and at one straight draught the full sweet sense of our one fine romancer's work—for sweet it then above all seemed to me; and I remember well how, while the process day after day drew itself admirably out, I found the actual exquisite taste of it, the strain of the revelation, justify up to the notch whatever had been weak in my delay. This prolonged hanging off from true knowledge had been the more odd, so that I couldn't have explained it, I felt, through the fact that The Wonder-Book and Twice-Told Tales had helped to enchant our childhood; the consequence at any rate seemed happy, since without it, very measurably, the sudden sense of recognition would have been less uplifting a wave. The joy of the recognition was to know at the time no lapse—was in fact through the years never to know one, and this by some rare action of a principle or a sentiment, I scarce know whether to call it a clinging consistency or a singular silliness, that placed the Seven Gables, the Blithedale Romance and the story of Donatello and Miriam (the accepted title of which I dislike to use, not the "marble" but very particularly the human Faun being throughout in question) somewhere on a shelf unvisited by harsh inquiry. The feeling had perhaps at the time been marked by presumption, by a touch of the fatuity of patronage; yet wasn't well-nigh the best charm of a relation with the works just named in the impulse, known from the first, somehow to stand in *between* them and harsh inquiry? If I had asked myself what I meant by that term, at which freedom of appreciation, in fact of intelligence, might have looked askance, I hope I should have found a sufficient answer in the mere plea of a sort of *bêtise* of tenderness. I recall how once, in the air of Rome at a time ever so long subsequent, a friend and countryman now no more, who had spent most of his life in Italy and who remains for me, with his accomplishment, his distinction, his extraordinary play of mind and his too early and too tragic death, the clearest case of "cosmopolitan culture" I was to have known, exclaimed with surprise on my happening to speak as from an ancient fondness for Hawthorne's treatment of the Roman scene: "Why, can you read *that* thing, and *here*?—to me it means nothing at all!" I remember well that under the breath of this disallowance of any possibility of association, and quite most of such a one as I had from far back positively cultivated, the gentle perforated book tumbled before me from its shelf very much as old Polonius, at the thrust of Hamlet's sword, must have collapsed behind the pictured arras. Of course I might have picked it up and brushed it off, but I seem to feel again that I didn't so much as want to, lost as I could only have been in the sense that the note of harsh inquiry, or in other words of the very stroke I had anciently wished to avert, *there* fell straight upon my ear. It represented everything I had so early known we must have none of; though there was interest galore at the same time (as there almost always is in lively oppositions of sensibility, with the sharpness of each, its special exclusions, well exhibited), in an "American" measure that could so reject our beautiful genius and in a Roman, as it were, that could so little see he had done anything for Rome. H. B. Brewster in truth, literary master of three tongues at least, was scarce American at all; homely superstitions had no hold on him; he was French, Italian, above all perhaps German; and there would have been small use, even had there been any importance, in my trying to tell him for instance why it had particularly been, in the gentle time, that I had settled once for all to take our author's case as simply exquisite and not budge from that taking. Which indeed scarce bears telling now, with matters of relative (if *but* of relative!) urgence on hand—consisting as it mainly did in the fact that his work was all charged with a *tone*, a full and rare tone of prose, and that this made for it an extraordinary value in an air in which absolutely nobody's else was or has shown since any aptitude for being. And the tone had been, in its beauty—for me at least—ever so appreciably American; which proved to what a use American matter could be put by an American hand: a consummation involving, it appeared, the happiest moral. For the moral was that an American could be an artist, one of the finest, without "going outside" about it, as I liked to say; quite in fact as if Hawthorne had become one just by being American *enough*, by the felicity of how the artist in him missed nothing, suspected nothing, that the ambient air didn't affect him as containing. Thus he was at once so clear and so entire—clear without thinness, for he might have seemed underfed, it was his danger; and entire without heterogeneity, which might, with less luck and to the discredit of our sufficing manners, have had to be his help. These remarks, as I say, were those I couldn't, or at any rate didn't, make to my Roman critic; if only because I was so held by the other case he offered me—that of a culture for which, in the dense medium around us, Miriam and Donatello and their friends hadn't the virtue that shines or pushes through. I tried to feel that this *constatation* left me musing—and perhaps in truth it did; though doubtless if my attachment to the arranger of those images had involved, to repeat, my not budging, my meditation, whatever it was, respected that condition.

It has renewed itself, however, but too much on this spot, and the scene viewed from Ashburton Place claims at the best more filling in than I can give it. Any illustration of anything worth illustrating has beauty, to my vision, largely by its developments; and developments, alas, are the whole flowering of the plant, while what really meets such attention as one may hope to beguile is at the best but a plucked and tossed sprig or two. That my elder brother was during these months away with Professor Agassiz, a member of the party recruited by that great naturalist for a prolonged exploration of Brazil, is one of the few blooms, I see, that I must content myself with detaching—the main sense of it being for myself, no doubt, that his absence (and he had never been at anything like such a distance from us,) left me the more exposed, and thereby the more responsive, to contact with impressions that had to learn to suffice for me in their uncorrected, when not still more in their inspiringly emphasised, state. The main sense for William himself is recorded in a series of letters from him addressed to us at home and for which, against my hope, these pages succeed in affording no space—they are to have ampler presentation; but the arrival of which at irregular intervals for the greater part of a year comes back to me as perhaps a fuller enrichment of my consciousness than it owed for the time to any other single source. We all still hung so together that this replete organ could yet go on helping itself, with whatever awkwardness, from the conception or projection of others of a like *general* strain, such as those of one's brothers might appear; thanks to which constant hum of borrowed experience, in addition to the quicker play of whatever could pass as more honestly earned, my stage of life knew no drop of the curtain. I literally came and went, I had never practised such coming and going; I went in particular, during summer weeks, and even if carrying my general difficulty with me, to the White Mountains of New Hampshire, with some repetition, and again and again back to Newport, on visits to John La Farge and to the Edmund Tweedys (*their* house almost a second summer home to us;) to say nothing of winter attempts, a little weak, but still more or less achieved, upon New York—which city was rapidly taking on the capital quality, the large worldly sense that dear old London and dear old Paris, with other matters in hand for them as time went on, the time they were "biding" for me, indulgently didn't grudge it. The matters they had in hand wandered indeed as stray vague airs across to us—this I think I have noted; but Boston itself could easily rule, in default even of New York, when to "go," in particular, was an act of such easy virtue. To go from Ashburton Place was to go verily round the corner not less than further afield; to go to the Athenæum, to the Museum, to a certain door of importances, in fact of immensities, defiant of vulgar notation, in Charles Street, at the opposite end from Beacon. The fruit of these mixed proceedings I found abundant at the time, and

I think quite inveterately sweet, but to gather it in again now—by which I mean set it forth as a banquet for imaginations already provided—would be to presume too far; not least indeed even on my own cultivated art of exhibition. The fruit of golden youth is all and always golden—it touches to gold what it gathers; this was so the essence of the case that in the first place everything was in some degree an adventure, and in the second any differences of degree guiding my selection would be imperceptible at this end of time to the cold eye of criticism. Not least moreover in the third place the very terms would fail, under whatever ingenuity, for my really justifying so bland an account of the period at large. Do I speak of it as a thumping sum but to show it in the small change, the handful of separate copper and silver coin, the scattered occasions reduced to their individual cash value, that, spread upon the table as a treasure of reminiscence, might only excite derision? *Why* was "staying at Newport" so absurdly, insistently romantic, romantic out of all proportion, as we say—why unless I can truly tell in proportion to what it became so? It consisted often in my "sitting" to John La Farge, within his own precincts and in the open air of attenuated summer days, and lounging thereby just passive to the surge of culture that broke upon me in waves the most desultory and disjointed, it was true, but to an absolute effect of unceasingly scented spray. Particular hours and old (that is young!) ineffable reactions come back to me; it's like putting one's ear, doctor-fashion, to the breast of time—or say as the subtle savage puts his to the ground—and catching at its start some vibratory hum that has been going on more or less for the fifty years since. Newport, the barren isle of our return from Europe, had thus become—and at no such great expense if the shock of public affairs, everywhere making interests start to their feet, be counted out of the process—a source of fifty suggestions to me; which it would have been much less, however, I hasten to add, if the call of La Farge hadn't worked in with our other most standing attraction, and this in turn hadn't practically been part of the positive affluence of certain elements of spectacle. Why again I should have been able to see the pictorial so freely suggested, that pictorial which was ever for me the dramatic, the social, the effectively human aspect, would be doubtless a baffling inquiry in presence of the queer and dear old phenomena themselves; those that, taken together, may be described at the best, I suppose, rather as a much-mixed grope or halting struggle, call it even a competitive scramble, toward the larger, the ideal elegance, the traditional forms of good society in possession, than as a presentation of great noble assurances.

Spectacle in any case broke out, spectacle accumulated, by our then measure, many thicknesses deep, flushing in the sovereign light, as one felt it, of the waning Rhode Island afternoons of August and September with the most "evolved" material civilisation our American world could then show; the vividest note of this in those years, unconscious, even to an artless innocence, of the wider wings still to spread, being the long daily *corso* or processional drive (with cavaliers and amazons not otherwise than conveniently intermixed,) which, with a different direction for different days, offered doubtless as good an example of that gregarious exercise at any cost distinguishing "fashionable life" as was anywhere on the globe to be observed. The price paid for the sticking together was what emphasised, I mean, the wondrous resolve to stick, however scant and narrow and unadjusted for processional effect the various fields of evolution. The variety moreover was short, just as the incongruities of composition in the yearning array were marked; but the tender grace of old sunset hours, the happier breadth of old shining sands under favour of friendly tides, the glitter *quand même* of "caparisoned" animals, appointed vehicles and approved charioteers, to say nothing of the other and more freely exchanged and interrelated brightnesses then at play (in the softer ease of women, the more moustachio'd swagger of men, the braver bonhomie of the social aspect at large), melted together for fond fancy into a tone, a rhythm, a representational virtue charged, as to the amenities, with authority. The amenities thus sought their occasion to multiply even to the sound of far cannonades, and I well remember at once reflecting, in such maturity as I could muster, that the luckier half of a nation able to carry a huge war-burden without sacrifice of amusement might well overcome the fraction that had to feed but on shrinkage and privation; at the same time that the so sad and handsome face of the most frequent of our hostesses, Mary Temple the elder as she had been, now the apt image of a stern priestess of the public altar, was to leave with me for the years to come the grand expression and tragic irony of its revulsion from those who, offering us some high entertainment during days of particular tension, could fiddle, as she scathingly said, while Rome was burning. Blest again the state of youth which could appreciate that admirable look and preserve it for illustration of one of the forms of ancient piety lost to us, and yet at the same time stow away as part of the poetry of the general drama just the luxury and pride, overhanging summer seas and projecting into summer nights great shafts of light and sound, that prompted the noble scorn. The "round of pleasure" all this with a grand good conscience of course—for it always in the like case has that, had it at least when arranging performances, dramatic and musical, at ever so much a ticket, under the advantage of rare amateur talent, in aid of the great Sanitary Commission that walked in the footsteps and renewed in various forms the example of Florence Nightingale; these exhibitions taking place indeed more particularly in the tributary cities, New York, Philadelphia, Boston (we were then shut up to those,) but with the shining stars marked for triumphant appearance announced in advance on the Newport scene and glittering there as beauties, as élégantes, as vocalists, as heroines of European legend. Hadn't there broken upon us, under public stress, a refluent wave from Paris, the mid-Empire Paris of the highest pitch, which was to raise our social water-mark to a point unprecedented and there strikingly leave it? We were learning new lessons in every branch—that was the sense of the so immensely quickened general pace; and though my examples may seem rather spectral I like to believe this bigger breathing of the freshness of the future to have been what the collective rumble and shimmer of the whole business most meant. It exhaled an artless confidence which yet momently increased; it had no great sense of a direction, but gratefully took any of which the least hint was given, gathering up by the way and after the fact whatever account of itself a vague voice might strike off. There were times when the account of itself as flooding Lawton's Valley for afternoon tea was doubtless what it would most comfortably have welcomed—Lawton's Valley, at a good drive's length from the seaward quarter, being the scene of villeggiatura of the Boston muse, as it were, and the Boston muse having in those after all battle-haunted seasons an authority and a finish of accent beyond any other Tyrtaean strain. The New York and perhaps still more the Philadelphia of the time fumbled more helplessly, even if aspiringly, with the Boston evidences in general, I think, than they were to be reduced to doing later on; and by the happy pretext, certainly, that these superior signs had then a bravery they were not perhaps on their own side indefinitely to keep up.

They rustled, with the other leafage of the umbrageous grove, in the summer airs that hung over the long tea-tables; afternoon tea was itself but a new and romantic possibility, with the lesson of it gratefully learnt at hands that dispensed, with the tea and sugar and in the charmingest voice perhaps then to be heard among us, a tone of talk that New York took for exotic and inimitable, yet all the more felt "good," much better than it might if left *all* to itself, for thus flocking in every sort of conveyance to listen to. The Valley was deep, winding and pastoral—or at least looks so now to my attached vision; the infancy of a finer self-consciousness seemed cradled there; the inconsequent vehicles fraternised, the dim, the more dejected, with the burnished and upstanding; so that I may really perhaps take most for the note of the hour the first tremor of the sense on the part of fashion that, if it could, as it already more or less suspected, get its thinking and reading and writing, almost everything in fact but its arithmetic, a bit dingily, but just by that sign cleverly, done for it, so occasion seemed easy, after all, for a nearer view, without responsibility, of the odd performers of the service. When these last were not literally all Bostonians they were New Yorkers who might have been mistaken for such—never indeed by Bostonians themselves, but only by other New Yorkers, the rich and guileless; so the effect as of a vague tribute to culture the most authentic (if I speak not too portentously) was left over for the aftertaste of simple and subtle alike. Those were comparatively thin seasons, I recognise, in the so ample career of Mrs. Howe, mistress of the Valley and wife of the eminent, the militant Phil-Hellene, Dr. S. G. of the honoured name, who reached back to the Byronic time and had dedicated his own later to still more distinguished liberating work on behalf of deaf mutes; for if she was thus the most attuned of interlocutors, most urbane of disputants, most insidious of wits, even before her gathered fame as Julia Ward and the established fortune of her elegant Battle-Hymn, she was perhaps to have served the State scarce better through final organised activities and shining optimisms and great lucky lyric hits than by having in her vale of heterogeneous hospitality undermined the blank assurance of her thicker contingent—after all too but to an *amusing* vague unrest—and thereby scattered the first rare seed of new assimilations. I am moved to add that, by the old terminology, the Avenue might have been figured, in the connection, as descending into the glen to meet the Point—which, save for a very small number of the rarest representatives of the latter, it could meet nowhere else. The difficulty was that of an encounter of birds and fishes; the two tribes were native to elements as opposed as air and water, the Avenue essentially nothing if not exalted on wheels or otherwise expertly mounted, and the Point hopelessly pedestrian and unequipped with stables, so that the very levels at which they materially moved were but upper and lower, dreadfully lower, parallels. And indeed the way to see the Point—which, without playing on the word, naturally became our highest law—was *at* the Point, where it appeared to much higher advantage than in its trudge through the purple haze or golden dust of supercilious parades. Of the advantage to which it did so appear, off in its own more languorous climate and on its own ground, we fairly cultivated a conviction, rejoicing by that aid very much as in certain old French towns it was possible to distinguish invidiously the Ville from the Cité. The Point was our *cité*, the primal aboriginal Newport—which, striking us on a first acquaintance as not other than dilapidated, might well have been "restored" quite as M. Viollet-le-Duc was even then restoring Carcassonne; and this all the more because our elder Newport, the only seat of history, had a dismantled grassy fort or archaic citadel that dozed over the waterside and that might (though I do take the vision, at close quarters, for horrible) be smartly waked up. The waterside, which was that of the inner bay, the ample reach toward Providence, so much more susceptible of quality than the extravagant open sea, the "old houses," the old elms, the old Quaker faces at the small-paned old windows, the appointedness of the scene for the literary and artistic people, who, by our fond constructive theory, lodged and boarded with the Quakers, always thrifty these, for the sake of all the sweetness and quaintness, for the sake above all somehow of *our* hungry felicity of view, by which I mean mine and that of a trusty friend or two, T. S. Perry in especial—those attributes, meeting a want, as the phrase is, of the decent imagination, made us perhaps overdramatise the sphere of the clever people, but made them at least also, when they unmistakably hovered, affect us as truly the finest touches in the picture. For they were in their way ironic about the rest, and that was a tremendous lift in face of an Avenue that not only, as one could see at a glance, had no irony, but hadn't yet risen, the magazines and the Point aiding, to so much as a suspicion of the effect, familiar to later generations, with which the word can conversationally come in. Oh the old clever people, with their difference of shade from that of the clever old ones—some few of these to have been discerned, no doubt, as of Avenue position: I read back into their various presences I know not what queer little functional value the exercise and privilege of which, uncontested, uncontrasted (save with the absence of everything but stables) represents a felicity for the individual that is lost to our age. It could count as functional then, it could count as felicitous, to have been reabsorbed into Boston, or to propose to absorb even, for the first time, New York, under cover of the mantle, the old artistic draped cloak, that had almost in each case trailed round in Florence, in Rome, in Venice, in conversations with Landor, in pencilled commemoration, a little niggling possibly but withal so sincere, of the "haunts" of Dante, in a general claim of having known the Brownings (ah "the Brownings" of those days!) in a disposition to arrange readings of these and the most oddly associated other poets about the great bleak parlours of the hotels. I despair, however, of any really right register of the art with which the cité ingratiated itself with me in this character of a vivid missionary Bohemia; I met it of course more than half way, as I met everything in the faintest degree ingratiating, even suggesting to it with an art of my own that it should become so—though in this matter I rather missed, I fear, a happy conversion, as if the authenticity were there but my sort of personal dash too absent.

I appear to myself none the less to have had dash for approaches to a confidence more largely seated; since I recall how, having commenced critic under Charles Norton's weighty protection, I was to find myself, on all but the very morrow, invited to the high glory, as I felt it, of aiding to launch, though on the obscurer side of the enterprise, a weekly journal which, putting forth its first leaves in the summer of '65 and under the highest auspices, was soon to enjoy a fortune and achieve an authority and a dignity of which neither newspaper nor critical review among us had hitherto so much as hinted the possibility. The New York Nation had from the first, to the enlivening of several persons consciously and ruefully astray in our desert, made no secret of a literary leaning; and indeed its few foremost months shine most for me in the light of their bestowal of one of the longest and happiest friendships of my life, a relation with Edwin Lawrence Godkin, the Nation incarnate as he was to become, which bore fruit of affection for years after it had ceased to involve the comparatively poorer exercise. Godkin's paper, Godkin's occasional presence and interesting history and vivid ability and, above all, admirably aggressive and ironic editorial humour, of a quality and authority new in the air of a journalism that had meant for the most part the heavy hand alone, these things, with the sudden sweet discovery that I might for my own part acceptedly stammer a style, are so many shades and shifting tints in the positive historic iridescence that flings itself for my memory, as I have noted, over the "period" of Ashburton Place. Wherever I dip, again, I pull out a plum from under the tooth of time—this at least so to my own rapt sense that had I more space I might pull both freely and at a venture. The strongest savour of the feast—with the fumes of a feast it comes back—was, I need scarce once more insist, the very taste of the War as ending and ended; through which blessing, more and more, the quantity of military life or at least the images of military experience seemed all about us, quite paradoxically, to grow greater. This I take to have been a result, first of the impending, and then of the effective, break-up of the vast veteran Army, swamping much of the scene as with the flow of a monster tide and bringing literally home to us, in bronzed, matured faces and even more in bronzed, matured characters, above all in the absolutely acquired and stored resource of overwhelming reference, reference usually of most substance the less it was immediately explicit, the more in fact it was faded and jaded to indifference, what was meant by having patiently served. The very smell of having so served was somehow, at least to my supersensitive nostril, in the larger and cooler air, where it might have been an emanation, the most masculine, the most communicative as to associated far-off things (according to the nature, ever, of elements vaguely exhaled), from the operation of the general huge gesture of relief—from worn toggery put off, from old army-cloth and other fittings at a discount, from swordbelts and buckles, from a myriad saturated articles now not even lying about but brushed away with an effect upon the passing breeze and all relegated to the dim state of some mere theoretic commemorative panoply that was never in the event to be objectively disposed. The generalisation grew richly or, as it were, quite adorably familiar, that life was ever so handsomely reinforced, and manners, not to say manner at large, refreshed, and personal aspects and types accented, and categories multiplied (no category, for the dreaming painter of things, could our scene afford not to grab at on the chance), just by the fact of the discharge upon society of such an amount of out-of-the-way experience, as it might roughly be termed—such a quantity and variety of possession and assimilation of unprecedented history. It had been unprecedented at least among ourselves, we had had it in our own highly original conditions—or "they," to be more exact, had had it admirably in theirs; and I think I was never to know a case in which his having been directly touched by it, or, in a word, having consistently "soldiered," learnt all about it and exhausted it, wasn't to count all the while on behalf of the happy man for one's own individual impression or attention; call it again, as everything came back to that, one's own need to interpret. The discharge upon "society" is moreover what I especially mean; it being the sense of how society in *our* image of the word was taking it all in that I was most concerned with; plenty of other images figured of course for other entertainers of such. The world immediately roundabout us at any rate bristled with more of the young, or the younger, cases I speak of, cases of "things seen" and felt, and a delectable difference in the man thereby made imputable, than I could begin here to name even had I kept the record. I think I fairly cultivated the perceiving of it all, so that nothing of it, under some face or other, shouldn't brush my sense and add to my impression; yet my point is more particularly that the body social itself was for the time so permeated, in the light I glance at, that it became to its own consciousness more interesting. As so many existent parts of it, however unstoried yet, to their minor credit, various thrilled persons could inhale the interest to their fullest capacity and feel that they too had been pushed forward—and were even to find themselves by so much the more pushable yet.

I resort thus to the lift and the push as the most expressive figures for that immensely *remonté* state which coincided for us all with the great disconcerting irony of the hour, the unforgettable death of Lincoln. I think of the springtime of '65 as it breathed through Boston streets—my remembrance of all those days is a matter, strangely enough, of the out-of-door vision, of one's constantly dropping down from Beacon Hill, to the brave edge of which we clung, for appreciation of those premonitory gusts of April that one felt most perhaps where Park Street Church stood dominant, where the mouth of the Common itself uttered promises, more signs and portents than one could count, more prodigies than one could keep apart, and where further strange matters seemed to charge up out of the lower districts and of the "business world," generative as never before of news. The streets were restless, the meeting of the seasons couldn't but be inordinately so, and one's own poor pulses matched—at the supreme pitch of that fusion, for instance, which condensed itself to blackness roundabout the dawn of April 15th: I was fairly to go in shame of its being my birthday. These would have been the hours of the streets if none others had been—when the huge general gasp filled them like a great earth-shudder and people's eyes met people's eyes without the vulgarity of speech. Even this was, all so strangely, part of the lift and the swell, as tragedy has but to be of a pure enough strain and a high enough connection to sow with its dark hand the seed of greater life. The collective sense of what had occurred was of a sadness too noble not somehow to inspire, and it was truly in the air that, whatever we had as a nation produced or failed to produce, we could at least gather round this perfection of a classic woe. True enough, as we were to see, the immediate harvest of our loss was almost too ugly to be borne—for nothing more sharply comes back to me than the tune to which the "esthetic sense," if one glanced but from *that* high window (which was after all one of many too), recoiled in dismay from the sight of Mr. Andrew Johnson perched on the stricken scene. We had given ourselves a figure-head, and the figure-head sat there in its habit as it lived, and we were to have it in our eyes for three or four years and to ask ourselves in horror what monstrous thing we had done. I speak but of aspects, those aspects which, under a certain turn of them, may be all but everything; gathered together they become a symbol of what is behind, and it was open to us to waver at shop-windows exposing the new photograph, exposing, that is, *the* photograph, and ask ourselves what we had been guilty of as a people, when all was said, to deserve the infliction of that form. It was vain to say that we had deliberately invoked the "common" in authority and must drink the wine we had drawn. No countenance, no salience of aspect nor composed symbol, could superficially have referred itself less than Lincoln's mould-smashing mask to any mere matter-of-course type of propriety; but his admirable unrelated head had itself revealed a type—as if by the very fact that what made in it for roughness of kind looked out only less than what made in it for splendid final stamp, in other words for commanding Style. The result thus determined had been precious for representation, and above all for fine suggestional function, in a degree that left behind every medal we had ever played at striking; whereas before the image now substituted representation veiled her head in silence and the element of the suggested was exactly the direst. What, however, on the further view, was to be more refreshing than to find that there were excesses of native habit which truly we couldn't bear? so that it was for the next two or three years fairly sustaining to consider that, let the reasons publicly given for the impeachment of the official in question be any that would serve, the grand inward logic or mystic law had been that we really couldn't go on offering each other before the nations the consciousness of such a presence. That was at any rate the style of reflection to which the humiliating case reduced me; just this withal now especially working, I feel, into that image of our generally quickened activity of spirit, our having by the turn of events more ideas to apply and even to play with, that I have tried to throw off. Everything I recover, I again risk repeating, fits into the vast miscellany—the detail of which I may well seem, however, too poorly to have handled.

Let it serve then for a scrap of detail that the appearance of William's further fortune enjoyed thereabouts a grasp of my attention scarce menaced even by the call on that faculty of such appearances of my own as I had naturally in some degree also to take for graces of the banquet. I associate the sense of his being, in a great cause, far away on the billow with that clearance of the air through the tremendous draught, from sea to sea, of the Northern triumph, which seemed to make a good-natured infinitude of room for all the individual interests and personal lives that might help the pot to bubble—if the expression be not too mean for the size of our confidence; that the cause on which the Agassiz expedition to South America embarked *was* of the greatest being happily a presumption altogether within my scope. It reawoke the mild divinatory rage with which I had followed, with so little to show for it, the military fortune of my younger brothers—feeding the gentle passion indeed, it must be added, thanks to the letter-writing grace of which the case had now the benefit, with report and picture of a vividness greater than any ever to be shed from a like source upon our waiting circle. Everything of the kind, for me, was company; but I dwelt, for that matter and as I put it all together, in company so constant and so enchanting that this amounted to moving, in whatever direction, with the mass—more and more aware as I was of the "fun" (to express it grossly) of living by my imagination and thereby finding that company, in countless different forms, could only swarm about me. Seeing further into the figurable world *made* company of persons and places, objects and subjects alike: it gave them all without exception chances to be somehow or other interesting, and the imaginative ply of finding interest once taken (I think I had by that time got much beyond looking for it), the whole conspiracy of aspects danced round me in a ring. It formed, by my present vision of it, a shining escort to one's possibly often hampered or mystified, but never long stayed and absolutely never wasted, steps; it hung about, after the fashion of winter evening adumbrations just outside the reach of the lamplight, while one sat writing, reading, listening, watching—perhaps even again, incurably, but dawdling and gaping; and most of all doubtless, if it supplied with colour people and things often by themselves, I dare say, neutral enough, how it painted thick, how it fairly smothered, any surface that did it the turn of showing positive and intrinsic life! Ah the things and the people, the hours and scenes and circumstances, the *inénarrables* occasions and relations, that I might still present in its light if I would, and with the enormous advantage now (for this I should unblushingly claim), of being able to mark for present irony or pity or wonder, or just for a better intelligence, or again for the high humour or extreme strangeness of the thing, the rare indebtedness, calculated by the long run, in which it could leave particular cases! This necessity I was under that everything should be interesting—for fear of the collapse otherwise of one's sustaining intention—would have confessed doubtless to a closest connection, of all the connections, with the small inkpot in which I seemed at last definitely destined to dip to the exclusion of any stream more Pactolean: a modest manner of saying that difficulty and slowness of composition were clearly by this time not in the least appointed to blight me, however inveterate they were likely to prove; that production, such as it was, floundered on in spite of them; and that, to put it frankly, if I enjoyed as much company as I have said no small part of it was of my very own earning. The freshness of first creations—since we are exalted, in art, to these arrogant expressions—never fails, I take it, to beguile the creator, in default of any other victim, even to the last extravagance; so that what happened was that one found all the swarm of one's intentions, one's projected images, quite "good enough" to mix with the rest of one's society, setting up with it terms of interpenetration, an admirable commerce of borrowing and lending, taking and giving, not to say stealing and keeping. Did it verily *all*, this freshness of felt contact, of curiosity and wonder, come back perhaps to certain small and relatively ridiculous achievements of "production" as aforesaid?—ridiculous causes, I mean, of such prodigious effects. I am divided between the shame on the one hand of claiming for them, these concocted "short stories," that they played so great a part, and a downright admiring tenderness on the other for their holding up their stiff little heads in such a bustle of life and traffic of affairs. I of course really and truly cared for them, as we say, more than for aught else whatever—cared for them with that kind of care, infatuated though it may seem, that makes it bliss for the fond votary never to so much as speak of the loved object, makes it a refinement of piety to perform his rites under cover of a perfect freedom of mind as to everything *but* them. These secrets of the imaginative life were in fact more various than I may dream of trying to tell; they referred to actual concretions of existence as well as to the supposititious; the joy of life indeed, drawbacks and all, was just in the constant quick flit of association, to and fro, and through a hundred open doors, between the two great chambers (if it be not absurd, or even base, to separate them) of direct and indirect experience. If it is of the great comprehensive *fusion* that I speak as the richest note of all those hours, what could truly have been more in the sense of it than exactly such a perfect muddle of pleasure for instance as my having (and, as I seem to remember, at his positive invitation) addressed the most presuming as yet of my fictional bids to my distinguished friend of a virtual lifetime, as he was to become, William Dean Howells, whom I rejoice to name here and who had shortly before returned from a considerable term of exile in Venice and was in the act of taking all but complete charge of the Boston "Atlantic"? The confusion was, to be plain, of more things than can hope to go into my picture with any effect of keeping distinct there—the felt felicity, literally, in my performance, the felt ecstasy, the still greater, in my receipt of Howells's message; and then, naturally, most of all, the at once to be recorded blest violence in the break upon my consciousness of his glittering response after perusal.

There was still more in it all than that, however—which is the point of my mild demonstration; I associate the passage, to press closer, with a long summer, from May to November, spent at the then rural retreat of Swampscott, forty minutes by train northward from Boston, and that scene of fermentation, in its turn, I invest with unspeakable memories. It was the summer of '66 and of the campaign of Sadowa across the sea—we had by that time got sufficiently away from our own campaigns to take some notice of those of other combatants, on which we bestowed in fact, I think, the highest competence of attention then anywhere at play; a sympathetic sense that bore us even over to the Franco-German war four years later and helped us to know what we meant when we "felt strongly" about it. No strength of feeling indeed of which the vibration had remained to us from the other time could have been greater than our woe-stricken vision of the plight of France under the portent of Sedan; I had been back to that country and some of its neighbourhoods for some fifteen months during the previous interval, and I recover again no share in a great collective pang more vividly than our particular appalled state, that of a whole company of us, while we gaped out at the cry of reiterated bulletins from the shade of an August verandah, and then again from amid boskages of more immediate consolation, during the Saratoga and the Newport seasons of 1870. I had happened to repair to Saratoga, of all inconsequent places, on my return from the Paris and the London of the weeks immediately preceding the war, and though it was not there that the worst sound of the first crash reached us, I feel around me still all the air of our dismay—which was, in the queerest way in the world, that of something so alien mixed, to the increase of horror, with something so cherished: the great hot glare of vulgarity of the aligned hotels of the place and period drenching with its crude light the apparent collapse of everything we had supposed most massive. Which forward stretch on the part of this chronicle represents, I recognise, the practice of the discursive well-nigh overmastering its principle—or would do so, rather, weren't it that the fitful and the flickering, the extravagant advance and the corrective retreat from it, the law and the lovely art of foreshortening, have had here throughout most to serve me. It is under countenance of that law that I still grasp my capricious clue, making a jump for the moment over two or three years and brushing aside by the way quite numberless appeals, claims upon tenderness of memory not less than pleas for charm of interest, against which I must steel myself, even though I account this rank disloyalty to each. There is no quarter to which I have inclined in my brief recovery of the high tide of impression flooding the "period" of Ashburton Place that might not have drawn me on and on; so that I confess I feel myself here drag my mantle, right and left, from the clutch of suppliant hands—voluminous as it may doubtless yet appear in spite of my sense of its raggedness. Wrapped in tatters it is therefore that, with three or four of William's letters of '67 and '68 kept before me, I make my stride, not only for the sake of what I still regard as their admirable interest, but for the way they bring back again to me everything they figured at the time, every flame of faith they rekindled, every gage they held out for the future. Present for me are still others than these in particular, which I keep over for another introducing, but even the pages I here preserve overflow with connections—so many that, extravagant as it may sound, I have to make an effort to breast them. These are with a hundred matters of our then actual life—little as that virtue may perhaps show on their face; but above all just with the huge small fact that the writer was by the blest description "in Europe," and that this had verily still its way of meaning for me more than aught else beside. For what sprang in especial from his situation was the proof, with its positive air, that a like, when all was said, might become again one's own; that such luck wasn't going to be for evermore perversely out of the question with us, and that in fine I too was already in a manner transported by the intimacy with which I partook of his having been. I shouldn't have overstated it, I think, in saying that I really preferred such a form of experience (of this particular one) to the simpler—given most of our current conditions; there was somehow a greater richness, a larger accession of knowledge, vision, life, whatever one might have called it, in "having him there," as we said, and in my individually getting the good of this with the peculiar degree of ease that reinforced the general quest of a special sufficiency of that boon to which I was during those years rigidly, and yet on the whole by no means abjectly, reduced.

Our parents had in the autumn of '66 settled, virtually for the rest of their days, at Cambridge, and William had concomitantly with this, that is from soon after his return from Brazil, entered upon a season of study at the Harvard Medical School, then keeping its terms in Boston and under the wide wing of—as one supposed it, or as I at any rate did—the Massachusetts General Hospital. I have to disengage my mantle here with a force in which I invite my reader to believe—for I push through a thicket of memories in which the thousand-fingered branches arrestingly catch; otherwise I should surrender, and with a passionate sense of the logic in it, to that long and crowded Swampscott summer at which its graceless name has already failed to keep me from having glanced. The place, smothered in a dense prose of prosperity now, may have been even in those days, by any high measure, a weak enough apology for an offered breast of Nature: nevertheless it ministered to me as the only "American country" save the silky Newport fringes with which my growing imagination, not to mention my specious energy, had met at all continuous occasion to play—so that I should have but to let myself go a little, as I say, to sit up to my neck again in the warm depth of its deposit. Out of this I should lift great handfuls of variety of vision; it was to have been in its way too a season of coming and going, and with its main mark, I make out, that it somehow absurdly flowered, first and last, into some intenser example of every sort of intimation up to then vouchsafed me, whether by the inward or the outward life. I think of it thus as a big bouquet of blooms the most mixed—yet from which it is to the point just here to detach the sole reminiscence, coloured to a shade I may not reproduce, of a day's excursion to see my brother up at the Hospital. Had I not now been warned off too many of the prime images brought, for their confusion, to the final proof, I should almost risk ever so briefly "evoking" the impression this mere snatch was to leave with me, the picture as of sublime activities and prodigious possibilities, of genial communities of consideration and acquisition, all in a great bright porticoed and gardened setting, that was to hang itself in my crazy cabinet for as long as the light of the hour might allow. I put my hand on the piece still—in its now so deeply obscured corner; though the true point of my reference would seem to be in the fact that if William studied medicine long enough to qualify and to take his degree (so as to have become as roundedly "scientific" as possible) he was yet immediately afterwards, by one of those quick shifts of the scene with which we were familiar, beginning philosophic study in Germany and again writing home letters of an interest that could be but re-emphasised by our having him planted out as a reflector of impressions where impressions were both strong and as different as possible from those that more directly beat upon us. I myself could do well enough with these last, I may parenthesise, so long as none others were in question; but that complacency shrank just in proportion as we were reached by the report of difference and of the foreign note, the report particularly favourable—which was indeed what any and every report perforce appeared to me. William's, from anywhere, had ever an authority for me that attended none others; even if this be not the place for more than a word of light on the apparent disconnection of his actual course. It comes back to me that the purpose of practising medicine had at no season been flagrant in him, and he was in fact, his hospital connection once over, never to practise for a day. He was on the other hand to remain grateful for his intimate experience of the laboratory and the clinic, and I was as constantly to feel that the varieties of his application had been as little wasted for him as those of my vagueness had really been for me. His months at Dresden and his winter in Berlin were of a new variety—this last even with that tinge of the old in it which came from his sharing quarters with T. S. Perry, who, his four years at Harvard ended and his ensuing grand tour of Europe, as then comprehensively carried out, performed, was giving the Universities of Berlin and Paris a highly competent attention. To whatever else of method may have underlain the apparently lawless strain of our sequences I should add the action of a sharp lapse of health on my brother's part which the tension of a year at the dissecting table seemed to have done much to determine, as well as the fond fact that Europe was again from that crisis forth to take its place for us as a standing remedy, a regular mitigation of all suffered, or at least of all wrong, stress. Of which remarks but a couple of letters addressed to myself, I have to recognise, form here the occasion; these only, in that order, have survived the accidents of time, as I the more regret that I have in my mind's eye still much of the matter of certain others; notably of one from Paris (on his way further) recounting a pair of evenings at the theatre, first for the younger Dumas and Les Idées de Madame Aubray, with Pasca and Delaporte, this latter of an exquisite truth to him, and then for something of the Palais Royal with *four* comedians, as he emphatically noted, who were each, wonderful to say, "de la force of Warren of the Boston Museum." He spent the summer of '67 partly in Dresden and partly at Bad-Teplitz in Bohemia, where he had been recommended the waters; he was to return for these again after a few months and was also to seek treatment by hydropathy at the establishment of Divonne, in the French back-country of Lake Leman, where a drawing sent home in a letter, and which I do my best to reproduce, very comically represents him as surrounded by the listening fair. I remember supposing even his Dresden of the empty weeks to bristle with precious images and every form of local character—this a little perhaps because of his treating us first of all to a pair of whimsical crayoned views of certain animated housetops seen from his window. It is the old names in the old letters, however, that now always most rewrite themselves to my eyes in colour—shades alas that defy plain notation, and if the two with which the following begins, and especially the first of them, only asked me to tell their story I but turn my back on the whole company of which they are part.

> . . . I got last week an excellent letter from Frank Washburn who writes in such a manly way. But the greatest delight I've had was the loan of 5 Weekly Transcripts from Dick Derby. It's strange how quickly one grows away from one's old surroundings. I never should have believed that in so few months the tone of a Boston paper would seem so outlandish to me. As it was, I was in one squeal of amusement, surprise and satisfaction until deep in the night, when I went to bed tired out with patriotism. The boisterous animal good-humour, familiarity, reckless energy and self-confidence, unprincipled optimism, esthetic saplessness and intellectual imbecility, made a mixture hard to characterise, but totally different from the tone of things here and, as the Germans would say, whose "Existenz so völlig dasteht," that there was nothing to do but to let yourself feel it. The Americans themselves here too amuse me much; they have such a hungry, restless look and seem so unhooked somehow from the general framework. The other afternoon as I was sitting on the Terrace, a gentleman and two young ladies came and sat down quite near me. I knew them for Americans at a glance, and the man interested me by his

exceedingly American expression: a reddish moustache and tuft on chin, a powerful nose, a small light eye, half insolent and *all* sagacious, and a sort of rowdy air of superiority that made me proud to claim him as a brother. In a few minutes I recognised him as General M'Clellan, rather different from his photographs of the War-time, but still not to be mistaken (and I afterwards learned he is here). Whatever his faults may be that of not being "one of us" is not among them.

This next is the note of a slightly earlier impression.

The Germans are certainly a most gemüthlich people. The way all the old women told me how "freundlich" their rooms were—"so freundlich mobilirt" and so forth—melted my heart. Whenever you tell an inferior here to do anything (*e.g.* a cabman) he or she replies "Schön!" or rather "Schehn!" with an accent not quick like a Frenchman's "Bien!" but so protracted, soothing and reassuring to you that you feel as if he were adopting you into his family. You say I've said nothing of the people of this house, but there is nothing to tell about them. The Doctor is an open-hearted excellent man as ever was, and wrapped up in his children; Frau Semler is a sickly, miserly, petty-spirited nonentity. The children are quite uninteresting, though the younger, Anna or Aennchen, aged five, is very handsome and fat. The following short colloquy, which I overheard one day after breakfast a few days since, may serve you as a piece of local colour. Aennchen drops a book she is carrying across the room and exclaims "Herr Jesus!"

Mother: "Ach, das sagen *Kinder* nicht, Anna!"

Aennchen (reflectively to herself, sotto voce): "Nicht fur Kinder!" . . .

What here follows from Divonne—of fourteen months later—is too full and too various to need contribution or comment.

You must have envied within the last few weeks my revisiting of the sacred scenes of our youth, the shores of Leman, the Écu de Genève, the sloping Corraterie, etc. My only pang in it all has been caused by your absence, or rather by the fact of my presence instead of yours; for I think your abstemious and poetic soul would have got much more good of the things I've seen than my hardening and definite-growing nature. I wrote a few words about Nürnberg to Alice from Montreux. I found that about as pleasant an impression as any I have had since being abroad—and this because I didn't expect it. The Americans at Dresden had told me it was quite uninteresting. I enclose you a few stereographs I got there—I don't know why, for they are totally irrelevant to the real effect of the place. This it would take Théophile Gautier to describe, so I renounce. It was strange to find how little I remembered at Geneva—I couldn't find the way I used to take up to the Academy, and the shops and houses of the Rue du Rhône visible from our old windows left me uncertain whether they were the same or new ones. Kohler has set up a new hotel on the Quai du Mont-Blanc—you remember he's the brother of our old Madame Buscarlet there; but I went for association's sake to the Écu. The dining-room was differently hung, and the only thing in my whole 24 hours in the place that stung me, so to speak, with memory, was that kind of chinese-patterned dessert-service we used to have. So runs the world away. I didn't try to look up Ritter, Chantre or any of ces messieurs, but started off here the next morning, where I have now been a week.

My impression on gradually coming from a German into a French atmosphere of things was rather unexpected and not in all respects happy. I have been in Germany half amused and half impatient with the slowness of proceeding and the uncouthness of taste and expression that prevail there so largely in all things, but on exchanging it for the brightness and shipshapeness of these quasi-French arrangements of life and for the tart fire-cracker-like speech of those who make them I found myself inclined to retreat again on what I had left, and had for a few days quite a home-sickness for the easy, ugly, substantial German ways. The "'tarnal" smartness in which the railway refreshment counters, for example, are dressed up, the tight waists and "tasteful" white caps of the female servants, the everlasting monsieur and madame, and especially the quickness and snappishness of enunciation, suggesting such an inward impatience, quite absurdly gave on my nerves. But I am getting used to it all, and the French people who sit near me here at table and who repelled me at first by the apparently cold-blooded artificiality of their address to each other, now seem less heartless and inhuman. I am struck more than ever I was with the hopelessness of us English, and *a fortiori* the Germans, ever competing with the French in matters of form or finite taste of any sort. They are sensitive to things that simply don't exist for us. I notice it here in manners and speech: how can a people who speak with no tonic accents in their words *help* being cleaner and neater in expressing themselves? On the other hand the limitations of

"The cold water cure at Divonne—excellent for melancholia."—From a letter of William James (page 525)

reach in the French mind strike me more and more; their delight in rallying round an official standard in all matters, in counting and dating everything from certain great names, their use and love of catchwords and current phrases, their sacrifice of independence of mind for the mere sake of meeting their hearer or reader on common ground, their metaphysical incapacity not only to deal with questions but to know what the questions are, stand out plainer and plainer the more headway I make in German. One wonders where the "Versöhnung" or conciliation of all these rival national qualities is going to take place. I imagine we English stand rather between the French and the Germans both in taste and in spiritual intuition. In Germany, while unable to avoid respecting that solidity of the national mind which causes such a mass of permanent work to be produced there annually, I couldn't help consoling myself by the thought that whatever, after all, they might *do*, the Germans were a plebeian crowd and could never *be* such gentlemen as we were. I now find myself getting over the French superiority by an exactly inverse process of thought. The Frenchman must sneer at us even more than we sneer at the Germans—and which sneer is final, his at us two, or ours at him, or the Germans' at us? It seems an insoluble question, which I fortunately haven't got to settle.

I've read several novels lately, some of the irrepressible George's: La Daniella and the Beaux Messieurs de Bois-Doré. (Was it thee, by the bye that wrotest the Nation notices on her, on W. Morris's new poem and on The Spanish Gypsy? They came to me unmarked, but the thoughts seemed such as you would entertain, and the style in some places like yours—in others not.) George Sand babbles her improvisations on so that I never begin to believe a word of what she says. I've also read The Woman in White, a couple of Balzac's, etc., and a volume of tales by Mérimée which I will send you if I can by Frank Washburn. He is a big man; but the things which have given me most pleasure have been some sketches of travel by Th. Gautier. What an absolute thing genius is! That this creature, with no more soul than a healthy poodle-dog, no philosophy, no morality, no information (for I doubt exceedingly if his knowledge of architectural terms and suchlike is accurate) should give one a finer enjoyment than his betters in all these respects by mere force of goodnature, clear eyesight and felicity of phrase! His style seems to me perfect, and I should think it would pay you to study it with love—principally in the most trivial of these collections of notes of travel. T. S. P. has a couple of them for you, and another, which I've read here and is called Caprices et Zigzags, is worth buying. It contains wonderful French (in the classic sense, I mean, with all those associations) descriptions of London. I'm not sure if you know Gautier at all save by the delicious Capitaine Fracasse. But these republished feuilletons are all of as charming a quality and I should think would last as long as the language.

There are 70 or 80 people in this établissement, no one of whom I have as yet particularly cottoned up to. It's incredible how even so slight a barrier as the difference of language with most of them, and still more as the absence of local and personal associations, range of gibes and other common ground to stand on, counts against one's scraping acquaintance. It's disgusting and humiliating. There is a lovely maiden of *etwa* 19 sits in sight of me at the table with whom I am falling deeply in love. She has never looked at me yet, and I really believe I should be quite incapable of conversing with her even were I "introduced," from a sense of the above difficulties and because one doesn't know what subjects or allusions may be possible with a jeune fille. I suppose my life for the past year would have furnished you, as the great American nouvelliste, a good many "motives" and subjects of observation —especially so in this place. I wish I could pass them over to you— such as they are you'd profit by them more than I and gather in a great many more. I should like full well an hour's, or even longer, interview with you, and with the Parents and the Sister and the Aunt and all; just so as to start afresh on a clean basis. Give my love to Wendell Holmes. I've seen ——— ——— several times; but what a cold-blooded cuss he is! Write me your impression of T. S. P., who will probably reach you before this letter. If Frank Washburn ever gets home be friendly to him. He is much aged by travel and experience, and is a most charming character and generous mind.

XIII

If I add to the foregoing a few lines more from my brother's hand, these are of a day separated by long years from that time of our youth of which I have treated. Addressed after the immense interval to an admirable friend whom I shall not name here, they yet so vividly refer—and with something I can only feel as the first authority—to one of the most prized interests of our youth that, under the need of still failing to rescue so many of these values from the dark gulf, I find myself insist the more on a place here, before I close, for that presence in our early lives as to which my brother's few words say so much. To have so promptly and earnestly spoken of Mary Temple the younger in this volume is indeed I think to have offered a gage for my not simply leaving her there. The opportunity not so to leave her comes at any rate very preciously into my hands, and I can not better round off this record than by making the most of it. The letter to which William alludes is one that my reader will presently recognise. It had come back to him thus clearly at the far end of time.

> I am deeply thankful to you for sending me this letter, which revives all sorts of poignant memories and makes her live again in all her lightness and freedom. Few spirits have been more free than hers. I find myself wishing so that she could know me as I am now. As for knowing her as *she* is now—??!! I find that she means as much in the way of human character for me now as she ever did, being unique and with no analogue in all my subsequent experience of people. Thank you once more for what you have done.

The testimony so acknowledged was a letter in a copious succession, the product of little more than one year, January '69 to February '70, sacredly preserved by the recipient; who was not long after the day of my brother's acknowledgment to do me the honour of communicating to me the whole series. He could have done nothing to accord more with the spirit in which I have tried to gather up something of the sense of our far-off past, his own as well as that of the rest of us; and no loose clue that I have been able to recover unaided touches into life anything like such a tract of the time-smothered consciousness. More charming and interesting things emerge for me than I can point to in their order—but they will make, I think, their own appeal. It need only further be premised that our delightful young cousin had had from some months back to begin to reckon with the progressive pulmonary weakness of which the letters tell the sad story. Also, I can scarce help saying, the whole world of the old New York, that of the earlier dancing years, shimmers out for me from the least of her allusions.

> I will write you as nice a letter as I can, but would much rather have a good talk with you. As I can't have the best thing I am putting up with the second-best, contrary to my pet theory. I feel as if I were in heaven to-day—all because the day is splendid and I have been driving about all the morning in a small sleigh in the fresh air and sunshine, until I found that I had in spite of myself, for the time being, stopped asking the usual inward question of why I was born. I am not going to Canada—I know no better reason for this than because I said I *was* going. My brother-in-law makes such a clamour when I propose departure that I am easily overcome by his kindness and my own want of energy. Besides, it is great fun to live here; the weather just now is grand, and I knock about all day in a sleigh, and do nothing but enjoy it and meditate. Then we are so near town that we often go in for the day to shop and lunch with some of our numerous friends, returning with a double relish for the country. We all went in on a spree the other night and stayed at the Everett House; from which, as a starting-point we poured ourselves in strong force upon Mrs. Gracie King's ball—a very grand affair, given for a very pretty Miss King, at Delmonico's. Our raid consisted of thirteen Emmets and a moderate supply of Temples, and the ball was a great success. It was two years since I had been to one and I enjoyed it so much that I mean very soon to repeat the experiment—at the next Assembly if possible. The men in society, in New York, this winter, are principally a lot of feeble-minded boys; but I was fortunate enough to escape them, as my partner for the German was a man of thirty-five, the solitary *man*, I believe, in the room. Curiously enough, I had danced my last German, two years before, in that very place and with the same person. He is a Mr. Lee, who has spent nearly all his life abroad; two of his sisters have married German princes, and from knocking

about so much he has become a thorough cosmopolite. As he is intelligent, with nothing to do but amuse himself, he is a very agreeable partner, and I mean to dance with him again as soon as possible. I don't know why I have tried your patience by writing so about a person you have never seen; unless it's to show you that I haven't irrevocably given up the world, the flesh and the devil, but am conscious of a faint charm about them still when taken in small doses. I agree with you perfectly about Uncle Henry—I should think he would be very irritating to the legal mind; he is not at all satisfactory even to mine. Have you seen much of Willy James lately? That is a rare creature, and one in whom my intellect, if you will pardon the misapplication of the word, takes more solid satisfaction than in almost anybody. I haven't read Browning's new book—I mean to wait till you are by to explain it to me—which reminds me, along with what you say about wishing for the spring, that we shall go to North Conway next summer, and that in that case you may as well make up your mind to come and see us there. I can't wait longer than that for the Browning readings. (Which would have been of The Ring and the Book.) Arthur Sedgwick has sent me Matthew Arnold's photograph, which Harry had pronounced so disappointing. I don't myself, on the whole, find it so; on the contrary, after having looked at it much, I like it—it quite harmonises with my notion of him, and I have always had an affection for him. You must tell me something that you are *sure* is true—I don't care much what it may be, I will take your word for it. Things get into a muddle with me—how can I give you "a start on the way of righteousness"? You know that way better than I do, and the only advice I can give you is not to stop saying your prayers. I hope God may bless you, and beyond those things I hardly know what is right, and therefore what to wish you. Good-bye.

"North Conway" in the foregoing has almost the force for me of a wizard's wand; the figures spring up again and move in a harmony that is not of the fierce present; the sense in particular of the August of '65 shuts me in to its blest unawarenesses not less than to all that was then exquisite in its current certainties and felicities; the fraternising, endlessly conversing group of us gather under the rustling pines—and I admire, precisely, the arrival, the bright revelation as I recover it, of the so handsome young man, marked with military distinction but already, with our light American promptitude, addressed to that high art of peace in which a greater eminence awaited him, of whom this most attaching member of the circle was to make four years later so wise and steady a confidant. Our circle I fondly call it, and doubtless then called it, because in the light of that description I could most rejoice in it, and I think of it now as having formed a little world of easy and happy interchange, of unrestricted and yet all so instinctively sane and secure association and conversation, with all its liberties and delicacies, all its mirth and its earnestness protected and directed so much more from within than from without, that I ask myself, perhaps too fatuously, whether any such right conditions for the play of young intelligence and young friendship, the reading of Matthew Arnold and Browning, the discussion of a hundred human and personal things, the sense of the splendid American summer drawn out to its last generosity, survives to this more complicated age. I doubt if there be circles to-day, and seem rather to distinguish confusedly gangs and crowds and camps, more propitious, I dare say, to material affluence and physical riot than anything we knew, but not nearly so appointed for ingenious and ingenuous talk. I think of our interplay of relation as attuned to that fruitful freedom of what we took for speculation, what we didn't recoil from as boundless curiosity—as the consideration of life, that is, the personal, the moral inquiry and adventure at large, so far as matter for them had up to then met our view—I think of this fine quality in our scene with no small confidence in its having been rare, or to be more exact perhaps, in its having been possible to the general American felicity and immunity as it couldn't otherwise or elsewhere have begun to be. Merely to say, as an assurance, that such relations shone with the light of "innocence" is of itself to breathe on them wrongly or rudely, is uncouthly to "defend" them—as if the very air that consciously conceived and produced them didn't all tenderly and amusedly take care of them. I at any rate figure again, to my customary positive piety, all the aspects now; that in especial of my young orphaned cousins as mainly composing the maiden train and seeming as if they still had but yesterday brushed the morning dew of the dear old Albany naturalness; that of the venerable, genial, erect great-aunt, their more immediately active guardian, a model of antique spinsterhood appointed to cares such as even renewals of wedlock could scarce more have multiplied for her, and thus, among her many ancient and curious national references—one was tempted to call them—most impressive by her striking resemblance to the portraits, the most benignant, of General Washington. She might have represented the mother, no less adequately than he represented the father, of their country. I can only feel, however, that what particularly drew the desired circle sharpest for me was the contribution to it that I had been able to effect by introducing the companion of my own pilgrimage, who was in turn to introduce a little later the great friend of *his* then expanding situation, restored with the close of the War to civil pursuits and already deep in them; the interesting pair possessed after this fashion of a quantity of common fine experience that glittered as so much acquired and enjoyed luxury—all of a sort that I had no acquisition whatever to match. I remember being happy in that I might repeatedly point our moral, under permission (for we were always pointing morals), with this brilliant advantage of theirs even if I might with none of my own; and I of course knew—what was half the beauty—that if we were just the most delightful loose band conceivable, and immersed in a regular revel of all the harmonies, it was largely by grace of the three quite exceptional young men who, thanks in part to the final sublime coach-drive of other days, had travelled up from Boston with their preparation to admire inevitably quickened. I was quite willing to offer myself as exceptional through being able to promote such exceptions and see them justified to waiting apprehension. There was a dangling fringe, there were graceful accessories and hovering shades, but, essentially, we of the true connection made up the drama, or in other words, for the benefit of my imagination, reduced the fond figment of the Circle to terms of daily experience. If drama we could indeed feel this as being, I hasten to add, we owed it most of all to our just having such a heroine that everything else inevitably came. Mary Temple was beautifully and indescribably *that*—in the technical or logical as distinguished from the pompous or romantic sense of the word; wholly without effort or desire on her part—for never was a girl less consciously or consentingly or vulgarly dominant—everything that took place around her took place as if primarily in relation to her and in her interest: that is in the interest of drawing her out and displaying her the more. This too without her in the least caring, as I say—in the deep, the morally nostalgic indifferences that were the most finally characteristic thing about her—whether such an effect took place or not; she liked nothing in the world so much as to see others fairly exhibited; not as they might best please her by being, but as they might most fully reveal themselves, their stuff and their truth: which was the only thing that, after any first flutter for the superficial air or grace in an acquaintance, could in the least fix her attention. She had beyond any equally young creature I have known a sense for verity of character and play of life in others, for their acting out of their force or their weakness, whatever either might be, at no matter what cost to herself; and it was this instinct that made her care so for life in general, just as it was her being thereby so engaged in that tangle that made her, as I have expressed it, ever the heroine of the scene. Life claimed her and used her and beset her—made her range in her groping, her naturally immature and unlighted way from end to end of the scale. No one felt more the charm of the actual—only the actual comprised for her kinds of reality (those to which her letters perhaps most of all testify), that she saw treated round her for the most part either as irrelevant or as unpleasant. She was absolutely afraid of nothing she might come to by living with enough sincerity and enough wonder; and I think it is because one was to see her launched on that adventure in such bedimmed, such almost tragically compromised conditions that one is caught by her title to the heroic and pathetic mark. It is always difficult for us after the fact not to see young things who were soon to be lost to us as already distinguished by their fate; this particular victim of it at all events might well have made the near witness ask within himself how her restlessness of spirit, the finest reckless impatience, was to be assuaged or "met" by the common lot. One somehow saw it nowhere about us as up to her terrible young standard of the interesting—even if to say this suggests an air of tension, a sharpness of importunity, than which nothing could have been less like her. The charming, irresistible fact was that one had never seen a creature with such lightness of forms, a lightness all her own, so inconsequently grave at the core, or an asker of endless questions with such apparent lapses of care. It is true that as an effect of the state of health which during the year '69 grew steadily worse the anxious note and serious mind sound in her less intermittently than by her former wont.

> This might be headed with that line of a hymn, "Hark, from the tombs etc.!"—but perhaps it won't prove as bad as that. It looks pretty doubtful still, but I have a sort of feeling that I shall come round this one time more; by which I don't mean to brag! The "it" of which I speak is of course my old enemy hemorrhage, of which I have had within the last week seven pretty big ones and several smaller, hardly worth mentioning. I don't know what has come over me—I can't stop them; but, as I said, I mean to try and beat them yet. Of course I am in bed, where I shall be indefinitely—not allowed to speak one word, literally, even in a whisper. The reason I write this is because I don't think it will hurt me at all—if I take it easy and stop when I feel tired. It is a pleasant break in the monotony of gruel and of thinking of the grave—and then too a few words from somebody who is strong and active in the good old world (as it seems to me now) would be very refreshing. But don't tell anyone I have written, because it will be sure to reach the ears of my dear relatives and will cause them to sniff the air and flounce! You see I am a good deal of a baby—in the sense of not wanting the reproaches of my relatives on this or any other subject. . . . All the Emmets are so good and kind that I found, when it came to the point, that there was a good deal to make life attractive, and that if the choice were given me I would much rather stay up here on the solid earth, in the air and sunshine, with an occasional sympathetic glimpse of another person's soul, than to be put down underground and say good-bye for ever to humanity, with all its laughter and its sadness. Yet you mustn't think me now in any *special* danger of dying, or even in low spirits, for it isn't so—the doctor tells me I am *not* in danger, even if the hemorrhages should keep on. However, "you can't fool a regular boarder," as Mr. Holmes would say, and I can't see why there is any reason to think they will heal a week hence, when I shall be still weaker, if they can't heal now. Still, they *may* be going to stop—I haven't had one since yesterday at 4, and now it's 3; nearly twenty-four hours. I am of a hopeful temperament and not easily scared, which is in my favour. If this *should* prove to be the last letter you get from me, why take it for a good-bye; I'll keep on the lookout for you in the spirit world, and shall be glad to see you when you come there, provided it's a better place than this.

Elly is in New York, enjoying herself immensely, and I haven't let her know how ill I have been, as there were to be several parties this last week and I was afraid it might spoil her fun. I didn't mean you to infer from my particularising Willy James's intellect that the rest of him isn't to my liking—he is one of the very few people in this world that I love. He has the largest heart as well as the largest head, and is thoroughly interesting to me. He is generous and affectionate and full of sympathy and humanity—though you mustn't tell him I say so, lest he should think I have been telling you a lie to serve my own purposes. Good-bye.

I should have little heart, I confess, for what is essentially the record of a rapid illness if it were not at the same time the image of an admirable soul. Surrounded as she was with affection she had yet greatly to help herself, and nothing is thus more penetrating than the sense, as one reads, that a method of care would have been followed for her to-day, and perhaps followed with signal success, that was not in the healing or nursing range of forty years ago.

It is a week ago to-day, I think, since I last wrote to you, and I have only had one more hemorrhage—the day after. I feel pretty sure they have stopped for the present, and I am sitting up in my room, as bright as possible. Yesterday when I walked across it I thought I should never be strong again, but now it's quite different, and so nice to be out of bed that my spirits go up absurdly. As soon as I am able I am to be taken to town for another examination, and then when I know my fate I will do the best I can. This climate is trying, to be sure, but such as it is I've got to take my chance in it, as there is no one I care enough for, or who cares enough for me, to take charge of me to Italy, or to the south anywhere. I don't believe any climate, however good, would be of the least use to me with people I don't care for. You may let your moustache grow down to your toes if you like, and I shall but smile scornfully at your futile precautions.

Of the following, in spite of its length, I can bring myself to abate nothing.

. . . . Well, "to make a long story short," as Hannah (her old nurse) says, I caught a cold, and it went to the weak spot, and I had another slight attack of hemorrhage; but I took the necessary steps at once, stayed in bed and didn't speak for six days, and then it stopped and I felt better than I had at all since I was first taken ill. But I began to tire so of such constant confinement to my room that they promised to take me to town as soon as I was well enough, and perhaps to the Opera. This of course would have been a wild excitement for me, and I had charming little plans of music by day and by night, for a week, which I meant to spend with Mrs. Griswold. Accordingly a cavalcade set out from here on Monday, consisting of myself escorted by sisters and friends, who were to see me safely installed in my new quarters and leave me. I arrived, bundled up, at Mrs. Griswold's, and had begun to consider myself already quite emancipated from bondage—so that I was discussing with my brother-in-law the propriety of my going that evening to hear Faust, this but the beginning of a mad career on which I proposed to rush headlong—when Dr. Bassett arrived, who is the medical man that I had meant to consult during my stay *incidentally* and between the pauses in the music. The first thing he said was: "What are you doing here? Go directly back to the place you came from and don't come up again till the warm weather. As for music, you mustn't hear of it or even think of it for two months." This was pleasant, but there was nothing to be done but obey; which I did a few hours later, with my trunk still unpacked and my immediate plan of life somewhat limited.

I say my immediate plan because my permanent found itself by no means curtailed, but on the contrary expanded and varied in a manner I had not even dared to hope. This came from what Dr. B. said subsequently, when he had examined my lungs; that is to say after he had laid his head affectionately first under one of my shoulders and then the other, and there kept it solemnly for about ten minutes, in a way that was irresistibly ludicrous, especially with Kitty as spectator. His verdict was that my lungs were *sound*, that he couldn't detect the least evidence of disease, and that hemorrhage couldn't have come from the lung itself, but from their membraneous lining, and that of the throat, whatever this may be. So he gave me to understand that I have as sound a pair of lungs at present as the next person; in fact from what he said one would have thought them a pair that a prize-fighter might covet. At the same time he sent me flying back to the country, with orders not to get excited, nor to listen to music, nor to speak with anybody I care for, nor to do anything in short that the unregenerate nature longs for. This struck my untutored mind as somewhat inconsistent, and I ventured a gentle remonstrance, which however was not even listened to, and I was ignominiously thrust into a car and borne back to Pelham. The problem still bothers me: either sound lungs are a very dangerous thing to have, or there is a foul conspiracy on foot to oppress me. Still, I cling to the consoling thought of my matchless lungs, and this obliterates my present sufferings.

Harry came to see me before he sailed for Europe; I'm very glad he has gone, though I don't expect to see him again for a good many years. I don't think he will come back for a long time, and I hope it will do him good and that he will enjoy himself—which he hasn't done for several years. I haven't read all of Faust, but I think I know the scenes you call divine—at least I know some that are exquisite. But why do you speak so disparagingly of King David, whom I always had a weakness for? Think how charming and lovable a person he must have been, poet, musician and so much else combined—with however their attendant imperfections. I don't think I should have cared to be *Queen* David exactly. I am possessed with an overpowering admiration and affection for George Eliot. I don't know why this has so suddenly come over me, but everything I look at of hers nowadays makes me take a deeper interest in her. I should love to see her, and I hope Harry will; I asked him to give my love to her. But I don't remember ever to have heard *you* speak of her. Good-bye. I wish conventionality would invent some other way of ending a letter than "yours truly"; I am so tired of it, and as one says it to one's shoemaker it would be rather more complimentary to one's friends to dispense with it altogether and just sign one's name without anything, after the manner of Miss Emerson and other free Boston citizens. But I am a slave to conventionality, and after all *am* yours truly. . . .

Singularly present has remained to "Harry," as may be imagined, the rapid visit he paid her at Pelham that February; he was spending a couple of days in New York, on a quick decision, before taking ship for England. I was then to make in Europe no such stay as she had forecast—I was away but for fifteen months; though I can well believe my appetite must have struck her as open to the boundless, and can easily be touched again by her generous thought of this as the right compensatory thing for me. That indeed is what I mainly recall of the hour I spent with her—so unforgettable none the less in its general value; our so beautifully agreeing that quite the same course would be the right thing for *her* and that it was wholly detestable I should be voyaging off without her. But the precious question and the bright aspect of her own still waiting chance made our talk for the time all gaiety; it was, strangely enough, a laughing hour altogether, coloured with the vision of the next winter in Rome, where we should romantically meet: the appearance then being of particular protective friends with Roman designs, under whose wing she might happily travel. She had at that moment been for many weeks as ill as will here have been shown; but such is the priceless good faith of youth that we perfectly kept at bay together the significance of this. I recall no mortal note—nothing but the bright extravagance of her envy; and see her again, in the old-time Pelham parlours, ever so erectly slight and so more than needfully, so transparently, fair (I fatuously took this for "becoming"), glide as swiftly, toss her head as characteristically, laugh to as free a disclosure of the handsome largeish teeth that made her mouth almost the main fact of her face, as if no corner of the veil of the future had been lifted. The house was quiet and spacious for the day, after the manner of all American houses of that age at those hours, and yet spoke of such a possible muster at need of generous, gregarious, neighbouring, sympathising Emmets; in spite of which, withal, the impression was to come back to me as of a child struggling with her ignorance in a sort of pathless desert of the genial and the casual. Three months before I returned to America the struggle had ended. I *was*, as happened, soon to see in London her admiration, and my own, the great George Eliot—a brief glimpse then, but a very impressive, and wellnigh my main satisfaction in which was that I should have my cousin to tell of it. I found the Charles Nortons settled for the time in London, with social contacts and penetrations, a give and take of hospitality, that I felt as wondrous and of some elements of which they offered me, in their great kindness, the benefit; so that I was long to value having owed them in the springtime of '69 five separate impressions of distinguished persons, then in the full flush of activity and authority, that affected my young provincialism as a positive fairytale of privilege. I had a Sunday afternoon hour with Mrs. Lewes at North Bank, no second visitor but my gentle introducer, the younger Miss Norton, sharing the revelation, which had some odd and for myself peculiarly thrilling accompaniments; and then the opportunity of dining with Mr. Ruskin at Denmark Hill, an impression of uneffaced intensity and followed by a like—and yet so unlike—evening of hospitality from William Morris in the medieval mise-en-scène of Queen Square. This had been preceded by a luncheon with Charles Darwin, beautifully benignant, sublimely simple, at Down; a memory to which I find attached our incidental wondrous walk—Mrs. Charles Norton, the too near term of her earthly span then smoothly out of sight, being my guide for the happy excursion—across a private park of great oaks, which I conceive to have been the admirable Holwood and where I knew my first sense of a matter afterwards, through fortunate years, to be more fully disclosed: the springtime in such places, the adored footpath, the first primroses, the stir and scent of renascence in the watered sunshine and under spreading boughs that were somehow before aught else the still reach of remembered lines of Tennyson, ached over in nostalgic years. The rarest hour of all perhaps, or at least the strangest, strange verily to the pitch of the sinister, was a vision, provided by the same care, of D. G. Rossetti in the vernal dusk of Queen's House Chelsea—among his pictures, amid his poetry itself, his whole haunting "esthetic," and yet above all bristling with his personality, with his perversity, with anything, as it rather awfully seemed to me, but his sympathy, though it at the same time left one oddly desirous of more of him. These impressions heaped up the measure, goodness knew, of what would serve for Minnie's curiosity—she was familiarly Minnie to us; the point remaining all along, however, that, impatient at having overmuch to wait, I rejoiced in possession of the exact vivid terms in which I should image George Eliot to her. I was much later on to renew acquaintance with that great lady, but I think I scarce exceed in saying that with my so interested cousin's death half the savour of my appreciation had lost itself. Just in those days, that month of April, the latter had made a weak ineffectual move to Philadelphia in quest of physical relief—which expressed at the same time even more one of those reachings out for appeasement of the soul which were never too publicly indulged in, but by which her power to interest the true subjects of her attraction was infinitely quickened. It represented wonderments, I might well indeed have said to myself, even beyond any inspired by the high muse of North Bank.

I suppose I ought to have something special to say after having been suddenly transplanted to a new place and among new people, yet there isn't much to tell. I came because they all thought at home that the climate might do me good; I don't feel, however, any difference in my sensations between this and New York—if I do it's in favour of New York. I wish it might turn out that an inland climate isn't after all necessary for me, as I like the other sort much better and really think I feel stronger in it too. My doctor told me that Boston would kill me in six months—though he is possibly mistaken. I am going to try it a little longer here, and then go back to Pelham, where I'm pretty sure I shall find myself better again. It may be that the mental atmosphere is more to me than any other, for I feel homesick here all the while, or at least what I call so, being away from what is most *like* home to me, and what if I were there I should call tired. The chief object I had in coming was to listen to Phillips Brooks; I have heard him several times and am not, I think, disappointed. To be sure he didn't say anything new or startling, but I certainly oughtn't to have expected that, though I believe I did have a secret hope that he was going to expound to me the old beliefs with a clearness that would convince me for ever and banish doubt. I had placed all my hopes in him as the one man I had heard of who, progressive in all other ways, had yet been able to keep his faith firm in the things that most earnest men have left far behind them. Yet in preaching to his congregation he doesn't, or didn't, touch the real difficulties at all. He was leading them forward instead of trying to make it clear to *me* that I have any good reason for my feelings. Still, it was something to feel that he has them too, and isn't afraid to trust them and live for them. I wonder what he really does believe or think about it all, and whether he knows the reaction that comes to me about Thursday, after the enthusiasm and confidence made by his eloquence and earnestness on Sunday. To-morrow will be Saturday, and I shall be glad when Sunday comes to wind me up again. I feel sadly run down to-night and as if I should like to see some honest old pagan and shake him by the hand. It will seem all right and easy again soon, I know, but is it always thus? Is there no more of that undoubting faith in the world that there used to be? But I won't talk any more about it now, or I shan't sleep; it is getting late and all themes but the least interesting must be put away.

"Quaint," as we now say, it at this end of time seems to me that Phillips Brooks, the great Episcopal light of the period, first in Philadelphia and then in Boston, and superior character, excellent, even ardent, thoughtful, genial, practical man, should have appeared to play before her a light possibly of the clear strain, the rich abundance, the straight incidence, that she so desired to think attainable. A large, in fact an enormous, softly massive and sociably active presence, of capacious attention and comforting suggestion, he was a brave worker among those who didn't too passionately press their questions and claims—half the office of such a minister being, no doubt, to abate the high pitch, and the high pitch being by the same token too much Minnie's tendency. She was left with it in the smug Philadelphia visibly on her hands; she had found there after all but a closed door, to which she was blandly directed, rather than an open, and the sigh of her falling back with her disappointment seems still to reach one's ears. She found them too much all round, the stiff blank barriers that, for whatever thumping, didn't "give;" and in fine I like not too faintly to colour this image of her as failing, in her avid young sincerity, to draw from the honest pastor of more satisfied souls any assurance that she could herself honestly apply. I confess that her particular recorded case, slender enough in its lonely unrest, suggests to me a force, or at least a play, of effective criticism more vivid to-day than either of the several rich monuments, honourably as these survive, to Phillips Brooks's positive "success." She had no occasion or no chance to find the delightful harmonising friend in him—which was part of the success for so many others. But her letter goes on after a couple of days—she had apparently not sent the previous part, and it brings her back, we can rejoicingly note, to George Eliot, whose poem, alluded to, must have been The Spanish Gipsy. This work may indeed much less have counted for her than the all-engulfing Mill on the Floss, incomparably privileged production, which shone for young persons of that contemporaneity with a nobleness that nothing under our actual star begins in like case to match. These are great recognitions, but how can I slight for them a mention that has again and again all but broken through in my pages?—that of Francis Boott and his daughter (she to become later on Mrs. Frank Duveneck and to yield to the same dismal decree of death before her time that rested on so many of the friends of our youth). When I turn in thought to the happiness that our kinswoman was still to have known in her short life, for all her disaster, Elizabeth Boott, delightful, devoted and infinitely under the charm, at once hovers for me; this all the more, I hasten to add, that we too on our side, and not least Mary Temple herself, were under the charm, and that *that* charm, if less immediately pointed, affected all our young collective sensibility as a wondrous composite thing. There was the charm for us—if I must not again speak in assurance but for myself—that "Europe," the irrepressible even as the *ewig Weibliche* of literary allusion was irrepressible, had more than anything else to do with; and then there was the other that, strange to say (strange as I, once more, found myself feeling it) owed nothing of its authority to anything so markedly out of the picture. The spell to which I in any case most piously sacrificed, most cultivated the sense of, was ever of this second cast—and for the simple reason that the other, serene in its virtue, fairly insolent in its pride, needed no rites and no care. It must be allowed that there was nothing composite in any spell proceeding, whether directly or indirectly, from the great Albany connection: this form of the agreeable, through whatever appeals, could certainly not have been more of a piece, as we say—more of a single superfused complexion, an element or principle that we could in the usual case ever so easily and pleasantly account for. The case of that one in the large number of my cousins whom we have seen to be so incomparably the most interesting was of course anything but the usual; yet the Albany origin, the woodnote wild, sounded out even amid her various voices and kept her true, in her way, to something we could only have called local, or perhaps family, type. Essentially, however, she had been a free incalculable product, a vivid exception to rules and precedents; so far as she had at all the value of the "composite" it was on her own lines altogether—the composition was of things that had lain nearest to hand. It mattered enormously for such a pair as the Bootts, intimately associated father and daughter, that what had lain nearest *their* hand, or at least that of conspiring nature and fortune in preparing them for our consumption, had been the things of old Italy, of the inconceivable Tuscany, that of the but lately expropriated Grand Dukes in particular, and that when originally alighting among us *en plein* Newport they had seemed fairly to reek with a saturation, esthetic, historic, romantic, that everything roundabout made precious. I was to apprehend in due course, and not without dismay, that what they really most reeked with was the delight of finding us ourselves exactly as we were; they fell so into the wondrous class of inverted romantics, several other odd flowers of which I was later on to have anxiously to deal with: we and our large crude scene of barbaric plenty, as it might have been called, beguiled them to appreciations such as made our tribute to themselves excite at moments their impatience and strike them as almost silly. It was *our* conditions that were picturesque, and I had to make the best of a time when they themselves appeared to consent to remain so but by the beautiful gaiety of their preference. This, I remember well, I found disconcerting, so that my main affectionate business with them became, under amusement by the way, that of keeping them true to type. What above all contributed was that they really couldn't help their case, try as they would to shake off the old infection; they were of "old world" production through steps it was too late to retrace; and they were in the practical way and in the course of the very next years to plead as guilty to this as the highest proper standard for them could have prescribed. They "went back," and again and again, with a charming, smiling, pleading inconsequence—any pretext but the real one, the fact that the prime poison was in their veins, serving them at need; so that, as the case turned, all my own earlier sense, on the spot, of Florence and Rome was to mix itself with their delightfully rueful presence there. I could then perfectly put up with that flame of passion for Boston and Newport in them which still left so perfect their adaptability to Italian installations that would have been impossible save for subtle Italian reasons.

I speak of course but of the whole original view: time brings strange revenges and contradictions, and all the later history was to be a chapter by itself and of the fullest. We had been all alike accessible in the first instance to the call of those references which played through their walk and conversation with an effect that their qualifying ironies and amusing reactions, where such memories were concerned, couldn't in the least abate; for nothing in fact lent them a happier colour than just this ability to afford so carelessly to cheapen the certain treasure of their past. They had enough of that treasure to give it perpetually away—in our subsequently to be more determined, our present, sense; in short we had the fondest use for their leavings even when they themselves hadn't. Mary Temple, with her own fine quality so far from composite, rejoiced in the perception, however unassisted by any sort of experience, of what their background had "meant"; she would have liked to be able to know just that for herself, as I have already hinted, and I actually find her image most touching perhaps by its so speaking of what she with a peculiar naturalness dreamed of and missed. Of clear old English stock on her father's side, her sense for what was English in life—so we used to simplify—was an intimate part of her, little chance as it enjoyed for happy verifications. In the Bootts, despite their still ampler and more recently attested share in that racial strain, the foreign tradition had exceedingly damped the English, which didn't however in the least prevent her being caught up by it as it had stamped itself upon the admirable, the infinitely civilised and sympathetic, the markedly *produced* Lizzie. This delightful girl, educated, cultivated, accomplished, toned above all, as from steeping in a rich old medium, to a degree of the rarest among her coevals "on our side," had the further, the supreme grace that she melted into American opportunities of friendship—and small blame to her, given such as she then met—with the glee of a sudden scarce believing discoverer. Tuscany could only swoon away under comparison of its starved sociabilities and complacent puerilities, the stress of which her previous years had so known, with the multiplied welcomes and freedoms, the exquisite and easy fellowships that glorified to her the home scene. Into not the least of these quick affinities had her prompt acquaintance with Mary Temple confidently ripened; and with no one in the aftertime, so long as that too escaped the waiting shears, was I to find it more a blest and sacred rite, guarded by no stiff approaches, to celebrate my cousin's memory. That really is my apology for this evocation —which might under straighter connections have let me in still deeper; since if I have glanced on another page of the present miscellany at the traps too often successfully set for my wandering feet my reader will doubtless here recognise a perfect illustration of our danger and will accuse me of treating an inch of canvas to an acre of embroidery. Let the poor canvas figure time and the embroidery figure consciousness—the proportion will perhaps then not strike us as so wrong. Consciousness accordingly still grips me to the point of a felt pressure of interest in such a matter as the recoverable history —history in the esthetic connection at least—of its insistent dealings with a given case. How in the course of time for instance was it not insistently to deal, for a purpose of application, with the fine prime image deposited all unwittingly by the "picturesque" (as I absolutely required to feel it) Boott situation or Boott *data*? The direct or vital value of these last, in so many ways, was experiential, a stored and assimilated thing; but the seed of suggestion proved after long years to have kept itself apart in order that it should develop under a particular breath. A not other than lonely and bereft American, addicted to the arts and endowed for them, housed to an effect of long expatriation in a massive old Florentine villa with a treasured and tended little daughter by his side, *that* was the germ which for reasons beyond my sounding the case of Frank Boott had been appointed to plant deep down in my vision of things. So lodged it waited, but the special instance, as I say, had lodged it, and it lost no vitality—on the contrary it acquired every patience—by the fact that little by little each of its connections above ground, so to speak, was successively cut. Then at last after years it raised its own head into the air and found its full use for the imagination. An Italianate bereft American with a little moulded daughter in the setting of a massive old Tuscan residence was at the end of years exactly what was required by a situation of my own—conceived in the light of the Novel; and I *had* it there, in the authenticated way, with its essential fund of truth, at once all the more because my admirable old friend had given it to me and none the less because he had no single note of character or temper, not a grain of the non-essential, in common with my Gilbert Osmond. This combination of facts has its shy interest, I think, in the general imaginative or reproductive connection—testifying as it so happens to do on that whole question of the "putting of people into books" as to which any ineptitude of judgment appears always in order. I probably shouldn't have had the Gilbert Osmonds at all without the early "form" of the Frank

Bootts, but I still more certainly shouldn't have had them with the *sense* of my old inspirers. The form had to be disembarrassed of that sense and to take in a thoroughly other; thanks to which account of the matter I am left feeling that I scarce know whether most to admire, for support of one's beautiful business of the picture of life, the relation of "people" to art or the relation of art to people. Adorable each time the mystery of which of these factors, as we say, has the more prevailingly conduced to a given effect—and too much adored, at any rate, I allow, when carrying me so very far away. I retrace my steps with this next.

> I have made several attempts lately to write you a letter, but I have given it up after two or three pages, because I have always been in a blue state of mind at the time, and have each time charitably decided before it was too late to spare you. But if I were to wait until things change to rose-colour I might perhaps wait till I die, or longer even, in which case your next communication from me would be a spiritual one. I am going to Newport in the early part of May to meet the Bootts—Henrietta has just come back from there delighted with her visit; why, heaven knows, I suppose, but I don't—except that she is in that blissful state of babyhood peculiar to herself where everything seems delightful. . . . I like George Eliot not through her poem so much, not nearly so much, as through her prose. The creature interests me personally, and I feel a desire to know something of her life; how far her lofty moral sentiments have served her practically—for instance in her dealings with Lewes. I see that she understands the character of a *generous* woman, that is of a woman who believes in generosity and who must be that or nothing, and who feels keenly, notwithstanding, how hard it is practically to follow this out, and how (looking at it from the point of view of comfort as far as this world goes) it "pays" not at all. We are having weather quite like summer and rather depressing; I don't feel very well and am always catching cold—that is I suppose I am, as I have a cough nearly all the time. As for Phillips Brooks, what you say of him is, no doubt, all true—he didn't touch the main point when *I* heard him, at all events, and that satisfaction you so kindly wish me is, I am afraid, not to be got from any man. The mystery of this world grows and grows, and sticks out of every apparently trivial thing, instead of lessening. I hope this feeling may not be the incipient stage of insanity. Paul told the truth when he said that now we see through

a glass, *very* darkly. I hope and trust that the rest may be equally true, and that some day we shall see face to face. You say it is easy to drown thought by well-doing, and is it not also the soundest philosophy (so long of course as one doesn't humbug oneself); since by simply thinking out a religion who has ever arrived at anything that did not leave one's heart empty? Do you ever see Willy James? Good-bye.

Needless enough surely to declare that such pages were essentially not love-letters: that they could scarce have been less so seems exactly part of their noble inevitability, as well as a proof singularly interesting and charming that confident friendship may obey its force and insist on its say quite as much as the sentiment we are apt to take, as to many of its occasions, for the supremely vocal. We have so often seen this latter beat distressfully about the bush for something still deficient, something in the line of positive esteem or constructive respect, whether offered or enjoyed, that an esteem and a respect such as we here apprehend, explicit enough on either side to dispense with those superlatives in which graceless reaction has been known insidiously to lurk, peculiarly refresh and instruct us. The fine special quietude of the relation thus promoted in a general consciousness of unrest—and even if it could breed questions too, since a relation that breeds none at all is not a living one—was of the highest value to the author of my letters, who had already sufficiently "lived," in her generous way, to know well enough in how different a quarter to look for the grand inconclusive. The directness, the ease, the extent of the high consideration, the felt need of it as a support, indeed one may almost say as an inspiration, in trouble, and the free gift of it as a delightful act of intelligence and justice, render the whole exhibition, to my sense, admirable in its kind. Questions luckily *could* haunt it, as I say and as we shall presently see, but only to illustrate the more all the equilibrium preserved. I confess I can imagine no tribute to a manly nature from a feminine more final even than the confidence in "mere" consideration here embodied—the comfort of the consideration being in the fact that the character with which the feminine nature was dealing lent it, could it but come, such weight. We seem to see play through the whole appeal of the younger person to the somewhat older an invocation of the weight suspended, weight of judgment, weight of experience and authority, and which may ever so quietly drop. How kindly in another relation it had been in fact capable of dropping comes back to me in the mention of my brother Wilky, as to whom this aspect of his admiring friendship for our young relative's correspondent, the fruit of their common military service roundabout Charleston, again comprehensively testifies. That comradeship was a privilege that Wilky strongly cherished, as well as what one particularly liked to think for him of his having known—he was to have known nothing more fortunate. In no less a degree was our elder brother to come to prize *his* like share in the association—this being sufficiently indicated, for that matter, in the note I have quoted from him. That I have prized my own share in it let my use of this benefit derived strongly represent. But again for Minnie herself the sadder admonition is sharp, and I find I know not what lonely pluck in her relapses shaken off as with the jangle of silver bells, her expert little efforts to live them down, Newport and other matters aiding and the general preoccupied good will all vainly at her service. Pitiful in particular her carrying her trouble experimentally back to the Newport of the first gladness of her girlhood and of the old bright spectacle.

> I know quite well I don't owe you a letter, and that the custom for maidens is to mete out strictly letter for letter; but if you don't mind it I don't, and if you *do* mind that kind of thing you had better learn not to at once—if you propose to be a friend of mine; or else have your feelings from time to time severely shocked. After which preamble I will say that there is a special reason in this case, though there might not be in another.

She mentions having seen a common friend, in great bereavement and trouble, who has charged her with a message to her correspondent "if you know of anything to comfort a person when the one they love best dies, for heaven's sake say it to her—*I* hadn't a word to say." And she goes on:

> I wrote to you that I was going to Newport, and I meant to go next Tuesday, but I had another hemorrhage last night, and it is impossible to say when I shall be able to leave here. I think I

was feeling ill when I last wrote to you, and ever since have been coughing and feeling wretchedly, until finally the hemorrhage has come. If that goes over well I think I shall be better. I am in bed now, on the old plan of gruel and silence, and I may get off without any worse attack this time. It is a perfect day, like summer —my windows are up and the birds sing. It seems quite out of keeping that I should be in bed. I should be all right if I could only get rid of coughing. The warm weather will set me up again. I wonder what you are doing to-day. Probably taking a solitary walk and meditating—on what? Good-bye.

But she went to Newport after a few days apparently; whence comes this.

I believe I was in bed when I last wrote to you, but that attack didn't prove nearly so bad a one as the previous; I rather bullied it, and after the fourth hemorrhage it ceased; moreover my cough is better since I came here. But I am, to tell the truth, a little homesick —and am afraid I am becoming too much of a baby. Whether it's from illness or from the natural bent I know not, but there is no comfort in life away from people who care for you—not an heroic statement, I am fully aware. I hear that Wilky is at home, and dare say he will have the kindness to run down and see me while I am here; at least I hope so. But I am not in the mood for writing to-day—I am tired and can only bore you if I kept on. It is just a year since we began to write, and aren't you by this time a little tired of it? If you are, say so like a man—don't be afraid of me. Now I am going to lie down before dressing for dinner. Good-bye.

This passage more than a month later makes me ask myself of which of the correspondents it strikes me as most characteristic. The gay clearness of the one looks out—as it always looked out on the least chance given—at the several apparent screens of the other; each of which is indeed disconnectedly, independently clear, but tells too small a part (at least for her pitch of lucidity) of what they together enclose, and what was *quand même* of so fine an implication. Delightful at the same time any page from her that is not one of the huddled milestones of her rate of decline.

How can I write to you when I have forgotten all about you?— if one *can* forget what one has never known. However, I am not quite sure whether it isn't knowing you too much rather than too little that seems to prevent. Do you comprehend the difficulty? Of course you don't, so I will explain. The trouble is, I think, that to me you have no distinct personality. I don't feel sure to whom I am writing when I say to myself that I will write to you. I see mentally three men, all answering to your name, each liable to read my letters and yet differing so much from each other that if it is proper for one of them it's quite unsuitable to the others. Do you see? If you can once settle for me the question of which gets my letters I shall know better what to say in them. Is it the man I used to see (I can't say know) at Conway, who had a beard, I think, and might have been middle-aged, and who discussed Trollope's novels with Kitty and Elly? This was doubtless one of the best of men, but he didn't *interest* me, I never felt disposed to speak to him, and used to get so sleepy in his society at about eight o'clock that I wondered how the other girls could stay awake till eleven. Is it *that* person who reads my letters? Or is it the young man I recently saw at Newport, with a priestly countenance, calm and critical, with whom I had certainly no fault to find as a chance companion for three or four days, but whom I should never have dreamt of writing to or bothering with my affairs one way or the other, happiness or no happiness, as he would doubtless at once despise me for my nonsense and wonder at me for my gravity? Does *he* get my letters?—or is it finally the being who has from time to time himself written to me, signing by the same name that the other gentlemen appropriate? If my correspondent is this last I know where I stand—and, please heaven, shall stand there some time longer. Him I won't describe, but he's the only one of the three I care anything about. My only doubt is because I always address him at Pemberton Square, and I think him the least likely of the three to go there much. But good-bye, whichever you are!

It was not at any rate to be said of her that she didn't live surrounded, even though she had to go so far afield—very far it may at moments have appeared to her—for the freedom of talk that was her greatest need of all. How happily and hilariously surrounded this next, of the end of the following August, and still more its sequel of the mid-September, abundantly bring back to me; so in the habit were the numerous Emmets, it might almost be said, of marrying the numerous young women of our own then kinship: they at all events formed mainly by themselves at that time the figures and the action of her immediate scene. The marriage of her younger sister was as yet but an engagement—to the brother-in-law of the eldest, already united to Richard Emmet and with Temple kinship, into the bargain, playing between the pairs. All of which animation of prospective and past wedding-bells, with whatever consolidation of pleasant ties, couldn't quench her ceaseless instinct for the obscurer connections of things or keep passionate reflections from awaiting her at every turn. This disposition in her, and the way in which, at the least push, the gate of thought opened for her to its widest, which was to the prospect of the soul and the question of interests on *its* part that wouldn't be ignored, by no means fails to put to me that she might well have found the mystifications of life, had she been appointed to enjoy more of them, much in excess of its contentments. It easily comes up for us over the relics of those we have seen beaten, this sense that it was not for nothing they missed the ampler experience, but in no case that I have known has it come up for me so much. In none other have I so felt the naturalness of our asking ourselves what such spirits would have done with their extension and what would have satisfied them; since dire as their defeat may have been we don't see them, in the ambiguous light of some of their possibilities, at peace with victory. This may be perhaps an illusion of our interest in them, a mere part of its ingenuity; and I allow that if our doubt is excessive it does them a great wrong—which is another way in which they were not to have been righted. We soothe a little with it at any rate our sense of the tragic.

> . . . The irretrievableness of the step (her sister E.'s marriage) comes over my mind from time to time in such an overwhelming way that it's most depressing, and I have to be constantly on my guard not to let Temple and Elly see it, as it would naturally not please them. After all, since they are not appalled at what they've done, and are quite sure of each other, as they evidently are, why should I worry myself? I am well aware that if all other women felt the seriousness of the matter to the extent I do, hardly any would *ever* marry, and the human race would stop short. So I ought perhaps to be glad so many people can find and take that "little ease" that Clough talks about, without consciously giving up the "highest thing." And may not this majority of people be

the truly wise and my own notions of the subject simply fanatical and impracticable? I clearly see in how small a minority I am, and that the other side has, with Bishop Blougram, the best of it from one point of view; but I can't help that, can I? We must be true to *ourselves*, mustn't we? though all the rest of humanity be of a contrary opinion, or else throw discredit upon the wisdom of God, who made us as we are and not like the next person. Do you remember my old hobby of the "remote possibility of the best thing" being better than a clear certainty of the second best? Well, I believe it more than ever, every day I live. Indeed I don't believe anything else—but is not that everything? And isn't it exactly what Christianity means? Wasn't Christ the only man who ever lived and died *entirely* for his faith, without a shadow of selfishness? And isn't that reason enough why we should all turn to Him after having tried everything else and found it wanting?—turn to Him as the only pure and *unmixed* manifestation of God in humanity? And if I believe this, which I think I do, how utterly inconsistent and detestable is the life I lead, which, so far from being a loving and cheerful surrender of itself once for all to God's service, is at best but a base compromise—a few moments or acts or thoughts consciously and with difficulty divested of actual selfishness. Must this always be so? Is it owing to the indissoluble mixture of the divine and the diabolical in us all, or is it because I myself am hopelessly frivolous and trifling? Or is it finally that I really don't *believe*, that I have still a doubt in my mind whether religion *is* the one exclusive thing to live for, as Christ taught us, or whether it will prove to be only *one* of the influences, though a great one, which educate the human race and help it along in that culture which Matthew Arnold thinks the most desirable thing in the world? In fine is it the meaning and end of our lives, or only a moral principle bearing a certain part in our development——?

Since I wrote this I have been having my tea and sitting on the piazza looking at the stars and thinking it most unfaithful and disloyal of me even to speak as I did just now, admitting the possibility of that faith not being everything which yet at moments is so divinely true as to light up the whole of life suddenly and make everything clear. I know the trouble is with *me* when doubt and despondency come, but on the other hand I can't altogether believe it wrong of me to have written as I have, for then what becomes of my principle of saying what one really thinks and leaving it to God to take care of his own glory? The truth will vindicate itself in spite of my voice to the contrary. If you think I am letting myself go this way without sufficient excuse I won't do it again;

> but I can't help it this time, I have nobody else to speak to about serious things. If by chance I say anything or ask a question that lies at all near my heart my sisters all tell me I am "queer" and that they "wouldn't be me for anything"—which is, no doubt, sensible on their part, but which puts an end to anything but conversation of the most superficial kind on mine. You know one gets lonely after a while on such a plan of living, so in sheer desperation I break out where I perhaps more safely can.

Such is the magic of old letters on its subtlest occasions that I reconstitute in every detail, to a vivid probability—even if I may not again proportionately project the bristling image—our scene of next mention; drawing for this upon my uneffaced impression of a like one, my cousin Katharine Temple's bright nuptials, in the same general setting, very much before, and in addition seeming to see the very muse of history take a fresh scroll in order to prepare to cover it, in her very handsomest hand, well before my eyes. Covered is it now for me with that abounding and interesting life of the generations then to come at the pair of preliminary flourishes ushering in the record of which I thus feel myself still assist.

> But a line to-day to tell you that Elly was safely married on Wednesday. She looked simply beautiful in her wedding garment, and behaved herself throughout with a composure that was as delightful as it was surprising. I send you a photograph of myself that I had taken a few weeks ago. It looks perhaps a trifle melancholy, but I can't help that—I did the best I could. But I won't write more—it wouldn't be enlivening. Everything looks grey and blue in the world nowadays. It will all be bright again in time, I have no doubt; there is no special reason for it; I think I am simply tired with knocking about. Yet my week in Newport might have been pleasant enough if the dentist hadn't taken that occasion to break my bones for me in a barbarous manner. You are very kind and friendly to me—you don't know how much happiness your letters give me. You will be surprised, I dare say, but I shall not, at the last day, when the accounts are all settled, to find how much this counts in your favour. Good-bye.

I find my story so attaching that I prize every step of its course, each note of which hangs together with all the others. The writer is expressed to my vision in every word, and the resulting image so worth preserving. Much of one's service to it is thus a gathering-in of the ever so faded ashes of the happiness that did come to her after all in snatches. Everything could well, on occasion, look "grey and blue," as she says; yet there were stretches, even if of the briefest, when other things still were present than the active symptoms of her state. The photograph that she speaks of above is before me as I write and blessedly helpful to memory—so that I am moved to reproduce it only till I feel again how the fondness of memory must strike the light for apprehension. The plan of the journey to California for the advantage of the climate there was, with other plans taken up and helplessly dropped, but beguiling for the day, to accompany her almost to the end.

> The Temple-Emmet caravan have advanced as far as Newport and now propose to retreat again to Pelham without stopping at Boston or anywhere else. My brother-in-law has business in New York and can't be away any longer. I haven't been well of late, or I should have run up to Boston for a day or two to take a sad farewell of all I love in that city and thereabouts before I cross the Rocky Mountains. This little trip has been made out for me by my friends; I have determined to go, and shall probably start with Elly and Temple in about ten days, possibly not for a fortnight, to spend the winter in San Francisco. I can't be enthusiastic about it, but suppose I might as well take all the means I can to get better: a winter in a warm climate *may* be good for me. In short I am going, and now what I want *you* to do about it is simply to come and see us before that. Kitty is going to send you a line to add her voice—perhaps that may bring you. You may never see me again, you know, and if I were to die so far away you'd be sorry you hadn't taken leave of me, wouldn't you?

The idea of California held, and with other pleasant matters really occupied the scene; out of which moreover insist on shining to me accessory connections, or connections that then were to be: intensely distinct for example the figure of Miss Crawford, afterwards Madame von Rabe, sister of my eminent friend F. Marion of the name and, in her essence, I think, but by a few shades less entire a figure than he—which is saying much. The most endowed and accomplished of men Frank Crawford, so that I have scarcely known another who had more aboundingly lived and wrought, about whom moreover there was singularly more to be said, it struck me, than at all found voice at the time he might have been commemorated. Therefore if the young lady alluded to in my cousin's anecdote was at all of the same personal style and proportion—well, I should draw the moral if it didn't represent here too speciously the mouth of a trap, one of those I have already done penance for; the effect of my yielding to which would be a shaft sunk so straight down into matters interesting and admirable and sad and strange that, with everything that was futurity to the occasion noted in our letter and is an infinitely mixed and a heavily closed past now, I hurry on without so much as a glance.

> The present plan is to send me to California in about three weeks by water, under the care of one of the Emmet boys and Temple's valet—for nurse; and by the time I get there, early in December, they will be settled in San Francisco for the winter. The idea of a twenty-one days' sea-voyage is rather appalling—what do you think of it? This day is but too heavenly here. I haven't been to church, but walking by myself, as happy as possible. When one sleeps well and the sun shines, what happiness to live! I wish you were here—wouldn't I show you Pelham at high tide, on a day that is simply intoxicating, with a fresh breeze blown through the red and yellow leaves and sunshine "on field and hill, in heart and brain," as Mr. Lowell says. I suppose you remember the pony I drove, and Punch, the little Scotch terrier that tried so to insinuate himself into your affections, on the piazza, the morning you left. The former has been "cutting up," the latter *cut* up, since then. You wouldn't believe me when I told you the pony was a highly nervous creature—but she behaved as one the other day when I took the Roman Miss Crawford, who has been staying near here, a ride. She shied at a dog that frightened her, and dragged the cart into a ditch, and tried to get over a stone wall, waggon and all. I of course had to hang on to the reins, but I suggested to Miss Crawford that she should get out, as the cart was pretty steady while the horse's forefeet were on top of the wall; which she did, into a mud-puddle, and soiled her pretty striped stockings and shoes in a horrible way. It ended by the dear little beast's consenting to get back upon all fours, but I found it very amusing and have liked her better ever since. . . . How does Mr. Holmes persevere about smoking? I pity him if he can't sleep, and wish *I* had a vicious habit so that I might give it up. But I must finish my tale of the

> quadruped Punch, who was called upon in the dead of night by five dogs of the neighbourhood and torn to pieces by them. The coachman heard him crying in the night, and in the morning we found him—that is to say we gathered him together, his dear little tail from one place and his head from another etc! So went out a very sweet little spirit—I wonder where it is now. Don't tell me he hadn't more of a soul than that Kaufmann, the fat oysterman.

I find bribes to recognition and recovery quite mercilessly multiply, and with the effort to brush past them more and more difficult; with the sense for me at any rate (whatever that may be worth for wisdom or comfort) of sitting rather queerly safe and alone, though as with a dangle of legs over the edge of a precipice, on the hither side of great gulfs of history. But these things, dated toward the end of that November, speak now in a manner for themselves.

> My passage for California is taken for the 4th of December; Elly and Temple have written to me to come at once—they are settled in San Francisco for the winter. My brother-in-law here has been promised that I shall be made so comfortable I shan't want to tear myself from the ship when I arrive. The captain is a friend of Temple's, and also of my uncle Captain Temple, and both of them are going to arrange so for me that I fully expect the ship to be hung with banners and flowers when I step on board. . . . I enjoyed my time in Boston far more than I had expected—in fact immensely, and wouldn't have missed it for anything; I feel now as if it had *necessarily* had to happen. I don't know how I should have done the winter, and especially started off for an indefinitely long absence in the west without the impetus that it gave me in certain directions—the settling down and shaking up, the dissipating of certain impressions that I had thought fixed and the strengthening of others that I hadn't been so sure of: an epoch in short. I dare say you have had such—in which a good deal of living was done in a short time, to be turned over and made fruitful in days to come. I saw Mr. Holmes once, and was very glad of that glimpse, short as it was. I went home by way of Newport, where I stayed two days—and where I was surprised to hear of Fred Jones's engagement to Miss Rawle of Philadelphia. Do you know her? When I got to New York I went to the Hones' to ask something about Fred and his affairs and found that Miss Rawle was staying next door with Mrs. Willy Duncan; so I went in to see her on the spur of the moment, very much as I had come from the boat, not

particularly presentable for a first call: however, I thought if she had a soul she wouldn't mind it—and such I found the case. . . . Lizzie Boott was as sweet and good to me as ever; I think she is at once the most unselfish and most unegotistical girl I know—they don't always go together.

What follows here has, in its order, I think, that it still so testifies to life—if one doesn't see in it indeed rather perhaps the instinct on the writer's part, though a scarce conscious one, to wind up the affairs of her spirit, as it were, and be able to turn over with a sigh of supreme relief for an end intimately felt as at hand. The moral fermentation breaking through the bustle of outward questions even at a time when she might have thrown herself, as one feels, on the great soft breast of equalising Nature, or taken her chance of not being too wrong, is a great stroke of truth. No one really could be less "morbid"; yet she would take no chance—it wasn't in her—of not being right with the right persons; among whom she so ranked her correspondent.

My address at San Francisco will be simply Care of C. Temple Emmet, Esq.; and I am surely off this time unless heaven interposes in a miraculous way between now and Saturday. I've no great courage about it, but after all it's much the same to me where I am; life is always full of interest and mystery and happiness to me, and as for the voyage, the idea of three weeks of comparative solitude between sea and sky isn't unattractive. . . . I know that by my question [as to why he had written, apparently, that she was, of her nature, "far off" from him] I am putting an end to that delightful immunity I have enjoyed so much with you from sickening introspection, analysis of myself and yourself, that exhausting and nauseating subjectivity, with which most of my other friends see fit to deluge me, thereby taking much that is refreshing out of life. Don't be afraid of "hurting my feelings" by anything you can say. Our friendship has always been to my mind a one-sided thing, and if you should tell me you find me in any way unsympathetic or unsatisfactory it won't disappoint me, and I won't even allow myself to think I'm sorry. I feel so clearly that God knows best, and that we ought neither of us surely to wish to distort his creatures from the uses he made them for, just to serve our own purposes—that is to get a little more sympathy and comfort. We must each of us, after all, live out our own lives apart from everyone else; and yet, this being once understood as a fundamental truth, there is nobody's sympathy and approval that would encourage me so much as yours. I mean that if one's heart and motives could be known by another as God knows them, without disguise or extenuation, and if it should *then* prove that on the *whole* you didn't think well of me, it would, more than anything else could, shake my confidence in my own instincts, which must after all forever be my guide. And yet, as I said before, I am quite prepared for the worst, and shall listen to it, if necessary, quite humbly. I am very much inclined to trust your opinion before my own.

An hour later. *Sold* again, by all that's wonderful—I had almost said by all that's damnable, though it isn't exactly that. My brother Dick has just walked in with a telegram from Temple: "I shall be back in December—don't send M." A tremendous revulsion of feeling and a general sigh of relief have taken place on this announcement, and it's all right, I'm sure, though when I wrote you an hour ago I thought the same of the other prospect.

One catches one's breath a little, frankly, at what was to follow the above within a few days—implying as it does that she had drawn upon herself some fairly direct statement of her correspondent's reserves of view as to her human or "intellectual" composition. To have *had* such reserves at such an hour, and to have responded to the invitation to express them—for invitation there had been—is something that our actual larger light quite helps us to flatter ourselves *we* shouldn't have been capable of. But what was of the essence between these admirable persons was exactly the tone of truth; the larger light was all to wait for, and the real bearings of the hour were as unapparent as the interlocutors themselves were at home in clearness, so far as they might bring that ideal about. And whatever turn their conversation took is to the honour always of the generous girl's passion for truth. As this long letter admirably illustrates that, I withdraw from it almost nothing. The record of the rare commerce would be incomplete without it; all the more perhaps for the wonder and pain of our seeing the noble and pathetic young creature have, of all things, in her predicament, to plead for extenuations, to excuse and justify herself.

I understood your letter perfectly well—it was better than I feared it might be, but bad enough. Better because I knew already all it told me, and had been afraid there might be some new and horrible development in store for me which I hadn't myself felt; but bad enough because I find it in itself, new or old, such a disgusting fact that I am intellectually so unsympathetic. It is a fault I feel profoundly conscious of, but one that, strange to say, I have only of late been conscious of *as* a fault. I dare say I have always known, in a general way, that I am very unobservant about things and take very little interest in subjects upon which my mind doesn't naturally dwell; but it had never occurred to me before that it is a fault that ought to be corrected. Whether because I have never been given to studying myself much, but have just let myself go the way my mind was most inclined to, more interested in the subject itself than in the fact that it interested me; or whether because one is averse to set oneself down as indolent and egotistic I don't know; at all events I have of late seen the thing in all its unattractiveness, and I wish I could get over it. Do you think that, now I am fully roused to the fact, my case is hopeless? Or that if I should try hard for the next twenty-five years I might succeed in modifying it? I am speaking now of a want of interest in *all* the rest of the world; of not having the desire to investigate subjects, naturally uninteresting to me, just because they are interesting to some other human being whom I don't particularly owe anything to except that he *is* a human being, and so his thoughts and feelings ought to be respected by me and sympathised with. Not to do this is, I know, unphilosophic and selfish, conceited and altogether inhuman. To be unselfish, to live for other people, to mould our lives as much as possible on the model of Christ's all-embracing humanity, seems most clearly to my mind the one thing worth living for; and yet it is still the hardest thing for me to do, and I think I do it less than anybody else who feels the necessity of it strongly at all.

I am glad you still go to an occasional ball—I should rather like to meet you at one myself; it's a phase of life we have seen so little of together. I have been feeling so well lately that I don't know what to make of it. I don't remember ever in my life being in such good spirits. Not that they are not in general pretty natural to me when there is the slightest excuse for them, but now everything seems bright and happy, my life so full of interest, my time so thoroughly filled and such a delicious calm to have settled down on my usually restless spirit. Such an enjoyment of the *present*, such a grateful contentment, is in each new day as I see it dawn in the east, that I can only be thankful and say to myself: "Make a note of this—you are happy; don't forget it, nor to be thankful for this beautiful gift of life." This is Sunday morning, and I wonder whether you are listening to Phillips Brooks. I understand how you feel about his preaching—that it is all feeling and no reason; I found it so myself last winter in Philadelphia: he was good for those within the pale, but not good to convince outsiders that they should come in. I am glad, however, that he preaches in this way—I think his power lies in it; for it seems to me, after all, that what comfort we get from religion, and what light we have upon it, come to us through feeling, that is through trusting our instinct as the voice of God, the Holy Ghost, though it may at the same time appear to us directly against what our intellect teaches us. I don't mean by this that we should deny the conclusions arrived at by our intellect—which on the contrary I believe we should trust and stand by to the bitter end, whenever this may be. But let us fearlessly trust our *whole* nature, showing our faith in God by being true to ourselves all through, and not dishonouring Him by ignoring what our heart says because it is not carried out by our intellect, or by wilfully blunting our intellectual perception because it happens to run against some cherished wish of our heart.

"But," you will say, "how can a man live torn to pieces this way by these contrary currents?" Well, I know it is hard to keep our faith *sure* of a standpoint where these apparent inconsistencies are all reconciled and the jangle and discord sound the sweetest harmony; but I do believe there *is* one, in God, and that we must only try to have that faith and never mind how great the inconsistency may seem, nor how perplexing the maze it leads us through. Let us never give up one element of the problem for the sake of coming to a comfortable solution of it in this world. I don't blame those eager minds that are always worrying, studying, investigating, to *find* the solution here below; it is a noble work, and let them follow it out (and without a bit of compromise) to whom God has given the work. But whether we find it or not I would have them and all of us feel that it is to *be* found, if God wills—and through no other means surely than by our being *true*. Blessed are they who have not seen and who have yet believed. But I am going out now for a walk! We have had the most delightful weather this whole week, and capital sleighing, and I have spent most of my time driving myself about with that same dear little pony. I went to town yesterday to a matinée of William Tell; it was delightful and I slept all night after it too. I am reading German a little every day, and it's beginning to go pretty well. Good-bye. Don't tire yourself out between work and dissipation.

I find myself quite sit up to her, as we have it to-day, while she sits there without inconvenience, after all that has happened, under the dead weight of William Tell; the relief of seeing her sublimely capable of which, with the reprieve from her formidable flight to the Pacific doubtless not a little contributing, helps to draw down again the vision, or more exactly the sound, of the old New York and Boston Opera as our young generation knew and artlessly admired it; admired it, by my quite broken memories of the early time, in Brignoli the sweet and vague, in Susini the deep and rich, in Miss Kellogg the native and charming, in Adelaide Phillipps the universal, to say nothing of other acclaimed warblers (they appear to me to have warbled then so much more than since) whom I am afraid of not placing in the right perspective. They warbled Faust a dozen times, it comes back to me, for once of anything else; Miss Kellogg and Brignoli heaped up the measure of that success, and I well remember the great yearning with which I heard my cousin describe her first enchanted sense of it. The next in date of the letters before me, of the last day but one of December '69, is mainly an interesting expression of the part that music plays in her mental economy—though but tentatively offered to her correspondent, who, she fears, may not be musical enough to understand her, understand how much "spiritual truth has been 'borne in' upon me by means of harmony: the relation of the part to the whole, the absolute value of the individual, the absolute necessity of uncompromising and unfaltering truth, the different ways in which we like our likes and our unlikes," things all that have been so made clearer to her. Of a singular grace in movement and attitude, a grace of free mobility and activity, as original and "unconventional" as it was carelessly natural, she never looked more possessed of her best resources than at the piano in which she delighted, at which she had ardently worked, and where, slim and straight, her shoulders and head constantly, sympathetically swaying, she discoursed with an admirable touch and a long surrender that was like a profession of the safest relation she could know. Comparatively safe though it might have been, however, in the better time, she was allowed now, I gather, but little playing, and she is deep again toward the end of January '70 in a quite other exposure, the old familiar exposure to the "demon," as she calls it, "of the Why, Whence, Whither?" Long as the letter is I feel it a case again for presentation whole; the last thoughts of her life, as they appear, breathe in it with such elevation. They seem to give us her last words and impulses, and, with what follows of the middle of February, constitute the moving climax of her rich short story.

> There have been times (and they will come again no doubt) when I could write to you about ordinary things in a way at least not depressing; but for a good while now I have felt so tired out, bodily and mentally, that I couldn't conscientiously ask you to share my mood. The life I live here in the country, and so very much alone, is capable of being the happiest or the unhappiest of existences, as it all depends so on oneself and is so very little interfered with by outside influences. Perhaps I am more than usually subject to extremes of happiness and of depression, yet I suppose everyone must have moments, even in the most varied and distracting life, when the old questioning spirit, the demon of the Why, Whence, Whither? stalks in like the skeleton at the feast and takes a seat beside him. I say everyone, but I must except those rare and happy souls who really believe in Christianity, who no longer strive after even goodness as it comes from one's own effort, but take refuge in the mysterious sacrifice of Christ, his merit sufficing, and in short throw themselves in the orthodox way on the consoling truth of the Atonement—to me hitherto neither comprehensible nor desirable. These people, having completely surrendered self, having lost their lives, as it were in Christ, must truly have found them, must know the rest that comes from literally casting their care of doubt and strife and thought upon the Lord.
>
> I say hitherto the doctrine of the vicarious suffering of Christ has been to me not only incomprehensible but also unconsoling; I didn't want it and didn't understand even intellectually the feeling of people who do. I don't mean to say that the life and death of Christ and the example they set for us have not been to me always the brightest spot in history—for they have; but they have stood rather as an example that we must try to follow, that we must by constant and ceaseless effort bring our lives nearer to—but always, to some extent at least, through ourselves, that is through ourselves with God's help, got by asking Him for it and by His giving it to us straight and with no mediation. When I have seen as time went by my own shortcomings all the more instead of the less frequent, I have thought: "Well, you don't try hard enough; you are

not really in earnest in thinking that you believe in the Christian life as the only true one." The more I tried, nevertheless, the less it seemed like the model life; the best things I did continued to be the more spontaneous ones; the greatest efforts had the least success; until finally I couldn't but see that if this was Christianity it was not the "rest" that Christ had promised his disciples—it was nothing more than a pagan life with a high ideal, only an ideal so high that nothing but failure and unhappiness came from trying to follow it. And one night when I was awake through all the hours it occurred to me: What if this were the need that Christianity came to fill up in our hearts? What if, after all, that old meaningless form of words that had been sounded in my unheeding ears all my days were suddenly to become invested with spirit and truth? What if this were the good tidings that have made so many hearts secure and happy in the most trying situations? For if morality and virtue were the test of a Christian, certainly Christ would never have likened the kingdom of heaven to a little child, in whose heart is no struggle, no conscious battle between right and wrong, but only unthinking love and trust.

However it may turn out, whether it shall seem true or untrue to me finally, I am at least glad to be able to put myself intellectually into the place of the long line of Christians who have felt the need and the comfort of this belief. It throws a light upon Uncle Henry's talk, which has seemed to me hitherto neither reasonable nor consoling. When I was with him it so far disgusted me that I fear I showed him plainly that I found it not only highly unpractical, but ignoble and shirking. I knew all the while that he disliked what he called my pride and conceit, but felt all the same that his views didn't touch my case a bit, didn't give me the least comfort or practical help, and seemed to me wanting in earnestness and strength. *Now* I say to myself: What if the good gentleman had all along really got hold of the higher truth, the purer spirituality? Verily there are two sides to everything in this world, and one becomes more charitable the older one grows. However, if I write at this length it is because I am feeling to-day too seedy for anything else. I had a hemorrhage a week ago, which rather took the life out of me; but as it was the only one I feel I should by this time be coming round again—and probably might if I hadn't got into a sleepless state which completely knocks me up. The old consolatory remark, "Patience, neighbour, and shuffle the cards," ought to impart a little hope to me, I suppose; but it's a long time since I've had any trumps in my hand, and you know that with the best luck the game always tired me. Willy James sometimes tells me to behave like a man and a gentleman if I wish to outwit fate. What a *real* person he is! He is to me in nearly all respects a head and shoulders above other people. How is Wendell Holmes? Elly is having the gayest winter in Washington and wants me to go to them there, which I had meant to do before the return of my last winter's illness. But it's not for me now.

Later.—I have kept my letter a day or two, thinking I might feel in tune for writing you a better one and not sending this at all. But alas I shall have to wait some time before I am like my old self again, so I may as well let this go. You see I'm not in a condition, mentally or physically, to take bright and healthy views of life. But if you really care you may as well see this mood as another, for heaven only knows when I shall get out of it. Can you understand the utter weariness of thinking about one thing all the time, so that when you wake up in the morning consciousness comes back with a sigh of "Oh yes, here it is again; another day of doubting and worrying, hoping and fearing has begun." If I don't get any sleep at all, which is too frequently the case, the strain is a "leetle" bit too hard, and I am sometimes tempted to take a drop of "pison" to put me to sleep in earnest. That momentary vision of redemption from thinking and striving, of a happy rest this side of eternity, has vanished away again. I can't help it; peaceful, desirable as it may be, the truth is that practically I don't believe it. It was such a sudden thing, such an entire change from anything that had ever come to me before, that it seemed almost like an inspiration, and I waited, almost expecting it to continue, to be permanent. But it doesn't stay, and so back swings the universe to the old place—paganism, naturalism, or whatever you call the belief whose watchword is "God and our own soul." And who shall say there is not comfort in it? One at least feels that here one breathes one's native air, welcoming back the old *human* feeling, with its beautiful pride and its striving, its despair, its mystery and its faith. Write to me and tell me whether, as one goes on, one must still be tossed about more and more by these conflicting feelings, or whether they finally settle themselves quietly one way or the other and take only their proper share at least of one's life. This day is like summer, but I should enjoy it more if last night hadn't been quite the most unpleasant I ever spent. I got so thoroughly tired about two in the morning that I made up my mind in despair to give the morphine another trial, and as one dose had no effect took two; the consequence of which is that I feel as ill to-day as one could desire. I can tell you, sir, you had better prize the gift of sleep as it deserves while you have it. If I don't never write to you no more you'll know it's because I really wish to treat you kindly. But one of these days you'll get another kind of letter, brim-full perhaps with health and happiness and thoroughly ashamed of my present self. I had a long letter yesterday from Harry James at Florence—enjoying Italy but homesick. Did you see those verses in the North American translated from the Persian? Good-bye.

The last of all is full both of realities and illusions, the latter insistently living through all the distress of the former. And I should like to say, or to believe, that they remained with her to the end, which was near.

Don't be alarmed at my pencil—I am not in bed but only bundled-up on the piazza by order of the doctor. . . . I started for New York feeling a good deal knocked up, but hoping to get better from the change; I was to stay there over Sunday and see Dr. Metcalfe, who has a high reputation and was a friend of my father's. I left a request at his office that he would come to me on Sunday P.M.; but in the meantime my cousin Mrs. Minturn Post, with whom I was staying, urged upon me her physician, Dr. Taylor, who came on Saturday night, just as I was going to bed, and, after sounding my lungs, told me very dreadful things about them. As his verdict was worse than Metcalfe's proved I will tell you what he said first. He began very solemnly: "My dear young lady, your right lung is diseased; all your hemorrhages have come from there. It must have been bad for at least a year before they began. You must go to Europe as soon as possible." This was not cheerful, as I had been idiot enough to believe some time ago such a different explanation. But of course I wanted to learn what he absolutely thought, and told him I wasn't a bit afraid. If there weren't tubercles was I curable and if there *were* was I hopeless? I asked him for the very worst view he had conscientiously to take, but didn't mean definitely to ask how long I should live, and so was rather unprepared for his reply of "Two or three years." I didn't however wish to make him regret his frankness, so I said, "Well, Doctor, even if my right lung were all gone I should make a stand with my left," and then, by way of showing how valiant the stand would be, fainted away. This, I should say, was owing a good deal to my previous used-up condition from want of sleep. It made him at any rate hasten to assure me that there was every possibility of my case being not after all so bad—with which he took his departure; to my great relief as I didn't think him at all nice. His grammar was bad, and he made himself generally objectionable.

The next night dear Dr. Metcalfe came, whom I love for the gentlest and kindest soul I have ever seen. To start with he's a gentleman, as well as an excellent physician, and to end with he and my father were fond of each other at West Point, and he takes a sort of paternal interest in me. He told me that my right lung is decidedly weaker than my left, which is quite sound, and that the hemorrhage has been a good thing for it and kept it from actual disease; and also that if I can keep up my general health I may get all right again. He has known a ten times worse case get entirely well. He urged me not to go to Washington, but decidedly to go to Europe; so this last is what I am to do with my cousin Mrs. Post if I am not dead before June. In a fortnight I'm to go back to New York to be for some time under Metcalfe's care. I feel tired out and hardly able to stir, but my courage is good, and I don't propose to lose it if I can help, for I know it all depends on myself whether I get through or not. That is if I begin to be indifferent to what happens I shall go down the hill fast. I have fortunately, through my mother's father, enough Irish blood in me rather to enjoy a good fight. I feel the greatest longing for summer or spring; I should like it to be always spring for the rest of my life and to have all the people I care for always with me! But who *wouldn't* like it so? Good-bye.

To the gallantry and beauty of which there is little surely to add. But there came a moment, almost immediately after, when all illusion failed; which it is not good to think of or linger on, and yet not pitiful not to note. One may have wondered rather doubtingly—and I have expressed that—what life would have had for her and how her exquisite faculty of challenge could have "worked in" with what she was likely otherwise to have encountered or been confined to. None the less did she in fact cling to consciousness; death, at the last, was dreadful to her; she would have given anything to live—and the image of this, which was long to remain with me, appeared so of the essence of tragedy that I was in the far-off aftertime to seek to lay the ghost by wrapping it, a particular occasion aiding, in the beauty and dignity of art. The figure that was to hover as the ghost has at any rate been of an extreme pertinence, I feel, to my doubtless too loose and confused general picture, vitiated perhaps by the effort to comprehend more than it contains. Much as this cherished companion's presence among us had represented for William and myself—and it is on *his* behalf I especially speak—her death made a mark that must stand here for a too waiting conclusion. We felt it together as the end of our youth.

THE END

THE MIDDLE YEARS

Henry James from a drawing kindly lent by Mr. W. Rothenstein

EDITOR'S NOTE

The following pages represent all that Henry James lived to write of a volume of autobiographical reminiscences to which he had given the name of one of his own short stories, The Middle Years. *It was designed to follow on* Notes of a Son and Brother *and to extend to about the same length. The chapters here printed were dictated during the autumn of 1914. They were laid aside for other work toward the end of the year and were not revised by the author. A few quite evident slips have been corrected and the marking of the paragraphs—which he usually deferred till the final revision—has been completed.*

In dictating The Middle Years *he used no notes, and beyond an allusion or two in the unfinished volume itself there is no indication of the course which the book would have taken or the precise period it was intended to cover.*

PERCY LUBBOCK.

I

IF THE author of this meandering record has noted elsewhere[1] that an event occurring early in 1870 was to mark the end of his youth, he is moved here at once to qualify in one or two respects that emphasis. Everything depends in such a view on what one means by one's youth—so shifting a consciousness is this, and so related at the same time to many different matters. We are never old, that is we never cease easily to be young, for *all* life at the same time: youth is an army, the whole battalion of our faculties and our freshnesses, our passions and our illusions, on a considerably reluctant march into the enemy's country, the country of the general lost freshness; and I think it throws out at least as many stragglers behind as skirmishers ahead—stragglers who often catch up but belatedly with the main body, and even in many a case never catch up at all. Or under another figure it is a book in several volumes, and even at this a mere instalment of the large library of life, with a volume here and there closing, as something in the clap of its covers may assure us, while another remains either completely agape or kept open by a fond finger thrust in between the leaves. A volume, and a most substantial, *had* felt its pages very gravely pressed together before the winter's end that I have spoken of, but a restriction may still bear, and blessedly enough, as I gather from memory, on my sense of the whole year then terminated—a year seen by me now in the light of agitations, explorations, initiations (I scarce know how endearingly enough to name them!) which I should call fairly infantine in their indifference to proportions and aims, had they not still more left with me effects and possessions that even yet lend themselves to estimation.

It was at any rate impossible to have been younger, in spite of whatever inevitable submissions to the rather violent push forward at certain particular points and on lines corresponding with them, than I found myself, from the first day of March 1869, in the face of an opportunity that affected me then and

[1] "Notes of a Son and Brother," 1914.

there as the happiest, the most interesting, the most alluring and beguiling, that could ever have opened before a somewhat disabled young man who was about to complete his twenty-sixth year. Treasures of susceptibility, treasures not only unconscious of the remotest approach to exhaustion, but, given the dazzling possibilities, positively and ideally intact, I now recognise—I in fact long ago recognised—on the part of that intensely "reacting" small organism; which couldn't have been in higher spirits or made more inward fuss about the matter if it had come into a property measured not by mere impressions and visions, occasions for play of perception and imagination, mind and soul, but by dollars and "shares", lands and houses or flocks and herds. It is to the account of that immense fantastication that I set down a state of mind so out of proportion to anything it could point to round about save by the vaguest of foolish-looking gestures; and it would perhaps in truth be hard to say whether in the mixture of spirit and sense so determined the fact of innocence or that of intelligence most prevailed. I like to recover this really prodigious flush—as my reader, clearly, must perceive I do; I like fairly to hang about a particular small hour of that momentous March day—which I have glanced at too, I believe, on some other and less separated page than this—for the sake of the extraordinary gage of experience that it seemed on the spot to offer, and that I had but to take straight up: my life, on so complacently near a view as I now treat myself to, having veritably consisted but in the prolongation of that act. I took up the gage, and as I look back the fullest as well as simplest account of the interval till now strikes me as being that I have never, in common honour, let it drop again. And the small hour was just that of my having landed at Liverpool in the gusty, cloudy, overwhelmingly English morning and pursued, with immediate intensities of appreciation, as I may call the muffled accompaniment for fear of almost indecently overnaming it, a course which had seated me at a late breakfast in the coffee-room of the old Adelphi Hotel ("Radley's," as I had to deplore its lately having ceased to be dubbed,) and handed me over without a scruple to my fate. This doom of inordinate exposure to appearances, aspects, images, every protrusive item almost, in the great beheld sum of things, I regard in other words as having settled upon me once for all while I observed for instance that in England the plate of buttered muffin and its cover were sacredly set upon the slop-bowl after hot water had been ingenuously poured into the same, and had seen that circumstance in a perfect cloud of accompaniments. I must have had with my tea and my muffin a boiled egg or two and a dab of marmalade, but it was from a far other store of condiments I most liberally helped myself. I was lucidly aware of so gorging—esoterically, as it were, while I drew out the gustatory process; and I must have said in that lost reference to this scene of my dedication which I mentioned above that I was again and again in the aftertime to win back the homeliest notes of the impression, the damp and darksome light washed in from the steep, black, bricky street, the crackle of the strong draught of the British "sea-coal" fire, much more confident of its function, I thought, than the fires I had left, the rustle of the thick, stiff, loudly unfolded and refolded "Times", the incomparable truth to type of the waiter, truth to history, to literature, to poetry, to Dickens, to Thackeray, positively to Smollett and to Hogarth, to every connection that could help me to appropriate him and his setting, an arrangement of things hanging together with a romantic rightness that had the force of a revelation.

To what end appropriation became thus eager and romance thus easy one could have asked one's self only if the idea of connectibility as stretching away and away hadn't of a sudden taken on such a wealth of suggestion; it represented at once a chain stretching off to heaven knew where, but far into one's future at least, one's possibilities of life, and every link and pulse of which it was going accordingly to be indispensable, besides being delightful and wonderful, to recognise. Recognition, I dare say, was what remained, through the adventure of the months to come, the liveliest principle at work; both as bearing on the already known, on things unforgotten and of a sense intensely cultivated and cherished from my younger time, and on the imagined, the unimagined and the unimaginable, a quantity that divided itself somehow into the double muster of its elements, an endless vista or waiting array, down the middle of which I should inconceivably pass—inconceivably save for being sure of some thrilled arrest, some exchange of assurance and response, at every step. Obviously half the charm, as I can but thinly describe it, of the substantially continuous experience the first passages of which I thus note was in the fact that, immensely moved by it as I was, and having so to deal with it—in the anticipatory way or to the whatevers and wherevers and whenevers within me that should find it in order—I yet felt it in no degree as strange or obscure, baffling or unrecognising on its own side; everything was so far from impenetrable that my most general notion was the very ecstasy of understanding and that really wherever I looked, and still more wherever I pressed, I sank in and in up to my nose. This in particular was of the perfect felicity, that while the fact of difference all round me was immense the embarrassment of it was nil—as if the getting into relation with the least waste had been prepared from so far back that a sort of divine economy now fairly ruled. It was doubtless a part of the total fatuity, and perhaps its sublimest mark, that I knew what everything meant, not simply then but for weeks and months after, and was to know less only with increase of knowledge. That must indeed have been of the essence of the general effect and the particular felicity—only not grotesque because, for want of occasion, not immediately exhibited: a consciousness not other than that of a person abruptly introduced into a preoccupied and animated circle and yet so miraculously aware of the matters conversed about as to need no word of explanation before joining in. To say of such a person that he hadn't lost time would, I knew, be feebly to express his advantage; my likeness to him, at any rate, probably fell short of an absurd one through the chapter of accidents, mostly of the happiest in their way too, which, restraining the personal impulse for me, kept appearances and pretensions down. The feast, as it more and more opened out, was all of the objective, as we have learned so comfortably to say; or at least of its convenient opposite only in so far as this undertook to interpret it for myself alone.

To return at all across the years to the gates of the paradise of the first larger initiations is to be ever so tempted to pass them, to push in again and breathe the air of this, that and the other plot of rising ground particularly associated, for memory and gratitude, with the quickening process. The trouble is that with these sacred spots, to later appreciation, the garden of youth is apt inordinately to bristle, and that one's account of them has to shake them together fairly hard, making a coherent thing of them, to profit by the contribution of each. In speaking of my earliest renewal of the vision of Europe, if I may give so grand a name to a scarce more than merely enlarged and uplifted gape, I have, I confess, truly to jerk myself over the ground, to wrench myself with violence from memories and images, stages and phases and branching arms, that catch and hold me as I pass them by. Such a matter as my recovery of contact with London for a few weeks, the contact broken off some nine years before, lays so many plausible traps for me that discretion half warns me to stand off the ground and walk round it altogether. I stop my ears to the advice, however, under the pleading reminder that just those days began a business for me that was to go ever so much further than I then dreamed and planted a seed that was, by my own measure, singularly to sprout and flourish—the harvest of which, I almost permit myself to believe, has even yet not all been gathered. I foresee moreover how little I shall be able to resist, throughout these Notes, the force of persuasion expressed in the individual *vivid* image of the past wherever encountered, these images having always such terms of their own, such subtle secrets and insidious arts for keeping us in relation with them, for bribing us by the beauty, the authority, the wonder of their saved intensity. They have saved it, they seem to say to us, from such a welter of death and darkness and ruin that this alone makes a value and a light and a dignity for them, something indeed of an argument that our story, since we attempt to tell one, has lapses and gaps without them. Not to be denied also, over and above this, is the downright pleasure of the illusion yet again created, the *apparent* transfer from the past to the present of the particular combination of things that did at its hour ever so directly operate and that isn't after all then drained of virtue, wholly wasted and lost, for sensation, for participation in the act of life, in the attesting sights, sounds, smells, the illusion, as I say, of the recording senses.

What began, during the springtime of my actual reference, in a couple of dusky ground-floor rooms at number 7 Half-Moon Street, was simply an establishment all in a few days of a personal relation with London that was not of course measurable at the moment—I saw in my bedazzled state of comparative freedom too many other relations ahead, a fairly intoxicated vision of choice and range—but that none the less set going a more intimately inner consciousness, a wheel within the wheels, and led to my departing, the actual, the general incident closed, in possession of a return-ticket "good", as we say, for a longer interval than I could then dream about, and that the first really earnest fumble of after years brought surprisingly to light. I think it must have been the very proportions themselves of the invitation and the interest that kept down, under the immense impression, everything in the nature of calculation and presumption; dark, huge and prodigious the other party to our relation, London's and mine, as I called it, loomed and spread—much too mighty a Goliath for the present in any conceivable ambition even of a fast-growing David. My earlier apprehension, fed at the season as from a thousand outstretched silver spoons—for these all shone to me with that effect of the handsomest hospitality—piled up the monster to such a height that I could somehow only fear him as much as I admired and that his proportions in fact reached away quite beyond my expectation. He was always the great figure of London, and I was for no small time, as the years followed, to be kept at my awestruck distance for taking him on that sort of trust: I had crept about his ankles, I had glanced adventurously up at his knees, and wasn't the moral for the most part the mere question of whether I should ever be big enough to so much as guess where he stopped?

Odd enough was it, I make out, that I was to feel no wonder of that kind or degree play in the coming time over such other social aspects, such superficially more colourable scenes as I paid, in repetition as frequent as possible, my respects and my compliments to: they might meet me with wreathed smiles and splendid promises and deep divinations of my own desire, a thousand graces and gages, in fine, that I couldn't pretend to have picked up within the circle, however experimentally widened, of which Half-Moon Street was the centre, and nothing therefore could have exceeded the splendour of these successive and multiplied assurances. What it none the less infinitely beguiles me to recognise to-day is that such exhibitions, for all their greater direct radiance, and still more for all their general implication of a store of meaning and mystery and beauty that they alone, from example to example, from prodigy to prodigy, had to open out, left me comparatively little crushed by the impression of their concerning me further than my own action perhaps could make good. It was as if I had seen that all there was for me of these great things I should sooner or later take; the amount would be immense, yet, as who should say, all on the same plane and the same connection, the aesthetic, the "artistic", the romantic in the looser sense, or in other words in the air of the passions of the intelligence. What other passions of a deeper strain, whether personal or racial, and thereby more superstitiously importunate, I must have felt involved in the question of an effective experience of English life I was doubtless then altogether unprepared to say; it probably came, however, I seem actually to make out, very much to this particular perception, exactly, that any penetration of the London scene would *be* experience after a fashion that an exercise of one's "mere intellectual curiosity" wherever else wouldn't begin to represent, glittering as the rewards to such curiosity amid alien peoples of genius might thoroughly appear. On the other hand it was of course going to be nothing less than a superlative help that one would have but to reach out straight and in the full measure of one's passion for these rewards, to find one's self carried all the way by one's active, one's contemplative concern with them—this delightful affair, fraught with increase of light, of joy and wonder, of possibilities of adventure for the mind, in fine, inevitably exhausting the relation.

II

LET ME not here withal appear to pretend to say how far I then foresaw myself likely to proceed, as it were, with the inimitable France and the incomparable Italy; my real point is altogether in the simple fact that they hovered before me, even in their scrappy foretastes, to a great effect of ease and inspiration, whereas I shouldn't at all have resented the charge of fairly hiding behind the lowly door of Mr. Lazarus Fox—so unmistakeably did it open into complications tremendous. This excellent man, my Half-Moon Street landlord—I surrender, I can't keep away from him—figures to me now as but one of the thousand forms of pressure in the collective assault, but he couldn't have been more carefully chosen for his office had he consciously undertaken to express to me in a concentrated manner most of the things I was "after". The case was rather indeed perhaps that he himself by his own mere perfection put me up to much of what I should most confidently look for, and that the right lines of observation and enjoyment, of local and social contact, as I may call it, were most of all those that started out from him and came back to him. It was as if nothing I saw could have done without him, as if nothing he was could have done without everything else. The very quarters I occupied under his protection happened, for that matter, to swarm—as I estimated swarming—with intensities of suggestion—aware as I now encourage myself to become that the first note of the numberless reverberations I was to pick up in the aftertime had definitely been struck for me as under the wave of his conducting little wand. He flourished it modestly enough, ancient worthy of an immemorial order that he was—old pensioned servant, of course, of a Cumberland (as I believe) family, a kind, slim, celibate, informing and informed member of which occupied his second floor apartments; a friend indeed whom I had met on the very first occasion of my sallying forth from Morley's Hotel in Trafalgar Square to dine at a house of sustaining, of inspiring hospitality in the Kensington quarter. Succumbing thus to my tangle of memories, from which I discern no escape, I recognise further that if the endlessly befriending Charles Nortons introduced me to Albert Rutson, and Albert Rutson introduced me to his feudal retainer, so it was in no small degree through the confidence borrowed from the latter's interest in the decent appearance I should make, an interest of a consistency not to have been prefigured by any at all like instance in my past, that I so far maintained my dizzy balance as to be able to ascend to the second floor under the thrill of sundry invitations to breakfast. I dare say it is the invitations to breakfast that hold me at this moment by their spell—so do they breathe to me across the age the note of a London world that we have left far behind; in consequence of which I the more yearningly steal back to it, as on sneaking tiptoe, and shut myself up there without interference. It is embalmed in disconnections, in differences, that I cultivate a free fancy for pronouncing advantageous to it: sunk already was the shaft by which I should descend into the years, and my inspiration is in touching as many as possible of the points of the other tradition, retracing as many as possible of the features of the old face, eventually to be blurred again even before my own eyes, and with the materials for a portrait thereby accessible but to those who were present up to the time of the change.

I don't pretend to date this change which still allows me to catch my younger observation and submission at play on the far side of it; I make it fall into the right perspective, however, I think, when I place it where I began to shudder before a confidence, not to say an impudence, of diminution in the aspects by which the British capital differed so from those of all the foreign together as to present throughout the straight contradiction to them. That straight contradiction, testifying invaluably at every turn, had been from far back the thing, romantically speaking, to clutch and keep the clue and the logic of; thanks to it the whole picture, every element, objects and figures, background and actors, nature and art, hung consummately together, appealing in their own light and under their own law—interesting ever in every case by instituting comparisons, sticking on the contrary to their true instinct and suggesting only contrast. They were the *opposite*, the assured, the absolute, the unashamed, in respect to whatever might be of a generally similar intention elsewhere: this was their dignity, their beauty and their strength—to look back on which is to wonder if one didn't quite consciously tremble, before the exhibition, for any menaced or mitigated symptom in it. I honestly think one did, even in the first flushes of recognition, more or less so tremble; I remember at least that in spite of such disconcertments, such dismays, as certain of the most thoroughly Victorian *choses vues* originally treated me to, something yet deeper and finer than observation admonished me to like them just as they were, or at least not too fatuously to dislike—since it somehow glimmered upon me that if they had lacked their oddity, their monstrosity, as it even might be, their unabashed insular conformity, other things that belong to them, as they belong to these, might have loomed less large and massed less thick, which effect was wholly to be deprecated. To catch that secret, I make out the more I think of it, was to have perhaps the smokiest, but none the less the steadiest, light to walk by; the "clue", as I have called it, was to be one's appreciation of an England that should turn its back directly enough, and without fear of doing it too much, on examples and ideas not strictly homebred—since she did her own sort of thing with such authority and was even then to be noted as sometimes trying other people's with a *kind* of disaster not recorded, at the worst, among themselves.

I must of course disavow pretending to have read this vivid philosophy into my most immediate impressions, and I may in fact perhaps not claim to have been really aware of its seed till a considerable time had passed, till apprehensions and reflections had taken place in quantity, immeasurable quantity, so to speak, and a great stir-up of the imagination been incurred. Undoubtedly is it in part the new—that is, more strictly, the elder—acuteness that I touch all the prime profit with; I didn't know at the time either how much appearances were all the while in the melting-pot or what wealth of reaction on them I was laying up. I cherish, for love of the unbroken interest, all the same, the theory of certain then positive and effective prefigurements, because it leaves me thus free for remarking that I knew where I was, as I may put it, from the moment I saw the state of the London to come brought down with the weight of her abdication of her genius. It not unnaturally may be said that it hasn't been till to-day that we *see* her genius in its fulness—throwing up in a hundred lights, matters we practically acknowledge, such a plastic side as we had never dreamed she possessed. The genius of accommodation is what we had last expected of her—accommodation to anything but her portentous self, for in *that* connection she was ever remarkable; and certainly the air of the generalised, the emulous smart modern capital has come to be written upon her larger and larger even while we look.

The unaccommodating and unaccommodated city remains none the less closely consecrated to one's fondest notion of her—the city too indifferent, too proud, too unaware, too stupid even if one will, to enter any lists that involved her moving from her base and that thereby, when one approached her from the alien *positive* places (I don't speak of the American, in those days too negative to be related at all) enjoyed the enormous "pull", for making her impression, of ignoring everything but her own perversities and then of driving these home with an emphasis not to be gainsaid. Since she didn't emulate, as I have termed it, so she practised her own arts altogether, and both these ways and these consequences were in the flattest opposition (*that* was the happy point!) to foreign felicities or foreign standards, so that the effect in every case was of the straightest reversal of them—with black for the foreign white and white for the foreign black, wet for the foreign dry and dry for the foreign wet, big for the foreign small and small for the foreign big: I needn't extend the catalogue. *Her* idiosyncrasy was never in the least to have been inferred or presumed; it could only, in general, make the outsider provisionally gape. She sat thus imperturbable in her felicities, and if that is how, remounting the stream of time, I like most to think of her, this is because if her interest is still undeniable—as that of overgrown things goes—it has yet lost its fineness of quality. Phenomena may be interesting, thank goodness, without being phenomena of elegant expression or of any other form of restless smartness, and when once type is strong, when once it plays up from deep sources, every show of its sincerity delivers us a message and we hang, to real suspense, on its continuance of energy, on its again and yet again consistently acquitting itself. So it keeps in tune, and, as the French adage says, *c'est le ton qui fait la chanson*. The mid-Victorian London was sincere—that was a vast virtue and a vast appeal; the contemporary is sceptical, and most so when most plausible; the turn of the tide could verily be fixed to an hour—the hour at which the new plausibility began to exceed the old sincerities by so much as a single sign. They could truly have been arrayed face to face, I think, for an attentive eye—and I risk even saying that my own, bent upon them, as was to come to pass, with a habit of anxiety that I should scarce be able to overstate, had its unrecorded penetrations, its alarms and recoveries, even perhaps its very lapses of faith, though always redeemed afresh by still fonder fanaticisms, to a pitch that shall perhaps present itself, when they expose it all the way, as that of tiresome extravagance. Exposing it all the way is none the less, I see, exactly what I plot against it—or, otherwise expressed, in favour of the fine truth of history, so far as a throb of that awful pulse has been matter of one's own life; in favour too of the mere returns derivable from more inordinate curiosity. These Notes would enjoy small self-respect, I think, if that principle, not to call it that passion, didn't almost furiously ride them.

III

I WAS at any rate in the midst of sincerities enough, sincerities of emphasis and "composition"; perversities, idiosyncrasies, incalculabilities, delightful all as densities at first insoluble, delightful even indeed as so much mere bewilderment and shock. When was the shock, I ask myself as I look back, not so deadened by the general atmospheric richness as not to melt more or less immediately into some succulence for the mind, something that could feed the historic sense almost to sweetness? I don't mean that it was a shock to be invited to breakfast—there were stronger ones than that; but was in fact the *trait de mœurs* that disconnected me with most rapidity and intensity from all I had left on the other side of the sea. To be so disconnected, for the time, and in the most insidious manner, was above all what I had come out for, and every appearance that might help it was to be artfully and gratefully cultivated. I recollect well how many of these combined as I sat at quite punctual fried sole and marmalade in the comparatively disengaged sitting-room of the second floor—the occupancy of the first has remained vague to me; disengaged from the mantle of gloom the folds of which draped most heavily the feet of the house, as it were, and thereby promoted in my own bower the chronic dusk favourable to mural decoration consisting mainly of framed and glazed "coloured" excisions from Christmas numbers of the Illustrated London News that had been at their hour quite modern miracles. Was it for that matter into a sudden splendour of the modern that I ascendingly emerged under the hospitality of my kind fellow-tenant, or was it rather into the fine classicism of a bygone age, as literature and the arts had handed down that memory? Such were the questions whisked at every turn under my nose and reducing me by their obscure charm but to bewildered brooding, I fear, when I should have been myself, to repay these attentions, quite forward and informing and affirmative.

There were eminent gentlemen, as I was sure they could only be, to "meet" and, alas, awfully to interrogate me—for vivid has remained to me, as the best of my bewilderment, the strangeness of finding that I could be of interest to *them*: not indeed to call it rather the proved humiliation of my impotence. My identity for myself was *all* in my sensibility to their own exhibition, with not a scrap left over for a personal show; which made it as inconvenient as it was queer that I should be treated as a specimen and have in the most unexpected manner to prove that I was a good one. I knew myself the very worst conceivable, but how to give to such other persons a decent or coherent reason for my being so required more presence of mind than I could in the least muster—the consequence of which failure had to be for me, I fear, under all that confused first flush, rather an abject acceptance of the air of imbecility. There were, it appeared, things of interest taking place in America, and I had had, in this absurd manner, to come to England to learn it: I had had over there on the ground itself no conception of any such matter—nothing of the smallest interest, by any perception of mine, as I suppose I should still blush to recall, had taken place in America since the War. How *could* anything, I really wanted to ask—anything comparable, that is, to what was taking place under my eyes in Half-Moon Street and at dear softly presiding Rutson's table of talk. It doubtless essentially belonged to the exactly right type and tone and general figure of my fellow-breakfasters from the Temple, from the Home Office, the Foreign Office, the House of Commons, from goodness knew what other scarce discernible Olympian altitudes, it belonged to the very cut of their hair and their waistcoats and their whiskers—for it was still more or less a whiskered age—that they should desire from me much distinctness about General Grant's first cabinet, upon the formation of which the light of the newspaper happened then to beat; yet at the same time that I asked myself if it was to such cold communities, such flat frustrations as were so proposed, that I had sought to lift my head again in European air, I found the crisis enriched by sundry other apprehensions.

They melted together in it to that increase of savour I have already noted, yet leaving me vividly admonished that the blankness of my mind as to the Washington candidates relegated me to some class unencountered as yet by any one of my conversers, a class only not perfectly ridiculous because perfectly insignificant. Also that politics walked abroad in England, so that one might supremely bump against them, as much as, by my fond impression, they took their exercise in America but through the back streets and the ways otherwise untrodden and the very darkness of night; that further all lively attestations were *ipso facto* interesting, and that finally and in the supreme degree, the authenticity of whatever one was going to learn in the world would probably always have for its sign that one got it at some personal cost. To this generalisation mightn't one even add that in proportion as the cost was great, or became fairly excruciating, the lesson, the value acquired would probably be a thing to treasure? I remember really going so far as to wonder if any act of acquisition of the life-loving, life-searching sort that most appealed to me wouldn't mostly be fallacious if unaccompanied by that tag of the price paid in personal discomfort, in some self-exposure and some none too impossible consequent discomfiture, for the sake of it. Didn't I even on occasion mount to the very height of seeing it written that these bad moments were the downright consecration of knowledge, that is of perception and, essentially, of exploration, always dangerous and treacherous, and so might afterwards come to figure to memory, each in its order, as the silver nail on the wall of the temple where the trophy is hung up? All of which remark, I freely grant, is a great ado about the long since so bedimmed little Half-Moon Street breakfasts, and is moreover quite wide of the mark if suggesting that the joys of recognition, those of imaginatively, of projectively fitting in and fitting out every piece in the puzzle and every recruit to the force of a further understanding weren't in themselves a most bustling and cheering business.

It was bustling at least, assuredly, if not quite always in the same degree exhilarating, to breakfast out at all, as distinguished from lunching, without its being what the Harvard scene made of it, one of the incidents of "boarding"; it was association at a jump with the ghosts of Byron and Sheridan and Scott and Moore and Lockhart and Rogers and *tutti quanti*—as well as the exciting note of a social order in which everyone wasn't hurled straight, with the momentum of rising, upon an office or a store. The mere vision in numbers of persons embodying and in various ways sharply illustrating a clear alternative to that passivity told a tale that would be more and more worth the reading with every turn of the page. So at all events I fantasticated while harassed by my necessity to weave into my general tapestry every thread that would conduce to a pattern, and so the thread for instance of the great little difference of my literally never having but once "at home" been invited to breakfast on types as well as on toast and its accessories could suggest an effect of silk or silver when absolutely dangled before me. That single occasion at home came back in a light that fairly brought tears to my eyes, for it was touching now to the last wanness that the lady of the winter morn of the Massachusetts Sabbath, one of those, as I recover it, of 1868, to reach whose board we had waded through snowdrifts, had been herself fondling a reminiscence, though I can scarce imagine supposing herself to offer for our consumption any other type than her own. It was for that matter but the sweet staleness of her reminiscence that made her a type, and I remember how it had had to do thereby all the work: *she*, of an age to reach so considerably back, had breakfasted out, in London, and with Mr. Rogers himself—that was the point; which I am bound to say did for the hour and on that spot supply richness of reference enough. And I am caught up, I find, in the very act of this claim for my prior scantness of experience by a memory that makes it not a little less perfect and which is oddly enough again associated with a struggle, on an empty stomach, through the massed New England whiteness of the prime Sunday hour. I still cherish the vision, which couldn't then have faded from me, of my having, during the age of innocence—I mean of my own—breakfasted with W. D. Howells, insidious disturber and fertiliser of that state in me, to "meet" Bayard Taylor and Arthur Sedgwick all in the Venetian manner, the delightful Venetian manner which toward the later 'sixties draped any motion on our host's part as with a habit still appropriate. *He* had risen that morning under the momentum of his but recently concluded consular term in Venice, where margin, if only that of the great loungeable piazza, had a breadth, and though Sedgwick and I had rather, as it were, to take the jump standing, this was yet under the inspiration of feeling the case most special. Only it had *been* Venetian, snow-shoes and all; I had stored it sacredly away as not American at all, and was of course to learn in Half-Moon Street how little it had been English either.

What must have seemed to me of a fine international mixture, during those weeks, was my thrilling opportunity to sit one morning, beside Mrs. Charles Norton's tea-urn, in Queen's Gate Terrace, opposite to Frederic Harrison, eminent to me at the moment as one of the subjects of Matthew Arnold's early fine banter, one of his too confidently roaring "young lions" of the periodical press. Has any gilding ray since that happy season rested here and there with the sovereign charm of interest, of drollery, of felicity and infelicity taken on by scattered selected objects in that writer's bright critical dawn?—an element in which we had the sense of sitting gratefully bathed, so that we fairly took out our young minds and dabbled and soaked them in it as we were to do again in no other. The beauty was thus at such a rate that people had references, and that a reference was then, to my mind, whether in a person or an object, the most glittering, the most becoming ornament possible, a style of decoration one seemed likely to perceive figures here and there, whether animate or not, quite groan under the accumulation and the weight of. One had scarcely met it before—that I now understood; at the same time that there was perhaps a wan joy in one's never having missed it, by all appearance, having on the contrary ever instinctively caught it, on the least glimmer of its presence. Even when present, or what in the other time I had taken for present, it had been of the thinnest, whereas all about me hereafter it would be by all appearance almost glutinously thick—to the point even of one's on occasion sticking fast in it; that is finding intelligibility smothered in quantity. I lost breath in fact, no doubt, again and again, with this latter increase, but was to go on and on for a long time before any first glimmer of reaction against so special a source of interest. It attached itself to objects often, I saw, by no merit or virtue—above all, repeatedly, by no "cleverness"—of their own, but just by the luck of history, by the action of multiplicity of circumstance. Condemned the human particle "over here" was to *live*, on whatever terms, in thickness—instead of being free, comparatively, or as I at once ruefully and exquisitely found myself, only to feel and to think in it. Ruefully because there were clearly a thousand contacts and sensations, of the strong direct order, that one lost by not so living; exquisitely because of the equal number of immunities and independences, blest independences of perception and judgment, blest liberties of range for the intellectual adventure, that accrued by the same stroke. These at least had the advantage, one of the most distinguished conceivable, that when enjoyed with a certain intensity they might produce the illusion of the other intensity, that of being involved in the composition and the picture itself, in the situations, the complications, the circumstances, admirable and dreadful; while no corresponding illusion, none making for the ideal play of reflection, conclusion, comparison, however one should incline to appraise the luxury, seemed likely to attend the immersed or engaged condition.

Whatever fatuity might at any rate have resided in these complacencies of view, I made them my own with the best conscience in the world, and I meet them again quite to extravagance of interest wherever on the whole extent of the scene my retrospect sets me down. It wasn't in the least at the same time that encountered celebrities only thus provoked the shifting play of my small lamp, and this too even though they were easily celebrated, by my measure, and though from the very first I owed an individual here and there among them, as was highly proper, the benefit of impression at the highest pitch. On the great supporting and enclosing scene itself, the big generalised picture, painted in layer upon layer and tone upon tone, one's fancy was all the while feeding; objects and items, illustrations and aspects might perpetually overlap or mutually interfere, but never without leaving consistency the more marked and character the more unmistakeable. The place, the places, bristled so for every glance with expressive particulars, that I really conversed with them, at happy moments, more than with the figures that moved in them, which affected me so often as but submissive articles of furniture, "put in" by an artist duly careful of effect and yet duly respectful of proportion. The great impression was doubtless no other then and there than what it is under every sky and before every scene that remind one afresh, at the given moment, of all the ways in which producing causes and produced creatures correspond and interdepend; but I think I must have believed at that time that these cross references kept up their game in the English air with a frankness and a good faith that kept the process, in all probability, the most traceable of its kind on the globe.

What was the secret of the force of that suggestion?—which was not, I may say, to be invalidated, to my eyes, by the further observation of cases and conditions. Was it that the enormous "pull" enjoyed at every point of the general surface the stoutness of the underlying belief in what was behind all surfaces?—so that the particular visible, audible, palpable fact, however small and subsidiary, was incomparably absolute, or had, so to speak, such a conscience and a confidence, such an absence of reserve and latent doubts about itself, as was not elsewhere to be found. Didn't such elements as that represent, in the heart of things, possibilities of scepticism, of mockery, of irony, of the return of the matter, whatever it might be, on itself, by some play or other of the questioning spirit, the spirit therefore weakening to entire comfort of affirmations? Didn't I see that humour itself, which might seem elsewhere corrosive and subversive, was, as an English faculty, turned outward altogether and never turned inward?—by which convenient circumstance subversion, or in other words alteration and variation were not promoted. Such truths were wondrous things to make out in such connections as my experience was then, and for no small time after, to be confined to; but I positively catch myself listening to them, even with my half-awakened ears, as if they had been all so many sermons of the very stones of London. *There*, to come back to it, was exactly the force with which these stones were to build me capaciously round: I invited them, I besought them, to say all they would, and—to return to my figure of a while back—it was soon so thoroughly as if they had understood that, once having begun, they were to keep year after year fairly chattering to me. Many of these pages, I fondly foresee, must consist but of the record of their chatter. What was most of all happening, I take it, was that under an absurd special stress I was having, as who should say, to improvise a local medium and to arrange a local consciousness. Against my due appropriation of those originally closest at my hand inevitable accidents had conspired—and, to conclude in respect to all this, if a considerable time was to be wanted, in the event, for ideal certainty of adjustment, half the terms required by this could then put forth the touching plea that they had quite achingly waited.

IV

It may perhaps seem strange that the soil should have been watered by such an incident as Mr. Lazarus Fox's reply, in the earliest rich dusk, to my inquiry as to whither, while I occupied his rooms, I had best betake myself most regularly for my dinner: "Well, there is the Bath Hotel, sir, a very short walk away, where I should think you would be very comfortable indeed. Mr. So-and-So dines at his club, sir—but there is also the Albany in Piccadilly, to which I believe many gentlemen go." I think I measured on the spot "all that it took" to make my friend most advisedly—for it was clearly what he did—see me seated in lone state, for my evening meal, at the heavy mahogany of the stodgy little hotel that in those days and for long after occupied the north-west corner of Arlington Street and to which, in common with many compatriots, I repeatedly resorted during the years immediately following. We *suffered*, however, on those occasions, the unmitigated coffee-room of Mr. Fox's prescription—it was part of a strange inevitability, a concomitant of necessary shelter and we hadn't at least gone forth to invoke its austere charm. I tried it, in that singular way, at the hour I speak of—and I well remember forecasting the interest of a social and moral order in which it could be supposed of me that, having tried it once, I should sublimely try it again. My success in doing so would indeed have been sublime, but a finer shade of the quality still attached somehow to my landlord's confidence in it; and this was one of the threads that, as I have called them, I was to tuck away for future picking-up again and unrolling. I fell back on the Albany, which long ago passed away and which I seem to have brushed with a touch of reminiscence in some anticipation of the present indulgence that is itself quite ancient history. It was a small eating-house of the very old English tradition, as I then supposed at least, just opposite the much greater establishment of the same name, which latter it had borrowed, and I remember wondering whether the tenants of the classic chambers, the beadle-guarded cluster of which was impressive even to the deprecated approach, found their conception of the "restaurant"—we still pronounced it in the French manner—met by the small compartments, narrow as horse-stalls, formed by the high straight backs of hard wooden benches and accommodating respectively two pairs of feeders, who were thus so closely face to face as fairly to threaten with knife and fork each other's more forward features.

The scene was sordid, the arrangements primitive, the detail of the procedure, as it struck me, wellnigh of the rudest; yet I remember rejoicing in it all—as one indeed might perfectly rejoice in the juiciness of joints and the abundance of accessory pudding; for I said to myself under every shock and at the hint of every savour that this was what it was for an exhibition to reek with local colour, and one could dispense with a napkin, with a crusty roll, with room for one's elbows or one's feet, with an immunity from intermittance of the "plain boiled", much better than one could dispense with that. There were restaurants galore even at that time in New York and in Boston, but I had never before had to do with an eating-house and had not yet seen the little old English world of Dickens, let alone of the ever-haunting Hogarth, of Smollett and of Boswell, drenched with such a flood of light. As one sat there one *understood*; one drew out the severe séance not to stay the assault of precious conspiring truths, not to break the current of in-rushing telltale suggestion. Every face was a documentary scrap, half a dozen broken words to piece with half a dozen others, and so on and on; every sound was strong, whether rich and fine or only queer and coarse; everything in this order drew a positive sweetness from never being—whatever else it was—gracelessly flat. The very rudeness was ripe, the very commonness was conscious—that is not related to mere other forms of the same, but to matters as different as possible, into which it shaded off and off or up and up; the image in fine was organic, rounded and complete, as definite as a Dutch picture of low life hung on a museum wall. "Low" I say in respect to the life; but that was the point for me, that whereas the smartness and newness beyond the sea supposedly disavowed the low, they did so but thinly and vainly, falling markedly short of the high; which the little boxed and boiled Albany attained to some effect of, after a fashion of its own, just by having its so thoroughly appreciable note-value in a scheme of manners. It was imbedded, so to speak, in the scheme, and it borrowed lights, it borrowed even glooms, from so much neighbouring distinction. The places across the sea, as they to my then eyes faintly after-glowed, had no impinging borders but those of the desert to borrow *from.* And if it be asked of me whether all the while I insist, for demonstration of the complacency with which I desire to revert, on not regretting the disappearance of such too long surviving sordidries as those I have evoked, I can but answer that blind emotion, in whichever sense directed, has nothing to say to the question and that the sense of what we just *could* confidently live by at a given far-away hour is a simple stout fact of relief.

Relief, again, I say, from the too enormous present accretions and alternatives—which we witlessly thought so innumerable then, which we artlessly found so much of the interest of *in* an immeasurable multiplicity and which I now feel myself thus grope for ghostly touch of in the name, neither more nor less, of poetic justice. I wasn't doubtless at the time so very sure, after all, of the comparative felicity of our state, that of the rare *moment* for the fond fancy—I doubtless even a bit greedily missed certain quantities, not to call them certain qualities, here and there, and the best of my actual purpose is to make amends for that blasphemy. There isn't a thing I can imagine having missed that I don't quite ache to miss again; and it remains at all events an odd stroke that, having of old most felt the thrill of the place in its mighty muchness, I have lived to adore it backward for its sweet simplicity. I find myself in fact at the present writing only too sorry when not able to minimise conscientiously this, that or the other of the old sources of impression. The thing is indeed admirably possible in a *general* way, though much of the exhibition was none the less undeniably, was absolutely large: how can I for instance recall the great cab-rank, mainly formed of delightful hansoms, that stretched along Piccadilly from the top of the Green Park unendingly down, without having to take it for unsurpassably modern and majestic? How can I think—I select my examples at hazard—of the "run" of the more successful of Mr. Robertson's comedies at the "dear little old" Prince of Wales's Theatre in Tottenham Court Road as anything less than one of the wonders of our age? How, by the same token, can I not lose myself still more in the glory of a time that was to watch the drawn-out procession of Henry Irving's Shakespearean splendours at the transcendent Lyceum? or how, in the same general line, not recognise that to live through the extravagant youth of the aesthetic era, whether as embodied in the then apparently inexhaustible vein of the Gilbert and Sullivan operas or as more monotonously expressed in those "last words" of the *raffiné* that were chanted and crooned in the damask-hung temple of the Grosvenor Gallery, was to seem privileged to such immensities as history would find left to her to record but with bated breath?

These latter triumphs of taste, however, though lost in the abysm now, had then a good many years to wait and I alight for illustrative support of my present mild thesis on the comparative humility, say, of the inward aspects, in a large measure, of the old National Gallery, where memory mixes for me together so many elements of the sense of an antique world. The great element was of course that I well-nigh incredibly stood again in the immediate presence of Titian and Rembrandt, of Rubens and Paul Veronese, and that the cup of sensation was thereby filled to overflowing; but I look at it to-day as concomitantly warm and closed-in and, as who should say, cosy that the ancient order and contracted state and thick-coloured dimness, all unconscious of rearrangements and reversals, blighting new lights and invidious shattering comparisons, still prevailed and kept contemplation comfortably confused and serenely superstitious, when not indeed at its sharpest moments quite fevered with incoherences. The place looks to me across the half century richly dim, yet at the same time both perversely plain and heavily violent—violent through indifference to the separations and selections that have become a tribute to modern nerves; but I cherish exactly those facts of benightedness, seeming as they do to have positively and blessedly conditioned the particular sweetness of wonder with which I haunted the Family of Darius, the Bacchus and Ariadne, or the so-called portrait of Ariosto. Could one in those days feel anything with force, whether for pleasure or for pain, without feeling it as an immense little act or event of life, and as therefore taking place on a scene and in circumstances scarce at all to be separated from its own sense and impact?—so that to recover it is to recover the whole medium, the material pressure of things, and find it most marked for preservation as an aspect, even, distinguishably, a "composition."

What a composition, for instance again I am capable at this hour of exclaiming, the conditions of felicity in which I became aware, one afternoon during a renewed gape before the Bacchus and Ariadne, first that a little gentleman beside me and talking with the greatest vivacity to another gentleman was extremely remarkable, second that he had the largest and most *chevelu* auburn head I had ever seen perched on a scarce perceptible body, third that I held some scrap of a clue to his identity, which couldn't fail to be eminent, fourth that this tag of association was with nothing less than a small photograph sent me westward across the sea a few months before, and fifth that the sitter for the photograph had been the author of Atalanta in Calydon and Poems and Ballads! I thrilled, it perfectly comes back to me, with the prodigy of this circumstance that I should be admiring Titian in the same breath with Mr. Swinburne—that is in the same breath in which *he* admired Titian and in which I also admired *him*, the whole constituting on the spot between us, for appreciation, that is for mine, a fact of intercourse, such a fact as could stamp and colour the whole passage ineffaceably, and this even though the more illustrious party to it had within the minute turned off and left me shaken. I was shaken, but I was satisfied—that was the point; I didn't ask more to interweave another touch in my pattern, and as I once more gather in the impression I am struck with my having deserved truly as many of the like as possible. I was welcome to them, it may well be said, on such easy terms—and yet I ask myself whether, after all, it didn't take on my own part some doing, as we nowadays say, to make them so well worth having. They themselves took, I even at the time felt, little enough trouble for it, and the virtue of the business was repeatedly, no doubt, a good deal more in what I brought than in what I took.

I apply this remark indeed to those extractions of the quintessence that had for their occasion either one's more undirected though never fruitless walks and wanderings or one's earnest, one's positively pious approach to whatever consecrated ground or shrine of pilgrimage that might be at the moment in order. There was not a regular prescribed "sight" that I during those weeks neglected—I remember haunting the museums in especial, though the South Kensington was then scarce more than embryonic, with a sense of duty and of excitement that I was never again to know combined in equal measure, I think, and that it might really have taken some element of personal danger to account for. There *was* the element, in a manner, to season the cup with sharpness—the danger, all the while, that my freedom might be brief and my experience broken, that I was under the menace of uncertainty and subject in fine to interruption. The fact of having been so long gravely unwell sufficed by itself to keep apprehension alive; it was our idea, or at least quite intensely mine, that what I was doing, could I but put it through, would be intimately good for me—only the putting it through was the difficulty, and I sometimes faltered by the way. This makes now for a general air on the part of all the objects of vision that I recover, and almost as much in those of accidental encounter as in the breathlessly invoked, of being looked at for the last time and giving out their message and story as with the still, collected passion of an only chance. This feeling about them, not to say, as I might have imputed it, *in* them, wonderfully helped, as may be believed, the extraction of quintessences—which sprang at me of themselves, for that matter, out of any appearance that confessed to the least value in the compound, the least office in the harmony. If the commonest street-vista was a fairly heart-shaking contributive image, if the incidents of the thick renascent light anywhere, and the perpetual excitement of never knowing, between it and the historic and determined gloom, which was which and which one would most "back" for the general outcome and picture, so the great sought-out compositions, the Hampton Courts and the Windsors, the Richmonds, the Dulwiches, even the very Hampstead Heaths and Putney Commons, to say nothing of the Towers, the Temples, the Cathedrals and the strange penetrabilities of the City, ranged themselves like the rows of great figures in a sum, an amount immeasurably huge, that one would draw on if not quite as long as one lived, yet as soon as ever one should seriously get to work. That, to a tune of the most beautiful melancholy—at least as I catch it again now—was the way all values came out: they were charged somehow with a useability the most immediate, the most urgent, and which, I seemed to see, would keep me restless till I should have done something of my very own with them.

This was indeed perhaps what most painted them over with the admonitory appeal: there were truly moments at which they seemed not to answer for it that I should get all the good of them, and the finest—what I was so extravagantly, so fantastically after—unless I could somehow at once indite my sonnet and prove my title. The difficulty was all in there being so much of them—I might myself have been less restless if they could only have been less vivid. This they absolutely declined at any moment and in any connection to be, and it was ever so long till they abated a jot of the refusal. Thereby, in consequence, as may easily be judged, they were to keep me in alarms to which my measures practically taken, my catastrophes anxiously averted, remained not quite proportionate. I recall a most interesting young man who had been my shipmate on the homeward-bound "China", shortly before—I could go at length into my reasons for having been so struck with him, but I forbear—who, on our talking, to my intense trepidation of curiosity, of where I might advisedly "go" in London, let me know that he always went to Craven Street Strand, where bachelor lodgings were highly convenient, and whence I in fact then saw them flush at me over the cold grey sea with an authenticity almost fierce. I didn't in the event, as has been seen, go to Craven Street for rooms, but I did go, on the very first occasion, for atmosphere, neither more nor less—the young man of the ship, building so much better than he knew, had guaranteed me such a rightness of that; and it belongs to this reminiscence, for the triviality of which I should apologize did I find myself at my present pitch capable of apologizing for anything, that I had on the very spot there one of those hallucinations as to the precious effect dreadful to lose and yet impossible to render which interfused the aesthetic dream in presence of its subject with the mortal drop of despair (as I should insist at least didn't the despair itself seem to have acted here as the preservative). The precious effect in the case of Craven Street was that it absolutely reeked, to my fond fancy, with associations born of the particular ancient piety embodied in one's private altar to Dickens; and that this upstart little truth alone would revel in explanations that I should for the time have feverishly to forego. The exquisite matter was not the identification with the scene of special shades or names; it was just that the whole Dickens procession marched up and down, the whole Dickens world looked out of its queer, quite sinister windows—for it was the socially sinister Dickens, I am afraid, rather than the socially encouraging or confoundingly comic who still at that moment was most apt to meet me with his reasons. Such a reason was just that look of the inscrutable riverward street, packed to blackness with accumulations of suffered experience, these, indescribably, disavowed and confessed at one and the same time, and with the fact of its blocked old Thames-side termination, a mere fact of more oppressive enclosure now, telling all sorts of vague loose stories about it.

V

WHY, HOWEVER, should I pick up so small a crumb from that mere brief first course at a banquet of initiation which was in the event to prolong itself through years and years?—unless indeed as a scrap of a specimen, chosen at hazard, of the prompt activity of a process by which my intelligence afterwards came to find itself more fed, I think, than from any other source at all, or, for that matter, from all other sources put together. A hundred more suchlike modest memories breathe upon me, each with its own dim little plea, as I turn to face them, but my idea is to deal somehow more conveniently with the whole gathered mass of my subsequent impressions in this order, a fruitage that I feel to have been only too abundantly stored. Half a dozen of those of a larger and more immediate dignity, incidents more particularly of the rather invidiously so-called social contact, pull my sleeve as I pass; but the long, backward-drawn train of the later life drags them along with it, lost and smothered in its spread—only one of them stands out or remains over, insisting on its place and hour, its felt distinguishability. To this day I feel again *that* roused emotion, my unsurpassably prized admission to the presence of the great George Eliot, whom I was taken to see, by one of the kind door-opening Norton ladies, by whom Mrs. Lewes's guarded portal at North Bank appeared especially penetrable, on a Sunday afternoon of April '69. Later occasions, after a considerable lapse, were not to overlay the absolute face value, as I may call it, of all the appearances then and there presented me—which were taken home by a young spirit almost abjectly grateful, at any rate all devoutly prepared, for them. I find it idle even to wonder what "place" the author of Silas Marner and Middlemarch may be conceived to have in the pride of our literature—so settled and consecrated in the individual range of view is many such a case free at last to find itself, free after ups and downs, after fluctuations of fame or whatever, which have divested judgment of any relevance that isn't most of all the relevance of a living and recorded *relation*. It has ceased then to know itself in any degree as an estimate, has shaken off the anxieties of circumspection and comparison and just grown happy to act as an attachment pure and simple, an effect of life's own logic, but in the ashes of which the wonted fires of youth need but to be blown upon for betrayal of a glow. Reflective appreciation may have originally been concerned, whether at its most or at its least, but it is well over, to our infinite relief—yes, to our immortal comfort, I think; the interval back cannot again be bridged. We simply sit with our enjoyed gain, our residual rounded possession in our lap; a safe old treasure, which has ceased to shrink, if indeed also perhaps greatly to swell, and all that further touches it is the fine vibration set up if the name we know it all by is called into question—perhaps however little.

It was by George Eliot's name that I was to go on knowing, was never to cease to know, a great treasure of beauty and humanity, of applied and achieved art, a testimony, historic as well as aesthetic, to the deeper interest of the intricate English aspects; and I now allow the vibration, as I have called it, all its play—quite as if I had been wronged even by my own hesitation as to whether to pick up my anecdote. That scruple wholly fades with the sense of how I must at the very time have foreseen that here was one of those associations that would determine in the far future an exquisite inability to revise it. Middlemarch had not then appeared—we of the faith were still to enjoy that saturation, and Felix Holt the radical was upwards of three years old; the impetus proceeding from this work, however, was still fresh enough in my pulses to have quickened the palpitation of my finding myself in presence. I had rejoiced without reserve in Felix Holt—the illusion of reading which, outstretched on my then too frequently inevitable bed at Swampscott during a couple of very hot days of the summer of 1866, comes back to me, followed by that in sooth of sitting up again, at no great ease, to indite with all promptness a review of the delightful thing, the place of appearance of which nothing could now induce me to name, shameless about the general fact as I may have been at the hour itself: over such a feast of fine rich natural tone did I feel myself earnestly bend. Quite unforgettable to me the art and truth with which the note of this tone was struck in the beautiful prologue and the bygone appearances, a hundred of the outward and visible signs of the author's own young rural and midmost England, made to hold us by their harmony. The book was not, if I rightly remember, altogether genially greeted, but I was to hold fast to the charm I had thankfully suffered it, I had been conscious of absolutely needing it, to work.

Exquisite the remembrance of how it wouldn't have "done" for me at all, in relation to other inward matters, not to strain from the case the last drop of its happiest sense. And I had even with the cooling of the first glow so little gone back upon it, as we have nowadays learned to say, had in fact so gone forward, floated by its wave of superlative intended benignity, that, once in the cool quiet drawing-room at North Bank I knew myself steeped in still deeper depths of the medium. G. H. Lewes was absent for the time on an urgent errand; one of his sons, on a visit at the house, had been suddenly taken with a violent attack of pain, the heritage of a bad accident not long before in the West Indies, a suffered onset from an angry bull, I seem to recall, who had tossed or otherwise mauled him, and, though beaten off, left him considerably compromised—these facts being promptly imparted to us, in no small flutter, by our distinguished lady, who came in to us from another room, where she had been with the hapless young man while his father appealed to the nearest good chemist for some known specific. It infinitely moved me to see so great a celebrity quite humanly and familiarly agitated—even with something clear and noble in it too, to which, as well as to the extraordinarily interesting dignity of her whole odd personal conformation, I remember thinking her black silk dress and the lace mantilla attached to her head and keeping company on either side with the low-falling thickness of her dark hair effectively contributed. I have found myself, my life long, attaching value to every noted thing in respect to a great person—and George Eliot struck me on the spot as somehow *illustratively* great; never at any rate has the impression of those troubled moments faded from me, nor that at once of a certain high grace in her anxiety and a frank immediate appreciation of our presence, modest embarrassed folk as we were. It took me no long time to thrill with the sense, sublime in its unexpectedness, that we were perhaps, or indeed quite clearly, helping her to pass the time till Mr. Lewes's return—after which he would again post off for Mr. Paget the pre-eminent surgeon; and I see involved with this the perfect amenity of her assisting us, as it were, to assist her, through unrelinquished proper talk, due responsible remark and report, in the last degree suggestive to me, on a short holiday taken with Mr. Lewes in the south of France, whence they had just returned. Yes indeed, the lightest words of great persons are so little as any words of others are that I catch myself again inordinately struck with her dropping it off-hand that the mistral, scourge of their excursion, had blown them into Avignon, where they had gone, I think, to see J. S. Mill, only to blow them straight out again—the figure put it so before us; as well as with the moral interest, the absence of the *banal*, in their having, on the whole scene, found pleasure further poisoned by the frequency in all those parts of "evil faces: oh the evil faces!" *That* recorded source of suffering enormously affected me—I felt it as beautifully characteristic: I had never heard an *impression de voyage* so little tainted with the superficial or the vulgar. I was myself at the time in the thick of impressions, and it was true that they would have seemed to me rather to fail of life, of their own doubtless inferior kind, if submitting beyond a certain point to be touched with that sad or, as who should say, that grey colour: Mrs. Lewes's were, it appeared, predominantly so touched, and I could at once admire it in them and wonder if they didn't pay for this by some lack of intensity on other sides. Why I didn't more impute to her, or to them, that possible lack is more than I can say, since under the law of moral earnestness the vulgar and the trivial would be then involved in the poor observations of my own making—a conclusion sufficiently depressing.

However, I didn't find myself depressed, and I didn't find the great mind that was so good as to shine upon us at that awkward moment however dimly anything but augmented; what was its sensibility to the evil faces but part of the large old tenderness which the occasion had caused to overflow and on which we were presently floated back into the room she had left?—where we might perhaps beguile a little the impatience of the sufferer waiting for relief. We ventured in our flutter to doubt whether we *should* beguile, we held back with a certain delicacy from this irruption, and if there was a momentary wonderful and beautiful conflict I remember how our yielding struck me as crowned with the finest grace it could possibly have, that of the prodigious privilege of humouring, yes literally humouring so renowned a spirit at a moment when we could really match our judgment with hers. For the injured young man, in the other and the larger room, simply lay stretched on his back on the floor, the posture apparently least painful to him—though painful enough at the best I easily saw on kneeling beside him, after my first dismay, to ask if I could in any way ease him. I see his face again, fair and young and flushed, with its vague little smile and its moist brow; I recover the moment or two during which we sought to make natural conversation in his presence, and my question as to what conversation *was* natural; and then as his father's return still failed my having the inspiration that at once terminated the strain of the scene and yet prolonged the sublime connection. Mightn't *I* then hurry off for Mr. Paget?—on whom, as fast as a cab could carry me, I would wait with the request that he would come at the first possible moment to the rescue. Mrs. Lewes's and our stricken companion's instant appreciation of this offer lent me wings on which I again feel myself borne very much as if suddenly acting as a messenger of the gods—surely I had never come so near to performing in that character. I shook off my fellow visitor for swifter cleaving of the air, and I recall still feeling that I cleft it even in the dull four-wheeler of other days which, on getting out of the house, I recognised as the only object animating, at a distance, the long blank Sunday vista beside the walled-out Regent's Park. I crawled to Hanover Square—or was it Cavendish? I let the question stand—and, after learning at the great man's door that though he was not at home he was soon expected back and would receive my message without delay, cherished for the rest of the day the particular quality of my vibration.

It was doubtless even excessive in proportion to its cause—yet in what else but that consisted the force and the use of vibrations? It was by their excess that one knew them for such, as one for that matter only knew things in general worth knowing. I didn't know what I had expected as an effect of our offered homage, but I had somehow not, at the best, expected a relation—and now a relation had been dramatically determined. It would exist for me if I should never again in all the world ask a feather's weight of it; for myself, that is, it would simply never be able not somehow to act. Its virtue was not in truth at all flagrantly to be put to the proof—any opportunity for that underwent at the best a considerable lapse; but why wasn't it intensely acting, none the less, during the time when, before being in London again for any length of stay, I found it intimately concerned in my perusal of Middlemarch, so soon then to appear, and even in that of Deronda, its intervention on behalf of which defied any chill of time? And to these references I can but subjoin that they obviously most illustrate the operation of a sense for drama. The process of appropriation of the two fictions was experience, in great intensity, and roundabout the field was drawn the distinguishable ring of something that belonged equally to this condition and that embraced and further vivified the imaged mass, playing in upon it lights of surpassing fineness. So it was, at any rate, that my "relation"—for I didn't go so far as to call it "ours"—helped me to squeeze further values from the intrinsic substance of the copious final productions I have named, a weight of variety, dignity and beauty of which I have never allowed my measure to shrink.

Even this example of a rage for connections, I may also remark, doesn't deter me from the mention here, somewhat out of its order of time, of another of those in which my whole privilege of reference to Mrs. Lewes, such as it remained, was to look to be preserved. I stretch over the years a little to overtake it, and it calls up at once another person, the ornament, or at least the diversion, of a society long since extinct to me, but who, in common with every bearer of a name I yield to the temptation of writing, insists on profiting promptly by the fact of inscription—very much as if first tricking me into it and then proving it upon me. The extinct societies that once were so sure of themselves, how can they *not* stir again if the right touch, that of a hand they actually knew, however little they may have happened to heed it, reaches tenderly back to them? The touch *is* the retrieval, so far as it goes, setting up as it does heaven knows what undefeated continuity. I must have been present among the faithful at North Bank during a

Sunday afternoon or two of the winter of '77 and '78—I was to see the great lady alone but on a single occasion before her death; but those attestations are all but lost to me now in the livelier pitch of a scene, as I can only call it, of which I feel myself again, all amusedly, rather as sacrificed witness. I had driven over with Mrs. Greville from Milford Cottage, in Surrey, to the villa George Eliot and George Lewes had not long before built themselves, and which they much inhabited, at Witley—this indeed, I well remember, in no great flush of assurance that my own measure of our intended felicity would be quite that of my buoyant hostess. But here exactly comes, with my memory of Mrs. Greville, from which numberless by-memories dangle, the interesting question that makes for my recall why things happened, under her much-waved wing, not in any too coherent fashion—and this even though it was never once given her, I surmise, to guess that they anywhere fell short. So gently used, all round indeed, was this large, elegant, extremely near-sighted and extremely demonstrative lady, whose genius was all for friendship, admiration, declamation and expenditure, that one doubted whether in the whole course of her career she had ever once been brought up, as it were, against a recognised reality; other at least perhaps than the tiresome cost of the materially agreeable in life and the perverse appearance, at times, that though she "said" things, otherwise recited choice morceaux, whether French or English, with a marked oddity of manner, of "attack", a general incongruity of drawing room art, the various contributive elements, hour, scene, persuaded patience and hushed attention, were perforce a precarious quantity.

It is in that bygone old grace of the unexploded factitious, the air of a thousand dimmed illusions and more or less early Victorian beatitudes on the part of the blandly idle and the supposedly accomplished, that Mrs. Greville, with her exquisite goodnature and her innocent fatuity, is embalmed for me; so that she becomes in that light a truly shining specimen, almost the image or compendium of a whole side of a social order. Just so she has happy suggestion; just so, whether or no by a twist of my mind toward the enviability of certain complacencies of faith and taste that we would yet neither live back into if we could, nor can catch again if we would, I see my forgotten friend of that moist autumn afternoon of our call, and of another, on the morrow, which I shall not pass over, as having rustled and gushed and protested and performed through her term under a kind of protection by the easy-going gods that is not of this fierce age. Amiabilities and absurdities, harmless serenities and vanities, pretensions and undertakings unashamed, still profited by the mildness of the critical air and the benignity of the social—on the right side at least of the social line. It had struck me from the first that nowhere so much as in England was it fortunate to *be* fortunate, and that against that condition, once it had somehow been handed down and determined, a number of the sharp truths that one might privately apprehend beat themselves beautifully in vain. I say beautifully for I confess without scruple to have found again and again at that time an attaching charm in the general exhibition of enjoyed immunity, paid for as it was almost always by the personal amenity, the practice of all sorts of pleasantness; if it kept the gods themselves for the time in goodhumour, one was willing enough, or at least I was, to be on the side of the gods. Unmistakeable too, as I seem to recover it, was the positive interest of watching and noting, roundabout one, for the turn, or rather for the blest continuity, of their benevolence: such an appeal proceeded, in this, that and the other particular case, from the fool's paradise really rounded and preserved, before one's eyes, for those who were so good as to animate it. There was always the question of how long they would be left to, and the growth of one's fine suspense, not to say one's frank little gratitude, as the miracle repeated itself.

All of which, I admit, dresses in many reflections the small circumstance that Milford Cottage, with its innumerable red candles and candle-shades, had affected me as the most embowered retreat for social innocence that it was possible to conceive, and as absolutely settling the question of whether the practice of pleasantness mightn't quite ideally pay for the fantastic protectedness. The red candles in the red shades have remained with me, inexplicably, as a vivid note of this pitch, shedding their rosy light, with the autumn gale, the averted reality, all shut out, upon such felicities of feminine helplessness as I couldn't have prefigured in advance and as exemplified, for further gathering in, the possibilities of the old tone. Nowhere had the evening curtains seemed so drawn, nowhere the copious service so soft, nowhere the second volume of the new novel, "half-uncut", so close to one's hand, nowhere the exquisite head and incomparable brush of the domesticated collie such an attestation of *that* standard at least, nowhere the harmonies of accident—of intention was more than one could say—so incapable of a wrong deflection. That society would lack the highest finish without some such distributed clusters of the thoroughly gentle, the mildly presumptuous and the inveterately mistaken, was brought home to me there, in fine, to a tune with which I had no quarrel, perverse enough as I had been from an early time to know but the impulse to egg on society to the fullest discharge of any material stirring within its breast and not making for cruelty or brutality, mere baseness or mere stupidity, that would fall into a picture or a scene. The quality of serene anxiety on the part for instance of exquisite Mrs. Thellusson, Mrs. Greville's mother, was by itself a plea for any privilege one should fancy her perched upon; and I scarce know if this be more or be less true because the anxiety—at least as I culled its fragrance—was all about the most secondary and superfluous small matters alone. It struck me, I remember, as a new and unexpected form of the pathetic altogether; and there was no form of the pathetic, any more than of the tragic or the comic, that didn't serve as another pearl for one's lengthening string. And I pass over what was doubtless the happiest stroke in the composition, the fact of its involving, as all-distinguished husband of the other daughter, an illustrious soldier and servant of his sovereign, of his sovereigns that were successively to be, than against whose patient handsome bearded presence the whole complexus of femininities and futilities couldn't have been left in more tolerated and more contrasted relief; pass it over to remind myself of how, in my particular friend of the three, the comic and the tragic were presented in a confusion that made the least intended of them at any moment take effectively the place of the most. The impression, that is, was never that of the sentiment operating—save indeed perhaps when the dear lady applied her faculty for frank imitation of the ridiculous, which she then quite directly and remarkably achieved; but that she could be comic, that she *was* comic, was what least appeased her unrest, and there were reasons enough, in a word, why her failure of the grand manner or the penetrating note should evoke the idea of their opposites perfectly achieved. She sat, alike in adoration and emulation, at the feet of my admirable old friend Fanny Kemble, the goodnature of whose consent to "hear" her was equalled only by the immediately consequent action of the splendidly corrective spring on the part of that unsurpassed subject of the dramatic afflatus fairly, or, as I should perhaps above all say, contradictiously provoked. Then aspirant and auditor, rash adventurer and shy alarmist, were swept away together in the gust of magnificent rightness and beauty, no scrap of the far-scattered prime proposal being left to pick up.

Which detail of reminiscence has again stayed my course to the Witley Villa, when even on the way I quaked a little with my sense of what *generally* most awaited or overtook my companion's prime proposals. What had come most to characterise the Leweses to my apprehension was that there couldn't be a thing in the world about which they weren't, and on the most conceded and assured grounds, almost scientifically particular; which presumption, however, only added to the relevance of one's learning how such a matter as their relation with Mrs. Greville could in accordance with noble consistencies be carried on. I could trust *her* for it perfectly, as she knew no law but that of innocent and exquisite aberration, never wanting and never less than consecrating, and I fear I but took refuge for the rest in declining all responsibility. I remember trying to say to myself that, even such as we were, our visit couldn't but scatter a little the weight of cloud on the Olympus we scaled—given the dreadful drenching afternoon we were after all an imaginable short solace there; and this indeed would have borne me through to the end save for an incident which, with a quite ideal logic, left our adventure an approved ruin. I see again our bland, benign, commiserating hostess beside the fire in a chill desert of a room where the master of the house guarded the opposite hearthstone, and I catch once more the impression of no occurrence of anything at all appreciable but their liking us to have come, with our terribly trivial contribution, mainly from a prevision of how they should more devoutly like it when we departed. It is remarkable, but the occasion yields me no single echo of a remark on the part of any of us—nothing more than the sense that our great author herself peculiarly suffered from the fury of the elements, and that they had about them rather the minimum of the paraphernalia of reading and writing, not to speak of that of tea, a conceivable feature of the hour, but which was not provided for. Again I felt touched with privilege, but not, as in '69, with a form of it redeemed from barrenness by a motion of my own, and the taste of barrenness was in fact in my mouth under the effect of our taking leave. We did so with considerable flourish till we had passed out to the hall again, indeed to the door of the waiting carriage, toward which G. H. Lewes himself all sociably, *then* above all conversingly, wafted us—yet staying me by a sudden remembrance before I had entered the brougham and signing me to wait while he repaired his omission. I returned to the doorstep, whence I still see him reissue from the room we had just left and hurry toward me across the hall shaking high the pair of blue-bound volumes his allusion to the uninvited, the verily importunate loan of which by Mrs. Greville had lingered on the air after his dash in quest of them; "Ah those books—take them away, please, away, away!" I hear him unreservedly plead while he thrusts them again at me, and I scurry back into our conveyance, where, and where only, settled afresh with my companion, I venture to assure myself of the horrid truth that had squinted at me as I relieved our good friend of his superfluity. What indeed was this superfluity but the two volumes of my own precious "last"—we were still in the blest age of volumes—presented by its author to the lady of Milford Cottage, and by her, misguided votary, dropped with the best conscience in the world into the Witley abyss, out of which it had jumped with violence, under the touch of accident, straight up again into my own exposed face?

The bruise inflicted there I remember feeling for the moment only as sharp, such a mixture of delightful small questions at once salved it over and such a charm in particular for me to my recognising that this particular wrong—inflicted all unawares, which exactly made it sublime—was the only rightness of our visit. Our hosts hadn't so much as connected book with author, or author with visitor, or visitor with anything but the convenience of his ridding them of an unconsidered trifle;

grudging as they so justifiedly did the impingement of such matters on their consciousness. The vivid demonstration of one's failure to penetrate there had been in the sweep of Lewes's gesture, which could scarce have been bettered by his actually wielding a broom. I think nothing passed between us in the brougham on revelation of the identity of the offered treat so emphatically declined—I see that I couldn't have laughed at it to the confusion of my gentle neighbour. But I quite recall my grasp of the *interest* of our distinguished friends' inaccessibility to the unattended plea, with the light it seemed to throw on what it was really to *be* attended. Never, never save as attended—by presumptions, that is, far other than any then hanging about one—would one so much as desire *not* to be pushed out of sight. I needn't attempt, however, to supply all the links in the chain of association which led to my finally just qualified beatitude: I had been served right enough in all conscience, but the pity was that Mrs. Greville had been. This I never wanted for her; and I may add, in the connection, that I discover now no grain of false humility in my having enjoyed in my own person adorning such a tale. There was positively a fine high thrill in thinking of persons—or at least of a person, for any fact about Lewes was but derivative—engaged in my own pursuit and yet detached, by what I conceived, detached by a pitch of intellectual life, from all that made it actual to myself. *There* was the lift of contemplation, there the inspiring image and the big supporting truth; the pitch of intellectual life in the very fact of which we seemed, my hostess and I, to have caught our celebrities sitting in that queer bleak way wouldn't have bullied me in the least if it hadn't been the centre of such a circle of gorgeous creation. It was the fashion among the profane in short either to misdoubt, before George Eliot's canvas, the latter's backing of rich thought, or else to hold that this matter of philosophy, and even if but of the philosophic vocabulary, thrust itself through to the confounding of the picture. But with that thin criticism I wasn't, as I have already intimated, to have a moment's patience; I was to become, I was to remain—I take pleasure in repeating—even a very Derondist of Derondists, for my own wanton joy: which amounts to saying that I found the figured, coloured tapestry *always* vivid enough to brave no matter what complication of the stitch.

VI

I TAKE courage to confess moreover that I am carried further still by the current on which Mrs. Greville, friend of the supereminent, happens to have launched me; for I can neither forbear a glance at one or two of the other adventures promoted by her, nor in the least dissociate her from that long aftertaste of them, such as they were, which I have positively cultivated. I ask myself first, however, whether or no our drive to Aldworth, on the noble height of Blackdown, had been preceded by the couple of occasions in London on which I was to feel I saw the Laureate most at his ease, yet on reflection concluding that the first of these—and the fewest days must have separated them—formed my prime introduction to the poet I had earliest known and best loved. The revelational evening I speak of is peopled, to my memory, not a little, yet with a confusedness out of which Tennyson's own presence doesn't at all distinctly emerge; he was occupying a house in Eaton Place, as appeared then his wont, for the earlier weeks of the spring, and I seem to recover that I had "gone on" to it, after dining somewhere else, under protection of my supremely kind old friend the late Lord Houghton, to whom I was indebted in those years for a most promiscuous befriending. He must have been of the party, and Mrs. Greville quite independently must, since I catch again the vision of her, so expansively and voluminously seated that she might fairly have been couchant, so to say, for the proposed characteristic act—there was a deliberation about it that precluded the idea of a spring; that, namely, of addressing something of the Laureate's very own to the Laureate's very face. Beyond the sense that he took these things with a gruff philosophy—and could always repay them, on the spot, in heavily-shovelled coin of the same mint, since it *was* a question of his genius—I gather in again no determined impression, unless it may have been, as could only be probable, the effect of fond prefigurements utterly blighted.

The fond prefigurements of youthful piety are predestined more often than not, I think, experience interfering, to strange and violent shocks; from which no general appeal is conceivable save by the prompt preclusion either of faith or of knowledge, a sad choice at the best. No other such illustration recurs to me of the possible refusal of those two conditions of an acquaintance to recognise each other at a given hour as the silent crash of which I was to be conscious several years later, in Paris, when placed in presence of M. Ernest Renan, from the surpassing distinction of whose literary face, with its exquisite finish of every feature, I had from far back extracted every sort of shining gage, a presumption general and positive. Widely enough to sink all interest—that was the dreadful thing—opened there the chasm between the implied, as I had taken it, and the attested, as I had, at the first blush, to take it; so that one was in fact scarce to know what might have happened if interest hadn't by good fortune already reached such a compass as to stick half way down the descent. What interest *can* survive becomes thus, surely, as much one of the lessons of life as the number of ways in which it remains impossible. What comes up in face of the shocks, as I have called them, is the question of a shift of every supposition, a change of base under fire, as it were; which must take place successfully if one's advance be not abandoned altogether. I remember that I saw the Tennyson directly presented as just utterly other than the Tennyson indirectly, and if the readjustment, for acquaintance, was less difficult than it was to prove in the case of the realised Renan the obligation to accept the difference—wholly as difference and without reference to strict loss or gain—was like a rap on the knuckles of a sweet superstition. Fine, fine, fine could he only be—fine in the sense of that quality in the texture of his verse, which had appealed all along by its most inward principle to one's taste, and had by the same stroke shown with what a force of lyric energy and sincerity the kind of beauty so engaged for could be associated. Was it that I had preconceived him in that light as pale and penetrating, as emphasising in every aspect the fact that he was fastidious? was it that I had supposed him more fastidious than really *could* have been—at the best for that effect? was it that the grace of the man *couldn't*, by my measure, but march somehow with the grace of the poet, given a perfection of this grace? was it in fine that style of a particular kind, when so highly developed, seemed logically to leave no room for other quite contradictious kinds?

These were considerations of which I recall the pressure, at the same time that I fear I have no account of them to give after they have fairly faced the full, the monstrous demonstration that Tennyson was not Tennysonian. The desperate sequel to that was that he thereby changed one's own state too, one's beguiled, one's aesthetic; for what *could* this strange apprehension do but reduce the Tennysonian amount altogether? It dried up, to a certain extent, that is, in my own vessel of sympathy—leaving me so to ask whether it was before or after that I should take myself for the bigger fool. There had been folly somewhere; yet let me add that once I recognised this, once I felt the old fond pitch drop of itself, not alone inevitably, but very soon quite conveniently and while I magnanimously granted that the error had been mine and nobody's else at all, an odd prosaic pleasantness set itself straight up, substitutionally, over the whole ground, which it swept clear of every single premeditated effect. It made one's perceptive condition purely profane, reduced it somehow to having rather the excess of awkwardness than the excess of felicity to reckon with; yet still again, as I say, enabled a compromise to work.

The compromise in fact worked beautifully under my renewal of impression—for which a second visit at Eaton Place offered occasion; and this even though I had to interweave with the scene as best I might a highly complicating influence. To speak of James Russell Lowell's influence as above all complicating on any scene to the interest of which he contributed may superficially seem a perverse appreciation of it; and yet in the light of that truth only do I recover the full sense of his value, his interest, the moving moral of his London adventure—to find myself already bumping so straight against which gives me, I confess, a sufficiently portentous shake. He comes in, as it were, by a force not to be denied, as soon as I look at him again—as soon as I find him for instance on the doorstep in Eaton Place at the hour of my too approaching it for luncheon as he had just done. There he is, with the whole question of him, at once before me, and literally superimposed by that fact on any minor essence. I quake, positively, with the apprehension of the commemorative dance he may lead me; but for the moment, just here, I steady myself with an effort and go in with him to his having the Laureate's personal acquaintance, by every symptom, and rather to my surprise, all to make. Mrs. Tennyson's luncheon table was an open feast, with places for possible when not assured guests; and no one but the American Minister, scarce more than just installed, and his extremely attached compatriot sat down at first with our gracious hostess. The board considerably stretched, and after it had been indicated to Lowell that he had best sit at the end near the window, where the Bard would presently join him, I remained, near our hostess, separated from him for some little time by an unpeopled waste. Hallam came in all genially and auspiciously, yet only to brush us with his blessing and say he was lunching elsewhere, and my wonder meanwhile hung about the representative of my country, who, though partaking of offered food, appeared doomed to disconnection from us. I may say at once that my wonder was always unable *not* to hang about this admired and cherished friend when other persons, especially of the eminent order, were concerned in the scene. The case was quite other for the unshared relation, or when it was shared by one or other of three or four of our common friends who had the gift of determining happily the pitch of ease; suspense, not to say anxiety, as to the possible turn or drift of the affair quite dropped—I rested then, we alike rested, I ever felt, in a golden confidence. This last was so definitely not the note of my attention to him, so far as I might indulge it, in the wider social world, that I shall not scruple, occasion offering, to inquire into the reasons of the difference. For I can only see the ghosts of my friends, by this token, as "my" J. R. L. and whoever; which means that my imagination, of the wanton life of which these remarks pretend but to form the record, had appropriated them, under the prime contact—from the moment the prime contact had successfully worked—once for all, and contributed the light in which they were constantly exposed.

Yes, delightful I shall undertake finding it, and perhaps even making it, to read J. R. L.'s exposure back into *its* light; which I in fact see begin to shine for me more amply during those very minutes of our wait for our distinguished host and even the several that followed the latter's arrival and his seating himself opposite the unknown guest, whose identity he had failed to grasp. Nothing, exactly, could have made dear Lowell more "my" Lowell, as I have presumed to figure him, than the stretch of uncertainty so supervening and which, in its form of silence at first completely unbroken between the two poets, rapidly took on for me monstrous proportions. I conversed with my gentle neighbour during what seemed an eternity—really but hearing, as the minutes sped, all that Tennyson didn't say to Lowell and all that Lowell wouldn't on any such compulsion as that say to Tennyson. I like, however, to hang again upon the hush—for the sweetness of the relief of its break by the fine Tennysonian growl. I had never dreamed, no, of a growling Tennyson—I had too utterly otherwise fantasticated; but no line of Locksley Hall rolled out as I was to happen soon after to hear it, could have been sweeter than the interrogative sound of "Do you know anything about *Lowell*?" launched on the chance across the table and crowned at once by Mrs. Tennyson's anxious quaver: "Why, my dear, this *is* Mr. Lowell!" The clearance took place successfully enough, and the incident, I am quite aware, seems to shrink with it; in spite of which I still cherish the reduced reminiscence for its connections: so far as my vision of Lowell was concerned they began at that moment so to multiply. A belated guest or two more came in, and I wish I could for my modesty's sake refer to this circumstance alone the fact that nothing more of the occasion survives for me save the intense but restricted glow of certain instants, in another room, to which we had adjourned for smoking and where my alarmed sense of the Bard's restriction to giving what he had as a bard only became under a single turn of his hand a vision of quite general munificence. Incredibly, inconceivably, he had *read*—and not only read but admired, and not only admired but understandingly referred; referred, time and some accident aiding, the appreciated object, a short tale I had lately put forth, to its actually present author, who could scarce believe his ears on hearing the thing superlatively commended; pronounced, that is, by the illustrious speaker, more to his taste than no matter what other like attempt. Nothing would induce me to disclose the title of the piece, which has little to do with the matter; my point is but in its having on the spot been matter of pure romance to me that I was there and positively so addressed. For it was a solution, the happiest in the world, and from which I at once extracted enormities of pleasure: my relation to whatever had bewildered me simply became perfect: the author of In Memoriam had "liked" my own twenty pages, and his doing so was a gage of his grace in which I felt I should rest forever—in which I have in fact rested to this hour. My own basis of liking—such a blessed supersession of all worryings and wonderings!—was accordingly established, and has met every demand made of it.

Greatest was to have been, I dare say, the demand to which I felt it exposed by the drive over to Aldworth with Mrs. Greville which I noted above and which took place, if I am not mistaken, on the morrow of our drive to Witley. A different shade of confidence and comfort, I make out, accompanied this experiment: I believed more, for reasons I shall not now attempt to recover, in the furthermost maintenance of our flying bridge, the final piers of which, it was indubitable, *had* at Witley given way. What could have been moreover less like G. H. Lewes's valedictory hurl back upon us of the printed appeal in which I was primarily concerned than that so recent and so directly opposed passage of the Eaton Place smoking-room, thanks to which I could nurse a certified security all along the road? I surrendered to security, I perhaps even grossly took my ease in it; and I was to breathe from beginning to end of our visit, which began with our sitting again at luncheon, an air—so unlike that of Witley!—in which it seemed to me frankly that nothing but the blest obvious, or at least the blest outright, could so much as attempt to live. These elements hung sociably and all auspiciously about us—it was a large and simple and almost empty occasion; yet empty without embarrassment, rather as from a certain high guardedness or defensiveness of situation, literally indeed from the material, the local sublimity, the fact of our all upliftedly hanging together over one of the grandest sweeps of view in England. Remembered passages again people, however, in their proportion, the excess of opportunity; each with that conclusive note of the outright all unadorned. What could have partaken more of this quality for instance than the question I was startled to hear launched before we had left the table by the chance of Mrs. Greville's having happened to mention in some connection one of her French relatives, Mademoiselle Laure de Sade? It had fallen on my own ear—the mention at least had—with a certain effect of unconscious provocation; but this was as nothing to its effect on the ear of our host. "De Sade?" he at once exclaimed with interest—and with the consequence, I may frankly add, of my wondering almost to ecstasy, that is to the ecstasy of curiosity, to what length he would proceed. He proceeded admirably—admirably for the triumph of simplification—to the very greatest length imaginable, as was signally promoted by the fact that clearly no one present, with a single exception, recognised the name or the nature of the scandalous, the long ignored, the at last all but unnameable author; least of all the gentle relative of Mademoiselle Laure, who listened with the blankest grace to her friend's enumeration of his titles to infamy, among which that of his most notorious work was pronounced. It was the homeliest, frankest, most domestic passage, as who should say, and most remarkable for leaving none of us save myself, by my impression, in the least embarrassed or bewildered; largely, I think, because of the failure—a failure the most charmingly flat—of all measure on the part of auditors and speaker alike of what might be intended or understood, of what, in fine, the latter was talking about.

He struck me in truth as neither knowing nor communicating knowledge, and I recall how I felt this note in his own case to belong to that general intimation with which the whole air was charged of the want of proportion between the great spaces and reaches and echoes commanded, the great eminence attained, and the quantity and variety of experience supposable. So to discriminate was in a manner to put one's hand on the key, and thereby to find one's self in presence of a rare and anomalous, but still scarcely the less beautiful fact. The assured and achieved conditions, the serenity, the security, the success, to put it vulgarly, shone in the light of their easiest law—that by which they emerge early from the complication of life, the great adventure of sensibility, and find themselves determined once for all, fortunately fixed, all consecrated and consecrating. If I should speak of this impression as that of glory without history, that of the poetic character more worn than paid for, or at least more saved than spent, I should doubtless much overemphasise; but such, or something like it, was none the less the explanation that met one's own fond fancy of the scene after one had cast about for it. For I allow myself thus to repeat that I was so moved to cast about, and perhaps at no moment more than during the friendly analysis of the reputation of M. de Sade. Was I not present at some undreamed-of demonstration of the absence of the remoter real, the real other than immediate and exquisite, other than guaranteed and enclosed, in landscape, friendship, fame, above all in consciousness of awaited and admired and self-consistent inspiration?

The question was indeed to be effectively answered for me, and everything meanwhile continued to play into this prevision—even to the pleasant growling note heard behind me, as the Bard followed with Mrs. Greville, who had permitted herself apparently some mild extravagance of homage: "Oh yes, you may do what you like—so long as you don't kiss me before the cabman!" The allusion was explained for us, if I remember—a matter of some more or less recent leave-taking of admirer and admired in London on his putting her down at her door after being taken to the play or wherever; between the rugged humour of which reference and the other just commemorated there wasn't a pin to choose, it struck me, for a certain old-time Lincolnshire ease or comfortable stay-at-home license. But it was later on, when, my introductress having accompanied us, I sat upstairs with him in his study, that he might read to us some poem of his own that we should venture to propose, it was then that mystifications dropped, that everything in the least dislocated fell into its place, and that image and picture stamped themselves strongly and finally, or to the point even, as I recover it, of leaving me almost too little to wonder about. He had not got a third of the way through Locksley Hall, which, my choice given me, I had made bold to suggest he should spout—for I had already heard him spout in Eaton Place—before I had begun to wonder that I didn't wonder, didn't at least wonder more consumedly; as a very little while back I should have made sure of my doing on any such prodigious occasion. I sat at one of the windows that hung over space, noting how the windy, watery autumn day, sometimes sheeting it all with rain, called up the dreary, dreary moorland or the long dun wolds; I pinched myself for the determination of my identity and hung on the reader's deep-voiced chant for the credibility of his: I asked myself in fine why, in complete deviation from everything that would have seemed from far back certain for the case, I failed to swoon away under the heaviest pressure I had doubtless ever known the romantic situation bring to bear. So lucidly all the while I considered, so detachedly I judged, so dissentingly, to tell the whole truth, I listened; pinching myself, as I say, not at all to keep from swooning, but much rather to set up some rush of sensibility. It was all interesting, it was at least all odd; but why in the name of poetic justice had one anciently heaved and flushed with one's own recital of the splendid stuff if one was now only to sigh in secret "Oh dear, oh dear"? The author lowered the whole pitch, that of expression, that of interpretation above all; I heard him, in cool surprise, take even more out of his verse than he had put in, and so bring me back to the point I had immediately and privately made, the point that he wasn't Tennysonian. I felt him as he went on and on lose that character beyond repair, and no effect of the organ-roll, of monotonous majesty, no suggestion of the long echo, availed at all to save it. What the case came to for me, I take it—and by the case I mean the intellectual, the artistic—was that it lacked the intelligence, the play of discrimination, I should have taken for granted in it, and thereby, brooding monster that I was, born to discriminate *à tout propos*, lacked the interest.

Detached I have mentioned that I had become, and it was doubtless at such a rate high time for that; though I hasten to repeat that with the close of the incident I was happily able to feel a new sense in the whole connection established. My critical reaction hadn't in the least invalidated our great man's being a Bard—it had in fact made him and left him more a Bard than ever: it had only settled to my perception as not before what a Bard might and mightn't be. The character was just a rigid idiosyncrasy, to which everything in the man conformed, but which supplied nothing outside of itself, and which above all was not intellectually wasteful or heterogeneous, conscious as it could only be of its intrinsic breadth and weight. On two or three occasions of the aftertime I was to hear Browning read out certain of his finest pages, and this exactly with all the exhibition of point and authority, the expressive particularisation, so to speak, that I had missed on the part of the Laureate; an observation through which the author of Men and Women appeared, in spite of the beauty and force of his demonstration, as little as possible a Bard. He particularised if ever a man did, was heterogeneous and profane, composed of pieces and patches that betrayed some creak of joints, and addicted to the excursions from which these were brought home; so that he had to *prove* himself a poet, almost against all presumptions, and with all the assurance and all the character he could use. Was not this last in especial, the character, so close to the surface, with which Browning fairly bristled, what was most to come out in his personal delivery of the fruit of his genius? It came out almost to harshness; but the result was that what he read showed extraordinary life. During that audition at Aldworth the question seemed on the contrary not of life at all—save, that is, of one's own; which was exactly not the question. With all the resonance of the chant, the whole thing was yet *still*, with all the long swing of its motion it yet remained where it was—heaving doubtless grandly enough up and down and beautiful to watch as through the superposed veils of its long self-consciousness. By all of which I don't mean to say that I was not, on the day at Aldworth, thoroughly reconciled to learning what a Bard consisted of; for that came as soon as I had swallowed my own mistake—the mistake of having supposed Tennyson something subtly other than one. I had supposed, probably, such an impossibility, had, to repeat my term, so absurdly fantasticated, that the long journey round and about the truth no more than served me right; just as after all it at last left me quite content.

VII

IT LEFT me moreover, I become aware—or at least it now leaves me—fingering the loose ends of this particular free stretch of my tapestry; so that, with my perhaps even extravagant aversion to loose ends, I can but try for a moment to interweave them. There dangles again for me least confusedly, I think, the vision of a dinner at Mrs. Greville's—and I like even to remember that Cadogan Place, where memories hang thick for me, was the scene of it—which took its light from the presence of Louisa Lady Waterford, who took hers in turn from that combination of rare beauty with rare talent which the previous Victorian age had for many years not ceased to acclaim. It insists on coming back to me with the utmost vividness that Lady Waterford was illustrational, historically, preciously so, meeting one's largest demand for the blest recovery, when possible, of some glimmer of the sense of personal beauty, to say nothing of personal "accomplishment", as our fathers were appointed to enjoy it. Scarce to be sated that form of wonder, to my own imagination, I confess—so that I fairly believe there was no moment at which I wouldn't have been ready to turn my back for the time even on the most triumphant actuality of form and feature if a chance apprehension of a like force as it played on the sensibility of the past had competed. And this for a reason I fear I can scarce explain—unless, when I come to consider it, by the perversity of a conviction that the conditions of beauty have improved, though those of character, in the fine old sense, may not, and that with these the measure of it is more just, the appreciation, as who should say, more competent and the effect more completely attained.

What the question seems thus to come to would be a consuming curiosity as to any cited old case of the spell in the very interest of one's catching it comparatively "out"; in the interest positively of the likelihood of one's doing so, and this in the face of so many great testifying portraits. My private perversity, as I here glance at it, has had its difficulties—most of all possibly that of one's addiction, in growing older, to allowing a supreme force to one's earlier, even one's earliest, estimates of physical felicity; or in other words that of the felt impulse to leave the palm for good looks to those who have reached out to it through the medium of our own history. If the conditions *grow* better for them why then should we have almost the habit of thinking better of our handsome folk dead than of our living?—and even to the very point of not resenting on the part of others similarly affected the wail of wonder as to what has strangely "become" of the happy types *d'antan.* I dodge that inquiry just now—we may meet it again; noting simply the fact that "old" pretenders to the particular crown I speak of—and in the sense especially of the pretension made rather for than by them—offered to my eyes a greater interest than the new, whom I was ready enough to take for granted, as one for the most part easily could; belonging as it exactly did on the other hand to the interest of their elders that *this* couldn't be so taken. That was just the attraction of the latter claim—that the grounds of it had to be made out, puzzled out verily on occasion, but that when they were recognised they had a force all their own. One would have liked to be able to clear the distinction between the new and the old of all ambiguity—explain, that is, how little the superficially invidious term was sometimes noted as having in common with the elderly: so much was it a clear light held up to the question that truly beautiful persons might be old without being elderly. Their juniors couldn't be new, unfortunately, without being youthful—unfortunately because the fact of youth, so far from dispelling ambiguity, positively introduced it. One made up one's mind thus that the only sure specimens were, and had to be, those acquainted with time, and with whom time, on its side, was acquainted; those in fine who had borne the test and still looked at it face to face. These were of one's own period of course—one looked at *them* face to face; one blessedly hadn't to consider them by hearsay or to refer to any portrait of them for proof: indeed in presence of the resisting, the gained, cases one found one's self practically averse to old facts or old traditions of portraiture, accompanied by no matter what names.

All of which leads by an avenue I trust not unduly majestic up to that hour of contemplation during which I could see quite enough for the major interest what was meant by Lady Waterford's great reputation. Nothing could in fact have been more informing than so to see what was meant, than so copiously to share with admirers who had had their vision and passed on; for if I spoke above of her image as illustrational this is because it affected me on the spot as so diffusing information. My impression was of course but the old story—to which my reader will feel himself treated, I fear, to satiety: when once I had drawn the curtain for the light shed by this or that or the other personal presence upon the society more or less intimately concerned in producing it the last thing I could think of was to darken the scene again. For this right or this wrong reason then Mrs. Greville's admirable guest struck me as flooding it; indebted in the highest degree to every art by which a commended appearance may have formed the habit of still suggesting commendation, she certainly—to my imagination at least—triumphed over time in the sense that if the years, in their generosity, went on helping her to live her grace returned the favour by paying life back to them. I mean that she reanimated for the fond analyst the age in which persons of her type could so greatly flourish—it being ever so pertinently of her type, or at least of that of the age, that she was regarded as having cast the spell of genius as well as of beauty. She painted, and on the largest scale, with all confidence and facility, and nothing could have contributed more, by my sense, to what I glance at again as her illustrational value than the apparently widespread appreciation of this fact—taken together, that is, with one's own impression of the work of her hand. There it was that, like Mrs. Greville herself, yet in a still higher degree, she bore witness to the fine old felicity of the fortunate and the "great" under the "old" order which would have made it so good then to live could one but have been in their shoes. She determined in me, I remember, a renewed perception of the old order, a renewed insistence on one's having come just in time to see it begin to stretch back: a little earlier one wouldn't have had the light for this perhaps, and a little later it would have receded too much.

The precious persons, the surviving figures, who held up, as I may call it, the light were still here and there to be met; my sense being that the last of them, at least for any vision of mine, has now quite gone and that illustration—not to let that term slip—accordingly fails. We all now illustrate together, in higgledy-piggledy fashion, or as a vast monotonous mob, our own wonderful period and order, and nothing else; whereby the historic imagination, under its acuter need of facing backward, gropes before it with a vain gesture, missing, or all but missing, the concrete *other*, always other, specimen which has volumes to give where hearsay has only snippets. The old, as we call it, I recognise, doesn't disappear all at once; the *ancien régime* of our commonest reference survived the Revolution of our most horrific in patches and scraps, and I bring myself to say that even at my present writing I am aware of more than one individual on the scene about me touched *comparatively* with the elder grace. (I think of the difference between these persons and so nearly all other persons as a grace for reasons that become perfectly clear in the immediate presence of the former, but of which a generalising account is difficult.) None the less it used to be one of the finest of pleasures to acclaim and cherish, in case of meeting them, one and another of the *complete* examples of the conditions irrecoverable, even if, as I have already noted, they were themselves least intelligently conscious of these; and for the enjoyment of that critical emotion to draw one's own wanton line between the past and the present. The happy effect of such apparitions as Lady Waterford, to whom I thus undisseverably cling, though I might give her after all much like company, was that they made one draw it just where they might most profit from it. They profited in that they recruited my group of the fatuously fortunate, the class, as I seemed to see it, that had had the longest and happiest innings in history—happier and longer, on the whole, even than their congeners of the old French time—and for whom the future wasn't going to be, by most signs, anything like as bland and benedictory as the past. They placed *themselves* in the right perspective for appreciation, and did it quite without knowing, which was half the interest; did it simply by showing themselves with all the right grace and the right assurance. It was as if they had come up to the very edge of the ground that was going to begin to fail them; yet looking over it, looking on and on always, with a confidence still unalarmed. One would have turned away certainly from the sight of any actual catastrophe, wouldn't have watched the ground nearly fail, in a particular case, without a sense of gross indelicacy. I can scarcely say how vivid I felt the drama so preparing might become—that of the lapse of immemorial protection, that of the finally complete exposure of the immemorially protected. It might take place rather more intensely before the footlights of one's inner vision than on the trodden stage of Cadogan Place or wherever, but it corresponded none the less to realities all the while in course of enactment and which only wanted the attentive enough spectator. Nothing should I evermore see comparable to the large fond consensus of admiration enjoyed by my beatific fellow-guest's imputed command of the very palette of the Venetian and other masters—Titian's, Bonifazio's, Rubens's, where did the delightful agreement on the subject stop? and never again should a noble lady be lifted so still further aloft on the ecstatic breath of connoisseurship.

This last consciousness, confirming my impression of a climax that could only decline, didn't break upon me all at once but spread itself through a couple of subsequent occasions into which my remembrance of the dinner at Mrs. Greville's was richly to play. The first of these was a visit to an exhibition of Lady Waterford's paintings held, in Carlton House Terrace, under the roof of a friend of the artist, and, as it enriched the hour also to be able to feel, a friend, one of the most generously gracious, of my own; during which the reflection that "they" had indeed had their innings, and were still splendidly using for the purpose the very fag-end of the waning time, mixed itself for me with all the "wonderful colour" framed and arrayed, that blazed from the walls of the kindly great room, lent for the advantage of a charity, and lost itself in the general chorus of immense comparison and tender consecration. Later on a few days spent at a house of the greatest beauty and interest in Northumberland did wonders to round off my view; the place, occupied for the time by genial tenants, belonged to the family of Lady Waterford's husband and fairly bristled, it might be said, with coloured designs from her brush. . .

OTHER AUTOBIOGRAPHICAL WRITINGS

1881–1910

From the Notebooks, 1881–82

Brunswick Hotel, Boston.
November 25th 1881.

If I should write here all that I might write, I should speedily fill this as yet unspotted blank-book, bought in London six months ago, but hitherto unopened. It is so long since I have kept any notes, taken any memoranda, written down my current reflections, taken a sheet of paper, as it were, into my confidence! Meanwhile so much has come and gone, so much that it is now too late to catch, to reproduce, to preserve. I have lost too much by losing, or rather by not having acquired, the note-taking habit. It might be of great profit to me; & now that I am older, that I have more time, that the labour of writing is less onerous to me, & I can work more at my leisure, I ought to endeavour to keep, to a certain extent, a record of passing impressions, of all that comes, that goes, that I see, & feel, & observe. To catch and keep something of life—that's what I mean. Here I am back in America, for instance, after six years of absence, & likely while here to see and learn a great deal that ought not to become mere waste material. Here I am, da vero, and here I am likely to be for the next five months. I am glad I have come—it was a wise thing to do. I needed to see again *les miens*, to revive my relations with them, and my sense of the consequences that these relations entail. Such relations, such consequences, are a part of one's life, and the best life, the most complete, is the one that takes full account of such things. One can only do this by seeing one's people from time to time, by being with them, by entering into their lives. Apart from this I hold it was not necessary I should come to this country. I am 37 years old, I have made my choice, & God knows that I have now no time to waste. My choice is the old world—my choice, my need, my life. There is no need for me to-day to argue about this; it is an inestimable blessing to me, and a rare good fortune, that the problem was settled long ago, & that I have now nothing to do but to act on the settlement.—My impressions here are exactly what I expected they would be, & I scarcely see the place, and feel the manners, the race, the tone of things, now that I am on the spot, more vividly than I did while I was still in Europe. My work lies there—and with this vast new world, je n'ai que faire. One can't do both—one must choose. No European writer is called upon to assume that terrible burden, and it seems hard that I should be. The burden is necessarily greater for an American—for he *must* deal, more or less, even if only by implication, with Europe; whereas no European is obliged to deal in the least with America. No one dreams of calling him less complete for not doing so. (I speak of course of people who do the sort of work that I do; not of economists, of social science people.) The painter of manners who neglects America is not thereby incomplete as yet; but a hundred years hence—fifty years hence perhaps—he will doubtless be accounted so. My impressions of America, however, I shall after all, not write here. I don't need to write them (at least not àpropos of Boston;) I know too well what they are. In many ways they are extremely pleasant; but, heaven forgive me! I feel as if my time were terribly wasted here! x x x x x x x x x x x x x x x x x x x x

It is too late to recover all those lost impressions—those of the last six years—that I spoke of in beginning; besides, they are not lost altogether, they are buried deep in my mind, they have become part of my life, of my nature. At the same time if I had nothing better to do, I might indulge in a retrospect that would be interesting and even fruitful—look back over all that has befallen me since last I left my native shores. I could remember vividly, & I have little doubt I could express happily enough, if I made the effort. I can remember without effort with what an irresistible longing I turned to Europe, with what ardent yet timid hopes, with what indefinite yet inspiring intentions, I took leave of *les miens.* I recall perfectly the maturing of my little plan to get abroad again and remain for years, during the summer of 1875; the summer the latter part of which I spent in Cambridge. It came to me there on my return from New York where I had been spending a bright cold unremunerative, uninteresting winter, finishing *Roderick Hudson* & writing for the *Nation.* (It was these two tasks that kept me alive.) I had returned from Europe the year before that, the beginning of September '74, sailing for Boston with Wendell

Holmes & his wife as my fellow passengers. I had come back then to "try New York"—thinking it my duty to attempt to live at home before I should grow older, and not take for granted too much that Europe alone was possible; especially as Europe for me then meant simply Italy, where I had had some very discouraged hours, and which, lovely and desirable though it was, didn't seem as a permanent residence, to lead to anything. I wanted some thing more active, and I came back and sought it in New York. I came back with a certain amount of scepticism, but with very loyal intentions, & extremely eager to be "interested." As I say, I was interested but imperfectly, and I very soon decided what was the real issue of my experiment. It was by no means equally soon, however, that I perceived how I should be able to cross the *Atlantic* again. But the opportunity came to me at last—it loomed before me one summer's day, in Quincy St. The best thing I could imagine then was to go and take up my abode in Paris. I went (sailing about October 20th 1875,) & I settled myself in Paris with the idea that I should spend several years there. This was not really what I wanted; what I wanted was London—and Paris was only a stopgap. But London appeared to me then impossible. I believed that I might arrive there in the fulness of years, but there were all sorts of obstacles to my attempting to live there then. I wonder greatly now, in the light of my present knowledge of England, that these obstacles should have seemed so large, so overwhelming & depressing as they did at that time. When a year later I came really to look them in the face, they absolutely melted away. But that year in Paris was not a lost year—on the contrary. On my way thither I spent something like a fortnight in London; lodging at Story's Hotel, in Dover Street. It was November—dark, foggy, muddy, rainy, & I knew scarcely a creature in the place. I don't remember calling on anyone but Lady Rose and H.J.W. Coulson, with whom I went out to lunch at Petersham, near Richmond. And yet the great city seemed to me enchanting, & I would have given my little finger to remain there rather than go to Paris. But I went to Paris, and lived for a year at 29 Rue de Luxembourg (now Rue Cambon.) I shall not attempt to write the history of that year—further than to say that it was time by no means mis-spent. I learned to know Paris & French affairs much better than before—I got a certain familiarity with Paris (added to what I had acquired before) which I shall never lose. I wrote letters to the *New York Tribune*, of which, though they were poor stuff, I may say that they were too good for the purpose; (of course they didn't succeed.) I saw a good deal of Charles Peirce that winter—as to whom his being a man of genius reconciled me to much that was intolerable in him. In the spring, at Madame Tourguéneff's I made the acquaintance of Paul Joukowsky. Non ragionam di lui—ma guarda e passa. I don't speak of Ivan Tourguéneff, most delightful & lovable of men, nor of Gustave Flaubert, whom I shall always be so glad to have known; a powerful, serious, melancholy, manly, deeply corrupted, yet not corrupting, nature. There was something I greatly liked in him, & he was very kind to me. He was a head & shoulders above the others, the men I saw at his house on Sunday afternoons—Zola, Goncourt, Daudet, &c; (I mean as a man—not as a talker &c.) I remember in especial one afternoon (a weekday) that I went to see him and found him alone. I sat with him a long time, something led him to repeat to me a little poem of Th. Gautier's—*Les Vieux Portraits* (what led him to repeat it was that we had been talking of French poets, and he had been expressing his preference for Theophile Gautier over Alfred de Musset—"il était plus fran[ç]ais," etc.) I went that winter a great deal to the Comédie Fran[ç]aise—though not so much as when I was in Paris in '72. Then I went every night—or almost. And I have been a great deal since; I may say that I know the Comédie Francaise. Of course I saw a great deal of the little American "set"—the American village encamped en plein Paris. They were all very kind, very friendly, hospitable &c; they knew up to a certain point their Paris. But ineffably tiresome and unprofitable. Their society had become a kind of obligation, and it had much to do with my suddenly deciding to abandon my plans of indefinite residence, take flight to London & settle there as best I could. I remember well what a crime Mrs. S. made of my doing so; & one or two other persons as to whom I was perfectly unconscious of having given them the right to judge my movements so intimately. Nothing is more characteristic of certain American women than the extraordinary promptitude with which they assume such a right. I remember how Paris had in a hundred ways, come to weary and displease me; I couldn't get out of the detestable *American* Paris. Then I hated the Boulevards, the horrible monotony of the new quarters. I saw, moreover, that I should be an eternal outsider. I went to London in November 1876. I should say that I had spent that summer chiefly in three places: at Etretat, at Varennes (with the Lee Childes,) and at Biarritz—or rather at Bayonne, where I took refuge being unable to find quarters at Biarritz. Then late in September I spent a short time at St. Germain, at the Pavillon Louis XIV. I was finishing the *American*. The pleasantest episode (by far) of that summer was my visit to the Childes; to whom I had been introduced by dear Jane Norton; who had been very kind to me during the winter; and who have remained my very good friends. Varennes is a little moated castel of the most picturesque character, a few miles from Montargis, "au coeur de l'ancienne France." I well recall the impression of my arrival —driving over from Montargis with Edward Childe in the warm August evening and reaching the place in the vague twilight, which made it look precisely like a *décor d'op[é]ra*. I have been back there since—and it was still delightful; but at that time I had not had my now very considerable experience of country visits in England; I had not seen all those other wonderful things. Varennes therefore was an exquisite sensation —a memory I shall never lose. I settled my self again in Paris—or attempted to do so; (I like to linger over these details, and to recall them one by one;) I had no intention of giving it up. But there were difficulties in the Rue de Luxembourg I couldn't get back my old apartment, which I had given up during the summer. I don't remember what suddenly brought me to the point of saying "Go to—I *will* try London." I think a letter from William had a good deal to do with it, in which he said "Why don't you?—that must be the place." A single word from outside often moves one (moves *me* at least) more than the same word infinitely multiplied, as a simple voice from within. I *did* try it, and it has succeeded beyond my most ardent hopes. As I think I wrote just now, I have become passionately fond of it; it is an anchorage for life. Here I sit scribbling in my bedroom at a Boston hotel—on a marble-topped table!—& conscious of a ferocious homesickness—a homesickness which makes me think of the day when I shall next see the white cliffs of old England loom through their native fog, as one of the happiest of my life! The history of the five years I have spent in London—a pledge, I suppose, of many future years—is too long, and too full to write. I can only glance at it here. I took a lodging at 3 Bolton St, Piccadilly; and there I have remained till to-day—there I have left my few earthly possessions, to await my return. I have *lived* much there, felt much, thought much, learned much, produced much; the little shabby furnished apartment ought to be sacred to me. I came to London as a complete stranger, and to-day I know much too many people. J'y suis absolument comme chez moi. Such an experience is an education—it fortifies the character & embellishes the mind. It is difficult to speak adequately or justly of London. It is not a pleasant place; it is not agreeable, or cheerful, or easy, or exempt from reproach. It is only magnificent. You can draw up a tremendous list of reasons why it should be insupportable. The fogs, the smoke, the dirt, the darkness, the wet, the distances, the ugliness, the brutal size of the place, the horrible *numerosity* of society, the manner in which this senseless bigness is fatal to amenity, to convenience, to conversation, to good manners—all this and much more you may expatiate upon. You may call it dreary, heavy, stupid, dull, inhuman, vulgar at heart and tiresome in form. I have felt these things at times so strongly that I have said—"Ah London, you too then are impossible?" But these are occasional moods; and for one who takes it as I take it, London is on the whole the most possible form of life. I take it as an artist and as a bachelor; as one who has the passion of observation and whose business is the study of human life. It is the biggest aggregation of human life—the most complete compendium of the world. The human race is better represented there than anywhere else, and if you learn to know your London you learn a great many things. I felt all this in that autumn of 1876, when I first took up my abode in Bolton St. I had very few friends, the season was of the darkest & wettest; but I was in a state of deep delight. I had complete liberty, and the prospect of profitable work; I used to take long walks in the rain. I took possession of London; I felt it to be the right place. I could get English books: I used to read in the evenings, before an English fire. I can hardly say how it was, but little by little I came to know people, to dine out, &c. I did, I was able to do, nothing at all to bring this state of things about; it came rather of itself. I had very few letters—I was afraid of letters. Three or four from Henry Adams, three or four from Mrs. Wister, of which I only, as I think, presented one (to George Howard.) Poor Motley, who died a few months later, & on whom I had no claim of *any* kind, sent me an invitation to the Athenaeum, which was renewed for several months, and which proved an unspeakable blessing. When one starts in the London world (& one cares enough about it, as I did, to make one's self agreeable, as I did) cela va de soi; it goes with constantly increasing velocity. I remained in London all the following summer—till Sept. 1st—& then went abroad. I spent some six weeks in Paris, which was rather empty and very lovely, and went a good deal to the theatre. Then I went to Italy, spending almost all my time in Rome (I had a little apartment flooded with sun, in the Capo le Case.) I came back to England before Xmas, and spent the following nine months or so in Bolton St. The club question had become serious and difficult; a club was indispensable, but I had of course none of my own. I went through Gaskell's, (& I think Locker's) kindness for some time to the Traveller's; then after that for a good while to the St. James's, where I could pay a monthly fee. At last, I forget exactly when, I was elected to the Reform; I think it was about April 1878. (F.H. Hill had proposed, and C.H. Robarts had seconded, me: or vice versa.) This was an excellent piece of good fortune, and the Club has ever since been, to me, a convenience of the first order. I could not have remained in London without it, and I have become extremely fond of it; a deep local attachment. I can now only briefly enumerate the landmarks of the rest of my residence in London. In the autumn of 1878 I went to Scotland, chiefly to stay at Tillypronie. (I afterwards paid a whole visit at Gillesbie, Mrs. Rogerson's, in Dumfriesshire.) This was my first visit to Scotland, which made a great impression on me. The following year, 1879, I went abroad again—but only to Paris. I staid in London during all August, writing my little book on Hawthorne, and on September 1st crossed over to Paris and remained there till within a few days of Xmas. I lodged again in the Rue de Luxembourg, in another house, in a delightful little entresol entre cour et jardin, which I had to give up after a few weeks however, as it had been let over my head. Afterwards I went to an hotel in the Rue St. Augustin (de Choiseul et d'Egypte—) where I was staying during the great snow-storm of that year, which will long be famous. It was in that October that I went again to Varennes; & I had other plans for seeing a little of France which I was unable to carry out. But I did a good deal of work: finished the ill-fated little *Hawthorne*, finished *Confidence*, began *Washington Square*, wrote a *Bundle of Letters.* I went that Christmas, and had been, I think, the Xmas before, to Ch. Milnes Gaskell's (Thorne's.) In the spring I went to Italy—partly to escape the "Season", which had become a terror to me. I couldn't keep out of it (I had become a highly-developed diner-out, &c,) & its interruptions, its repetitions, its fatigues, were horribly wearisome, & made work extremely difficult. I went to Florence and spent a couple of months, during which I took a short run down to Rome and to Naples, where I had not been since my first visit to Italy, in 1869. I spent three days with Paul Joukowsky at Posilippo, and a couple of days alone at Sorrento. Florence was divine, as usual, and I was a great deal with the Bootts, at that exquisite Bellosguardo. At the Hotel de l'Arno, in a room in that deep recess, in the front, I began the *Portrait of a Lady*—that is I took up, and worked over, an old beginning, made long before. I returned to London to meet William, who came out in the early part of June, & spent a month with me in Bolton St, before going to the continent. That summer and autumn I worked, tant bien que mal, at my novel which began to appear in *Macmillan* in October (1880.) I got away from London more or less—to Brighton, detestable in August, to Folkestone, Dover, St. Leonard's &c. I tried to work hard, and I paid very few visits. I had a plan of coming to America for the winter, and even took my passage; but I gave it up. William came back from abroad & was with me again for a few days, before sailing for home. I spent November & December quietly in London, getting on with the *Portrait*, which went steadily, but very slowly, every part being written twice. About Xmas I went down into Cornwall, to stay with the John Clarks, who were wintering there, & then to the Pakenhams, who were (and still are,) in the Government House at Plymouth.

(Xmas day, indeed, I spent at the Pakenhams'—a bright, military dinner, at which I took in Elizabeth Thompson (Mrs. Butler,) the military paintress: a gentle, pleasing woman, very deaf.) Cornwall was charming, and my dear Sir John drove me far away to Penzance, & thence to the Land's End, where we spent the morning of New Year's day—a soft moist morning, with the great Atlantic heaving gently round the nethermost point of Old England (I was wrong just above in saying that I went *first* to the Clarks—I went on there from Devonport.) I came back to London for a few weeks, and then, again, I went abroad. I wished to get away from the London crowd, the London hubbub, all the entanglements & interruptions of London life; and to quietly bring my novel to a close. So I planned to betake myself to Venice. I started about February 10th and I came back the middle of July following. I have always to pay toll in Paris—it's impossible to pass through. I was there for a fortnight, which I didn't much enjoy. Then I travelled down through France, to Avignon, Marseilles, Nice, Mentone & San Remo, in which latter place I spent three charming weeks, during most of which time I had the genial society of Mrs. Lombard & Fanny L. who came over from Nice for a fortnight. I worked there capitally, and it made me very happy. I used in the morning, to take a walk among the olives, over the hills, behind the queer little black, steep town. Those old paved roads that rise behind and above San Remo, and climb and wander through the dusky light of the olives, have an extraordinary sweetness. Below and beyond, were the deep ravines, on whose sides old villages were perched, and the blue sea, glittering through the grey foliage. Fanny L. used to go with me—enjoying it so much that it was a pleasure to take her. I went back to the inn to breakfast (that is, lunch) and scribbled for 3 or 4 hours in the afternoon. Then, in the fading light, I took another stroll, before dinner. We went to bed early, but I used to read late. I went with the Lombards, one lovely day, on an enchanting drive—to the strange little old mountain town of Ceriana. I shall never forget that; it was one of the things one remembers; the grand clear hills, among which we wound higher and higher; the long valleys, swimming seaward, far away beneath; the bright Mediterranean, growing paler and paler as we rose above it; the splendid stillness, the infinite light, the clumps of olives, the brown villages, pierced by the carriage road, where the vehicle bumped against opposite doorposts. I spent ten days at Milan after that, working at my tale & scarcely speaking to a soul; Milan was cold, dull, & less attractive than it had been to me before. Thence I went straight to Venice, where I remained till the last of June—between three and four months. It would take long to go into that now; and yet I can't simply pass it by. It was a charming time; one of those things that don't repeat themselves; I seemed to myself to grow young again. The lovely Venetian spring came and went, and brought with it an infinitude of impressions, of delightful hours. I became passionately fond of the place, of the life, of the people, of the habits. I asked myself at times whether it wouldn't be a happy thought to take a little pied-à-terre there, which one might keep forever. I looked at unfurnished apartments; I fancied myself coming back every year. I *shall* go back; but not every year. Herbert Pratt was there for a month, and I saw him tolerably often; he used to talk to me about Spain, about the East, about Tripoli, Persia, Damascus; till it seemed to me that life would be manquée altogether if one shouldn't have some of that knowledge. He was a most singular, a most interesting type, and I shall certainly put him into a novel. I shall even make the portrait close, and he won't mind. Seeing picturesque lands, simply for their own sake, and without making any use of it—that, with him, is a passion—a passion of which if one lives with him a little (a little, I say; not too much) one feels the contagion. He gave me the nostalgia of the sun, of the south, of colour, of freedom, of being one's own master, and doing absolutely what one pleases. He used to say "I know such a sunny corner, under the South wall of old Toledo. There's a wild fig growing there; I have lain on the grass, with my guitar. There was a musical muleteer, &c." I remember one evening when he took me to a queer little wine shop, haunted only by gondoliers & facchini, in an out of the way corner of Venice. We had some excellent muscat wine; he had discovered the place and made himself quite at home there. Another evening I went with him to his rooms—far down on the Grand Canal, overlooking the Rialto. It was a hot night; the cry of the gondoliers came up from the Canal. He took out a couple of

Persian books and read me extracts from Firdausi and Saadi. A good deal might be done with Herbert Pratt. He, however, was but a small part of my Venice. I lodged on the Riva, 4161, 4° p°. The view from my windows was "una bellezza;" the far-shining lagoon, the pink walls of San Giorgio, the downward curve of the Riva, the distant islands, the movement of the quay, the gondolas in profile. Here I wrote, diligently every day & finished, or virtually finished, my novel. As I say, it was a charming life; it seemed to me at times, too improbable, too festive. I went out in the morning—first to Florian's, to breakfast; then to my bath, at the Stabilimento Chitarin; then I wandered about, looking at pictures, street life &c, till noon, when I went for my real breakfast to the Café Quadri. After this I went home and worked till six o'clock—& sometimes only till five. In this latter case I had time for an hour or two en gondole before dinner. The evenings I strolled about, went to Florian's, listened to the music in the Piazza, & two or three nights a week went to Mrs. Bronson's. That was a resource—but the milieu was too American. Late in the spring came Mrs. V. R., from Rome, who was an even greater resource. I went with her one day to Torcello, & Burano; where we took our lunch and ate it on a lovely canal at the former place. Toward the last of April I went down to Rome and spent a fortnight—during part of which I was laid up with one of those terrible attacks in my head. But Rome was very lovely; I saw a great deal of Mrs. V. R.: had (with her) several beautiful drives. One in particular I remember; out beyond the Ponte Normentano, a splendid Sunday. We left the carriage & wandered into the fields, where we sat down for some time. The exquisite stillness, the divine horizon, brought back to me out of the buried past all that ineffable, incomparable impression of Rome. (1869, 1873.) I returned to Venice by Ancona and Rimini. From Ancona I drove to Loreto, and, on the same occasion, to Recanati, to see the house of Giacomo Leopardi, whose infinitely touching letters I had been reading while in Rome. The day was lovely and the excursion picturesque; but I was not allowed to enter Leopardi's house. I saw, however, the dreary little hill-town where he passed so much of his life, with its enchanting beauty of site, and its strange, bright loneliness. I saw the streets—I saw the views he looked upon. . . . Very little can have changed. I spent only an evening at Rimini, where I made the acquaintance of a most obliging officer, who seemed delighted to converse with a forestiero, and who walked me (it was a Sunday evening) all over the place. I passed near *Urbino*: that is I passed a station, where I might have descended to spend the night, to drive to Urbino the next day. But I didn't stop! If I had been told that a month before, I should have repelled the foul insinuation. But my reason was strong. I was so nervous about my interrupted work that every day I lost was a misery, and I hurried back to Venice and to my MS. But I made another short absence, in June—a 5 days' giro to Vicenza, Bassano, Padua. At Vicenza I spent 3 of these days—it was wonderfully sweet; old Italy, and the old feeling of it. Vivid in my memory is the afternoon I arrived, when I wandered into the Piazza and sat there in the warm shade, before a caffè, with the smooth slabs of the old pavement around me, the big palace & the tall campanile opposite, &c. It was so soft, so mellow, so quiet, so genial, so Italian; very little movement, only the waning of the bright day, the approach of the summer night. Before I left Venice the heat became intense, the days and nights alike impossible. I left it at last, and closed a singularly happy episode; but I took much away with me. x x x x x x x x x x x x x x x x x x x

I went straight to the Lake of Como and over the Splügen spent only a lovely evening (with the next morning) at Cadenabbia. I mounted the Splügen under a splendid sky, and I shall never forget the sensation of rising, as night came (I walked incessantly, after we began to ascend) into that cool pure Alpine air, out of the stifling *calidarium* of Italy. I shall always remember a certain glass of fresh milk which I drank that evening, in the gloaming, far up, (a woman at a wayside hostel had it fetched from the cow) as the most heavenly draft that ever passed my lips. I went straight to Lucerne, to see Mrs. Kemble, who had already gone to Engelberg. I spent a day on the lake, making the giro; it was a splendid day, & Switzerland looked more sympathetic than I had ventured to hope. I went up to Engelberg, & spent nearly a week with Mrs. Kemble & Miss Butler, in that grim, ragged, rather vacuous, but by no means absolutely unbeautiful valley. I spent an enchanting day

with Miss Butler—climbing up to the Trubsee, toward the Joch pass. The Trubsee is a little steel-grey tarn, in a high cool valley, at the foot of the Tiltis, whose great silver-gleaming snows overhang it and light it up. The whole place was a wilderness of the alpine rose—& the alpine stillness, the splendour of the weather, the beauty of the place, made the whole impression immense. We had a man with us who carried a lunch; & we partook of it at the little cold inn. The whole thing brought back my old Swiss days; I hadn't believed they could revive even to that point. x x x x x x x x x x x x x x x
x x x x x x x x x x x x x x x x x x x x

New York, 115 East 25th St. Dec. 20th 1881. I had to break off the other day in Boston—the interruptions in the *morning* here are intolerable. That period of the day has none of the social sanctity here that it [has] in England, & which keeps it singularly free from intrusion. People—by which I mean ladies—think nothing of asking you to come & see them before lunch. Of course one can decline, but when many propositions of that sort come, a certain number stick. Besides, I have had all sorts of things to do, chiefly not profitable to recall. I have been three weeks in New York, and all my time has slipped away in mere movement. I try as usual to console myself with the reflection that I am getting impressions. This is very true; I have got a great many. I did well to come over; it was well worth doing. I indulged in some reflections a few pages back which were partly the result of a melancholy mood. I *can* do something here—it is not a mere complication. But it is not of that I must speak first in taking up my pen again—I shall return to those things later. I should like to finish briefly the little retrospect of the past year's doings, which I left ragged on the opposite page. x x x

x x x x x x x x I came back from Switzerland to meet Alice, who had been a month in England, & whom I presently saw at the Star & Garter, at Richmond. I spent two or three days with her, and saw her afterwards at Kew, then I went down to Sevenoaks and to Canterbury for the same purpose, spending a night at each place. I paid during July & August several visits. One to Burford Lodge, (Sir Trevor Lawrence's;) memorable on which occasion was a certain walk we took (on a Sunday afternoon,) through the grounds of the Deepdene, an artificial but to me a most enchanting and most suggestive English place—full of foreign reminiscences; the sort of place that an Englishman of 80 years ago, who had made the grand tour and lingered in Italy would naturally construct. I went to Leatherhead, & I went twice to Mentmore. (On one of these occasions Mr. Gladstone was there.) I went to Fredk. Macmillan's at Walton-on-Thames, & had some charming moments on the river. Then I went down into Somerset & spent a week at Midelney Place, the Cely Trevilians'. It is the impression of this visit that I wish not wholly to fade away. Very exquisite it was (not the visit, but the impression of the country;) it kept me a-dreaming, all the while I was there. It seemed to me very old England; there was a peculiarly mellow and ancient feeling in it all. Somerset is not especially beautiful; I have seen much better English scenery. But I think I have never been more *penetrated*—I have never more loved the land. It was the old houses that fetched me—Montacute, the admirable; Barrington, that superb Ford Abbey, & several smaller ones. Trevilian showed me them all; he has a great care for such things. These delicious old houses, in the long August days, in the South of England air, on the soil over which so much has passed & out of which so much has come, rose before me like a series of visions. I thought of a thousand things; what becomes of the things one thinks of at these times? They are not lost, we must hope; they drop back into the mind again, and they enrich and embellish it. I thought of stories, of dramas, of all the life of the past,—of things one can hardly speak of; speak of, I mean, at the time. It is art that speaks of those things; & the idea makes me adore her more & more. Such a house as Montacute, so perfect, with its grey personality, its old-world gardens, its accumulations of expression, of tone—such a house is really, au fond, an ineffaceable image; it can be trusted to rise before the eyes in the future. But what we think of with a kind of serrement de coeur is the gone-&-left-behind-us emotion with which at the moment we stood and looked at it. The picture may live again; but *that* is part of the past. x x x x x x

Cambridge, Dec. 26th. x x x x x x

I came here on the 23*d*, to spend Xmas, Wilky having come

on from the West (the first time in several years,) to meet me. Here I sit writing in the old back sitting room which William & I used to occupy & which I now occupy alone—or sometimes with poor Wilky, whom I have not seen in some eleven years, & who is wonderfully unchanged for a man with whom life has not gone easy. The long interval of years drops away, & the edges of the chasm "piece together" again, after a fashion. The feeling of that younger time comes back to me in which I sat here scribbling, dreaming, planning, gazing out upon the world in which my fortune was to seek, & suffering tortures from my damnable state of health. It was a time of suffering so keen that that fact might seem to give its dark colour to the whole period; but this is not what I think of to-day. When the burden of pain has been lifted, as many memories & emotions start into being as the little insects that scramble about when, in the country, one displaces a flat stone. Ill-health, physical suffering, in one's younger years is a grievous trial; but I am not sure that we do not bear it most easily then. In spite of it we feel the joy of youth; and that is what I think of to-day among the things that remind me of the past. The freshness of impression and desire, the hope, the curiosity, the vivacity, the sense of the richness and mystery of the world that lies before us,—there is an enchantment in all that which it takes a heavy dose of pain to quench and which in later hours, even if *success* have come to us, touches us less nearly. Some of my doses of pain were very heavy; very weary were some of my months and years. But all that is sacred; it is idle to write of it to-day. x x x x x x x x x

What comes back to me freely, delightfully, is the visions of those untried years. Never did a poor fellow have more; never was an ingenuous youth more passionately and yet more patiently eager for what life might bring. Now that life has brought something, brought a measurable part of what I dreamed of then, it is touching enough to look back. I know at last what I wanted then—to see something of the world. I have seen a good deal of it, and I look at the past in the light of this knowledge. What strikes me is the definiteness, the unerringness of those longings. I wanted to do very much what I have done, and success, if I may say so, now stretches back a tender hand to its younger brother, desire. I remember the days, the hours, the books, the seasons, the winter skies and darkened rooms of summer. I remember the old walks, the old efforts, the old exaltations and depressions. I remember more than I can say here to-day.

x x x x x x x x x x x x x x x x x x x

Again, in New York the other day, I had to break off: I was trying to finish the little history of the past year. There is not much more to be said about it. I came back from Midelney, to find Alice in London, and spent ten days with her there, very pleasantly, at the end of August. Delightful to me is London at that time, after the horrors of the Season have spent themselves, and the long afternoons make a cool grey light in the empty West End. Delightful to me, too, it was to see how *she* enjoyed it—how interesting was the impression of the huge, mild city. London is mild then; that is the word. And then I went to Scotland—to Tillypronie, to Cortachy, to Dalmeny, to Laidlawstiel. I was to have wound up, on my way back, with Castle Howard; but I retracted, on account of Lord Airlie's death. I can't go in to all this; there were some delightful moments, and Scotland made, as it had made before, a great impression. Perhaps what struck me as much as anything was my drive, in the gloaming, over from Kirriemuir to Cortachy; though taking the road afterward by daylight, I saw it was commonplace. In the late Scotch twilight, & the keen air, it was romantic: at least it was romantic to ford the river at the entrance to Cortachy, to drive through the dim avenues and up to the great lighted pile of the castle, where Lady A., hearing my wheels on the gravel (I was late) put her handsome head from a window in the clock-tower, asked if it was I, and wished me a bonny good-evening. I was in a Waverley Novel. Then my drive (with her) to Glamys; and my drive (with Miss Stanley) to Airlie Castle, enchanting spot! Dalmeny is delicious, a magnificent pile of woods beside the Forth; & the weather, while I was there, was the loveliest I have ever known in the British isles. But the company was not interesting, and there was a good deal of dreariness in the ball we all went to at Hopetoun for the coming of age of the heir. A charming heir he was, however, and a very pretty picture of a young nobleman stepping into his place in Society—handsome, well-mannered, gallant, graceful, with 40 000 £ a year and the world at his feet. Laidlawstiel, on a bare hill among hills, just above the Tweed, is in the midst of Walter Scott's country. Reay walked with me over to Achistiel one lovely afternoon; it is only an hour away. The house has been greatly changed since the "Sheriff's" day; but the place, the country, are the same, and I found the thing deeply interesting. It took me back. While I was at the Reays' I took up one of Scott's novels —*Redgauntlet*; it was years since I had read one. They have always a charm for me—but I was amazed at the badness of *R.*; *l'enfance de l'art.*

x x x x x x x x x x x x x x x x

Now and here, I have only one feeling—the desire to get at work again. It is nearly six months that I have been resting on my oars—letting the weeks go, with nothing to show for them but these famous "impressions"! Prolonged idleness exasperates & depresses me, and though now that I am here, it is a pity not to move about and (if the chance presents itself) see the country, the prospect of producing nothing for the rest of the winter is absolutely intolerable to me. If it comes to my having to choose between remaining stationary somewhere and getting at work, or making a journey during which I shall be able to do no work, I shall certainly elect for the former. But probably I shall be able to compromise: to see something of the country & yet work a little. My mind is full of plans, of ambitions; they crowd upon me, for these are the productive years of life. I have taken aboard by this time a tremendous quantity of material; I really have never taken stock of my cargo. After long years of waiting, of obstruction, I find myself able to put into execution the most cherished of all my projects —that of beginning to work for the stage. It was one of my earliest—I had it from the first. None has given me brighter hopes—none has given me sweeter emotions. It is strange never the less that I should never have done anything—& to a certain extent it is ominous. I wonder at times that the dream should not have faded away. It comes back to me now, however, & I ache with longing to settle down at last to a sustained attempt in this direction. I think there is really reason enough for my not having done so before: the little work at any time that I could do, the uninterrupted need of making money on the spot, the inability to do two things at once, the absence of opportunities, of openings. I may add to this the feeling that I could afford to wait, that, looked at as I look at it, the drama is the ripest of all the arts, the one to which one must bring most of the acquired as well as most of the natural, and that while I was waiting I was studying the art, and clearing off my field. I think I may now claim to have studied the art as well as it can be studied in the contemplative way. The French stage I have mastered: I say that without hesitation. I have it in my pocket, and it seems to me clear that this is the light by which one must work to-day. I have laid up treasures of wisdom about all that. What interesting hours it has given me—what endless consideration it has led to! Sometimes, as I say, it seems to me simply deplorable that I should not have got at work before. *But it was impossible at the time*, and I knew that my chance would come. Here it is: let me guard it sacredly now. Let nothing divert me from it; but now the loss of time, which has simply been a maturing process, will become an injurious one. Je me résume, as George Sand's heroes say. I remember certain occasions; several acute visitations of the purpose of which I write come back to me vividly. Some of them, the earliest, were brought on merely by visits to the theatre—by seeing great actors, &c—at fortunate hours; or by reading a new piece of Alex. Dumas, of Sardou, of Augier. No, my dear friend, nothing of all that is lost. Ces [é]motions-là ne se perdent pas; elle[s] rentrent dans le fonds même de notre nature; elle[s] font partie de notre volonté. The *volonté* has not expired; it is only perfect to-day. Two or three of the later occasions of which I speak have been among the things that *count* in the formation of a purpose; they are worth making a note of here. What has always counted, of course, has been the Comédie Française; it is on that, as regards this long day-dream, that I have lived. But there was an evening there that I shall long remember; it was in September 1877. I had come over from London; I was lodging in the Avenue d'Antin—the house with a *tir* behind it. I went to see *Jean Dacier*, with Coquelin as the hero; I shall certain[ly not] forget that impression. The piece is, on the whole, I suppose, bad; but it contains some very effective scenes, and the two principal parts gave Coquelin & Favart a magnificent chance. It is Coquelin's *great* chance, and he told me afterwards in London that it is the part he values most. He is everything in it by turns, and I don't think I ever followed an actor's creation more intently. It threw me into a great state of excitement; I thought seriously of writing to Coquelin, telling him I had been his school-mate &c. It held up a glowing light to me—seemed to point to my own path. If I could have sat down to work then I probably should not have stopped soon. But I didn't; I couldn't; I was writing things for which I needed to be paid from month to month. (I like to remind myself of these facts—to justify my innumerable postponements.[)] I remember how, on leaving the theatre—it was a lovely evening—I walked about a long time under the influence not so much of the piece as of Coquelin's acting of it, which had made the thing so human, so brilliant, so valuable. I was agitated with what it said to me that I might do—what I ought to attempt; I walked about the Place de la Concorde, along the Seine, up the Champs Elysées. That was nothing, however, to the state I was thrown into by meeting Coquelin at breakfast at Andrew Lang's, when the Comédie Française came to London. The occasion, for obvious reasons, was unpropitious, but I had some talk with him which rekindled and revived all my latent ambitions. At that time too my hands were tied; I could do nothing, and the feeling passed away in smoke. But it stirred me to the depths. Coquelin's personality, his talk, the way the *artist* overflowed in him,—all this was tremendously suggestive. I could say little to him there—not a tittle of what I wished; I could only listen, and translate to him what *they* said—an awkward task! But I listened to some purpose, and I have never lost what I gained. It excited me power fully; I shall not forget my walk, afterwards, down from South Kensington to Westminster. I met Jack Gardner, & he walked with me to leave a card at the Speaker's House. All day, & for days afterward, I remained under the impression. It faded away, in time, & I had to give myself to other things. But this brings it back to me; and I may say that those two little moments were landmarks. There was a smaller incident, later, which it gives me pleasure to recall, as it gave me extreme pleasure at the time. John Hare asked me (I met him at dinner, at the Comyns Carrs',)—urged me, I may say—to write a play, and offered me his services in the event of my doing so. I shall take him at his word. When I came back from Scotland in October last I was full of this work; my hands were free; my pocket lined; I would have given a £100 for the liberty [to] sit down and hammer away. I imagined such a capital winter of work. But I had to come hither instead. If that however involves a loss of part of my time, it needn't involve the loss of all!

Feb. 9th 1882. x x x x x x x x x x x x
102 Mt. Vernon St. Boston. x x
When I began to make these rather ineffectual records I had no idea that I should have in a few weeks to write such a tale of sadness as to-day. I came back from Washington on the 30th of last month (reached Cambridge the next day,) to find that I should never again see my dear mother. On Sunday Jan. 29th, as Aunt Kate sat with her in the closing dusk (she had been ill with an attack of bronchial asthma, but was apparently recovering happily,) she passed away. It makes a great difference to me! I knew that I loved her—but I didn't know how tenderly till I saw her lying in her shroud in that cold North Room, with a dreary snow-storm outside, & looking as sweet & tranquil & noble as in life. These are hours of exquisite pain; thank heaven this particular pang comes to us but once. On Sunday evening (at 10 o'clock—in Washington) I was dressing to go to Mrs. Robeson's—who has written me a very kind letter, when a telegram came in from Alice (William's.) "Your mother exceedingly ill. Come at once." It was a great alarm, but it didn't suggest the loss of all hope; & I made the journey to New York with whatever hope seemed to present itself. In New York at 5 o'clock I went to Cousin H.P.'s—& there the telegram was translated to me. Eliza Ripley was there—& Katie Rodgers—& as I went out I met Lily Walsh. The rest was dreary enough. I went back to the Hoffman House, where I had engaged a room on my way up town & remained there till 9.30, when I took the night-train to Boston. I shall never pass that place in future without thinking of the wretched hours I spent there. At home the worst was over; I found Father & Alice & A.K. extraordinarily calm—almost happy. Mother seemed still to be there—so beautiful, so full of all that we loved in her, she looked in death. We buried her on Wednesday Feb. 1st; Wilkie

arrived from Milwaukee a couple of hours before. Bob had been there for a month—he was devoted to mother in her illness. It was a splendid winter's day—the snow lay deep & high. We placed her for the present in a temporary vault in the Cambridge cemetery—the part that lies near the river. When the spring comes on we shall go & choose a burial place. I have often walked there in the old years—in those long, lonely, rambles that I used to take about Cambridge, & I had, I suppose, a vague idea that some of us would some day lie there, but I didn't see just that scene. It is impossible to me to say—to begin to say—all that has gone down into the grave with her. She was our life, she was the house, she was the key-stone of the arch. She held us all together, & without her we are scattered reeds. She was patience, she was wisdom, she was exquisite maternity. Her sweetness, her mildness, her quiet natural beneficence were unspeakable, & it is infinitely touching to me to write about her here as that *was*. When I think of all that she had been, for years—when I think of her hourly devotion to each & all of us—& that when I went to Washington the last of December I gave her my last kiss, I heard her voice for the last time,—there seems not to be enough tenderness in my being to register the extinction of such a life. But I can reflect, with perfect gladness, that her work was done—her long patience had done its utmost. She had had heavy cares & sorrows, which she had borne without a murmur, & the weariness of age had come upon her. I would rather have lost her forever than see her begin to suffer as she would probably have been condemned to suffer, & I can think with a kind of holy joy of her being lifted now above all our pains and anxieties. Her death has given me a passionate belief in certain transcendent things—the immanence of being as nobly created as hers—the immortality of such a virtue as that—the reunion of spirits in better conditions than these. She is no more of an angel to-day than she had always been; but I can't believe that by the accident of her death all her unspeakable tenderness is lost to the beings she so dearly loved. She is with us, she is of us—the eternal stillness is but a form of her love. One can hear her voice in it—one can feel, forever, the inextinguishable vibration of her devotion. I can't help feeling that in those last weeks I was not tender enough with her—that I was blind to her sweetness & beneficence. One can't help wishing one had only known what was coming, so that one might have enveloped her with the softest affection. When I came back from Europe I was struck with her being worn & shrunken, & now I know that she was very weary. She went about her usual activities, but the burden of life had grown heavy for her, & she needed rest. There is something inexpressibly touching to me in the way in which, during these last years, she went on from year to year without it. If she could only have lived she should have had it, & it would have been a delight to see her have it. But she has it now, in the most complete perfection! Summer after summer she never left Cambridge—it was impossible that father should leave his own house. The country, the sea, the change of air & scene, were an exquisite enjoyment to her; but she bore with the deepest gentleness & patience the constant loss of such opportunities. She passed her nights & her days in that dry, flat, hot, stale & odious Cambridge, & had never a thought while she did so but for Father & Alice. It was a perfect mother's life—the life of a perfect wife. To bring her children into the world—to expend herself, for years, for their happiness & welfare—then, when they had reached a full maturity & were absorbed in the world & in their own interests—to lay herself down in her ebbing strength & yield up her pure soul to the celestial power that had given her this divine commission. Thank God one knows this loss but once; and thank God that certain supreme impressions remain! x x x x x x x x x x x x

x x x x x x x All my plans are altered—my return to England vanishes for the present. I must remain near father; his infirmities make it impossible I should leave him. This means an indefinite detention in this country—a prospect far enough removed from all my recent hopes of departure.

August 3d 1882. 3 Bolton St. W. From time to time one feels the need of summing-up. I have done it little in the past, but it will be a good thing to do it more in the future. The prevision with which I closed my last entry in these pages was not verified. I sailed from America on the date I had in my mind when I went home—May 10th. Father was materially better and had the strongest wish that I should depart; he and Alice had moved into Boston, and were settled very comfortably in a small, pretty house (101 Mt. Vernon St.) Besides, their cottage at Manchester was rapidly being finished; shortly before sailing I went down to see it. Very pretty—bating the American scragginess; with the sea close to the piazzas, and the smell of bayberries in the air. Rest, coolness, peace, society enough, charming drives; they will have all that.—

Very soon after I had got back here my American episode began to fade away, to seem like a dream; a very painful dream, much of it. While I was there, it was Europe, it was England, that was dreamlike—but now all this is real enough. The Season is over thank God; I came in for as much of it as could crowd itself into June and July. I was out of the mood for it, preoccupied, uninterested, bored, eager to begin work again; but I was obliged, being on the spot, to accommodate myself to the things of the day, and always with my old salve to a perturbed spirit, the idea that I was seeing the world. It seemed to me on the whole a poor world this time; I saw and did very little that was interesting. I am extremely glad to be in London again; I am deeply attached to London; I always shall be; but decidedly I like it best when it is "empty," as during the period now beginning. I know too many people—I have gone in too much for society. x x x x x x x x x x x x x x x x x

Grand Hotel, Paris, November 11th. Thanks to "society," which, in the shape of various surviving remnants of the season, to a succession of transient Americans and to several country visits, continued to mark me for its own during the greater part of the month of August, I had not even time to finish that last sentence, written more than three months ago. I can hardly take up at this date the history of these three months: a simple glance must suffice. I remained in England till the 12th of September. Bob, whom I had found reclining on my sofa in Bolton St when I arrived from America toward the last of May—(I hadn't even time, above, to mention my little disembarkation in Ireland and the few days I spent there—) Bob, who as I say was awaiting me at my lodgings in London—greatly to my surprise, and in a very battered & depressed condition, thanks to his unhappy voyage to the Azores—sailed for home again in the last days of August, after having spent some weeks in London, at Malvern and at Llandudno, in Wales. The last days, before sailing, he spent with me. About the 10th of September William arrived from America, on his way to the continent to pass the winter. After being with him for a couple of days, I came over to Paris via Folkestone (I came down there & slept, before crossing,) while he crossed to Flushing, from Queenborough. All summer I had been trying to work, but my interruptions had been so numerous that it was only during the last weeks that I succeeded, even moderately, in doing something. My record of work for the whole past year is terribly small, and I opened this book, just now, with the intention of taking several solemn vows in reference to the future. But I don't even know whether I shall accomplish that. However, I am not sure that such solemnities are necessary, for God knows I am eager enough to work, and that I am deeply conscious of the need of it, both for fortune and for happiness. x x x x x x x x x x x x x I scarcely even remember the three or four visits to which, in the summer, I succeeded in restricting my "social activity." A pleasant night at Losely—Rhoda Broughton was there. Another day I went down there to lunch, to take Howells (who spent all August in London) and Bob. Two days at Mentmore, a Saturday-to-Monday episode (very dull) at Miss de Rothschild's, at Wimbledon; a very pleasant day at the Arthur Russells', at Shiere. This last was charming; I think I went nowhere else—having wriggled out of Midelney, from my promised visit to Mrs. Pakenham, and from pledges more or less given to Tilliepronie. Toward the last, in London, I had my time pretty well to myself, and I felt, as I have always felt before, the charm of those long, still days, in the empty time, when one can sit and scribble, without notes to answer and visits to pay. Shall I confess, however, that the evenings had become dull? x x x x x x x x x x x x x x x I had meant to write some account of my last months in America, but I fear the chance for this has already passed away. I look back at them, however, with a great deal of tenderness. Boston is absolutely nothing to me—I don't even dislike it. I like it, on the contrary; I only dislike to live there. But all those weeks I spent there, after Mother's death, had an exquisite stillness and solemnity. My rooms in Mt. Vernon St. were bare and ugly; but they were comfortable—even, in a certain way, pleasant. I used to walk out, and across the Common, every morning, and take my breakfast at Parker's. Then I walked back to my lodgings and sat writing till four or five o'clock; after which I walked out to Cambridge over that dreary Bridge whose length I had measured so often in the past, and, four or five days in the week, dined in Quincy St. with Father and Alice. In the evening I walked back, in the clear American starlight—I got in this way plenty of exercise. It was a simple, serious, wholesome time. Mother's death appeared to have left behind it a soft beneficent hush in which we lived for weeks, for months, and which was full of rest and sweetness. I thought of her, constantly, as I walked to Boston at night along those dark vacant roads, where, in the winter air, one met nothing but the coloured lamps and the far-heard jingle of the Cambridge horse-cars. My work at this time interested me too, and I look back upon the whole three months with a kind of religious veneration. My work interested me even more than the importance of it would explain—or than the success of it has justified. I tried to write a little play (*D. M.*) & I wrote it; but my poor little play has not been an encouragement. I needn't enter into the tiresome history of my ridiculous negotiations with the people of the Madison Square Theatre, of which the Proprietors behaved like asses and sharpers combined; this episode, by itself, would make a brilliant chapter in a realistic novel. It interested me immensely to write the piece, and the work confirmed all my convictions as to the fascination of this sort of composition. But what it has brought [me] to know, both in New York and in London, about the manners and ideas of managers & actors and about the conditions of production on our unhappy English stage, is almost fatally disgusting and discouraging. I have learned, very vividly, that if one attempts to work for it one must be prepared for *disgust*, deep and unspeakable disgust. But though I am disgusted, I do not think I am discouraged. The reason of this latter is that I simply can't afford to be. I have determined to take a year—even two years, if need be, more, in experiments, in studies, in attempts. The dramatic form seems to me the most beautiful thing possible; the misery of the thing is that the baseness of the English-speaking stage affords no setting for it. How I am to reconcile this with the constant solicitation that presses upon me, both from within and from without, to get at work upon another novel, is more than I can say. It is surely the part of wisdom, however, not to begin another novel at once—not to commit myself to a work of longue haleine. I must do *short* things, in such measure as I need, which will leave me intervals for dramatic work. I say this rather glibly—and yet I sometimes feel a woful hunger to sit down to another novel. If I can only *concentrate* myself: this is the great lesson of life. I have hours of unspeakable reaction against my smallness of production; my wretched habits of work—or of no-work; my levity, my vagueness of mind, my perpetual failure to focus my attention, to absorb myself, to look things in the face, to invent, to produce, in a word. I shall be 40 years old in April next: it's a horrible fact! I believe however that I have learned how to work and that it is in moments of forced idleness, almost alone, that these melancholy reflections seize me. When I am really at work, I'm happy, I feel strong, I see many opportunities ahead. It is the only thing that makes life endurable. I must make some great efforts during the next few years, however, if I wish not to have been on the whole a failure. I shall have been a failure unless I do something *great*!

Wolcott Balestier

THEY HAVE a place apart in the record of the dead, the young names which represent less for the big indifferent public than for a knot of friends who remember and regret, and yet on behalf of which we discreetly plead for some attenuation, in the general memory, of the common fate. So far as they *are* spared by oblivion they form a ghostly but enviable little band—the company of those who were estimated early and rescued early, who created expectations and cherished hopes, and for whom there remains no question of disappointment or of failure. We can think of them as it most pleases us to think, allude to them with unchallengeable faith, and give our imagination the luxury of filling out the vague disc of the possible. Charles Wolcott Balestier, who died in Dresden on the 6th of December 1891, just before he had reached his thirtieth year, participates in this dim distinction and becomes one of the mute appealers to whom we are indulgent in proportion as we recognise that what there is to "show" for them accounts but imperfectly for our plea. We make the plea for the plea's sake, and because that is fairer than not to make it. He had not had time, though he had so many of the other conditions, and this particular use of a little of the time that we ourselves feel half-ashamed to have gained—as if we had gained it at his expense—presents itself as an act of common generosity.

Wolcott Balestier loved literature better than anything but his friends, and he had found opportunity to testify to this in a career as eagerly active as it was short. He left behind him a youthful unpublished novel, which is, conspicuously, to see the light; three very short tales, and the vivid mark of his collaboration with Mr. Rudyard Kipling in *The Naulahka*. His memory therefore may take its stand on a certain quantity of performance; but I confess that it is not mainly under the impression of this little sum of literary achievement that I find myself moved to speak of him. What he wrote, what he would have published, will be largely and sympathetically scrutinised, but there are persons for whom it will remain both only the smaller part of what he did and the pledge of a talent smothered at the very moment it had begun to expand. He was conscious that he had only begun, and it would be an unkindness to his memory to represent that in spite of the extreme vividness of "Reffey," and of "Captain, my Captain!" his slender relics were very sacred in his own eyes. They are interesting, and in glimpses original, but their greatest merit is perhaps that by making him for the hour an actuality they give us a pretext for attempting to preserve some little record of his beneficence. He was a man of business of altogether peculiar genius, and it was in this light that he figured, with singular intensity, to a large number of charmed, befriended people during the part of his brief life in which I judge that he had lived more than in all its preceding time, the three crowded London years that began in December 1888. This was the period of my acquaintance with him; my personal relations with him became close, and I speak of him, of course, essentially as I had the good fortune to know him. I freely confess that I should not add my voice to the commemorative hum if it were a question of taking any less affectionate a point of view.

I speak of his having "figured" in London, because he was from the first, in his bright young ingenuity, his suggestion of immediate capacity, an apparition essentially salient. This was what he remained to the end, unmistakably an influence exotic and curious, dropped down from without, not thrown up from within. He made London, on the ground on which he dealt with it, so extraordinarily his own that the contrast between the spirit and the matter, the agent and the medium, could only grow more striking and, if I may frankly say so, more amusing. Nothing feeds more actively some of our reflections than the sight of that animated symbol, the "cultured American," entangled for the first time in the dense meshes of the great London net. The manner in which his native faculty deals with them is often an instructive spectacle. We see it, however, for the most part, exercised in a merely contemplative or "sightseeing" way, in the interest of leisure and shopping, or at the most of patriotism and consolation. But Wolcott Balestier, at twenty-seven, with a very complicated and characteristic American past already behind him—born at Rochester, N.Y., in 1861, he had haunted colleges, administered libraries, started "businesses," explored territories, conducted theatricals, edited periodicals and published "works"—this penetrating representative of a peculiarly transatlantic interest in books alighted in the formidable city, in the dusky void of Christmas week, on no merely passive errand. He had a specific mission, business to transact for an American publishing firm, but I trust I do no injustice to the perfection with which he transacted it if I say that such things could, in the nature of the case, give him only his pretext and his introduction. What he had really come for, as it turned out, was to find a field large enough for his admirable spirit. The field was largest in London because London was an extension without being a substitution. It "took in," as it were, the great agglomerations he had left beyond the sea and added others to them. It had, in a word—it always has—the advantage of being the biggest box at the theatre, the highest seat of observation of the English-speaking multitude as a whole—with nothing less than which was Wolcott Balestier prompted to concern himself.

I met him, accidentally, soon after his arrival, and was struck with his happy perceptions and with his acute appreciation of London. Young and fresh as he was, he rejoiced in the dim vastness of the great city—this was a quality which he found altogether inspiring. He delighted in space and number, and dealt with the latter element in particular in a way which, at his age, was already masterly. He never was so happy as when he had too many things to do, and he could view the infinite multiplication of detail with pure exhilaration. This is partly what I mean by his admirable spirit, which was his love of handling large things, of handling everything in a large way. In the poor little three years to which the best of his activity was restricted he of course had established but imperfectly his independence; but they were sufficient to give the measure of his capacity. It was those who knew him best who "chaffed" him most about his Napoleonic propensities—his complete incapacity to recognise difficulties, his immediate adoption of his own or, in other words, of an original solution. It never could have occurred to him that there was not a way round an obstacle so long as a way was inventible, and the invented way, which in almost all cases was the one he embraced—he suspected stupidity, with which he had no patience, in the ready-made—always proved in fact the most amusing. This was a high recommendation to him, for, observant and genial as he was, he liked to enjoy transactions for themselves, as one is happy in the exercise of any implanted faculty, quite apart from purpose and profit. The Copyright Bill had not yet been passed, and it appeared to him that there might be much to be done in helping the English author in America to a temporary *modus vivendi*. This was an idea at the service of which he put all his ingenuity—an ingenuity sharpened by his detestation of the ignoble state of the law. This acute and sympathetic interest in the fruits of literary labour, as they concern the labourer, generalised and systematised itself with extraordinary rapidity, and became, by the time he had been six months in London, a very remarkable and singularly interesting passion, a passion which, for those who had the advantage of seeing it in exercise, quickly assumed all the authority of genius.

It was a faculty altogether individual and one of the most original I have ever known. It consisted, in its simplest expression, of an extraordinary agility in putting himself in the place of the man, and quite as easily, when the need was, of the woman, of letters; and it sprang from an intense and curious appreciation of the literary character and an odd, charmed, amused acceptance of the dominion of the book. Nothing could be quite ultimate for a spirit so humorous, but Wolcott Balestier found in the importunity of the book the elements of a kind of cheerful fatalism, a state of mind that went hand in hand, in a whimsical way, with the critical instinct. To see the book through—almost even through the press—was a perpetual pastime to him, and one that varied of course according to what the book might be. It was far greater in some cases than in others; but in the free play of his ingenuity he could *faire un sort*, prepare a kind of respectable future, for almost anything newly printed and published, take a peep from any point of view that passed muster as literary. In this way, in our scribbling hour, he multiplied immensely his relations with the pen-driving class, even in the persons of some of its most pathetic representatives, of whom he became, in the shortest space of time, the clever providence and kindly adviser. Signs were not wanting from many of these after his death, signs of their mourning for him as the most trusted of friends. And all this, on the young man's part, in a spirit so disinterested and so sincerely sympathetic that one hardly knew what name to give to the genius of the market when the genius of the market appeared in a form so human.

He had the greatest appetite for success and had begun to be a man of business of the very largest conceptions, but I have never seen this characteristic combined with so visible an indifference to the usual lures and ideals of commerce. As the faithful representative of others he could only be jealous of their interests, but a high and imaginative talent for affairs could not well have been associated with less reverence for mere acquisition. He had in fact none at all—he seemed to me to care nothing for money. What he cared for was the drama of business, the various human game. To make money, up to a certain point, would have been convenient to him, and if he proposed to do so it was simply because this meant freedom, freedom to make a very different use of his time when (at no very distant day, as he hoped), the hour should strike. Much as he was absorbed in the literary affairs of other people, he was excusable for keeping a commodious chamber of his brain open to his own; and he had the most definite purpose of hammering away at the modern, the very modern novel, as soon as he should get out of the glare of the market-place and be able to command the conditions. He had already given pledges in this direction—had published two boyish fictions before coming to England, and in the intervals of his busy first year in London had put together a long story of much maturer, of really confident promise. An intimate personal alliance with Mr. Rudyard Kipling had led to his working in concert with that extraordinary genius, a lesson precious doubtless and wasted, like so many of his irrepressible young experiments—wasted, I mean, in the sense of its being a morning without a morrow.

Wolcott Balestier's death came too soon, in my judgment, to permit of a just calculation of what he might have done; we must recognise the limits of the evidence that his talent was real and remarkably capable of growth—evidence confirmed, on the part of those who knew him, by the sense of his acuteness and his ambition. He was all for the novel of observation, the undiscourageable study of the actual; he professed an intense relish for the works of Mr. Howells, and there is little reason to doubt that if he had lived to give what was in him the followers of some of the ancient ways would have had many a bone to pick with him. The prospect of picking such bones was, for himself, a thing to add zest to the existence he was not destined to enjoy. His imagination, so far as he had given a hint of it, was all American, and a long stay in the far west, a familiarity with mining-camps and infant cities, had given it, for the time at least, the turn of the new convention. He was prejudiced in favour of American humour—it was his only prejudice that I can remember; fortunately it is not one that is fatal to intellectual growth. He liked little raw new places only one degree less than he liked London, where he had established himself, in the heart of Westminster, under the Abbey towers, just within the old archway of that Dean's Yard which makes a kind of provincial backwater, like the corner of a cathedral close, in a roaring "imperial" neighbourhood. But when once it had begun to go, his talent would probably have had many moods and seasons. I remember thinking (on first observing what dreams he had of becoming a literary artist), that as the presumption is always against the duplication of a special gift, it was not particularly probable that the subtle secret of creation had been vouchsafed to a man who, in his natural mastery of affairs, might already account himself fortunately equipped. What community was there, in the same mind, between the noisy world of affairs and the hushed little chamber of literary art? That question was eventually answered —there could be none unless such a mind should be a rare exception. This was indeed the fact with Wolcott Balestier, and it made him, in my experience, unique.

I have known literary folk who were full, for themselves, of the commercial spirit, but I have in no other case known a commercial connection with literature to have had a twinship with an artistic one. Wolcott Balestier, however, was commercial, as I may say, for others; it was for himself that he cherished the hope of achieving some painted picture of life. Moreover the technical term seems invidious as applied to a part played so easily and gracefully, with such friendly personal perceptions. This function cost him nothing intellectually—it was too instinctive and, incidentally, as I have said, too suggestive. It had advantages from the point of view of what he intended when a better day should have begun; it meant perpetual contact with the world of men and women and innumerable opportunities for observation. In this he ironically exulted, and indeed it made him enviable. He had a particular aptitude for the personal part of affairs, for arranging things in talk and face to face. He had instincts and ideals of rapidity, and a talent for dispensing with the matter of course (which seemed to him flat and prosaic), calculated often to bewilder the children of a postponing habit. And it was given to him moreover to encounter the human, not to say the supposedly literary spirit, bared of factitious graces, in the simple severity of some of its appetites. He saw many realities and had already learned not to blink many uglinesses. Young as he was he had perceived what was of the essence. He was a well of discretion, and it was charming and interesting in him that even when he was most humorously communicative his talk was traversed by little wandering airs of the unsaid; nevertheless he was not without nameless anecdotes and illustrations of this same tenacity of grasp—all the more striking that in general no man could be less prejudiced in favour of the publishing interest. Such an incident as the quick foundation of the "English Library"—an association for the larger diffusion on the Continent of English and American books—not only was a remarkable example of his fertility of resource (his idea always became a fact as soon as he could personally represent it and act for it), but brought with it an extension of experience of the sort which was really most remunerative to him and as to which he could be independently and delightfully descriptive. It was partly on business connected with this happy undertaking and partly exactly to do nothing at all—to rest from a torment of detail and a strain of responsibility—that he made, sadly unwell when he started, in November 1891, that excursion to Germany from which he was not to return. He had only once or twice in his life been gravely ill, but those who were fond of him were never persuaded by his gallantry of optimism about himself, reinforced as it was by a thoroughly consistent and characteristic ingenuity in neglecting dull precautions, to think of his slender structure as really adequate to the service—the formidable service—of his generously restless spirit. It was not, in fact, and the disparity made him touching—makes his present image so in memory, though he doubtless would have carried on the brave deception much longer had it not been for the miserable typhoidal infection, from an undiscoverable source, that he bore with him from London and to which, in happy unconsciousness, he succumbed.

It is vain to attempt to exclude the egotistical note from a memorial like the present, and the better course is frankly to enjoy the benefit of it. I may therefore mention that during the last year of his life in particular I saw him so often and so closely that, as I write, my page is overscored with importunate reminiscence and picture. These things are the possession of the private eye, but one would fain reflect something of their clearness in one's words. A wet winter night in a windy Lancashire town, for instance—a formidable "first night" at a troubled provincial theatre to which he had made a long and loyal pilgrimage for purposes of "support" at a grotesquely nervous hour—such an occasion comes back to me, vividly, with the very quality of the support afforded, lavish and eager and shrewd; with the pleasantness of the little commemorative inn-supper, half histrionic and wholly confident, and with the dragged-out drollery of the sequel next day, our sociable, amused participation in a collective theatrical flitting, effected in pottering Sunday trains, besprinkled with refreshment-room impressions and terminating, that night, at an all but inaccessible Birmingham, in independent repose and relaxed criticism. He had taken, the summer before his death, a house on the Isle of Wight—on the south shore, well on the way to the Freshwater end—and I cannot withhold the emphasis of an allusion to a couple of August days spent there with him. One of them had a rare perfection and made the purest medium for the high finish—as if it were a leaf out of an old-fashioned drawing-book—of the little pencilled island. It was given all to a long drive to Freshwater, much of the way over the firm grass of the great downs, and a lunch there and a rambling lazy lounge on the high cliffs, with the full sense of summer, for once, in a summerless year, and a still lazier return in the golden afternoon, amid all sorts of delicacies of effect of sea and land. He loved the little temporary home he had made on the edge of the sea and even the great wind-storms of the early autumn, and no season of his life, probably, in spite of haunting illness, had given him more contented hours. Now he lies in the last place he could have dreamed of, the bristling alien cemetery, contracted and charmless, of the foreign city to which he had made his feverish way only to die. There was something in him so actively modern, so open to new reciprocities and assimilations, that it is not fanciful to say that he would have worked originally, in his degree, for civilisation. He had the real cosmopolitan spirit, the easy imagination of differences and hindrances surmounted. He struck me as a bright young forerunner of some higher common conveniences, some greater international transfusions. He had just had time to begin, and that is exactly what makes the exceeding pity of his early end.

1892

Dumas the Younger

ONE OF the things that most bring home his time of life to a man of fifty is the increase of the rate at which he loses his friends. Some one dies every week, some one dies every day, and if the rate be high among his coevals it is higher still in the generation that, on awaking to spectatorship, he found in possession of the stage. He begins to feel his own world, the world of his most vivid impressions, gradually become historical. He is present, and closely present, at the process by which legend grows up. He sees the friends in question pictured as only death can picture them—a master superior to the Rembrandts and Titians. They have been of many sorts and many degrees, they have been private and public, but they have had in common that they were the furniture of this first fresh world, the world in which associations are formed. That one by one they go is what makes the main difference in it. The landscape of life, in foreground and distance, becomes, as the painters say, another composition, another subject; and quite as much as the objects directly under our eyes we miss the features that have educated for us our sense of proportion.

Among such features for the author of these lines the younger Dumas, who has just passed away, was in the public order long one of the most conspicuous. Suffused as he is already with the quick historic haze, fixed, for whatever term, in his ultimate value, he appeals to me, I must begin by declaring, as a party to one of these associations that have the savour of the prime. I knew him only in his work, but he is the object of an old-time sentiment for the beginning of which I have to go back absurdly far. He arrived early—he was so loudly introduced by his name. I am tempted to say that I knew him when he was young, but what I suppose I mean is that I knew him when I myself was. I knew him indeed when we both were, for I recall that in Paris, in distant days and undeveloped conditions, I was aware with perhaps undue and uncanny precocity of his first successes. There emerges in my memory from the night of time the image of a small boy walking in the Palais

Royal with innocent American girls who were his cousins and wistfully hearing them relate how many times (they lived in Paris) they had seen Madame Doche in "La Dame aux Camélias" and what floods of tears she had made them weep. It was the first time I had heard of pockethandkerchiefs as a provision for the play. I had no remotest idea of the social position of the lady of the expensive flowers, and the artless objects of my envy had, in spite of their repeated privilege, even less of one; but her title had a strange beauty and her story a strange meaning—things that ever after were to accompany the name of the author with a faint yet rich echo. The younger Dumas, after all, was then not only relatively but absolutely young; the American infants, privileged and unprivileged, were only somewhat younger; the former going with their *bonne*, who must have enjoyed the adventure, to the "upper boxes" of the old Vaudeville of the Place de la Bourse, where later on I remember thinking Madame Fargueil divine. He was quite as fortunate moreover in his own designation as in that of his heroine; for it emphasised that bloom of youth (I don't say bloom of innocence—a very different matter) which was the signal-note of the work destined, in the world at large, to bring him nine-tenths of his celebrity.

Written at twenty-five "La Dame aux Camélias" remains in its combination of freshness and form, of the feeling of the springtime of life and the sense of the conditions of the theatre, a singular, an astonishing production. The author has had no time to part with his illusions, but has had full opportunity to master the most difficult of the arts. Consecrated as he was to this mastery he never afterwards showed greater adroitness than he had then done in keeping his knowledge and his *naïveté* from spoiling each other. The play has been blown about the world at a fearful rate, but it has never lost its happy juvenility, a charm that nothing can vulgarise. It is all champagne and tears—fresh perversity, fresh credulity, fresh passion, fresh pain. We have each seen it both well done and ill done, and perhaps more particularly the latter—in strange places, in barbarous tongues, with Marguerite Gautier fat and Armand Duval old. I remember ages ago in Boston a version in which this young lady and this young gentleman were represented as "engaged": that indeed for all I know may still be the form in which the piece most enjoys favour with the Anglo-Saxon public. Nothing makes any difference—it carries with it an April air: some tender young man and some coughing young woman have only to speak the lines to give it a great place among the love-stories of the world. I recollect coming out of the Gymnase one night when Madame Pierson had been the Marguerite—this was very long since—and giving myself up on the boulevard to a fine critical sense of what in such a composition was flimsy and what was false. Somehow, none the less, my fine critical sense never prevented my embracing the next opportunity to expose it to the same irritation; for I have been, I am happy to think to-day, a playgoer who, whatever else he may have had on his conscience, has never had the neglect of any chance to see this dramatist acted. Least of all, within a much shorter period, has it undermined one's kindness to have had occasion to admire in connection with the piece such an artist for instance as Eleonora Duse. We have seen Madame Duse this year or two in her tattered translation, with few advantages, with meagre accessories and with one side of the character of the heroine scarcely touched at all—so little indeed that the Italian version joins hands with the American and the relation of Marguerite and Armand seems to present itself as a question of the consecrated even if not approved "union." For this interesting actress, however, the most beautiful thing is always the great thing, and her performance—if seen on a fortunate evening—lives in the mind as a fine vindication of the play. I am not sure indeed that it is the very performance Dumas intended; but he lived long enough to have forgotten perhaps what that performance was. He might on some sides, I think, have accepted Madame Duse's as a reminder.

If I have stopped to be myself so much reminded, it is because after and outside of "La Dame aux Camélias" Dumas really never figured among us all again—a circumstance full of illustration of one of the most striking of our peculiarities, the capacity for granting a prodigious ear to some one manifestation of an author's talent and caring nothing whatever for the others. It is solely the manifestation and never the talent that interests us, and nothing is stranger than the fact that no critic has ever explained on our behalf the system by which we hurl ourselves on a writer to-day and stare at him to-morrow as if we had never heard of him. It gives us the air of perpetually awaking from mistakes, but it renders obscure all our canons of judgment. A great force makes a great success, but a great force is furthermore no less a great force on Friday than on Monday. Was the reader a sorry dupe on the first day, or is the writer a wanton sacrifice on the second? That the public is intelligent on both occasions is a claim it can scarcely make: it can only choose between having its acuteness impugned or its manners condemned. At any rate if we have in England and the United States only the two alternatives of the roar of the market and the silence of the tomb the situation is apt to be different in France, where the quality that goes into a man's work and gives it an identity is the source of the attention excited. It happens that the interest in the play of the genius is greater there than the "boom" of the particular hit, the concern primarily for the author rather than the subject, instead of, as among ourselves, primarily for the subject rather than the author. Is this because the French have been acute enough to reflect that authors comprehend subjects, but that subjects can unfortunately not be said to comprehend authors? Literature would be a merry game if the business were arranged in the latter fashion. However such a question may be answered, Dumas was in his own country, to the end, the force that, save in connection with his first play, he failed to become elsewhere; and if he was there much the most original worker in his field one of the incidental signs of his originality was that, despite our inveterate practice, in theatrical matters, of helping ourselves from our neighbour's plate, he was inveterately not a convenience to us. We picked our morsels from the plates of smaller people—we never found on that of the author of "Le Fils Naturel" any we could swallow. He was not to our poor purpose, and I cannot help thinking that this helps a little to give his artistic measure. It would be a bad note for him now if we had found him amenable to that graceless game of which we show signs to-day of having grown ashamed, but which flourished for years in two imperturbable communities as the art of theatrical adaptation. A Dumas adaptable is a Dumas inconceivable; and in point of fact he was touched by the purveyors of the English-speaking stage only to prove fatal to them. If the history of so mean a traffic as the one here glanced at were worth writing it would throw light on some odd conceptions of the delicacy in the abused name of which it was carried on. It is all to the honour of our author's seriousness that he was, in such conditions, so unmanageable; though one must of course hasten to add that this seriousness was not the only reason of it. There were several others, not undiscoverable, and the effect of the whole combination was, in view of the brilliant fortune of his productions at home and the eager foraging of English and American speculators, to place him on a footing all his own. He was of active interest among us only to individual observers—simply as one of the most devoted of whom I trace these few pages of commemoration.

It takes some analysis, yet is not impossible, to explain why among the men of his time to whom the creative gift had been granted his image, for sundry such admirers, always presented him as somehow the happiest consciousness. They were perhaps not always aware of it, but now that he is gone they have a revelation of the place he occupied in the envious mind. This envy flowed doubtless, to begin with, from the sense of his extraordinarily firm grasp of his hard refractory art; the grasp that had put him into possession of it without fumblings or gropings made him canter away on the back of it the moment he had touched the stirrup. He had the air through all his career of a man riding a dangerous horse without ever being thrown. Every one else had a fall—he alone never really quitted the saddle, never produced a play that was not to stay to be revived and in the case of his comparative failures enjoy some sort of revenge, even to that of travelling in the repertory of great actresses round the globe. Such travels, moreover, much as they may please his shade, are far from having been the only felicities of his long career. The others strike me as so numerous that I scarcely indeed know where to begin to reckon them. Greatly even if oddly auspicious for instance was just his stark sonship to his prodigious father, his having been launched with that momentum into the particular world in which he was to live. It was a privilege to make up for the legal irregularity attaching to his birth; we think of it really almost to wonder that it didn't lift him on a still higher wave. His limitations, which one encounters with a sort of violence, were not to be overlooked; it expresses them in some degree to say that he was bricked up in his hard Parisianism, but it is also incontestable that some of them were much concerned in producing his firm and easy equilibrium. We understand, however, the trap they set for him when we reflect that a certain omniscience, a great breadth of horizon, may well have seemed to him to be transmitted, in his blood, from such a boundless fountain of life. What mattered to him the fact of a reach of reference that stopped at the *banlieue*, when experience had sat at his cradle in the shape not at all of a fairy godmother but of an immediate progenitor who was at once fabulous and familiar? He had been encompassed by all history in being held in such arms—it was an entrance into possession of more matters than he could even guess what to do with. The profit was all the greater as the son had the luxury of differing actively from the father, as well as that of actively admiring and, in a splendid sense, on all the becoming sides, those of stature, strength and health, vividly reproducing him. He had in relation to his special gift, his mastery of the dramatic form, a faculty of imagination as contracted as that of the author of "Monte Cristo" was boundless, but his moral sense on the other hand, as distinguished from that of his parent, was of the liveliest, was indeed of the most special and curious kind. The moral sense of the parent was to be found only in his good humour and his good health—the moral sense of a musketeer in love. This lack of adventurous vision, of the long flight and the joy of motion, was in the younger genius quite one of the conditions of his strength and luck, of his fine assurance, his sharp edge, his high emphasis, his state untroubled above all by things not within his too irregularly conditioned ken. The things close about him were the things he saw—there were alternatives, differences, opposites, of which he lacked so much as the suspicion. Nothing contributes more to the prompt fortune of an artist than some such positive and exclusive temper, the courage of his convictions, as we usually call it, the power to neglect something thoroughly, to abound aggressively in his own sense and express without reserve his own saturation. The saturation of the author of "Le Demi-Monde" was never far to seek. He was as native to Paris as a nectarine to a south wall. He would have fared ill if he had not had a great gift and Paris had not been a great city.

It was another element of the happy mixture that he came into the world at the moment in all our time that was for a man of letters the most amusing and beguiling—the moment exactly when he could see the end of one era and the beginning of another and join hands luxuriously with each. This was an advantage to which it would have taken a genius more elastic to do full justice, but which must have made him feel himself both greatly related and inspiringly free. He sprang straight from the lap of full-grown romanticism; he was a boy, a privileged and initiated youth, when his father, when Victor Hugo, when Lamartine and Musset and Scribe and Michelet and Balzac and George Sand were at the high tide of production. He saw them all, knew them all, lived with them and made of them his profit, tasting just enough of the old concoction to understand the proportions in which the new should be mixed. He had above all in his father, for the purpose that was in him, a magnificent springboard—a background to throw into relief, as a ruddy sunset seems to make a young tree doubly bristle, a profile of another type. If it was not indispensable it was at any rate quite poetic justice that the successor to the name should be, in his conditions, the great casuist of the theatre. He had seen the end of an age of imagination, he had seen all that could be done and shown in the way of mere illustration of the passions. That the passions are always with us is a fact he had not the smallest pretension to shut his eyes to—they were to constitute the almost exclusive subject of his study. But he was to study them not for the pleasure, the picture, the poetry they offer; he was to study them in the interest of something quite outside of them, about which the author of "Antony" and "Kean," about which Victor Hugo and Musset, Scribe and Balzac and even George Sand had had almost nothing to say. He was to study them from the point of view of the idea of the right and the wrong, of duty and conduct, and he was to this end to spend his artistic life with them and give a new turn to the theatre. He was in short to become, on the basis of a determined observation of the manners of his time and country, a professional moralist.

There can scarcely be a better illustration of differences of national habit and attitude than the fact that while among his own people this is the character, as an operative force, borne by the author of "Le Demi-Monde" and "Les Idées de Madame Aubray," so among a couple of others, in the proportion in which his reputation there has emerged from the vague, his most definite identity is that of a mere painter of indecent people and indecent doings. There are, as I have hinted, several reasons for the circumstance already noted, the failure of the attempt to domesticate him on the English-speaking stage; but one states the case fairly, I think, in saying that what accounts for half of it is our passion, in the presence of a work of art, for confounding the object, as the philosophers have it, with the subject, for losing sight of the idea in the vehicle, of the intention in the fable. Dumas is a dramatist as to whom nine playgoers out of ten would precipitately exclaim: "Ah, but you know, isn't he dreadfully immoral?" Such are the lions in the path of reputation, such the fate, in an alien air, of a master whose main reproach in his native clime is the importunity and the rigour of his lesson. The real difference, I take it, is that whereas we like to be good the French like to be better. We like to be moral, they like to moralise. This helps us to understand the number of our innocent writers—writers innocent even of reflection, a practice of course essentially indelicate, inasmuch as it speedily brings us face to face with scandal and even with evil. It accounts doubtless also for the number of writers on the further side of the Channel who have made the journey once for all and to whom, in the dangerous quarter they have reached, it appears of the very nature of scandal and evil to be inquired about. The whole undertaking of such a writer as Dumas is, according to his light, to carry a particular, an esthetic form of investigation as far as it will stretch—to study, and study thoroughly, the bad cases. These bad cases were precisely what our managers and adapters, our spectators and critics would have nothing to do with. It defines indeed the separation that they should have been, in the light in which he presented them, precisely what made them for his own public exceptionally edifying. One of his great contentions is, for instance, that seduced girls should under all circumstances be married—by somebody or other, failing the seducer. This is a contention that, as we feel, barely concerns us, shut up as we are in the antecedent conviction that they should under no circumstances be seduced. He meets all the cases that, as we see him, we feel to have been spread out before him; meets them successively, systematically, at once with a great earnestness and a great wit. He is exuberantly sincere: his good faith sometimes obscures his humour, but nothing obscures his good faith. So he gives us in their order the unworthy brides who must be denounced, the prenuptial children who must be adopted, the natural sons who must be avenged, the wavering ladies who must be saved, the credulous fiancés who must be enlightened, the profligate wives who must be shot, the merely blemished ones who must be forgiven, the too vindictive ones who must be humoured, the venal young men who must be exposed, the unfaithful husbands who must be frightened, the frivolous fathers who must be pulled up and the earnest sons who must pull them. To enjoy his manner of dealing with such material we must grant him in every connection his full premise: that of the importunity of the phenomenon, the ubiquity of the general plight, the plight in which people are left by an insufficient control of their passions. We must grant him in fact for his didactic and dramatic purpose a great many things. These things, taken together and added to some others, constitute the luxurious terms on which I have spoken of him as appearing to the alien admirer to have practised his complicated art.

When we speak of the passions in general we really mean, for the most part, the first of the number, the most imperious in its action and the most interesting in its consequences, the passion that unites and divides the sexes. It is the passion, at any rate, to which Dumas as dramatist and pamphleteer mainly devoted himself: his plays, his prefaces, his manifestos, his few tales roll exclusively on the special relation of the man to the woman and the woman to the man, and on the dangers of various sorts, even that of ridicule, with which this relation surrounds each party. This element of danger is what I have called the general plight, for when our author considers the sexes as united and divided it is with the predominance of the division that he is principally struck. It is not an unfair account of him to say that life presented itself to him almost wholly as a fierce battle between the woman and the man. He sides now with one and now with the other; the former combatant, in her own country, however, was far from pronouncing him sympathetic. His subject at all events is what we of English race call the sexes and what they in France call the sex. To talk of love is to talk, as we have it, of men and women; to talk of love is, as the French have it, to *parler femmes.* From every play of our author's we receive the impression that to *parler femmes* is its essential and innermost purpose. It is not assuredly singular that a novelist, a dramatist *should* talk of love, or even should talk of nothing else: what, in addition to his adroitness and his penetration, makes the position special for Dumas is that he talks of it—and in the form of address most associated with pure diversion—altogether from the anxious point of view of the legislator and the citizen.

"Diane de Lys," which immediately followed "La Dame aux Camélias," is, so far as I can recall it, a picture pure and simple, a pretty story, as we say, sufficiently romantic and rather long-winded; but with "Le Demi-Monde" began his rich argumentative series, concluding only the other day with "Denise" and "Francillon," the series in which every theme is a proposition to be established and every proposition a form of duty to be faced. The only variation that I can recollect in the list is the disinterested portraiture of "Le Père Prodigue," with its remarkable presentation, in the figure of Albertine de la Borde, of vice domesticated and thrifty, keeping early hours and books in double-entry, and its remarkable illustration, I may further add, of all that was the reverse of infallible in the author's power to distinguish between amiable infirmities and ugly ones. The idea on which "Le Père Prodigue" rests belongs more distinctively to the world of comedy than almost any other situation exhibited in the series; but what are we to say of the selection, for comic effect, of a fable of which the principal feature is a son's not unfounded suspicion of the attitude of his own father to his own wife? The father is the image of a nature profusely frivolous, but we scent something more frivolous still in the way his frivolity is disposed of. At the time the play was produced the spectator thought himself warranted in recognising in this picture the personal character (certainly not the personal genius) of the elder Dumas. If the spectator *was* so warranted, that only helps, I think, to make "Le Père Prodigue" a stumbling-block for the critic—make it, I mean, an exhibition of the author off his guard and a fact to be taken into account in an estimate of his moral reach; a moral reach, for the rest, at all events, never impugned by any obliquity in facing that conception of the duty imposed which it is the main source of the writer's interest in the figured circumstances that they may be held to impose it, and which he was apt to set forth more dogmatically, or at least more excitedly, in an occasional and polemical pamphlet. These pamphlets, I may parenthetically say, strike me as definitely compromising to his character as artist. What shines in them most is the appetite for a discussion, or rather the appetite for a conclusion, and the passion for a simplified and vindictive justice. But I have never found it easy to forgive a writer who, in possession of a form capable of all sorts of splendid application, puts on this resource the slight of using substitutes for it at will, as if it is good but for parts of the cause. If it is good for anything it is good for the whole demonstration, and if it is not good for the whole demonstration it is good for nothing—nothing that *he* is concerned with. If the picture of life doesn't cover the ground what in the world *can* cover it? The fault can only be the painter's. Woe, in the esthetic line, to any example that requires the escort of precept. It is like a guest arriving to dine accompanied by constables. Our author's prefaces and treatises show a mistrust of disinterested art. He would have declared probably that his art was not disinterested; to which our reply would be that it had then no right to put us off the scent and prepare deceptions for us by coming within an ace of being as good as if it were.

The merits of the play—that is of the picture, in these hands—are sometimes singularly independent of the lesson conveyed. The merits of the lesson conveyed are in other cases much more incontestable than those of the picture, than the production of the air of life or the happiest observance of the conditions of the drama. The conclusion, the prescription, of "Denise" strikes me (to give an instance) as singularly fine, but the subject belongs none the less to the hapless order of those that fail to profit by the dramatic form though they have sacrificed the highest advantages of the literary. A play—even the best—pays so tremendously by what it essentially can not do for the comparatively little it practically can, that a mistake in the arithmetic of this positive side speedily produces a wide deviation. In other words the spectator, and still more the reader, sees such a theme as that of "Denise," which may be described as the evolution of a view, presented most in accordance with its nature when the attempt is not made to present it in accordance with the nature of the theatre. It is the nature of the theatre to give its victims, in exchange for melancholy concessions, a vision of the immediate not to be enjoyed in any other way; and consequently when the material offered it to deal with is not the immediate, but the contingent, the derived, the hypothetic, our melancholy concessions have been made in vain and the inadequacy of the form comes out. In "Francillon," partly perhaps because the thing has nothing to do with anybody's duty—least of all with the heroine's, which would be surely to keep off the streets—the form happens to be remarkably adequate. The question is of the liberty of the protagonist, the right of a wronged and indignant wife to work out her husband's chastisement in the same material as his sin, work it out moreover on the spot, as a blow is repaid by a blow, exacting an eye for an eye and a tooth for a tooth. The play has all the kinds of life that the theatre can achieve, because in the first place Dumas, though acting as the wife's advocate, has had the intelligence to give us a solution which is only a scenic sequence and not a real, still less a "philosophic," one; and because in the second it deals with emotions and impulses, which can be shown by the short measure, and not with reflections and aspirations, which can be shown but by the long.

I am not pretending to take things in turn, but a critic with a generous memory of the spell of Dumas should not, however pressed, neglect to strain a point for "Le Demi-Monde." I doubt my competence, however, to consider that admirable work scientifically—I find myself too condemned to consider it sentimentally. A critic is lost, as a critic, from the moment his feeling about the worse parts of the matter he investigates fails to differ materially from his feeling about the better. That is an attitude even less enlightened than being unconscious of the blemishes; all the same it must serve me for the present case. I am perfectly aware that Olivier de Jalin is a man of no true delicacy; in spite of which I take when I see them represented the liveliest interest in his proceedings. I am perfectly aware that Madame d'Ange, with her *calme infernal*, as George Sand calls it, is tainted and tortuous; in spite of which my imagination quite warms to Madame d'Ange. Perhaps I should indeed rather say that this interest and this sympathy have for their object the great total of the play. It is the member of the series in which Dumas first took up the scales in one hand and the sword in the other, and it is a wonderful piece of work, wonderful in kind of maturity, for a man of thirty. It has all the easy amplitude we call authority. I won't pretend to say what I think, here, of the author's justice, and if I happen to think ill of it I won't pretend to care. I see the thing through too many old memories, old echoes, old charms. In the light of the admirable acting of ancient days, of the faded image of the exquisite Desclée, of a dim recollection even of the prehistoric Rose Chéri and of Mademoiselle Delaporte, it represents too many of the reasons why I saw him always ideally triumphant. To practise an art which for its full, its rich effect depended on interpretation, and to be able to do one's work with an eye on interpretation of that quality—this had in common with supreme bliss the element at any rate of being attainable only by the elect. It partook of a peace the world cannot give. To be a moralist with the aid of Croizette, a philosopher with the aid of Delaunay, an Academician, even, with the aid of Bartet—such things suggested an almost equivocal union of virtue and success. One had never seen virtue so agreeable to one's self, nor success so useful to others. One had never seen a play that was a model so alive in spite of it. Models in the theatre were apt to be dead and vivacities vulgar. One had never above all seen on the stage a picture so conformable to deep pictorial art, a drama so liberally, gradually, scientifically flushed with its action. Beautiful in "Le Demi-Monde" is the way the subject quietly, steadily, strongly expands from within.

It was always the coercive force that his tone gave one the strongest sense of life, and it remains the interesting thing that this element in Dumas abounds in spite of not being fed from the source that we usually assume to be the richest. It was not fed from the imagination, for his imagination, by no means of the great plastic sort, has left us a comparatively small heritage of typical figures. His characters are all pointed by observation, they are clear notes in the concert, but not one of them has known the little invisible push that, even when shyly and awkwardly administered, makes the puppet, in spite of the string, walk off by himself and quite "cut," if the mood take him, that distant relation his creator. They are always formal with this personage and thoroughly conscious and proud of him; there is a charm of mystery and poetry and oddity, a glory of unexpectedness, that they consistently lack. Their life, and that, in each case, of the whole story (quite the most wonderful part of this) is simply the author's own life, his high vitality, his very presence and temperament and voice. They do more for him even than they do for the subject, and he himself is at last accordingly the most vivid thing in every situation. He keeps it at arm's length because he has the instinct of the dramatist and the conscience of the artist, but we feel all the while that his face is bigger than his mask. Nothing about his work is more extraordinary than this manner in which his personality pervades without spoiling it the most detached and most impersonal of literary forms. The reasons for such an impunity are first that his precautions, the result of a great intelligence, were so effective, and second that his personality, the result of a great affiliation, was so robust. It may be said that the precautions were not effective if the man himself was what one most enjoyed in the play. The only answer to that can be that I speak merely for myself and for the fresher sensibility of the happy time. Other admirers found certainly other things; what I found most was a tall figure in muscular motion and the sense of a character that had made admirably free with life. If it was mainly as an unabashed observer that he had made free, and if the life supplied was much of it uncommonly queer, that never diminished the action of his hard masculinity and his fine intellectual brutality. There was an easy competence in it all, and a masterful experience, and a kind of vicarious courage. In particular there was a real genius for putting all persons—especially all bad ones—very much in their place. Then it was all, for another bribe, so copious and so close, so sustained and so quiet, with such fascinating unities and complex simplicities and natural solutions. It was the breath of the world and the development of an art.

All the good, however, that I recollect thinking of Dumas only reminds me how little I desired that my remarks in general should lead me into vain discriminations. There are some indeed that are not vain—at least they help us to understand. He has a noble strain of force, a fulness of blood that has permitted him to be tapped without shrinking. We must speak of him in the present tense, as we always speak of the masters. The theatre of his time, wherever it has been serious, has on the ground of general method lived on him; wherever it has not done so it has not lived at all. To pretend to be too shocked to profit by him was a way of covering up its levity, but there was no escaping its fate. He was the kind of artistic influence that is as inevitable as a medical specific: you may decline it from a black bottle to-day—you will take it from a green bottle to-morrow. The energy that went forth blooming as Dumas has come back grizzled as Ibsen, and would under the latter form, I am sure, very freely acknowledge its debt. A critic whose words meet my eyes as I write very justly says that: "Just as we have the novel before Balzac and the novel after Balzac, the poetry that preceded Victor Hugo and the poetry that followed him, so we have the drama before Alexandre Dumas and the drama after him." He has left his strong hand upon it; he remodelled it as a vehicle, he refreshed it as an art. His passion for it was obviously great, but there would be a high injustice to him in not immediately adding that his interest in the material it dealt with, in his subject, his question, his problem, was greater still than this joy of the craftsman. That might well be, but there are celebrated cases in which it has not been. The largest quality in Dumas was his immense concern about life—his sense of human character and human fate as commanding and controllable things. To do something on their behalf was paramount for him, and *what* to do in his own case clear: what else but act upon the conscience as violently as he could, and with the remarkable weapons that Providence had placed within his grasp and for which he was to show his gratitude by a perfectly intrepid application? These weapons were three: a hard rare wit, not lambent like a flame, but stiff and straight like an arrow from a crossbow; a perception not less rare of some of the realities of the particular human tendency about which most falsities have clustered; and lastly that native instinct for the conditions of dramatic presentation without which any attempt to meet them is a helpless groping.

It must always be remembered of him that he was the observer of a special order of things, the moralist of a particular relation as the umpire of a yacht-race is the legislator of a particular sport. His vision and his talent, as I have said, were all for the immediate, for the manners and the practices he himself was drenched with: he had none of the faculty that scents from afar, that wings away and dips beyond the horizon. There are moments when a reader not of his own race feels that he simplifies almost absurdly. There are too many things he didn't after all guess, too many cases he didn't after all provide for. He has a certain odour of bad company that almost imperils his distinction. This was doubtless the deepest of the reasons why among ourselves he flourished so scantly: we felt ourselves to be of a world in which the elements were differently mixed, the proportions differently marked, so that the tables of our law would have to be differently graven. His very earnestness was only a hindrance—he might have had more to say to us if he had consented to have less application. This produced the curious dryness, the obtrusive economy of his drama—the hammered sharpness of every outline, the metallic ring of every sound. His terrible knowledge suggested a kind of uniform —gilt buttons, a feathered hat and a little official book; it was almost like an irruption of the police. The most general masters are the poets, with all the things they blessedly don't hold for so very certain and all the things they blessedly and preferably invent. It is true that Dumas was splendid, in his way, exactly because he was not vague: his concentration, all confidence and doctrine and epigram, is the explanation of his extraordinary force. That force is his abiding quality: one feels that he was magnificently a man—that he stands up high and sees straight and speaks loud. It is his great temperament, undiminished by what it lacks, that endears him to his admirers. It made him still of the greater race and played well its part in its time—so well that one thinks of him finally as perhaps not, when all is said, of the very happiest group, the group of those for whom in the general affection there is yet more to come. He had an immense reverberation—he practised the art that makes up for being the most difficult by being the most acclaimed. There is no postponed poetic justice for those who have had everything. He was seconded in a manner that must have made success a double delight. There are indications that the dramatist of the future will be less and less elated. He may well become so if he is to see himself less and less interpreted.

1895

The Late James Payn

It is difficult to express with just the happy shade of truth how little the knowledge of James Payn as the most lovable of men happened oppressively to involve taking the writer into account. It is, at all events, a simple and veracious statement of my own affectionate acquaintance with him that it scarcely ever came up between us directly that either of us were writers. I hardly know what would have occurred on any occasion if either he or I had suddenly become very literary. It was a feature of a long and an unclouded intercourse that I had positively to remind myself at need that books were in him quite as much as friendship and talk and hospitality and whist. Books, indeed, as he saw them, liked them and produced them, were exactly the equally immediate, sociable, personal things—things to be kept and used within the radius of healthy amusement; they were not mysteries and sanctities, embarrassments and problems—they might perfectly be overlooked, but not relegated and enshrined. As it happened then, we overlooked them—though I, perhaps, had most to try.

As I can speak of him only from my personal point of view, that of a comparatively late comer into a general circle very much wound up and going, which therefore rather imposed spectatorship, or, to put it crudely, observation, I may say that much of the interest of knowing him sprang exactly from this pleasant vision of him as the man of letters not on the stretch, the workman who had hit off a happy economy. He told of practice and ease—ease of feeling, I mean (precious boon!) about his trade and his daily job.

I recall how, on first becoming aware that, more quickly than I had either hoped or feared, I was knee-deep in London life, people and things put on a colour to me just in proportion as my imagination fitted them into some scheme, some theory of historic conditions and of the general English picture—some idea of tradition that, though it seemed to me I could put my finger on it, they (the real participants) were carrying out with an unconsciousness sometimes charming, often amusing, always magnificent. Payn, essentially, was unconscious, and so it was that he struck me as being, besides the gentlest, drollest, most human spirit, a man of a period, a survival, a witness with an answer to one's particular curiosity. Great was that, inevitably, of an American rather continentalised and really, at last, seeing with his eyes and touching with his hands the unadulterated English school. Payn was of that lineage the natural, unaggressive, almost unwitting specimen.

Without the aid of years or other creaking machinery, he "went back"—went back as a link, in imagination and sympathy, to the taste and tone that I had supposed I should have come too late to catch. He seemed ever to belong to a literary fashion more remote than his time of life made possible—which was the effect of his turn of mind and his love of a "good story." He presented the old feeling for that incontestable blessing with a fond familiarity that often made me envy him. I envied altogether his comfortable, sociable relation to letters and to his *métier*, which he had got so perfectly into harness. What he "went back" to above all was Dickens and the world of Dickens—I mean of Dickens and the whole Dickens period and pitch at the uncriticised stage. This particular colour kept him to the end, with his personal freshness both of sympathy and indifference (it was as if the latter, in particular, in certain directions, were renewed each morning), a vivid and consistent "case."

I had, at all events, a friendly vision of all this that he kindly never did anything to spoil. He was always the author of "Lost Sir Massingberd," which, without his being so very much my senior, he had miraculously managed to make contemporary with the picture of that remembered morning of life when I brushed the dew from *Chambers's Journal*. What made him and kept him enviable was that he was the man of ingenious and active imagination who could yet remain untormented from within. From without it was doubtless another matter—sensitive and tender, he was quite accessible enough to the world's worries to show his friends that he could always be droll at the expense of them. This power, towards the close of his life, fate subjected to tests enough; and yet when I last saw him his wit was unvanquished.

Therefore it is that I feel I keep nearer to him in memory by not breaking ground on his writings than by attempting to speak of them. The best were those in which he most gave his whimsical humour its head. These were admirable and, on a sifting, ought to be gathered together. But whether for comedy or drama, he gave even to the end of his sad last few years—in perpetual confinement and pain—the impression of the command of an independent faculty of laughter and sighs, a blessed chamber of the brain that could remain clear, show at last, at the top of the lighthouse, the lamp trimmed and the spark red, while darkness crept steadily on. His imagination had not made so much of the human bustle that to miss it was to miss all things. He wrought, like a good workman, to the latest hour, and as the world shrank more to what was devotedly close to him he had more and more affection to take and more and more gentleness to show.

April 9, 1898

From the Notebooks, 1905

Coronado Beach, Cal.
Wednesday March 29th
1905.

I needn't take precious time with marking & re-marking here how the above effort to catch up with my "impressions" of the early winter was condemned to speedy frustration & collapse. I struggled, but it all got beyond me,—any opportunity for the process of this little pressing, this sacred little record & register—but the history is written in my troubled & anxious, my always so strangely, more or less aching, doubting, yearning, yet also more or less triumphant, or at least, uplifted heart. *Basta!* I sit here, after long weeks, at any rate, in front of my arrears with an inward accumulation of material of which I feel the wealth, & as to which I can only invoke my familiar demon of patience, who always comes, doesn't he? when I call. He is here with me, in front of this green Pacific—he sits close & I feel his soft breath, which cools & steadies & inspires, on my cheek. Everything sinks in: nothing is lost; everything abides & fertilizes & renews its golden promise, making me think, with closed eyes of deep & grateful longing when, in the full summer days of L.H., my long dusty adventure over, I shall be able to [plunge?] my hand, my arm, *in*, deep & far, & up to the shoulder—into the heavy bag of remembrance—of suggestion—of imagination—of art—& fish out every little figure & felicity, every little fact & fancy that can be to my purpose. These things are all packed away, now, thicker than I can penetrate, deeper than I can fathom, & there let them rest, for the present, in their sacred cool darkness, till I shall let in upon them the mild still light of dear old L.H.—in which they will begin to gleam & glitter & take form like the gold & jewels of a mine. X X X X X X X X X

The question, however, is with, is of, what I want now, & how I need to hark back, & hook on, to those very 1st little emotions & agitations & stirred sensibilities of the first Cambridge hours & days & even weeks—though it's really a matter, for any *acuteness*, for any quality, of *but* the hours, the very first, during which the charm of the brave handsome autumn (I woo it, stretching a point with soft names,) lingered & hung about, & made something of a little medium for the sensibility to act in. That was a good moment, genuine so far as it went & just enough, no doubt, under an artful economy, to conjure with. What it is a question of at present is the putting together, with some blessed little nervous intensity of patience, of a Third Part to the "New England: An Autumn Impression" now begun in the *N.A. Review*. I drop out Boston—to come in later (next,) into "Three Cities," the three being B., Philadelphia & Washington. There is absolutely no room *here* to squeeze in a stinted, starved little Boston picture. Oh, the division is good, I see—the "three" will do beautifully, and so for winding up the little "New England," will Cambridge & its accessories. I feel as if I could *spread* on C., & that is my danger, as it's my danger everywhere. For *my* poor little personal C., of the far-off unspeakable first years, hangs there behind, like a pale pathetic ghost, hangs there behind, fixing me with tender, pleading eyes, eyes of such exquisite, pathetic appeal, & holding up the silver mirror, just faintly dim, that is like a sphere peopled with the old ghosts. How can I speak of Cambridge at all, e.g., without speaking of dear J. R. L. & even of the early *Atlantic*, by ah, such a delicate, ironic implication?—[to] say nothing of the *old* Shady Hill & the old Quincy St. & those days that bring tears, & the figure, for Shady Hill, the figure & presence, of J. N., & of S. N., & even of G. W. C., & the reminiscence of that night of Dickens, & the *emotion*, abiding, that it left with me. How it *did* something for my thought of him & his work—& would have done more without the readings, the hard charmless readings, (or *à peu près*) that remained with me. (This is of course an impossible side-issue, but one just catches there the tip of the tail of *such* an old emotion of the throbbing prime!) The point for me (for fatal, for impossible expansion,) is that I knew there, *had* there, in the ghostly old C. that I sit & write of here by the strange Pacific, on the other side of the continent, *l'initiation première* (the divine, the unique;) there & in Ashburton Place (which I just came in time to have that October or November glimpse of before seeing its site swept bare a month ago.) Ah, the "epoch-making" weeks of the spring of 1865!—from the 1st days of April or so on to the summer (partly spent at Newport &c, partly at North Conway!) Something—some fine, superfine, supersubtle mystic breath of that *may* come in perhaps in the Three Cities, in relation to any reference to the remembered Boston *of* the "prime." Ah, that pathetic, heroic, little *personal* prime of my own, which stretches over into the following summer at Swampscott—'66, that of the Seven Weeks War, & of unforgettable gropings & findings & sufferings & strivings & play of sensibility & of inward passion there. The hours, the moments, the days, come back to me—on into the early autumn before the move to Cambridge & with the sense, still, after such a lifetime, of particular little thrills & throbs & daydreams there. I can't help, either, just touching with my pen-point (here, here, *only* here,) the recollection of that (probably August) day when I went up to Boston from Swampscott & called in Charles St for news of O. W. H., then on his 1st flushed & charming visit to England, & saw his mother in the cool dim matted drawingroom of that house (passed, *never*, since, without the *sense*,) & *got* the news, of all his London, his general English, success & felicity, & *vibrated* so with the wonder & romance & curiosity & dim, weak tender (oh tender!) envy of it, that my walk up the hill, afterwards, up Mount Vernon St & probably to Athenaeum was all coloured & gilded & humming with it, & the emotion, exquisite of its kind, so remained with me that I always think of that occasion, that hour, as a sovereign contribution to the germ of that inward romantic principle which was [to] determine, so much later on, (ten years!) my own vision-haunted migration. I recall, I can *feel*, now the empty August St, the Mt. Vernon St. of the closed houses & absent "families" & my slow, upward, sympathetic, excited stroll there, & my sense of the remainder of the day in town,—before the old "cars" for the return home —so innocently to make a small adventure: "vision"-haunted as I was already even then: linking on to which somehow, moreover, too, is the memory of lying on my bed at Swampscott, later than that, somewhat, & toward the summer's end, & reading, in ever so thrilled a state, George Eliot's *Felix Holt*, just out & of which I was to write, & *did* write, a review in the *Nation*. (I had just come back from a bad little "sick" visit to the Temples somewhere—I have forgotten the name of the place—in the White Mountains; & the Gourlays were staying with us at S., & I was miserably stricken [by] my poor broken, at least unbearable, & unsurvivable, *back* of those (& still, under fatigue, even of these) years.[)] To read over the opening pages of *Felix Holt* makes, even now, the whole time softly & shyly live again. Oh, strange little intensities of history, of ineffaceability; oh delicate little odd links in the long chain, kept unbroken for the fingers of one's tenderest touch! Sanctities, pieties, treasures, abysses! X X X X X X X

But these are wanton lapses & impossible excursions; irrelevant strayings of the pen, in defiance of every economy. My subject awaits me, all too charged & too bristling with the most artful economy possible. What I seem to feel is that the Cambridge *tendresse* stands in the path like a waiting lion—or, more congruously, like a cooing dove that I shrink from scaring away. I want a little of the *tendresse*, but it trembles away over the whole field—or would if it could. Yet to present these accidents is what it is to be a *master*: that & that only. Isn't the highest deepest note of the whole thing the never-to-be-lost memory of that evening hour at Mount Auburn—at the Cambridge Cemetery when I took my way alone,—after much waiting for the favouring hour—to that unspeakable group of graves? It was late, in November; the trees all bare, the dusk to fall early, the air all still (at Cambridge, in general, *so* still;) with the western sky more & more turning to that terrific deadly pure polar pink that shows behind American winter woods. But I can't go over this—I can only, oh, so gently, so tenderly, brush it & breathe upon it—breathe upon it & brush it. It was the moment; it was the hour; it was the blessed flood of emotion that broke out at the touch of one's sudden *vision* & carried me away. I seemed then to know why I had done *this*; I seemed then to know why I had *come*—& to feel how not to have come would have been miserably, horribly to miss it. It made everything right—it made everything priceless. The moon was there, early, white & young, & seemed reflected in the white face of the great empty Stadium, forming one of the boundaries of Soldiers' Field, that looked over at me, stared over at me, through the clear twilight, from across the Charles. Everything was there; everything *came*; the recognition, stillness, the strangeness, the pity & the sanctity & the terror, the breath-catching passion & the divine relief of tears. William's inspired transcript, on the exquisite little Florentine urn of Alice's ashes, William's divine gift to us, & to *her*, of the Dantean lines—

Dopo lungo esilio & martir
Venne a questa pace—

took me so at the throat by its penetrating *rightness*, that it was as if one sank down on one's knees in a kind of anguish of gratitude before something for which one had waited with a long, deep *ache*. But why do I write of the all unutterable & the all abysmal? Why does my pen not drop from my hand on approaching the infinite pity & tragedy of all the past? It does, poor he[l]pless pen, with what it meets of the ineffable, what it meets of the cold Medusa-face of life, of all the life *lived*, on every side. Basta, basta! X X X X

An American Art-Scholar: Charles Eliot Norton

I GLADLY embrace the occasion to devote a few words to the honoured memory of my distinguished friend the late Charles Eliot Norton, who, dying at Cambridge, Massachusetts, on the 21st of October last, after having reached his eightieth year, had long occupied—and with an originality of spirit and a beneficence of effect all his own—the chair of the History of the Fine Arts at Harvard University, as well as, in the view of the American world surrounding that seat of influence, the position of one of the most accomplished of scholars and most efficient of citizens. This commemorative page may not disclaim the personal tone, for I can speak of Charles Norton but in the light of an affection which began long years ago, even though my part in our relation had to be, for some time, markedly that of a junior; of which tie I was to remain ever after, despite long stretches of material separation, a conscious and grateful beneficiary. I can speak of him therefore as I happened myself to see and know him—with interest and sympathy acting, for considerable periods together, across distances and superficial differences, yet with the sense of his extremely individual character and career suffering no abatement, and indeed with my impression of the fine consistency and exemplary value of these things clear as never before.

I find this impression go back for its origin very far—to one autumn day when, an extremely immature aspirant to the rare laurel of the critic, I went out from Boston to Cambridge to offer him a contribution to the old, if I should not rather say the then middle-aged, "North American Review," of which he had recently undertaken the editorship. I already knew him a little, enough to have met casual kindness at his hands; but my vision of his active presence and function, in the community that had happily produced and that was long to enjoy him, found itself, I think, completely constituted at that hour, with scarce an essential touch to be afterwards added. He largely developed and expanded as time went on; certain more or less local reserves and conservatisms fell away from him; but his temper and attitude, all his own from the first, were to give a singular unity to his life. This intensity of perception on his young visitor's part may perhaps have sprung a little from the fact that he accepted on the spot, as the visitor still romantically remembers, a certain very first awkward essay in criticism, and was to publish it in his forthcoming number; but I little doubt whether even had he refused it the grace of the whole occasion would have lost anything to my excited view, and feel sure that the interest in particular would have gained had he charmingly put before me (as he would have been sure to do) the ground of his discrimination. For his eminent character as a "representative of culture" announced itself exactly in proportion as one's general sense of the medium in which it was to be exerted was strong; and I seem verily to recall that even in the comparative tenderness of that season I had grasped the idea of the precious, the quite far-reaching part such an exemplar might play. Charles Norton's distinction and value—this was still some years before his professorate had taken form—showed early and above all the note and the advantage that they were to be virtues of American application, and were to draw their life from the signal American opportunity; to that degree that the detailed record of his influence would be really one of the most interesting of American social documents, and that his good work is best lighted by a due acquaintance with the conditions of the life about him, indispensable for a founded recognition of it. It is not too much to say that the representative of culture—always in the high and special sense in which he practised that faith—had before him in the United States of those days a great and arduous mission, requiring plentiful courage as well as plentiful knowledge, endless good humour as well as assured taste.

What comes back to me then from the early day I have glanced at is exactly that prompt sense of the clustered evidence of my friend's perfect adaptation to the civilising mission, and not least to the needfully dauntless and unperturbed side of it. His so pleasant old hereditary home, with its ample acres and numerous spoils—at a time when acres merely marginal and, so to speak, atmospheric, as well as spoils at all felicitously gathered, were rare in the United States—seemed to minister to the general assurance, constituting as they did such a picture of life as one vaguely supposed recognisable, right and left, in an old society, or, otherwise expressed, in that "Europe" which was always, roundabout one, the fond alternative of the cultivated imagination, but of which the possible American copy ever seemed far to seek. To put it in a nutshell, the pilgrimage to the Shady Hill of those years had, among the "spoils," among pictures and books, drawings and medals, memories and relics and anecdotes, things of a remote but charming reference, very much the effect of a sudden rise into a finer and clearer air and of a stopgap against one's own coveted renewal of the more direct experience. If I allude to a particular, to a personal yearning appreciation of those matters, it is with the justified conviction—this justification having been all along abundantly perceptible—that appreciation of the general sort only waited to be called for, though to be called for with due authority. It was the sign of our host, on the attaching spot, and almost the principal one, that he spoke, all round and with the highest emphasis, as under the warrant of authority, and that at a time when, as to the main matter of his claim and his discourse, scarce anyone pretended to it, he carried himself valiantly under that banner. The main matter of his discourse offered itself just simply as the matter of *civilisation*—the particular civilisation that a young roaring and money-getting democracy, inevitably but almost exclusively occupied with "business success," most needed to have brought home to it. The New England air in especial was no natural conductor of any appeal to an esthetic aim, but the interest of Professor Norton's general work, to say nothing of the interest of his character for a closer view, is exactly that the whole fruitful enterprise was to prove intimately a New England adventure; illustrating thus at the same time and once more the innate capacity of New England for leavening the great American mass on the finer issues.

To have grown up as the accomplished man at large was in itself at that time to have felt, and even in some degree to have suffered, this hand of differentiation; the only accomplished men of the exhibited New England Society had been the ministers, the heads of the congregations—whom, however, one docks of little of their credit in saying that their accomplishments and their earnestness had been almost wholly in the moral order. The advantage of that connection was indeed what Norton was fundamentally to have enjoyed in his descent, both on his father's and his mother's side (pre-eminently on the latter, the historic stock of the Eliots) from a long line of those stalwart pastoral worthies who had notably formed the aristocracy of Massachusetts. It was largely, no doubt, to this heritage of character and conscience that he owed the strong and special strain of confidence with which he addressed himself to the business of perfect candour toward his fellow-citizens—his pupils in particular; they, to whom this candour was to become in the long run the rarest and raciest and most endearing of "treats," being but his fellow-citizens in the making. This view of an urgent duty would have been a comparatively slight thing, moreover, without the special preoccupations, without the love of the high humanities and curiosities and urbanities in themselves, without the conception of science and the ingrained studious cast of mind, which had been also an affair of heredity with him and had opened his eyes betimes to educative values and standards other than most of those he saw flourish near at hand. He would defer to dilettantism as little as to vulgarity, and if he ultimately embraced the fine ideal of taking up the work that lay close to him at home, and of irrigating the immediate arid tracts and desert spaces, it was not from ignorance of the temptation to wander and linger where the streams already flowed and the soil had already borne an abiding fruit.

He had come to Italy and to England early in life; he had repeated his visits to these countries with infinite relish and as often as possible—though never, as a good New Englander, without certain firm and, where they had to be, invidious discriminations; he was attached to them by a hundred intellectual and social ties; but he had been from the first incapable of doubting that the best activity and the liveliest interest lay where it always, given certain conditions, lies in America—in a measure of response to intellectual and esthetic "missionary" labour more traceable and appreciable, more distinguishably attested and registered, more directly and artlessly grateful, in a word, than in the thicker elemental mixture of Europe. On the whole side of taste and association his choice was thus betimes for conscious exile and for a considerably, though doubtless not altogether irremediably, deprived state; but it was at the same time for a freedom of exhortation and a play of ironic comment less restricted, after all, in the clear American air, than on ground more pretentiously enclosed—less restricted, that is, from the moment personal conviction might be absolute and indifference to every form of provincial bewilderment equally patient and complete. The incontestable *crânerie* of his attitude—a thing that one felt to be a high form of sincerity—always at last won success; the respect and affection that more and more surrounded him and that finally made his situation sole of its kind and pre-eminently happy, attest together the interesting truth that unqualified confidence in one's errand, the serenest acceptance of a responsibility and the exercise of a critical authority never too apt to return critically upon itself, only require for beneficent action that they be attended at once with a fund of illustration and a fund of good humour.

Professor Norton's pre-eminent work in the interpretation of Dante—by which I mean his translation, text and notes, of the "Divine Comedy" and the "New Life," an achievement of infinite piety, patience and resource; his admirable volume on Church-Building in the Middle Ages (to say nothing of his charming earlier one, "Study and Travel in Italy," largely devoted to the cathedral of Orvieto); his long and intimate friendship with Ruskin, commemorated by his publication, as joint-executor to Ruskin's will, of the best fruits of the latter's sustained correspondence with him; his numerous English friendships, in especial—to say nothing of his native—all with persons of a highly representative character: these things give in part the measure of his finest curiosities and of his appetite, in all directions, for the best sources and examples and the best company. But it is probable that if his Harvard lectures are in form for publication, and if his general correspondence, and above all his own easily handsomest show in it, comes to be published, as most emphatically it should be, they will testify not in the least to any unredeemed contraction of life, but to the largest and happiest and most rewarded energy. An exhilarated invocation of close responsibility, an absolute ease of mind about one's point of view, a thorough and never-failing intellectual wholeness, are so far from weakening the appeal to young allegiances that, once they succeed at all, they succeed the better for going all their length. So it was that, with admirable urbanity of form and uncompromising straightness of attack, the Professor of the History of the Fine Arts at Harvard for a quarter of a century let himself go; thinking no trouble wasted and no flutter and no scandal other than auspicious if only he might, to the receptive and aspiring undergraduate mind, brand the ugly and the vulgar and the inferior wherever he found them, tracking them through plausible disguises and into trumpery strongholds; if only he might convert young products of the unmitigated American order into material for men of the world in the finer sense of that term; if only in short he might render more supple their view, liable to obfuscation from sights and sounds about them, of the true meaning of a liberal education and of the civilised character and spirit in the civilised State.

What it came to thus was that he availed himself to the utmost of his free hand for sowing and planting ideals—ideals that, though they might after all be vague and general things, lacking sometimes a little the clearer connections with practice, were yet a new and inspiring note to most of his hearers, who could be trusted, just so far as they were intelligent and loyal, not to be heavily embarrassed by them, not to want for fields of application. It was given him, quite unprecedentedly, to be popular, to be altogether loved and cherished, even while "rubbing it into" whomever it might concern that such unfortunates were mainly given over to mediocrity and vulgarity, and that half the crude and ugly objects and aspects, half the low standards and loose ends surrounding them and which they might take for granted with a facility and a complacency alike deplorable, represented a platitude of imagination that dishonoured the citizen on whom a University worthy of the name should have left its stamp. Happy, it would thus in fact seem, beyond any other occasion for educative influence, the immense and delightful opportunity he enjoyed, the clear field and long reach attached to preaching an esthetic crusade, to pleading for the higher amenities in general, in a new and superficially tutored, yet also but superficially prejudiced, country, where a consequently felt and noted rise of the tide of manners may be held to have come home to him, or certainly to have visited his dreams. His effect on the community at large, with allowances of time, was ever indubitable—even though such workers have everywhere to take much on trust and to remember that bushels of doctrine, and even tons of example, make at the most ounces and grains of responsive life. It can only be the very general and hopeful view that sustains and rewards—with here and there, at wide intervals, the prized individual instance of the sown seed actively emerging and flowering.

If not all ingenious disciples could give independent proof, however, all could rally and feel the spirit; all could crowd to a course of instruction which, largely elective and optional, yet united more listeners than many others put together, and in which the subject itself, the illustration of European artistic endeavour at large, or in other words the record of man's most comprehensive sacrifice to organised beauty, tended so to take up on familiar ground the question of manners, character, conscience, tone, to bristle with questions addressed to the actual and possible American scene. That, I hasten to add, was of course but one side of the matter; there were wells of special science for those who chose to draw from them, and an inner circle of pupils whose whole fruitful relation to their philosopher and friend—the happy and easy privilege of Shady Hill in general, where other charming personal influences helped, not counting as least in this—can scarce have failed to prepare much practical evidence for observation still to come. The ivory tower of study would ever, by his natural bent, I think, have most solicited Charles Norton; but he liked, as I say, he accepted without a reserve, the function of presiding over young destinies; he believed in the personal and the social communication of light, and had a gift for the generous and personal relation that perhaps found its best issue, as I have already hinted, in his admirable letters. These were not of this hustled and hustling age, but of a cooler and steadier sphere and rhythm, and of a charming mannerly substantial type to which he will have been, I think, among correspondents truly animated by the social spirit and a due cosmopolite ideal, one of the last systematically to sacrifice. With the lapse of years I ceased to be, I admit, a near spectator of his situation; but my sense of his activity—with more intimate renewals, besides, occasionally taking place—was to be, all along, so constantly fed by echo and anecdote and all manner of indirect glimpses, that I find myself speak quite with the confidence and with all the attachment of a continuous "assistant."

With which, if I reflect on this, I see how interesting a *case* above all my distinguished friend was ever to remain to me—a case, I mean, of such a mixture of the elements as would have seemed in advance, critically speaking, quite anomalous or at least highly incalculable. His interest was predominantly in Art, as the most beneficial of human products; his ostensible plea was for the esthetic law, under the wide wing of which we really move, it may seem to many of us, in an air of strange and treacherous appearances, of much bewilderment and not a little mystification; of terribly fine and complicated issues in short, such as call for the highest interpretative wisdom. But if nothing was of a more delightful example than Professor Norton's large and nourished serenity in all these connections, a serenity seasoned and tempered, as it were, by infinite interest in his "subject," by a steadying faith in exact and extensive knowledge, so to a fond and incorrigible student of character the case, as I have called it, and the long and genial career, may seem to shine in the light of quite other importances, quite other references, than the presumed and the nominal. Nothing in fact *can* be more interesting to a haunter of other intellectual climes and a worshipper at the esthetic shrine *quand même* than to note once more how race and implanted quality and association always in the end come by their own; how for example a son of the Puritans the most intellectually transmuted, the most liberally emancipated and initiated possible, could still plead most for substance when proposing to plead for style, could still try to lose himself in the labyrinth of delight while keeping tight hold of the clue of duty, tangled even a little in his feet; could still address himself all consistently to the moral conscience while speaking as by his office for our imagination and our free curiosity. All of which vision of him, however, is far from pointing to a wasted effort. The great thing, whatever turn we take, is to find before us perspectives and to have a weight to throw; in accordance with which wisdom the world he lived in received for long no firmer nor more gallant and generous impress than that of Charles Eliot Norton.

1908

The Turning Point of My Life

WHEN A distinguished friend, whose sympathy I have a pampered sense of almost inveterately enjoying, lately remarked to me that every man's life had had its "turning-point," and that there were cases, particular lives, as to which some account of what had turned on it, and how and why the turn had come, couldn't fail to be interesting, I glanced back at my own career in the light of this generalisation—only perhaps, however, to look too blank and unrecognising. This made the light, thanks to the source of it, glow more brightly—that is with an even more than customary kindness; my own case and my own life were in other words a matter into which my friend could sufficiently enter to remind me of their having had upon a time at least the appearance of one of the momentous junctures in question; occasions of the taking of the ply that is never again to be lost, occasions of the true vocation or the right opportunity recognised more or less in a flash, determinations in short of character and purpose, and above all of a sharper and finer consciousness. It so happened that I had in the deepest depths of the past spent a year at that admirable institution the Harvard Law School, and that, withdrawing from it prematurely—though under no precipitation that I may not now comfortably enough refer to;—I brought away with me certain rolls of manuscript that were quite shamelessly not so many bundles of notes on the perusal of so many calf-skin volumes. These were notes of quite another sort, small sickly seed enough, no doubt, but to be sown and to sprout up into such flowers as they might, in a much less trimmed and ordered garden than that of the law. My friend had reason enough to remember two or three of the first literary nosegays they were to enable me to gather—boldly disposed on his own editorial table as he was one day to find them; and he now suggested to me the inference that, since the tribute with which I was so promptly to affront him had, in principle, forced its way up through a soil that so little favored it, I must there, in the cold shade of queer little old Dane Hall, have stood at the parting of my ways, recognised the false steps, even though few enough, already taken, and consciously committed myself to my particular divergence. Let me say at once that I welcomed the suggestion—for the kindly grace of it, the element of antique charm and bedimmed romance that it placed, straight away, at the disposal of my memory; by which I mean that I wondered whether I mightn't find, on ingenious reflection, that my youth *had* in fact enjoyed that amount of drama. I couldn't, I felt, be sure; but the question itself, and its accompaniments, appealed to me; giving me, the ancient, the classic thrill known to all those who have felt the ground made firm for talking about themselves. So at any rate seems to stand before me, wreathed with flowers, smiling Opportunity; with the reminder in her eyes of the numberless men and women who, on smaller provocation, have leaped to her embrace. It is well enough to talk, overflowingly, of the things one had thrown off and that seem so to have ceased to be part of oneself; but real bliss of publication, I make out, must be for those one has kept in—that is if they have at all richly accumulated and are too tightly packed to be gouged out (or, to put it more delicately, too shy or too proud to consent to be touched).

1909

Is There a Life After Death?

PART I

I CONFESS at the outset that I think it the most interesting question in the world, once it takes on all the intensity of which it is capable. It does that, insidiously but inevitably, as we live longer and longer—does it at least for many persons; I myself, in any case, find it increasingly assert its power to attach and, if I may use the word so unjustly compromised by trivial applications, to amuse. I say "assert its power" so to occupy us, because I mean to express only its most general effect. That effect on our spirit is mostly either one of two forms; the effect of making us desire death, and for reasons, absolutely *as* welcome extinction and termination; or the effect of making us desire it as a renewal of the interest, the appreciation, the passion, the large and consecrated consciousness, in a word, of which we have had so splendid a sample in this world. Either one or the other of these opposed states of feeling is bound finally to declare itself, we judge, in persons of a fine sensibility and whose innermost spirit experience has set vibrating at all; for the condition of indifference and of knowing neither is the condition of living altogether so much below the human privilege as to have little right to pass for unjustly excluded or neglected in this business of the speculative reckoning.

That an immense number of persons should not recognize the appeal of our speculation, or even be aware of the existence of our question, is a fact that might seem to demand, in the whole connection, some particular consideration; but our anxiety, our hope, or our fear, hangs before us, after all, only because it more or less torments us, and in order to contribute in any degree to a discussion of the possibility we have to be consciously in presence of it. I can only see it, the great interrogation or the great deprecation we are ultimately driven to, as a part of our general concern with life and our general, and extremely various—because I speak of each man's general—mode of reaction under it; but to testify for an experience we must have reacted in one way or another. The weight of those who don't react may be felt, it is true, in one of the scales; for it may very well be asked on their behalf whether they are distinguishable as "living" either before or after. Only the special reaction of others, or the play of *their* speculation, however, will, in due consideration, have put it there. How *can* there be a personal and a differentiated life "after," it will then of course be asked, for those for whom there has been so little of one before?—unless indeed it be pronounced conceivable that the possibility may vary from man to man, from human case to human case, and that the quantity or the quality of our practice of consciousness may have something to say to it. If I myself am disposed to pronounce this conceivable—as verily I expect to find myself before we have done—I must glance at a few other relations of the matter first.

My point for the moment is that the more or less visibly diminishing distance which separates us at a certain age from death is, however we are affected toward the supposition of an existence beyond it, an intensifier of the feeling that most works in us, and that in the light of the lamp so held up our aggravated sense of life, as I may perhaps best call it, our impression of what we have been through, is what essentially fosters and determines, on the whole ground, our desire or our aversion. So, at any rate, the situation strikes me, and one can speak of it but for one's personal self. The subject is portentous and any individual utterance upon it, however ingenious or however grave, but comparatively a feeble pipe or a pathetic quaver; yet I hold that as we can scarce have too many visions, too many statements or pictures of the conceived social Utopia that the sincere fond dreamer, the believer in better things, may find glimmer before him, so the sincere and struggling son of earth among his fellow-strugglers reports of the positive or negative presumption in the savor of his world, that is not to be of earth, and thus drops his testimony, however scant, into the reservoir. It all depends, in other words, the weight or the force or the interest of this testimony does, on what life has predominantly said to us. And there are those—I take them for the constant and vast majority—to whom it in the way of intelligible suggestion says nothing. Possibly immortality itself—or another chance at least, as we may freely call it—will say as little; which is a fair and simple manner of disposing of the idea of a new start in relation to them. Though, indeed, I must add, the contemplative critic scarce—save under one probability—sees why the universe should be at the expense of a new start for those on whom the old start appears (though but to our purblind sight, it may, of course, be replied) so to have been wasted. The probability is, in fact, that what we dimly discern as waste the wisdom of the universe may know as a very different matter. We don't think of slugs and jellyfish as the waste, but rather as the amusement, the attestation of wealth and variety, of gardens and sea-beaches; so why should we, under stress, in respect to the human scene and its discussable sequel, think differently of dull people?

This is but an instance, or a trifle, however, among the difficulties with which the whole case bristles for those on whom the fact of the lived life has insisted on thrusting it, and which it yet leaves them tormentedly to deal with. The question is of the *personal* experience, of course, of another existence; of its being I my very self, and you, definitely, and he and she, who resume and go on, and not of unthinkable substitutes or metamorphoses. The whole interest of the matter is that it is my or your sensibility that is involved and at stake; the thing figuring to us as momentous just because that sensibility and its tasted fruits, as we owe them to life, are either remunerative enough and sweet enough or too barren and too bitter. Only because posthumous survival in some other conditions involves what we know, what we have enjoyed and suffered, as our particular personal adventure, does it appeal to us or excite our protest; only because of the *associations* of consciousness do we trouble and consult ourselves—do we wish the latter prolonged and wonder if it may not be indestructible, or decide that we have had enough of it and invoke the conclusion that we have so had it once for all. We pass, I think, through many changes of impression, many shifting estimates, as to the force and value of those associations; and there is no single, there is no decisive sense of them in which, throughout our earthly course, it is easy or needful to rest.

Whatever we may begin with we almost inevitably go on, under the discipline of life, to more or less resigned acceptance of the grim fact that "science" takes no account of the soul, the principle we worry about, and that, as however nobly thinking and feeling creatures, we are abjectly and inveterately shut up in our material organs. We flutter away from that account of ourselves, on sublime occasion, only to come back to it with the collapse of our wings, and during much of our life the grim view, as I have called it, the sense of the rigor of our physical basis, is confirmed to us by overwhelming appearances. The mere spectacle, all about us, of personal decay, and of the decay, as seems, of the whole being, adds itself formidably to that of so much bloom and assurance and energy—the things we catch in the very fact of their material identity. There are times when *all* the elements and qualities that constitute the affirmation of the personal life here affect us as making against any apprehensible other affirmation of it. And that general observation and evidence abide with us and keep us company; they reinforce the verdict of the dismal laboratories and the confident analysts as to the interconvertibility of our genius, as it comparatively is at the worst, and our brain—the poor palpable, ponderable, probeable, laboratory-brain that we ourselves see in certain inevitable conditions—become as naught.

It brings itself home to us thus in all sorts of ways that we are even at our highest flights of personality, our furthest reachings out of the mind, of the very stuff of the abject actual, and that the sublimest idea we can form and the noblest hope and affection we can cherish are but flowers sprouting in that eminently and infinitely diggable soil. It may be as favorable to them—as well as to quite other moral growths—as we are free to note; but we see its power to put them forth break down and end, and ours to receive them from it to do the same—we watch the relentless ebb of the tide on which the vessel of experience carries us, and which to our earthly eyes never flows again. It is to the personality that the idea of renewed being attaches itself, and we see nothing so much written over the personalities of the world as that they are finite and precarious and insusceptible. All the ugliness, the grossness, the stupidity, the cruelty, the vast extent to which the score in question is a record of brutality and vulgarity, the so easy non-existence of consciousness, round about us as to most of the things that make for living desirably at all, or even for living once, let alone on the enlarged chance—these things fairly rub it into us that to *have* a personality need create no presumption beyond what this remarkably mixed world is by itself amply sufficient to meet. A renewal of being, we ask, for people who understand being, even here, where renewals, of sorts, are possible, that way, and that way, apparently, alone?—leaving us vainly to wonder, in presence of such obvious and offensive matter for decay and putrescence, what there is for renewal to take hold of, or what element may be supposed fine enough to create a claim for disengagement. The mere fact in short that so much of life as we know it dishonors, or at any rate falls below, the greater part of the beauty and the opportunity even of this world, works upon us for persuasion that none other can be eager to receive it.

With which all the while there co-operates the exhibited limitation of our faculty for persistence, for not giving way, for not doing more than attest the inextinguishable or extinguishable spark in the mere minimum of time. The thinkable, the possible, we are fairly moved to say, in the way of the resistances and renewals of our conceded day, baffle us and are already beyond our command; I mean in the sense that the spirit even still in activity never shows as recovering, before our present eyes, an inch of the ground the body has once fairly taken from it. The personality, the apparently final eclipse of which by death we are discussing, fails, we remark, of any partial victory over partial eclipses, and keeps before us, once for all, the same sharp edge of blackness on the compromised disk of light. Even while "we" nominally go on those parts of us that have been overdarkened become as dead; our extinct passions and faculties and interests, that is, refuse to revive; our personality, by which I mean our "soul," declining in many a case, or in most, by inches, is aware of itself at any given moment as it is, however contracted, and not as it *was*, however magnificent; we may die piecemeal, but by no sign ever demonstrably caught does the "liberated" spirit react from death piecemeal. The answer to that may of course be that such reactions as can be "caught" are not claimed for it even by the fondest lovers of the precarious idea; the most that is claimed is that the reaction takes place *somewhere*—and the farther away from the conditions and circumstances of death the more probably. The apparently significant thing is none the less that during slow and successive stages of material extinction *some* nearness—of the personal quantity departing to the personal quantity remaining, and in the name of personal association and personal affection, and to the abatement of utter personal eclipse—might be supposable; and that this is what we miss.

Such, at least, is one of the faces, however small, that life put on to persuade us of the utterly contingent nature of our familiar inward ease—ease of being—and that, to our comfort or our disconcertment, this familiarity is a perfectly restricted thing. And so we go on noting, through our time and amid the abundance of life, everything that makes, to our earthly senses, for the unmistakable absoluteness of death. Every hour affords us some fresh illustration of it, drawn especially from the condition of others; but one, if we really heed it, recurs and recurs as the most poignant of all. How can we not make much of the terrible fashion in which the universe takes upon itself to emphasize and multiply the disconnectedness of those who vanish from our sight?—or they perhaps not so much from ours as we from theirs; though indeed if once we lend ourselves to the hypothesis of posthumous renovation at all, the fact that our ex-fellow-mortals would appear thus to have taken up some very much better interest than the poor world they have left might pass for a positively favorable argument. On the basis of their enjoying another state of being, we have certainly to assume that this is the case, for to the probability of a quite different case the inveteracy of their neglect of the previous one, through all the ages and the spaces, the grimness of their utter refusal, so far as we know it, of a retrospective personal sign, would seem directly to point. (I can only treat here as absolutely not established the value of those personal signs that ostensibly come to us through the trance medium. These often make, I grant, for attention and wonder and interest—but for interest above all in the medium and the trance. Whether or no they may in the given case seem to savor of another state of being on the part of those from whom they profess to come, they savor intensely, to my sense, of the medium and the trance, and, with their remarkable felicities and fitnesses, their immense call for explanation, invest that personage, in that state, with an almost irresistible attraction.)

Here it is, at any rate, that we break ourselves against that conception of immortality *as* personal which is the only thing that gives it meaning or relevance. That it shall be personal and yet shall so entirely and relentlessly have yielded to dissociation, this makes us ask if such terms for it are acceptable to thought. Is to be as dissociated as that consistent with personality as we understand *our* share in the condition?—since on any contingency save *by* that understanding of it our interest in the subject drops. I practically know what I am talking about when I say, "I," hypothetically, for my full experience of another term of being, just as I know it when I say "I" for my experience of this one; but I shouldn't in the least do so were I not *able* to say "I"—had I to reckon, that is, with a failure of the signs by which I know myself. In presence of the great question I cling to these signs more than ever, and to conceive of the actual achievement of immortality by others who may have had like knowledge I have to impute to such others a clinging to similar signs. Yet with that advantage, as it were, for any friendly re-participation, whether for our sake or for their own, in that consciousness in which they bathed themselves on earth, they yet appear to find no grain of relief to bestow on our anxiety, no dimmest spark to flash upon our ignorance. This fact, as after middle life we continue to note it, contributes to the confirmation, within us, of our seeming awareness of extinct things *as* utterly and veritably extinct, with whatever splendid intensity we may have known them to live; an awareness that settles upon us with a formidable weight as time and the world pile up around us all their affirmation of *other* things, and all importunate ones—which little by little acts upon us as so much triumphant negation of the past and the lost; the flicker of some vast sardonic, leering "Don't you see?" on the mask of Nature.

We tend so to feel *that* become for us the last word on the matter that all Nature and all life and all society and all so-called knowledge, with everything these huge, grim indifferences strive to make, and to some degree succeed in making, of ourselves, take the form and have the effect of a mass of machinery for ignoring and denying, the universe through, everything that is not of their own actuality. So it is, therefore, that we keep on and that we reflect; we begin by pitying the remembered dead, even for the very danger of our indifference to them, and we end by pitying ourselves for the final demonstration, as it were, of their indifference to us. "They must be dead, indeed," we say; "they must be as dead as 'science' affirms, for this consecration of it on such a scale, and with these tremendous rites of nullification, to take place." We think of the particular cases of those who could have been backed, as we call it, not to fail, on occasion, of somehow reaching us. We recall the forces of passion, of reason, of personality, that lived in them, and what such forces had made them, to our sight, capable of; and then we say, conclusively, "Talk of triumphant identity if *they*, wanting to triumph, haven't done it!"

Those in whom we saw consciousness, to all appearance, the consciousness of *us*, slowly *déménager*, piece by piece, so that they more or less consentingly parted with it—of *them* let us take it, under stress, if we must, that their ground for interest (in us and in other matters) "unmistakably" reached its limit. But what of those lights that went out in a single gust and those life passions that were nipped in their flower and their promise? Are these spirits thinkable as having emptied the measure the services of sense could offer them? Do we feel capable of a brutal rupture with registered promises, started curiosities, waiting initiations? The mere acquired momentum of intelligence, of perception, of vibration, of experience in a word, would have carried them on, we argue, to *something*, the something that never takes place for us, if the laboratory-brain were *not* really all. What it comes to is then that our faith or our hope may to some degree resist the fact, once accomplished, of watched and deplored death, but that they may well break down before the avidity and consistency with which everything insufferably *continues* to die.

PART II

I have said "we argue" as we take in impressions of the order of those I have glanced at and of which I have pretended to mention only a few. I am not, however, putting them forward for their direct weight in the scale; I speak of them but as the inevitable obsession of those who with the failure of the illusions of youth have had to learn more and more to reckon with reality. For if I referred previously to their bearing us increase of company I mean this to be true with the qualification that applies to our whole attitude, or that of many of us, on our question—the fact that it is subject to the very shifting admonitions of that reality, which may seem to us at times to mean one thing and at times quite another. Yet rather than attempt to speak, to this effect, even for "many of us," I had best do so simply for myself, since it is only for one's self that one can positively answer. It is a matter of individual experience, which I have seen multiply, to satiety, the obsessions I have named and then suffer them to be displaced by others—only once more to reappear again and once more to give way. I speak as one who has had time to take many notes, to be struck with many differences, and to see, a little typically perhaps, what may eventually happen; and I contribute thus, and thus only, my grain of consideration to the store.

I began, I may accordingly say, with a distinct sense that our question didn't appeal to me—as it appeals, in general, but scantly to the young—and I was content for a long time to let it alone, only asking that it should, in turn, as irrelevant and insoluble, let *me*. This it did, in abundance, for many a day—which is, however, but another way of saying that death remained for me, in a large measure, unexhibited and unaggressive. The exhibition, the aggression of life was quite ready to cover the ground and fill the bill, and to my sense of that balance still inclined even after the opposite pressure had begun to show in the scale. Resented bereavement is all at first—and may long go on appearing more than anything else—one of the exhibitions of life; the various forms and necessities of our resentment sufficiently meet then the questions that death brings up. That aspect changes, however, as we seem to see what it is to die—and to have died—in contradistinction to suffering (which means to warmly *being*) on earth; and as we so see what it is the difficulties involved in the thought of its not being absolute tend to take possession of us and rule us. Treating my own case, again, as a "given" one, I found it long impossible not to succumb—so far as one began to yield at all to irresistible wonder—to discouragement by the mere pitiless dryness of all the appearances. This was for years quite blighting to my sensibility; and the appearances, as I have called them—and as they make, in "science" particularly, the most assured show—

imposed themselves; the universe, or all of it that I could make out, kept proclaiming in a myriad voices that I and my poor form of consciousness were a quantity it could at any moment perfectly do without, even in what I might be pleased to call our very finest principle. If without me then just so without others; all the more that if it was not so dispensing with them the simply *bête* situation of one's forever and forever failing of the least whiff of a positive symptom to the contrary would not so ineffably persist.

During which period, none the less, as I was afterward to find, the question subtly took care of itself for me—waking up as I did gradually, in the event (very slowly indeed, with no sudden start of perception, no bound of enthusiasm), to its facing me with a "mild but firm" refusal to regard itself as settled. That circumstance once noted, I began to inquire—mainly, I confess, of myself—why it should be thus obstinate, what reason it could at all clearly give me; and this led me in due course to my getting, or at least framing my reply: a reply not perhaps so multitudinous as those voices of the universe that I have spoken of as discouraging, but which none the less, I find, still holds its ground for me. What had happened, in short, was that all the while I had been practically, though however dimly, trying to take the measure of my consciousness—on this appropriate and prescribed basis of its being so finite—I had learned, as I may say, to live in it more, and with the consequence of thereby not a little undermining the conclusion most unfavorable to it. I had doubtless taken thus to increased living in it by reaction against so grossly finite a world—for it at least *contained* the world, and could handle and criticise it, could play with it and deride it; it had *that* superiority: which meant, all the while, such successful living that the abode itself grew more and more interesting to me, and with this beautiful sign of its character that the more and the more one asked of it the more and the more it appeared to give. I should perhaps rather say that the more one turned it, as an easy reflector, here and there and everywhere over the immensity of things, the more it appeared to take; which is but another way of putting, for "interest," the same truth.

I recognize that the questions I have come after this fashion to ask my consciousness are questions embarrassed by the conditions of this world; but it has none the less left me at last with a sense that, beautiful and adorable thing, it is capable of sorts of action for which I have not as yet even the wit to call upon it. Of what I suggestively find in it, at any rate, I shall speak; but I must first explain the felt connection between this enlarged impression of its quality and *portée* and the improved discussibility of a life hereafter. I hope, then, I shall not seem to push the relation of that idea to the ampler enjoyment of consciousness beyond what it will bear when I say that the ground is gained by the great extension so obtained for one's precious inward "personality"—one's personality not at all in itself of course, or on its claims of general importance, but as conceivably hanging together for survival. It is not that I have found in growing older any one marked or momentous line in the life of the mind or in the play and the freedom of the imagination to be stepped over; but that a process takes place which I can only describe as the accumulation of the very treasure itself of consciousness. I won't say that "the world," as we commonly refer to it, grows more attaching, but will say that the universe increasingly does, and that this makes us present at the enormous multiplication of our possible relations with it; relations still vague, no doubt, as undefined as they are uplifting, as they are inspiring, to think of, and on a scale beyond our actual use or application, yet filling us (through the "law" in question, the law that consciousness gives us immensities and imaginabilities wherever we direct it) with the unlimited vision of being. This mere fact that so small a part of one's visionary and speculative and emotional activity has even a traceably indirect bearing on one's doings or purposes or particular desires contributes strangely to the luxury—which is the magnificent waste—of thought, and strongly reminds one that even should one cease to be in love with life it would be difficult, on such terms, not to be in love with living.

Living, or feeling one's exquisite curiosity about the universe fed and fed, rewarded and rewarded—though I of course don't say definitely answered and answered—becomes thus the highest good I can conceive of, a million times better than not living (however *that* comfort may at bad moments have solicited us); all of which illustrates what I mean by the consecrated "interest" of consciousness. It so peoples and animates and extends and transforms itself; it so gives me the chance to take, on behalf of my personality, these inordinate intellectual and irresponsible liberties with the idea of things. And, once more—speaking for myself only and keeping to the facts of my experience—it is above all as an artist that I appreciate this beautiful and enjoyable independence of thought and more especially this assault of the boundlessly multiplied personal relation (my own), which carries me beyond even any "profoundest" observation of this world whatever, and any mortal adventure, and refers me to realizations I am condemned as yet but to dream of. For the artist the sense of our luxurious "waste" of postulation and supposition is of the strongest; of him is it superlatively true that he knows the aggression as of infinite numbers of modes of being. His case, as I see it, is easily such as to make him declare that if he were not constantly, in his commonest processes, carrying the field of consciousness further and further, making it lose itself in the ineffable, he shouldn't in the least feel himself an artist. As more or less of one myself, for instance, I deal with being, I invoke and evoke, I figure and represent, I seize and fix, as many phases and aspects and conceptions of it as my infirm hand allows me strength for; and in so doing I find myself—I can't express it otherwise—in communication with *sources*; sources to which I owe the apprehension of far more and far other combinations than observation and experience, in their ordinary sense, have given me the pattern of.

The truth is that to live, to this tune, intellectually, and in order to do beautiful things, with questions of being as such questions may for the man of imagination aboundingly come up, is to find one's view of one's share in it, and above all of its appeal to *be* shared, in an infinite variety, enormously enlarged. The very provocation offered to the artist by the universe, the provocation to him to *be*—poor man who may know so little what he's in for!—an artist, and thereby supremely serve it; what do I take that for but the intense desire of being to get itself personally shared, to show itself for personally sharable, and thus foster the sublimest faith? If the artist's surrender to invasive floods is accordingly nine-tenths of the matter that makes his consciousness, that makes mine, so persuasively interesting, so I should see people of our character peculiarly victimized if the vulgar arrangement of our fate, as I have called it, imputable to the power that produced us, should prove to be the true one. For I think of myself as enjoying the very maximum reason to desire the renewal of existence—existence the forms of which I have had admirably and endlessly to *cultivate*—and as therefore embracing it in thought as a possible something that shall be better than what we have known here; only then to ask myself if it be credible that the power just mentioned is simply enjoying the unholy "treat" or brutal amusement of encouraging that conviction in us in order to say with elation: "Then you shall have it, the charming confidence (for I shall wantonly let it come to that), only so long as that it shall beautifully mature; after which, as soon as the prospect has vividly and desirably opened out to you, you shall become as naught."

"Well, you *will* have had them, the sense and the vision of existence," the rejoinder on that may be; to which I retort in turn: "Yes, I shall have them exactly for the space of time during which the question of my appetite for what they represent may clear itself up. The complete privation, as a more or less prompt sequel to that clearance, is worthy but of the wit of a sniggering little boy who makes his dog jump at a morsel only to whisk it away; a practical joke of the lowest description, with the execrable taste of which I decline to charge our prime originator."

I do not deny of course that the case may be different for those who have had another experience—there are so many different experiences of consciousness possible, and with the result of so many different positions on the matter. Those to whom such dreadful things have happened that they haven't even the refuge of the negative state of mind, but have been driven into the exasperated positive, so that they but long to lay down the burden of being and never again take it up—these unfortunates have an equal chance of expressing their attitude and of making it as eloquent and as representative as they will. Their testimony may easily be tremendous and their revelation black. Will they belong, however, to the class of those the really main condition of whose life is to work and work their inner spirit to a productive or illustrative end, and so to feel themselves find in it a general warrant for anything and everything, in the way of particular projections and adventures, that they may dream that spirit susceptible of? This comes again to asking, doubtless, whether it has been their fate to perceive themselves, in the fulness of time, and for good or for ill, living preponderantly by the imagination and having to call upon it at every turn to see them through. By which I don't mean to say that no sincere artist has ever been overwhelmed by life and found his connections with the infinite cut, so that his history may *seem* to represent for him so much evidence that this so easily awful world is the last word to us, and a horrible one at that: cases confounding me could quite too promptly be adduced. The point is, none the less, that in proportion as we (of the class I speak of) enjoy the greater number of our most characteristic inward reactions, in proportion as we do curiously and lovingly, yearningly and irrepressibly, interrogate and liberate, try and test and explore, our general productive and, as we like conveniently to say, creative awareness of things—though the individual, I grant, may pull his job off on occasion and for a while and yet never have done so at all—in that proportion does our function strike us as establishing sublime relations. It is this effect of working it that is exquisite, it is the character of the response it makes, and the merest fraction or dimmest shade of which is ever reported again in what we "have to show"; it is in a word the artistic consciousness and privilege in itself that thus shines as from immersion in the fountain of being. Into that fountain, to depths immeasurable, our spirit dips—to the effect of feeling itself, *quâ* imagination and aspiration, all scented with universal sources. What is that but an adventure of our personality, and how can we after it hold complete disconnection likely?

I do not so hold it, I profess, for my own part, and, above all, I freely concede, do not in the least want to. Consciousness has thus arrived at interesting me too much and on too great a scale—that is all my revelation or my secret; on too great a scale, that is, for me not to ask myself what she can mean by such blandishments—to the altogether normally hampered and benighted random individual that I am. Does she mean nothing more than that I shall have found life, by her enrichment, the more amusing here? But I find it, at this well-nigh final pass, mainly amusing in the light of the possibility that the idea of an exclusively present world, with all its appearances wholly dependent on our physical outfit, may represent for us but a chance for experiment in the very interest of our better and freer being and to its very honor and reinforcement; but a chance for the practice and initial confidence of our faculties and our passions, of the precious personality at stake—precious to *us* at least—which shall have been not unlike the sustaining frame on little wheels that often encases growing infants, so that, dangling and shaking about in it, they may feel their assurance of walking increase and teach their small toes to know the ground. I like to think that we here, as to soul, dangle from the infinite and shake about in the universe; that this world and this conformation and these senses are our helpful and ingenious frame, amply provided with wheels and replete with the lesson for us of how to plant, spiritually, our feet. That conception of the matter rather comes back, I recognize, to the theory of the spiritual discipline, the purification and preparation on earth for heaven, of the orthodox theology—which is a resemblance I don't object to, all the more that it is a superficial one, as well as a fact mainly showing, at any rate, how neatly extremes may sometimes meet.

My mind, however that may be, doesn't in the least resent its association with all the highly appreciable and perishable matter of which the rest of my personality is composed; nor does it fail to recognize the beautiful assistance—alternating indeed frequently with the extreme inconvenience—received from it; representing, as these latter forms do, much ministration to experience. The ministration may have sometimes affected my consciousness as clumsy, but has at other times affected it as exquisite, and it accepts and appropriates and consumes everything the universe puts in its way; matter in tons, if necessary, so long as such quantities are, in so mysterious and complicated a sphere, one of its conditions of activity. Above all, it takes kindly to that admirable philosophic view which makes of matter the mere encasement or sheath, thicker, thinner, coarser, finer, more transparent or more obstructive, of a spirit it has no more concern in producing than the baby-frame has in producing the intelligence of the baby—much as that intelligence may be so promoted.

I "like" to think, I may be held too artlessly to repeat, that this, that, and the other appearances are favorable to the idea of the independence, behind everything (*its* everything), of my individual soul; I "like" to think even at the risk of lumping myself with those shallow minds who are happily and foolishly able to believe what they would prefer. It isn't really a question of belief—which is a term I have made no use of in these remarks; it is on the other hand a question of desire, but of desire so confirmed, so thoroughly established and nourished, as to leave belief a comparatively irrelevant affair. There is one light, moreover, under which they come to the same thing—at least in presence of a question as insoluble as the one before us. If one acts from desire quite as one would from belief, it signifies little what name one gives to one's motive. By which term action I mean action of the mind, mean that I can encourage my consciousness to acquire that interest, to live in that elasticity and that affluence, which affect me as symptomatic and auspicious. I can't do less if I desire, but I shouldn't be able to do more if I believed. Just so I shouldn't be able to do more than cultivate belief; and it is exactly to cultivation that I subject my hopeful sense of the auspicious; with such success—or at least with such intensity—as to give me the splendid illusion of doing something myself for my prospect, or at all events for my own possibility, of immortality. There again, I recognize extremes "neatly meet"; one doesn't talk otherwise, doubtless, of one's working out one's salvation. But this coincidence too I am perfectly free to welcome—putting it, that is, that the theological provision happens to coincide with (or, for all I know, to have been, at bottom, insidiously built on) some such sense of appearances as my own. If I am talking, at all events, of what I "like" to think I may, in short, say all: I like to think it open to me to establish speculative and imaginative connections, to take up conceived presumptions and pledges, that have for me all the air of not being decently able to escape redeeming themselves. And when once such a mental relation to the question as that begins to hover and settle, who shall say over what fields of experience, past and current, and what immensities of perception and yearning, it shall *not* spread the protection of its wings? No, no, no—I reach beyond the laboratory-brain.

1910

APPENDIX

"Henry James at Work"

by
Theodora Bosanquet

Henry James at Work

I

I KNEW nothing of Henry James beyond the revelation of his novels and tales before the summer of 1907. Then, as I sat in a top-floor office near Whitehall one August morning, compiling a very full index to the Report of the Royal Commission on Coast Erosion, my ears were struck by the astonishing sound of passages from *The Ambassadors* being dictated to a young typist. Neglecting my Blue-book, I turned round to watch the operator ticking off sentences which seemed to be at least as much of a surprise to her as they were to me. When my bewilderment had broken into a question, I learnt that Henry James was on the point of coming back from Italy, that he had asked to be provided with an amanuensis, and that the lady at the typewriter was making acquaintance with his style. Without any hopeful design of supplanting her, I lodged an immediate petition that I might be allowed the next opportunity of filling the post, supposing she should ever abandon it. I was told, to my amazement, that I need not wait. The established candidate was not enthusiastic about the prospect before her, was even genuinely relieved to look in another direction. If I set about practising typewriting on a Remington machine at once, I could be interviewed by Henry James as soon as he arrived in London. Within an hour I had begun work on the typewriter. By the time he was ready to interview me, I could tap out paragraphs of *The Ambassadors* at quite a fair speed.

He asked no questions at that interview about my speed on a typewriter or about anything else. The friend to whom he had applied for an amanuensis had told him that I was sufficiently the right young woman for his purpose and he relied on her word. He had, at the best, little hope of any young woman beyond docility. We sat in armchairs on either side of a fireless grate while we observed each other. I suppose he found me harmless and I know that I found him overwhelming. He was much more massive than I had expected, much broader and stouter and stronger. I remembered that someone had told me he used to be taken for a sea-captain when he wore a beard, but it was clear that now, with the beard shaved away, he would hardly have passed for, say, an admiral, in spite of the keen gray eyes set in a face burned to a colourable sea-faring brown by the Italian sun. No successful naval officer could have afforded to keep that sensitive mobile mouth. After the interview I wondered what kind of impression one might have gained from a chance encounter in some such observation cell as a railway carriage. Would it have been possible to fit him confidently into any single category? He had reacted with so much success against both the American accent and the English manner that he seemed only doubtfully Anglo-Saxon. He might perhaps have been some species of disguised cardinal, or even a Roman nobleman amusing himself by playing the part of a Sussex squire. The observer could at least have guessed that any part he chose to assume would be finely conceived and generously played, for his features were all cast in the classical mould of greatness. He might very well have been a merciful Cæsar or a benevolent Napoleon, and a painter who worked at his portrait a year or two later was excusably reminded of so many illustrious makers of history that he declared it to be a hard task to isolate the individual character of the model.

If the interview was overwhelming, it had none of the usual awkwardness of such curious conversations. Instead of critical angles and disconcerting silences, there were only benign curves and ample reassurances. There was encouraging gaiety in an expanse of bright check waistcoat. He invited me to ask any questions I liked, but I had none to ask. I wanted nothing but to be allowed to go to Rye and work his typewriter. He was prepared, however, with his statements and, once I was seated opposite to him, the strong, slow stream of his deliberate speech played over me without ceasing. He had it on his mind to tell me the conditions of life and labour at Rye, and he unburdened himself fully, with numberless amplifications and qualifications but without any real break. It would be a dull business, he warned me, and I should probably find Rye a dull place. He told me of rooms in Mermaid Street, "very simple, rustic and antique—but that is the case for everything near my house, and this particular little old house is very near mine, and I know the good woman for kind and worthy and a convenient cook and in short——." It was settled at once that I should take the rooms, that I should begin my duties in October.

II

Since winter was approaching, Henry James had begun to use a panelled, green-painted room on the upper floor of Lamb House for his work. It was known simply as the green room. It had many advantages as a winter workroom, for it was small enough to be easily warmed and a wide south window caught all the morning sunshine. The window overhung the smooth, green lawn, shaded in summer by a mulberry tree, surrounded by roses and enclosed behind a tall, brick wall. It never failed to give the owner pleasure to look out of this window at his charming English garden where he could watch his English gardener digging the flower-beds or mowing the lawn or sweeping up fallen leaves. There was another window for the afternoon sun, looking towards Winchelsea and doubly glazed against the force of the westerly gales. Three high bookcases, two big writing-desks and an easy chair filled most of the space in the green room, but left enough clear floor for a restricted amount of the pacing exercise that was indispensable to literary composition. On summer days Henry James liked better to work in the large "garden room" which gave him a longer stretch for perambulation and a window overlooking the cobbled street that curved up the hill past his door. He liked to be able to relieve the tension of a difficult sentence by a glance down the street; he enjoyed hailing a passing friend or watching a motor-car pant up the sharp little slope. The sight of one of these vehicles could be counted on to draw from him a vigorous outburst of amazement, admiration, or horror for the complications of an age that produced such efficient monsters for gobbling protective distance.

The business of acting as a medium between the spoken and the typewritten word was at first as alarming as it was fascinating. The most handsome and expensive typewriters exercise as vicious an influence as any others over the spelling of the operator, and the new pattern of a Remington machine which I found installed offered a few additional problems. But Henry

James's patience during my struggles with that baffling mechanism was unfailing—he watched me helplessly, for he was one of the few men without the smallest pretension to the understanding of a machine—and he was as easy to spell from as an open dictionary. The experience of years had evidently taught him that it was not safe to leave any word of more than one syllable to luck. He took pains to pronounce every pronounceable letter, he always spelt out words which the ear might confuse with others, and he never left a single punctuation mark unuttered, except sometimes that necessary point, the full stop. Occasionally, in a low "aside" he would interject a few words for the enlightenment of the amanuensis, adding, for instance, after spelling out "The Newcomes," that the words were the title of a novel by one Thackeray.

The practice of dictation was begun in the nineties. By 1907 it was a confirmed habit, its effects being easily recognizable in his style, which became more and more like free, involved, unanswered talk. "I know," he once said to me, "that I'm too diffuse when I'm dictating." But he found dictation not only an easier but a more inspiring method of composing than writing with his own hand, and he considered that the gain in expression more than compensated for any loss of concision. The spelling out of the words, the indication of commas, were scarcely felt as a drag on the movement of his thought. "It all seems," he once explained, "to be so much more effectively and unceasingly *pulled* out of me in speech than in writing." Indeed, at the time when I began to work for him, he had reached a stage at which the click of a Remington machine acted as a positive spur. He found it more difficult to compose to the music of any other make. During a fortnight when the Remington was out of order he dictated to an Oliver typewriter with evident discomfort, and he found it almost impossibly disconcerting to speak to something that made no responsive sound at all. Once or twice when he was ill and in bed I took down a note or two by hand, but as a rule he liked to have the typewriter moved into his bedroom for even the shortest letters. Yet there were to the end certain kinds of work which he was obliged to do with a pen. Plays, if they were to be kept within the limits of possible performance, and short stories, if they were to remain within the bounds of publication in a monthly magazine, must be written by hand. He was well aware that the manual labour of writing was his best aid to a desired brevity. The plays—such a play as *The Outcry*, for instance—were copied straight from his manuscript, since he was too much afraid of "the murderous limits of the English theatre" to risk the temptation of dictation and embroidery. With the short stories he allowed himself a little more freedom, dictating them from his written draft and expanding them as he went to an extent which inevitably defeated his original purpose. It is almost literally true to say of the sheaf of tales collected in *The Finer Grain* that they were all written in response to a single request for a short story for *Harper's Monthly Magazine*. The length was to be about 5,000 words and each promising idea was cultivated in the optimistic belief that it would produce a flower too frail and small to demand any exhaustive treatment. But even under pressure of being written by hand, with dictated interpolations rigidly restricted, each in turn pushed out to lengths that no chopping could reduce to the word limit. The tale eventually printed was *Crapy Cornelia*, but, although it was the shortest of the batch, it was thought too long to be published in one number and appeared in two sections, to the great annoyance of the author.

III

The method adopted for full-length novels was very different. With a clear run of 100,000 words or more before him, Henry James always cherished the delusive expectation of being able to fit his theme quite easily between the covers of a volume. It was not until he was more than half way through that the problem of space began to be embarrassing. At the beginning he had no questions of compression to attend to, and he "broke ground," as he said, by talking to himself day by day about the characters and construction until the persons and their actions were vividly present to his inward eye. This soliloquy was of course recorded on the typewriter. He had from far back tended to dramatize all the material that life gave him, and he more and more prefigured his novels as staged performances, arranged in acts and scenes, with the characters making their observed entrances and exits. These scenes he worked out until he felt himself so thoroughly possessed of the action that he could begin on the dictation of the book itself—a process which has been incorrectly described by one critic as re-dictation from a rough draft. It was nothing of the kind. Owners of the volumes containing *The Ivory Tower* or *The Sense of the Past* have only to turn to the Notes printed at the end to see that the scenario dictated in advance contains practically none of the phrases used in the final work. The two sets of Notes are a different and a much more interesting literary record than a mere draft. They are the framework set up for imagination to clothe with the spun web of life. But they are not bare framework. They are elaborate and abundant. They are the kind of exercise described in *The Death of the Lion* as "a great gossiping eloquent letter—the overflow into talk of an artist's amorous design." But the design was thus mapped out with the clear understanding that at a later stage and at closer quarters the subject might grow away from the plan. "In the intimacy of composition pre-noted proportions and arrangements do most uncommonly insist on making themselves different by shifts and variations, always improving, which impose themselves as one goes and keep the door open always to something *more* right and *more* related. It is subject to that constant possibility, all the while, that one does pre-note and tentatively sketch."*

The preliminary sketch was seldom consulted after the novel began to take permanent shape, but the same method of "talking out" was resorted to at difficult points of the narrative as it progressed, always for the sake of testing in advance the values of the persons involved in a given situation, so that their creator should ensure their right action both for the development of the drama and the truth of their relations to each other. The knowledge of all the conscious motives and concealments of his creatures, gained by unwearied observation of their attitudes behind the scenes, enabled Henry James to exhibit them with a final confidence that dispensed with explanations. Among certain stumbling blocks in the path of the perfect comprehension of his readers is their uneasy doubt of the sincerity of the conversational encounters recorded. Most

* *The Ivory Tower* (Collins, 1917), p. 341.

novelists provide some clue to help their readers to distinguish truth from falsehood, and in the theatre, although husbands and wives may be deceived by lies, the audience is usually privy to the plot. But a study of the Notes to *The Ivory Tower* will make it clear that between the people created by Henry James lying is as frequent as among mortals and not any easier to detect.

For the volumes of memories, *A Small Boy and Others*, *Notes of a Son and Brother*, and the uncompleted *Middle Years*, no preliminary work was needed. A straight dive into the past brought to the surface treasure after treasure, a wealth of material which became embarrassing. The earlier book was begun in 1911, after Henry James had returned from a year in the United States, where he had been called by his brother's fatal illness. He had come back, after many seasons of country solitude, to his former love of the friendly London winter, and for the first few months after his return from America he lodged near the Reform Club and came to the old house in Chelsea where I was living and where he had taken a room for his work. It was a quiet room, long and narrow and rather dark—he used to speak of it as "my Chelsea cellar." There he settled down to write what, as he outlined it to me, was to be a set of notes to his brother William's early letters, prefaced by a brief account of the family into which they were both born. But an entire volume of memories was finished before bringing William to an age for writing letters, and *A Small Boy* came to a rather abrupt end as a result of the writer's sudden decision that a break must be made at once if the flood of remembrance was not to drown his pious intention.

It was extraordinarily easy for him to recover the past; he had always been sensitive to impressions and his mind was stored with records of exposure. All he had to do was to render his sense of those records as adequately as he could. Each morning, after reading over the pages written the day before, he would settle down in a chair for an hour or so of conscious effort. Then, lifted on a rising tide of inspiration, he would get up and pace up and down the room, sounding out the periods in tones of resonant assurance. At such times he was beyond reach of irrelevant sounds or sights. Hosts of cats—a tribe he usually routed with shouts of execration—might wail outside the window, phalanxes of motor-cars bearing dreaded visitors might hoot at the door. He heard nothing of them. The only thing that could arrest his progress was the escape of the word he wanted to use. When that had vanished he broke off the rhythmic pacing and made his way to a chimney-piece or book-case tall enough to support his elbows while he rested his head in his hands and audibly pursued the fugitive.

IV

In the autumn of 1907, when I began to tap the Remington typewriter at Henry James's dictation, he was engaged on the arduous task of preparing his Novels and Tales for the definitive New York edition, published in 1909. Since it was only between breakfast and luncheon that he undertook what he called "inventive" work, he gave the hours from half-past ten to half-past one to the composition of the prefaces which are so interesting a feature of the edition. In the evenings he read over again the work of former years, treating the printed pages like so many proof-sheets of extremely corrupt text. The revision was a task he had seen in advance as formidable. He had cultivated the habit of forgetting past achievements almost to the pitch of a sincere conviction that nothing he had written before about 1890 could come with any shred of credit through the ordeal of a critical inspection. On a morning when he was obliged to give time to the selection of a set of tales for a forthcoming volume, he confessed that the difficulty of selection was mainly the difficulty of reading them at all. "They seem," he said, "so bad until I *have* read them that I can't force myself to go through them except with a pen in my hand, altering as I go the crudities and ineptitudes that to my sense deform each page." Unfamiliarity and adverse prejudice are rare advantages for a writer to bring to the task of choosing among his works. For Henry James the prejudice might give way to half reluctant appreciation as the unfamiliarity passed into recognition, but it must be clear to every reader of the prefaces that he never lost the sense of being paternally responsible for two distinct families. For the earlier brood, acknowledged fruit of his alliance with Romance, he claimed indulgence on the ground of their youthful spontaneity, their confident assurance, their rather touching good faith. One catches echoes of a plea that these elderly youngsters may not be too closely compared, to their inevitable disadvantage, with the richly endowed, the carefully bred, the highly civilized and sensitized children of his second marriage, contracted with that wealthy bride, Experience. Attentive readers of the novels may perhaps find the distinction between these two groups less remarkable than it seemed to their writer. They may even wonder whether the second marriage was not rather a silver wedding, with the old romantic mistress cleverly disguised as a woman of the world. The different note was possibly due more to the substitution of dictation for pen and ink than to any profound change of heart. But whatever the reason, their author certainly found it necessary to spend a good deal of time working on the earlier tales before he considered them fit for appearance in the company of those composed later. Some members of the elder family he entirely cast off, not counting them worth the expense of completely new clothes. Others he left in their place more from a necessary, though deprecated, respect for the declared taste of the reading public than because he loved them for their own sake. It would, for instance, have been difficult to exclude *Daisy Miller* from any representative collection of his work, yet the popularity of the tale had become almost a grievance. To be acclaimed as the author of *Daisy Miller* by persons blandly unconscious of *The Wings of the Dove* or *The Golden Bowl* was a reason among many for Henry James's despair of intelligent comprehension. Confronted repeatedly with *Daisy*, he felt himself rather in the position of some *grande dame* who, with a jewel-case of sparkling diamonds, is constrained by her admirers always to appear in the simple string of moonstones worn at her first dance.

From the moment he began to read over the earlier tales, he found himself involved in a highly practical examination of the scope and limits of permissible revision. Poets, as he pointed out, have often revised their verse with good effect. Why should the novelist not have equal license? The only sound reason for not altering anything is a conviction that it cannot be improved. It was Henry James's profound conviction that he could improve his early writing in nearly every sentence. Not to revise would have been to confess to a loss of faith in himself, and it was not likely that the writer who had fasted for forty years in the wilderness of British and American misconceptions without yielding a scrap of intellectual integrity to editorial or publishing tempters should have lost faith in himself. But he was well aware that the game of revision must be played with a due observance of the rules. He knew that no novelist can safely afford to repudiate his fundamental understanding with his readers that the tale he has to tell is at least as true as history and the figures he has set in motion at least as independently alive as the people we see in offices and motorcars. He allowed himself few freedoms with any recorded appearances or actions, although occasionally the temptation to correct a false gesture, to make it "right," was too strong to be resisted. We have a pleasant instance of this correction in the second version of *The American*. At her first appearance, the old Marquise de Bellegarde had acknowledged the introduction of Newman by returning his handshake "with a sort of British positiveness which reminded him that she was the daughter of the Earl of St. Dunstan's." In the later edition she behaves differently. "Newman came sufficiently near to the old lady by the fire to take in that she would offer him no handshake. . . . Madame de Bellegarde looked hard at him and refused what she did refuse with a sort of British positiveness which reminded him that she was the daughter of the Earl of St. Dunstan's." There were good reasons why the Marquise should have denied Newman a welcoming handshake. Her attitude throughout the book was to be consistently hostile and should never have been compromised by the significantly British grip. Yet it is almost shocking to see her snatching back her first card after playing it for so many years. She was to perform less credible actions than shaking hands with an innocent American, as her progenitor knew very well. He invited his readers, in the preface to *The American*, to observe the impossible behaviour of the noble Bellegarde family, but he realized that since they had been begotten in absurdity the Bellegardes could under no stress of revision achieve a very solid humanity. The best he could do for them was to let a faint consciousness flush the mind of Valentin, the only detached member of the family. In the first edition Valentin warned his friend of the Bellegarde peculiarities with the easy good faith of the younger Henry James under the spell of the magic word "Europe." "My mother is strange, my brother is strange, and I verily believe I am stranger than either. Old trees have queer cracks, old races have odd secrets." To this statement he added in the revised version: "We're fit for a museum or a Balzac novel." A comparable growth of ironic perception was allowed to Roderick Hudson, whose comment on Rowland's admission of his heroically silent passion for Mary Garland, "It's like something in a novel," was altered to: "It's like something in a bad novel."

V

But the legitimate business of revision was, for Henry James, neither substitution nor re-arrangement. It was the demonstration of values implicit in the earlier work, the retrieval of neglected opportunities for adequate "renderings." "It was," as he explained in his final preface, "all sensibly, as if the clear matter being still there, even as a shining expanse of snow spread over a plain, my exploring tread, for application to it, had quite unlearned the old pace and found itself naturally falling into another, which might sometimes more or less agree with the original tracks, but might most often, or very nearly, break the surface at other places. What was thus predominantly interesting to note, at all events, was the high spontaneity of these deviations and differences, which become thus things not of choice but of immediate and perfect necessity: necessity to the end of dealing with the quantities in question at all." On every page the act of re-reading became automatically one with the act of re-writing, and the revised parts are just "those rigid conditions of re-perusal, registered; so many close notes, as who should say, on the particular vision of the matter itself that experience had at last made the only possible one." These are words written with the clear confidence of the artist who, in complete possession of his "faculties," had no need to bother himself with doubts as to his ability to write better at the end of a lifetime of hard work and varied experience than at the beginning. He knew he could write better. His readers have not always agreed with his own view. They have denounced the multiplication of qualifying clauses, the imposition of a system of punctuation which, although rigid and orderly, occasionally fails to act as a guide to immediate comprehension of the writer's intention, and the increasing passion for adverbial interpositions. "Adjectives are the sugar of literature and adverbs the salt," was Henry James's reply to a criticism which once came to his ears.

It must be admitted that the case for the revised version relies on other merits than simplicity or elegance to make its claim good. It is not so smooth, nor so easy, nor, on the whole, so pretty as the older form. But it is nearly always richer and more alive. Abstractions give place to sharp definite images, loose vague phrases to close-locked significances. We can find a fair example of this in *The Madonna of the Future*, a tale first published in 1879. In the original version one of the sentences runs: "His professions, somehow, were all half professions, and his allusions to his work and circumstances left something dimly ambiguous in the background." In the New York Edition this has become: "His professions were practically somehow, all masks and screens, and his personal allusions as to his ambiguous background mere wavings of the dim lantern." In some passages it would be hard to deny a gain of beauty as well as of significance. There is, for instance, a sentence in the earlier account of Newman's silent renunciation of his meditated revenge, in the Cathedral of Notre Dame: "He sat a long time; he heard far-away bells chiming off, at long intervals, to the rest of the world." In the definitive edition of *The American* the passage has become: "He sat a long time; he heard far-away bells chiming off into space, at long intervals, the big bronze syllables of the Word."

A paragraph from *Four Meetings*, a tale worked over with extreme care, will give a fair idea of the general effect of the revision. It records a moment of the final Meeting, when the helplessly indignant narrator is watching poor Caroline ministering to the vulgar French cocotte who has imposed herself on the hospitality of the innocent little New Englander.

"At this moment," runs the passage of 1879, "Caroline Spencer came out of the house bearing a coffee pot on a little tray. I noticed that on her way from the door to the table she gave me a single quick vaguely appealing glance. I wondered what it signified; I felt that it signified a sort of half-frightened longing to know what, as a man of the world who had been in France, I thought of the Countess. It made me extremely uncomfortable. I could not tell her that the Countess was very possibly the runaway wife of a little hairdresser. I tried, suddenly, on the contrary, to show a high consideration for her."

The "particular vision" registered on re-perusal reveals states of mind much more definite than these wonderings and longings and vague appeals.

"Our hostess moreover at this moment came out of the house, bearing a coffee-pot and three cups on a neat little tray. I took from her eyes, as she approached us, a brief but intense appeal—the mute expression, as I felt, conveyed in the hardest little look she had yet addressed me, of her longing to know what as a man of the world in general and of the French world in particular, I thought of these allied forces now so encamped on the stricken field of her life. I could only 'act,' however, as they said at North Verona, quite impenetrably—only make no answering sign. I couldn't intimate, much less could I frankly utter, my inward sense of the Countess's probable past, with its measure of her virtue, value and accomplishments, and of the limits of consideration to which she could properly pretend. I couldn't give my friend a hint of how I myself personally 'saw' her interesting pensioner—whether as the runaway wife of a too-jealous hair-dresser or of a too-morose pastry-cook, say; whether as a very small bourgeoise, in fine, who had vitiated her case beyond patching up, or even some character of the nomadic sort, less edifying still. I couldn't let in, by the jog of a shutter, as it were, a hard informing ray and then, washing my hands of the business, turn my back for ever. I could on the contrary but save the situation, my own at least, for the moment, by pulling myself together with a master hand and appearing to ignore everything but that the dreadful person between us *was* a 'grande dame.'"

Anyone genuinely interested in "the how and the whence and the why these intenser lights of experience come into being and insist on shining," will find it a profitable exercise to read and compare the old and the new versions of any of the novels or tales first published during the 'seventies or 'eighties. Such a reader will be qualified to decide for himself between the opinion of a bold young critic that "all the works have been subjected to a revision which in several cases, notably *Daisy Miller* and *Four Meetings*, amounts to their ruin," and their writer's confidence that "I shouldn't have breathed upon the old catastrophes and accidents, the old wounds and mutilations and disfigurements wholly in vain. . . . I have prayed that the finer air of the better form may sufficiently seem to hang about them and gild them over—at least for readers, however few, at all *curious* of questions of air and form."

VI

Explanatory prefaces and elaborate revisions, short stories and long memories, were far from being the complete tale of literary labour during the last eight years of Henry James's life. A new era for English drama was prophesied in 1907. Led by Miss Horniman, advocates of the repertory system were marching forward, capturing one by one the intellectual centres of the provinces. In London, repertory seasons were announced in two West-end theatres. Actor-managers began to ask for "non-commercial" plays and when their appeal reached Henry James it met with a quick response. The theatre had both allured and repelled him for many years, and he had already been the victim of a theatrical misadventure. His assertions that he wrote plays solely in the hope of making money should not, I think, be taken as the complete explanation of his dramas. It is pretty clear that he wrote plays because he wanted to write them, because he was convinced that his instinct for dramatic situations could find a happy outlet in plays, because writing for the stage is a game rich in precise rules and he delighted in the multiplication of technical difficulties, and because he lived in circles more addicted to the intelligent criticism of plays than to the intelligent criticism of novels. The plays he wrote in the early 'nineties are very careful exercises in technique. They are derived straight from the light comedies of the Parisian stage, with the difference that in the 'nineties, for all their advertised naughtiness, there were even stricter limits to the free representation of Parisian situations on English stages than there are to-day. In *The Reprobate*, a play successfully produced a few years ago by the Stage Society, the lady whose hair has changed from black to red and from red to gold is the centre of the drama, she holds the key to the position, but all her complicating effect depends upon the past —pasts being allowed on every stage comparative license of reference. The compromising evidence is all a matter of old photographs and letters, and the play loses in vividness whatever it may gain in respectability. Nobody knew better than the author that *The Reprobate* was not a good play. Terror of being cut forbade him to work on a subject of intrinsic importance. With another hour guaranteed, a playwright might attempt anything, but "he does not get his hour, and he will probably begin by missing his subjects. He takes, in his dread of complication, a minor one, and it's heavy odds that the minor one, with the habit of small natures, will prove thankless."

Other early plays had been converted into novels or tales and so published. One of these, written originally for Miss Ellen Terry but never produced by her, had appeared as an incongruous companion to *The Turn of the Screw* in the volume entitled *The Two Magics*. A few attentive readers had seen the dramatic possibilities of *Covering End*, and when it was suggested to Henry James that he should convert it into a three-act comedy for production by Mr. Forbes Robertson (as he was then) and Miss Gertrude Elliot, he willingly consented. Flying under a new flag, as *The High Bid*, the play was produced in London in February, 1909, but only for a series of matinées, the prodigious success of *The Passing of the Third Floor Back* precluding the possibility of an evening for any other production under the same management. Under the inspiration of the repertory movement, other material was re-cast for acting. *The Other House* was re-dictated as a tragedy. *Owen Wingrave* became *The Saloon*, a one-act play produced by Miss Gertrude Kingston in 1910. Finally an entirely new three-act comedy, *The Outcry*, was written round the highly topical subject of the sale of art treasures to rich Americans. It was not produced during Henry James's life. At the time when it should have been rehearsed he was ill and the production was postponed. On his recovery, he went to the United States for a year, and when he came back the day of repertory performances had died in a fresh night of stars.

When *The Outcry* was given by the Stage Society in 1917, it was evident that the actors were embarrassed by their lines, for by 1909, when the play was written, the men and women of Henry James could talk only in the manner of their creator. His own speech, assisted by the practice of dictating, had by that time become so inveterately characteristic that his questions to a railway clerk about a ticket or to a fishmonger about a lobster, might easily be recognized as coined in the same mint as his addresses to the Academic Committee of the Royal Society of Literature. Apart from this difficulty of enunciating the lines, *The Outcry* has all the advantages over the earlier plays. The characters are real and they act from adequate motives. The solution of the presented problem, which requires, like most of the author's solutions, a change of heart, is worked out with admirable art, without any use of the mechanical shifts and stage properties needed in *The Reprobate.* It is not very difficult to believe that if Henry James had been encouraged twenty years earlier to go on writing plays he might have made a name as a dramatist, but the faithful may be forgiven for rejoicing that the playwright was sacrificed to the novelist and critic.

VII

Many men whose prime business is the art of writing find rest and refreshment in other occupations. They marry or they keep dogs, they play golf or bridge, they study Sanskrit or collect postage stamps. Except for a period of ownership of a dachshund, Henry James did none of these things. He lived a life consecrated to the service of a jealous, insatiable, and supremely rewarding goddess, and all his activities had essential reference to that service. He had a great belief in the virtues of air and exercise, and he was expert at making a walk of two or three miles last for as many hours by his habit of punctuating movement with frequent and prolonged halts for meditation or conversation. He liked the exhilaration of driving in a motor-car, which gave him, he said, "a sense of spiritual adventure." He liked a communicative companion. Indeed the cultivation of friendships may be said to have been his sole recreation. To the very end of his life he was quick to recognize every chance of forming a friendly relation, swift to act on his recognition, and beautifully ready to protect and nourish the warm life of engendered affection. His letters, especially those written in his later years, are more than anything else great generous gestures of remembrance, gathering up and embracing his correspondents much as his talk would gather up his hearers and sweep them along on a rising flood of eloquence.

But that fine capacity for forming and maintaining a "relation" worked, inevitably, within definite limits. He was obliged to create impassable barriers between himself and the rest of mankind before he could stretch out his eager hands over safe walls to beckon and to bless. He loved his friends, but he was condemned by the law of his being to keep clear of any really entangling net of human affection and exaction. His contacts had to be subordinate, or indeed ancillary, to the vocation he had followed with a single passion from the time when, as a small boy, he obtained a report from his tutor as showing no great aptitude for anything but a felicitous rendering of La Fontaine's fables into English. Nothing could be allowed to interfere for long with the labour from which Henry James never rested, unless perhaps during sleep. When his "morning stint of inventive work" was over, he went forth to the renewed assault of the impressions that were always lying in wait for him. He was perpetually and mercilessly exposed, incessantly occupied with the task of assimilating his experience, freeing the pure workable metal from the base, remoulding it into new beauty with the aid of every device of his craft. He used his friends not, as some incompletely inspired artists do, as in themselves the material of his art, but as the sources of his material. He took everything they could give and he gave it back in his books. With this constant preoccupation, it was natural that the people least interesting to him were the comparatively dumb. To be "inarticulate" was for him the cardinal social sin. It amounted to a wilful withholding of treasures of alien experience. And if he could extract no satisfaction from contemplating the keepers of golden silence, he could gain little more from intercourse with the numerous persons he dismissed from his attention as "simple organisms." These he held to be mere waste of any writer's time, and it was characteristic that his constant appreciation of the works of Mrs. Wharton was baffled by the popularity of *Ethan Frome*, because he considered that the gifted author had spent her labour on creatures too easily comprehensible to be worth her pains. He greatly preferred *The Reef*, where, as he said, "she deals with persons really fine and complicated."

We might arrive at the same conclusion from a study of the prefaces to the New York Edition. More often than not, the initial idea for a tale came to Henry James through the medium of other people's talk. From a welter of anecdote he could unerringly pick out the living nucleus for a reconstructed and balanced work of art. His instinct for selection was admirable, and he could afford to let it range freely among a profusion of proffered subjects, secure that it would alight on the most promising. But he liked to have the subjects presented with a little artful discrimination, even in the first instance. He was dependent on conversation, but it must be educated and up to a point intelligent conversation. There is an early letter written from Italy in 1874, in which he complains of having hardly spoken to an Italian creature in nearly a year's sojourn, "save washerwomen and waiters. This, you'll say, is my own stupidity," he continues, "but granting this gladly, it proves that even a creature addicted as much to sentimentalizing as I am over the whole *mise en scène* of Italian life, doesn't find an easy initiation into what lies behind it. Sometimes I am overwhelmed with the pitifulness of this absurd want of reciprocity between Italy itself and all my rhapsodies about it." Other wanderers might have found more of Italy in washerwomen and waiters, here guaranteed to be the true native article, than in all the nobility of Rome or the Anglo-Americans of Venice, but that was not Henry James's way. For him neither pearls nor diamonds fell from the lips of waiters and washerwomen, and princesses never walked in his world disguised as goose-girls.

Friendships are maintained by the communication of speech and letters. Henry James was a voluminous letter-writer and exhaustively communicative in his talk upon every subject but one, his own work, which was his own real life. It was not because he was indifferent to what people thought of his books that he evaded discussion about them. He was always touched and pleased by any evidence that he had been intelligently read, but he never went a step out of his way to seek this assurance. He found it safest to assume that nobody read him, and he liked his friends none the worse for their incapacity. Meanwhile, the volumes of his published works—visible, palpable, readable proof of that unceasing travail of the creative spirit which was always labouring behind the barrier of his silence—piled themselves up year after year, to be dropped on to the tables of booksellers and pushed on to the shelves of libraries, to be bought and cherished by the faithful, ignored by the multitude, and treated as a test of mental endurance by the kind of person who organized the Browning Society. Fortunately for literature, Henry James did not lend himself to exploitation by any Jacobean Society. Instead of inventing riddles for prize students, he scattered about his pages a number of pregnant passages containing all the clues that are needed for keeping up with him. It was his theory that if readers didn't keep up with him—as they admittedly didn't always—the fault was entirely in their failure of attention. There are revelations in his books, just as he declared them to be in the works of Neil Paraday. "Extract the opinion, disengage the answer—these are the real acts of homage."

VIII

From his familiar correspondence we need not hope to extract as considered an opinion or as definite an answer as from the novels, but his letters are extraordinarily valuable as side-lights, helping us to see how it happened that any man was able to progress along so straight a path from one end of his life to another. The two volumes of memories are clear evidence of the kind of temperamental make-up with which Henry James was gifted, the two volumes of letters show how his life contributed to preserve and enhance his rare capacity for taking and keeping impressions. They show him too as unusually impervious to everything which is not an impression of visual images or a sense of a human situation. He was very little troubled by a number of ideas which press with an increasing weight upon the minds of most educated persons. Not until the outbreak of the Great War was he moved to utter a forcible "opinion" about affairs outside his personal range. He was delightfully free from the common delusion that by grouping individuals in arbitrary classes and by twisting harmless adjectives into abstract nouns it is possible for us to think of more than one thing at a time and to conceive of qualities apart from their manifestation. What he saw he possessed; what he understood he criticized, but he never reckoned it to be any part of his business to sit in judgment on the deeds of men working in alien material for inartistic ends, or to speculate about the nature of the universe or the conflict or reconciliation of science with religion. He could let Huxley and Gladstone, the combatant champions of Darwinism and orthodox theology, enrich the pages of a single letter without any reference to their respective beliefs. "Huxley is a very genial, comfortable being . . . But of course my talk with him is mere amiable generalities." Of Gladstone there is a little more, but again the personal impression is the thing sought. "I was glad of a chance to feel the 'personality' of a great political leader—or as G. is now thought here even, I think, by his partisans, ex-leader. That of Gladstone is very fascinating—his urbanity extreme—his eye that of a man of genius—and his apparent self-surrender to what he is talking of without a flaw. He made a great impression on me." One would like to know what the subject was to which Gladstone had surrendered himself in his talk with this entranced young American, who must surely, for his part, have been as much reduced conversationally to "mere amiable generalities" as on the occasion of his meeting Huxley. It is difficult to think of a single likely point of contact between the minds of Gladstone and Henry James. But that, for delicacy of registration, was an advantage. The recording instrument could perform its work without the hindrance of any distraction of attention from the man himself to the matter of his speech, which did not presumably contain any germ for cultivation into fiction.

His nationality saved Henry James from the common English necessity of taking a side in the political game; and in the United States nobody of his world had expected him to be interested in politics. There is a pleasant account in *The Middle Years* of his blankness when he was asked at a London breakfast-table for "distinctness about General Grant's first cabinet, upon the formation of which the light of the newspaper happened then to beat." The question was embarrassing. "There were, it appeared, things of interest taking place in

America, and I had had, in this absurd manner, to come to England to learn it: I had had over there on the ground itself no conception of any such matter—nothing of the smallest interest, by any perception of mine, as I suppose I should still blush to recall, had taken place in America since the War." Nothing of any great public interest, by any perception of his, was to take place in Europe until the outbreak of another war at that time far beyond the range of speculation. But if cabinets and parties and politics were and remained outside the pale of his sensibility, he was none the less charmed by the customs of a country where Members of Parliament and Civil Servants could meet together for a leisurely breakfast, thus striking "the exciting note of a social order in which everyone wasn't hurled straight, with the momentum of rising, upon an office or a store."

IX

Henry James came to England to admire. But his early reverence for the men and women of an island with so fine and ancient a historic tone as Great Britain soon faded. He had forgotten, in the first passion of acquaintance, that the English are born afresh in every generation and are about as new as young Americans, differing from them chiefly in having other forms of domestic and ecclesiastical architecture and smoother lawns to take for granted. He looked at old stone castles and Tudor brickwork, at great hanging eaves and immemorial gardens, and then he looked at the heirs of this heritage and listened intently for their speech. This was disappointing, partly because they spoke so little. "I rarely remember," he wrote when he had lived through several London months, "to have heard on English lips any other intellectual verdict (no matter under what provocation) than this broad synthesis 'so immensely clever.' What exasperates you is not that they can't say more but that they wouldn't if they could."

How different was this inarticulate world from the fine civilization of Boston, from the cultivated circle that gathered round Charles Eliot Norton at Shady Hill. To that circle he appealed for sympathy, complaining that he was "sinking into dull British acceptance and conformity. . . . I am losing my standard—my charming little standard that I used to think so high; my standard of wit, of grace, of good manners, of vivacity, of urbanity, of intelligence, of what makes an easy and natural style of intercourse! And this in consequence of having dined out during the past winter 107 times!" Great men, or at the least men with great names, swam into his ken and he condemned them. Ruskin was "weakness pure and simple." In Paris he found that he could "easily—more than easily—see all round Flaubert intellectually." A happy Sunday evening at Madame Viardot's provoked a curious reflection on the capacity of celebrated Europeans to behave absurdly and the incapacity of celebrated Americans to indulge in similar antics. "It was both strange and sweet to see poor Turgenev acting charades of the most extravagant description, dressed out in old shawls, and masks, going on all fours, etc. The charades are their usual Sunday evening occupation and the good faith with which Turgenev, at his age and with his glories, can go into them is a striking example of the truth of that spontaneity which Europeans have and we have not. Fancy Longfellow, Lowell, or Charles Norton doing the like and every Sunday evening!"

Whether or not all celebrated Americans behave with invariable decorum, the astonished spectator of Turgenev's performance had no temptation to "do the like." His appearance among a company of artists and writers gathered together in a country village during the late summer of 1886 has been characteristically recorded by Mr. Edmund Gosse. "Henry James was the only sedate one of us all—benign, indulgent, but grave, and not often unbending beyond a genial chuckle. . . . It is remembered with what affability he wore a garland of flowers at a birthday feast, and even, nobly descending, took part one night in a cakewalk. But mostly, though not much our senior, he was serious, mildly avuncular, but very happy and unupbraiding."

By that time Henry James was at his ease in England. The inhabitants were no longer either gods or imbeciles. Through the general British fog he had perceived gleams of intelligence shining on his bewilderment. He was no longer wholly dependent on Boston for refreshment. He could fall back upon the company of Mr. Edmund Gosse and he had found a friend in R. L. Stevenson. The little handful of Islanders possessed of a genuine interest in the art of letters and the criticism of life emerged from the obscurity, and he made out that, on the whole, there were perhaps about as many civilized people in England as in his native land. Yet he was a little troubled about his position. He wondered, while he reviewed the past, whether the path he had so carefully chosen for himself was the right one, whether he might not have missed more by leaving the United States than he had gained by coming to England. He lamented, in a letter written to his brother William in 1899, that he had not had the kind of early experience that might have attached him to his own country. He earnestly advised a different treatment for his nephews. "What I most of all feel, and in the light of it conjure you to keep doing for them, is their being *à même* to contract local saturations and attachments in respect to their *own* great and glorious country, to learn, and strike roots into, its infinite beauty, as I suppose, and variety. . . . Its being their 'own' will double their *use* of it."

It was only after a visit to America in 1904 that he found, on his return to Rye, that he had a home and a country. He was able after this discovery to write to Mrs. Wharton that "your only drawback is not having the homeliness and the inevitability and the happy limitation and the affluent poverty, of a Country of your Own (comme moi, par exemple!)"; and he could declare after taking the Oath of Allegiance to the King of England in 1915 that "I was really too associated before for any nominal change to matter. The process has only shown me what I virtually *was*—so that it's rather disappointing in respect to acute sensation. I *haven't* any." Associated he certainly was, allied by innumerable sympathies and affections to the adopted country. But he was never really English or American or even Cosmopolitan. And it is too difficult to suppose that even if he had passed all his youth in New England and contracted all the local saturations and attachments he urged for his nephews he could ever have melted comfortably into American uniformity. He, who took nothing in the world for granted, could surely never have taken New England for granted.

To-day, with the complete record before us—the novels,

criticisms, biographies, plays, and letters—we can understand how little those international relations that engaged Henry James's attention mattered to his genius. Wherever he might have lived and whatever human interactions he might have observed, he would in all probability have reached much the same conclusion that he arrived at by the way of America, France, and England. When he walked out of the refuge of his study into the world and looked about him, he saw a place of torment, where creatures of prey perpetually thrust their claws into the quivering flesh of the doomed, defenceless children of light. He had the abiding comfort of an inner certainty (and perhaps he did bring that from New England) that the children of light had an eternal advantage; he was aware to the finest fibre of his being that the "poor sensitive gentlemen" he so numerously treated possessed a treasure that would outlast all the glittering paste of the world and the flesh; he knew that nothing in life mattered compared with spiritual decency.

We may conclude that the nationalities of his betrayed and triumphant victims are not an important factor. They may equally well be innocent Americans maltreated by odious Europeans, refined Europeans fleeced by unscrupulous Americans, or young children of any race exposed to evil influences. The essential fact is that wherever he looked Henry James saw fineness apparently sacrificed to grossness, beauty to avarice, truth to a bold front. He realized how constantly the tenderness of growing life is at the mercy of personal tyranny and he hated the tyranny of persons over each other. His novels are a repeated exposure of this wickedness, a reiterated and passionate plea for the fullest freedom of development, unimperilled by reckless and barbarous stupidity.

He was himself most scrupulously careful not to exercise any tyrannical power over other people. The only advice he ever permitted himself to offer to a friend was a recommendation to "let your soul live." Towards the end of his days his horror of interfering, or seeming to interfere, with the freedom of others became so overpowering that it was a misery for him to suspect that the plans of his friends might be made with reference to himself. Much as he enjoyed seeing them, he so disliked to think that they were undergoing the discomfort of voyages and railway journeys in order to be near him that he would gladly have prevented their start if he could. His Utopia was an anarchy where nobody would be responsible for any other human being but only for his own civilized character. His circle of friends will easily recall how finely Henry James had fitted himself to be a citizen of this commonwealth.

CHRONOLOGY

NOTE ON THE TEXTS

NOTES

INDEX

Chronology

1843 Born April 15 at 21 Washington Place, New York City, the second child (after William, born January 11, 1842) of Henry James of Albany and Mary Robertson Walsh of New York. Father lives on inheritance of $10,000 a year, his share of litigated $3,000,000 fortune of his Albany father, William James, an Irish immigrant who came to the United States immediately after the Revolution.

1843–45 Accompanied by Mary's sister, Catharine Walsh, and servants, the James parents take infant children to England and later to France. Reside at Windsor, where father has nervous collapse ("vastation") and experiences spiritual illumination. He becomes a Swedenborgian (May 1844), devoting his time to lecturing and religious-philosophical writings. James later claimed his earliest memory was a glimpse, during his second year, of the Place Vendôme in Paris with its Napoleonic column.

1845–47 Family returns to New York. Garth Wilkinson James (Wilky) born July 21, 1845. Family moves to Albany at 50 N. Pearl St., a few doors from grandmother Catharine Barber James. Robertson James (Bob or Rob) born August 29, 1846.

1847–55 Family moves to a large house at 58 W. 14th St., New York. Alice James born August 7, 1848. Relatives and father's friends and acquaintances—Horace Greeley, George Ripley, Charles Anderson Dana, William Cullen Bryant, Bronson Alcott, and Ralph Waldo Emerson ("I knew he was great, greater than any of our friends")—are frequent visitors. Thackeray calls during his lecture tour on the English humorists. Summers at New Brighton on Staten Island and Fort Hamilton on Long Island's south shore. On steamboat to Fort Hamilton in August 1850, hears Washington Irving tell his father of Margaret Fuller's drowning in shipwreck off Fire Island. Frequently visits Barnum's American Museum on free days. Taken to art shows and theaters; writes and draws stage scenes. Described by father as "a devourer of libraries." Taught in assorted private schools and by tutors in lower Broadway and Greenwich

Village. Father claims in 1848 that American schooling fails to provide "sensuous education" for his children and plans to take them to Europe.

1855–58 Family (with Aunt Kate) sails for Liverpool, June 27. James is intermittently sick with malarial fever as they travel to Paris, Lyon, and Geneva. After Swiss summer, leaves for London where Robert Thomson (later Robert Louis Stevenson's tutor) is engaged. Early summer 1856, family moves to Paris. Another tutor engaged and children attend experimental Fourierist school. Acquires fluency in French. Family goes to Boulogne-sur-Mer in summer, where James contracts typhoid. Spends late October in Paris, but American economic crash of 1857 returns family to Boulogne where they can live more cheaply. Attends public school (fellow classmate is Coquelin, the future French actor).

1858–59 Family returns to America and settles in Newport, Rhode Island. Goes boating, fishing, and riding. Attends the Reverend W. C. Leverett's Berkeley Institute, and forms friendship with classmate Thomas Sergeant Perry. Takes long walks and sketches with the painter John La Farge.

1859–60 Father, still dissatisfied with American education, returns family to Geneva in October. James attends a pre-engineering school, Institution Rochette, because parents, with "a flattering misconception of my aptitudes," feel he might benefit from less reading and more mathematics. After a few months withdraws from all classes except French, German, and Latin, and joins William as a special student at the Academy (later the University of Geneva) where he attends lectures on literary subjects. Studies German in Bonn during summer 1860.

1860–62 Family returns to Newport in September where William studies with William Morris Hunt, and James sits in on his classes. La Farge introduces him to works of Balzac, Merimée, Musset, and Browning. Wilky and Bob attend Frank Sanborn's experimental school in Concord with children of Hawthorne and Emerson and John Brown's daughter. Early in 1861, orphaned Temple cousins come to live in Newport. Develops close friendship with cousin Mary (Minnie) Temple. Goes on a week's walking tour in July in New Hampshire with Perry. William abandons art in autumn 1861 and enters Lawrence Scientific School at

Harvard. James suffers back injury in a stable fire while serving as a volunteer fireman. Reads Hawthorne ("an American could be an artist, one of the finest").

1862–63 Enters Harvard Law School (Dane Hall). Wilky enlists in the Massachusetts 44th Regiment, and later in Colonel Robert Gould Shaw's 54th, one of the first black regiments. Summer 1863, Bob joins the Massachusetts 55th, another black regiment, under Colonel Hollowell. James withdraws from law studies to try writing. Sends unsigned stories to magazines. Wilky is badly wounded and brought home to Newport in August.

1864 Family moves from Newport to 13 Ashburton Place, Boston. First tale, "A Tragedy of Error" (unsigned), published in *Continental Monthly* (Feb. 1864). Stays in Northampton, Massachusetts, early August–November. Begins writing book reviews for *North American Review* and forms friendship with its editor, Charles Eliot Norton, and his family, including his sister Grace (with whom he maintains a long-lasting correspondence). Wilky returns to his regiment.

1865 First signed tale, "The Story of a Year," published in *Atlantic Monthly* (March 1865). Begins to write reviews for the newly founded *Nation* and publishes anonymously in it during next fifteen years. William sails on a scientific expedition with Louis Agassiz to the Amazon. During summer James vacations in the White Mountains with Minnie Temple and her family; joined by Oliver Wendell Holmes Jr. and John Chipman Gray, both recently demobilized. Father subsidizes plantation for Wilky and Bob in Florida with black hired workers. (The idealistic but impractical venture fails in 1870.)

1866–68 Continues to publish reviews and tales in Boston and New York journals. William returns from Brazil and resumes medical education. James has recurrence of back ailment and spends summer in Swampscott, Massachusetts. Begins friendship with William Dean Howells. Family moves to 20 Quincy St., Cambridge. William, suffering from nervous ailments, goes to Germany in spring 1867. "Poor Richard," James's longest story to date, published in *Atlantic Monthly* (June–Aug. 1867). William begins intermittent criticism of Henry's storytelling and style (which will continue throughout their careers). Momentary meeting with Charles Dickens at Norton's house. Vacations in Jefferson, New Hampshire, summer 1868. William returns from Europe.

1869–70 Sails in February for European tour. Visits English towns and cathedrals. Through Nortons meets Leslie Stephen, William Morris, Dante Gabriel Rossetti, Edward Burne-Jones, John Ruskin, Charles Darwin, and George Eliot (the "one marvel" of his stay in London). Goes to Paris in May, then travels in Switzerland in summer and hikes into Italy in autumn, where he stays in Milan, Venice (Sept.), Florence, and Rome (Oct. 30–Dec. 28). Returns to England to drink the waters at Malvern health spa in Worcester because of digestive troubles. Stays in Paris en route and has first experience of Comédie Française. Learns that his beloved cousin, Minnie Temple, has died of tuberculosis.

1870–72 Returns to Cambridge in May. Travels to Rhode Island, Vermont, and New York to write travel sketches for *The Nation*. Spends a few days with Emerson in Concord. Meets Bret Harte at Howells's home April 1871. *Watch and Ward*, his first novel, published in *Atlantic Monthly* (Aug.–Dec. 1871). Serves as occasional art reviewer for the *Atlantic*, January–March 1872.

1872–74 Accompanies Aunt Kate and sister Alice on tour of England, France, Switzerland, Italy, Austria, and Germany from May through October. Writes travel sketches for *The Nation*. Spends autumn in Paris, becoming friends with James Russell Lowell. Escorts Emerson through the Louvre. (Later, on Emerson's return from Egypt, will show him the Vatican.) Goes to Florence in December and from there to Rome, where he becomes friends with actress Fanny Kemble, her daughter Sarah Butler Wister, and William Wetmore Story and his family. In Italy sees old family friend Francis Boott and his daughter Elizabeth (Lizzie), expatriates who have lived for many years in Florentine villa at Bellosguardo. Takes up horseback riding on the Campagna. Encounters Matthew Arnold in April 1873 at Story's. Moves from Rome hotel to rooms of his own. Continues writing and now earns enough to support himself. Leaves Rome in June, spends summer in Bad Homburg. In October goes to Florence, where William joins him. They also visit Rome, William returning to America in March. In Baden-Baden (June–August) and returns to America on September 4, with *Roderick Hudson* all but finished.

1875 *Roderick Hudson* serialized in *Atlantic Monthly* from January (published by Osgood at the end of the year). *A Passionate Pilgrim and Other Tales* published January 31. Tries living and writing in New York, in rooms at 111 E. 25th St. Earns $200 a month from novel installments and continues reviewing, but finds New York too expensive. *Transatlantic Sketches*, published in April, sells almost 1,000 copies in three months. In Cambridge in July decides to return to Europe; arranges with John Hay, assistant to the publisher, to write Paris letters for the *New-York Tribune.*

1875–76 Arriving in Paris in November, he takes rooms at 29 Rue de Luxembourg (since renamed Cambon). Becomes friend of Ivan Turgenev and is introduced by him to Gustave Flaubert's Sunday parties. Meets Edmond de Goncourt, Émile Zola, G. Charpentier (the publisher), Catulle Mendès, Alphonse Daudet, Guy de Maupassant, Ernest Renan, Gustave Doré. Makes friends with Charles Sanders Peirce, who is in Paris. Reviews (unfavorably) the early Impressionists at the Durand-Ruel gallery. By midsummer has received $400 for *Tribune* pieces, but editor asks for more Parisian gossip and James resigns. Travels in France during July, visiting Normandy and the Midi, and in September crosses to San Sebastian, Spain, to see a bullfight ("I thought the bull, in any case, a finer fellow than any of his tormentors"). Moves to London in December, taking rooms at 3 Bolton St., Piccadilly, where he will live for the next decade.

1877 *The American* published. Meets Robert Browning and George du Maurier. Leaves London in midsummer for visit to Paris and then goes to Italy. In Rome rides again in Campagna and hears of an episode that inspires "Daisy Miller." Back in England, spends Christmas at Stratford with Fanny Kemble.

1878 Publishes first book in England, *French Poets and Novelists* (Macmillan). Appearance of "Daisy Miller" in *Cornhill Magazine*, edited by Leslie Stephen, is international success, but by publishing it abroad loses American copyright and story is pirated in the United States. *Cornhill* also prints "An International Episode." *The Europeans* is serialized in *Atlantic.* Now a celebrity, he dines out often, visits country houses, gains weight, takes long walks, fences, and does weight lifting to reduce. Elected to Reform Club. Meets Tennyson, George Meredith, and James McNeill Whistler. William marries Alice Howe Gibbens.

1879 Immersed in London society ("dined out during the past winter 107 times!"). Meets Edmund Gosse and Robert Louis Stevenson, who will later become his close friends. Sees much of Henry Adams and his wife, Marian (Clover), in London and later in Paris. Takes rooms in Paris, September–December. *Confidence* is serialized in *Scribner's* and published by Chatto & Windus. *Hawthorne* appears in Macmillan's "English Men of Letters" series.

1880–81 Stays in Florence (March–May) to work on *The Portrait of a Lady.* Meets Constance Fenimore Woolson, American novelist and grandniece of James Fenimore Cooper. Returns to Bolton Street in June, where William visits him. *Washington Square* serialized in *Cornhill Magazine* and published in the United States by Harper & Brothers (Dec. 1880). *The Portrait of a Lady* serialized in *Macmillan's Magazine* (Oct. 1880–Nov. 1881) and *Atlantic Monthly*; published by Macmillan and Houghton, Mifflin (Nov. 1881). Publication both in United States and in England yields him the then-large income of $500 a month, though book sales are disappointing. Leaves London in February for Paris, the south of France, the Italian Riviera, and Venice, and returns to London in July. Sister Alice visits with her friend Katharine Loring. James goes to Scotland in September.

1881–83 In November revisits America after absence of six years. Lionized in New York. Returns to Quincy Street for Christmas and sees ailing brother Wilky for the first time in ten years. In January visits Washington and Henry and Clover Adams and meets President Chester A. Arthur. Summoned to Cambridge by mother's death, January 29 ("the sweetest, gentlest, most beneficent human being I have ever known"). All four brothers are together for the first time in fifteen years at her funeral. Alice and father move from Cambridge to Boston. Prepares a stage version of "Daisy Miller" and returns to England in May. William, now a Harvard professor, comes to Europe in September. Proposed by Leslie Stephen, James becomes member, without the usual red tape, of the Atheneum Club. Travels in France in October to write *A Little Tour in France* (published 1884) and has last visit with Turgenev, who is dying. Returns to England in December and learns of father's illness. Sails for America but Henry James Sr. dies December 18, 1882, before his arrival. Made executor of father's will. Visits brothers Wilky and Bob in Milwaukee in January. Quarrels with William over division of property—James wants to restore Wilky's share. Macmillan publishes a collected pocket edition of James's novels and tales in fourteen volumes. *Siege of London* and *Portraits of Places* published. Returns to Bolton Street in September. Wilky dies in November. Constance Fenimore Woolson comes to London for the winter.

1884–86 Goes to Paris in February and visits Daudet, Zola, and Goncourt. Again impressed with their intense concern with "art, form, manner" but calls them "mandarins." Meets John Singer Sargent and persuades him to settle in London. Returns to Bolton Street. Sargent introduces him to young Paul Bourget. During country visits encounters many British political and social figures, including W. E. Gladstone, John Bright, and Charles Dilke. Alice, suffering from nervous ailment, arrives in England for visit in November but is too ill to travel and settles near her brother. *Tales of Three Cities* ("The Impressions of a Cousin," "Lady Barberina," "A New England Winter") and "The Art of Fiction" published in 1884. Alice goes to Bournemouth in late January. James joins her in May and becomes an intimate of Robert Louis Stevenson, who resides nearby. Spends August at Dover and is visited by Bourget. Stays in Paris for the next two months. Alice takes rooms in London in the fall of 1885. James moves into a flat at 34 De Vere Gardens in Kensington in early March 1886. *The Bostonians* serialized in *Century* (Feb. 1885–Feb. 1886; published 1886), *The Princess Casamassima* serialized in *Atlantic Monthly* (Sept. 1885–Oct. 1886; published 1886).

1886–87 Leaves for Italy in December for extended stay, mainly in Florence and Venice. Sees much of Constance Fenimore Woolson and stays in her villa. Writes "The Aspern Papers" and other tales. Returns to De Vere Gardens in July and begins work on *The Tragic Muse*. Pays several country visits. Dines out less often ("I know it all—all that one sees by 'going out'—today, as if I had made it. But if I had, I would have made it better!").

1888 *The Reverberator*, *The Aspern Papers*, *Louisa Pallant*, *The Modern Warning*, and *Partial Portraits* published. Elizabeth Boott Duveneck dies. Robert Louis Stevenson leaves for the South Seas. Engages fencing teacher to combat "symptoms of a portentous corpulence." Goes abroad in October to Geneva (where he visits Woolson), Genoa, Monte Carlo, and Paris.

1889–90 Catharine Walsh (Aunt Kate) dies in March 1889. William comes to England to visit Alice in August. James goes to Dover in September and then to Paris for five weeks. Writes account of Robert Browning's funeral in Westminster Abbey. Dramatizes *The American* for the Compton Comedy Company. Meets and becomes close friends with American journalist William Morton Fullerton and young American publisher Wolcott Balestier. Goes to Italy for the summer, staying in Venice and Florence, and takes a brief walking tour in Tuscany with W. W. Baldwin, an American physician practicing in Florence. Woolson moves to Cheltenham, England, to be near James. *Atlantic Monthly* rejects his story "The Pupil," but it appears in England in April 1891. Writes series of drawing-room comedies for theater. Meets Rudyard Kipling. *The Tragic Muse* serialized in *Atlantic Monthly* (Jan. 1889–May 1890; published 1890). *A London Life* (including "The Patagonia," "The Liar," "Mrs. Temperly") published in 1889.

1891 *The American* produced at Southport is a success during road tour. After residence in Leamington, Alice returns to London, cared for by Katharine Loring. Doctors discover she has breast cancer. James circulates comedies (*Mrs. Vibert*, later called *Tenants*, and *Mrs. Jasper*, later named *Disengaged*) among theater managers who are cool to his work. Unimpressed at first by Ibsen, writes an appreciative review after seeing a performance of *Hedda Gabler* with Elizabeth Robins, a young Kentucky actress; persuades her to take the part of Mme. de Cintré in the London production of *The American*. Recuperates from flu in Ireland. James Russell Lowell dies. *The American* opens in London, September 26, and runs for seventy nights. Wolcott Balestier dies, and James attends his funeral in Dresden in December.

1892 Alice James dies on March 6. James travels to Siena to be near the Paul Bourgets, and Venice (June–July) to visit the Daniel Curtises, then to Lausanne to meet William and his family, who have come abroad for his sabbatical. Attends funeral of Tennyson at Westminster Abbey. Augustin Daly agrees to produce *Mrs. Jasper*. *The American* continues to be performed on the road by Edward Compton. *The Lesson of the Master* (with a collection of stories including "The Marriages," "The Pupil," "Brooksmith," "The Solution," and "Sir Edmund Orme") published.

1893 Fanny Kemble dies in January. Continues to write unproduced plays. In March goes to Paris for two months. Sends Compton first act and scenario for *Guy Domville*. Meets William and family in Lucerne and stays a month, returning to London in June. Spends July completing *Guy Domville* in Ramsgate. George Alexander, actor-manager, agrees to produce the play. Daly stages first reading of *Mrs. Jasper*, and James withdraws it, calling the rehearsal a mockery. *The Real Thing and Other Tales* (including "The Wheel of Time," "Lord Beaupré," "The Visit") published.

1894 Constance Fenimore Woolson dies in Venice, January. Shocked and upset, James prepares to attend funeral in Rome but changes his mind on learning she is a suicide. Goes to Venice in April to help her family settle her affairs. Receives one of four copies, privately printed by Loring, of Alice's diary. Finds it impressive but is concerned that so much gossip he told Alice in private has been included (later burns his copy). Robert Louis Stevenson dies in Samoa. *Guy Domville* goes into rehearsal. *Theatricals: Two Comedies* and *Theatricals: Second Series* published.

1895 *Guy Domville* opens January 5 at St. James's Theatre in London. At play's end James is greeted by a fifteen-minute roar of boos, catcalls, and applause. Horrified and depressed, abandons the theater. Play earns him $1,300 after five-week run. Feels he can salvage something useful from playwriting for his fiction ("a key that, working in the same *general* way fits the complicated chambers of *both* the dramatic and the narrative lock"). Writes scenario for *The Spoils of Poynton*. Visits Lord Wolseley and Lord Houghton in Ireland. In the summer goes to Torquay in Devon and stays until November while electricity is being installed in De Vere Gardens flat. Begins friendship with W. E. Norris, who resides at Torquay. Writes a one-act play ("Mrs. Gracedew") at request of Ellen Terry. *Terminations* (containing "The Death of the Lion," "The Coxon Fund," "The Middle Years," "The Altar of the Dead") published.

1896–97 Finishes *The Spoils of Poynton* (serialized in *Atlantic Monthly* April–Oct. 1896 as *The Old Things*; published 1897). *Embarrassments* ("The Figure in the Carpet," "Glasses," "The Next Time," "The Way It Came") published. Takes a house on Point Hill, Playden, opposite the old town of Rye, Sussex, for August–September. Ford Madox Hueffer (later Ford Madox Ford) visits him. Converts play *The Other House* into novel and works on *What Maisie Knew* (published Sept. 1897). George du Maurier dies early in October. Because of increasing pain in wrist, hires stenographer William MacAlpine in February and then purchases a typewriter; soon begins direct dictation to MacAlpine at the machine. Invites Joseph Conrad to lunch at De Vere Gardens, beginning their friendship. Goes to Bournemouth in July. Serves on jury in London before going to Dunwich, Suffolk, to spend time with Temple-Emmet cousins. In late September 1897 signs a twenty-one-year lease for Lamb House in Rye for £70 a year ($350). Takes on extra work to pay for setting up his house and writes the life of William Wetmore Story ($1,250 advance) and will furnish an "American Letter" for new magazine *Literature* (precursor of *Times Literary Supplement*) for $200 a month. Howells visits.

1898 "The Turn of the Screw" (serialized in *Collier's* Jan.–April; published with "Covering End" under the title *The Two Magics*) proves his most popular work since "Daisy Miller." Sleeps in Lamb House for first time on June 28. Soon after is visited by William's son, Henry James Jr. (Harry), followed by a stream of visitors: future Justice Oliver Wendell Holmes, Annie Adams Fields, Sarah Orne Jewett, Paul Bourget, Edward Warren, Daniel Curtis and Ariana Curtis, Edmund Gosse, and Howard Sturgis. His witty friend Jonathan Sturges, a young, crippled New Yorker, stays for two months during autumn. *In the Cage* published. Meets neighbors Stephen Crane and H. G. Wells.

1899 Finishes *The Awkward Age* and plans trip to the Continent. Fire in Lamb House delays departure. To Paris in March and then visits the Paul Bourgets at Hyères. Stays with the Curtises in their Venice palazzo, where he meets and becomes friends with Jessie Allen. In Rome meets young American-Norwegian sculptor Hendrik C. Andersen; buys one of his busts. Returns to England in July and Andersen comes for three days in August. William, his wife, Alice, and daughter, Peggy, arrive at Lamb House in October. First meeting of brothers in six years. William now has confirmed heart condition. James B. Pinker becomes literary agent and for first time James's professional relations are systematically organized; he reviews copyrights, finds new publishers, and obtains better prices for work ("the germ of a new career"). Purchases Lamb House for $10,000 with an easy mortgage.

1900 Unhappy at whiteness of beard which he has worn since the Civil War, he shaves it off. Alternates between Rye and London. Begins *The Sacred Fount.* Works on and then sets aside *The Sense of the Past* (never finished). Begins *The Ambassadors. The Soft Side*, a collection of twelve tales, published. Niece Peggy comes to Lamb House for Christmas.

1901 Obtains permanent room at the Reform Club for London visits and spends eight weeks in town. Sees funeral of Queen Victoria. Decides to employ a typist, Mary Weld, to replace the more expensive overqualified shorthand stenographer, MacAlpine. Completes *The Ambassadors* and begins *The Wings of the Dove. The Sacred Fount* published. Has meeting with George Gissing. William James, much improved, returns home after two years in Europe. Young Cambridge admirer Percy Lubbock visits. Discharges his alcoholic servants of sixteen years (the Smiths). Mrs. Paddington becomes new housekeeper.

1902 In London for the winter but gout and stomach disorder force him home earlier. Finishes *The Wings of the Dove* (published in August). William James Jr. (Billy) visits in October and becomes a favorite nephew. Writes "The Beast in the Jungle" and "The Birthplace."

1903 *The Ambassadors*, *The Better Sort* (a collection of eleven tales), and *William Wetmore Story and His Friends* published. After another spell in town, returns to Lamb House in May and begins work on *The Golden Bowl.* Meets and establishes close friendship with Dudley Jocelyn Persse, a nephew of Lady Gregory. First meeting with Edith Wharton in December.

1904–5 Completes *The Golden Bowl* (published Nov. 1904). Rents out Lamb House for six months, and sails in August for America after twenty-year absence. Sees new Manhattan skyline from New Jersey on arrival and stays with Colonel George Harvey, president of Harper's, in Jersey shore house with Mark Twain as fellow guest. Goes to William's country house at Chocorua in the White Mountains, New Hampshire. Reexplores Cambridge, Boston, Salem, Newport, and Concord, where he visits brother Bob. In October stays with Edith Wharton in the Berkshires and motors with her through Massachusetts and New York. Later visits New York City, Philadelphia (where he delivers lecture "The Lesson of Balzac"), and then Washington, D.C., as a guest in Henry Adams's house. Meets (and is critical of) President Theodore Roosevelt. Returns to Philadelphia to lecture at Bryn Mawr. Travels to Richmond, Charleston, Jacksonville, Palm Beach, and St. Augustine. Then lectures in St. Louis, Chicago, South Bend, Indianapolis, Los Angeles (with a short vacation at Coronado Beach near San Diego), San Francisco, Portland, and Seattle. Returns to explore New York City ("the terrible town"), May–June. Lectures on "The Question of Our Speech" at Bryn Mawr commencement. Elected to newly founded American Academy of Arts and Letters (William declines). Returns to England in July; lectures had more than covered expenses of his trip. Begins revision of novels for the New York Edition.

1906–8 Writes "The Jolly Corner" and *The American Scene* (published 1907). Writes eighteen prefaces for the New York Edition (twenty-four volumes published 1907–9). Visits Paris and Edith Wharton in spring 1907 and motors with her in Midi. Travels to Italy for the last time, visiting Hendrik Andersen in Rome, and goes on to Florence and Venice. Engages Theodora Bosanquet as his typist in autumn. Again visits Edith Wharton in Paris, spring 1908. William comes to England to give a series of lectures at Oxford and receives an honorary Doctor of Science degree. James goes to Edinburgh in March to see a tryout by the Forbes-Robertsons of his play *The High Bid*, a rewrite in three acts of the one-act play originally written for Ellen Terry (revised earlier as the story "Covering End"). Play gets only five special matinees in London. Shocked by slim royalties from sales of the New York Edition.

1909 Growing acquaintance with young writers and artists of Bloomsbury, including Virginia and Vanessa Stephen and others. Meets and befriends young Hugh Walpole in February. Goes to Cambridge in June as guest of admiring dons and undergraduates and meets John Maynard Keynes. Feels unwell and sees doctors about what he believes may be heart trouble. They reassure him. Late in year burns forty years of his letters and papers at Rye. Suffers severe attacks of gout. *Italian Hours* published.

1910 Very ill in January ("food-loathing") and spends much time in bed. Nephew Harry comes to be with him in February. In March is examined by Sir William Osler, who finds nothing physically wrong. James begins to realize that he has had "a sort of nervous breakdown." William, in spite of now severe heart trouble, and his wife, Alice, come to England to give him support. Brothers and Alice go to Bad Nauheim for cure, then travel to Zurich, Lucerne, and Geneva, where they learn Robertson (Bob) James has died in America of heart attack. James's health begins to improve but William is failing. Sails with William and Alice for America in August. William dies at Chocorua soon after arrival, and James remains with the family for the winter. *The Finer Grain* published.

1911 Honorary degree from Harvard in spring. Visits with Howells and Grace Norton. Sails for England on July 30. On return to Lamb House, decides he will be too lonely there and starts search for a London flat. Theodora Bosanquet obtains work rooms adjoining her flat in Chelsea and he begins autobiography, *A Small Boy and Others*. Continues to reside at the Reform Club. *The Outcry* published.

1912 Delivers "The Novel in *The Ring and the Book*," on the 100th anniversary of Browning's birth, to the Royal Society of Literature. Receives honorary Doctor of Letters from Oxford University on June 26. Spends summer at Lamb House. Sees much of Edith Wharton ("the Firebird"), who spends summer in England. (She secretly arranges to have Scribner's put $8,000 into James's account.) Takes 21 Carlyle Mansions, in Cheyne Walk, Chelsea, as London quarters. Writes a long admiring letter for William Dean Howells's seventy-fifth birthday. Meets André Gide. Contracts bad case of shingles and is ill four months, much of the time not able to leave bed.

1913 Moves into Cheyne Walk flat. Two hundred and seventy friends and admirers subscribe for seventieth birthday portrait by Sargent and present also a silver-gilt Charles II porringer and dish ("golden bowl"). Sargent turns over his payment to young sculptor Derwent Wood, who does a bust of James. Autobiography *A Small Boy and Others* published. Goes with niece Peggy to Lamb House for the summer.

1914 *Notes of a Son and Brother* published. Works on *The Ivory Tower*. Returns to Lamb House in July. Niece Peggy joins him. Horrified by the war ("this crash of our civilisation," "a nightmare from which there is no waking"). In London in September participates in Belgian Relief, visits wounded in St. Bartholomew's and other hospitals; feels less "finished and useless and doddering" and recalls Walt Whitman and his Civil War hospital visits. Accepts chairmanship of American Volunteer Motor Ambulance Corps in France. *Notes on Novelists* (essays on Balzac, Flaubert, and Zola) published.

1915–16 Continues work with the wounded and war relief. Has occasional lunches with Prime Minister Asquith and family, and meets Winston Churchill and other war leaders. Discovers that he is considered an alien and has to report to police before going to coastal Rye. Decides to become a British national and asks Asquith to be one of his sponsors. Receives Certificate of Naturalization on July 26. H. G. Wells satirizes him in *Boon* ("leviathan retrieving pebbles") and James, in the correspondence that follows, writes: "Art *makes* life, makes interest, makes importance." Burns more papers and photographs at Lamb House in autumn. Has a stroke December 2 in his flat, followed by another two days later. Develops pneumonia and during delirium gives his last confused dictation (dealing with the Napoleonic legend) to Theodora Bosanquet, who types it on the familiar typewriter. Alice, William's widow, arrives December 13 to care for him. On New Year's Day, George V confers the Order of Merit. Dies February 28. Funeral services held at the Chelsea Old Church. The body is cremated and the ashes are later buried in Cambridge Cemetery family plot.

Note on the Texts

This volume contains Henry James's books *A Small Boy and Others* (1913), *Notes of a Son and Brother* (1914), and the unfinished *The Middle Years* (1917), along with eight essays and selections from James's notebooks written from 1881 to 1910.

It was relatively late in his career that James began to dwell on, and write about, his own past. He had always been interested in what he calls in the Preface to "The Aspern Papers" the "*visitable* past," and prized contact with members of the older generation who had known Byron or Shelley, Dickens or Thackeray, Hawthorne or Thoreau. But as he grew older and more of his friends and intimates died—especially in the decade from 1885, when he lost his friends Clover Hooper, Lizzie Boott, James Russell Lowell, Wolcott Balestier, his sister Alice, Fanny Kemble, Constance Fenimore Woolson, and Robert Louis Stevenson—he became ever more aware that his past experiences were a subject of interest, not only to himself but to others. He wrote a succession of memorial essays, and after a delay of some years, the biographical volume *William Wetmore Story and His Friends* (1903), produced at the urging of the family of William Wetmore Story (1819–1895), an expatriate American sculptor in Rome. In that book he cited letters and connected them with reflective commentary, a method he would use in *Notes of a Son and Brother.*

In 1910 James's brother William and his wife, Alice Howe Gibbens James, traveled to England because of alarming reports about the medical and psychological state of the novelist in his Sussex home (James was suffering from angina and most probably depression). But William's own heart condition became a more pressing concern, and in late summer all three sailed back to America—only for William to die on August 26, 1910, at his house in Chocorua, New Hampshire.

James stayed on with his brother's family, and later told his nephew Henry (Harry) that the idea of a "Family Book" emerged in talk with William's widow, as he gave voice to memories of the family and of the brothers' youth. James wrote that Alice declared, "Oh Henry, why don't you *write* these things?"—so that "after a bit I found myself wondering vaguely whether I *mightn't* do something of the sort" (*Henry James: Letters*, ed. Leon Edel, 4 vols. [1974–84], IV, pp. 801–2; November 15–18, 1913). Given the initial necessity of gathering and transcribing letters, it took some time before a book began to emerge. Back in England, on November 19, 1911, James told Alice that he was in agreement with her son Henry about the treatment of the letters:

> I am entirely at one with him about the kind of use to be made by me of all these early things, the kind of setting they must have, the kind of encompassment that the book, as my book, my play of reminiscence & almost of brotherly autobiography, & filial autobiography not less, must enshrine them in. The book I see & feel will be difficult & unprecedented & perilous—but if I bring it off it will be exquisite & unique; bring it off as I inwardly project it & oh so devoutly desire it. (*Henry James: A Life in Letters*, ed. Philip Horne [1999], pp. 503–4)

But the workings of memory complicated the task. On July 16, 1912, James told his nephew that

> in doing this book I am led, by the very process and action of my idiosyncrasy, on and on into more evocation and ramification of old images and connections, more intellectual and moral autobiography (though all closely and, as I feel it, exquisitely associated and involved,) than I shall quite know what to do with—to do with, that is, in this book. (*Letters of Henry James*, ed. Percy Lubbock [1920], 2 vols., II, p. 240)

On August 7, 1912, James told his agent James Brand Pinker that he realized he had material for "two books, two distinct ones, taking the place of the one multifarious and comprehensive one that I originally saw." And on September 9, he wrote Pinker that "in going over more searchingly my work of the past winter I can't help recognising in it—that is in a mere portion of it, for the moment—the stuff, already highly finished and, as it were, deliverable—of a beautiful little book of about 70000 words, complete in itself, carrying the record concerned in it up to my twelfth year (!!!) and of the most enchanting effect!" (*Henry James: A Life in Letters*, p. 515). This would become *A Small Boy and Others*, a title that "exactly describes the volume" (letter to Pinker, September 29, 1912). On October 9 Pinker told Scribner that James now intended to defer using William James's letters—the book would draw directly on James's childhood memories, without including correspondence—and sent *A Small Boy and Others* by the same post, complete but for twenty to twenty-five pages.

A Small Boy and Others was a departure from the original undertaking as agreed with William's family, and on September 23–24 James told his anxious nephew, who was himself planning to edit his father's letters in a more conventional way, of the process that had led him to go against their expectations:

> This whole record of early childhood simply *grew* so as one came to write it that one could but let it take its way—and it was a miracle

> to me (and still is as I go on further) how the memories revived and pressed upon me, and how they *keep* a-doing of it in the "letters" book. But this earlier thing makes a Book in itself, and I think a very charming and original and unprecedented one of its kind, and which has the merit of giving a whole introductory or initiatory Family picture as an approach to the later stage. (*Henry James: Letters*, IV, p. 794)

A Small Boy and Others was published in the United States and Britain by James's usual publishers at the time, who had cooperated in the publication of the *New York Edition of the Novels and Tales of Henry James* in 24 volumes (1907–9). Charles Scribner's Sons published the book on March 29, 1913, in a print run for the first impression of 2,750 copies in greenish brown sateen, sold at $2.50 (for the second impression in August 1914 another 525 were printed). On April 19, 1913, James wrote to Scribner's expressing his regret that they had not inserted a notice saying that *Notes of a Son and Brother* was "In Preparation," because "this indication would have been in a considerable degree explanatory of the First Instalment character of the Book, accounting for certain omissions, postponements and other provisional matters" (quoted in *A Bibliography of Henry James: Third Edition*, ed. Leon Edel and Dan H. Laurence, revised with the assistance of James Rambeau [Oxford: Clarendon Press, 1982], p. 149). Scribner's at once put a cancel leaf in the remaining copies: "By Henry James | A Small Boy and Others | In preparation | Notes of a Son and Brother." Macmillan & Co. in London published the book on April 1, 1913, in a print run of 1,000 copies in dark blue, sold at 12 shillings. Although there are mostly incidental variants between the American and English editions, James did not significantly revise the text of *A Small Boy and Others*. The text printed here is taken from the 1913 Charles Scribner's Sons edition of *A Small Boy and Others*.

James had already written much of what became the second volume before he decided on the final division of material, so *Notes of a Son and Brother* was completed without great delay. Charles Scribner's Sons published the book on March 7, 1914, in a first and sole print run of 3,000 copies in dull olive-brown smooth sateen, sold at $2.50. Macmillan & Co. in London published the book on March 13, 1914, in a print run of 1,250 copies, sold at 12 shillings. Although there are a few differences between the two editions, James did not significantly revise *Notes of a Son and Brother*. The 1914 Scribner's edition contains the text printed here.

Notes of a Son and Brother concluded with the death of James's cousin Minnie Temple in 1870, which he describes in its closing words as "the end of our youth." Before its publication James had started work on an additional volume about his early experiences in England.

On April 7, 1914, he wrote to his nephew Harry that, conditions permitting,

> I probably *shall* perpetrate a certain number more passages of retrospect & reminiscences—though quite disconnectedly from these 2 recent volumes, which are complete in themselves & of which the original intention is now a performed and discharged thing. (quoted in *Notes of a Son and Brother* and *The Middle Years: A Critical Edition* [2011], ed. Peter Collister, p. xxii)

James went on to "confess that something of the appeal of the period from 1869 to the beginning of my life in London [in late 1876] (the rest of *that* making a history by itself altogether,) *does* a good deal hang about me." On June 3 he told his American friend Gaillard T. Lapsley how touched he was by Lapsley's sister Eleanor's appreciative letter about his memoirs: "I am trying my hand at another even now, & the most I can do is to assure her that it shall be very slow, very difficult, very delayed" (quoted in *Henry James: A Life in Letters*, p. 540). Though he dictated some chapters during the autumn of 1914, he laid it aside for other work as the war grew more intense. He was also unable to continue with a novel set in contemporary America, *The Ivory Tower*. In this final phase he also attempted to complete—probably because as a romance of time travel it seemed so removed from the painful present-day world—a novel of the supernatural he had begun and had to abandon in 1900, *The Sense of the Past*, though this, too, remained incomplete at his death on February 28, 1916.

Theodora Bosanquet, a young Englishwoman with literary talent and ambition, had been James's amanuensis from 1907 onward. When James died she helped one of his young friends, his literary executor Percy Lubbock, to salvage and organize his abandoned works—including what remained of the third volume of memoirs. As Lubbock's headnote to *The Middle Years* explains, James had given it a title taken from one of his most poignant short stories—itself that of an author who dies leaving much undone. Lubbock took an active editorial role in regard to paragraph and chapter divisions, as is evident from the manuscript in the Houghton Library at Harvard University (bMS Am 1237.9). The text printed here is that of the first English edition, published by Collins on October 18, 1917, in a print run of 1,000 copies, sold at 5 shillings. Scribner's in New York published the book on November 23, 1917, in a print run of 1,275 copies, sold at $1.25. There are not significant textual revisions between the two editions, though the editions contain different frontispieces. (Two edited extracts of *The Middle Years* had been published in *Scribner's Magazine* in October and November 1917.)

The "Other Autobiographical Writings, 1881–1910" by James chosen for this volume are taken from the following sources.

From the Notebooks, 1881–82; From the Notebooks, 1905: The texts here are drawn, with the kind permission of Cambridge University Press, from a new edition in preparation by Philip Horne, forthcoming as part of the *Complete Fiction of Henry James*; they are based on manuscripts in the Houghton Library at Harvard University, MS Am 1094 (from volume 2 and volume 7, respectively), and contain emendations of certain inaccuracies in earlier published editions of James's notebooks.

Wolcott Balestier: Introductory "Biographical Sketch" in Wolcott Balestier, *The Average Woman* (Leipzig: Heinemann and Balestier, 1892), vii–xxxi. James's essay was first published in *Cosmopolitan Magazine*, XIII, May 1892, 43–47.

Dumas the Younger: *Notes on Novelists; with Some Other Notes* (London: J. M. Dent & Sons, 1914), pp. 362–84; this collection was also brought out by Charles Scribner's Sons, not revised by James, one day later than the Dent edition. The essay had been published in the *Boston Herald*, February 23, 1896, III, 33: 1–4 and the *New York Herald* of the same date, VI, 5: 1–4; and, under the heading "On the Death of Dumas the Younger," in the *New Review*, XIV (March 1896), 288–302.

The Late James Payn: *Illustrated London News*, April 9, 1898 (v. 112: 500). For passages in the manuscript not included in the published text, see notes 688.20 and 688.38.

An American Art-Scholar: Charles Eliot Norton: *Notes on Novelists; with Some Other Notes* (London: J. M. Dent & Sons, 1914), pp. 412–23. First published in *Burlington Magazine*, January 1909 (v. 14: 201–4).

The Turning Point of My Life: *The Complete Notebooks of Henry James*, ed. Leon Edel and Lyall H. Powers (Oxford: Oxford University Press, 1987), pp. 437–38, based on bMS Am 1237.9, Houghton Library, Harvard University. The Edel and Powers edition gives the erroneous date "1900–1901"; the entry was written in late 1909 or early 1910.

Is There a Life After Death?: The anthology *In After Days: Thoughts on the Future Life* (New York: Harper & Brothers, 1910), pp. 199–233. James's essay was first published in *Harper's Bazaar*, January–February 1910 (v. 44: 26, 128–29).

Appendix: "Henry James at Work" by Theodora Bosanquet: *The Hogarth Essays*, ed. Virginia Woolf and Leonard Woolf (Garden City, NY: Doubleday Doran & Co., 1928), 243–76. It was first published in London by the Hogarth Press in 1924.

This volume presents the texts of the original printings chosen for inclusion here, but it does not attempt to reproduce nontextual features of their typographic design. The texts are presented without change, except for the correction of typographical errors. Spelling, punctuation, and capitalization are often expressive features and are not altered, even when inconsistent or irregular. The following is a list of typographical errors corrected, cited by page and line number: 14.28, Waverley; 149.18, appeciated; 231.16, areh-refinemnet,; 237.22, that; 254.6 (and *passim*), Katherine; 323.13, instrinsic; 331.1, of the of the; 397.7, vegatable; 422.26, gynmastic; 489.35, revéille; 533.25, dont; 533.26, it Things; 592.38, i had; 598.6, others'; 645.22, eat; 684.24, from black; 698.35, esthethic; 707.1, it it; 716.30, contribute; 726.23, the the; 738.2, *Dasiy*.

Notes

In the notes below, the reference numbers denote page and line of this volume (the line count includes chapter headings). Biblical quotations are keyed to the King James Version. Quotations from Shakespeare are keyed to *The Riverside Shakespeare*, ed. G. Blakemore Evans (Boston: Houghton Mifflin, 1974). For further biographical context, see *A Small Boy and Others: A Critical Edition*, ed. Peter Collister (Charlottesville: University of Virginia Press, 2011); *Notes of a Son and Brother* and *The Middle Years: A Critical Edition*, ed. Peter Collister (Charlottesville: University of Virginia Press, 2011); Leon Edel, *Henry James: The Untried Years, 1843–1870* (Philadelphia: Lippincott, 1953) and *Henry James: The Conquest of London, 1870–1881* (Philadelphia: Lippincott, 1962); Alfred Habegger, *The Father: A Life of Henry James, Sr.* (New York: Farrar, Straus and Giroux, 1994); Philip Horne, *Henry James: A Life in Letters* (New York: Viking, 1999); R.W.B. Lewis, *The Jameses: A Family Narrative* (New York: Doubleday, 1991); and Sheldon M. Novick, *Henry James: The Young Master* (New York: Random House, 1996). The editor would like gratefully to acknowledge the wise advice of Oliver Herford and Michael Anesko; and the kind permission of Bay James to quote unpublished Henry James material.

A SMALL BOY AND OTHERS

3.2 From a daguerreotype taken in 1854] At the New York City studio of American photographer Mathew Brady (1822–1896); see p. 56.

6.38–39 "criticism of life"] The English poet and critic Matthew Arnold (1822–1888), admired by James, declared in his essay "The Study of Poetry" (1880) that "poetry is the criticism of life."

7.7–10 the novels . . . Mrs. Trollope and Mrs. Gore, of Mrs. Marsh, Mrs. Hubback and the Misses Kavanagh and Aguilar] Popular British novelists: Frances Trollope (1779–1863), author of travel books and thirty-five novels, including *The Vicar of Wrexhill* (1837) and *The Old World and the New* (1849), and mother of novelist Anthony Trollope; Catherine Gore (1798–1861), prolific writer whose novels include *The Hamiltons* (1834) and *The Banker's Wife, or Court and City* (1843); Anne Marsh Caldwell (1791–1874), author of *Emilia Wyndham* (1846); Catherine Anne Hubback (1818–1877), niece of Jane Austen whose own novels include *The Younger Sister* (1850) and *Malvern, or The Three Marriages* (1855); Julia Kavanagh (1824–1877), author of *Madeleine, A Tale of Auvergne* (1848), *Adèle* (1858), and many other works; Grace Aguilar (1816–1847), writer on

Jewish subjects and author of popular novel *Home Influence: A Tale for Mothers and Daughters* (1847) and six posthumously published novels.

7.17–19 so-called Stephen Dewhurst . . . Literary Remains of Henry James] Henry James Sr. wrote a short fictionalized autobiography in the persona of Stephen Dewhurst. Unpublished during his lifetime, it was collected in a volume edited by William James, *The Literary Remains of the Late Henry James* (1885).

9.26–29 in a collection of other pages than these . . . work of imagination).] In James's novel *The Portrait of a Lady* (1881), young Isabel Archer refuses to go back to the Dutch House after spending a single day at school there. The Albany house where Isabel lives was based on James's grandmother's house.

10.20 "glimmering squares"] From the third stanza of Tennyson's elegiac "Tears, Idle Tears" in *The Princess* (1847): "Ah, sad and strange as in dark summer dawns / The earliest pipe of half-awakened birds / To dying ears, when unto dying eyes / The casement slowly grows a glimmering square; / So sad, so strange, the days that are no more."

11.33–34 our uncle . . . son of Mr. Martin Van Buren] Smith Thompson Van Buren (1817–1876), son of the eighth American president, married James's aunt Ellen King James (1813–1849) in 1842.

14.22–29 in certain notes on New York . . . vanished social order.] See "New York Revisited" in *The American Scene* (1907): "The shabby red house, with its mere two storys, its lowly 'stoop,' its dislocated iron-work of the forties, the early fifties, the record, in its face, of blistering summers and of the long stages of the loss of self-respect, made it as consummate a morsel of the old liquor-scented, heated-looking city, the city of no pavements, but of such a plenty of politics, as I could have desired."

15.16 the celebrated Casimir] French playwright and poet Jean-François Casimir Delavigne (1793–1843), author of the comedy *L'École des vieillards* (1823; *The school for old men*).

15.19–20 the royal crown of Frédégonde or Brunéhaut] Long-feuding Merovingian Frankish queens Fredegund (d. 597), wife of Chilperic of Neustria who ruled as regent for her son Chlotar II, and Brunhilde (d. 613), wife of Sigebert of Austrasia.

15.26 Louis Philippe] French king (1773–1850, ruled 1830–48).

15.27 Gavarni] Pseudonym of French graphic artist, illustrator, and caricaturist Sulpice-Guillaume Chevalier (1804–1866).

15.30 Béranger] Widely read French poet Pierre-Jean Béranger (1780–1857).

15.34 Nash's lithographed Mansions of England in the Olden Time] Four-volume edition (1839–49) of lithographs by the English artist Joseph Nash (1809–1878).

22.39–40 Fort Lafayette, the Bastille of the Civil War] Fortress built on an island off Brooklyn at the entrance to New York Harbor, which was used as a military prison during the Civil War.

23.20 Dr. Beattie's poem] *The Minstrel* (1771) by Scottish poet and philosopher James Beattie (1735–1803).

24.22 town of Coppet] Town in Switzerland in the canton of Vaud, at the western end of Lake Geneva near the border with France.

24.32–33 Chateaubriand declaiming Les Natchez at Madame Récamier's] *Les Natchez* (1826) was a popular romance of American Indian life by François-René de Chateaubriand (1768–1848), French writer and statesman who was a friend and admirer of Juliette Récamier (1777–1849), hostess of an eminent Paris salon.

25.25 *il se fit fort*] French: he declared himself able.

28.2 *féronnière*] French: frontlet (decorative band on forehead).

30.12 the "German"] The German cotillion, popular social dance in nineteenth-century America.

31.5–6 Ultima Thule] Medieval geographers' term for a place at the northernmost limit of the known world.

31.6–7 supposedly ample scheme of the regular ninth "wide" street.] North of Fourteenth Street in Manhattan, wide streets (Fourteenth Street, Twenty-Third Street, Thirty-Fourth Street, and thereafter at irregular intervals) alternate irregularly with narrower streets.

31.20 *trait de mœurs*] French: feature of manners.

35.2–3 Rond-Point . . . Jardin d'Hiver] A point on the Champs-Elysées from which avenues radiate; large public greenhouse and winter garden, from 1846 a fashionable venue for entertainments and gathering place for Parisians.

35.4–5 the ancient lodges of the *octroi* . . . Barrière de l'Étoile?] Temple-like buildings at one of the customs posts where a tax (*octroi*) levied on goods entering Paris was collected.

35.7–8 the assault on Sumner by the South Carolina ruffian of the House.] In his antislavery speech, "The Crime Against Kansas," delivered in the Senate May 19–20, 1856, Senator Charles Sumner (1811–1874) of Massachusetts described Senator Andrew Butler of South Carolina as having chosen "the harlot, Slavery" as his "mistress." On May 22 South Carolina congressman Preston Brooks (1819–1857), a cousin of Senator Butler, approached Sumner as he sat at his desk in the Senate chamber, accused him of libeling South Carolina and Butler, and beat him unconscious with a cane. After a measure to expel him from the House failed to win the necessary two-thirds majority, Brooks resigned his seat and was reelected by his district. Sumner did not return regularly to the Senate until December 1859.

37.11 *souvenir*] French: memory.

38.24 *fond*] French: here, basis.

38.30–31 raid and the capture of John Brown, of Harper's Ferry fame] Abolitionist John Brown (1800–1859) and a group of his followers seized the U.S. armory at Harpers Ferry, Virginia (now West Virginia), on October 16, 1859, with the purpose of arming slaves and starting an insurrection. Fifteen people were killed during the raid. Brown was captured, convicted of treason, and hanged on December 2, 1859.

38.35 pages of "Punch,"] English illustrated comic magazine founded in 1841.

39.2 John Leech's] English illustrator John Leech (1817–1864), *Punch*'s most popular cartoonist.

39.3 Lords Brougham, Palmerston and John Russell] Henry Peter Brougham, 1st Baron Brougham and Vaux (1778–1868), English lawyer, man of letters, and politician who served as Lord Chancellor, 1830–34; Henry John Temple, 3rd Viscount Palmerston (1784–1865), British prime minister, 1855–58, 1859–65; John Russell, 1st Earl Russell (1792–1878), British prime minister, 1846–52, 1865–66.

39.13–14 he had decently provided] See Chronology, 1843.

40.5–7 Tom Hicks . . . Darley] American artist Thomas Hicks (1823–1891), Irish-born American artist Paul Duggan (d. 1861), American artist and writer Christopher Pearse Cranch (1813–1892), and American artist and illustrator F.O.C. Darley (1822–1888).

40.10 landscapist Cropseys and Coles and Kensetts] The American Hudson River School painters Jasper Francis Cropsey (1823–1900), Thomas Cole (1801–1848), and John Frederick Kensett (1816–1872).

40.11 bust-producing Iveses and Powerses and Moziers] American sculptors Chauncey Ives (1810–1894), Hiram Powers (1805–1873), and Joseph Mozier (1812–1870).

40.15–16 George Curtis and Parke Godwin and George Ripley and Charles Dana and N. P. Willis] American journalist, travel writer, and editor George William Curtis (1824–1892); American journalist and editor Parke Godwin (1816–1904); American journalist, literary critic, and social reformer George Ripley (1802–1880); American journalist, poet, playwright, travel writer, and magazine editor Nathaniel Parker Willis (1806–1867).

41.6–8 wife of the painter of the piece, Mr. Osgood . . . friend of the unhappy Mr. Poe.] American poet Frances Sargent Osgood (née Locke, 1811–1850), whom Poe befriended in 1845 and wrote three poems to, as well as praising her in a short essay in *Godey's Lady's Book*; she was the wife of American artist Samuel Stillman Osgood (1808–1885), who painted Poe's portrait.

41.9 Queen Constance on the "huge firm earth"] See Queen Constance's lines in Shakespeare, *King John*, III.i.71–73: "my grief's so great / That no supporter but the huge firm earth / Can hold it up."

41.20–21 the shipwreck of Margaret Fuller . . . (Fire Island] Traveling back to the United States on the merchant freighter *Elizabeth* after a three-year stay in Italy, American writer, social reformer and feminist Margaret Fuller (1810–1850), author of *Woman in the Nineteenth Century* (1845), was drowned after the ship ran aground in a storm on a sandbar off Fire Island on July 19, 1850.

41.31–32 National Academy, then confined to scant quarters] New York arts institution founded in 1825, which held its exhibitions at Broadway and Leonard Street in Lower Manhattan before moving in 1850 to 663 Broadway, opposite Bond Street.

41.32–33 small full-length portrait of Miss Fuller] By Thomas Hicks, painted in 1848.

42.1 new bride of the artist] Hicks married Angelina D. King (1834–1917) in 1855.

43.8–9 Barnum's great American Museum by the City Hall] Exhibition hall with "lecture-room" theater at the corner of Broadway and Ann Street founded by American entrepreneur P. T. Barnum (1810–1891), a popular attraction for its educational displays and curiosities from its opening in 1841 to 1865, when it was destroyed by fire.

43.21 Phiz's illustrations to Dickens] "Phiz" was the pseudonym of English artist Hablot Knight Browne (1815–1882), who illustrated many of Charles Dickens's novels.

43.29 Godey's Lady's Book] American monthly magazine, 1830–98, influential on taste and fashion.

43.32–34 Joey Bagstock's . . . Dombey and Son] Major Joseph Bagstock is a grotesque character in Dickens's novel *Dombey and Son* (1846–48).

45.8 *repaire*] French: den, haunt.

46.3 to the extent of here reproducing] On the frontispiece to *A Small Boy and Others*; see p. 3.

46.13 *abords*] French: outskirts.

46.37–38 Where . . . *d'antan?*] Phrase recalling the line "Where are the snows of yesteryear?" ("Où sont les neiges d'antan?") from the poem "Ballade des Dames du Temps Jadis" by French poet François Villon (1431–after 1463).

49.14–16 Théâtre Français . . . coreligionary Rachel] The Théâtre Français or Comédie Française, official home of the classical French theater, founded in 1600; the French actors known as Madame Judith (Julie Bernat, 1827–1912) and as Mlle. Rachel (Élisa Rachel Félix, 1821–1858), who were both Jewish.

49.33–34 Robinson . . . "Hot Corn"] A series of loosely interrelated short stories by American journalist Solon Robinson (1803–1880) were first published in the *New-York Tribune*, then collected in *Hot Corn: Life Scenes in New York Illustrated* (1854). Set in Manhattan's Five Points slum, the book was a popular success and the basis of several stage adaptations such as C. W. Taylor's *Little Katy; or, The Hot Corn Girl.*

51.11–12 The Seven Gables] Novel *The House of the Seven Gables* (1851), published the year after his *Scarlet Letter* by American novelist Nathaniel Hawthorne (1804–1864).

51.16 The Lamplighter] Best-selling novel (1854) by American novelist Maria Susanna Cummins (1827–1866).

51.33 The Initials] Novel (1850) by Irish-born novelist Jemima Montgomery, Baroness von Tautphoeus (1807–1893), who spent most of her life in Bavaria.

52.4 Boon Children] Child actors Isabella (b. 1842) and Charlotte (b. 1848?) Boone.

52.7–8 history of the long-legged Mr. Hamilton and his two Bavarian beauties] In *The Initials*, the young Englishman Alfred Hamilton boards with the Rosenberg family in Munich and becomes entangled romantically with Rosenberg's two daughters from his first marriage: the younger daughter Cresencz falls in love with Hamilton, who then falls in love with the older daughter Hildegarde, whom he marries at the end of the novel.

52.35–53.2 The little Batemans . . . later and more grateful appreciation.] The sisters Kate (1842–1917) and Ellen Bateman (1844–1936) performed as child actors managed by P. T. Barnum from 1849 to 1856. Two other Bateman sisters, Virginia (1853–1940) and Isabel (1854–1934), also made their theatrical debuts as children. Kate, who had a long acting career as an adult, played the villainous Marquise de Bellegarde in James's stage adaptation (1891) of his novel *The American* directed by Virginia's husband Edward Compton (1854–1918). Virginia Compton played the heroine Claire de Cintré until she was replaced by Elizabeth Robins.

54.36–38 small periodical . . . The Charm] Illustrated children's monthly, 1852–54, published by English publisher, writer, and photographer Joseph Cundall (1818–1895).

56.12–13 establishment of Mr. Brady] At 205 Broadway (see note 3.2).

57.11 great Mr. Thackeray had come to America to lecture] English writer William Makepeace Thackeray (1811–1863), author of *Vanity Fair* (1848), visited the United States on a lecture tour, October 1852–May 1853.

58.9–10 our distinguished friend's secretary, who was also a young artist] English painter Eyre Crowe (1824–1910), who worked as Thackeray's secretary and amanuensis and accompanied him on his American tour. He painted Henry James Sr.' s portrait.

59.10 Colonel Newcome] One of the central characters in Thackeray's novel *The Newcomes* (1855).

61.15 the New York Hotel] At 721 Broadway, between Washington Place and Waverly Place.

63.8 "our" house, just acquired by us] At 58 West Fourteenth Street.

64.5–6 ancient name of the Parade-ground still hung about the central space] The Washington Military Parade Grounds and an adjoining public park opened to the public in 1826 on what is now Washington Square.

65.19 *badaud*] French: gawker, bystander.

66.35–36 Mr. William Burton] British-born actor and theater manager William Evans Burton (1804–1860), proprietor of the popular Chambers Street Theatre and its successor, Burton's New Theatre.

66.37 the Park] City Hall Park, bounded by Chambers Street on its northern side.

67.11 the Dromios] The identical twins Dromio of Syracuse and Dromio of Ephesus in Shakespeare's *Comedy of Errors.*

67.11 agreeable Mrs. Holman] English-born singer, actor, and opera company manager Harriet Holman (1822–1897).

67.14 Miss Mary Taylor] American comic actor and singer (1827–1866).

67.18 Miss Malvina] Malvina Pray (born Anna Pray, 1830–1906), dancer and comic actor later known as Malvina Pray Florence after her marriage to the American actor William J. Florence (1831–1891), with whom she frequently performed.

67.21–22 Paul Pry, as Mr. Toodles and as Aminadab Sleek in The Serious Family] Comic roles often performed by Burton: Paul Pry, the titular character of an 1825 farce by English playwright John Poole (1786–1872); Timothy Toodles in *The Toodles* (1848), Burton's adaptation of *The Farmer's Daughter of the Severnside; or, The Broken Heart* (1831) by English comic playwright Richard John Raymond; Aminadab Sleek in *The Serious Family* (1849), play by English playwright Morris Barnett (1800–1856) adapted from *Le mari à la campagne* (*The Husband in the Country*, 1844) by French playwright Jean-François Bayard (1796–1853).

67.27 Mr. Blake] Canadian comic actor and theater manager Rufus William Blake (1805–1863).

67.30 Mrs. Blake] American actor Caroline Blake (1797–1881), a member of the Placide theatrical family.

67.34–37 Brougham's Lyceum . . . migratory life as Wallack's Theatre] Brougham's Broadway Lyceum, established by Irish-born playwright and theater manager James Brougham (1814–1880) in 1850 on Broadway near

Broome Street, was bought by actor and theater manager James William Wallack Sr. (1794–1864) in 1852 and renamed Wallack's Theatre; it was replaced by a second Wallack's Theatre, at the corner of Thirteenth Street and Broadway, built in 1861, and a third, at Broadway and Thirtieth Street, which opened in 1881.

68.3 English version of Le Père de la Débutante] *The First Night* (1849), adaptation of French play *Le Père de la Débutante* (1837; *The debutante's father*) by Jean-François Bayard and Emmanuel Théaulon (1787–1841).

68.10 Mr. Placide.] American actor Henry Placide (1799–1870).

68.14–15 Miss Kate Horn in Nan the Good-for-Nothing] Irish-born actor Kate Horn (1826–1896), known after her marriage in 1852 as Kate Buckland, was one of the stock company at Brougham's Broadway Lyceum and starred in a production of *Good For Nothing* (1851), farce by English comic actor and playwright John Baldwin Buckstone (1802–1879).

68.15–16 displaced by the brilliant Laura Keene] English-born actor and theater manager (born Mary Francis Moss, 1826–1873), who began her long American career in 1852–53 at Wallack's Theatre.

68.17 Goldsmith's Hardcastle pair] Mr. and Mrs. Hardcastle in *She Stoops to Conquer* (1773), comedy by Irish novelist and playwright Oliver Goldsmith (1728–1774).

68.18 Dogberry] Bumbling chief constable in Shakespeare's *Much Ado About Nothing*.

68.20–21 Mr. Lester—the Lester Wallack that was to be] American actor and theater manager John Lester Wallack (1820–1888), son of James William Wallack Sr. (see note 67.34–37).

68.25 at the Broadway] The Broadway Theatre at 356–58 Broadway, which opened in 1847 and was demolished in 1859.

68.30–32 sisters Gougenheim . . . roguish "Joey"] English-born actor Adelaide Gougenheim (b. 1828) and her sister Josephine, known as "Joey," who performed together.

68.33–38 Mrs. Nagle . . . Lysander or Demetrius;] English-born actor Mary Nagle (née Logue, c. 1833) and her American husband Joseph E. Nagle (b. 1828); but the actors who played Lysander and Demetrius in the February 1854 production of *A Midsummer Night's Dream* that James is recalling were James Lanergan and Joseph Grosvenor.

68.38 Davidge] English-born comic actor William Pleater Davidge (1814–1888).

68.39 Madame Ponisi] Stage name of English actor born Elizabeth Hanson (1818–1899).

69.1 white-veiled heroine of The Cataract of the Ganges] *The Cataract of the Ganges; or, The Rajah's Daughter* (1823), equestrian melodrama by English playwright William Thomas Moncrieff (1794–1857); Ponisi starred as Zamine in the production at the Broadway Theatre, December 1853–January 1854.

69.17–18 Green Bushes . . . Madame Céleste, who came to us straight out of London] John Baldwin Buckstone's play *The Green Bushes, or a Hundred Years Ago* (1845); French actor, dancer, and theater manager Céline Céleste (1810 or 1811–1882) starred as an American Indian in the play's premiere run in London and in several revivals.

69.24–25 Mr. Bourcicault, as he then wrote his name] Irish-born playwright and actor Dion Boucicault (1820–1890), who for a time used the spelling "Bourcicault."

69.29–30 London Assurance . . . "Fanny" Wallack, I think] Boucicault's comedy *London Assurance* (1841); American actor Fanny Wallack (1822–1856).

69.33 Love in a Maze] Comedy (1851) by Boucicault.

69.36 Mrs. Russell . . . Mrs. Hoey] English-born actor born Josephine Shaw (1824–1896).

70.1 Miss Julia Bennett] English actor and theater manager Julia Bennett Barrow (1824–1903).

70.2 the Haymarket] London's Theatre Royal Haymarket.

70.9 Edwin Booth's] American classical and Shakespearean actor (1833–1893).

70.9–10 Portia, Desdemona and Julie de Mortemer] Major roles in Shakespeare's *The Merchant of Venice* and *Othello*, and in *Richelieu* (1839), play by English novelist, playwright, and politician Edward Bulwer-Lytton (1803–1873).

70.19–27 A Morning Call . . . Porte Ouverte ou Fermée] The one-act "comedietta" *A Morning Call* (1851) was an adaptation by English playwright Charles Dance (1794–1863) of *Il faut qu'une porte soit ouverte ou fermée* (1845; *A door must either be open or closed*) by French dramatist, poet, and novelist Alfred de Musset (1810–1857).

70.20 Mr. Lester] See note 68.20–21.

70.26 Musset's elegant proverb] Musset's play is an example of the "dramatic proverb," French genre originating in the seventeenth century in which a short play's action illustrates the proverb of its title.

71.38–39 Captain Cuttle . . . form of the big Burton] William E. Burton (see note 66.35–36) played Captain Cuttle in numerous performances of James Brougham's adaptation of Charles Dickens's novel *Dombey and Son* (1846–48), starting with its inaugural run at Burton's Chambers Street Theatre in the summer of 1848.

72.1–2 he whom I remember as a monstrous Micawber] Burton played Mr. Micawber in the stage adaptation of Dickens's novel *David Copperfield* (1850) by William Knight Northall, which premiered at the Chambers Street Theatre late in 1850.

72.6 illustrations of Phiz] See note 43.21.

72.12–14 Miss Cushman . . . Nancy of Oliver Twist:] American actor Charlotte Cushman (1816–1876) was well-known for her portrayal of Nancy in a stage adaptation of Dickens's *Oliver Twist* (1837–39), which she first performed at the Park Theatre in 1839.

72.17–18 Bosio and Badiali, Ronconi and Steffanone] Italian opera singers: soprano Angiolina Bosio (1830–1859); baritone Cesare Badiali (1810–1865); baritone Giorgio Ronconi (1810–1890); soprano Balbina Steffenone, also spelled "Steffanone" (1825–1896).

72.22 Castle Garden] On the Battery at the south end of Manhattan. Originally a fort called Castle Clinton (built 1808–11, named 1817), the building was named Castle Garden when it was made into an opera house and amusement hall in 1823. From 1855 to 1892, before Ellis Island was opened, it served as an immigration processing station, and from 1896 to 1914 housed the New York Aquarium.

72.22–23 rarest of infant phenomena, Adelina Patti] Celebrated soprano (1843–1919) born to Italian parents in Spain who sang in her first public concert at the age of eight in New York. In Dickens's novel *Nicholas Nickleby* (1838–39), eight-year-old performer Ninetta Crummles is known as the "Infant Phenomenon."

72.28–29 Tripler Hall or at Niblo's] The theaters Tripler Hall (later Metropolitan Hall) on Broadway near Bond Street, and Niblo's Garden, at Broadway and Prince Street.

72.32 Henrietta Sontag, Countess Rossi] German soprano Henriette Sontag (1805–1854).

73.5 "Casta Diva,"] Aria from act 1 of *Norma* (1831), opera by Vincenzo Bellini (1801–1835).

73.18–19 Signor Blitz, the peerless conjurer] English-born magician, ventriloquist, and entertainer Antonio Blitz (1810–1877).

73.30 Smike of Miss Weston] Male character in a stage adaptation of Dickens's *Nicholas Nickleby* played by American actor Lizzie Weston (née Elizabeth Jackson, d. 1899).

73.31–33 afterwards Mrs. E. L. Davenport and then . . . Mrs. Charles Matthews] Weston was married not to the American actor Edward Loomis Davenport (1816–1877) but to the actor Adolphus Hoyt "Dolly" Davenport (1828–1873). Almost immediately after the couple was granted a divorce in February 1858, Weston married Charles Mathews (1803–1878), an English comic actor and theater manager then on tour in the United States. Davenport was later reported to have horsewhipped Mathews in a public altercation.

73.38–40 Dotheboys Hall . . . Brodie.] Grim Yorkshire school in *Nicholas Nickleby*; "John Brodie" refers to the character John Browdie.

75.33 Cruikshank's splendid form of the work] English caricaturist George Cruikshank (1792–1878) was best known for his illustrations for Dickens's novels.

78.39 *fils de famille*] French: literally "son of the family," a young man coming from a respected family.

81.13–14 pious institution of his founding] The Alexander Robertson School, founded in 1789 with funding from James's great-grandfather Alexander Robertson (1733–1816), run by New York City's Second Presbyterian Church.

81.27–28 the worst visitation of cholera New York was to know.] The cholera epidemic of 1849 resulted in more than five thousand deaths in New York City.

82.30 "stock"] A stiff neckcloth.

82.31–35 then great subject of Jenny Lind . . . "Miss Lind";] Internationally renowned Swedish soprano Jenny Lind (1820–1887) sang in America in 1850–52 on a tour organized by P. T. Barnum; she married German pianist and composer Otto Goldschmidt (1829–1907) in February 1852.

83.18 Barmecide banquet] Or Barmecide feast: an imaginary meal or illusion of abundance, phrase derived from the name of the royal house (also spelled Barmakids) in a tale in *The Thousand and One Nights.*

83.38–40 Madame Ristori . . . wrong emphasis of the then acclaimed Mrs. Rousby] Both the eminent Italian actor Adelaide Ristori (1822–1906) and English actor Clara Rousby (1848–1879), known primarily for her beauty, performed at the Lyceum Theatre, on Fourteenth Street west of Sixth Avenue, during the 1874–75 season. James devoted a review to Ristori in 1875 as "before all things stately."

84.4 John Toole] English comic actor and theater manager (1830–1906).

84.11 cousin Helen] Helen Rodgers Perkins (née Wyckoff, 1807–1887).

84.13–14 a small New York Orestes ridden by Furies;] In Greek mythology, and notably in Aeschylus's tragic trilogy the *Oresteia* (458 B.C.E.), Orestes is tormented by the Furies after he murders his mother, Clytemnestra, in revenge for her murder of his father, Agamemnon.

84.17 admirable Aunt] Catharine Walsh (1812–1889), the sister of James's mother.

88.3–5 the great Daumier, say, or Henri Monnier . . . Monsieur Prudhomme] French artist Honoré Daumier (1808–1879), about whom James wrote an essay, "Daumier, Caricaturist," in 1890. French caricaturist Henri Monnier (1799–1877) is best known for his satirical bourgeois character

M. Joseph Prudhomme, also the main character in a play (1852) and a fictional autobiography (1857) written by Monnier.

89.26 Wanderjahre] German: traveling years, a reference to *Wilhelm Meisters Wanderjahre* (1821, 1829), novel by Johann Wolfgang von Goethe (1749–1832).

91.15–17 Mr. Dick . . . Miss Trotwood] In *David Copperfield*, Richard Babley, known as Mr. Dick, is a simple-minded man who lives with and is cared for by Betsey Trotwood.

97.5–7 Barnum . . . Museum] See note 43.8–9.

98.5–6 celebrity of the hour, then "dancing" . . . Lola Montes, Countess of Lansfeldt] Irish-born dancer and actor Lola Montez (1818–1861) was mistress of Ludwig I of Bavaria (1786–1868), who ennobled her and allowed her to exert political influence until his abdication during the political unrest of 1848. Montez danced at the Old Broadway Theatre in the ballet *Betley, The Tyrolean*, December 1851–January 1852, and also performed there as herself in the stage biography *Lola Montes in Bavaria* (1852) by C.P.T. Ware.

98.21–22 Love, or the Countess and the Serf, by J. Sheridan Knowles] Play (1839) by Irish playwright, novelist, and actor James Sheridan Knowles (1784–1862).

98.23 Emily Mestayer] American actor (1813 or 1814–1882).

98.35 that Boston Museum] Theater at the Boston Museum and Gallery of Fine Arts, which was home to a stock company, 1843–94.

99.2 the Booths] The Booth theatrical family, most notably Edwin (see note 70.9).

99.30–32 Barnumite scenic memories . . . Eliza of Uncle Tom's Cabin] Emily Mestayer played the fugitive slave Eliza in the dramatic adaptation (1852) by Henry J. Conway (1800–1860) of Harriet Beecher Stowe's *Uncle Tom's Cabin* (1852) that was staged in the lecture-room theater at Barnum's American Museum in the fall of 1853.

100.36–37 fine free rendering . . . National Theatre] Purdy's National Theatre, formerly called Chatham's Theatre, on what is now Park Row south of the Bowery, staged two distinct adaptations of *Uncle Tom's Cabin*: first the version by Charles W. Taylor (c. 1800–1874) in August 1852 (which closed after eleven performances), then the version by George L. Aiken (1830–1876) in 1852–53. James is referring to Aiken's adaptation.

101.31–32 "Cassy," . . . Mrs. Bellamy] Eliza's mother in *Uncle Tom's Cabin*, played in the production at Barnum's American Museum by Mrs. William Hoare Bellamy (d. 1857), Scottish-born actor.

101.38–39 the real water of Mr. Crummles's pump] In Dickens's *Nicholas Nickleby*.

102.10–11 "free play of mind"] Cf. the phrase "free disinterested play of mind" in "The Function of Criticism at the Present Time" in *Essays in Criticism* (1865) by English poet and critic Matthew Arnold (1822–1888).

102.28 Kenwigs tradition of pantalettes and pigtails] Children of the Kenwigs family in *Nicholas Nickleby.*

103.34–39 Ravels, French acrobats . . . offshoots of Martinettis and others] The family of French acrobat Gabriel Ravel (including his son Jean and grandchildren Gabriel, Antoine, Angelique, Jerome, and François), accompanied by other acrobats, mimes, and performers, were a popular attraction at the Park and Niblo's Garden theaters. Members of Paul Martinetti's family of acrobats were among the European performers who joined them or performed in successor troupes, sometimes billed under the Martinetti name.

104.9 Raoul or the Night-Owl] Conflation of titles of two pantomimes staged by the Ravels' troupe: *Mazulme, or The Night Owl*; and *Raoul, or The Magic Star.*

104.31–32 Martinetti Jocko] Paul Martinetti played the role of Jocko in hundreds of performances of *Jocko, or, The Brazilian Ape.*

105.10–11 Signor Léon Javelli] French-born tightrope walker and mime (1821–1854), a member of the Ravels' troupe.

106.3 Franconi's] Franconi's Hippodrome, 1853–54, at Broadway and 23rd Street.

106.9 Crystal Palace, second of its name] Glass-and-metal exhibition hall on what is now Bryant Park, 1853–58, inspired by and named for the Crystal Palace built in London's Hyde Park for the Great Exhibition of 1851.

106.9–10 not *passibus æquis*] Latin: [not] with equal steps. See Virgil, *Aeneid,* II.724.

106.11–12 Paris Palais de l'Industrie of 1855] Palace of Industry, 1855–97, built for the Universal Exposition in Paris in 1855.

106.16 "talma"] Long cape, sometimes hooded, named for the French actor François Joseph Talma (1763–1826).

106.23–24 Thorwaldsen's enormous Christ and the Disciples] Sculptures (1821–27) of Christ and the twelve apostles by Danish sculptor Bertel Thorvaldsen (1770–1844) created for the Church of Our Lady in Copenhagen.

106.36–37 Kiss's mounted Amazon attacked by a leopard or whatever] *Mounted Amazon Attacked by a Panther* (1837–41), bronze statue by German sculptor August Kiss (1802–1865).

108.11–13 Gus Barker . . . cut short, in a cavalry dash] Augustus Barker, a captain in the Fifth Regiment, New York Cavalry, was shot by a Confederate sniper behind Union lines near Kelly's Ford, Virginia, September 17, 1863, and died the following day.

111.34 *étape*] French: stopping-place.

112.12 M. Arsène Houssaye, Philosophes et Comédiennes] Book (1851; *Philosophers and actresses*) by French critic, editor, poet, and novelist Arsène Houssaye (1815–1896), administrator of the Comédie Française 1849–59 (see note 49.14–16).

112.30 *chronique galante* of the eighteenth century] Or *histoire galante*, French mostly fictional genre that focused on the private and often the amorous life of its protagonists.

112.35–36 the Confessions . . . of the celebrated "Rosseau."] The *Confessions* by Jean-Jacques Rousseau (1712–1778) (see *Notes of a Son and Brother*, p. 462).

115.39–40 That was all the witchcraft the occasion used] Cf. Shakespeare, *Othello*, I.iii.169: "This only is the witchcraft I have us'd."

118.19 *falot*] French: wan, said of a light.

120.8 ranz-des-vaches] Swiss French dialect: literally "rows of cows," a melody played or sung to assist in the herding of cattle.

122.6–10 Count Adam Gurowski . . . so polyglot] Polish writer Adam Gurowski (1805–1866), who spent his last seventeen years in the United States, worked for the *New-York Tribune* and as a translator for the State Department, and was known for speaking eight languages.

124.13–19 Alphonse Daudet's chronicle of "Jack,"] The novel *Jack* (1876) by James's friend the French writer Alphonse Daudet (1840–1897); "petits pays chauds" ("little hot countries") refers to children from abroad who attended the boarding school depicted in the novel.

124.29 *dictées*] French: dictations.

128.22 Serjeant Buzfuz's exposure of Mr. Pickwick.] In Dickens's *The Pickwick Papers* (1836–37), Serjeant Buzfuz is the prosecuting attorney for Mrs. Bardell, Samuel Pickwick's landlady, in the lawsuit she has brought against Pickwick for breach of promise of marriage.

128.26 novels of the once-admired Theodore of that name] American lawyer, traveler, and writer Theodore Winthrop (1828–1861), killed fighting for the Union during the Civil War, whose writings include three novels posthumously published in 1862: *Cecil Dreeme*, *John Brent*, and *Edwin Brothertoft*.

130.4 *barbiche*] French: goatee.

130.24–25 aspects of that season as Mr. Jenks's image presides;] Peter Collister, in his edition of *A Small Boy and Others*, includes as an appendix a passage he found in the Houghton Library in a sheaf of forty-seven typescript pages catalogued as "*Notes of a Son and Brother*, TS. with autograph revision. Scattered fragments of an early draft" (bMS Eng 1213 [72]). The passage in question, Collister persuasively suggests, might have been intended for Chapter 15 or 16 of *A Small Boy and Others*, since they evoke an episode in James's New York schooldays. "Johnny" here has not been clearly identified.

> I might happily offer him the tribute of a gay cornucopia of sweets bought of no less a purveyor than Dean, the celebrated confectioner, then near at hand? I had sallied forth with timely art, leaving Johnny, more distressed than elate, I inferred, upon the scene, and I hovered, to waylay him, where I knew he must presently pass. I recognised in fact before long his approach, but perceived also, to my dismay, that, flushed and disordered, with his spectacles awry, he was bathed in angry tears and came along in a passion of grief or of resentment, talking to himself aloud and beating the air with the pair of books he carried. Painful the shock of the sight and dire for me, as I feel it again, the instant of indecision—during which I stood gaping with my packet of candies. The next moment I had chosen, or at least had acted—for choice was sharply impossible as to whether I should most aggravate his woe by interrupting or by ignoring it. Vivid to me even now is the whole opposition of aspects—that of the feared "false note" of my offering and that, which affected me as the uglier, of his seeing me, token in hand, let him unconsoledly pass. I had doubtless never yet had so many fine grains for the scales of analysis to weigh. But what I best recall is his momentary lapse, on my sudden thrust; his stare, through his tears or as from far off, not in the least at me, for whom he hadn't a glance, but only at the object placed in his grasp—any word from my lips quite impossible with it; and the resumed anguish of his walk, in which he seems to have passed from me for ever, making his points now with both hands monologuing and asseverating in the saddest public manner and [amid?] the bland brightness of Broadway. *That* was the abiding image and the queer little tragedy, that even of such material in part, the overschooled, the spectacled, the sensitive, the already wounded, the already sacrificed, had the great grim hecatombs been composed.

A child's diary of mid-nineteenth-century New York states that "Down Broadway, below Eighth Street is Dean's candy store, and they make molasses candy that is the best in the city" (*Diary of a Little Girl in Old New York* [1849–1850] by Catherine Elizabeth Havens, New York: Henry Collins Brown, 1920). Jenks's school was at 689 Broadway, just below Fourth Street, and James emphasizes how much time the pupils spent on Broadway; so it seems a more likely location for this episode than James's next school, that of "Messrs. Forest and Quackenboss, who carried on business at the northwest corner of Fourteenth Street and Sixth Avenue."

130.32 Doctor Anthon] American classical scholar and longtime Columbia College professor Charles Anthon (1797–1867).

130.34–35 sterner discipline of Andrews and Stoddard] Latin textbook (*A Grammar of the Latin Language, for Use of Schools and Colleges*, 1836) by American educators Ethan Allen Andrews (1787–1858) and Solomon Stoddard (1800–1847).

130.39 rival, the Columbia College school] The Columbia Grammar and Preparatory School, founded in 1764.

131.28 *trempe*] French: stamp, character.

137.10–11 Romulus . . . Remus] Romulus and Remus, the brothers who according to legend were the founders of Rome, were found and suckled by a she-wolf, after being abandoned to die as newborn infants.

142.25–26 *tutti quanti*] Italian: all such, all of those.

143.31 elder Jarves] Probably English-born American portrait painter John Wesley Jarvis (1780–1839).

143.37 Mayor . . . I think Mr. Varick.] Richard Varick (1753–1831), mayor of New York City, 1789–1801. They were married on July 28, 1840, not by Varick but by Isaac Leggett Varian (1793–1864), the city's mayor, 1835–42.

144.26 *en règle.*] French: in proper form, by the book.

145.20 through an injury received in youth)] One of Henry James Sr.' s legs had been amputated above the knee after being burned in a fire when he was twelve or thirteen.

145.32 Bloomingdale] Area in the western side of Upper Manhattan.

146.19 *jarret tendu*] French: with leg extended.

146.23 outbreak of the Civil War, as a General of volunteers] In 1861 the dancing instructor Edward Ferrero (1831–1899) raised the 51st New York Infantry Regiment (also known as the "Shepard Rifles") and as its commander was given the rank of colonel.

147.28 mousquetaire de Louis Quinze] Musketeer during the reign of French king Louis XV (1710–1774).

148.5–6 the visit of the great Grisi and the great Mario] In 1854 the Italian opera singers Guilia Grisi (1811–1869), a soprano, and her longtime companion Giovanni Matteo de Candia (1810–1883), the tenor known as Mario, toured the United States.

148.11–12 Norma and Lucrezia Borgia] *Norma*, see note 73.5; *Lucrezia Borgia* (1833), opera by Italian composer Gaetano Donizetti (1797–1848).

148.18 débardeur] French: stevedore; here a carnival costume based on the stevedore's work-clothes made popular through the lithographs of Gavarni (see note 15.27).

149.32–33 as unwittingly as M. Jourdain expressed himself in prose] In Molière's comedy *Le Bourgeois gentilhomme* (1670; *The Bourgeois gentleman*), M. Jourdain is delighted to discover that he has been unwittingly speaking in prose his entire life.

150.1–2 Franconia stories . . . Rollo series] American clergyman and educator Jacob Abbott (1803–1879) was a prolific writer of children's books, including many novels about a young boy named Rollo and the ten-volume "Franconia" series. For some of his books he collaborated with his brother John (1805–1877).

151.18 Mr. Channing] Unitarian theologian and social reformer William Ellery Channing (1780–1842).

151.26–27 Ladies of the Sacred Heart . . . Bloomingdale, if they were not already in part established there] The Catholic Society of the Sacred Heart established their school and teachers' convent on their Upper Manhattan campus (between West 130th and West 135th streets) in 1847.

155.3 that heir of all the ages] From Tennyson's 1842 poem "Locksley Hall."

156.5 *pas seul*] French: solo dance.

156.5 garment of "Turkey red"] Cotton garment dyed bright red.

156.7 *dessous*] French: underwear.

157.30 Doctor Anthon's?] The Columbia College Preparatory School, presided over by Charles Anthon (see notes 130.32, 130.39).

161.27 Mr. Benjamin Haydon] English history painter and writer Benjamin Robert Haydon (1786–1846).

161.30 Düsseldorf collection in Broadway;] The Düsseldorf Gallery, at 548 Broadway.

161.31 canvas of the Martyrdom of John Huss] *Hus vor dem Scheiterhaufen* (1850; *Hus at the Stake*) by German artist Karl Friedrich Lessing (1808–1880), depicting the execution of Jan Hus (1369?–1415), Czech religious reformer condemned to death as a heretic.

162.3 Düsseldorf school] School of Romantic painting focusing on landscape and genre scenes that emerged from the Academy of Art in Düsseldorf under the directorship of German painter Friedrich Wilhelm Schadow (1789–1862).

162.19–20 masterpiece of Mr. Leutze . . . Washington crossing the Delaware] Painting (1851) by German-born American artist Emanuel Leutze (1816–1868).

163.9–10 Bryan's Gallery of Christian Art] The art collection of more than two hundred works acquired in Europe by American collector Thomas J. Bryan (1802–1870), exhibited at several locations before being given to the New-York Historical Society in 1867.

163.16 grave suspicion] As to the provenance and authenticity of many of the works Bryan collected.

163.33–34 the ample canvas of Mr. Cole] Thomas Cole's *View of Florence from San Miniato* (1837), oil painting now in the collection of the Cleveland Museum of Art.

164.34 French painter, M. Lefèvre] Robert-Jacques-François Lefèvre (1755–1830).

166.31 *agrément*] French: pleasure, delight.

167.14–16 Civil War . . . laid down before Petersburg a young life] Vernon King, an officer in Robert Gould Shaw's black regiment the 54th Massachusetts Infantry (see note 402.14–16), was killed on June 15, 1864, during the Union assault on Petersburg, Virginia, June 15–18.

167.26 *dame de compagnie*] French: a female paid companion.

168.22 flourishing farce of Betsy Baker] *Betsy Baker; or, Too Attentive by Half* (1849), farce by English playwright John Maddison Morton (1811–1891).

170.16 *modiste*] French: milliner.

171.20 *vie de province*] French: provincial life.

171.33 "bonne Lorraine"] French: a good female servant from Lorraine.

175.38 petits pays chauds] See note 124.13–19.

175.40 *à la portée*] French: within reach.

176.30–31 Rodolphe Toeppfer's Voyages en Zigzag, the two goodly octavo volumes] Illustrated book (1844) and its sequel *Nouveaux voyages en zigzag* . . . (1854) by Swiss writer and cartoonist Rodolphe Töppfer (1799–1846).

177.6–7 association makes that faded Swiss master of landscape Calame] Some of the engraved illustrations in Töppfer's *Voyages en zigzag* are based on works by Swiss artist Alexandre Calame (1810–1864).

177.8 Ruysdael] Dutch painter and etcher Jacob van Ruysdael (1628 or 1629–1682).

178.3 malle-poste] French: mail coach.

178.10 "rien que pour saluer ces dames,"] French: only to greet these ladies.

179.8–9 The Order of Release of a young English painter, J. E. Millais] *The Order of Release 1746* (1852–53) by the English Pre-Raphaelite painter John Everett Millais (1829–1896).

181.14 Lambs' Tales from Shakespeare] The children's adaptation *Tales from Shakespeare* (1807) by English essayist and critic Charles Lamb (1775–1834) and his sister Mary Lamb (1764–1847).

183.37–184.2 Madame Tussaud's . . . Chamber of Horrors] The Baker Street Bazaar, where the collection of wax figures by Strasbourg-born artist Marie Tussaud (1761–1850), first displayed in London in 1802, were permanently exhibited starting in 1835. Its Chamber of Horrors contained figures as well as torture instruments and items relating to notorious crimes.

184.1 Mrs. Manning] Marie Manning (1821–1849), a Swiss lady's maid who with the help of her husband murdered her lover, Frederick O'Connor, in an attempt to take possession of his financial assets. Both Mannings were hanged for the crime, known as the "Bermondsey Horror," on November 13, 1849.

184.2 Burke and Hare] William Burke (1792–1829) and William Hare (c. 1792–1859?) robbed graves and committed murders to sell corpses to Edinburgh medical schools.

185.2 night of the Deux-Décembre] December 2, 1851, date of the coup d'état in which French ruler Louis-Napoléon (1808–1873) seized power and dismissed the French National Assembly.

185.2 micawberish] Baselessly optimistic; in Dickens's *David Copperfield*, Micawber is a debtor who lives in cheerful optimism about his future prospects (see also note 72.1–2).

185.28 *ramage*] French: warbling.

185.29 wood-note wild] Cf. *L'Allegro* (1631), lines 133–34, where English poet John Milton imagines going to the theater to hear "sweetest Shakespear fancies childe, / Warble his native Wood-notes wilde."

186.15–16 George Cruikshank's Artful Dodger and his Bill Sikes and his Nancy] Criminal characters in Dickens's novel *Oliver Twist* (1838), as illustrated by George Cruikshank (see note 75.33).

186.24 quite a Hogarth, side] William Hogarth (1697–1764), English painter and printmaker best known as a satirist, in works like *Gin Lane* (1751).

186.28 *per contra*] Latin: on the other hand.

189.3 B. R. Haydon] See note 161.27.

189.7–8 Banishment of Aristides] Painting first exhibited in 1846.

189.14 hapless artist's Autobiography] Haydon committed suicide in 1846. *Life of Benjamin Robert Haydon, Historical Painter, from his Autobiography and Journals*, edited by English playwright Tom Taylor (1817–1880), was published posthumously in 1853.

189.28 English collection, the Vernon bequest to the nation] English businessman and art collector Robert Vernon (1774–1849) gave his collection of British art to the nation in 1847.

189.34–35 Maclise, Mulready and Landseer, to David Wilkie and Charles Leslie.] Irish painter and illustrator Daniel Maclise (1806–1870); Irish artist William Mulready (1786–1863); English painter Sir Edwin Landseer (1802–1873), whose specialty was paintings of animals; Scottish painter Sir David Wilkie (1785–1841); Charles Robert Leslie (1794–1859), English artist born to American parents.

189.38 Maclise's Play-scene in Hamlet] *The Play Scene in "Hamlet"* (1842), painting now in the collection of Tate Britain, depicting the performance of the play-within-the-play in *Hamlet*.

190.1–2 Leslie's Sancho Panza and his Duchess] The painting *Sancho Panza in the Apartment of the Duchess* (1843–44), now in the collection of Tate Britain, illustrating a scene in Cervantes's *Don Quixote* (1605–15).

190.8 the Pre-Raphaelite efflorescence] The Pre-Raphaelite Brotherhood was founded in London in 1848 by the English artists Dante Gabriel Rossetti (1828–1882), William Holman Hunt (1827–1910), and John Everett Millais, and soon included other artists. Rejecting the dominant modes of contemporary painting as taught by England's Royal Academy, they created highly realistic, meticulously detailed paintings of religious and literary, often medieval, subjects.

190.17 Holman Hunt's Scapegoat] Holman Hunt's 1854 painting of the biblical animal from the book of Leviticus—also referred to in James's 1904 novel *The Golden Bowl* (Ch. 36).

190.24–26 M. Léon Coigniet . . . Ruins of Carthage] *Marius Among the Ruins of Carthage* (1824), painting by French artist Léon Cogniet (1794–1880).

191.6–7 Mr. Albert Smith's once-famous representation of the Tour of Mount Blanc.] Popular theatrical entertainment *Mr. Albert Smith's Ascent of Mont Blanc*, first performed at the Egyptian Hall in London in 1852, by the English mountaineer and author Albert Smith (1816–1860), based on his experience climbing the mountain in 1851.

191.23–25 Princess's, then under the management of Charles Kean . . . Shakespearean revivalist] In 1850 English actor Charles Kean (1811–1868) leased the Princess's Theatre in Oxford Street, London, and staged revivals of Shakespeare plays there through 1859.

191.26–27 Alfred Wigan, the extraordinary and too short-lived Robson . . . Mrs. Stirling] English actors Alfred Wigan (1814–1878), Frederick Robson (1821–1864), and Fanny Stirling (1815–1895); "Mr. Ryder" (see page 191) is English actor John Ryder (1814–1885).

191.31–32 Queen Katharine's dream-vision . . . on the way to the scaffold.] References to the masque-like vision of "six personages, clad in white robes" (*Henry VIII*, IV.ii), Wolsey's elegiac speech (III.ii.203–27), and Buckingham's speech as he goes to face "the long divorce of steel" (II.i.56–136).

192.22–24 Hogarth and Zoffany . . . the Mrs. Cibbers and the Mrs. Pritchards] English actors portrayed by German-born English artist Johann Zoffany (c. 1733–1810): Susannah Maria Cibber (1714–1766) in *David Garrick as Jaffier and Susannah Cibber as Belvidera in* Venice Preserv'd (1762–63), and Hannah Vaughan Pritchard (1711–1768) in *David Garrick as Macbeth and Hannah Pritchard as Lady Macbeth* (c. 1768). Another painting of Cibber on the stage, *Susannah Cibber as Cordelia* (1755), is not by Hogarth or Zoffany but by Pieter van Bleeck (fl. 1723–1764).

192.27–31 Still Waters Run Deep . . . Charles de Bernard's novel of Un

Gendre] *Still Waters Run Deep* (1855) was a stage adaptation by Tom Taylor (see note 189.14) of *Le Gendre* (1841; *The son-in-law*), novella by Charles de Bernard, pseudonym of novelist and journalist Charles-Bernard du Grail de la Villette (1805–1850), discussed by James in "The Minor French Novelists" (1876).

192.28–29 old friend Fanny Kemble's] In 1893 James published an essay on "Frances Anne Kemble" (1809–1895), an English actor and writer he had first met in 1873.

193.8 Planché's extravaganza of The Discreet Princess] *The Discreet Princess; or, The Three Glass Distaffs* (1855), billed as a "fairy extravaganza," by English playwright and actor James Robinson Planché (1796–1880).

193.14 parody of Charles Kean in The Corsican Brothers;] Popular stage adaptation (1852) by Dion Boucicault (see note 69.24–25) of an 1844 story by Alexandre Dumas *père* (1802–1870), in which Kean played both lead roles, those of the play's titular brothers.

193.15–17 his Daddy Hardacre . . . Balzac's Eugénie Grandet.] Robson played the title role in *Daddy Hardacre* (1857), two-act play by English playwright John Palgrave Simpson (1807–1887) based on *Eugénie Grandet* (1833), novel by French novelist Honoré de Balzac (1799–1850).

193.32–35 Charles Matthews in Sheridan's Critic and in a comedy botched from the French . . . called Married for Money;] Mathews (see note 73.31–33) starred in a revival of *The Critic* (1779), play by Irishborn dramatist Richard Brinsley Sheridan (1751–1816), and in *Married for Money* (1855), based on *Le jeune mari* (1826; *The young husband*) by French playwright Édouard-Joseph-Ennemond Mazères (1796–1866).

195.2 *fin*] French: clever, sharp, shrewd.

196.23 *communs*] French: outbuildings.

197.8 Victor Cherbuliez] Swiss born French novelist (1829–1899), published in the *Revue des Deux Mondes*, whose *Paule Méré* (1865) is mentioned in James's *Daisy Miller* (1878).

197.11 Sainte-Beuve of the Causeries] Charles-Augustin Sainte-Beuve (1804–1869), French literary historian and critic whose weekly newspaper essays were known as "Causeries du lundi" ("Monday Chats"). On September 20, 1867, James wrote to his friend T. S. Perry that "deep in the timorous recesses of my being is a vague desire to do for our dear old English letters and writers something of what Ste. Beuve & the best French critics have done for theirs."

197.24 *taille*] French: waist.

197.25 Miss Rebecca Sharp] Morally questionable heroine of Thackeray's novel *Vanity Fair* (1847–48).

197.28–29 l'ingénieux petit] French: the clever little.

198.34–35 the great free hand soon to be allowed to Baron Haussmann] From 1853, French civil administrator Georges-Eugène Haussmann (1809–1891) directed the radical transformation of Paris under Louis-Napoléon (Napoléon III), which included the destruction of many of the city's medieval streets and the creation of wide boulevards.

199.9 Jardin d'Hiver] See note 35.2–3.

199.19–20 two matched lodges of the octroi] See note 35.4–5.

199.23–24 Avenue of the Empress, now, so much more thinly, but of the Wood itself] The Avenue de l'Impératrice, at the time of James's writing called Avenue du Bois de Boulogne, and since 1929 Avenue Foch.

199.25 the Empress herself] The Spanish-born Eugénie, Empress of France, 1853–71 (born Eugénia Maria de Montijo de Guzmán, Countess of Teba, 1826–1920).

199.29–36 baby Prince Imperial . . . Prince's baptism at Notre Dame, the fête of Saint-Napoléon] The baptism of the only son of Napoléon III and Empress Eugenie, Napoléon Eugène Louis Jean Joseph Bonaparte (1856–1879), took place at the cathedral of Notre-Dame in Paris on June 14, 1856, followed the next day with a celebration to coincide with the birthday of Napoléon Bonaparte.

199.32 *cent-gardes*] French: Emperor's bodyguards, created in 1854.

199.38 Eugène Rougon of Emile Zola] *Son Excellence Eugène Rougon* (1876; *His excellency Eugène Rougon*), the sixth of the twenty Rougon-Macquart novels by French writer Émile Zola (1840–1902), which James said in 1876 showed "brutal indecency."

200.6 biggest and brightest illumination] Fireworks display.

200.27–28 Guignol and of Gringalet . . . Polichinelle and his puppets] Puppet-show characters Guignol and his son, Gringalet; Polichinelle is the French name for Italian *commedia dell'arte* character Pulcinella.

201.7 *ours*] French: bear.

201.25 many-windowed *premier*] French: first floor, above the ground floor.

201.39 *bavards*] French: chatty, garrulous people.

202.2 marchand-de-bois] French: wood-seller.

202.11 ouvrière] French: female worker, seamstress.

204.5 jeune homme] French: young man.

204.15 unmenaced, the inviolate Café Foyot] A bomb planted by anarchists exploded inside the Café Foyot on April 4, 1894.

204.26 Les Français Peints par Eux-Mêmes] Illustrated multivolume edition (1840–42; *The French painted by themselves*). See also note 204.31–35.

204.26–27 of Gavarni, of Grandville, of Henri-Monnier] Gavarni, see note 15.27; Grandville, pseudonym of French caricaturist and illustrator Jean-Ignace-Isidore Gérard (1803–1847). Henri-Monnier, see note 88.3–5.

204.31–35 Balzac . . . exposition there of the contrasted types of L'Habituée des Tuileries and L'Habituée du Luxembourg] There were five entries by Balzac in *Les Français Peints par Eux-Mêmes*, but the essay on the contrasting types frequenting the Tuileries and the Jardin du Luxembourg was written by French writer and traveler Jacques Arago (1790–1855).

204.35 *serré*] French: packed, clotted.

205.15 Couture's Romains de la Décadence, recently acclaimed] History painting (*The Romans During the Decadence*, 1847) by French artist Thomas Couture (1815–1879), exhibited to high critical praise at the 1847 Paris Salon.

205.22 William Hunt] American painter (1824–1879) who taught William James, as well as James himself and the American artist John La Farge (1835–1910); see *Notes of a Son and Brother*, pp. 292–94.

205.27 Edouard Frère] French painter Pierre Édouard Frère (1819–1886).

205.29–30 Troyon, Rousseau, Daubigny, even Lambinet] French artists affiliated with the Barbizon school of landscape painters: Constant Troyon (1810–1865), Théodore Rousseau (1812–1867), Charles-François Daubigny (1817–1878), and Émile Charles Lambinet (1813–1877). The memory of a painting by Lambinet is cherished by Lambert Strether, the hero of James's novel *The Ambassadors* (1903).

205.39 beautiful Page with a Falcon] *The Falconer* (1844–45).

206.36 Paul Delaroche] French painter of historical subjects (1797–1856).

206.39–40 La Barque du Dante] Painting (1822) by French artist Eugène Delacroix (1798–1863).

207.3 Les Enfants d'Edouard] Delaroche's painting (*The Children of Edward*, 1830) depicting the sons of English king Edward IV imprisoned in the Tower of London and about to be murdered.

207.16–17 commemorative show of Delaroche] The posthumous exhibition (1857) of Delaroche's works at the Palais des Beaux-Arts in Paris.

207.24–25 Lady Jane Grey . . . Charles the First] Delaroche's paintings *The Execution of Lady Jane Grey* (1833) and *Charles I Insulted by Cromwell's Soldiers* (1836).

207.36 Decamps] French artist Alexandre-Gabriel Decamps (1803–1860).

210.26–32 Géricault's Radeau de la Méduse . . . Guérin's Burial of Atala, Prudhon's Cupid and Psyche, David's helmetted Romanisms, Madame Vigée-Lebrun's "ravishing" portrait of herself and her little girl] Paintings by French artists: *The Raft of the Medusa* (1818–19) by Théodore Géricault (1791–1824);

Burial of Atala (1808) by Anne-Louis Girodet de Roucy-Trioson (1767–1824); possibly *Psyche and Cupid* (1798) by François Gérard (1770–1837), or *The Abduction of Psyché* (1808) by Pierre-Paul Prud'hon (1758–1823); the neoclassical depictions of Roman antiquity by Jacques-Louis David (1748–1825); one of two self-portraits by Louise Élisabeth Vigée-Lebrun (1755–1842) with her daughter in the collection of the Louvre.

211.24–26 vast Veronese, at Murillo's moon-borne Madonna, at Leonardo's almost unholy dame] *The Wedding at Cana* (1563) by Italian artist Paolo Caliari, known as Veronese (1528–1588); *Immaculate Conception* (1678) by Spanish painter Bartolomé Esteban Murillo (1617–1682); *La Gioconda* (c. 1503–1519) or the Mona Lisa by Italian artist Leonardo da Vinci (1452–1519), described by Walter Pater in *The Renaissance* (1873): "like the vampire, she has been dead many times, and learned the secrets of the grave." The Murillo and Veronese figure in the first and second chapters respectively of James's *The American* (1877).

213.23 *féerie*] French: enchanted spectacle.

213.25 Le Diable d'Argent] Play (*The Money Devil*, 1820) by French writers Armand d'Artois (1788–1867), Edmond Rochefort (1790–1871), and Emmanuel Théaulon (1787–1841).

213.28 *donnée*] French: theme, subject.

214.8 Rachel] See note 49.14–16.

214.9–13 Mademoiselle Mars . . . Mlle. Georges . . . Déjazet and Frédéric Lemaître and Mélingue and Samson] French actors: Anne-Françoise-Hippolyte Boutet (1779–1847), known as Mademoiselle Mars; Marguerite-Joséphine Weimer (1787–1867), known as Mademoiselle George; Virginie Déjazet (1798–1875), also a theater owner; Frédérick Lemaître (1800–1876), famous for his portrayal of the criminal Robert Macaire; Étienne Marin Mélingue (1808–1875), also a painter and sculptor; Joseph-Isidore Samson (1793–1871), also a playwright.

214.24 *spectacle coupé*] A performance consisting of excerpts from several plays.

214.24–25 Mesdames Rose Chéri, Mélanie, Delaporte and Victoria (afterwards Victoria-La-fontaine)] French actors: Rose-Marie Cizos (1824–1861), known as Rose Chéri; Dinah Félix (1836–1909), known as Madame Mélanie or Madame Mélanie-Émilie, the youngest sister of the actor Rachel; Marie Delaporte (1838–1910); and Victoria Valous (1841–1918), known as Victoria Lafontaine after her marriage.

214.27 baignoire] French: box in the lowest tier of a theater.

214.27–28 Madame de Girardin's Une Femme qui Déteste son Mari] Comedy (*A Wife Who Hates Her Husband*, first staged in 1856) by the French poet, newspaper writer, novelist, and playwright Delphine de Girardin (1804–1855).

214.38 *tenue*] French: bearing.

215.9 *physique ingrat*] French: unprepossessing physical appearance.

215.18 the then still admired Ponsard, Ce qui Plaît aux Femmes] Play (1860; *What pleases women*) by French dramatist François Ponsard (1814–1867).

215.22 Mademoiselle Fargeuil, the heroine?] French actor Anaïs Fargueil (1819–1896) played the role of the Countess in the 1860 production of Ponsard's play.

215.29–30 *revendeuse*] French: female retailer or secondhand dealer.

215.37–216.1 veteran of the stage, Mademoiselle Pierson . . . a very juvenile beauty] French actor Blanche Pierson (1842–1919), who made her stage debut at the age of eleven.

216.7–8 she had given all Sardou's earlier successes the help of her shining firmness] Fargueil acted in several early plays of French playwright Victorien Sardou (1831–1908), including *Les femmes fortes* (1860; *The strong women*), *Nos intimes* (1861; *Our intimates*), and *Les diables noirs* (1863; *The black devils*).

216.10–11 Patrie . . . Ambigu] Sardou's historical drama *Patrie* (1869) was first performed at the Théâtre de l'Ambigu in Paris.

216.34 *assouplissement*] French: softening-up, making supple.

217.8 thinness of the school of Scribe] Followers of French playwright Eugène Scribe (1791–1861), author of hundreds of plays alone or in collaboration, noted for his handling of stagecraft and plot construction.

217.10 the younger Dumas and Augier] French writer Alexandre Dumas *fils* (1824–1895); French playwright and poet Émile Augier (1820–1889), author of *L'aventurière* (1848; *The adventuress*); *Le mariage d'Olympe* (1855; *Olympe's marriage*), *Lions et renards* (1869; *Lions and foxes*), and many other plays.

218.4–5 Daudet's lean asylum for the *petits pays chauds*] See note 124.13–19.

218.33–34 Charles Fourier and in his scheme of the "phalanstery"] Utopian French social theorist Charles Fourier (1772–1837) proposed a new model of social organization made up of autonomous collectives of 1,620 people (one phalanx) living in communal buildings called "phalansteries."

219.7 Hawthorne's co-operative Blithedale] In Nathaniel Hawthorne's novel *The Blithedale Romance* (1852), a fictional communal experiment based largely on Brook Farm, 1841–47, cooperative near West Roxbury, Massachusetts, whose members included prominent Transcendentalists, and for a time Hawthorne himself.

219.10 where Balzac had ended his life] At his final home in the rue Fortunée in Paris, now rue Balzac in the 8th arrondissement.

219.23 *externes*] Day students.

219.27 *pensionnat*] French: boarding school; a *pension* is a boardinghouse.

219.35 a Daudet *méridional*] A person from southern France like those in Daudet's writings.

220.16 Talma] French actor François-Joseph Talma (1763–1826).

220.28 *mouchards*] French: spies, informants.

220.36 Le Cid] Tragedy (1637) by French playwright Pierre Corneille (1606–1684); "Nous nous levons alors" ("Then we leapt up") is from IV.iii.27.

221.14–15 *quand même*] French: all the same.

221.34 bonnes] French: female domestic servants.

222.19–20 the late M. Henry Houssaye, the shining hellenist and historian] French historian (1848–1911) who wrote several books on classical Greece.

223.4 *beaux jours*] French: heyday, prime.

223.10 *jeunesse*] French: youth.

223.11 Castalian spring] In Greek legend, a sacred spring near Delphi whose waters possessed the power of poetic inspiration.

223.16–17 *invraisemblable*] French: improbable.

224.19 Pension Vauquer] Shabby boardinghouse, main setting in Balzac's novel *Père Goriot* (1834).

225.16 déjeuner] French: lunch.

225.35 "Punch"] See note 38.35.

226.13 *vitrines*] French: windows.

227.28 Pradier] Swiss neoclassical sculptor James Pradier (1790–1852).

228.34 *matinal*] French: of the early morning.

229.34 *en tête*] French: at the head.

230.24 chiffonier] French: ragpicker.

230.26–31 La Dame aux Camélias . . . Fechter] Novel (1848; *The lady of the camelias*) and play (1852) by Dumas *fils* (see note 217.10); actors Eugénie Doche (1821–1900) and Charles Fechter (1824–1879) starred in the original production of the play. James's story "The Siege of London" (1883) was inspired by his reaction against Dumas *fils*'s play *Le Demi-Monde* in 1877.

231.15 *bavardise*] French: chatter.

232.11 dragées de baptême] Sugar-coated almonds customarily given at baptisms for good luck.

232.16–17 "Election" cake known to us in New York] Spiced cake prepared for Election Day in the United States, a tradition dating back to the early years of the nation.

235.36 Electra of a lucidest Orestes] In Greek mythology, Electra was the sister of Orestes (see note 84.13–14). But James may be thinking of Sophocles's *Antigone* (c. 441 B.C.E.), where the eponymous heroine insists on properly burying the body of her brother Polynices against the decree of the ruler, her uncle Creon.

236.9–10 Lucy Snowe . . . Jane Eyre] Heroines of, respectively, *Villette* (1853) and *Jane Eyre* (1847) by English novelist Charlotte Brontë (1816–1855).

237.26 "financial crisis"] The Panic of 1857, severe U.S. economic crisis linked to speculation in land and railroads, among other factors.

239.24 *haute ville*] French: upper town.

239.39 *cour d'honneur*] French: grand courtyard for a building.

240.2 *perron.*] French: flight of steps.

240.9–10 *musée de province*] French: provincial museum.

240.29 *internes*] Boarding students.

240.37 awful Mutiny in India] The Indian rebellion of 1857–58, which began with a series of mutinies by Indian soldiers of the East India Company.

242.1 *babas*] Rum soaked sponge cakes.

242.4 C. B. Coquelin] French actor Constant-Benoît Coquelin (1841–1909); James published an essay on him in 1887.

242.10 *diseur*] French: reciter.

242.33–34 *entre cour et jardin*] French: between courtyard and garden.

243.24 Men's Wives] Title of a group of three stories (1843) by Thackeray; the characters listed at 243.25–30 are all taken from Thackeray's fiction, sometimes appearing in more than one novel.

243.39–40 Arthur Pendennis] Protagonist of Thackeray's *History of Arthur Pendennis* (1848–50); he is also the narrator of *The Newcomes* and *The Adventures of Philip* (1862).

245.13 *ruelles*] French: alleyways, narrow streets.

245.14–15 the first Napoleon's so tremendously mustered camp of invasion] Napoleon stationed a large army near Boulogne from 1803 to 1805 in preparation for an invasion of England that was never carried out.

247.12 *vieux temps*] French: the old days.

248.12–13 with all Matthew Arnold's "ennui of the middle ages,"] See Arnold's essay "Spinoza and the Bible" in *Essays in Criticism*, where he writes of "a street blank with all the ennui of the Middle Ages."

NOTES OF A SON AND BROTHER

258.40 Tite-Live . . . Schiller and Lessing] The Roman historian Livy (59 B.C.E.–17 C.E.); German playwright and poet Johann Cristoph Friedrich von Schiller (1759–1805); Gotthold Ephraim Lessing (1729–1781), German playwright and philosopher-critic.

259.2 talma] See note 106.16.

259.17 *causeur*] French: talker, conversationalist.

259.23–24 Rachel] See note 49.14–16.

259.28–29 "Que ces vains ornemens, que ces voiles me pèsent!"] "How these vain ornaments, these veils weigh upon me!" From *Phèdre* (1677), tragedy by French dramatist Jean Racine (1639–1699), I.iii.

259.33–34 first of his father's Nouvelles Genevoises, La Bibliothèque de mon Oncle] Collection of short stories about Genevan life (1832; *My uncle's library*) by Rodolphe Töppfer (see note 176.30–31), followed by the collection *Nouvelles genevoises* (1841; *News from Geneva*).

261.14 *magnifique gendarme*] French: magnificent policeman.

261.19 H. F. Amiel] Swiss diarist, critic, and professor at the University of Geneva Henri-Frédéric Amiel (1821–1881). His *Journal* was translated in 1885 by James's friend Mary Ward, who persuaded her uncle Matthew Arnold to write an essay on him.

261.24 Victor Cherbuliez] See note 197.8.

262.13 Vaud] Canton in southwestern Switzerland.

262.34 the Bâlois] People from Basel.

263.25–28 It was the hour . . . liberation of Lombardy; the cession of Nice and Savoie were in the air] The Austrian defeat in the Franco-Austrian War (1859; also known as the Second War of Italian Independence and the Austro-Sardinian War) resulted in the ceding of Lombardy to the Italian Kingdom of Piedmont-Sardinia, which had been allied with France in the war. Piedmont-Sardinia, enlarged after several northern Italian states elected to join it after the war, ceded Savoy and Nice to France under the terms of the Treaty of Turin (1860).

264.29–30 the two Cornhill Magazines] English literary monthly periodical, 1860–1975, first edited by William Makepeace Thackeray, in which were serialized numerous Victorian novels, including, as James mentions on p. 268, *Framley Parsonage* (1860–61) by English novelist Anthony Trollope (1815–1882). Thackeray's own *Roundabout Papers* comprises essays first published in the magazine, 1860–63. One later editor (1883–1896) was English novelist James Payn (1830–1898); see James's memorial essay on Payn in this volume, pp. 687–89.

269.8–9 the prolonged "coming-out" of The Newcomes] Thackeray's novel (see note 59.10) was serialized in the *Cornhill Magazine* from 1853 to 1855.

270.15 Once a Week . . . George Meredith and Charles Reade and J. E. Millais and George du Maurier] The illustrated English weekly magazine *Once a Week*, 1859–80, featured serialized fiction by English novelist and poet George Meredith (1828–1909) and English novelist and playwright Charles Reade (1814–1884), as well as illustrations by John Everett Millais (see note 179.8–9) and James's good friend the French-born cartoonist and writer George du Maurier (1834–1896).

270.23 Evan Harrington] George Meredith's novel (1860–61).

272.36–38 Schiller's Thirty Years' War . . . Goethe's Wahlverwandtschaften] Historical study (1790–92) by Schiller (see note 258.40); *Elective Affinities* (1809), novel by Goethe.

273.24 Hermann and Dorothea] Narrative poem (1798) by Goethe.

273.30 The House of the Seven Gables] See note 51.11–12.

274.28 the Drachenfels] Hill overlooking the Rhine from nearly one thousand feet at its summit, site of castle ruins.

275.34–35 he had solved the question simply *ambulando*] Latin: by walking. (Full phrase *solvitur ambulando*: it is solved by walking.)

276.22–23 of the Lieder or the Werther sort] Romantic and melancholic, as fitting the mood of German-language art song (*Lieder*) or, as in the case of the titular hero of Goethe's novel *Die Leiden des jungen Werthers* (1774; *The sorrows of young Werther*), suicidal.

276.24–25 for an Uhland or a Heine] German poet Ludwig Uhland (1787–1862); German-Jewish poet Heinrich Heine (1797–1856).

276.32–35 letter . . . commemorative purpose.] James freely edited the family letters included in *Notes of a Son and Brother*, sometimes rewriting, deleting, or adding passages. His nephew Henry James III objected, and James defended his practice (November 15–18, 1913): "when I laid hands upon the letters to use as so many touches and tones in the picture I frankly confess I seemed to see them in a better, or at all events in another light, here and there, than those rough and rather illiterate copies I had from you showed at their face value." The issue remains controversial.

277.39 cocher] French: coachman.

279.20 Lord Macaulay] English historian, essayist, and poet Thomas Babington Macaulay, 1st Baron Macaulay (1800–1859), author of *Essays Critical and Historical* (1843) and the widely read four-volume *History of England* (1849–55).

279.28–30 Mary Chaworth, Byron's "first love," . . . Mr. Musters] The fifteen-year-old George Gordon, Lord Byron (1788–1824) fell in love with

Mary Ann Chaworth (1786–1832), his neighbor in Nottinghamshire and a distant relation, during the summer of 1803. In 1805 she married John Musters.

280.3 "grey paper with blunt type"] From "Soliloquy of the Spanish Cloister" (1842), poem by English poet Robert Browning (1812–1889), lines 57–58: "my scrofulous French novel / On gray paper with blunt type!"

280.17 Ristori to play Mary Stuart] Ristori (see note 83.38–40) played the heroine of *Maria Stuart* (1801), historical drama by Schiller.

280.18 Jenny Wren] Character in Dickens's *Our Mutual Friend* (1864–65), a dolls' dressmaker.

282.18 Zoffingen group] In 1860 William James was elected to the Genevan section of the Zofingia Society, an academic student fraternity named for Zofingen, the village in north-central Switzerland where it was founded.

282.20 Mary Helen] James's cousin Mary Helen James Grymes (1840–1881).

287.20 Mr. James T. Fields] James Thomas Fields (1817–1881), poet, editor of the *Atlantic Monthly*, 1861–1870, Boston's most eminent publisher. He and his wife Annie Adams Fields (1834–1915), whom James remembered in a 1915 essay on them as equally "addicted to the cultivation of talk and wit," held a regular salon on Charles Street.

288.1 *parti-pris*] French: preconceived view or bias.

289.2 *gens*] French: servants.

289.9–10 Edmond About and then in Alphonse Daudet] French novelist and journalist Edmond About (1828–1885), author of *Le Roi des montagnes* (*The King of the Mountains*, 1856); Daudet, see note 124.13–19.

289.31 Revue des Deux Mondes] French literary monthly, founded in Paris in 1829.

289.39 *cadres*] French: plans, outlines.

290.5 *études de mœurs*] French: studies of manners and morals

290.6 *larbin*] French: flunkey.

290.9 Petite Comtesse] Novel (1856; *The little countess*) by French novelist and playwright Octave Feuillet (1821–1890).

291.13 quatrième] Fourth floor above the ground floor.

291.15 façade of the new Louvre] As part of the expansion of the Louvre, 1852–57, under Napoléon III, new buildings were constructed along the rue de Rivoli.

291.21–22 statues of heroes, Napoleon's young generals, Hoche, Marceau, Desaix or whoever] Three of the statues of eight French generals and marshals mounted on the Louvre's Pavillon du Rohan: Louis Lazare Hoche (1768–1797), François Séverin Marceau-Desgraviers (1769–1796), and Louis Charles Antoine Desaix (1768–1800).

292.24–25 William Hunt] See note 205.22.

293.22–23 Couture's and Frère's] See notes 205.15 and 205.27.

294.1 John La Farge] New York–born artist (1835–1910), a reader of Browning and Balzac. In the late 1870s he gave up painting for decorative work and suffered various reversals, including arrest in 1885 on bogus charges of grand larceny and, finally, mental collapse.

297.12 *Lectures and Miscellanies James*] Henry James Sr.' s *Lectures and Miscellanies* (1852).

297.14 Henry T. Tuckerman] American poet (1813–1871).

302.38 *élèves*] French: students.

303.4 Michael Angelo's "Captive" in the Louvre] One of two sculptures by Michelangelo entitled *Captive* in the Louvre: *The Dying Slave* and *The Rebellious Slave*, both made for the tomb of Pope Julius II in 1513–16 (both have uplifted faces).

303.27 *porte d'honneur*] Main entrance (literally, door or gate of honor in French).

309.1–2 *empressement*] French: willingness, eagerness.

309.33–35 adorable Fromentin . . . "Dominique"] French artist, writer, and art critic Eugène Fromentin (1820–1876), who wrote about and painted pictures of his travels in North Africa. His novel *Dominique* was serialized in the *Revue des Deux Mondes* in 1862.

310.2 a Catholic college in Maryland] Mount St. Mary's College.

310.9 Men and Women] Poetry collection (1855) by Robert Browning.

310.20 Eugénie Grandet] See note 193.15–17.

310.24–26 Mérimée . . . La Vénus d'Ille;] Short story ("The Venus of Ille," 1837) by French writer Prosper Mérimée (1803–1870). James's translation is not known to survive.

311.24 Haydon] See note 161.27.

312.17–18 *profil perdu*] French: "lost profile," a pose in which the head is turned so that much if not all of the face is not visible.

312.26 *raffiné*] French: refined, cultivated.

316.37–39 commemorative cluster of La Farge's earlier productions, gathered in on the occasion of his death] "La Farge Memorial Exhibition," Museum of Fine Arts, Boston, January 1–31, 1911.

319.25 *crânerie*] French: pluck, daring, jauntiness.

320.27 Thomas Sargeant Perry] James first befriended Perry (1845–1928), who became a wide-ranging literary historian, translator, and academic, at the Rev. W. C. Leverett's school in Newport.

322.29 excursions and alarms] Cf. English poet John Dryden (1631–1700) in his 1679 preface to Shakespeare's *Troilus and Cressida*: "the latter part of the tragedy is nothing but a confusion of Drums and Trumpets, Excursions and Alarms."

330.2–3 "on espère alors qu'on désespère toujours,"] French: one hopes even while one despairs (cf. Molière's *Le Misanthrope* [1666], I.ii: "Belle Philis, on désespère, / Alors qu'on espère toujours").

331.10–11 Poor Tom seems a-cold too.] Cf. Shakespeare, *King Lear*, III.iv.147: "Poor Tom's a-cold."

331.12 Professor Eliot, at the School] Charles William Eliot (1834–1926), chemistry professor and later president of Harvard.

331.23 Agassiz lecture (12 lectures on "Methods in Nat. Hist.")] The lectures of Swiss-born naturalist Louis Agassiz (1807–1873) given at the Lowell Institute in Boston were collected as *Methods of Study in Natural History* (1863).

331.25–26 Professor F. J. Child] American scholar and folklorist Francis James Child (1825–1896), editor of *English and Scottish Ballads* (8 vols., 1857–58) and from 1876 the first professor of English at Harvard.

332.24 Jeffries Wyman's lectures] American naturalist and anatomist Jeffries Wyman (1814–1874), professor of anatomy at Harvard.

332.26 nourris] French: stuffed with matter, substantial.

332.30 "crowded life"] Cf. Samuel Johnson, *The Vanity of Human Wishes* (1749), lines 1–4: "Let observation with extensive view, / Survey mankind, from China to Peru; / Remark each anxious toil, each eager strife, / And watch the busy scenes of crowded life."

332.33 native hue of resolution] *Hamlet*, III.i.83.

333.21–22 the "co-educational" school . . . established by Mr F. B. Sanborn at Concord, Massachusetts] Franklin Benjamin Sanborn (1831–1917), educator, biographer and abolitionist, an associate of John Brown (see note 38.30–31) who was invited to run the school by Ralph Waldo Emerson.

333.37 alas irreproducible.] The drawing was in fact included in both the American and English editions of *Notes of a Son and Brother*, and is in the present edition; see p. 335.

337.3 the Tappans'] The Boston home on Beacon Street of the family of William Aspinwall Tappan (1819–1905).

339.12–16 Commodores Perry . . . Benjamin Franklin.] On his father's side, Perry was the grandson of Oliver Hazard Perry (1785–1819), the American naval officer who was the hero of the battle of lake Erie, September 10, 1813, and the grand-nephew of Matthew Perry (1794–1858), the American naval officer who led the expedition, 1852–54, that established commercial relations with Japan, which had been closed to the West. On his mother's side, Perry was the great-great-grandson of Benjamin Franklin.

339.38 President Felton's death . . . week] Harvard president Cornelius Felton (b. 1807), influential classical scholar, died on February 26, 1862.

340.2 Dr. Peabody's] American clergyman and writer Andrew Preston Peabody (1811–1893), Harvard's Plummer Professor of Christian Morals.

340.34–35 Ganot's Physique] The physics textbook *Traité élémentaire de physique expérimental et appliquée et de météorologie* (1851) by French writer Adolphe Ganot (1804–1887), which went through many editions and was translated into English.

340.39 Charmante jeune fille] French: charming young girl.

341.15–31 Est-ce que . . . James William.] French: Do you ever dream of me as I dream of you?—oh I really don't think so! many times each day the image of a kind of angel dressed in white with long black ringlets framing a face such that most mortals glimpse it only in their dreams, thrusts itself on my ravished senses; a tall slim creature who gets ready to go to bed in a little green room where the gas makes it look like daylight. Eh, yeah, yeah, yeah! It's enough to make you die of grief. But I bet that even so not a single spark vibrates for me in the fibers of your callous heart. Alas, forgotten by my parents and my fellows, I see only, wherever I look, an abyss of despair, a black gulf peopled with demons that will sooner or later swallow me. You never write me except to extract from me luxury items. My vast mother hates me, only my brother remains attached to me, and more out of a spirit of opposition than anything else. My God, what will become of me? Anyway I will close this letter, which has grown so long in spite of me. Your brother, James William.

342.9 Wendell Phillips] American lawyer, orator, and abolitionist Wendell Phillips (1811–1884).

342.28 s'est promené à l'envi sur ma peau] French: strolled at will on my skin.

342.39–40 Governor Andrew] American lawyer and politician John Albion Andrew (1818–1867), governor of Massachusetts, 1861–66.

343.15–16 John Wilkes Booth, the "young American Roscius"] A member of the Booth theatrical family, actor John Wilkes Booth (1838–1865), later the assassin of President Lincoln, was lauded for his Shakespearean roles in the early 1860s. "Roscius" was a byword of praise for any successful actor, after the Roman actor Quintus Roscius Gallus (126?–62? B.C.E.).

343.19 Sévigné] Marie de Rabutin-Chantal, Marquise de Sévigné (1626–1696), celebrated for her prolific correspondence with her daughter, first published in 1725.

343.23 Jack Tar] Generic name for Royal Navy sailors.

347.36 Schiller's Robbers] Schiller's first play, *Die Räuber* (1781; *The robbers*).

350.12 Prof. Goodwin] American classicist William Watson Goodwin (1831–1912), professor of Greek.

350.13 the great Edward] American politician, diplomat, and Unitarian clergyman Edward Everett (1794–1865).

350.15 General Sickles] Daniel Edgar Sickles (1819–1914), a Democratic congressman from New York City, shot and killed Philip Barton Key (1818–1859), the U.S. attorney for the District of Columbia and the son of Francis Scott Key (1779–1843), author of "The Star-Spangled Banner," in Washington on February 27, 1859, shortly after he learned that Key was having an affair with his wife. Sickles was acquitted of murder in April 1859, becoming the first defendant to successfully use the defense of temporary insanity in an American court. He later served as a Union general in the Civil War and lost a leg at Gettysburg.

353.1–5 Swedenborg's works . . . Arcana Coelestia, Heaven and Hell] Emanuel Swedenborg (1688–1772), Swedish theologian, philosopher, and mystic. The eight-volume treatise *Arcana Cœlestia . . .* (*Heavenly Mysteries*, 1749–58); *Heaven and its Wonders and Hell From Things Heard and Seen* (1758), commonly known as *Heaven and Hell.*

366.20–21 nihil in vita . . . quod non prius in intellectu] Latin: there is nothing in life not already in the mind (a scholastic maxim originating in Thomas Aquinas, *Disputed Questions on Truth*).

367.16–17 book, which Greeley announces] After he was given a copy of Thomas Carlyle's *Past and Present* (1843) by Ralph Waldo Emerson, who had facilitated the publication of the book's American edition by Little & Brown in May 1843, Horace Greeley (1811–1872) praised the book in the newspaper he owned and edited, the *New-York Tribune.*

367.35–39 Jonathan Edwards . . . Schelling] Jonathan Edwards (1703–1758), New England clergyman and philosopher associated with the "Great Awakening"; German idealist philosopher Friedrich Wilhelm Joseph Schelling (1775–1854).

368.40 John Sterling] Scottish essayist and poet (1806–1844), the subject of Carlyle's biography *The Life of Sterling* (1851).

369.16 Theodore Parker] American Unitarian minister, author, and abolitionist (1810–1860).

369.34 Mill] English Utilitarian philosopher John Stuart Mill (1806–1873).

371.9 Balzac's *villes de province*] Provincial towns as depicted in the novels and tales of Balzac.

372.6–7 an accident received in early youth] See note 145.20.

372.39 G.P.R. James] English novelist and diplomat George Payne Rainsford James (1799–1860; no relation), a prolific writer who immigrated to the U.S. in 1850; his works include *Richelieu: A Tale of France* (1829) and *Ticonderoga, or The Black Eagle* (1854).

373.38 *de part et d'autre*] French: on both sides.

374.16 Dr. J. J. Garth Wilkinson] English Swedenborgian writer and physician James John Garth Wilkinson (1812–1899).

374.23 Sir Benjamin] English public-health official, civil engineer and politician Benjamin Hall (1802–1867), president of the General Board of Health, 1854–55. The bell in the Houses of Parliament, Big Ben, is named after him.

374.32 as a Niobe or as a Rachel] In Greek mythology, mother who grieves over the loss of all her children; the biblical figure of Rachel from the book of Genesis, who is said to be "weeping for her children" in Jeremiah 31:15 and Matthew 2:18.

374.33–35 much-enduring Hero is borne to the marble Invalides . . . Alma] Armand-Jacques Leroy de Saint-Arnaud (1798–1854), marshal of France, commanded French forces at the battle of Alma, September 20, 1854, an Anglo-French victory in the Crimean War. He died at sea nine days later and was buried at the Invalides in Paris.

375.11 Neuberg] German-born English businessman and man of letters Joseph Neuberg (1806–1867), who upon his retirement worked for Carlyle as a secretary and translated some of his work into German.

375.28 his recent pamphlet . . . Latter-Day-Tracts] Carlyle's *Latter-Day Pamphlets* (1850).

377.19–20 ever denied by such solemn pedants as Mr. Atkinson and Miss Martineau] The anti-religious book *Letters on the Laws of Man's Nature and Development* (1851) was cast as a series of letters between English freethinker Henry George Atkinson (1812–1890), an advocate of mesmerism and phrenology, and English writer and activist Harriet Martineau (1802–1876).

378.5–6 Arthur Helps] English historian, playwright, and civil servant Edmund Arthur Helps (1813–1875), clerk of the Privy Council, 1860–75. James reviewed his *Social Pressure* in 1875.

378.13–14 Dr. Cheever's or Brownson's] American Congregationalist minister, journalist, and poet George Barrell Cheever (1807–1890); Orestes Brownson (1803–1876), American Unitarian minister who converted to Roman Catholicism in 1844.

379.17 *acceuil*] French: reception.

381.2 là-bas] French: over there.

381.23 Ellery Channing] William Ellery Channing (1817–1901), poet, nephew, and namesake of Unitarian theologian and social reformer William Ellery Channing (1780–1842).

381.37 John Forbes] French-born American railroad magnate and abolitionist John Murray Forbes (1813–1898).

382.4–5 Tommy Titmouse] Young hero of English children's book (c. 1786), "a little boy, who became a great man by minding his learning, doing as he was bid, and being good-natured and obliging to every body."

391.16 a joyful Nunc Dimittis] Luke 2:29, from the Vulgate: "Nunc dimittis servum tuum, Domine," in the Book of Common Prayer: "Now lettest thou thy servant depart in peace."

391.23–24 Hooper band] The family of American physician Robert William Hooper (1810–1885), including his daughter Marian ("Clover," 1843–1885), photographer and friend of James, who in 1872 married the writer and historian Henry Adams (1838–1918).

394.7 *bête*] French: stupid.

394.15 *en herbe*] French: budding, in embryo.

395.23–24 that war keep smooth his wrinkled front] Cf. *Richard III*, I.i.9: "Grim-visaged War hath smooth'd his wrinkled front."

395.24–25 They must fight in Italy] In 1860 the push for Italian unification was spurred on by the recent enlargement of Piedmont-Sardinia after the Franco-Austrian War (see note 263.25–28) and the conquering of Sicily and Naples by forces led by Italian nationalist soldier Giuseppe Garibaldi (1807–1882).

396.37–39 barbaric yawp . . . not yet a "cosmos" as that gentleman avowedly is] See sections 52 and 24, respectively, of Walt Whitman's "Song of Myself" from *Leaves of Grass*, first published in 1855.

400.20 as Dryden says, or Collins] English poets John Dryden and William Collins (1721–1759); cf. *Liberty* (1735–36) by James Thomson (1700–1748), lines 614–16: "the savage crew, / That prowl amid the darkness they themselves / Have thrown around the laws."

401.7 Tartarus] In Greek mythology, place of punishment in the afterlife.

402.14–16 unsuccessful attack on Fort Wagner from which the gallant young leader of the movement was not to return.] On July 10, 1863, Union troops landed on Morris Island at the southern entrance to Charleston Harbor but failed to capture Fort Wagner at the island's northern end the following day. On July 18, Union forces led by the 54th Massachusetts Infantry, a black regiment commanded by Robert Gould Shaw (1837–1863), were repulsed with heavy losses in an unsuccessful assault on the fort. Shaw was killed during the fighting and was buried by the Confederates in a mass grave with his men.

402.35 his regiment] The 55th Massachusetts Infantry, like the 54th a black regiment with white commissioned officers.

403.5 Frank Shaw] Francis George Shaw (1809–1882), abolitionist, father of Robert Gould Shaw.

407.32 *gaudia certaminis*] Latin: joys of battle. (Byron's "Ode to Napoleon Bonaparte," line 29, "The rapture of the strife," has a note referring to "'Certaminis gaudia'—the expression of Attila in his harangue to his army, previous to the battle of Chalons, given in Cassiodorus.")

408.14 *recueil*] French: gathering, anthology, compendium.

410.15 *arva beata*] Latin: blessed fields (from Horace, *Epode* 16: "arva beata / petamus arva divites et insulas": "we seek fields, blessed fields / and rich islands").

410.21 conquered sage] Mistranscription of the original letter's "Concord sage," epithet for Ralph Waldo Emerson.

411.6 the Nortons' dinner!] At Shady Hill, the home of Charles Eliot Norton (1827–1908) and his wife Susan Ridley Norton (née Sedgwick, 1838–1872). Norton was an author and professor of art history at Harvard, 1873–97, as well as a founder of *The Nation* in 1865 and a frequent contributor to *The Atlantic Monthly* and other publications. See James's memorial essay on Norton in this volume, pp. 695–703.

411.13 Arthur Sedgwick] American lawyer (1844–1915) who worked on the editorial staff of *The Nation* and of the *New York Evening Post* (into which *The Nation* was merged).

414.34 Jane Norton?] Older sister (1824–1877) of Charles Eliot Norton.

416.3 the Gurneys] American professor of history at Harvard Ephraim Whitman Gurney (1829–1886), editor of the *North American Review*, 1868–1870, and his wife (from 1868) Ellen Sturgis Gurney (née Hooper, 1837–1887; sister of Marian, see note 391.23–24).

416.7 Godkin and his wife] Dublin-born author, editor, and publisher Edwin Lawrence Godkin (1831–1902), founder and editor of *The Nation*, 1865–81, and of the *New York Evening Post*, 1881–99. The American Frances Elizabeth Godkin (née Foote, 1835–1875) was the first of his two wives.

417.13–19 in '69 . . . William had in '68 been appointed to an instructorship in Psychology] The letter is not from 1869 but 1873; William James began teaching at Harvard as an instructor of anatomy and physiology in 1872, and was named professor of psychology in 1889.

417.32–33 Renouvier . . . Wordsworth] French philosopher Charles Bernard

Renouvier (1815–1903); in February 1873 William wrote to Henry, "I have read hardly anything of late, some of the immortal Wordsworth's excursion [*The Excursion*, 1814] having been the best."

422.7–10 the spring of '70 . . . Forrest, the American actor, of high renown] The letter is actually of March 4, 1873; Edwin Forrest (1806–1872).

423.5–6 the Bulwers, the Pelhams, the Coningsbys . . . N. P. Willises] English novelist and playwright Edward Bulwer Lytton (1803–1873), author of the "fashionable" novel *Pelham* (1828); the eponymous protagonist of *Coningsby* (1844) by English novelist and prime minister Benjamin Disraeli (1804–1881); N. P. Willis, see note 40.15–16.

424.8–9 William . . . his experience at the Somerville Asylum] Horatio Alger's son William (1822–1905), poet and successful Unitarian preacher, had suffered a severe mental breakdown in Paris in 1871 and spent several months in the McLean Asylum in Somerville, Massachusetts.

424.9 Charles Grinnell] American lawyer and author (1841–1916).

424.12 *aussi*] French: also.

424.12–13 J. G. hasn't caught a Rosamund Vincy in Miss M.] The Jameses' friend John Chipman Gray (1839–1915), a lawyer and Harvard Law School professor, married Anna Lyman Mason (1839–1915) in 1873. He had been a suitor of James's cousin Mary Temple (b. 1845), known as Minnie or Minny, who died of tuberculosis in March 1870. Their correspondence is the basis of the final chapter of *Notes of a Son and Brother*, see pp. 531–70. Rosamund Vincy is the self-centered beauty who marries Dr. Lydgate in *Middlemarch* (1871–72) by George Eliot (pseud. Mary Ann Evans, 1819–1880).

424.15 Gail Hamilton] Pseudonym of American essayist and journalist Mary Abigail Dodge (1833–1896), to whom, as editor of *Wood's Household Magazine*, 1872–73, James had sent his story "The Sweetheart of M. Briseux"—subsequently published in the *Galaxy* in June 1873.

424.17 Osgood] The Boston publisher James Ripley Osgood (1836–1892), whose May 1885 bankruptcy while *The Bostonians* was appearing was costly for James.

424.26 materials of a story] The basis of James's story "Crawford's Consistency" (*Scribner's Monthly*, August 1876), which he did not collect in his lifetime.

424.29 Matthew Henry W.] American lawyer Matthew Henry Webster (1803 or 1804–1846).

424.35 Joseph Henry of the Smithsonian] American physicist Joseph Henry (1797–1878), inaugural secretary (director) of the Smithsonian Institution, 1846–78.

426.17 a good basis. . . .] Peter Collister has pointed out that James omits his father's last words of this sentence in the original letter: "a good basis for a novel."

426.27–29 the novel of Madame Sand's . . . cherished Revue] *Francia*, first serialized in the *Revue des Deux Mondes* in 1871, by the French novelist George Sand (pseud. of Aurore Dupin, 1804–1876).

426.30 siege of Paris had been raised] In March 1871 a coalition of radical left-wing factions came to power and established the "Commune" in Paris in the aftermath of France's defeat in the Franco-Prussian War. The conservative national government, under Adolphe Thiers (1797–1877), besieged and took control of the city in May at the cost of many thousands of lives. Most of those killed were summarily executed after the fighting ended.

427.5–6 Tamaris and Valvèdre and Mademoiselle La Quintinie] Novels by George Sand published in 1862, 1861, and 1863, respectively.

427.10 Edmond de Goncourt] French naturalist novelist, art critic, and man of letters (1822–1896) whose books were written in collaboration with his brother Jules (1830–1870) until the latter's death.

427.11–12 *robe de satin fleur-de-pêcher*] French: dress of peach-blossom satin.

427.13 Blanche Amory] Character in Thackeray's *History of Arthur Pendennis* (see note 243.39–40).

427.14 *s'était fait faire*] French: had made for herself.

427.16 Dîner Magny] The Dîners Magny were fortnightly gatherings of writers and artists at the restaurant Magny in the Latin Quarter of Paris. Regular participants from 1862 through about 1875 included the writers Gustave Flaubert (1821–1880), the Goncourt brothers, Théophile Gautier (1811–1872), Charles-Augustin Sainte-Beuve, and Ivan Turgenev (1818–1883).

427.32 *y regarder*] French: to look there.

427.36–37 La Famille de Germandre, La Ville Noire, Nanon and L'Homme de Neige] Novels by Sand published in 1861, 1860, 1872, and 1859, respectively.

428.27–28 Valentine and Jacques and suchlike . . . La Mare au Diable] Sand's early novels *Valentine* (1832) and *Jacques* (1834), *La Mare au Diable* (*The Devil's Pool*) was published in 1846.

428.31 Chauncey Wright] American philosopher of science and mathematician (1830–1875), lecturer at Harvard, and a defender of Darwinism. James saw Wright within a week of the latter's death, and according to one account rushed to see his friend within minutes of his death.

429.9 yet to be writ in water.] Cf. the epitaph of English poet John Keats (1795–1821), "Here lies one whose name was writ in water," adapted from lines in Beaumont and Fletcher's play *Philaster, or Love Lies A-Bleeding* (c. 1610): "All your better deeds / Shall be in water writ."

429.28 Mount Desert] Mount Desert Island off the Maine coast.

429.33 The Eustace Diamonds] Novel (1871–73) by Anthony Trollope.

429.38–39 North American . . . Chauncey Wright's on Mivart] The July 1871 issue of the *North American Review* contained an essay by Wright that attacked the anti-Darwinian arguments of English Jesuit biologist St. George Mivart (1827–1900).

429.40 Mr. Stirling on Buckle] Scottish Hegelian philosopher James Hutchison Stirling (1820–1909) writing on English historian Henry Thomas Buckle (1821–1862), author of the unfinished *History of Civilization in England* (1856, 1861).

430.38–431.1 notice of Gustave Droz's Babolain (by T.S.P., I suppose)] Novel (1872) by French writer and artist Gustave Droz (1832–1895), reviewed by Thomas Sergeant Perry (see note 320.27). The following month, August 1871, James reviewed Droz's "excellent novel" *Autour d'une source* in English translation (as *Around a Spring*) for *The Atlantic Monthly.*

431.4 souffle] French: breath.

431.13 J. Eliot Cabot, most accomplished of Bostonians] American man of letters James Elliot Cabot (1821–1903), literary executor of Ralph Waldo Emerson. James reviewed his memoir of Emerson in 1887 as "a biography intelligently and carefully composed."

432.4 in se] Latin: in itself.

432.6 brutum fulmen] Futile threat, from Latin: insensible thunderbolt.

437.31 physical mishap] James's back injury suffered while fighting a fire in Newport; see Chronology, 1860–62.

443.1 Maison Vauquer, in Le Père Goriot] See note 224.19.

443.9 *de mieux*] French: of the best.

444.9 *plats*] French: dishes.

444.20 *in petto*] Italian: in the breast; privately, inwardly.

446.11 great sculptor] Irish-born American artist Augustus Saint-Gaudens (1848–1907), whose 1897 bronze relief sculpture depicting Robert Gould Shaw and the men of the 54th Massachusetts Infantry is installed across from the Massachusetts State House on Beacon Street in Boston.

446.16 camp life at Readville] Camp Meigs, army training camp at Readville, Massachusetts, south of Boston.

446.17–18 44th of the same State] Before joining the 55th Massachusetts Infantry, Garth Wilkinson James served with the 44th Massachusetts Infantry. James's visit to Readville occurred in the fall of 1862.

451.17–18 autocrat of that breakfast-table] A reference to *The Autocrat of the Breakfast-Table* (1858), a series of humorous and reflective essays by Oliver Wendell Holmes (1809–1894), originally published in *The Atlantic Monthly.*

452.3–4 the quips and cranks, the wreathed smiles] Cf Milton, "L'Allegro," lines 26–28: "Jest and youthful Jollity, / Quips and cranks, and wanton wiles, / Nods, and becks, and wreathed smile."

455.25–26 John May, son . . . distinguished Abolitionist of New York State] Joseph May (1836–1918), son of the Unitarian minister, abolitionist, and feminist Samuel Joseph May (1797–1871), who moved to Syracuse in 1845 and lived there the rest of his life.

455.33 by his name of Salter] Charles Christie Salter (1839–1870), who after graduating from divinity school was ordained as a Unitarian pastor.

458.16–22 silent Vanderpool . . . quasi-conservative New Jersey finish] Beach Vanderpool Jr., son of a mayor of Newark.

458.30–31 *commensal*] French: table companion.

459.19 John Bancroft] John Chandler Bancroft (1835–1901), who would go on to a successful career in business; he was also a European-trained painter and art collector, a friend of George Du Maurier (see note 270.15).

459.35–36 eminent historian of our country and earlier and later diplomatist] American historian George Bancroft (1800–1891), author of *History of the United States* (10 vols., 1834–74) and U.S. ambassador to Germany, 1867–74.

461.20 "Metternich!" or "Talleyrand!"] Renowned diplomats Klemens Wenzel von Metternich (1773–1859), foreign minister of Austria, 1809–48, and Charles Maurice de Talleyrand-Périgord (1754–1838), foreign minister of France, 1797–99, 1799–1807, 1814–15.

462.22–23 after the fashion of Rousseau in a passage of the Confessions)] See book 4 of Jean-Jacques Rousseau's *Confessions*, where he describes performing an inept musical composition of his own at the home of the Lausanne lawyer M. de Treytorrens.

464.30–465.3 the swim into my ken of Sainte-Beuve . . . Causeries du Lundi] Cf Keats's sonnet "On First Looking Into Chapman's Homer": "Then felt I like some watcher of the skies / When a new planet swims into his ken"; for Sainte-Beuve, see note 197.11.

465.11–12 Dr. Theophilus Parsons, "Governor" Washburn and Professor Joel Parker] The law professors at Harvard while James was a student there: Parsons (1797–1882) was called by Oliver Wendell Holmes Jr. "almost if not quite, a man of genius"; Emory Washburn (1800–1877) had been governor of Massachusetts, 1854–55; Parker (1795–1875) was often found dry and difficult.

466.7 *faire mon droit*] French: to study law.

469.34 Parker's] The Parker House, Boston hotel.

470.8–9 *point de repère*] French: landmark.

470.38–39 Miss Maggie Mitchell and Miss Kate Bateman] American actor Margaret Julia Mitchell (1832–1918); Kate Bateman, see note 52.35–53.2.

471.1–2 half-buried Puritan curse not so very long before devoted to such perversities.] The staging of plays in Boston was illegal for several decades after the Massachusetts legislature banned all theatrical productions in 1750.

471.20 Mr. Joe Jefferson] American actor and playwright Joseph Jefferson (1829–1905).

472.3 Pendennis's Miss Fotheringay] Young actor in Thackeray's novel, with whom Pendennis falls in love.

472.11 *réduit*] French: tiny room, retreat.

472.19 the despatch of manuscripts] Sheldon Novick in *Henry James: The Young Master* (1996) has identified the review in question, James's first published work, as a review entitled "Miss Maggie Mitchell in 'Fanchon the Cricket'" in an evening Boston newspaper, *The Daily Traveller*, on January 6, 1863.

475.3 *portée*] French: range.

477.1 G. A. J.] George Abbott James (1838–1917; no relation), who went on to practice law in Boston and married Elizabeth Cabot Lodge, sister of U.S. senator and author Henry Cabot Lodge; his sister married John Chandler Bancroft (see note 459.19).

479.25–26 after the fashion of the hare in the famous receipt.] "First catch your hare," proverbial beginning of a recipe for jugged hare sometimes misattributed to one or other of the British cookbook writers Isabella Beeton (1836–1865) and Hannah Glasse (1708–1770).

481.5 G. W. J.] Garth Wilkinson James.

482.26 l'ingénieux petit] French: the clever little.

482.38 U.S.C.T., Colonel A. P. Hallowell . . . commanding;] United States Colored Troops; the regiment was commanded by Colonel Norwood Penrose Hallowell (1839–1914).

482.40–483.2 siege of Charleston . . . camp-covered "Folly Island" of his letters.] Folly Island off Charleston was a staging area for Union troops during the siege of Charleston in 1863.

483.3 Seymour's raid on Florida] Union advances into Florida led by Brigadier General Truman Seymour (1824–1891), halted by the Confederate victory in the battle of Olustee, February 20, 1864.

483.6 General Ames's] Brigadier General Adelbert Ames (1835–1933), later a senator and governor of Mississippi during Reconstruction.

483.13 Gen'l Hartwell] Major General Alfred Stedman Hartwell (1836–1912).

483.21–22 Brigadier-Generals Potter, Rufus Hatch] Union army officers Edward Elmer Potter (1823–1889) and John Porter Hatch (1822–1901). (Rufus Hatch [1832–1893] was a financier.)

486.38–39 under Foster] Major General John Gray Foster (1823–1874), at the time commander of the Department of North Carolina.

487.7 Halleck] Major General Henry Wager Halleck (1814–1872), general in chief of the Union armies, 1862–64.

487.9–11 near Goldsboro' . . . Foster!] Foster led the victorious Union forces in fighting near Goldsboro, North Carolina, in December 1862, achieving the strategic objective of destroying a railroad bridge over the Neuse River.

488.12–13 Charles Lowell's virtue and value and death] Colonel Charles Russell Lowell Jr. (1835–1864), a Harvard graduate, was fatally wounded at Cedar Creek, Virginia, on October 19, 1864, while leading the 2nd Massachusetts Cavalry.

488.16–17 inspired kinsman's Harvard Commemoration Ode] "Ode Recited at the Harvard Commemoration, July 21, 1865," by American poet James Russell Lowell (1819 1891), Charles Russell Lowell Jr.'s uncle and later a good friend of James.

488.18 Two gallantest nephews] Charles Russell Lowell Jr.'s brother, First Lieutenant James Jackson Lowell (1837–1862), who had been at Harvard Law School, was fatally wounded in Virginia at the battle of Glendale on June 30, 1862.

488.26 Cabot] Wilky's friend Cabot Russell.

488.26 Mr. Amos Lawrence of Boston] Merchant and abolitionist Amos Adams Lawrence (1814–1886).

488.30–31 Perkins . . . Massachusetts 2nd] William Edward Perkins (b. 1838) rose to the rank of captain with the Massachusetts 2nd Infantry and was wounded at Chancellorsville.

492.11 Tillapenny River] The Tulifinny River in South Carolina.

492.33–34 The taking of Fort McAllister] Fort McAllister, near Savannah, Georgia, was captured by Sherman's forces on December 13, 1864.

492.36 Oguchee and Ossahaw] Ogeechee River and Ossabaw Sound.

493.11 Forrest is killed] An inaccurate report of the death of Confederate Brigadier General Nathan Bedford Forrest (1821–1877), cavalry division commander in the Army of Tennessee.

493.12 Rousseau] Major General Lovell Harrison Rousseau (1818–1869), commander of the District of Nashville, 1863–65.

493.12 Thomas . . . Hood] In the battle of Nashville, December 15–16, 1864, a Union force of 55,000 men under Major General George Henry Thomas (1816–1870) defeated the army of Confederate Major General John Bell Hood (1831–1879) and forced it to retreat into northern Mississippi.

493.20 Hardee] Confederate Lieutenant General William J. Hardee (1815–1873), who commanded the First Corps of the Army of Tennessee.

494.14–15 Honey Hill] Honey Hill, South Carolina, site of a battle fought on November 30, 1864, a Confederate victory.

494.19 Gen'l Stephen Lee] Confederate Lieutenant General Stephen Dill Lee (1833–1908).

495.19–20 Billy Perkins and Sam Storrow in the 2nd Mass.] Perkins, see note 488.30–31; First Lieutenant Samuel Storrow (1843–1865).

495.28–29 General Gillmore's staff as A.D.C.] Major General Quincy Adams Gillmore (1825–1888), commander of the Department of the South, July 1863–May 1864, Feb.–June 1865; A.D.C.: aide-de-camp.

496.8 Governor Aiken of S.C.] William Aiken Jr. (1806–1887), governor of South Carolina, 1844–46, and a Democratic U.S. congressman, 1851–57.

497.5 R. J.' s] Robertson James's.

503.28 The Wonder-Book and Twice-Told Tales] *A Wonder-Book for Boys and Girls* (1852), a retelling of Greek myths; and the story collection *Twice-Told Tales* (1837), so called because they had already been published in magazines.

503.36–37 story of Donatello and Miriam] The guilty couple in Hawthorne's novel *The Marble Faun* (1860), whose British title was *Transformation.*

504.8 *bêtise*] French: foolishness.

504.21–23 Polonius . . . arras] In Shakespeare, *Hamlet*, III.iv.

505.25–26 *constatation*] French: statement of fact.

505.39 prolonged exploration of Brazil] William James accompanied Louis Agassiz on his scientific expedition to Brazil, 1865–66, recounted in Agassiz's *Journey in Brazil* (1868).

507.20 my "sitting" to John La Farge] Only one portrait of James by La Farge is known to survive, now in the Century Club, New York.

509.16–18 the great Sanitary Commission . . . Nightingale] The United States Sanitary Commission, founded in June 1861, was a civilian organization dedicated to improving conditions in Union army camps and caring for sick and wounded soldiers. It was based on similar British efforts in the Crimean

War and especially the work of English nurse, social reformer, and public-health advocate Florence Nightingale (1820–1910).

509.38 Lawton's Valley] Summer residence in South Portsmouth, Rhode Island, of poet, editor, and social reformer Julia Ward Howe (1819–1910), whose best-known work is "The Battle Hymn of the Republic" (1862). In March 1864 James wrote to Perry of a "grand Sanitary concert" in Newport, where "your humble servant performed the duties of one: attired like an English footman, he showed folks to their seats."

510.3 Tyrtaean] Martial and patriotic songs, after the seventh-century B.C.E. Spartan poet Tyrtaeus.

510.37–40 wife of the eminent, the militant Phil-Hellene, Dr. S. G. . . . deaf-mutes] Julia Ward Howe's husband, Dr. Samuel Gridley Howe (1801–1876), had, like Byron, traveled to Greece as a young man in support of the Greek war of independence, working as a surgeon. He was later the founding director of the Perkins School for the Blind in Watertown, Massachusetts, and an advocate for prison reform, abolition, and better care for the mentally ill and disabled.

511.32 M. Viollet-le-Duc was even then restoring Carcassonne] French architect Eugène Viollet-le-Duc (1814–1879), the guiding spirit of the Gothic Revival movement in France, began his controversial restoration of Carcassonne's medieval fortifications in 1853.

512.27–28 conversations with Landor] English poet Walter Savage Landor (1775–1864), author of *Imaginary Conversations* (1824–53).

515.13 *remonté*] French: agitated.

516.8–9 in its habit as it lived] Cf *Hamlet*, III.iv.135: "My father, in his habit as he lived!"

518.11 *inénarrables*] French: indescribable.

518.23 any stream more Pactolean] A reference to the river Pactolus, on the Aegean coast of Turkey. According to Greek legend, King Midas of Phrygia could turn whatever he touched into gold. Seeking to be rid of his power after fatally transforming his daughter into a golden statue, he washed himself in the Pactolus, giving it a golden gleam.

520.1–2 the campaign of Sadowa across the sea] The battle of Sadowa (also called the battle of Königgrätz), July 3, 1866, Prussian victory over the Austrians in the decisive battle of the Austro-Prussian War, at Sadová in the present-day Czech Republic.

520.10–11 plight of France under the portent of Sedan] Overwhelming French defeat in the Franco-Prussian War, September 1, 1870, which decided the outcome of the war, leading to the siege of Paris.

523.39–40 Les Idées de Madame Aubray, with Pasca and Delaporte]

Inaugural 1867 production of the play by Dumas *fils*, with French actor Alix-Marie-Angèle Séon, known as Madame Pasca (1835–1914), and French actor Marie Delaporte (1838–1910).

524.3–4 Warren of the Boston Museum."] American comic actor William Warren (1812–1888); for Boston Museum, see note 98.35.

524.9 Lake Leman] Lake Geneva.

524.34 "Existenz so völlig dasteht,"] German: existence [is] so fully present.

525.10 gemüthlich] German: comfortable, pleasant.

525.12 "so freundlich mobilirt"] German: furnished in such a friendly way.

525.14 "Schön!"] German: fine.

525.26–28 das sagen *Kinder* . . . Kinder!"] German: *Children* don't say that. . . . Not for children!

525.33–34 Écu . . . Corraterie] In Geneva, the Hôtel de l'Écu and the rue de la Corraterie.

526.5 Théophile Gautier] William James on pages 529–530 of this volume refers to Gautier's collection of travel writing *Caprices et Zigzags* (1852) and his novel *Capitaine Fracasse* (1863).

526.16 Ritter, Chantre] Swiss writer and theologian Charles Ritter (1838–1908); French archaeologist and anthropologist Ernest Chantre (1843–1924), Geneva school friends of William James.

529.22–23 George's: La Daniella and the Beaux Messieurs de Bois-Doré] Novels by George Sand published in 1857 and 1858, respectively.

529.23–26 Was it thee . . . Nation notices on her, on W. Morris's new poem and on The Spanish Gypsy?] Epic poem *The Earthly Paradise* (1868–70) by English writer, artist, designer, and social reformer William Morris (1834–1896); *The Spanish Gypsy* (1868), book-length poem by George Eliot. James published reviews of these books and of George Sand's latest novel, *Mademoiselle Merquem*, in *The Nation* in July 1868.

529.29 The Woman in White] Novel (1860) by English novelist Wilkie Collins (1824–1889).

529.42 T. S. P.] Thomas Sergeant Perry.

530.5 établissement] French *établissement*: establishment.

530.11 *etwa*] German: about.

531.5–6 friend whom I shall not name here] John Chipman Gray (see note 424.12–13).

532.29–30 Mrs. Gracie King's . . . a very pretty Miss King] Elizabeth

Denning King (née Duer, 1821–1900) and her daughter Maria "May" Van Rensselaer (1848–1925).

532.30 Delmonico's] Prestigious New York restaurant in the nineteenth and early twentieth centuries, originally located in Lower Manhattan; the restaurant referred to here was at Fourteenth Street and Fifth Avenue.

532.40 a Mr. Lee] David Bradley Lee (1834–1903), who made his fortune in the wholesale grocery business; one sister inherited $4,000,000 from her (elderly) prince and remarried; the other was a Baroness.

533.16 North Conway] In the White Mountains of New Hampshire.

533.19 The Ring and the Book.] Blank-verse novel in twelve books (1868–69) by Robert Browning based on a seventeenth-century Roman murder case. James lectured on it in 1912.

533.40 so handsome young man] John Chipman Gray.

535.10 the companion of my own pilgrimage] Oliver Wendell Holmes Jr. (1841–1935); his "great friend" was John Chipman Gray.

537.5–6 that line of a hymn, "Hark, from the tombs etc.!"] Opening of "A Funeral Thought" (1707), by English hymnist Isaac Watts (1674–1748).

538.1 Elly] Her sister Ellen James Temple (1850–1920), the second youngest of the four Temple sisters, who married Christopher Temple Emmet (1822–1884), a railroad baron, in 1869.

539.14 to hear Faust] Opera (1859) by French composer Charles Gounod (1818–1893), based on Goethe's play.

540.26 Miss Emerson] Ellen Tucker Emerson (1839–1909), daughter of Ralph Waldo Emerson. The original letter reads: "of Ellen Emerson."

541.36 Mrs Lewes] George Eliot.

543.16 Phillips Brooks] Episcopal clergyman Phillips Brooks (1835–1893), at the time the rector of the Church of the Holy Trinity in Philadelphia.

544.31 Mill on the Floss] Novel (1860) by George Eliot.

544.36–37 Francis Boott and his daughter . . . later on Mrs. Frank Duveneck] American composer (1813–1904) who spent much of his middle life in Italy; Boston-born artist Elizabeth Boott (1846–1888), who married American artist Frank Duveneck (1848–1919) in Paris in 1886.

545.8–9 *ewig Weibliche*] German: eternal feminine (from the final lines of Goethe's *Faust*).

545.26 the woodnote wild] See note 185.29.

545.38 but lately expropriated Grand Dukes] The last grand dukes of Tuscany, Leopold II (1797–1870) and his son Ferdinand IV (1835–1908), were exiled in 1859 during the Second War of Italian Independence (see note 263.25–28).

545.39 *en plein*] French: in the middle of.

548.34–35 my Gilbert Osmond] In *The Portrait of a Lady.*

549.27 Lewes] English philosopher and literary and dramatic critic George Henry Lewes (1817–1878) was the longtime partner of Mary Ann Evans (George Eliot). The founder and editor of *The Fortnightly Review*, Lewes was the author of many books, including *The Life and Works of Goethe* (1855), *The Physiology of Common Life* (1859), and *The Problems of Life and Mind* (1874–79).

549.41–550.1 Paul . . . glass, *very* darkly.] Cf. 1 Corinthians 13:12.

554.37–38 that "little ease" that Clough talks about] In the poem "Blank Misgivings of a Creature Moving About in Worlds Not Realised" (1841), sec. 10, by English poet Arthur Hugh Clough (1819–1861).

555.3 with Bishop Blougram] In "Bishop Bloughram's Apology" (1855), dramatic monologue in verse by Robert Browning, uttered by a worldly prelate.

557.35–36 my eminent friend F. Marion] American writer Francis Marion Crawford (1854–1909), author of *Dr. Claudius* (1883), *A Roman Singer* (1884), *Zoroaster* (1885), and many other novels.

558.23–24 "on field and hill, in heart and brain," as Mr. Lowell says.] The second line of James Russell Lowell's poem "Palinode: Autumn" (1854).

559.36–37 Fred Jones's engagement with Miss Rawle of Philadelphia.] In 1870 Frederic Rhinelander Jones (1846–1918), the brother of novelist Edith Wharton, married his first wife Mary Cadwalader Rawle (1850–1935), later a close friend of James as well as of Wharton and Theodore Roosevelt.

559.38 the Hones'] The home at 247 Fifth Avenue of insurance executive Robert Hone (c. 1819–c. 1890), son of New York mayor and diarist Philip Hone, and his wife Eliza Russell Hone (née Rodman, 1819–1876).

559.40 Mrs. Willy Duncan] Jane Percy Duncan (née Sargent, 1833–1905), a cousin of the painter John Singer Sargent.

563.35–36 Blessed are they . . . believed.] Cf. Christ's words to the doubting apostle Thomas at John 20:29.

563.40 a matinée of William Tell] Opera (1829) by Italian composer Gioachino Rossini (1792–1868), based on Schiller's 1804 play.

564.9–11 Brignoli . . . Phillipps] Italian tenor Pasquale Brignoli (1824–1884), Italian bass Agostino Susini (1825–1883), American soprano Clara Louise Kellogg (1842–1916), and American contralto Adelaide Phillips (1833–1882).

566.16–17 likened the kingdom of heaven to a little child] Cf. Matthew

19:14: "But Jesus said, Suffer little children, and forbid them not, to come unto me: for of such is the kingdom of heaven."

THE MIDDLE YEARS

573.1 lent by Mr. W. Rothenstein] English artist William Rothenstein (1872–1945), who made the drawing in 1897.

575.4 *one of his own short stories*] James's story "The Middle Years" was first published in 1893.

575.15 *PERCY LUBBOCK.*] See Note on the Texts.

578.22–23 glanced at too . . . on some other and less separated page] At the beginning of "London" (1888), collected in *Essays on London and Elsewhere* (1893).

579.19 Smollett] Scottish novelist and historian Tobias Smollett (1721–1771), author of *The Adventures of Roderick Random* (1748).

585.1–2 Albert Rutson] Albert Osliff Rutson (1836–1890), barrister and Liberal politician, private secretary to Liberal politician Henry Austin Bruce, 1st Baron Aberdare (1815–1895), who was at this time home secretary, 1868–73, under Gladstone.

586.7 *choses vues*] French: things seen (a reference to Victor Hugo's posthumously collected memoirs, *Choses vues*).

587.39–40 French adage says, *c'est le ton qui fait la chanson.*] It's the tone that makes the song (i.e., it isn't what you say but how you say it).

589.11–12 *trait de mœurs*] French: feature of manners.

591.35 Moore and Lockhart and Rogers] Irish poet Thomas Moore (1779–1852); Scottish writer John Gibson Lockhart (1794–1854), best known for his biography of Sir Walter Scott, his father-in-law; English poet Samuel Rogers (1763–1855).

592.29–30 Bayard Taylor] American poet and travel writer (1825–1878), author of *Poems of the Orient* (1854), *Poems of Home and Travel* (1855), and such travel books as *Eldorado* (1850), *A Journey to Central Africa* (1854), and *By-ways of Europe* (1869). James had written an unpublished review of Taylor's novel *John Godfrey's Fortunes* (1865), admonishing him that "to write a good novel is . . . not in any degree an off-hand piece of business."

593.6–8 Frederic Harrison . . . Arnold's early fine banter] English legal scholar and historian Frederic Harrison (1831–1923) published a satire directed at Arnold, "Culture: A Dialogue," in the *Fortnightly Review* in 1867, which Arnold called "very good-tempered and witty" in *Culture and Anarchy* (1869), though elsewhere in the book he takes issue with Harrison's views.

593.8–9 his too confidently roaring "young lions" of the periodical press.]

Arnold wrote ironically of the "magnificent roaring of the young lions of the 'Daily Telegraph'" in his preface to *Essays in Criticism* (1865). He was especially hostile to one of the *Daily Telegraph*'s journalists, the English writer George Augustus Sala (1828–1895).

595.29–30 sermons of the very stones of London.] Cf. Shakespeare, *As You Like It*, II.i.15–17: "And this our life, exempt from public haunt, / Finds tongues in trees, books in the running brooks, / Sermons in stones, and good in everything." James may also be thinking of John Ruskin's *The Stones of Venice* (1851–53).

599.37–38 more successful of Mr. Robertson's comedies] The comedies of English playwright Thomas William Robertson (1829–1871) include his breakthrough success *Society* (1865), *Ours* (1866), *Caste* (1867), and *School* (1869).

600.2–3 Henry Irving's Shakespearean splendours at the transcendent Lyceum?] English Shakespearean actor Henry Irving (1838–1905), manager of the Lyceum Theater, 1878–1902, dominated the London stage for many decades. James reviewed him, with reservations, several times.

600.9 the Grosvenor Gallery] Commercial art gallery in London, 1877–90, which exhibited important works by English Aesthetic movement artists; James knew its founders, Sir Coutts (1824–1913) and Lady Blanche Lindsay (1845–1912).

600.35–36 Family of Darius . . . portrait of Ariosto.] *The Family of Darius Before Alexander* (1565–67) by Paolo Veronese; *Bacchus and Ariadne* (1520–23) and most likely the *Portrait of Gerolamo Barbarigo* (c. 1510) by Titian (c. 1490–1576).

601.10 *chevelu*] French: hairy.

602.3 South Kensington] From 1857 the South Kensington Museum, since 1899 the Victoria and Albert Museum.

606.25–34 Felix Holt the radical . . . review of the delightful thing] James reviewed George Eliot's novel *Felix Holt, The Radical* (1866) in *The Nation*, August 16, 1866.

608.2 Mr. Paget the pre-eminent surgeon] English surgeon and scientist James Paget (1814–1899), a baronet from 1871.

608.11–12 Avignon . . . J. S. Mill] John Stuart Mill owned a house in St-Véran, near Avignon in southern France.

608.18 *impression de voyage*] French: impressions from one's travels.

610.10 Deronda] George Eliot's novel *Daniel Deronda* (1876).

611.6 Mrs. Greville] Sabine Matilda Greville (née Thellusson, 1823–1882), a friend of Victorian writers such as Carlyle, Tennyson, and Swinburne.

613.29 an illustrious soldier] Sir Dighton Macnaghton Probyn (1833–1924), a general in the British army, who had won the Victoria Cross.

614.5–6 Fanny Kemble] See note 192.28–29.

617.11 the Laureate] Tennyson was the British Poet Laureate from 1850 to his death in 1892.

617.20–21 old friend the late Lord Houghton] Richard Monckton Milnes (1809–1885), poet, writer, literary patron, biographer of John Keats, and a member of parliament from 1837 to 1863, when he was made Baron Houghton.

618.6 M. Ernest Renan] French historian, philosopher, and philologist (1823–1892), best known for his *Life of Jesus* (1863).

619.29 his London adventure] Lowell was U.S. ambassador to Great Britain, 1880–85.

620.10 Hallam] Alfred, Lord Tennyson's oldest son (1852–1928).

621.11 Locksley Hall] Tennyson's 1842 poem (see note 155.3).

622.1 In Memoriam] Tennyson's elegiac poem-sequence (1850).

625.22 *à tout propos*] French: at every turn.

627.10 Louisa Lady Waterford] English artist Louisa Anne Stuart, Marchioness of Waterford (1818–1891), a friend of Ruskin.

628.8 *d'antan*] French: of former times. See note 46.37–38.

631.11–12 Bonifazio's] Italian artist Bonifazio de' Pitati, also known as Bonifazio Veronese (c. 1487–1553).

OTHER AUTOBIOGRAPHICAL WRITINGS

635.21 da vero] Italian (usually *davvero*): really, indeed.

635.23 *les miens*] French: my people, my family.

635.30 37] James was thirty-eight.

636.3 je n'ai que faire.] French: I have nothing to do.

637.16 Quincy St.] At the home of James's parents at 20 Quincy Street, Cambridge, beside Harvard Yard.

637.33 Lady Rose and H.J.W. Coulson] James's relative Charlotte Emmett Rose (née Temple, 1813–1883), an aunt to his Temple cousins; English lawyer Henry John Wastell Coulson (b. 1848).

638.6 Charles Peirce] American pragmatist philosopher and mathematician Charles Sanders Peirce (1839–1914).

638.8 at Madame Tourguéneff's] At the house of the widow of Nikolai Turgenev (1789–1871), an exiled Russian political radical and author who was the uncle of Russian writer Ivan Turgenev.

638.9 Paul Joukowsky] Pavel Zhukovsky (1845–1912), Russian painter, long resident in Italy.

638.9 Non ragionam di lui—ma guarda e passa.] Italian: "Let us not talk of him, but look and pass." Cf. Dante, *Inferno*, canto 3.

638.16 Goncourt, Daudet] See notes 427.10 and 124.13–19.

638.20 a little poem of Th. Gautier's—*Les Vieux Portraits*] Théophile Gautier's "Pastel" (1836), which refers to forgotten "old portraits" in the last of its four stanzas.

638.23 Alfred de Musset] See note 70.19–27.

638.23 "il était plus français,"] French: he was more French.

638.29 en plein Paris.] French: in the middle of Paris.

638.35 Mrs. S.] Eleanor Burrill Strong (née Fearing, b. 1831), who after separating from her husband spent most of her life in Europe. James said of her: "She has a spark of feu sacré [sacred fire], an ability to interest herself and s'enthousiasmer [become enthusiastic] which is sincere & pleasing."

639.6 the Lee Childes] The French-born American Edward Lee Childe (1836–1911), a nephew of Robert E. Lee, and his wife Blanche (née de Triqueti, 1837–1886), herself an author.

639.12 Jane Norton] See note 414.34. Norton died in 1877.

639.15–16 "au coeur de l'ancienne France."] French: in the heart of old France.

640.11–12 J'y suis absolument comme chez moi.] French: I am absolutely at home there.

641.5 Mrs. Wister] Sarah Butler Wister (1835–1908), the older of the two daughters of Fanny Kemble (see note 192.28–29).

641.6 George Howard] English Liberal politician and artist George James Howard, from 1889 9th Earl of Carlisle (1843–1911).

641.6 Motley] American diplomat and historian John Lothrop Motley (1814–1877), author of *The Rise of the Dutch Republic* (1856).

641.11 cela va de soi] French: it happens by itself.

641.21 Gaskell's . . . Locker's] English politician and lawyer Charles George Milnes Gaskell (1842–1919), one of whose country residences was Thornes House, Wakefield, Yorkshire; English poet Frederick Locker-Lampson (1821–1895).

641.25–26 F.H. Hill . . . C.H. Robarts] English journalist Frank Harrison Hill (1830–1910), editor-in-chief of the *London Daily News*, 1870–86; English lawyer Charles Henry Robarts (1840–1904).

641.33 Mrs. Rogerson's] Christina Rogerson (née Stewart, c. 1839–1911).

641.40–642.1 entre cour et jardin] French: between courtyard and garden.

642.21 the Bootts] See note 544.36–37.

642.28 tant bien que mal] French: as best I could.

642.38–39 John Clarks . . . Pakenhams] English diplomat John Forbes Clark (1821–1910) and his wife Charlotte, Lady Clark (née Coltman, 1823–1897); English military officer Thomas Henry Pakenham (1826–1913) and his American wife Elizabeth Staples Pakenham (née Clarke, 1836–1919).

643.2–3 Elizabeth Thompson (Mrs. Butler,)] English painter Elizabeth Southerden Thompson, Lady Butler (1846–1933).

643.21 Mrs. Lombard & Fanny L.] Mother and daughter from Cambridge who were friends of the James family.

644.18 Herbert Pratt] Herbert James Pratt (1841–1915), American traveler who had trained as a doctor at Harvard and in Vienna; he was a friend of William James.

644.35 facchini] Italian: porters, coachmen.

645.1 Firdausi and Saadi] Persian poets Hakīm Abu'l-Qāsim Ferdowsī Tūsī (c. 940–1020), author of a Persian national epic, and Abū-Muḥammad Muṣliḥ al-Dīn bin Abdallāh Shīrāzī (c. 1200–1292), revered for his wisdom and known for his aphorisms.

645.4 "una bellezza;"] Italian: a beauty.

645.18 Mrs. Bronson's] Casa Alvisi, the Venetian home of American expatriate Katherine Bronson (née De Kay, 1834–1901), a frequent meeting place for English and American expatriates and visitors in Venice, notably Robert Browning; James published an essay on "Casa Alvisi" in 1902.

645.19–20 Mrs. V. R.] American expatriate Anne Van Rensselaer (née Whittemore, b. 1840).

645.34 Giacomo Leopardi] Italian Romantic poet (1798–1837), an invalid in a conservative provincial milieu, but with a modern poetic and philosophical vision.

646.29 *calidarium*] Latin: a steamy room in an ancient Roman bath.

646.37–38 Mrs. Kemble & Miss Butler] Fanny Kemble (see note 192.28–29) and her daughter Frances Butler Leigh (1838–1910).

647.3 Tiltis] Mount Titlis, a mountain in the Urner Alps of Switzerland, on the border between the cantons of Obwalden and Berne, overlooking Engelberg. The Trübsee is a mountain lake at its foot.

647.38–40 Sir Trevor Lawrence's . . . the Deepdene] English horticulturalist and Conservative politician James John Trevor Lawrence, 2nd Baronet

(1831–1913). He had some three thousand types of orchid at Burford Lodge. The Deepdene was a grand house remodeled to resemble a large Roman villa.

648.5 Leatherhead] Estate of Russell Sturgis (1805–1887), American-born senior partner of the banking house of Baring Brothers, and father of James's friend the novelist Howard Overing Sturgis (1855–1920).

648.5 Mentmore.] Mentmore Towers, English country house belonging at the time to Hannah Primrose, Countess of Rosebery (1851–1890), daughter of Baron Mayer Amschel de Rothschild (1818–1874) and wife from 1878 of English politician Archibald Philip Primrose, 5th Earl of Rosebery (1847–1929), leader of the Liberal Party and prime minister, 1894–95.

648.6–7 Fredk. Macmillan's] James's English publisher, Frederick Macmillan (1851–1936), who had an American wife.

648.9 Midelney Place, the Cely Trevilians'.] Country house of English lawyer Edwin Brooke Cely Trevilian (1833–1914), who married Kate Carter of New York in 1880.

648.17 Montacute] Elizabethan mansion in Somerset, at the time still owned by the Phelips family, which has been claimed as the inspiration for the country house in James's *The Spoils of Poynton* (1897).

648.32 au fond] French: at its heart, at bottom.

648.34 serrement de coeur] French: pang, oppression of the heart.

650.19–20 Lord Airlie's death] David Ogilvy, 10th Earl of Airlie (1826–1881), died in Denver, Colorado.

651.11 *l'enfance de l'art.*] French: the infancy of the art.

652.19 Je me résume] French: I am summarizing.

652.24 of Sardou, of Augier.] See notes 216.7–8 and 217.10, respectively.

652.25–27 Ces émotions-là ne se perdent pas . . . notre volonté.] French: "Those emotions are not lost; they are absorbed back into the very basis of our being; they become a part of our will."

652.36 *tir*] French: firing range.

652.36 *Jean Dacier*] Tragedy (1877) by French playwright Charles Lomon (1852–1923).

652.39 Coquelin] See note 242.4.

652.40 Favart] French actor Marie Favart (1833–1908), whose technique James admired.

653.19 Andrew Lang's] Scottish poet and scholar (1844–1912), translator of Homer's *Odyssey* (1879), author of *Myth, Ritual and Religion* (1887), and compiler of numerous compilations of fairy tales, beginning with *The Blue Fairy Book* (1889).

653.31 Jack Gardner] American businessman and art collector John Lowell Gardner II (1837–1898), husband of the art collector and friend of James, Isabella Stewart Gardner (1840–1924).

653.38–39 John Hare asked me . . . write a play] English actor and manager born John Fairs (1844–1921), head of the Garrick Theatre, 1889–1895. In 1890 James wrote *Tenants* (first entitled *Mrs Vibert*) for Hare, who accepted but then did not produce it.

653.39 Comyns Carrs'] English critic, gallery owner, playwright, magazine editor, and theatrical producer Joseph William Comyn Carr (1849–1916) and his wife, the novelist and designer Alice Laura Vansittart Comyns Carr (née Strettell, 1850–1927).

654.15 Aunt Kate] Catherine Walsh (see note 84.17).

654.24 Mrs. Robeson's] Mary Isabelle Robeson (née Ogston, d. 1910), wife of George Maxwell Robeson (1829–1897), U.S. secretary of the navy, 1869–77, and U.S. congressman from New Jersey, 1879–83.

654.29–31 cousin H.P.'s . . . Eliza Ripley . . . Katie Rodgers . . . Lily Walsh.] Helen (Wyckoff) Perkins (see note 84.11) and other members of James's extended family on his mother's side.

654.36 A.K.] Aunt Kate.

654.39–655.1 Wilkie arrived from Milwaukee] Wilkie had moved to Milwaukee in the fall of 1871 when he accepted a position there with the Chicago, Milwaukee and St. Paul Railway.

655.1 Bob] James's younger brother Robertson.

657.38–39 his unhappy voyage to the Azores] Beset with health and financial problems, and struggling with alcoholism, Robertson set off for the Azores in March 1881, then traveled on to Lisbon and eventually spent the summer in England, some of it with James.

658.20 Rhoda Broughton] Welsh-born novelist (1840–1920), noted for her wit and at first considered racy, author of the best-selling *Cometh up as a Flower* (1867) and *Red as a Rose Is She* (1870), among many other works.

658.24–25 Arthur Russells'] Lord Arthur John Edward Russell (1825–1892), English member of parliament, and his wife Lady Russell (née Laura de Peyronnet, 1836–1910).

659.20 *D.M.*] Stage adaptation of *Daisy Miller*, never produced, but published in 1883.

661.1 *Wolcott Balestier*] American writer and editor (1861–1891), author of the novels *A Potent Philtre* (1884), *A Fair Device* (1884), *A Victorious Defeat*

(1886), and, in collaboration with Rudyard Kipling, *The Naulahka: A Story of West and East* (1892).

661.28–29 youthful unpublished novel . . . to see the light] *Benefits Forgot,* written 1885–90 and published in book form in 1894.

661.29 three very short tales] "A Common Story," "Reffey," and "Captain, My Captain!": stories collected posthumously in *The Average Woman* (1892), a volume with this essay as an introduction.

664.5 The Copyright Bill] The U.S. International Copyright Act of 1891, which extended a degree of protection to authors whose works were copyrighted in other nations, including Great Britain.

664.7 helping the English author in America] Balestier arranged for the American publication of Kipling's first novel, *The Light That Failed* (1890).

664.31–32 *faire un sort*] French: make a fortune.

667.22 the quick foundation of the "English Library"] As a rival to the continental Tauchnitz editions for English-speaking travelers.

668.14–15 A wet winter night in a windy Lancashire town] Balestier attended the premiere of James's play *The American* in Southport on January 3, 1891.

669.3–4 the bristling alien cemetery] James traveled to Dresden for the funeral on December 10, 1891, which he called in a letter "these monstrous rites for the poor yesterday-so-much-living boy—in this far-away, alien city."

671.3 Madame Doche in "La Dame aux Camélias"] See note 230.26–31.

671.17 Madame Fargeuil] See note 215.22.

671.37–38 with Marguerite Gautier fat and Armand Duval old.] Young lovers, the former dying of consumption, who are the main characters of *The Lady of the Camellias.*

672.7 Madame Pierson] See note 215.37–216.1.

672.18–20 Eleonora Duse . . . tattered translation] Celebrated Italian actor Eleonora Duse (1858–1924), who had played Marguerite in London in May–June 1895 using an anonymous Italian translation of *The Lady of the Camellias.*

674.39–40 the legal irregularity attaching to his birth] Dumas was the child of Alexandre Dumas *père* and his mistress the dressmaker Marie-Laure-Catherine Labay (1794–1868); his father legally recognized him in 1831.

675.11 *banlieue*] French: the suburbs.

676.14 Lamartine and Musset and Scribe and Michelet] French poet, historian, novelist, and politician Alphonse de Lamartine (1790–1869); Musset, see note 70.19–27; Scribe, see note 217.8; French historian Jules Michelet (1798–1874).

676.33 the author of "Antony" and "Kean,"] The plays *Antony* (1831) and *Kean* (1836) by Dumas *père*, not *fils*.

679.12 *parler femmes*] French: to speak of women.

682.12–13 *calme infernal*, as George Sand calls it] In a short prefatory essay to Sand's play *Françoise* (1856).

682.24–25 exquisite Desclée] French actor Aimée Desclée (1836–1874).

682.25–26 Rose Chéri] See note 214.24–25.

682.26 Mademoiselle Delaporte] See note 214.24–25.

682.33–34 Croizette . . . Bartet—] Russian-born French actor Sophie Croizette (1847–1901); French actor Marie Thomas Delaunay, also known as Marie Dorval (1798–1849); French actor Julia Bartet (1854–1941): all performed at the Comédie-Française. In February 1889 James recalled visiting Bartet "in her *loge*, the other day in Paris."

688.20 uncriticised stage.] In the manuscript, after this sentence, James had written, "He himself could no more have criticised them than he could have subscribed to Ibsen, and of the undisturbed felicity of which they were so long the source no man, probably, had ever drunk more deep." For this omission in the published text (and the deleted passage given in the following note), see Frederick Wegener, "Henry James on James Payn: A Forgotten Critical Text," *New England Quarterly*, vol. 67, no. 1 (March 1994): 115–29.

688.38 was unvanquished.] A manuscript passage cut from the published text here reads: "He made it no ghost of a condition that a confrère should read his novels, but there were, none the less, liberties that a neighbour's restless fancy could take with them, and I liked to think, especially at a period when we often leaned elbows on the same luncheon table (table of easy mid-day laughter quenched outright the day, a sharp date, he dropped out) of the convenient, compact corner of his life in which he tangled and untangled. He could come round from Waterloo Place [location of the *Cornhill Magazine*'s offices] with a good conscience, he could chaff and be chaffed—he had given another twist to the skein. It was precisely that that made it all romance—we talked of it no more than, within the pale, we would really have talked of the haunted chamber or the personated heir."

690.13 Basta!] Italian: enough!

690.22 L.H.] Lamb House, James's home in Rye, Sussex, from 1897 until his death.

691.23 J. R. L.] James Russell Lowell (see note 488.16–17).

691.27 J. N., & of S. N., & even of G. W. C.] Jane Norton (see note 414.34), her niece Sara Norton (1864–1922, daughter of Charles Eliot Norton), and George William Curtis (see note 40.15–16).

691.31 à peu près)] French: more or less, just about.

692.9–10 Seven Weeks War] Or Austro-Prussian War, June–July 1866, a victory for Prussia against the Austro-Hungarian Empire and its German allies from Bavaria, Saxony, Hanover, and smaller states.

692.17 O. W. H.] Oliver Wendell Holmes Jr.

692.38 George Eliot's *Felix Holt*] See note 606.25–34.

694.5–7 Dantean lines . . . questa pace—] Italian: "After long exile and martyrdom / Came to this peace," based on Dante's lines "ed essa da martiro / e da essilio venne a questa pace" (*Paradiso*, canto 10, lines 128–29).

696.5 certain very first awkward essay in criticism] James's review of *Essays on Fiction* by English economist, lawyer, and writer Nassau W. Senior (1790–1864) was published in the *North American Review*, October 1864.

699.8 *crânerie*] French: pluck, daring.

699.21–22 his admirable volume on Church-Building in the Middle Ages] Norton's *Historical Studies of Church-Building in the Middle Ages: Venice, Siena, Florence* (1880).

704.2 distinguished friend] Probably William Dean Howells.

713.13 *déménager*] French: to quit the premises, move out.

716.6 *portée*] French: range.

723.4 THEODORA BOSANQUET] English writer and literary critic (1880–1961) who worked for James as secretary and amanuensis from 1907 until James's death in 1916.

Index

Abbott, Jacob and John: *Franconia* and *Rollo* stories, 150–51
About, Edmond, 289
Academy (Geneva), 255, 257, 260–61, 263
Academy of Music (New York City), 147–48
Adams, Henry, 641
Aeschylus: *Oresteia*, 84
African-American soldiers, 402, 446, 481–82, 494, 496
Agassiz, Louis, 331–32, 337–39, 348, 505, 517
Aguilar, Grace, 7
Aiken, William, 496
Airlie, Lord, 650
Albany, N.Y., 33, 37, 54–55, 114, 118, 370, 422, 424, 469, 534; HJ's relatives from, 6, 8–13, 28, 39, 44, 61, 74, 104, 106, 108, 110–13, 120, 145–46, 148, 166, 178, 226, 281, 298, 300–301, 312, 323, 326, 344–46, 418–19, 545
Alger, Horatio, 423–24
Ames, Adelbert, 483
Amiel, Henri-Frédéric, 261
Ancona, Italy, 645
Anderson, Robert, 497
Andrew, John, 342
Andrews & Stoddard (Latin textbook), 130
Ansleaux, Napoléon, 248–50
Anthon, Charles, 130, 157
Appomattox, surrender at, 502
Arctic (steamship), 169
Arnold, Matthew, 102, 248, 533–34, 555, 593
Ashburner family, 416
Astor House, 8–9
Astor, John Jacob, 419
Athenaeum (Boston), 506, 692
Athenaeum (London), 641
Atkinson, Charles, 430
Atkinson, Henry George, 377
Atlantic (steamship), 168
Atlantic Monthly, The, 287, 408, 519
Augier, Émile, 217, 652
Auteuil, 200
Avignon, France, 608, 643
Axel, Madame, 104

Bader, Clarisse, 184
Badiali, Cesare, 72
Balestier, Charles Wolcott, 661–69; *The Naulahka*, 661
Balzac, Honoré de, 204, 219, 268, 371, 529, 676, 684, 735; *Eugénie Grandet*, 193, 310; *Le Père Goriot*, 224, 442–43, 456
Bancroft, George, 461
Bancroft, John Chandler, 459–61
Barbara, 420
Barker, Augustus (Gus), 13, 16, 108–11, 117, 311, 327, 333
Barker, Elizabeth Hazard (Lily), 117, 334, 341
Barker, Jeannette James (aunt), 108
Barker, Robert, 117–18
Barnet, Morris: *The Serious Family*, 67
Barnum, Phineas T., 43, 97–99, 103, 381
Barnum's American Museum, 43, 97–98, 103
Bartet, Julia, 682
Basel, Switzerland, 270
Bassano, Italy, 646
Bassett, Dr., 539, 543
Bateman, Ellen, 52–53
Bateman, Kate, 52–53, 470
Bayonne, France, 639
Bayou, Miss (teacher), 10, 14
Bean family (New York City), 40–41
Beattie, James: "The Minstrel," 23
Beaufort, N.C., 491, 494
Beaverkill property, 78, 82, 90
Bellamy, Mrs. William Hoare, 101
Bellini, Vincenzo: *Norma*, 73, 148
Bennett, Julia, 70
Béranger, Pierre-Jean de, 15
Berlin, Germany, 523
Bernard, Charles de: *Le Gendre*, 192
Biarritz, France, 639

Bible, 357, 362
Birmingham, England, 668
Blake, Caroline, 67–68
Blake, William Rufus, 67–68
Blitz, Antonio, 73
Bloomingdale, 145, 151
Bois de Boulogne, 199–200
Bonaparte, Napoléon-Eugène (Prince Imperial), 199
Bonn, Germany, 264, 270–77, 279–80, 283–85, 288
Bonnefond, Georges, 220–23, 225
Bonningue, Félicie, 184
Bonningue, Marie, 184
Bookstore, 53–55
Boone children (actors), 52–53
Booth family (actors), 99
Booth, Edwin, 70
Booth, John Wilkes, 343, 347
Boott, Elizabeth. *See* Duveneck, Elizabeth (Lizzy) Boott
Boott, Francis, 544–49, 642
Bosanquet, Theodora: *Henry James at Work*, 725–49
Bosio, Angiolina, 72
Boston, Mass., 41, 99, 151, 192, 205, 218, 236, 385, 408, 421, 431, 442, 505, 513, 519, 524, 535, 540, 543, 546, 598, 691, 695; and Civil War, 446, 480–82, 488, 502, 515; cultural scene in, 468–71, 564, 745–46; HJ's later visits to, 635–36, 639, 647, 654; James family resides in, 370–71, 407, 500–502, 657–59; and John La Farge, 302, 316–19; and Minnie Temple, 557, 559; versus New York City, 506, 509–10, 512; visited by Henry James, Sr., 370–71, 373, 376–77, 379, 381; while WJ and HJ at Harvard, 331–32, 334, 343, 347, 435, 439, 521, 692
Boston Museum (theater), 98
Boston Weekly Transcript, 524
Boswell, James, 49, 598
Boucicault, Dion: *The Corsican Brothers*, 193; *London Assurance*, 69; *Love in a Maze*, 69
Boulogne-sur-Mer, France, 201, 226, 237–50, 328
Brady, Mathew, 56–57
Brevoort Hotel, 36
Brewster, Henry Bennet, 504–5
Brighton, England, 642
Brighton, Mass., 463, 472
Brignoli, Pasquale, 564
British Museum, 54
Broadway Theatre, 68, 98
Bronson, Katherine De Kay, 645
Brontë, Charlotte: *Jane Eyre*, 236; *Villette*, 236
Brooklyn, N.Y., 22, 41, 55, 145
Brooks, Phillips, 543–44, 549, 563
Brooks, Preston S., 35
Brougham, Henry Peter, 39
Brougham (theater owner), 67–69, 71, 168
Broughton, Rhoda, 658
Brown, John, 38, 390
Brown, Sarah, 390
Brown College, 324
Browning, Elizabeth Barrett, 512
Browning, Robert, 512, 626; "Bishop Blougram's Apology," 555; *Men and Women*, 310, 625; *The Ring and the Book*, 533–34
Browning Society, 743
Brownson, Orestes, 378
Bryan's Gallery of Christian Art, 163
Bryant, William Cullen, 40
Buckle, Henry T., 429–30
Buckstone, John Baldwin: *Green Bushes*, 69; *Nan the Good-for-Nothing*, 68
Bulwer-Lytton, Edward: *Pelham*, 423
Burton, William, 66–68, 71–72; *The Toodles*, 67
Buscarlet, Madame, 526
Butler, Frances, 646–47
Byron, Lord (George Gordon), 279, 423, 591

Cabot, J. Elliott, 431
Calame, Alexandre, 177
Caldwell, Anne Marsh, 7
Calvinism, 367
Cambridge, Mass., 326, 380, 442, 500, 695; cultural scene in, 461, 463, 469–72; and Harvard University, 329, 333, 339–40, 347, 434–36, 440, 448, 451; HJ's later visits to, 636–37, 648, 654–56, 659; James family resides in, 413, 521, 690–94; Shady Hill, 411–16, 429, 457, 501–2, 691, 697, 701, 745

Campagne Gerebsoff, 173–75
Cannon, Anne C., 60–62, 146
Canterbury, England, 647
Carcassonne, France, 511
Carlyle, Thomas, 368–69, 375–78, 380–81; *Past and Present*, 367
Carr, J. Comyns, 653
Casimir-Périer, Jean-Paul-Pierre, 15
Castle Garden, 72
Catherine de Médici, 245
Catholics, 144, 309–10, 345, 347
Céleste, Céline, 69
Ceriana, Italy, 643
Cervantes, Miguel de: *Don Quixote*, 305, 461
Chambers's Journal, 688
Chancellorsville, battle of, 326–27
Channing, William Ellery, 151
Channing, William Ellery (nephew), 381–82
Chantre, Ernest, 526
Charleston, S.C., 438, 446, 482–83, 486, 491, 495–98, 551
Charm, The, 54–55
Charriau, Monsieur (dancing teacher), 146
Chateaubriand, François-Auguste-René de: *Les Natchez*, 24
Châtelaine, Switzerland, 174–75
Chaworth, Mary, 279
Cheever, George Barrell, 378
Chelsea Female Institute, 14
Cherbuliez, Victor, 197, 261
Chéri, Rose, 214–15, 682
Chicago, Ill., 49
Chichester, Sophia, 361
Child, Francis J., 331, 349, 451, 455
Childe, Edward Lee, 639
Christian art, 163
Cibber, Susannah Maria, 192
Cirque d'Eté and Cirque d'Hiver, 213
Civil War, 22, 34–35, 39, 146, 154, 294, 300, 325, 339, 386–87, 452, 500, 513, 517, 525, 535, 590, 745; Robertson James's service during, 402, 482–86, 496–97, 517; and Boston, 446, 480–82, 488, 502, 515; Harvard University during, 434, 437, 440–43, 448, 488; HJ's relatives involved in, 108, 167, 234–35, 326–27; Lowell's poetry about, 488; Whitman's poetry about, 445, 447–48; Wilky James's service during, 402–5, 407, 446, 480–98, 517, 551
Clarendon Hotel, 58
Clark, John, 642–43
Clark, Mrs. (teacher), 389–90
Clinton family (Albany), 33
Clough, Arthur Hugh, 554–55
Coe, Benjamin, 126–28
Cogniet, Léon: *Marius among the Ruins of Carthage*, 190
Cole, Thomas, 40; *View of Florence from San Miniato*, 163–64
Colgate (fellow student), 137
Collège Communal (Boulogne), 239–40, 248
Collins, Wilkie: *The Woman in White*, 529
Collins, William, 400
Cologne, Germany, 288, 290
Columbia College, 130, 324
Comédie Française, 638, 652–53
Concord, Mass., 333–34, 381–82, 387–91
Cooper, James Fenimore, 324
Coquelin, Benoît-Constant, 242, 652–53
Corneille, Pierre: *Le Cid*, 220
Cornhill Magazine, 264, 268–69, 460
Coronado Beach, Calif., 690
Coster, Hal, 73
Coster family (New York City), 142, 156
Coulson, H.J.W., 637
Couture, Thomas, 293, 305; *Page with a Falcon*, 205–6; *Romains de la décadence*, 205
Craig, Sam D., 475–76
Cranch, Christopher P., 40
Crawford, Frank Marion, 557
Croizette, Sophie, 682
Cromwell, Oliver, 487
Cropsey, Jasper F., 40
Crowe, Eyre, 58–59
Cruikshank, George, 75–76, 127, 186
Crystal Palace (London), 16–17, 106, 179
Crystal Palace (New York City), 106
Cummins, Maria Susanna: *The Lamplighter*, 51
Curtis, George Ticknor, 40

Cushman, Charlotte, 72
Cusin, Amélie, 184, 197–98

Daly, Mrs. (teacher), 14–15
Dana, Charles A., 40
Danse, Augustine, 184–85, 197–98, 201
Dante Alighieri, 430, 512, 694, 699
Darley, Felix, 40
Darwin, Charles, 542, 744
Daubigny, Charles-François, 205
Daudet, Alphonse, 218–20, 289, 638; *Jack*, 124
Daumier, Honoré, 88
David, Jacques-Louis, 211; *The Lictors Returning to Brutus the Bodies of His Sons*, 210; *The Oath of the Horatii*, 210
Davidge, William, 68–69
Davis, Jefferson, 496
Davy (slave), 153–54
Decamps, Alexandre-Gabriel, 207
De Coppet, Louis, 24–26
Déjazet, Virginie, 214
Delacroix, Eugène: *La barque de Dante*, 206–7
Delaporte, Marie, 214, 523, 682
Delaroche, Paul, 206; *Charles I Insulted by Cromwell's Soldiers*, 207; *The Children of Edward IV*, 207; *The Execution of Lady Jane Grey*, 207
Delaunay, Marie, 682
Delavigne, Mademoiselle (teacher), 15–16
Delmonico's restaurant, 532
De Peyster brothers (Beekman, George, Henry), 156
De Peyster family (New York City), 142, 155
Derby, Richard H., 524
Desaix de Veygoux, Louis-Charles, 291
Desclée, Aimée, 682
"Dewhurst, Stephen" (Henry James Sr. pseudonym), 7
Diable d'Argent, Le, 213
Dickens, Charles, 76, 127, 268, 283, 342, 344, 346, 362, 579, 598, 604, 688, 691; *Bleak House*, 75; *David Copperfield*, 72, 75, 91, 93, 185, 411; *Dombey and Son*, 43, 71, 75; *Hard Times*, 75; *Little Dorrit*, 75; *Martin Chuzzlewit*, 75; *Nicholas Nickleby*, 73–74, 102; *Oliver Twist*, 72, 75, 186; *Pickwick Papers*, 128, 411
Diderot, Denis: *Les fils naturels*, 673
Disraeli, Benjamin: *Coningsby*, 423
Doche, Eugénie, 230, 671
Dodge, Mary Abigail Hamilton, 424
Dolmidge, Mr. (teacher), 126–27
Donizetti, Gaetano: *Lucrezia Borgia*, 148
Dover, England, 642
Dresden, Germany, 416, 523–24, 526, 661, 669
Droz, Gustave: *Babolain*, 431
Dryden, John, 400
Dubreuil, Madame (dancing teacher), 147
Dubreuil, Monsieur (opera singer), 147–48
Duggan, Paul, 40
Dumas, Alexandre (*fils*), 215, 217, 652, 670–86; *La dame aux camélias*, 230, 671–72, 679; *Le demi-monde*, 675, 677, 679, 682–83; *Denise*, 679, 681; *Diane de Lys*, 679; *Francillon*, 679, 681; *Le père prodigue*, 679–80; *Les idées de Madame Aubray*, 523, 677
Dumas, Alexandre (*père*), 674, 680; *Antony*, 676; *The Count of Monte Cristo*, 675; *Kean*, 676
Du Maurier, George, 270, 460
Duncan, Jane Percy, 559
Duse, Eleonora, 672
Düsseldorf, Germany, 233, 460
Düsseldorf school of painting, 161–63
Dutch House, 9
Duveneck, Elizabeth (Lizzy) Boott, 544–49, 560, 642

École des Beaux-Arts, 207
Edinburgh, Scotland, 180
Edwards, Jonathan, 367
Eliot, Charles William, 331–32, 341
Eliot, George, 268, 359, 540–42, 607–9, 611, 614; *Adam Bede*, 267; *Daniel Deronda*, 610, 616; *Felix Holt*, 606, 692–93; *Middlemarch*, 424, 605–6; *The Mill on the Floss*, 544; *Silas Marner*, 605; "The Spanish Gypsy," 529, 544, 549
Elliot, Gertrude, 739
Emancipation Proclamation, 496

Emerson, Edith, 390–91
Emerson, Edward Waldo, 331–32
Emerson, Ellen, 390–91
Emerson, Ralph Waldo, 9, 41, 151, 365–69, 372–83, 385–86, 390, 399, 410
Emmet, Catherine Elizabeth James (cousin), 29–30
Emmet, Christopher Temple, 554, 557, 559–60
Emmet, Ellen (Elly) Temple, 538, 553–54, 556–57, 559, 567
Emmet, Katharine (Kitty) Temple, 1 2, 29, 312–13, 539, 553, 556–57
Emmet, Richard Stockton, 312, 531, 554, 561
Emmet, Robert, 29–30
Emmet family, 312, 532, 537, 553, 557–61
English ancestors, 7
English Library, 667
Episcopalians, 543
Étretat, France, 639
Eugénie, Empress, 199, 228
Everett, Edward, 350
Everett, William, 350

Fanchon the Cricket, 471
Fanny (nurse), 54
Fargueil, Anaîs, 215–16, 671
Favart, Marie (Pierette Pingaud), 652
Fechter, Charles, 230
Felton, Cornelius C., 339–40
Ferrero, Edward, 143, 146–48, 150, 171
Feuillet, Octave, 290
Fezandié, Félix-Eugène, 218–19, 225
Fezandié, Madame, 219, 225
Fields, Annie Adams, 408–10
Fields, James T., 287, 408, 410–11
Flaubert, Gustave, 214, 427, 638, 746
Florence, Italy, 163–66, 227, 512, 546, 548, 568, 642
Folkestone, England, 642, 658
Forbes family, 342
Forbes, John, 381
Forrest, Edwin, 422–26
Forrest, Nathan B., 493
Forrest, William, 131–32, 137, 141
Fort Hamilton (Brooklyn), 22, 41, 55
Fort McAllister, 492
Fort Moultrie, 497
Fortress Monroe, 495
Fort Sumter, 437–38, 495–97
Fort Wagner, 402, 446, 492
Fortin, Amélie, 184
Foster, John G., 487, 489–92
Fourier, Charles, 218
Four Lovers, The (pantomime), 105
Fox, Lazarus, 584, 597
Français peints par eux-mêmes, Les, 204
Franconi's circus, 106
Franco-Prussian War, 520
Franklin, Benjamin, 131, 330, 339
Free Academy, 150
French Revolution, 196, 214, 220
French Theater, 83
Frère, Édouard, 205, 293
Fromentin, Eugène: *Dominique*, 309
Fuller, Margaret, 41, 151, 368, 385

Galerie d'Apollon (Louvre), 208–10
Gallipolis, Ohio, 185
Galopin, Monsieur (teacher), 259–60
Ganot, Adolphe, 340
Gardner, John L., 653
Gaskell, Charles Milnes, 641–42
Gautier, Théophile, 526; *Le Capitaine Fracasse*, 530; *Caprices et zigzags*, 529; "Pastel," 638
Gavarni, Paul (Guillaume-Sulpice Chevalier), 15–16, 204
Geneva, Switzerland, 19, 166–67, 170, 173–76, 184, 255–67, 277, 385, 395–96, 400, 526
Genoa, Italy, 277–78
Georges, Mademoiselle (Marguerite Weimer), 214
Gerebsoff, Madame, 173
Géricault, Jean-Louis, 211; *The Raft of the "Medusa,"* 210
Gettysburg, battle of, 445–46
Gilbert, W. S., 600
Gillmore, Quincy Adams, 495–96, 498
Girardin, Delphine de: *Une femme que déteste son mari*, 214–15
Gladstone, William E., 648, 744
Godefroi, Annette, 171
Godey's Lady's Book, 43–44
Godkin, Edwin Lawrence, 416, 513
Godkin, Frances, 416
Godwin, Parke, 40
Goethe, Johann Wolfgang von: *Faust*, 540; *Hermann und Dorothea*, 273;

The Sorrows of Young Werther, 276; *Die Wahlverwandtschaften*, 272
Goldsboro, N.C., 487, 491
Goldsmith, Oliver, 68
Goncourt, Edmond de, 427, 638
Goodwin, William, 350
Gore, Catherine Grace, 7
Gosse, Edmund, 746–47
Gougenheim, Adelaide and Josephine, 68–69
Gounod, Charles: *Faust*, 539, 564
Gourlay family, 693
Gramercy Park, 167
Grandville (Jean-Jacques Gérard), 204
Grant, Ulysses S., 235, 502, 590, 744
Gray, Francis Calley, 331
Gray, John Chipman, 424
Greeley, Horace, 367
Greville, Sabine Thellusson, 611–17, 622, 624, 627, 629
Grinnell, Charles, 424
Grisi, Giulia, 148
Griswold, Mrs., 539
Grosvenor Gallery, 600
Grymes, Alfred, 282
Grymes, Mary Helen Vanderburgh James (cousin), 120, 281–82
Guérin, Pierre-Narcisse: *The Burial of Atala*, 210
Gunter, Thomas, 180
Gurney, Ellen, 416, 429
Gurney, Ephraim, 416, 429
Gurowski, Adam, 122
Guyard, Marie, 184
Gymnase (theater), 214, 672

Hall, Benjamin, 374–75
Halleck, Henry W., 487
Hallowell, A. P., 482
Hallowell, Norwood P., 492
Hamilton House (Fort Hamilton), 22
Hampton Court, 602
Hannah (nurse), 538
Hardee, William J., 493–94
Hare, John, 653–54
Harlem, 145
Harper's Monthly Magazine, 729
Harrison, Frederic, 593
Hartford, Conn., 150
Hartwell, Alfred, 483, 497
Harvard University, 233, 324, 326, 429, 523, 591; and Charles Eliot Norton, 413, 695, 699–700; during Civil War, 434, 437, 440–43, 448, 488; HJ attends law school, 434–37, 440–41, 443, 448, 455, 464, 473, 704–5; HJ attends other lectures at, 451–52, 456–59, 465–70; WJ as instructor in psychology, 417; WJ attends medical school, 521–22; WJ as undergraduate, 329–32, 337–40, 348, 350
Hatch, John Porter, 483, 494
Hathorn, George C., 145–46
Haussmann, Georges-Eugène, 198
Havemeyer (fellow student), 137
Hawthorne, Nathaniel, 297, 381–82, 641–42; *The Blithedale Romance*, 219, 503; *The House of the Seven Gables*, 51, 273, 503; *The Marble Faun*, 503–5; *The Scarlet Letter*, 51; *Twice-Told Tales*, 503; *The Wonder-Book for Boys and Girls*, 503
Haydon, Benjamin, 161, 311; *Autobiography*, 189; *The Banishment of Aristides*, 189
Haymarket Theatre, 70
Hedge, Frederic, 381
Hegel, G. W. F., 432
Heine, Heinrich, 276
Helps, Arthur, 378
Henry, Joseph, 424
Hicks, Thomas, 40–42
Higginson, Francis Lee, 332
Higginson, Samuel Storrow, 331
Higginson, Thomas Wentworth, 288
Hill, Frank H., 641
Hilton Head, S.C., 494–95
Hoboken, N.J., 145
Hoche, Lazare, 291
Hoe (fellow student), 137
Hoey, Josephine Shaw Russell, 69
Hogarth, William, 186, 192, 579, 598
Holman, Harriet Phillips, 67
Holmes, Fanny Bowditch, 637
Holmes, Oliver Wendell, Jr., 530, 567, 636–37, 692
Holmes, Oliver Wendell, Sr., 537, 558–59
Homer, 395
Hones family, 559

Honorine (guide), 228–30
Hood, John B., 493
Hooper family (Newport), 391
Horn, Kate, 68
Horniman, Annie, 738
Houssaye, Arsène, 222–23; *Philosophes et comédiennes*, 112
Houssaye, Henry, 222–23
Howard Atheneum, 470, 472
Howard, George, 641
Howe, Julia Ward, 510–11
Howe, Samuel Gridley, 510
Howells, William Dean, 519, 592, 658, 666
Hubback, Catherine, 7
Hudson River, 111, 114
Hudson River Railroad, 17–18, 111
Hudson River School, 163–64
Hugo, Victor, 676, 684; *Les Misérables*, 491
Humpert, Dr. (landlord), 270, 273–76, 283
Humpert, Theodor, 276
Humpert family, 273–74, 283
Hunt, Louisa Perkins, 341, 391
Hunt, William Holman: *The Scapegoat*, 190
Hunt, William Morris, 205, 292, 294, 298, 302–6, 311, 341; *Girl at the Fountain*, 303
Hunt family (New York City), 142, 155
Huxley, Thomas Henry, 744

Ibsen, Henrik, 684
Illustrated London News, The, 589
Indian Rebellion of 1857, 240–41
Institution Charlier, 13, 108, 117
Institution Fezandié, 201, 218–25, 241
Institution Haccius, 176, 264
Institution Maquelin, 255, 264, 267, 277
Institution Rochette, 255–61, 270, 275
Institution Vergnès, 121, 123–26, 137, 150
International Copyright Act of 1891, 664
Irish ancestors, 6–8, 418, 420–21, 569
Irving, Henry, 600
Irving, Washington, 40–41
Ives, Chauncey B., 40

James, Alice (sister): death of, 694; and death of mother, 654; with HJ in London, 647, 650; moves to Boston with father, 656–57, 659; visits Europe with Aunt Kate, 426, 429–30; WJ's references to, 525, 530; youth of, 57–58, 170, 184, 197, 225, 281–84, 331, 337–38, 340–41, 343, 349–50, 396, 409, 421
James, Alice Howe Gibbens (sister-in-law), 654
James, Augustus (uncle), 29, 36–37, 110, 112–15, 226
James, Catharine Barber (grandmother), 7–12, 28, 75, 109, 111, 323
James, Catharine Margaret (aunt). *See* Temple, Catharine Margaret James
James, Catherine Elizabeth (cousin). *See* Emmet, Catherine Elizabeth James
James, Edward (uncle), 61, 110, 112
James, Elizabeth Bay (aunt), 29, 113–15
James, Ellen King (aunt). *See* Van Buren, Ellen King James
James, Garth Wilkinson (Wilky) (brother), 552; Civil War service, 402–5, 407, 446, 480–98, 517, 551; and death of mother, 654–55; returns to Cambridge, 648–49; at Sanborn's school in Concord, 333, 388–91; WJ's references to, 331–32, 334, 337–38, 348, 350; youth of, 17, 57, 144, 164, 170, 173–76, 180–81, 195, 197, 218–19, 225, 239, 248, 255, 264, 267, 270, 273, 275–77, 281–84, 289, 291, 374, 421
James, George Abbott, 285–86
James, George Payne Rainsford, 372–73
James, Gertrude (cousin). *See* Pendleton, Gertrude James
James, Henry, Jr.:
A SMALL BOY AND OTHERS, 731; daguerreotype with father, 3, 56–57; ancestors, 6–8; Albany relatives, 8–9, 11, 13, 39, 44, 61, 74, 106, 108, 110–12, 118, 148, 178; education in New York City, 10, 14–17, 40, 83, 121,

123–32, 137, 150; outings with father, 11, 44–46, 48–49, 63, 114, 145; summers on Staten Island, 17, 21–27, 51–52, 55–56, 114, 169, 172; New York City rambles, 17–19, 30–31, 43, 62–65, 97–98, 106–7, 125, 140–41; summers in Brooklyn, 22, 41, 55; learns to dance from mother, 28; early observations of paintings, 40–43, 161–65; boyhood reading, 40, 51, 52–55, 99–102, 150–51, 176–77, 243; first theater experiences, 52–53, 66–73, 98–102, 104, 168; growing awareness of Europe, 54, 117, 139, 163, 166, 172; childhood clothing, 57; first music experiences, 72–73; entertainments taken to, 97–98, 103–6; visits Sing Sing prison, 108–10; church-going, 143–44; neighbors of, 149–57; firsthand contact with slavery, 152–55; early literary efforts, 158–60, 195–96; first visits to London, 168, 177, 179–94, 197–98; childhood illnesses, 169–71, 174, 238, 243, 246; first visits to Paris, 170, 177–79, 181, 196–233; first visit to Geneva, 173–76; views paintings in London, 179, 188–90; education in London, 180–81, 183–84, 188, 195–97, 201, 207, 218; attends theater in London, 190–94; education in Paris, 195–97, 201, 218–25; views paintings in Paris, 203–12; Galerie d'Apollon nightmare, 209–10; attends circuses in Paris, 213; attends theater in Paris, 214–17; family excursions to Boulogne-sur-Mer, 237–50; education in Boulogne, 239–41, 248–50

NOTES OF A SON AND BROTHER, 731; education in Geneva, 255–61; reading of, 257, 268–73, 307, 310, 359, 408, 427–28, 431, 460, 503–5, 513, 533–34; summer in Bonn, 264, 270–85, 288; attends theater in Bonn, 280; literary efforts, 287, 310, 315, 423; visits Paris again, 288–92; return to America, 288–93, 295; growing awareness of Europe, 289–92, 295–96, 299, 307, 344, 374, 389, 457, 545; in Newport, 289, 293, 295–320, 324–26, 346, 351; artistic sensibility, 303, 311–12, 317–18, 355; college education, 323–24, 326–27; letters from William at Harvard, 329–43, 348–50; on his father's ideas and character, 351–57, 360–84, 392–94; religious education, 355–60, 362, 365; and Civil War, 404, 407, 437–38, 442, 445–48, 480–99, 502, 513; attends dinner at Norton home, 411–13; theater recollections, 422–26, 470–72; at Harvard Law School, 434–78; injury of, 437–39; attends literature lectures at Harvard, 451, 455, 465–70; with William at Harvard, 451–57; moves to Boston, 500–502, 506, 510, 512; growing interest in Americans in Europe, 504–5; on Lincoln, 515–16; letters from William studying medicine in Germany, 523–26, 529–30; friendship with Minnie Temple, 531–70; on opera, 539, 564

THE MIDDLE YEARS, 731, 744; drawing of Henry James, 573; returns to England, 577–631; early awareness of Europe, 581; attends theater in London, 599–600; looks at paintings in London, 600–602; reading of, 605–10; at Milford Cottage in Surrey, 611–16, 622; observes London literary scene, 617–26

OTHER WORKS: *The Ambassadors*, 725; *The American*, 734–36; "Bundle of Letters," 642; *Confidence*, 642; "Covering End," 739; "Crapy Cornelia," 729; "Daisy Miller," 659, 733, 738; "The Death of the Lion," 730, 743; *The Finer Grain*, 729; "Four Meetings," 736–38; *The Golden Bowl*, 733; *Hawthorne*, 641–42; *The High Bid*, 739; *The Ivory Tower*, 730–31; "The Madonna of the Future," 736; *The Other House*, 739; "Owen Wingrave," 739; *The Outcry*, 729, 739–40; *The Portrait of a Lady*, 548, 642; *The Reprobate*, 738–40; *Roderick Hudson*, 636, 735; *The Saloon*, 739; *The Sense of the Past*,

730; "The Turn of the Screw," 739; *Washington Square*, 642; *The Wings of the Dove*, 733
James, Henry, Sr. (father), 12, 22, 35, 48–49, 55, 58, 136, 159, 173, 175, 179, 186, 237, 255, 264, 273, 280, 288, 296, 322, 325, 394, 408, 425–26, 521, 533, 566; and Alice James, 429–30, 656–57, 659; ancestors and relatives, 7–8, 29–30, 61, 114, 300, 418–22; daguerreotype with HJ, 3, 56–57; decision to return to America, 290, 292–93; educational views of, 121, 126, 133–34, 176, 180, 184, 188, 195, 210, 218, 256, 260, 323–24, 327, 389–91, 435–37; emphasis on inward life, 38–39, 47, 295, 297; friendship with Caroline Sturgis Tappan, 385, 389–91, 395–403, 407; friendship with Emerson, 9, 41, 365–69, 372–83, 390, 410; friendship with Nortons, 411–13, 415–16; friendship with Tweedys, 166, 298, 300; and HJ's reading, 53–54, 189, 257, 267–70, 310; ideas and character of, 351–57, 360–84, 392–93; interest in opera, 148; interest in painting, 162, 165; interest in theater, 65, 70, 104, 168; *Lectures and Miscellanies*, 297; *Literary Remains*, 7, 356, 361, 369; literary views of, 423–24, 430–31; outings with HJ, 11, 44–46, 48–49, 63, 114, 145; philosophical views of, 431–32; relationship with wife, 56, 353–54, 363–65, 376, 409–10, 429–30, 654–55; religious views of, 144; stories told by, 33; visits to Boston, 370–71, 373, 376–77, 379, 381; and WJ, 281–83, 285–87, 321, 323–24, 327–28, 331–33, 337–38, 340–42, 347, 417, 530
James, Howard (uncle), 61, 110, 112
James, Jeannette (aunt). *See* Barker, Jeannette James
James, John Barber (uncle), 36–37, 61, 110, 112, 119–20
James, John Vanderburgh (J. J.) (cousin), 119–20, 148
James, Marie Bay (later Marie Bay James Coster) (cousin), 115–16
James, Mary Helen Vanderburgh (cousin). *See* Grymes, Mary Helen Vanderburgh James
James, Mary Walsh (mother), 9, 12, 33, 41, 46, 52, 54–55, 108, 117, 143, 146, 173, 175, 236–37, 255, 264, 273, 295, 361, 369, 372, 374, 379, 413, 521; ancestors and relatives, 8, 29, 43, 76, 82–83, 92, 166; death of, 654–55, 658–59; decision to return to America, 290; educational views of, 121, 126, 133, 176, 188, 210, 218, 256, 260, 324, 327, 389; HJ's love for, 655–56; and HJ's reading, 75, 257, 267–69, 310; interest in opera, 72–73, 148; interest in theater, 65, 70, 104, 162, 168, 214; outings with HJ, 225–27; relationship with husband, 56, 353–54, 363–65, 376, 409–10, 429–30, 654–55; religious views of, 144; teaches HJ to dance, 28; and WJ, 281, 283, 330–33, 337–38, 340–41, 343, 349, 530
James, Robertson (Bob) (brother): Civil War service, 402, 482–86, 496–97, 517; and death of mother, 655; at Sanborn's school in Concord, 333, 388–91; visits HJ in London, 657–58; youth of, 57, 170, 197, 255, 264, 267, 277–79, 291, 297, 330, 337, 343, 374
James, William (brother), 5–6, 10, 23, 44, 48, 54, 57, 108, 144, 168, 170, 173, 201, 233–34, 273, 277, 291, 323–24, 327–28, 347, 374, 392, 407, 421, 440, 451, 455–57, 489, 649, 747; artwork by, 253, 265, 335, 405, 527; attends theater in Paris, 214–15; Bonn education of, 279; and death of Alice James, 694; and death of mother, 654–55; drawing ability of, 160–61, 188, 207, 278, 311–12; edits father's *Literary Remains*, 7, 356, 361, 369; Emerson at birth of, 9; expedition to Brazil, 505–6, 517; Geneva education of, 174, 255, 257, 261–64; at Harvard Medical School, 521–22; instructor in psychology at Harvard, 417; intellect of, 354, 418, 452–54; letters from, 281–88, 330–35, 337–43, 348–50, 429, 441, 506, 523–

27, 529–30, 639, 731; London education of, 180–83, 195; London walks with HJ, 185; and Minnie Temple, 531, 533, 538, 550, 566, 570; New York City education of, 14, 17, 56, 121, 123–33; New York City friends of, 78, 97, 155, 158; outings with father, 45, 53; Paris education of, 190, 210, 218–19, 225, 239, 248; Paris walks with HJ, 203; proposed artistic career, 286–88, 292–93, 295, 302, 321; reading of, 40, 460; studies medicine in Berlin, 523; undergraduate at Harvard, 329–32, 337–40, 348, 350; visits HJ in London, 642, 658; visits Paris art museums, 204, 206–7, 210–12
James, William (grandfather), 7–8, 39, 64, 118, 283, 370, 418–19, 569
Jarvis, John Wesley, 143
Javelli, Léon, 105
Jefferson, Joseph, 471
Jenks, Richard Pulling, 24, 125–26, 129–30, 137, 150, 157
Jesus Christ, 555, 562, 565–66
Jews, 144
Johnson, Andrew, 516
Jones, Fred, 559
Judith, Madame (Julie Bernat), 49

Kane, Lydia Sibyl, 425–26
Kaufmann (oysterman), 559
Kavanagh, Julia, 7
Kean, Charles, 191–93
Kean, Ellen Tree, 192
Keene, Laura, 68, 70
Kellogg, Clara Louise, 564
Kemble, Frances (Fanny), 192, 614, 646
Kensett, John Frederick, 40
King, Anne, 167, 232–33, 235–36, 261
King, Arthur, 167, 235
King, Charlotte, 166–67, 178, 232–36
King, Clarence William, 167, 235
King, Gracie, 532
King, Vernon, 167, 232–36
Kingston, Gertrude, 739
Kinston, N.C., 488, 490–91
Kipling, Rudyard, 665; *The Naulahka*, 662
Kiss, August, 106
Knowles, J. Sheridan: *Love, or the Countess and the Serf*, 98
Kohler, Monsieur, 526

Ladies of the Sacred Heart, 151
La Farge, John, 294, 298, 302, 305–19, 339, 460, 506–7; *The Lost Profile*, 312–13
La Fontaine, Jean: *Fables*, 195, 741
Lafontaine, Victoria, 214
Lamartine, Alphonse de, 676
Lamb, Charles and Mary: *Tales from Shakespeare*, 181
Lamb House (Rye), 726–27
Lambinet, Émile, 205
Landor, William Savage, 512
Landseer, Edwin, 189
Lang, Andrew, 653
Lawrence, Amos, 480
Lawrence, Trevor, 647
Lee, David Bradley, 532
Lee, Francis L., 446, 487
Lee, Robert E., 502
Lee, Stephen, 494
Leech, John, 39
Lefèvre, Robert-Jacques-François, 164–65
Lemaître, Frédéric, 214
Leonardo da Vinci: *Mona Lisa*, 211
Leopardi, Giacomo, 645–46
Lerambert, C. F., 195–97, 201, 218
Leslie, Charles: *Sancho Panza*, 189–90
Lessing, Gotthold Ephraim, 258
Lessing, Karl Friedrich: *Hus at the stake*, 161
Leutze, Emanuel: *Washington Crossing the Delaware*, 162–63
Leverett, William C., 303–4
Lewes, George Henry, 549, 607–8, 611, 614–16, 622
Lewes, Thornton, 607, 609
Lincoln, Abraham, 347–48, 437, 494, 496, 502, 515–16
Lind, Jenny, 82
Liverpool, England, 168, 578
Livy, 258
Locker, Frederic, 641
Lockhart, John, 591
Logan, John A., 494
Lombard, Fanny, 643
Lombard, Mrs., 643

Lomon, Charles: *Jean Dacier*, 652
London, England, 16, 19, 37, 53, 55, 106, 139, 161, 168–69, 171, 353, 361, 368–69, 374–75, 400–401, 506, 530, 659, 692, 725; art museums in, 179, 188–90, 600–602; HJ's education in, 180–81, 183–84, 188, 195–97, 201, 207, 218; HJ's first visits to, 54, 168, 177, 179–94, 197–98; HJ's later visits to, 520, 541–42, 581–631, 637–43, 647–48, 650, 652–53, 657–58; literary scene in, 605–11, 617–26, 746–47; theater in, 69–70, 105, 190–94, 599–600, 738–40; and Wolcott Balestier, 662–68
Longfellow, Henry Wadsworth, 297, 381, 421, 746
Louis XV, 147
Louis-Philippe, 15, 36
Louisville, Ky., 151
Louvre Museum, 208–12, 291–92, 303
Lowell, Charles Russell, 488
Lowell, James Russell, 297, 430, 619–21, 691, 746; "Harvard Commemoration Ode," 488; "Palinode: Autumn," 558
Lubbock, Percy, 575
Lucca, Italy, 166
Luxembourg Gallery, 190, 203–5, 212, 233
Lyceum Theater, 67–69, 600
Lyons, France, 170–71, 178

Macaulay, Thomas Babington, 279, 362
Maclise, Daniel: *Play Scene in "Hamlet,"* 189
Macmillan, Frederick, 648
Macmillan's Magazine, 642
Madison Square Theater, 659
Manet, Édouard, 312
Maquelin, Monsieur (teacher), 267, 277
Marceau-Desgraviers, François-Sévérin, 291
Mario, Giovanni Matteo, 148
Marlborough House, 189
Mars, Mademoiselle (Anne-Françoise Boutet), 214
Marseilles, France, 233, 236, 643
Martineau, Harriet, 377
Martinetti family (performers), 103–4
Mason family, 166, 227–28
Mason, Anne Lyman, 424
Mason, Gertrude, 228–30
Mason, Helen, 228–30
Mason, Herbert, 330
Mason, Lydia, 228–30
Mason, Serena, 228–30
Masonic Temple (Boston), 376
Massachusetts General Hospital, 522
Mathews, Charles: *Married for Money*, 193–94
May, John, 455
McClellan, George B., 235, 488, 525
McElroy, Joseph, 143
Mélanie, Madame (actress), 214
Mélingue, Étienne, 214
Mentone, France, 643
Mercer, Reverend, 303
Meredith, George: *Evan Harrington*, 270
Mérimée, Prosper, 312, 529; *La Vénus d'Ille*, 310
Merridew's British Library, 243, 246–47
Mesnard, Monsieur (teacher), 221–22
Mestayer, Emily, 98–99
Metcalfe, John T., 568–69
Methodists, 267
Metropolitan Hotel, 31, 104
Metternich, Klemens von, 461
Metz, France, 171
Mexican-American War, 35–36
Michelangelo Buonarroti: *The Dying Captive*, 303
Michelet, Jules, 676
Milan, Italy, 643
Mill, John Stuart, 369, 608
Millais, John Everett, 270; *Autumn Leaves*, 190; *The Blind Girl*, 190; *The Order of Release 1746*, 179; *The Vale of Rest*, 190
Milnes, Richard Monckton (later Baron Houghton), 617
Milton, Mass., 342
Milwaukee, Wis., 655
Mitchell, Margaret (Maggie), 470–71
Mobile, Ala., 491
Molière (Jean-Baptiste Poquelin): *Le bourgeois gentilhomme*, 149

Moncrieff, W. T.: *The Cataract of the Ganges*, 69
Monnier, Henri, 88, 204
Montez, Lola, 98
Montreux, Switzerland, 525
Moore, Thomas, 591
Morris, William, 542; "The Earthly Paradise," 529
Morrison (army officer), 490
Morton, John Maddison: *Betsy Baker*, 168
Motley, John Lothrop, 641
Mozier, Joseph, 40
Mulready, William, 189
Murillo, Bartolomé, 211
Museum of Fine Arts (Boston), 316–19, 506, 524
Musset, Alfred de, 676; *Il faut qu'une porte soit ouverte ou fermé*, 70

Nadali, Jean, 171, 178, 210–11
Nagle, Joseph, 68
Nagle, Mary, 68
Nantua, France, 171
Napier (fellow student), 241
Naples, Italy, 233, 642
Napoléon I (Napoléon Bonaparte), 146, 245, 255, 291, 663
Napoléon III (Louis Napoléon), 220, 263
Nash, Joseph: *The Mansions of England in the Olden Time*, 15
Nation, 380, 430, 513, 529, 636, 693
National Academy of Design, 41
National Gallery (London), 189–90, 600
National Theater, 100–101
Nepos, Cornelius, 131
Neuberg, Joseph, 375
New Bern, N.C., 486, 488
New Brighton (Staten Island), 17, 21–27, 51–52, 55–56, 114, 169, 172
Newburgh, N.Y., 8
Newport, R.I., 167, 234–36, 338, 343, 346, 381, 385, 402, 404, 460–61, 489, 500, 509, 511, 520, 546; James family resides in, 289, 293, 295–320, 324–26, 329–30, 333, 348, 351, 434, 441, 503, 506–8, 522, 545, 692; and Minnie Temple, 545–46, 549, 551–53, 556–57, 559; Portsmouth Grove, 444–46, 449
New York City, 9, 21, 24, 27, 35–37, 46, 76–77, 84–85, 87–90, 95, 108, 111, 113–14, 117, 119, 122, 142, 149, 159, 166, 171, 176, 182, 227–28, 231–32, 298, 306, 310, 373, 375, 379–80, 404, 418, 446, 469, 475, 477, 498, 513, 538, 540, 543, 557, 568–69; art galleries in, 40–43, 161–65, 205; bookstores in, 53–55; cholera outbreak, 81; churches in, 143–44; dance studios in, 143, 146–48, 150; entertainment in, 97–98, 103–6; HJ's education in, 10, 12–17, 40, 83, 121, 123–32, 137, 150, 174–75, 184–85, 218, 241, 296, 324; HJ's later visits to, 636–37, 647, 650, 654; hotels in, 8, 31, 33, 61, 145, 226; literary scene, 40–41; music and opera in, 72–73, 82, 147–48; neighborhoods of, 17–19, 30–31, 43, 60, 62–65, 97–98, 106–7, 125, 140–41, 365; "old New York," 32, 60, 169, 532, 564; photographers in, 56–57; restaurants in, 44–45, 53, 598; society in, 29; theater in, 52–53, 65–73, 98–102, 104, 162, 168, 190, 214, 659; versus Boston, 506, 509–10, 512
New York Edition, 732, 736, 742
New York Evening Post, 419
New York Hotel, 31, 33, 61, 145
New-York Tribune, 48–49, 638
New York University, 127–28
Niblo's Garden, 72, 103–5
Nice, France, 26, 643
Nightingale, Florence, 509
Norcom brothers (Eugene, Reginald, Albert), 151–52, 154
Norcom family (New York City), 142, 151–54
North American Review, 429, 501, 568, 691, 695
North Conway, N.H., 533, 553, 692
Norton, Charles Eliot, 411–14, 429, 501–2, 513, 541, 585, 695–703, 745–46; *Church-Building in the Middle Ages*, 699; *Study and Travel in Italy*, 699
Norton, Grace, 541, 605
Norton, Jane, 414–17, 429, 639, 691
Norton, Susan Sedgwick, 411, 416–17, 429, 541–42, 585, 593, 605, 691

Norton family, 411–17, 457
Notre-Dame cathedral, 199
Nuremberg, Germany, 525

Ogden family (New York City), 151
Olympic Theatre, 191–92
Once a Week, 270–71, 281, 460
Orvieto, Italy, 699
Osborne, Louis, 264–65, 267
Osborne family, 267
Osgood, Frances Locke, 41
Osgood, James, 424
Osgood, Samuel Stillman, 41

Pacific (steamship), 169
Padua, Italy, 646
Paget, James, 608–9
Pakenham, Elizabeth Staples, 642–43, 658
Pakenham, Thomas Henry, 642–43
Palais de l'Industrie, 106, 179
Palais de Luxembourg, 190, 203–5, 212, 233
Palais Royal, 229, 292, 524, 670–71
Palmerston, Viscount (Henry John Temple), 39
Pantheon art gallery, 161, 188–90
Paris, France, 19, 34–37, 106, 115, 148, 161, 184–85, 190, 237, 248, 264, 270, 277, 389, 395–96, 398, 400, 426, 430, 498, 506, 509, 746; art museums in, 203–12, 291–92, 303; HJ's education in, 195–97, 201; HJ's first visits to, 34–35, 57, 170, 177–79, 181, 196–233, 288–92, 310; HJ's later visits to, 520, 618, 637–39, 641, 643, 655, 657–58; literary scene in, 670–86; theater in, 49, 193, 214–17, 259, 638, 652–53, 738; WJ's later visits to, 281, 285, 523–24
Parker, Joel, 465, 469–70
Parker, Theodore, 369
Parkhurst, William H., 43–44
Park Street Church, 515
Park Theater, 72
Parsons, Theophilus, 465–66, 468
Pasca, Madame, 523
Pascoe, Mrs. (landlady), 330
Passy, 200
Patti, Adelina, 72
Pavilion (New Brighton), 21–22, 27, 52
Payn, James, 687–89
Peabody, Arthur P., 340
Peirce, Charles Sanders, 638
Pendleton, Gertrude James (cousin), 29, 226–27, 231
Pendleton, James M., 29–30, 226, 231
Pensionnat Roediger, 174–76
Pension Sillig (Vevey), 119–20
Penzance, England, 643
Perkins, Helen Wyckoff, 76–79, 81, 84–85, 154
Perkins, Leonard, 84–85
Perkins, William E., 488, 495
Perry, Matthew C., 339
Perry, Oliver H., 339
Perry, Thomas Sergeant, 320, 337–39, 431, 512, 523, 529–30
Peters, Mr. (of Philadelphia), 277–78
Petersburg, Va., 167, 235, 483
Phelps (fellow student), 137
Philadelphia, Pa., 44, 277, 379, 509–10, 543–44, 559, 563, 691
Phillipps, Adelaide, 564
Phillips, Wendell, 342
Phiz (Hablot K. Browne), 43, 72, 127
Pierson, Blanche, 215–16, 672
Placide, Henry, 68
Planché, James Robertson: *The Discreet Princess*, 193
Plato, 395
Plumley, Miss (teacher), 390
Poe, Edgar Allan, 41, 297, 483; "Annabel Lee," 40; "The Gold-Bug," 40; "Lenore," 40; "The Murders in the Rue Morgue," 40; "The Pit and the Pendulum," 40; "The Raven," 40
Ponisi, Elizabeth Hanson, 68–69
Ponsard, François: *Ce qui plaît aux femmes*, 215–16
Poole, John: *Paul Pry*, 67
Portland, Me., 474
Portsmouth Grove, R.I., 444–46, 449
Posilippo, Italy, 642
Post, Mary Minturn, 425, 568–69
Potter, Edward F., 483
Powers, Hiram, 40
Pradier, Jean-Jacques, 227
Pratt, Herbert, 644–45
Pray, Malvina, 67

Pre-Raphaelites, 190
Prince of Wales's Theatre, 599
Princess's Theatre, 191
Pritchard, Hannah Vaughan, 192
Probyn, Dighton Macnaghten, 613
Probyn, Letitia Thellusson, 613
Providence, R.I., 324, 474, 511
Prud'hon, Pierre-Paul: *Cupid and Psyche*, 210
Pruyn family (Albany), 33
Punch, 38, 225, 460
Puritans, 370–71, 468, 471, 487, 702
Pynsent's confectionery, 141

Quackenbos, Mr. (teacher), 131–32, 137
Quakers, 511–12
Quincy, Henry Parker, 330

Rabe, Annie Crawford von, 557–58
Rachel, Madame (Élisa Félix), 49, 214–15, 259, 374
Racine, Jean: *Phèdre*, 259
Ravel family (acrobats), 103–4
Rawle, Mary Cadwalader, 559
Reade, Charles: *The Cloister and the Hearth*, 270; *A Good Fight*, 270
Readville, Mass., 446, 480–81
Récamier, Jeanne-Françoise Bernard, 24
Reform Club, 641, 731
Reichhardt-Stromberg, Mathilde, 117, 279
Rembrandt Harmensz van Rijn, 600, 670
Renan, Ernest, 618
Renouvier, Charles, 417
Revolutionary War, 8, 303
Revolution of 1848 (France), 36–37
Revue des Deux Mondes, 289–90, 299–300, 306–7, 309, 331, 373, 408, 426–27, 436
Rhinebeck, N.Y., 110–11, 113–14, 159, 226
Richmond, Va., 235, 483
Rimini, Italy, 645–46
Ripley, Eliza, 654
Ripley, George, 40
Ristori, Adelaide, 83, 280
Ritter, Charles, 526
Robarts, Charles H., 641
Robertson, Alexander, 8, 81–82, 143
Robertson, Forbes, 739
Robertson, Thomas William, 599
Robeson, Alice, 342
Robeson, Andrew, 332
Robeson, Mary Isabelle, 654
Robin Hood, 182
Robinson, Solon, 51; *Hot Corn*, 49–50
Robinson family (New York City), 142
Robson, Frederick, 191, 193
Rochester, N.Y., 662
Rochette, Monsieur (teacher), 255
Rodgers, Katharine, 654
Roediger, Monsieur (teacher), 175
Rogers, Miss (teacher), 14
Rogers, Samuel, 591–92
Rogerson, Christina Stewart, 641
Rome, Italy, 164, 166, 503–5, 509, 512, 541, 546, 641–42, 645, 742
Romulus and Remus, 137
Ronconi, Giorgio, 72
Ropes, John Codman, 330
Rose, Charlotte Temple, 637
Rossetti, Dante Gabriel, 542
Rossini, Giacchino: *William Tell*, 563–64
Rothschild, Miss de, 658
Rousby, Clara (actress), 83–84
Rousseau, Jean-Jacques: *Confessions*, 112, 462
Rousseau, Lovell H., 493
Rousseau, Théodore, 205
Rowney (artists' supplies), 188
Royal Academy, 190
Royal Society of Literature, 740
Rubens, Peter Paul, 189, 600, 631
Ruskin, John, 541, 699, 746
Russel, Cabot Jackson, 402–4, 446, 488
Russel, William C., 404
Russell, Arthur, 658
Russell, John, 39
Rutson, Albert, 585, 590
Ruysdael, Jacob van, 177
Ryder, John, 191
Rye, England, 726, 747

Sade, Donatien-Alphonse-François de, 623–24
Sade, Laure de, 622–23
Sadowa, battle of, 520
Saint-Cloud, 199

Sainte-Beuve, Charles-Augustin: *Causeries du lundi*, 197, 464–65
Saint-Gaudens, Augustus: Shaw Memorial, 446
St. Leonards-on-Sea, England, 642
St. Mivart, George, 429
St. Nicholas Hotel, 31
St. Paul's Cathedral, 183
Salter, Charles, 350, 455–56
Samson, Joseph, 214
Sanborn, Franklin B., 333, 386, 388–89, 391
Sand, George, 426–29, 652, 676, 682; *Les beaux messieurs de Bois-Doré*, 529; *La Daniella*, 529; *La famille de Germandre*, 427–28; *Francia*, 427, 429; *L'homme de neige*, 427–28; *Jacques*, 428; *Mademoiselle La Quintinie*, 427; *La mare au diable*, 428; *Nanon*, 427; *La petite Fadette*, 471; *Tamaris*, 427; *Valentine*, 428; *Valvèdre*, 427; *La ville noire*, 427
San Francisco, Calif., 557–60
Sanitary Commission, U.S., 509
San Remo, Italy, 643
Saratoga, N.Y., 520
Sardou, Victorien, 652; *Patrie*, 216
Saturday Review, 167
Sauvage, Prosper, 242
Savannah, Ga., 492–93, 495
Schelling, Friedrich von, 367
Schenectady, N.Y., 323–24
Schiller, Friedrich von, 258; *Mary Stuart*, 280; *The Robbers*, 347; *Thirty Years' War*, 272
Scotch Presbyterian Church, 142–43
Scott, Walter, 269, 591, 650; *Redgauntlet*, 651
Scott, Winfield, 35, 41, 127
Scottish ancestors, 7–8, 143
Scribe, Eugène, 217, 676
Sedan, battle of, 520
Sedgwick, Arthur, 411, 533, 592
Sedgwick, Miss (teacher), 15
Sedgwick family, 416
Semler, Christian, 525
Senter family (New York City), 142
Sepoy Mutiny, 240–41
Sévigné, Marie de, 343
Seymour, Truman, 483
Shady Hill (Norton home), 411–16, 429, 457, 501–2, 691, 697, 701, 745
Shakespeare, William, 62, 67, 99, 181, 193, 362, 600; *As You Like It*, 177; *The Comedy of Errors*, 66; *Hamlet*, 189, 504; *Henry VIII*, 191–92; *King John*, 41; *Macbeth*, 192; *The Merchant of Venice*, 70; *A Midsummer Night's Dream*, 68; *Much Ado about Nothing*, 68; *Othello*, 70
Shaw, Francis G., and family, 22, 403
Shaw, Robert Gould, 402, 446
Sheridan, Richard Brinsley, 591; *The Critic*, 193
Sherman, William T., 492–95
Sickles, Daniel, 350
Sillig, Monsieur (teacher), 120
Simpson (fellow student), 138–40, 296
Sing Sing prison, 108–10, 117
Smith, Albert: *Tour of Mont Blanc*, 191
Smithsonian Institution, 424
Smollett, Tobias, 579, 598
Société de Zofingue, 262–63, 282
Somerville Asylum, 424
Sontag, Henriette, 72
Sorrento, Italy, 166, 642
South Kensington Museum (now Victoria and Albert Museum), 602
Springfield, Mass., 474
Stage Society, 738–39
Stanley, Miss, 650
Staten Island, N.Y., 17, 21–27, 51–52, 55–56, 114, 169, 172
Stearns, Mrs. (dressmaker), 391
Steffanone, Balbina, 72
Sterling, John, 368–69
Stevenson, Robert Louis, 180, 747
Stewart's department store, 44, 66
Stirling, Fanny, 191
Stirling, J. H., 430
Stokes (fellow student), 137
Storrow, Samuel, 495
Stowe, Harriet Beecher: *Uncle Tom's Cabin*, 99–102, 153–54
Strasbourg, France, 288
Stromberg, Theodor, 279
Strong, Eleanor Fearing, 638
Stuart, Gilbert, 424
Stuyvesant Institute, 162

Sullivan, Arthur, 600
Sumner, Charles, 34–35, 38, 380
Susini, Agostino, 564
Swampscott, Mass., 349, 519, 522, 606, 692–93
Swedenborg, Emanuel, 144, 352–53, 361–62, 382; *Arcana Coelestia*, 353; *Heaven and Hell*, 353
Sweetser, Mr. and Mrs. (landlords), 340, 342
Swinburne, Algernon Charles: "Atalanta in Calydon," 601
Sylvia (slave), 153–54

Talleyrand-Périgord, Charles-Maurice de, 461
Talma, François-Joseph, 220
Tappan, Caroline Sturgis, 385–86, 389–91, 395–403, 407
Tappan, Ellen, 340
Tappan, Mary Aspinwall, 337, 340
Tappan, William Aspinwall, 337, 340
Tautphoeus, Jemima Montgomery: *The Initials*, 51, 53, 99
Taylor, Bayard, 592
Taylor, Billy, 418, 420
Taylor, Dr., 568–69
Taylor, Mary Cecilia, 67–68
Taylor, Tom: *Still Waters Run Deep*, 192
Taylor's ice-cream parlor, 44–45, 53
Temple, Catharine Margaret James (aunt), 12, 114
Temple, Ellen. *See* Emmet, Ellen (Elly) Temple
Temple, Henrietta (later Henrietta Temple Pell-Clarke), 12, 549
Temple, Katharine. *See* Emmet, Katharine (Kitty) Temple
Temple, Mary (Minnie), 12, 298, 300–302, 531–70
Temple, Robert Emmet, Jr. (Bob), 12, 343–47
Temple, Robert Emmet, Sr., 12, 36, 114
Temple, William James, 12, 326–27, 330, 343, 346
Temple family, 166, 312, 532, 554, 557–61, 693
Tennyson, Alfred, 542, 617–20, 625–26; "In Memoriam," 622; "Locksley Hall," 621, 624
Tennyson, Emily Sellwood, 620–21
Tennyson, Hallam, 620
Terry, Ellen, 739
Thackeray, William Makepeace, 58, 183, 344, 346, 579; *The English Humorists*, 57; *Men's Wives*, 243; *The Newcomes*, 59, 239, 243, 269, 728; *Pendennis*, 243–44, 427, 472; *Roundabout Papers*, 268; *Vanity Fair*, 197–98
Thames Tunnel, 183
Théâtre Français, 49, 215, 222, 259
Thellusson, Marie Macnaghten, 613
Thies, Louis, 331
Thomas, George H., 493
Thomas family (New York City and Paris), 265, 267
Thompson, Elizabeth, 643
Thompson's ice-cream parlor, 44–45, 53
Thomson, Robert, 180–81, 183–84, 195, 197, 207
Théaulon, Emmanuel: *Le père de la débutante*, 68
Thorvaldsen, Bertel: *Christ and the Twelve Disciples*, 106
Times (London), 180, 579
Titian (Tiziano Vecelli), 189, 472, 670; *Bacchus and Ariadne*, 600–601; *Portrait of Ariosto*, 600
Toledo, Spain, 644
Toole, John, 84
Töppfer, Charles, 258–59
Töppfer, Rodolphe, 258; *Nouvelle Genevoises*, 259; *Voyages en Zigzag*, 176–77
Tours, France, 166, 227
Tower of London, 183
Townsend family (Albany), 33
Travellers' Club, 641
Trevilian, Edwin Cely, 648
Trinity Church (Newport), 303
Trinity Church (New York City), 44
Tripler Hall, 72
Trollope, Anthony, 359, 553; *The Eustace Diamonds*, 429; *Framley Parsonage*, 268
Trollope, Frances, 7
Trouville, France, 166, 227
Troyon, Constant, 205
Tuckerman, Henry T., 297

Tuileries, 199, 204, 228, 289
Turgenev, Ivan, 424, 431, 746
Turgenev, Madame (widow of Nikolai Turgenev), 638
Turin, Italy, 278
Turner, J.M.W., 163
Tussaud, Marie, 183–84
Tweedy, Edmund, 166, 298, 341–42, 506
Tweedy, Mary Temple, 166, 298, 300, 341–42, 400, 506, 508–9

Uhland, Ludwig, 276
Union College, 323–24
Union Square, 43, 60, 62, 64, 101, 123, 147
Unitarians, 349, 381, 441
University of Aberdeen, 345
University of Cambridge, 350
Upham, Catharine, 331–32, 334, 348–49, 441–42, 444, 451, 458
Urbino, Italy, 646

Van Buren, Ellen King James (aunt), 11
Van Buren family (New York City), 142
Van Buren, Martin, 11
Van Buren, Smith Thompson, 11
Vanderpool, Beach, 458–59
Van Rensselaer, Anne, 645
Van Rensselaer family (Albany), 33
Van Winkle, Edgar, 157
Van Winkle family (New York City), 142, 151, 156–57
Varennes, France, 639, 642
Varian, Isaac Leggett, 143
Varick, Richard, 143
Venice, Italy, 430, 512, 519, 592, 631, 643–46, 742
Ventnor, England, 369, 372
Verchère, Monsieur (teacher), 258
Vergnès, Monsieur (teacher), 124
Veronese, Bonifazio, 631
Veronese, Paolo, 211; *Family of Darius*, 600
Versailles, France, 167
Vevey, Switzerland, 119–20
Viardot, Pauline, 746
Vicenza, Italy, 646
Victor Emmanuel II, 263, 278
Victoria, Queen, 29
Vigée Le Brun, Élisabeth, 210
Viollet-le-Duc, Eugène-Emmanuel, 511
Virgil, 258
Voltaire (François-Marie Arouet), 146, 456
Vredenburg, Mrs. (teacher), 17, 23

Wallack, Fanny, 69
Wallack, Lester, 67–68, 70
Walsh, Alexander Robertson, 81–82
Walsh, Catharine (later Catharine Walsh Marshall) (Aunt Kate), 43–44, 54, 76, 82, 84, 92, 95–96, 146, 214, 225, 264, 281, 283, 331, 337–38, 342–43, 426, 429, 530, 654
Walsh, Elizabeth Robertson, 76, 79, 82
Walsh, Hugh, 8
Walsh, John A. Robertson, 82–83
Walsh, Lily, 654
Walsh, Robertson, 83, 296
Ward, Samuel Gray, 333, 341
Ward, Thomas, 331, 333–34
Ward brothers (Johnny, Charley, Freddy), 150–52, 156–57
Ward family (New York City), 142, 149–52, 155–56
War of 1812, 339
Warren, William, 524
Washburn, Emory, 465–68
Washburn, Frank, 524, 529–30
Washington, D.C., 494, 497, 567, 569, 590, 654–55, 691
Washington, George, 162, 535
Washington Square, 63–64, 127, 143
Waterford, Lady (Louisa Beresford), 627–29, 631
Waterford, Marques of (Henry Beresford), 631
Waterloo, battle of, 221, 490–91
Waterman, Miss (teacher), 390
Webster, Daniel, 34, 38, 466
Webster, Matthew Henry, 424–26
Welles, Gideon, 497
Wellington, Duke of (Arthur Wellesley), 189
Westminster Abbey, 183
Weston, Elizabeth (Lizzie), 73
Wharton, Edith, 747; *Ethan Frome*, 741–42; *The Reef*, 742
Whig Party, 35
Whitehall, N.C., 491

Whitman, Walt, 51, 396, 445, 447–48
Wigan, Alfred, 191–93
Wilkie, David, 189
Wilkinson, Emma, 378
Wilkinson, James John Garth, 374, 380, 399; *The Human Body and Its Connection with Man*, 375; *War, Cholera, and the Ministry of Health*, 374–75
William (coachman), 343
Williamsburg (Brooklyn), 145
Willis, Nathaniel Parker, 40, 423
Wilmington, N.C., 491
Windsor Palace, 602
Winsor & Newton (artists' supplies), 188
Winthrop, Theodore, 128
Wister, Sarah Butler, 641
Wood, Mrs., 349
Worcester, Mass., 474
Wordsworth, William, 417
World War I, 743
Wright, Chauncey, 428–29
Wright, Lavinia D., 15–17, 27–28, 31
Wyckoff, Albert, 76, 78–79, 84, 87–90, 93, 97, 142, 155
Wyckoff, Alexander, 81, 84, 94
Wyckoff, Helen. *See* Perkins, Helen Wyckoff
Wyckoff, Henry, 84, 90–96
Wyckoff, Mary (Great-Aunt Wyckoff), 78–81, 84
Wyman, Jeffries, 332, 348, 350

Yale College, 324, 326
Young, Mrs. William, 498

Zhukovsky, Vassili (Paul Joukowsky), 638, 642
Zoffany, Johann, 192
Zola, Émile, 638; *Son Excellence Eugène Rougon*, 199–200
Zoological Gardens (London), 183
Zurich Polytechnic School, 255–56

THE LIBRARY OF AMERICA SERIES

The Library of America fosters appreciation and pride in America's literary heritage by publishing, and keeping permanently in print, authoritative editions of America's best and most significant writing. An independent nonprofit organization, it was founded in 1979 with seed funding from the National Endowment for the Humanities and the Ford Foundation.

1. Herman Melville: *Typee, Omoo, Mardi*
2. Nathaniel Hawthorne: *Tales and Sketches*
3. Walt Whitman: *Poetry and Prose*
4. Harriet Beecher Stowe: *Three Novels*
5. Mark Twain: *Mississippi Writings*
6. Jack London: *Novels and Stories*
7. Jack London: *Novels and Social Writings*
8. William Dean Howells: *Novels 1875–1886*
9. Herman Melville: *Redburn, White-Jacket, Moby-Dick*
10. Nathaniel Hawthorne: *Collected Novels*
11. Francis Parkman: *France and England in North America*, Vol. I
12. Francis Parkman: *France and England in North America*, Vol. II
13. Henry James: *Novels 1871–1880*
14. Henry Adams: *Novels, Mont Saint Michel, The Education*
15. Ralph Waldo Emerson: *Essays and Lectures*
16. Washington Irving: *History, Tales and Sketches*
17. Thomas Jefferson: *Writings*
18. Stephen Crane: *Prose and Poetry*
19. Edgar Allan Poe: *Poetry and Tales*
20. Edgar Allan Poe: *Essays and Reviews*
21. Mark Twain: *The Innocents Abroad, Roughing It*
22. Henry James: *Literary Criticism: Essays, American & English Writers*
23. Henry James: *Literary Criticism: European Writers & The Prefaces*
24. Herman Melville: *Pierre, Israel Potter, The Confidence-Man, Tales & Billy Budd*
25. William Faulkner: *Novels 1930–1935*
26. James Fenimore Cooper: *The Leatherstocking Tales*, Vol. I
27. James Fenimore Cooper: *The Leatherstocking Tales*, Vol. II
28. Henry David Thoreau: *A Week, Walden, The Maine Woods, Cape Cod*
29. Henry James: *Novels 1881–1886*
30. Edith Wharton: *Novels*
31. Henry Adams: *History of the U.S. during the Administrations of Jefferson*
32. Henry Adams: *History of the U.S. during the Administrations of Madison*
33. Frank Norris: *Novels and Essays*
34. W.E.B. Du Bois: *Writings*
35. Willa Cather: *Early Novels and Stories*
36. Theodore Dreiser: *Sister Carrie, Jennie Gerhardt, Twelve Men*

37a. Benjamin Franklin: *Silence Dogood, The Busy-Body, & Early Writings*

37b. Benjamin Franklin: *Autobiography, Poor Richard, & Later Writings*

38. William James: *Writings 1902–1910*
39. Flannery O'Connor: *Collected Works*
40. Eugene O'Neill: *Complete Plays 1913–1920*
41. Eugene O'Neill: *Complete Plays 1920–1931*
42. Eugene O'Neill: *Complete Plays 1932–1943*
43. Henry James: *Novels 1886–1890*
44. William Dean Howells: *Novels 1886–1888*
45. Abraham Lincoln: *Speeches and Writings 1832–1858*
46. Abraham Lincoln: *Speeches and Writings 1859–1865*
47. Edith Wharton: *Novellas and Other Writings*
48. William Faulkner: *Novels 1936–1940*
49. Willa Cather: *Later Novels*
50. Ulysses S. Grant: *Memoirs and Selected Letters*
51. William Tecumseh Sherman: *Memoirs*
52. Washington Irving: *Bracebridge Hall, Tales of a Traveller, The Alhambra*
53. Francis Parkman: *The Oregon Trail, The Conspiracy of Pontiac*
54. James Fenimore Cooper: *Sea Tales: The Pilot, The Red Rover*
55. Richard Wright: *Early Works*
56. Richard Wright: *Later Works*
57. Willa Cather: *Stories, Poems, and Other Writings*
58. William James: *Writings 1878–1899*
59. Sinclair Lewis: *Main Street & Babbitt*
60. Mark Twain: *Collected Tales, Sketches, Speeches, & Essays 1852–1890*
61. Mark Twain: *Collected Tales, Sketches, Speeches, & Essays 1891–1910*
62. *The Debate on the Constitution: Part One*
63. *The Debate on the Constitution: Part Two*
64. Henry James: *Collected Travel Writings: Great Britain & America*
65. Henry James: *Collected Travel Writings: The Continent*

66. *American Poetry: The Nineteenth Century*, Vol. 1
67. *American Poetry: The Nineteenth Century*, Vol. 2
68. Frederick Douglass: *Autobiographies*
69. Sarah Orne Jewett: *Novels and Stories*
70. Ralph Waldo Emerson: *Collected Poems and Translations*
71. Mark Twain: *Historical Romances*
72. John Steinbeck: *Novels and Stories 1932–1937*
73. William Faulkner: *Novels 1942–1954*
74. Zora Neale Hurston: *Novels and Stories*
75. Zora Neale Hurston: *Folklore, Memoirs, and Other Writings*
76. Thomas Paine: *Collected Writings*
77. *Reporting World War II: American Journalism 1938–1944*
78. *Reporting World War II: American Journalism 1944–1946*
79. Raymond Chandler: *Stories and Early Novels*
80. Raymond Chandler: *Later Novels and Other Writings*
81. Robert Frost: *Collected Poems, Prose, & Plays*
82. Henry James: *Complete Stories 1892–1898*
83. Henry James: *Complete Stories 1898–1910*
84. William Bartram: *Travels and Other Writings*
85. John Dos Passos: *U.S.A.*
86. John Steinbeck: *The Grapes of Wrath and Other Writings 1936–1941*
87. Vladimir Nabokov: *Novels and Memoirs 1941–1951*
88. Vladimir Nabokov: *Novels 1955–1962*
89. Vladimir Nabokov: *Novels 1969–1974*
90. James Thurber: *Writings and Drawings*
91. George Washington: *Writings*
92. John Muir: *Nature Writings*
93. Nathanael West: *Novels and Other Writings*
94. *Crime Novels: American Noir of the 1930s and 40s*
95. *Crime Novels: American Noir of the 1950s*
96. Wallace Stevens: *Collected Poetry and Prose*
97. James Baldwin: *Early Novels and Stories*
98. James Baldwin: *Collected Essays*
99. Gertrude Stein: *Writings 1903–1932*
100. Gertrude Stein: *Writings 1932–1946*
101. Eudora Welty: *Complete Novels*
102. Eudora Welty: *Stories, Essays, & Memoir*
103. Charles Brockden Brown: *Three Gothic Novels*
104. *Reporting Vietnam: American Journalism 1959–1969*
105. *Reporting Vietnam: American Journalism 1969–1975*
106. Henry James: *Complete Stories 1874–1884*
107. Henry James: *Complete Stories 1884–1891*
108. *American Sermons: The Pilgrims to Martin Luther King Jr.*
109. James Madison: *Writings*
110. Dashiell Hammett: *Complete Novels*
111. Henry James: *Complete Stories 1864–1874*
112. William Faulkner: *Novels 1957–1962*
113. John James Audubon: *Writings & Drawings*
114. *Slave Narratives*
115. *American Poetry: The Twentieth Century*, Vol. 1
116. *American Poetry: The Twentieth Century*, Vol. 2
117. F. Scott Fitzgerald: *Novels and Stories 1920–1922*
118. Henry Wadsworth Longfellow: *Poems and Other Writings*
119. Tennessee Williams: *Plays 1937–1955*
120. Tennessee Williams: *Plays 1957–1980*
121. Edith Wharton: *Collected Stories 1891–1910*
122. Edith Wharton: *Collected Stories 1911–1937*
123. *The American Revolution: Writings from the War of Independence*
124. Henry David Thoreau: *Collected Essays and Poems*
125. Dashiell Hammett: *Crime Stories and Other Writings*
126. Dawn Powell: *Novels 1930–1942*
127. Dawn Powell: *Novels 1944–1962*
128. Carson McCullers: *Complete Novels*
129. Alexander Hamilton: *Writings*
130. Mark Twain: *The Gilded Age and Later Novels*
131. Charles W. Chesnutt: *Stories, Novels, and Essays*
132. John Steinbeck: *Novels 1942–1952*
133. Sinclair Lewis: *Arrowsmith, Elmer Gantry, Dodsworth*
134. Paul Bowles: *The Sheltering Sky, Let It Come Down, The Spider's House*
135. Paul Bowles: *Collected Stories & Later Writings*
136. Kate Chopin: *Complete Novels & Stories*
137. *Reporting Civil Rights: American Journalism 1941–1963*
138. *Reporting Civil Rights: American Journalism 1963–1973*
139. Henry James: *Novels 1896–1899*
140. Theodore Dreiser: *An American Tragedy*
141. Saul Bellow: *Novels 1944–1953*
142. John Dos Passos: *Novels 1920–1925*

143. John Dos Passos: *Travel Books and Other Writings*
144. Ezra Pound: *Poems and Translations*
145. James Weldon Johnson: *Writings*
146. Washington Irving: *Three Western Narratives*
147. Alexis de Tocqueville: *Democracy in America*
148. James T. Farrell: *Studs Lonigan: A Trilogy*
149. Isaac Bashevis Singer: *Collected Stories I*
150. Isaac Bashevis Singer: *Collected Stories II*
151. Isaac Bashevis Singer: *Collected Stories III*
152. Kaufman & Co.: *Broadway Comedies*
153. Theodore Roosevelt: *The Rough Riders, An Autobiography*
154. Theodore Roosevelt: *Letters and Speeches*
155. H. P. Lovecraft: *Tales*
156. Louisa May Alcott: *Little Women, Little Men, Jo's Boys*
157. Philip Roth: *Novels & Stories 1959–1962*
158. Philip Roth: *Novels 1967–1972*
159. James Agee: *Let Us Now Praise Famous Men, A Death in the Family*
160. James Agee: *Film Writing & Selected Journalism*
161. Richard Henry Dana Jr.: *Two Years Before the Mast & Other Voyages*
162. Henry James: *Novels 1901–1902*
163. Arthur Miller: *Collected Plays 1944–1961*
164. William Faulkner: *Novels 1926–1929*
165. Philip Roth: *Novels 1973–1977*
166. *American Speeches: Part One*
167. *American Speeches: Part Two*
168. Hart Crane: *Complete Poems & Selected Letters*
169. Saul Bellow: *Novels 1956–1964*
170. John Steinbeck: *Travels with Charley and Later Novels*
171. Capt. John Smith: *Writings with Other Narratives*
172. Thornton Wilder: *Collected Plays & Writings on Theater*
173. Philip K. Dick: *Four Novels of the 1960s*
174. Jack Kerouac: *Road Novels 1957–1960*
175. Philip Roth: *Zuckerman Bound*
176. Edmund Wilson: *Literary Essays & Reviews of the 1920s & 30s*
177. Edmund Wilson: *Literary Essays & Reviews of the 1930s & 40s*
178. *American Poetry: The 17th & 18th Centuries*
179. William Maxwell: *Early Novels & Stories*
180. Elizabeth Bishop: *Poems, Prose, & Letters*
181. A. J. Liebling: *World War II Writings*
182s. *American Earth: Environmental Writing Since Thoreau*
183. Philip K. Dick: *Five Novels of the 1960s & 70s*
184. William Maxwell: *Later Novels & Stories*
185. Philip Roth: *Novels & Other Narratives 1986–1991*
186. Katherine Anne Porter: *Collected Stories & Other Writings*
187. John Ashbery: *Collected Poems 1956–1987*
188. John Cheever: *Collected Stories & Other Writings*
189. John Cheever: *Complete Novels*
190. Lafcadio Hearn: *American Writings*
191. A. J. Liebling: *The Sweet Science & Other Writings*
192s. *The Lincoln Anthology: Great Writers on His Life and Legacy from 1860 to Now*
193. Philip K. Dick: *VALIS & Later Novels*
194. Thornton Wilder: *The Bridge of San Luis Rey and Other Novels 1926–1948*
195. Raymond Carver: *Collected Stories*
196. *American Fantastic Tales: Terror and the Uncanny from Poe to the Pulps*
197. *American Fantastic Tales: Terror and the Uncanny from the 1940s to Now*
198. John Marshall: *Writings*
199s. *The Mark Twain Anthology: Great Writers on His Life and Works*
200. Mark Twain: *A Tramp Abroad, Following the Equator, Other Travels*
201. Ralph Waldo Emerson: *Selected Journals 1820–1842*
202. Ralph Waldo Emerson: *Selected Journals 1841–1877*
203. *The American Stage: Writing on Theater from Washington Irving to Tony Kushner*
204. Shirley Jackson: *Novels & Stories*
205. Philip Roth: *Novels 1993–1995*
206. H. L. Mencken: *Prejudices: First, Second, and Third Series*
207. H. L. Mencken: *Prejudices: Fourth, Fifth, and Sixth Series*
208. John Kenneth Galbraith: *The Affluent Society and Other Writings 1952–1967*
209. Saul Bellow: *Novels 1970–1982*
210. Lynd Ward: *Gods' Man, Madman's Drum, Wild Pilgrimage*
211. Lynd Ward: *Prelude to a Million Years, Song Without Words, Vertigo*
212. *The Civil War: The First Year Told by Those Who Lived It*
213. John Adams: *Revolutionary Writings 1755–1775*
214. John Adams: *Revolutionary Writings 1775–1783*
215. Henry James: *Novels 1903–1911*
216. Kurt Vonnegut: *Novels & Stories 1963–1973*

217. *Harlem Renaissance: Five Novels of the 1920s*
218. *Harlem Renaissance: Four Novels of the 1930s*
219. Ambrose Bierce: *The Devil's Dictionary, Tales, & Memoirs*
220. Philip Roth: *The American Trilogy 1997–2000*
221. *The Civil War: The Second Year Told by Those Who Lived It*
222. Barbara W. Tuchman: *The Guns of August & The Proud Tower*
223. Arthur Miller: *Collected Plays 1964–1982*
224. Thornton Wilder: *The Eighth Day, Theophilus North, Autobiographical Writings*
225. David Goodis: *Five Noir Novels of the 1940s & 50s*
226. Kurt Vonnegut: *Novels & Stories 1950–1962*
227. *American Science Fiction: Four Classic Novels 1953–1956*
228. *American Science Fiction: Five Classic Novels 1956–1958*
229. Laura Ingalls Wilder: *The Little House Books, Volume One*
230. Laura Ingalls Wilder: *The Little House Books, Volume Two*
231. Jack Kerouac: *Collected Poems*
232. *The War of 1812: Writings from America's Second War of Independence*
233. *American Antislavery Writings: Colonial Beginnings to Emancipation*
234. *The Civil War: The Third Year Told by Those Who Lived It*
235. Sherwood Anderson: *Collected Stories*
236. Philip Roth: *Novels 2001–2007*
237. Philip Roth: *Nemeses*
238. Aldo Leopold: *A Sand County Almanac & Other Writings on Ecology and Conservation*
239. May Swenson: *Collected Poems*
240. W. S. Merwin: *Collected Poems 1952–1993*
241. W. S. Merwin: *Collected Poems 1996–2011*
242. John Updike: *Collected Early Stories*
243. John Updike: *Collected Later Stories*
244. Ring Lardner: *Stories & Other Writings*
245. Jonathan Edwards: *Writings from the Great Awakening*
246. Susan Sontag: *Essays of the 1960s & 70s*
247. William Wells Brown: *Clotel & Other Writings*
248. Bernard Malamud: *Novels and Stories of the 1940s & 50s*
249. Bernard Malamud: *Novels and Stories of the 1960s*
250. *The Civil War: The Final Year Told by Those Who Lived It*
251. *Shakespeare in America: An Anthology from the Revolution to Now*
252. Kurt Vonnegut: *Novels 1976–1985*
253. *American Musicals 1927–1949: The Complete Books & Lyrics of Eight Broadway Classics*
254. *American Musicals 1950–1969: The Complete Books & Lyrics of Eight Broadway Classics*
255. Elmore Leonard: *Four Novels of the 1970s*
256. Louisa May Alcott: *Work, Eight Cousins, Rose in Bloom, Stories & Other Writings*
257. H. L. Mencken: *The Days Trilogy, Expanded Edition*
258. Virgil Thomson: *Music Chronicles 1940–1954*
259. *Art in America 1945–1970: Writings from the Age of Abstract Expressionism, Pop Art, and Minimalism*
260. Saul Bellow: *Novels 1984–2000*
261. Arthur Miller: *Collected Plays 1987–2004*
262. Jack Kerouac: *Visions of Cody, Visions of Gerard, Big Sur*
263. Reinhold Niebuhr: *Major Works on Religion and Politics*
264. Ross Macdonald: *Four Novels of the 1950s*
265. *The American Revolution: Writings from the Pamphlet Debate, Volume I, 1764–1772*
266. *The American Revolution: Writings from the Pamphlet Debate, Volume II, 1773–1776*
267. Elmore Leonard: *Four Novels of the 1980s*
268. *Women Crime Writers: Four Suspense Novels of the 1940s*
269. *Women Crime Writers: Four Suspense Novels of the 1950s*
270. Frederick Law Olmsted: *Writings on Landscape, Culture, and Society*
271. Edith Wharton: *Four Novels of the 1920s*
272. James Baldwin: *Later Novels*

This book is set in 10 point ITC Galliard, a face designed for digital composition by Matthew Carter and based on the sixteenth-century face Granjon. The paper is acid-free lightweight opaque that will not turn yellow or brittle with age. The binding is sewn, which allows the book to open easily and lie flat. The binding board is covered in Brillianta, a woven rayon cloth made by Van Heek–Scholco Textielfabrieken, Holland. Composition by Dedicated Book Services. Printing and binding by Edwards Brothers Malloy, Ann Arbor. Designed by Bruce Campbell.

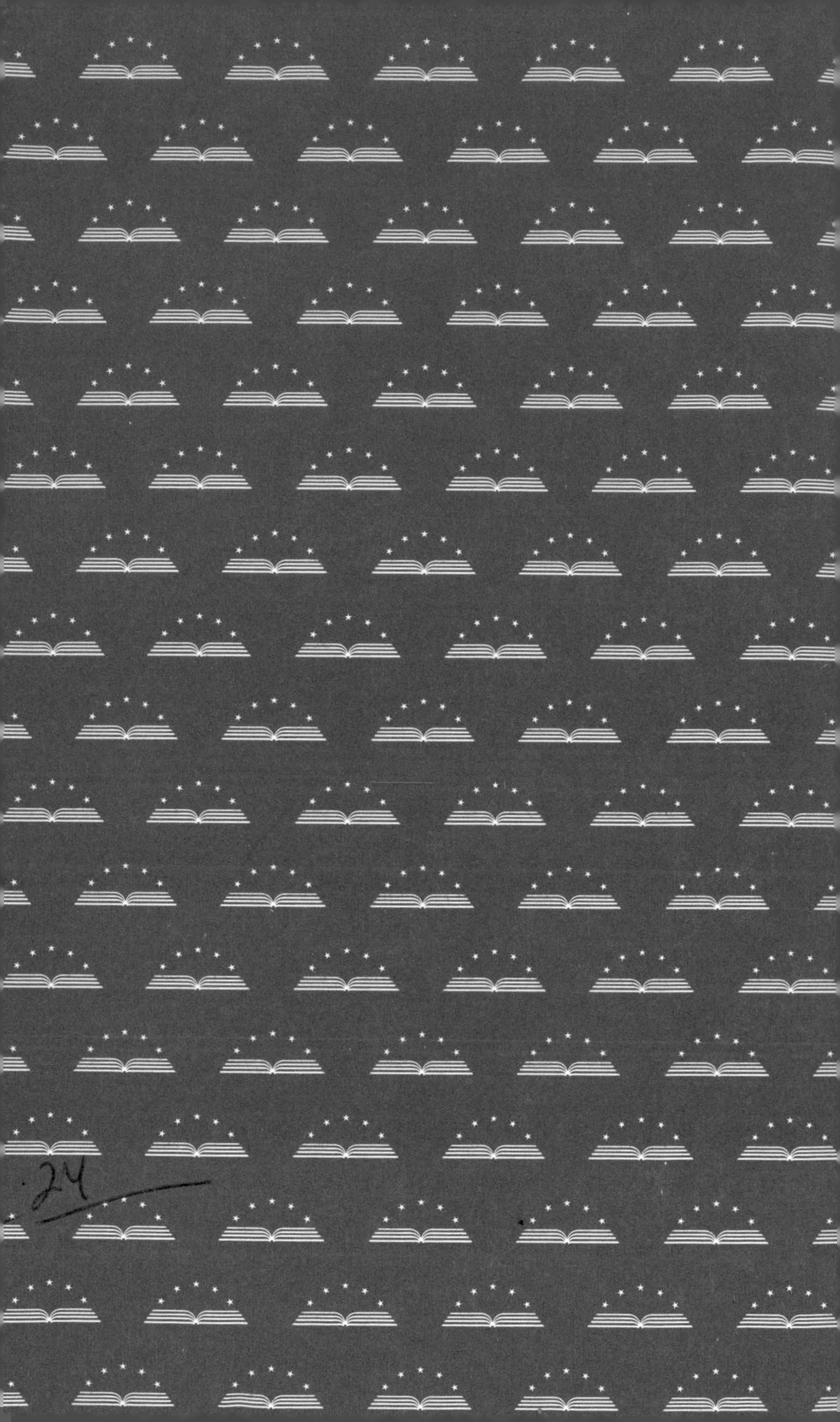